MAN'S FATE AND GOD'S CHOICE

MAN'S FATE AND GOD'S CHOICE

An Agenda for Human Transformation

Bhimeswara Challa

KALPAZ

Man's Fate and God's Choice : An Agenda for Human Transformation

Rs. 500

ISBN: 978-81-7835-881-9

Published in 2011 in India by
Kalpaz Publications
C-30, Satyawati Nagar,
Delhi-110052
E-mail: kalpaz@hotmail.com
Phone : 9212729499

Lasser Type Setting by: Rudra Computer Graphics, Delhi
Printed at : Salasar Imaging System, Delhi

To the 'Hundredth Monkey' — potentially anyone from the mass of mankind — who can tilt the scales and save the world

Contents

Preface

To paraphrase Shakespeare, 'all is not well'; indeed 'something is rotten' in the state of humankind; and our time too appears 'out of joint'.

The world of today has much in common with the fictional *Denmark* of *Hamlet* — chaos, disorder, distrust, bloodletting, breakdown of the 'great chain of being', and collapse of the natural and moral order. Like Hamlet, the tormented prince we too wail inside our wounded minds: "To be or not to be: that is the question; whether 'tis nobler in the mind to suffer the slings and arrows of outrageous fortune, Or to take arms against a sea of troubles, and by opposing end them? To die, to sleep; No more…" Those famous words have inspired a wealth of literature. German philosopher Schopenhauer summed up: "The essential purport of the world-famous monologue in *Hamlet* is, in condensed form, that our state is so wretched that complete non-existence would be decidedly preferable to it. Now if suicide actually offered us this, so that the alternative '*to be or not to be*' lay before us in the full sense of the words, it could be chosen unconditionally as a highly desirable termination…"

The choice transformation or termination — is more stark and real today than in that Shakespearean world. The thought of 'termination' is finding growing acceptance in the mainstream of mankind. Such is the daunting intractability of modern life that, for a growing number of people, the only way to 'terminate' a problem is to terminate life. Many are not even sure if they are already into 'posthumous existence', as the terminally ill Keats once described, a kind of life in the twilight zone, a kind of 'living dead'. Everyone is fleeing, running away, but few know *what* it is that they are escaping from; even less where they are headed to, or what they are looking for. Always in doubt about our true identity, our instinctive orientation, our distilled difference, we oscillate between the reality of our animal origin and our aspiration to be a 'god'. The medieval Persian poet Saadi wrote, "What a strange elixir is Man, he is a compound of the animal and the angel, moving towards the former makes him lower than the animals and by moving towards the latter he can surpass the angels". Trouble is, we want to be both, deathless like an angel and carefree like an animal. And, while trying to emulate the angels, in our behavior we are inching towards a state of being 'lower than animals'.

Animal or angel, 'civilized brute' or simply human, we all struggle, in moments of 'quiet desperation', with questions such as 'Who in the world am I?' 'Why am I?', and 'What should I be?'. These are no longer philosophical questions to be pondered over in solititude; on how each of us faces them — not necessarily find answers — could hinge the fate of humankind. Clearly, we are in a time like no other in the history of the human species. Some even say that the primary reason we are out of sync with Nature is because we are the only species that operates on a different sense of 'time-frequency' than the rest of the biosphere. In their view, we need to return not only to the natural world but also to 'natural time' to lead a harmonious life. Man has always been a seeker, be it of liberation or salvation or Self-realization or the *Elixir Vitae*, eternal life. Man's yearning to know the meaning and mission of his being has spawned a wide spectrum of knowledge, from the esoteric to the occult, from the religious to the scientific. But with no breakthrough or beacon, and a good deal of confusion in the cranium, we wander in the wilderness of the wasteland, searching for a place where we can 'find' ourselves, a place where we need not be anyone or anything else, or where we can cease to be pretenders, which is what we are much of our life. Our highest good is tainted by our oversized ego. What has happened is that instead of embarking on the spiritual journey of self-discovery, we have become self-righteously self-destructive, always trying to find short cuts to pleasure, profit, and power, and trying to look for scapegoats for our own faults and failings.

What is new is that for the first time in the history of the earth, a single species, the human, has acquired the awesome power to chart the course of its own evolution and alter the course of practically all other species. And also to quicken what Jonathan Schell (*The Fate of the Earth*, 1982) calls 'the death of the earth'. The irony and tragedy is that with that kind of power man is perhaps the most miserable creature on earth; to borrow the words from the song *Epitaph* by the rock band *King Crimson*, 'every man is torn apart with nightmares and dreams' and no one cares 'as silence drowns the screams'. Many things have gone awry in our long march from the life of a hunter-gatherer to the post-modern man or posthumous man, and we can only speculate if it is all in tune with divine will or if it is purely a product of human will. Perhaps our greatest failing is that, despite our obvious interdependence, we have failed to imbibe a strong sense of *species-hood*, of solidarity, of respect for each other, of a shared destiny. Indeed, take away the capacity for interbreeding and reproduction, and we would hardly qualify as a 'species' in the way we relate to each other. But instead, what unites us all is a 'sense of *victim-hood*', the entrenched conviction that we are being wronged by our fellow-men, by our fate, and by the gods.

That state of mind, or rather of consciousness, warps our vision and distorts our behavior. Our actions contradict our own acumen, run against our own narrow self-interest. That we are dependent on Nature, that earth is our only home, is evident even to a school child, and yet we wage a suicidal war on the ecosystems and biosphere that sustain our life; and, to top it all, we feel that it is our God-given right. At this juncture in the 'life of life' on earth, the human is at once the prey and the predator: prey to his own mind and predator to everyone else. He is hands down the deadliest animal on the planet, feared by all and fearful of his own shadow. He is the greatest polluter of the planet. The Nobel prize winning chemist Paul Crutzen says that man now plays a 'central role in geology and ecology'. Whether it is still Earth or it has already become '*Eaarth*', as environmentalist Bill McKibben calls it, clearly our planet is in peril. That humankind is unwilling to unequivocally accept this state of peril is itself a sure sign that we are in peril. To be fair, what we are doing to the planet we are doing no less to our own kind. Wanton wrongdoing, wickedness, intrigue, habitual humiliation and hurting of others, and reflexive violence have become inseparable from our daily life, possibly beyond our control. While the scriptures proclaim that we are essentially spiritual beings encased in a human body and awaiting liberation, in actuality, human beings have been reduced to unconnected brute empirical entities, each trying to outsmart the other to expand its own *lebensraum*, and fated to worshipping false gods and the 'good life', endless economic growth, and obscene opulence. While the scriptures say that "you shall not hate your brother in your heart', hatred is the overarching emotion today. It is behind family friction, conflicts with neighbors, national turmoil, ethnic strife, and religious antagonism. It is hatred that kills millions in acts of violence and vengeance; and it is hatred that has led to hundreds of millions of deaths in devastating wars throughout time.

Something seismic, something utterly mysterious has happened in the human spirit and psyche at the deepest levels, and equally mystifying is that we do not have the foggiest idea what it could possibly be. But on one sentiment and statement almost everyone concurs: *we are in trouble*. We are in trouble because all of our relationships begin and continue, not rooted in trust and love, but as forms of mutual exploitation, in the words of American poet W.H. Auden, 'a mental or physical barter'. Every individual is in some sort of trouble; every relationship is in trouble; every institution is in trouble. Every day brings bad news — accident, destruction, massacre, soul-numbing violence. A little-noticed development is the radical, even revolutionary, change in the mindset of man towards morality and mortality. And that has completely altered every facet of human life; but it is so insidious and incremental, we can hardly notice it. We yearn to be moral, but almost compulsively we behave immorally; bad thoughts and things seduce us easily, and the good ones fail to appeal and we shun them as if prompted by an alien force. We want to conquer personal mortality, but we do everything possible to hasten the mortality of our species, among other things by poisoning and pillaging our very life support system. Even more perplexing is our attitude towards death. Normally the knowledge of the inevitability of an event affects how we spend the intervening time. But not with mortality. The impermanence of life makes no difference to the way we live; we manifest the same pettiness, backbiting, and malice. In a twisted sense, man has crossed the final frontier that for millenniums has been a spiritual goal, namely, the freedom from fear of evil and death. He has done this not by cleansing his soul and controlling his mind, but by lowering the threshold of evil, making it, in Hannah Arendt's phrase, banal, radical and seamlessly embedded into every aspect of his everyday life, indeed indistinguishable from everything human.

For many, too many people, life is harsh, brutal, unfair, and simply unbearable and untenable — it takes too much to 'just live'; and too little to 'just die', and just be done with all their problems, passions, and prejudices. We assume that *other* people are the cause of our misery, the source of 'hell' on earth. Many have come to feel, as Walt Whitman, the great American poet, complained to his 'Boswell' Horace Traubel, that they are *non grata*, 'not welcome in the world'. Scriptures and sages might say what they might — death is chasing clothes; suffering cleanses; grief is a gift of God, and so on — but the truth of the matter is that we have become at once a narcissistic and nihilistic species, individually and collectively. Our self-love often takes the form of a craving for admiration and lack of empathy for others; and the noblest of human emotions, love, unreciprocated, turns into vengeful wrath and a murderous weapon. Such are the plethora of paradoxes, perplexities, inexplicabilities, injustices, inequities, illusions, and delusions of the human form of life, and so intertwined is suffering with our earthly lot that, despite our scriptural and scientific claims to superiority and suzerainty over the rest of life on this planet, one wonders if human life is what other species are supposed to be — reborn to 'suffer' for their sins in their earlier lives.

There are no more elevating principles, soaring ideals, and enriching ideas that inspire the young and the restless. Since there is nothing 'worth dying for', everything becomes worth killing for, including their own selves. The most virulent pandemics in the world are suicide and homicide, which really are the two sides of the same coin, if not the same side. To paraphrase Dostoevsky, people kill, in their mind, not people but a 'principle' — religion, revenge, love, honor, property; nothing is too banal or silly or sacred to make one take away one's own or an other's life. Seemingly normal people are turning into sadistic and mass murderers. It is hard to tell if we are dying by murder or dying *to* murder. To paraphrase Shakespeare, we can well say 'murder, thy name is man'.

Man has hopelessly lost his way somewhere in his struggle for survival and supremacy on earth. At the beginning of *The Divine Comedy*, Dante, who was then just turning thirty-five, wrote, "Midway upon the journey of our life, I found myself within a forest dark; for the straightforward pathway had been lost. Ah me! how hard a thing it is to say what was this forest savage, rough, and stern; which in the very thought renews the fear..." (Henry Longfellow's translation). That was the year 1300. Most people of this century feel they too are stranded in the 'forest savage'. The tragic irony is that just when our power over Nature is at its zenith, our power over our own nature is at its lowest ebb. Yet there are some who predict that mankind is poised on the crest of its final evolution, the emergence of a new paradigm of global consciousness. They argue that the crisis that the world faces is the crisis of consciousness, and that everything else — whether it is financial or religious fanaticism — is but its fall-out. And they sense signs of an emergent revolution in consciousness. For long, science has been dangling, before our greedy gaze, the carrot of making man an 'immortal superman' or a Neo-tech 'God-man' with, in Mark Hamilton's words, a 'slim and sexy body, superior intelligence, millionaire wealth, exceptional health and longevity'; and it is now being claimed that significant breakthroughs have been made in that direction, and that it could be a reality sooner than we dare to dream. In short, it is hoped that science will do what religion could not do: literally liberate man from the clutches of biology, from the limits and limitations of what 'being human' may be. But others fear that in trying to be a superhuman species and without fear of death and God, humanity will collapse from within, because our 'intelligence' or the 'inside of us' is not appropriate to exercise that kind of power.

Whatever the future has in store, there is a universal sense of unease, gloom, and doom in the world, a 'gut-feeling' that time is running out, and even faster, our legitimacy, ingenuity, and options to solve any of the pressing problems we face. And that some sort of a meltdown —monetary, ecological, strategic or something still unimaginable — is round the corner. Often when we step aside and look at our lives and our experiences, we feel certain that in some mystical way it must be making sense, but we are beset with too many problems and too much chaos for us to ever get a handle on life. Our drifting existence finds comfort in gurus, guns, and gadgets. There are no guiding stars or shining symbols or enlightened anchors; everything that ever claimed to provide guidance has let us down. Religion is resurgent but vengeful; science is 'out of control', has an agenda of its own; and all models of governance at all levels have become irksome and oppressive, and we have yet to invent one that suits human nature. What Thomas Carlyle prophetically called 'dismal science', *economics* — which is production, distribution, and consumption of goods and services — dominates our lives, our consciousness, today. Of the two 'isms' that have injected economics into everyday life — Marxism and capitalism — the former never really lived and the latter, after having made man a money-making and money-spending machine, is now collapsing, unable to contain the greed and avarice it itself unleashed. No successor 'ism' is in sight and no one can tell where the blend of economics and emotions molded in the cauldron of the marketplace is leading man towards.

At a more fundamental level we must rethink what the rightful place of affluence is in human affairs. Clearly we cannot even envision a world without wealth. Even setting aside the point that not all wealth is monetary — it can be moral and spiritual too — it is worth noting that even the scriptures assign a role for wealth in life. One of the five *purusharthas*, the goals of human life, is the pursuit of *artha* ('wealth') but it must be carried out in a *dharmic* way, that is righteously, and a part of it must be shared with the needy. The Buddha said that we should not eat a single meal without sharing it. Judaism and Christianity extol charity and the latter, by equating service to the poor and the unwanted in society with service to God, became a missionary religion. The generous giving of alms (*zakat*) is one of the pillars of Islam; it even lays down that one should offer to charity, two and half percent of the wealth accumulated by him in a year. It is meant to be a way of purification of wealth — and of the mind of the giver too. In today's world, in which economic disparities are glaring and the very rich are the 'super-human', the obscenely opulent and the very poor are equally 'sub-human', whose bodies and life are crippled fo want of what economists call 'purchasing power'. Since nothing, absolutely nothing, is equal, either in Nature or in life, we must turn our effort towards equity and affirmative actions. And since money and wealth have come to be the measure of life and the primary source of inequity and injustice, we must find a way to create a more fair and reasonable playing field of economic opportunities and fulfillment. And further, one does not have to be monetarily rich to give; the greatest giving is of one's self. Any future paradigm of social justice or spiritual growth must give a pride of place to sharing and giving.

Another overarching imperative is to properly channel the power of science-based technology. The fusion of technology with science has at once awesomely empowered and terminally enfeebled the human species; it has given man the destructive power to cripple earth itself; and it has crippled the human psyche too. Technology, as French philosopher Jacques Ellul puts it, has become a 'total phenomenon for civilization, the defining force of a new social order in which efficiency is no longer an option but a necessity imposed on all human activity'. Such is the sting of what Ellul called 'technological tyranny', that man is defenseless before every new technology and novelty that feeds on his foibles. The combination of economic 'determinism' and technological enslavement has affected the functioning of the human brain, and has put at risk our moral reasoning capacity and even our rational decision making. Whether it is the 'vulcanization' of the brain, as some call it, or the 'boosting' of brain power, designed to enhance its strength, sharpness, resilience, and versatility, the fact is that the kind of pulls, pressures, and temptations that modern man is now subjected to are so raw and novel that the human brain is unable to manage the very circumstances it has created.

At the end of the day, despite our ignorance about the essentials of life, delusions of our glory and grandeur and denials of our depravity, we all know what the '*trouble*' is; we also know what has to be done. We just seem too paralyzed to do what we want to do and, what is more troubling, to *not* do what we hate to do. The '*why*' of everything malevolent and '*why not*' of what we want, haunt our lives. And the troubling thought keeps humming: is this the end or the beginning of the end, or the end of the beginning? And can any of us or all of us make any difference? Are we innocent or ignorant, villains or victims? Are we playing our doomed parts ordained by the gods of remorseless fate, or are we thwarting the intent of God, inebriated as we are by our own 'god-like' powers of creation and destruction? Is nemesis finally catching up, forcing us to pay for our crimes, callousness, cruelty, selfishness, and sins? Adding immediacy to our disquiet and angst looms the Mayan prophecy of 21st December 2012. Opinions vary on what the date portends. Some say it is doomsday, the end of the world. Others say that more probably it will, in some way, force us to confront the truth that the human–planetary equation is out of balance, presaging a seminal shift in human consciousness, ending the era of psychological 'individuation' that began some 26,000 years ago. Instead of debating what a particular dawn of a day might portend, we should start participating and living in the moment, not fearing the future, and start purifying ourselves inside out, and embody in us genuine compassion. This is no time to try to fix things in our mind; it is the time to tune-in to our heart.

Our track record shows that mind-generated human intelligence has not managed well the paradoxes endemic to the human condition; and its increased reliance on machines like the computer as its own proxy has only worsened it. It has not found a way to harmonize the *dwandas* or the pairs of opposites that are inherent in nature and in life in general: pain and pleasure, joy and sorrow, virtue and vice, good and bad, success and failure, finite and infinite, and, above all, competition and cooperation. As a result, fault lines have developed between knowledge and knower, knowing and doing. Those who possess knowledge hardly have the right mindset, leading to wrong actions. And those who are 'hands-on' cannot see beyond the short term. Knowledge, like much else in the human world, is increasingly fractured. To carry any credibility or respect everyone today must get himself accepted as an 'expert' or a 'specialist'. From cooking to killing, we have people who advertize themselves as experts and specialists and sub-specialists, who often contradict and undermine each other, based on the same set of 'facts'. What we desperately need are '*specialist* non-specialists' and 'global citizens', who look at a part in the context of the whole, and who view the world as one wholesome organism. And we must stop perceiving 'facts', 'proof' and 'truth' as interchangeable. The real 'fact', 'proof', and 'truth' is that we know nothing or nothing about 'knowing *That* by knowing which everything is known' as the Upanishad says. Such is the state of our 'factual' knowledge and insightful intelligence that the best brains in the business cannot even agree on the 'facts' of any problem that we confront. For example, on anthropogenic global warming (AGM), that is, global warming caused by human actions, some experts say that, contrary to what we are led to believe, the globe is actually cooling. We are at a loss to know how to react to the news that the past month — June, 2010 — was the hottest month ever recorded. Some say that human behavior is endangering earth; others say that the earth can take care of itself, with or without man. We cannot agree whether the nuclear weapon is a terrible weapon of war, or a gift of god to prevent war and to check on our appetite for mass murder. We cannot agree on any affirmation; we agree by elimination. This was the *modus operandi* that even the Upanishads adopted to explain the concept of *Brahman* — the famous double negative, *neti, neti* (not this, not this). Some modern thinkers too echo the Upanishadic line of thought, its point of departure. According to Karl Popper, we cannot conclusively affirm a hypothesis, but we can conclusively negate it. The human mind is more at ease at elimination, whether it is an idea or an individual. And it 'eliminates' any possible threats to its suffocating hold on the human consciousness. Man's search for another source of cognition or intelligence has also thus far failed.

All this angst leads us to a startling but obvious conclusion. The starting point for any candid and quiet introspection has to be the recognition, or confession, if you will, that the malaise and malady of man is, in the main, the mind itself. The human mind is the deadliest weapon in the world, not the nuclear or biological bomb. The theosophist Alexander Wilder said that 'the chief problem of life is man'. And man has become 'the problem' because the mind governs man. Malice, the visceral will and dark desire to wish ill of others sans self-gain, enslaves us and rules our mind. In fact, behind every crisis the world faces — be it broken homes or convulsive climate change, nuclear Armageddon or noxious neighborhoods, 'clash of civilizations' or ethnic savagery, random violence or rabid religiosity — it is the canker of malice, far more noxious and deeper than envy or jealousy, that is the undercurrent, the driving force. Our ceaseless search for another villain is a ruse of the mind itself. Although the human mind has been called 'superior to everything born or begotten', it has also been described ironically as not only feeble and fickle but also mischievous and malicious, a refrain common to all scriptures. It has been called the 'greatest gift of God', as well as a crippling burden. While we yearn for 'peace of mind', what we give to others is a '*piece of our* mind' when their actions do not fit in with the will of our mind. The mind brooks no delay or denial, contradiction or correction; it does not let us admit our mistakes or take responsibility; for all our omissions and commissions it placates us through the three 'E's — evasion, explanation, and excuse. The human mind is the force in the universe that makes the oppressor believe he is the oppressed; the controller think he is the controlled. It makes the nasty person think that he is nice, much like a tiger thinking it is a lamb. It wants to prevail, not participate; wants to control, not cooperate. It has not learned how to handle both dependency and dominance. It does not let us feel guilt or shame for hurting or humiliating others. The Buddha said, "All wrong-doing arises because of mind. If mind is transformed, can wrong-doing remain?" One of the most powerful tools man has is the 'tool of tools', the mind, and that is where we have gone terribly wrong. Whatever were the driving forces or stumbling blocks, we are unable to 'choose' well or wisely, both as individuals and as a species. Every choice in the end is mental, and the inherent attributes of the mind stick to the choices we make, or think we make. While pundits debate about 'the art of choosing' (*à la* Sheena Iyengar) and improving our decision making capacity, the instrument chosen is the one that has got us into trouble in the first place — the mind itself. And those who say humankind is prematurely drifting towards apocalyptic disaster, as well as those who say we are headed towards the ultimate Utopia, are united on the means — the mind. Those who say that man is terminally adrift, rely on *mind control*, while the latter, who say that a great awakening is upwelling from the deepest depths of man, bank on boosting *mind-power*. Although it is sometimes said, like in Vedanta, that the mind is the source of our bondage as well as of our liberation, what we actually experience is that that which is the problem cannot be the solution, as Einstein noted about human intelligence. It is this conundrum that has bedeviled man's attempt to master himself. Nothing seems right in our lives because, quite simply, the one thing that drives our actions and reactions, perceptions and prejudices and predispositions, is flawed: our intelligence. And our intelligence is flawed because its source of supply is the wrong one: the mind. We cannot change the 'mind-set', the innate character of the mind; but we can — and must — change the *mindset*, the 'view from within', to borrow the words from the Chilean philosopher Francisco Varela. What we can and must change are the assumptions, beliefs, dispositions that predetermine a person's responses to and interpretations of situations. At this pivotal point in human history, we must discard not only the dated paradigms but also the dated questions; we must dare to ask new questions.

These new questions must touch the very core of our being, and the thrust of our thought ought to be to understand how to awaken ourselves from our cosmic amnesia, and move into the embrace of the universal essence that underlies and pervades all life. Although it might seem a deficiency, man, unlike any other species, being borne incomplete, offers the potential to become radically different in the break between birth and death. That 'wet-clay' state, that very incompleteness, that lack of finality, makes radical transformation not only possible, but also enables man to be simultaneously a participant and a partner. It is in us to make the difference — positive or negative. Indeed, transformation is the meaning and mission — and measure — of human life. The problem is that we cannot truly change without giving up something; we cannot be transformed unless we terminate. But we have to remain the same in some way; and retain something we must, while being transformed. A caterpillar cannot become a butterfly if it wants to stay firmly on the ground. And the fact is that the butterfly is *in situ*; already in the creepy creature. It is not 'visible' before, in the words of Primo Levi, the 'mystery of metamorphosis', but the blueprint and the potential was always there and present. The trouble is that we do not know what is truly inside us; what is the nature of our 'self'. As a result, we do not know what to give up or terminate, and what to hold on to, and to let what we already are to manifest. In Vedantic terms, our true 'self' is the eternal Self, the divine essence, which is the 'butterfly', and it has always been there. The caterpillar is the idea of, or sole identification with, being only human; and that has to be liquefied and disintegrated through spiritual *sadhana* or practice. Then, the already present butterfly camouflaged by the illusion can emerge from the cocoon of consciousness and, as Robert Frost wrote, 'fly and all but sing'.

To evolve into a higher — and nobler — paradigm of life, to orchestrate our own 'mystery', we need to change the complex of controls, compass and coordinates, the thinking and the tools we have thus far used to reach this point in our evolution. We have to go to an altogether different dimension of life, to a higher cusp of consciousness. As the Czech philosopher Stanislav Grof noted, "A radical inner transformation and rise to a new level of consciousness might be the only real hope we have in the current global crisis brought on by the dominance of the Western mechanistic paradigm". It means changing, in Alexander Wilder's words, the 'potencies of man's interior being', the forces that drive and determine everything we think, feel, say, and do. It means that for any meaningful change in the content and character of the human condition, we need a new 'genre of inner identity', a complete break from almost everything we have come to accept, value, and cherish. The touchstone is that we must feel, instinctively and effortlessly, *pain*, not pleasure, at someone else's pain. That depth of empathy is clearly not possible without cathartic consciousness change, which, in turn, means that we must dethrone our brain/mind-driven intelligence from its pedestal and from where it dominates our lives. Consciousness and unconsciousness are relative states; states of wakefulness or somnolence. In truth, no one is fully conscious or fully unconscious, even in death. Even within a single life — from infancy to childhood to adolescence to youth to old age — we function in different states of consciousness or unconsciousness. What man has to strive for is to be 'awake', as the Buddha described himself when asked who he was. We must awaken the Buddha within, or allow the baby Buddha struggling to come out from the darkness of our 'womb'. Then everything and everyone will appear as different parts of the same universal body, and we will then cease to be a marauding menace on earth. Compassion will become our first impulse and response to every situation, provocation, and circumstance. And love will be reborn in the human world.

Even that kind of caring and compassionate consciousness change would not, and need not, make us all saints, mahatmas, or heroes, but it will empower and enable us to do *differently* the myriad things we do every day and all our lives, and, as American historian Howard Zinn said, "small acts, multiplied by millions of people, can transform the world". That kind of human effort has to show up not as a bunch of spectacular scientific breakthroughs, but in the myriad choices we make in our lives over the next few decades — from where and how we live, to what we eat, buy, and use, from how we generate and use energy, to how we discard and recycle our waste. Those choices and acts will determine whether man will hasten his own extinction or reach the plateau of a nobler planetary civilization. If he has to achieve the latter, man must go beyond both scriptures and science; for, the scriptures are intelligible only to the initiated, and science, as it is put into effect, is no longer a search for truth but a travesty of truth. We must go beyond brainpower and mind control, beyond even a new way of thinking; because thinking too is mental, and scripture too is filtered through the mind. We have to shift our focus from mind control to cleansing of the consciousness.

In sum, transform, or turn terminal, that is the defining choice before mankind at the turn of this millennium. But transformation has to be radically different from what science and technology are attempting through technologies like cryonics, nanotechnology, cloning, etc. With the kind of consciousness that man has, that kind of 'transformation' could be catastrophic. Conscience cannot save us; we need a cathartic consciousness change. We need a new source of 'intelligence', a new mode of cognition, far removed from the dominance of the brain/mind. The mind cannot be 'destroyed'; it cannot be 'overcome'; it cannot be 'controlled', as we, the humans of this age, at least, are exorted to do by scriptures and sages. It needs to be outflanked. The only way is to bring back our heart to the center stage of conscious intelligence, from its present 'fringe function' of a life-sustaining pump. Fortunately, new research is reinforcing the ancient wisdom that the heart is an autonomous source of energy, memory, and intelligence, quite distinct from the brain-mind. Indeed, some eminent psychologists like Julian Jaynes have posited that the dominance of the mind over man dates barely three thousand years, and before that, both mind and heart played independent but complementary roles in human affairs. Something went wrong or maybe our survival demanded it; the mind became the master and the heart was reduced to a mere powerful muscle that kept us ticking. Long after sheer survival ceased to be the primary challenge for man, the human mind, having tasted and enjoyed absolute power, refuses to yield. As a result, the very tools we have so far relied upon — our unique ability to think, to analyze, to comprehend, to plan and prepare, to at once look back and ahead — have brought us to the edge of the abyss. With mind in control, we have not been able to harmonize or manage our passions, predispositions, and priorities, nor our thoughts, emotions, and impulses. Our genetic, ethnic, and cultural diversity has become a drag, not an asset. And we have messed up our equation with Nature and God. As the Worldwatch Institute noted (*State of the World 1997*), "In just a few centuries we have gone from living off nature's interest to depleting the natural capital that has accumulated over millions of years of evolution". Biologist Edward O. Wilson (*The Future of Life*, 2002) said that what humanity is inflicting on itself and on earth is "the result of a mistake in capital investment". As for God, we have turned Him into a superintendent of the supermarket whose only function is to ensure instant home delivery of what we order, and when there is any demur or delay, we threaten to create a new, '*Tomorrow's God*'.

But much as we might squirm and quibble, we cannot cut ourselves loose from either God or Nature. The historic human tendency has been to abuse Nature and ignore God when things go right, and to turn to them for help when things go wrong. The time has come yet again to turn to Nature, a kind of the return of the Prodigal Son. The living world of insects and animals is rich with models and paradigms of transformation, like the anthill, the beehive, and the butterfly. Even if it may seem an affront to our intelligence, imagination, and creativity, we must draw upon their 'experiences' to shape our own path. And if we do not, the metaphor of the 'lemming suicide' will most likely catch up. While human transformation and consciousness change have been the elusive age-old spiritual goals, the promise now lies in the fact that science is capable of joining forces. Recent discoveries in fields like quantum physics are prompting scientists to talk of hitherto taboo ideas like a single unifying force in the universe, and of a seamless existence and a soul. There is an air of fragrant optimism that, at last, science and spirit *together* can achieve what neither could do alone, and catapult man to perhaps the ultimate level of evolution. This arguably could be the greatest challenge man has ever faced. It is nothing less than to reconfigure human 'presence' on earth. So monumental and momentous is the task, that to seize this uncommon opportunity it will not suffice to have a handful of 'New Age' spiritualists or evangelical environmentalists or disparate 'civil society' initiatives. We need a coalition of 'critical mass' agents of change. What that magical number is, crossing which the momentum for transformational change becomes unstoppable, we do not know, but each of us must believe and behave as if we are that one extra person — the hundredth monkey, if you will — whose addition will catalyze species-scale consciousness connectivity.

In sketching on such a huge kaleidoscopic canvas, and not to lose one's way in the woods, it is imperative to have some clear points of reference. This book encompasses five principal ideas. *One*, it is a brutally candid and unflinching gaze at what ails the human condition; why we are such slaves of our senses, and why our behavior is so brazen and bizarre. It goes behind behavior and notes that behavior just does not burst out of nowhere; it incubates inside, nurtured by our thoughts. And thought, as the Indian sage Ramana Maharshi said, is the origin of sin. *Two*, it suggests that since we cannot alter the basic character of the mind, we should move to transform our mindset, that is, change the body of our assumptions, beliefs, and values that govern our lives. *Three*, it suggests that for any meaningful betterment of the human context of life on earth, what is needed is not simply a new way of understanding, but a change in *the way we understand* the way we understand, *the way we think about* the way we think, and that requires our finding a new source of cognition and intelligence, and that can only be the human heart. *Four*, only transformation through consciousness change could be the hope to avoid the sixth mass extinction that scientists are predicting, paving the way, in turn, to our premature posthumous existence. *Five*, and the most important idea, as the Bhagavad Gita exhorts, there is no greater *dharma* than *swadharma*. In life, every species, be it a plant or an ant or an animal, or even God, has a *swadharma*, and for the human, as the dominant form of life on earth, the *swadharma* must be to do God's work on earth: to sustain, synergize, and harmonize *all* life, human and non-human alike. That should be the ultimate aim of human transformation.

With these parameters serving as the framework, the book addresses a plethora of questions: What is our *swadharma* on earth, and how close or how far are we in tune with it? Has human culture and conduct brought man to the edge of extinction or to the launch pad of his final evolution? Why does man, who prides himself as the sole rational and spiritual being on this planet, behave so irrationally when it comes to issues that impact on the survival of his own species? Why is the human such a slave to his senses, and so prone to anger, malice, and violence, so addicted to sex, money, and power? Why is the human species at once so fratricidal and suicidal? Is evil endemic to the human condition or is it simply circumstantial? Is our goodness merely a matter of genes, just another form of selfishness? What should be done to make compassion and cooperation the reflexive response of the human condition, and take it away from the confines of kinship and friendship? What should we do to transform human diversity into an enriching asset, not a debilitating drag? If there is soon going to be a 'robot in every home', as Bill Gates predicts, what are the evolutionary implications? If medicine could cure the 'disease of death', as Richard Dawkins hopes it will, what kind of human society would that lead to? What should we do to break down, not build up, the barriers between people of race, religion, ethnicity, and nationality? What is so unique about the human species? Are we better than 'bugs and bacteria' simply because we have evolved a more complex neurobiology? What are the implications of the current thrust of scientific transformative effort to make man an 'immortal superman'? Without a corresponding consciousness change, would man become an intolerable menace on earth? If so, how could such a consciousness change be induced? Is the way the human mind receives, comprehends, and analyzes the dynamics that drive the human way of life intrinsically capable of coping with the looming threats to human existence like nuclear war and climate change? How could the human loosen himself from the grip of his own mind on consciousness, and activate the latent energy of his heart to counterbalance his mind? If man needs a fundamental transformation of the very meaning of '*being* human', what agenda should he subscribe to?

To adequately address these intertwined questions, the book breaks up into eight chapters.

Chapter 1 offers a preview, a bird's-eye view of the book. It begins by setting the two basic parameters of this introspective inquiry at this turn of a millennium — why does man seem to be predisposed towards the immoral path, when being moral can give him all that he wants, and is God getting, in the Churchillian phrase, weary of mankind? The reality is that 'something seismic has happened at the very core of our being', which has changed our perceptions of the fundamentals and is blurring the boundaries between life and death. Man has become disillusioned, alienated, angry, at once narcissistic and nihilistic, and no longer lives in the 'natural milieu'; and the mind has become the monarch of man. The human condition has gone from being a 'paradoxical promise' to a 'perilous paradox'. We seem utterly — and fatefully — incapable of realizing that all humans share the same fate on a lone and crowded planet. The chapter goes on to discuss the dynamics of change and transformation, and notes that for the first time humanity confronts the kind of 'existential' risks it has never experienced before, and unlike the case with previous 'risks', it cannot learn from its mistakes. While change is inherent and constant, man is now 'making it happen', but in the wrong direction, focused on the body and driven solely by the power of technology. Instead of consciousness change, he is attempting to become a superman; instead of spiritual transformation, he is aiming for physical immortality. An 'immortal superman' with the present consciousness would be an intolerable burden and menace to earth and Nature — and an affront to God. How Nature/God would react is not hard to guess — the scriptures have foretold the course of this most immoral age and how it will end. But if we can mend our ways and transform ourselves in the right direction, we might still get a reprieve and last longer than a century or two, as scientists like Martin Rees predict. What we do for the rest of this century could determine the fate and future of this human species — and of life on earth. That is the great challenge of this generation of human beings — and the 'point of departure' for the subsequent chapters.

Chapter 2 deals with the myriad aspects germane to 'being human', and the fall from paradoxical promise to perilous paradox. It puts the multiple identities of man in perspective. It begins with the fountainhead of all inquiry — *Who am I?* — and goes on to discuss a range of issues such as: human nature; human evolution or involution; the place of man in space and time; the debate about prehistoric man (god-like or ape-like); the dialectics of the real and unreal; greatness and goodness. It examines in some depth the question why man seems so predisposed to injustice, inequity, exploitation, hatred, and divisiveness. It gives particular attention to the contours and context of human behavior, and why and how it has become both suicidal and homicidal and a threat to life on earth. The chapter points out the growing toxicity in human life due to the alarming presence of chemicals in everything human, and the pollution of the living environment, potentially capable of transforming us into a 'mutant species'.

Chapter 3 begins by reviewing the gamut of subjects under the rubric of freedom and bondage — is man born free but chained through his culture, crippling his innate potential goodness, or is he too dangerous an animal to be let loose? What makes us aspire for salvation and be addicted to slavery? Bondage and inequality run through life, and most men, in Thoreau's words, lead lives of 'quiet desperation'. The state of the world reflects the state of a 'bonded man'; a symptom of the bondage is that good men seem to suffer and the bad seem to have all the luck. In that context, the chapter pays particular attention to the galloping 'banality' of personal, collective, and moral and economic evil, and our acceptance of that as the inevitable, if not necessary part of modern life, and to the attendant question "What is God 'doing about it'?" A plausible explanation explored here leads to the twin doctrines of *karma* and *dharma*. The author looks at the three kinds of *karma*, and examines the infiniteness of *dharma*, the subtleties of *swadharma*, one's own righteous path, and the *yuga dharma*, the moral way of this age. Among the topics the chapter covers are: the 'end of the world' scriptural scenarios and the 'gloom and doom' prophecies, the Hindu idea of *avatars*, direct divine incarnations, the last of which is due at the end of this age, the *Kali Yuga*; man's mindless (or maybe mindful) assault on Nature and its calamitous consequences; our inability to manage 'our aggregate existence', or the humane governance of human diversity; the complex of information-knowledge-ignorance, and the perils of assembling information without wisdom; the various aspects of 'external' and 'internal governance'; the paradox of a 'globalized globe' and of billions living lives of extreme poverty, alienation, and abandonment; the decline of the primacy of the Nation-State and its impact; the irony of our claiming to be a 'god' and constant comparison with animals; the rise of the 'economic man' and the decline of 'moral man'; the hold of power, sex, and control over the human mind; the vice-like grip of violence on the human mind and our growing insensitivity to human suffering; the human history of war-making and massacres, and horrors and genocides, and their colossal cost for the human conscience; man's indefatigable quest for immortality.

Chapter 4 delves deep into one of the most complex and increasingly important subjects of human thought, the two dominant strands in space and time — sacred and secular. In this setting, the chapter deals with the much-debated clash of religion and science, and describes the current state of both domains of knowledge, noting that the clash that is dissipating the human spirit is not between religion and science, but between one religion and another. Even though they are not in open conflict, religion and science have not worked out a way to work together, thus hampering both and diminishing overall human advancement. Both work on separate agendas, religion deriving legitimacy through revelation, and science focused on its own glory. The chapter highlights some of the emerging trends in both science and religion, and their implications for the future of mankind. Religion, rather the way it is perceived and practiced, has become a major source of the very evil that it warns man to be wary of. The chapter goes on to argue that the greater danger stems from the fusion of technology with science, which has at once lethally empowered man as well as terminally enfeebled him. Technologies like nanotechnology and biotechnology are now trying to change not just the human environment, but the human organism itself. In a mood of disenchantment with both religion and science, many are turning to 'spirituality' as a way to be fully human. This chapter, towards the end, explores the ramifications of this trend and puts this in the context of the major thrust of this book — the need for spiritual transformation through mutation of consciousness, which is fundamentally different from the physical transformation through mutation of the body that science is attempting.

Chapter 5 focuses on the prerequisites for any meaningful change in human behavior through consciousness change. Consciousness remains, in many ways, the final frontier of human quest, an enigma wrapped in a riddle. We still do not know much about it, but we know enough to know that consciousness is the master key that can unlock many closed doors in the human condition and conduct. It is consciousness that separates one individual from another, the early humans from the modern man, one age from another, one species from another, and a baby from an adult. True transformation requires consciousness change. To get rid of all that ails us, to cleanse ourselves of all the toxins that we have accumulated, most of all our sense of separation and our entrenched ego, we need consciousness change. It is the content of our present consciousness that makes non-reciprocal love and spontaneous compassion so rare. It is this consciousness that warps our decision making, and prioritization and making of choices. All the afflictions and frailties of the brain/mind are attached to the consciousness, and in turn determine the nature of human behavior. To get rid of them, we need consciousness change. To contain the pandemics of suicide, homicide, fratricide, ecocide, and biocide, we need to attack them where they germinate and incubate — the consciousness. To make cooperation, not confrontation, altruism, not animosity, our natural and ordinary impulses, we need to change the very content of our consciousness.

Chapter 6 of the book elaborates perhaps the most important aspect: if consciousness change is to become a reality, it is imperative for the human consciousness to transit from mind-centeredness to heart-centeredness. It argues that despite consistently describing the mind as feeble, fickle, mischievous, and wayward, we have essentially become mental beings, and our behavior reflects that state. The central message is that for human behaviour to change constructively our consciousness must change. And for consciousness to change, the grip of the mind must be eased, and for that to happen, the human heart has to be brought back, as a source of energy and intelligence, from the margins to the mainstream. '*A Path with Heart*', borrowing the title of Jack Kornfield's book, has long been the spiritual path to salvation, and the scriptures, from the Upanishads to the Bible, have extolled the heart as the seat of the soul and the abode of God. It has also been said that the primary source of intelligence of prehistoric man was not in the head but in the heart, and earlier, even further down, below in the navel. Psychologists like Julian Jaynes say that till a few millenniums ago, human consciousness was 'bicameral', that is, it was powered by two kinds of intelligences, of the brain-mind and the heart-mind. All our troubles began when the heart regressed, and the mind virtually colonized the consciousness. The heart is the source of love, compassion, and much of what is good in the human personality. In what is described as frontier research, tools and techniques are being developed to re-energize heart intelligence. The truth of the matter is that our eyes can mislead, our ears can lead us astray, our mouth can betray us, and our mind can make us a monster, but our heart will always be faithful and unflinching in its integrity. The chapter suggests that restoring the heart to its rightful place ought to be at the top of the human agenda of this century, and offers a framework towards this end.

Chapter 7 addresses the central issue: what should man do to be fundamentally different from what he has become now, to remain essentially human and yet be post-human? To achieve that, man must shed the baggage of his post-industrial past, and acquire a new consciousness that is not exclusively mind-fixated, but constitutes a blend of two complementary intelligences — of the mind and of the heart. Transformation is neither new nor confined to human aspiration. Nature and life are nothing but transformations. Every passage from infancy through adolescence to youth, to old age and to death is transformation. We want something 'more', something different that lets us choose or discard what we like or dislike, like eternal youth and deathlessness. This section identifies and elaborates the two classical paths to transformation: the scientific and the spiritual, and suggests that we should lay out a new, the third, path: that of consciousness change and of the heart. A large part of this chapter goes into some detail about 'the phenomenon of God', covering a broad range of issues such as the scriptural view; the traditional mainstream scientific view that denies divine existence and role; the recent developments that are inducing some people to change their view; the different scenarios of the relationship of God and man; the dynamics of freewill, fate, and surrender; faith, divinity, and doubt; transcendence, immanence, and indifference of God The chapter closes with an examination of the triad of Transformation, Nature and Science.

The final ***Chapter 8*** brings the 'story' to its climax. It looks at the living world for inspiration, metaphors, and models for human transformation. The living world has all the knowledge and know-how for man to attain the fullness of his potential. The section identifies three scenarios applicable to the human condition: the way of the ant and the bee; the way of the 'lemming suicide'; and the way of the caterpillar turning into a butterfly. Clearly, we have much in common with the caterpillar, but we want to be the butterfly. Can man emulate this model, and if so, what could be the necessary elements? What could be the intermediate stage, the human equivalent of the 'pupa'? This chapter notes that there are alarming parallels between the 'suicidal' lemmings of the Arctic, and the present 'suicidal' human condition. And it argues that the kind of transformation that man must undergo, to ensure his own continued existence beyond a century or two, is impossible without a fundamental consciousness change, and that is virtually impossible without divine grace. Man must combine two opposites: he must endeavor and struggle as if nothing is impossible for human will, and he must surrender to God as if He alone can save and steer man. But for God to extend His hand, we must create the right context and conditions here on earth. That is the privilege and opportunity for this generation of men and women. Can we measure up? At first sight, things look grim and gloomy. But some see hopeful signs, a resurgence, albeit sparse, of spirituality, of mysticism, of the emergence of a new paradigm of global consciousness. And science is breaking new ground through discoveries like that of a possible 'God-gene', and, most of all, the techniques to re-energize heart intelligence as a counterbalance to that of the mind. Individuals do matter, but for a species-scale transformation, the book posits, we must marshal a 'critical mass' and a coalition of forces. That is the challenge — and the choice.

On a personal note, I have a confession to offer: this book is a mystery to myself. How it came about, I do not know or remember. Purely factually, it is but a part of a much larger length of prose, running to over thousand five hundred pages, which I hope, God willing, will see the light of day sometime in the future. Nothing in my life fits in with the profile of an author of this book: there is no 'long foreground somewhere' to borrow the words of Emerson in his famous letter to Walt Whitman. My professional experience at first glance appears far removed, if not antithetical, to what the book encompasses. And, I am one of those who are truly troubled by the gathering dirt, decay, and drift in the human way of life, and who not only see misery and ask 'Why?', but also see promise in the rainbow and ask '*Why not?* I have been a writer of sorts for much of my life, whether it was writing novels in my mother tongue (*Telugu*), writing for the United Nations, or publishing articles in reputed journals on a broad range of subjects. I have had the uncommon opportunity to live and work literally at every layer and level of human society, all the way from the grassroots to the global. One of God's gifts that I believe I possess is a natural ability to step aside and look at the different dimensions of the human condition, and discern what ails modern man, and offer some ideas on how to fix it. While living in the world, I can be an observer and a participant, an insider who can look from the outside, or an outsider who can cut through to the core. My association with the Indian Administrative Service (I.A.S.) and the International Civil Service (UN) gave me that rare chance to don those roles. But in the end, my real 'qualification' is that, to paraphrase Tennessee Williams, 'having found life unsatisfactory, I wanted to do the only thing I know: brood and write'.

Samuel Johnson once said that to write one book a man 'will turn over a half a library'. At least, judging by the voluminous notes and its kaleidoscopic coverage, this book came close to that. Disraeli said that the best way to get acquainted with a subject is to write about it, and, as E.M. Forster said, the only way to truly know what I think is to 'see what I say'. As much as the book is a journey of ideas and options on human transformation, it is also a personal voyage of self-discovery, to 'ascend' to the deepest depths of my heart, to feel, in Wordsworth's words, the 'breathings of my heart'. It is a means to save myself from 'tempered melancholy', said to be the central theme of the works of Joseph Conrad, or 'to withdraw myself from myself', as Byron puts it, and offer an utterance to my solitary soul.

If 'no one is a stranger' on the voyage of life, any potential reader would be my soul-mate, those who yearn, as Richard Bach (*David Livingston Seagull*) said, to 'make life come to life'. This book has been written in the spirit that '*manava seve madhava seva*' (service to humanity is service to God), and if it triggers the tiniest tremor in the turbulent mindsets of a few of my fellow-men, then the long and exasperating travail behind this work would not go without leaving a trail behind. This book hopefully constitutes a humble offering to the Almighty, and any ripple effect it might cause in the ocean of global consciousness is a small service to make man a better being on earth. The opening to that offering is provided by Lord Krishna Himself, in the Bhagavad Gita: "*Yat karoshi yad ashnasi; yaj juhoshi dadasi yat; yat tapas yasi kaunteya; tat kurushva mad-arpanam*" (Chapter 9.27), which roughly translates as 'Whatever you do, eat, sacrifice, offer as gift, perform as austerity, O Kaunteya — do all this as dedication to Me'.

So, if nothing is too trivial or temporal to be a divine dedication, why not then a book… why not from a *mere* me?

Finally, we know that a book does not just happen. Apart from the actual author and the publisher, there are always unseen forces and invisible actors who facilitate the process and the product. Being invisible should not deny the right to be remembered; death should not annihilate deserved gratitude. In my case, I would be guilty of ingratitude — one of the *Panchamahapapams*, the five great sins — if I did not mention my beloved parents and siblings who gave me boundless love, without which any urge for creativity would have long been smothered. In terms of its content, it has been a singularly solitary effort, from conception to conclusion. Any creative effort is greatly influenced by the immediacy of the 'world' around, where just one element, just one person, can make all the difference. In my case, that 'one' has been my wife Nirmala, without whose critical support this labor would not have come to fruit. Coming to those who were more directly involved, I wish to take this opportunity to thank the language editors Kranthi Buddhiraju and S. Vijay Ramchander for their contributions. I would specially like to gratefully acknowledge the extraordinary commitment, diligence, and dedication of the latter. My assistant S.P. Babu Aradhya was also helpful in the preparation of the manuscript.

Bhimeswara Challa

Hyderabad

1

Man in Context

God Gotten Weary of Man!

The turn of any millennium is always a time for thoughtfulness, a rugged moment for intrepid introspection, a hinge of history for an honest audit of human conduct, for a moral inventory of our presence on earth, a juncture for a steadfast look at a nebulous — and numinous — stage in the life of our blessed (and baffling) species. Although it is but a twinkle in the cosmic calendar and a trifling stretch in the geological calculus, a thousand years is a huge hiatus in human history and deserves a moment to pause and ponder. In the long, tempestuous tale of man's search for the substratum, his endeavors to understand the nature of the basic 'reality', the 'meaning of his being' and to bend fate, as it were, to his wanton whim and will, this is a period of pregnant profundity, the twilight of a dusky dawn. We are stranded between the crumbling past and a convulsive future, the ground underneath giving way, in our attempt to know why things are as they are. Whether we are simply the secular and stray descendents of a tiny cell of primordial protoplasm, or an arbitrary product guided by no objective value, or the special creation of an All-Wise and All-Merciful God and with a manifest mission that has somehow gone terribly awry, what the human presence has wrought on earth has come to a boil. We do not know what the future holds. Is it likely that a new species could evolve from *Homo sapiens* with improved or additional senses, with the ability to perceive and experience new dimensions, and with the capacity to develop a higher or different intelligence? Could it be that new species would manifest in a completely different form and shape with an entirely new life pattern?

In the 'magical' drama of the origin and evolution of life on earth, spread over a span of nearly four billion years, the present period is indeed a pivot without parallel when, as astronomer Martin Rees tells us, a lone species — the human, for now — has grasped the earth's future in its hands, casting on it a responsibility never before borne by any other species. In his book, *Our Final Century* (2004), Rees argues that humankind, with the devices it has on hand, is potentially the maker of its own demise and the demise of the cosmos. He says that "what happens here on Earth, in this century, could conceivably make the difference between a near eternity filled with ever more complex and subtle forms of life, and one filled with nothing but base matter." He adds that the odds are fewer than 50:50 that humans will survive till the end of this century; and brings the matter closer home — and heart— by reminding us that the decisions that man makes in the next few decades are possibly the most important that man has ever made.

Even if the time-frame is debatable, clearly we are poised at a pivotal point, and by the time this millennium passes and the year 3,000 CE arrives the human race would have either perished or would have become a radically different form of life on earth. Some astrobiologists calculate that the planet has already has begun the long process of devolving into a burned-out cinder, eventually to be swallowed by the sun. Whatever is the course of the future, it is becoming unmistakably obvious that we are in the middle of much more than a mere quantitative change in rates of growth, pace of application of technology, information explosion, or declining moral standards. While we talk of post-human as the next, perhaps the final, phase in evolution, the fact is that the base itself is eroded: we humans have already become other than *only* human for at least half a century, both in terms of our creative and destructive potential. With the result, we need new tools to govern our own behavior and new yardsticks on what or who a 'moral man' is or ought to be. We must bring into clearer focus what Scottish historian Adam Ferguson called in his essay *History of Civil Society* (1767) 'a principle for affection for mankind' and the conviction that "an individual is no more than a part of the whole that demands his regard"[1].

The Socratic axiom that "an unexamined life is not worth living" is even more germane to the life and loves of a species that prides itself as the most 'intelligent' on this planet and that now has turned to be the most menacing mammal. Man, having largely succeeded in his labor to extricate himself from the rigors and limits inherent in the laws of Nature, has now shifted his greedy gaze towards the natural (or divine) determinants of earthly life — disability, decay, disease, and finally death. The other 'D' of human life is a congenital delusionary disorder. Deluded by his visions of anthropocentric grandeur, man is audaciously aiming at individual immortality, space colonization, and species-scale eternity, and has summoned science to his aid. For science, the defining driving force now on earth, has the primeval power to make things indistinguishably different from what they originally were, to transform their basic features, make them vanish and reappear as an altogether different substance — the attributes that hitherto God alone had. Man is now turning that 'transformational' power towards himself, trying to direct his own destiny. But unlike God's power, the power of science is, although awesome, still finite. And it can, in a trifle, like God, destroy not only incrementally but also exponentially.

The tantalizing prospect is this: can science be a tool not to hasten the passage of humankind into the dustbin of evolution, but rather be, as physicist Paul Davies (*God and the New Physics*, 1992), who in the past had denied divine possibility, put it, 'a surer path to God than religion'? And be a channel for the spiritual goal of self-discovery? For now, the copulation of man's greedy gaze and god-like power sets up the epic stage for a titanic struggle between human ambition and Nature's stoicism and divine forbearance. Most people have a 'gut feeling' that the world we have grown accustomed to is drawing to a rather messy end, and the Mayan apocalyptic date of 2012 is too close for comfort. There is erudite talk of a 'flat world' and of what really constitutes 'life', but it is the reality of living that has become flat without fizz, utilitarian sans idealism, a ritual devoid of the sense of the sacred, leaving a silent scream in the souls of sullen and stricken men. While the world is gluing electronically, it is fractured emotionally. Many seek solace through frenetic activity and seamless sensual pleasure through all kinds of devices and drugs, gurus and gadgets, religion and recreation, sermons and spiritualism.

And such is the extravagant extent of human rapacity, that life on earth is approaching or passing through, according to many experts, the sixth great wave of mass extinctions (the last, some 65 million years ago, was that of the dinosaurs). Scientists project that as much as 20 to 30 percent of species on earth could well vanish by the end of this century, triggered this time primarily by the predatory activity of a single biological species: the *Homo sapiens*. But it also means that, unlike the previous extinctions, we have the wherewithal to preempt or abort this one by the way we live each of our otherwise matter-of-fact lives. This could be the meaning — and the mission — we are all searching for. However much we might wish to lead prosaic lives of perfect peace and perpetual prosperity, this day and age is a moment with celestial import and doomsday odds. The gods of fate have cast us all a part to play sans the reassurance of rehearsal or reprieve; and in so doing, destiny has ceded a chunk of its own zealous domain. In everything we do in the immediacy of our lives, as individuals and as a collective unit, we must never let this central thought slip out of our mind.

Looking at man as he is and the world as it is, a clutch of questions grab us by our throat and brook no dillydally or shilly-shally, nor the proverbial 'Nelson's eye'. At this stage in the passage of the paradigm of life on earth, is the human, in the words of scientist Gordon Rodley, a 'monstrous, meaningless accident' and mankind fated to fail by the weight of its own frailty? Is Man's Fate — and what might befall him — just man's fate; does it matter for anyone else? And is God's choice only His preserve? At what point are we in God's watchful reckoning or Nature's forgiving indulgence? Are we mere puppets on a cosmic string or a blessed species blinded and brooding on the brink? Is man, in the words of the great Indian spiritual humanist Swami Vivekananda (*Parliament of Religions*, Chicago, 1893), "a tiny boat in a tempest, raised one moment on the foaming crest of a billow and dashed down into a yawning chasm the next, rolled to and fro at the mercy of his own good and bad actions, a powerless, helpless wreck, in an ever-raging, ever-rushing, uncompromising current of cause and effect, a little moth placed under the wheel of causation, which rolls on crushing everything in its way, and waits not for the widow's tears or the orphan's cry?"[2] Is man, as the German philosopher and self-styled 'immoralist' Friedrich Nietzsche puts it, a mere condition to be overcome — for the good of the world? And is that 'overcoming' really to become extinguished, winging its way to a nobler species? At a time when the future seems grey and grim such questions seem increasingly pertinent. Such is our comprehensive incomprehension — or the lack of it — of what is happening around us that, while visualizing the world that awaits our grandchildren, we are puzzled if we should shudder or smile, feel scared or be elated. The great 19th century theosophist and occultist Helena Blavatsky wrote "Our age is a paradoxical anomaly. It is preeminently materialistic and as preeminently pietistic."[3] That clash between the two, intensified over the last century, now threatens to blight our future. Clearly, so much in this world is so unfair, unjust and, one might even say, unforgivable that we are almost forced to give up trying to make sense of the 'why' of it. Often, the 'why not' seems more appropriate to the vagaries of life.

The scriptures might say 'it is all in the mind', and science might say that it is the undue agitation of some specific parts of the brain, but the daily reality is that we are confronted by perplexes that seem hopeless, vexed by ills and crushed by wrongs that we can barely perceive or prevent, forces we can scarcely comprehend or control. We often get a gnawing sense that we are surrounded by, in the words of William Wordsworth, "the fleet waters of a drowning world"[4] and that, tormented, many feel they "have no rightful way to live."[5] No rightful way to live and no place to escape to from the ruthless ritual of life. A huge chunk of humanity is afflicted with a sinking sense of visceral emptiness, a volcanic void deep inside and no help appears within reach from any quarter. Suffering, either 'deep, unspeakable ', in the words of George Eliot, or as chronic and low-grade, is what defines and unites much of mankind. The feeling that 'no one cares', or even that someone is inwardly gleeful at our suffering, causes disillusionment and bitterness, much like an inmate of a concentration camp who, on his release, discovers that no one awaited him or really missed him. But *suffering*, as the Buddha told us, is the central fact of human life and it is its denial that causes more suffering.

After thousands of years of contemplation, reflection, analysis, evocation, and spiritual seeking, of 'rationally' ruminating over the most profound problems of identity, life, and afterlife, and despite our greater understanding of the 'micro-behavior' of Nature, man still finds himself at war, within and without, nowhere near the shores of sanity, safety or stability, none the better or wiser for the effort. The real 'problem' we are trying to fix is *us*, all of us. What man does not understand, and cannot come to grips with, is his own 'behavior', rather his misbehavior; his deportment, rather his depravity. He seems more able to tame the turbulence of the elements but not the sway of his senses. And every man is in conflict with another man for material gain and divine favor. Whenever we try to free our lives from circumstances and constraints that hurt and limit us, we inevitably create others of the same or of a more abstruse order that shackle us tighter.

New knowledge reveals new mysteries. Every 'solution' seems to contain the seeds of another problem because both are filtered through the same sieve: the human mind. As a sequel we appear afloat and adrift, rootless and rudderless, not sure which path to tread or what to do for that mercurial and much-sought-after 'peace of mind'. Mindful that we are equally the children of the earth and the sky, the sun and the moon, air and water, dust and darkness, and that order in human affairs is intertwined with oneness of life, many a thoughtful person is searching for a symbiotic synergy between man and Nature, and between God and man, as a way to move forward. Restive but with reverence, they yearn to experience the ecstasy of resonance with the rhythms of empty space, to savor the silken whisper of fragrance of the wind and of the rumblings of the rafting rivulet as a way to the divine. Such wistfulness is also a part of a larger, and deeper, longing for self-transcendence, a hunger for a comforting shoulder, a quickening quest for 'meaning' that has endured all through history, cutting across all cultures and civilizations, myth, magic, and mythology.

Still, too many of us live in a fractured state of doubt, dismay, dread and denial, afraid of what the morning might bring to our kith and kin and what we might see in the mirror of our soul that might haunt us. Theories abound, but we really are unawake why so much of our existence is so disagreeable, distasteful, and destructive. We know a lot more of what matters in life than we are prepared to do what it takes to make it matter. We want to prevail; we want to succeed; we want to 'progress'. What we have achieved since the twentieth century is what British author F.J.P. Veale famously called 'advance to barbarism'; the savagery of a Genghis Khan'. What we do not want at any cost is being called a 'loser'. Indeed the most unwelcome putdown, the dreaded name-calling, worse than being called a rogue or rascal, is the use of that 'L' word. We are getting tired not of evil but of being good, not of greed but of

God. The cause, pundits tell us, is because our mental capacity for moral imagination or indignation, evolved through Darwinian 'natural selection', is not able to cope with the pressures and temptations of modern life. Man's very sense of the divine has increasingly become a reckless thought, propelling us to do things we would not otherwise do. Much of mankind, turning ancient wisdom upside down, has convinced itself that it does not pay to be caring, considerate and compassionate except to the shrinking circle of 'the near and dear'. Such is the state of 'quiet desperation', to borrow a phrase from Henry David Thoreau, that, exhausted with what existence entails we pine for a quick getaway to the safe shadow of a 'green mansion', to somehow end it all, no matter if it means suicide or homicide. The promise of our genius, the premise of our genus, is converted into a toxic peril.

The immediate task is to turn back that peril into a promise, even if it is paradoxical. We must explore how to become more fully human and still be saved from the fate of being merely human. Or put differently, inject humaneness into everything human. The challenge is prodigious and we must remember that out of any deep agony can spring enchanting ecstasy and that any in-depth inquiry, like any inquest, might show up surprises that might not always tally with the expected intent. Yet we must bring to bear the audacity of unvanquished courage and steel ourselves to face the strangest, most unusual, most inexplicable experiences that might come our way. But the reckoning must be right, the coordinates correct and the goal crystal clear. And we must not fight shy of reviewing the most basic of all, our hallowed assumptions about the nature of reality, of human worth and human way of life. While there could be many intermediate stops on the journey, the finishing line has to be to "consciously reinvent the human as a dimension of the emergent universe"[6] and evolve into a mode of being, a form of life, in which we are deeply able to feel in our bones a cascading compassion and responsibility for all of life. Nothing less would do either to save man or the world. We need a new 'moral fire' within to propel us to unveil a fuller and kinder model of human essence that brings man closer to another man and thus to God. That is the trembling task; this is the convulsive challenge and the chaste choice that lays before Man — the queerest creature of all on earth that walks on two legs, to paraphrase G.K. Chesterton (*The Everlasting Man*, 1925).

So much of our life is a show and style, sound and fury, grounded on pride and pretence, vanity and venality, that if we were to go anywhere in our age-old aspiration to make life more luminous than the daily grind of drudgery and drift, we must be prepared to be more skeletal and more candid in our confessions about the true nature of our innermost thoughts, dark passions and deep feelings, and be prepared to explore the more obscure and frightening reaches of our souls. For what comes under the rubric of 'human way of life' has had its mixed moment on earth; and the moment is now to invent a new framework for and a frame of reference of living. It means letting go many things that have become almost 'living' parts of our organic life and which give us such a soothing sense of smug but sterile satisfaction. It also means, at once, to let go a huge chunk of us at the core, to renounce many trappings of modern life and to let something unknown, something still wrapped in the veils of virginity, to emerge from the womb of our being. We need to reappraise and reconfigure concepts like 'progress', 'success' and 'goodness', as we have come to instinctively understand them.

It is not to abandon or to turn the clock of history back. We need 'progress'; otherwise life becomes a zero-sum game. We need 'success'; otherwise we will lapse into inertia. The world needs 'good persons' if only to prove that human behavior is not beyond reform. But simply the status quo is untenable; it does no good to anyone, not to man or Nature or even to God. One of the little-noticed facts of evolution is that the environment of human habitation is changing so fast that it is outpacing the ability of the human organism to adapt. A new field of science called *epigenetics* is showing that the environment we are polluting and the lifestyle choices we routinely make, and our reflexive addictions to violence and to 'good life' can not only mar our lives but influence our very genetic code — and, ominously, that of the next generation (*Why Genes Are Not Destiny*; Time, 18 January 2010). In other words, our life is not the business of us alone; the way we go on with our daily activities, the myriad choices we make, whether volitionally or by default, carry consequences not only for us but for the very future survival and sustainability of the human race. If this 'finding' were further corroborated, it would cast on us an awesome responsibility, and to fulfill that we have to add a new dimension to how we spend every minute of our life.

While there is lot of levity and lasciviousness in contemporary life, there is also a simmering sentiment for an undefined 'something' lofty and elevating, a gnawing disquiet at what human life has come to be, burdened with a motley blend of helplessness and hope, apprehension and aspiration, of angst and anticipation. With all our incisive insights into how life began and the world works, human nature remains enigmatic, human personality problematic, human behavior erratic, and human destiny clouded. And man has become what one might describe as self-righteously self-destructive and guiltlessly, almost flippantly, murderous. Even more than God, man is the mystery wrapped in a riddle. The theosophist Alexander Wilder, a contemporary of Blavatsky, wrote that the problem of life is man. Ana Maria O'Neill, the Puerto Rican writer (*Ethics for the Atomic Age*, 1948) wrote that once man is put together, everything else will fall into place. The big question is, when is that 'once' going to be? Meanwhile, practically every institution man has 'put together' (with what Freeman Dyson calls 'ape-brain' and 'tool-making hands') — family to society, marriage to marketplace, City-State to Nation-State — has largely failed to measure up to its intent to make the whole more than the sum of the parts, and to provide us the space for self-fulfillment without impeding others. Human culture, which is what we assume strikingly distinguishes us from other species, has not found the *modus operandi* to harmonize the human, as a solitary being and a social being; and as a social being and a spiritual being. We are unable to harmonize externally because there is no harmony internally. The human mind is a good 'advocate' but a poor 'judge'; it is good at espousing causes, not at ensuring that that cause serves the overall good. As a result, to paraphrase H.G. Wells (*Mind at the End of its Tether*, 1945), a harsh queerness is coming into things human. So many horrific things happen with such banality and repetitiveness in our lives that our mind is benumbed. In our thirst for excitement and entertainment, the horrible breaks the tedium, the awful makes boredom more bearable and a day is deemed barren without an atrocity perpetrated by one of *us*. So much dirt, grime, and mildew has accumulated on the human slate, that we must wipe it crystal clear to even look at ourselves as we are, which means cleansing ourselves since we too are on the slate; indeed we *are* the slate, and the dirt and the chalk are nothing but us.

It is not only the individual that needs deep cleansing. Our collective soul needs it too. Our way of life has made human society into a conglomeration of competitive entities, each one trying to expand its 'sphere of influence' and power and control. That stems from our obsession with comparison. Nothing in life is valued for its own sake; but only in the context of someone else having it or not having it or wanting it. Man's much-flaunted faculties of freedom and freewill — 'the right to live as we wish' (Epictetus) — have not given him either security or stability, or freedom from fear. Indeed it is fear that frames much of our tenure on earth — fear of old age, of illness, of bereavement, of accident, of loss of livelihood, of the Grim Reaper's inexorable entry. We 'fear'— or 'favor' — many things not for their own sake but for their expected consequences. And, following the advice of the Italian philosopher Machiavelli to rulers, we would rather be feared than be loved, we are enthralled by the illusion of a mastered destiny but, as individuals, we are laid waste and haunted by the fear of the future.

Nor has the freedom of choice in our elevated awareness of 'good' and 'evil' — a special gift of God — helped us to lead moral lives that add value to other's lives. It is a harsh verdict, but our sense of the divine down the ages has not helped much, if any, in our moral progress. Nor has allegiance to theism or agnosticism or atheism made any difference. That is because we do not have in the deepest depths of our being what it takes to use that awareness wisely or to simply be able to see, as the philosopher Immanuel Kant noted, the good only in goodwill, or the bad only in actions, not as a person. Or, more ominously, as the Grand Inquisitor in Fyodor Dostoevsky's *The Brothers Karamazov* (1880) upbraids the returning Jesus, and thunders: are freedom and free choice too burdensome for humanity? They are burdensome because in bestowing us, by endowing us with them, God has pretty much turned himself, in Julian Huxley's phrase, into a smiling Cheshire cat, pretty much leaving us alone to fight our own inner battles.

And in choosing, we must discard something we cling to like our skin, like the belief in our irreplaceability and the invincibility of our intellect. Greedy as we are, we want choice without choosing; we want to feel the miraculous without miracle, order without authority, God without religion, or religion without revelation. However crushing free will is, all history tells us two things: that tyranny in the guise of security has not stilled the human spirit; and deep inside lurks a tyrant in every human. In that quandary, face to face with what free spirit, free speech and unfettered action have entailed, man today seems willing to experiment with anything that proffers to save him from himself, from euphoria-inducing drugs to 'sacred' self-annihilation. He talks of a 'spiritual' path as the way forward, but since that means giving up much of what he has become, he therefore contents himself with being a 'spiritual tourist' rather than a steadfast seeker.

Whether as a 'tourist' or an 'immigrant' or a 'seeker', what we really want is a future without worry and want. Although a much-used phrase, we are ambivalent about 'future': deep inside we cannot relate to that which is so hazy and we cannot, in our vision, go beyond our 'own world'. As for anything beyond that, be it humankind or the earth, even our imagination falters. That is why, despite an avalanche of scientific 'evidence', we cannot bring ourselves to believe that anything can truly endanger the earth. The present generation of mankind is going through a tumultuous period of apocalyptic danger and epochal opportunity, of abysmal moral decadence and seething spiritual renaissance. Bound and bare, naked in our vulnerability, we live; we wander in the wasteland of the wanton world, laden with meaningless chores and multiple 'duties'. But, as J.R.R. Tolkien said, not all who wander are lost; but *we* are lost, the present crop of men that inhabit the world. T.S. Eliot's description of the modern man as 'hollow man', as a stuffed man, appears apt at this juncture. In becoming modern or post-modern, the bedrock of which is 'rationality', man has discovered the world but lost himself in the labyrinths of life. An issue that has for long been the subject of animated debate is whether our moral capacity is contingent on reasoning or religion, intelligence or intuition. Many people simply assume that morality comes from God, crafted during creation or implanted in our mind by religion. Some say that our brain contains unconscious biases that explain our moral behavior. Some others have argued that reason is not enough and that we have to reckon with what Aristotle called *akrasia*, weakness of will, that knowing is not the same as doing. The human spirit has become 'helplessly cold', hopelessly led astray by avarice, ill-will and evil. Self-absorbed on this long trail, we have forgotten that the Spirit or the Self in all is one, that we are a part not only of a colossal cosmic context but also of an unimaginably bigger process of creation — and that we have a role and responsibility in that adventure.

The root cause is that the physiological state of man has shifted from an abundant reliance on the sacred and the supernatural, and intuition (sometimes described as 'spontaneous-cum-reflected judgment' or as direct vision or pure perception of Truth), to an almost absolute obeisance to logic, reason, and the laws of science, which we have come to view as emancipators and liberators of mankind. What has been called by the 20th century Russian-American philosopher Ayn Rand 'ethical egoism' and 'rational selfishness' has not created the harmonious human, nor has it allowed the spiritual side to surface. We have developed a mindset that disconnects many things that need to be connected; for example, passion and compassion, prayer and piety, conscience and conduct, belief and behavior, power and forbearance. One of the greatest intellectual and moral crises of our age, one with enormous practical implications, is the fact that most people simply do not believe that there are any universal principles of ethical conduct, or moral imperatives of right and wrong, or, if there are any such principles, that we can know them well enough to induce generic adherence. With growing skepticism about any ecumenical and theological basis to life, the only universal norm appears to be to contend and conspire against one another for 'comparative advantage' of the competitive crumbs of crass consumerism, for the remains of the ruins of a 'good life'. We want liberty and love, freedom and fortune, health and happiness — all of them more than someone or everyone else. None of them has any value in isolation from the opposite and from that of another person. Everything abominable is now honorable under the given circumstances; no atrocity is beyond human depravity; all legitimacy is contextual; and nothing is ruled out for personal gain or to seek divine favor; there are no more any moral or ethical thresholds that one trembles to cross. Human self-righteousness is rivaled only by human fallibility; unrighteousness by condescension; insensitivity by intolerance. And may we pause for a moment to ponder — more horror has been committed throughout human history by self-righteous men, religious or otherwise, than by men we condemn as 'evil'. Were there to be no more morrows for mankind and a monument erected in its melancholic memory, a large chunk of its dark side will be written dipped in the blood let loose by these men.

Unwilling or unable to own up our responsibility or face the consequences of our actions, we moan 'Oh, God!' and ask, 'what does He truly want from us?' And 'why does He not do *something*?' And then there are those like Winston Churchill, a man of war for much of his life, who, in the waning years of his eventful life, wondered, in his farewell speech to the House of Commons (1955), what would happen "if God wearied of mankind."[7] In the great Indian epic Mahabharata, its chronicler, the sage Vyasa, himself deemed a divine *amsa* or a spark, asks a haunting question that goes to the heart of the human malaise, which echoes unanswered down the ages. He laments that no one listens to him when he espouses the importance of *dharma* (moral conduct), and asks, when man can get virtually everything he aspires in life — *artha* (wealth) and *kama* (all worldly wants) and *moksha* (final liberation) — through righteousness, "why then should any one fail to follow *dharma*?"[8]

It was not only sages like Vyasa who are not listened to. No one listens to anyone, and one of the crying needs of the hour is to be heard with sensitivity, not necessarily when one desperately needs help, but as a human soul yearning for attention. As the stoic Greek philosopher Epictetus said, 'Nature has given us two ears and one mouth so that we can listen twice as much as we speak'. We speak with multiple mouths while being seemingly devoid of ears. We end up doing things we do not want to, manipulated as if by a malevolent force. Apostle Paul, one of the greatest and earliest Christian missionaries and the author of several epistles incorporated into the New Testament, spoke, as it were, for all of mankind: "I do not understand what I do. For what I want to do I do not do, but what I hate I do."[9] The two questions or laments, Churchill's and Vyasa's, reinforced by the wrenching 'reflection' of St. Paul, are the central points of reference — the deepening moral decadence, the gap between belief and behavior, and the potential divine displeasure — that frame this introspective inquest.

We may be barely cognizant of its contours but something utterly awesome, something seminal and seismic has happened — and is happening, even as we blink — at the very core of our being, and at the deepest depths of human consciousness. It relates to the most fundamental issues of birth, life, living, dying, and death. We can only surmise about the state of divine 'weariness' about man, but the fact is that man himself is getting weary of his own tenuous and tiresome existence, weary of the kind of things he has to do just to be counted among the living, weary of the pain, sorrow, and the loss of personal dignity that seem so irrevocably embedded in the ethos of contemporary life.

Perhaps we are already, without our knowing, in a state of collective 'posthumous life' as a prelude to a post-human future, a kind of 'living dead' trying to survive the materialistic apocalypse. We have 'controlled' birth to suit our convenience; we 'love' or hate life, without knowing what it means; we dread 'living' but still do everything possible to prolong that 'dread'; we detest death, yet deep inside, long for its embrace to make up for what we seem to miss in life. And yet paradoxically nothing for the human is as unsettling as dying. The irony and tragedy is that while man craves for certainties in life, he wants to change the only certainty, death. And this despite what the Scriptures tell us that death is similar to the transition from the dream state to the waking state or, as described in Tibetan Buddhism, waking 'from the dream state of having lived'. While we envy the gods for their immortality, the gods, it is said, envy our mortality. But we want to give up our only 'comparative advantage' and get prolonged misery in return.

But death, even after mastering man, is not 'living on its laurels'. It too, for want of a better word, is 'evolving' inside our consciousness in a way that defies our capacity for comprehension, our ability to put that 'development' in the perspective of the overall balance and continuum of life on earth. We seem infected with some kind of a 'death-wish disorder', which is to wish our own death by taking other people's lives and inviting a death sentence. We have no inkling if this urge is to escape from the agony and anguish of life or Nature's way of getting back at man for all the insults he has heaped upon it. The irony is that while we do everything possible — and seemingly impossible — to ward off death, we are now turning to death itself as the panacea for all our life's ills, to find redemption from the 'inhuman' world, to 'lighten' its crushing heaviness, and to settle earthly scores. It is through killing that we are trying to circumvent or overcome every human predicament: disappointment, disagreement, or unfulfilled demand.

Our mind has grasped that no one can touch us beyond death; that no human being, once dead, can do us any harm. Many are choosing to voluntarily leave the ranks of what Christopher Isherwood called 'the marvelous minority — the Living', and join the majority — the Dead. So reflexive has this 'disorder' become that it is almost impossible to anticipate what one should not say or do to another person to ensure that it will not provoke suicide or homicide or, increasingly, a cocktail of the two. Death in that sense is not snuffing out a life; it is simply 'problem-solving'. Human self-centeredness and malevolence have become so pervasive that self-destruction and suicide as a source of permanent settlement to life's temporary problems seems to have attained 'criticality' in our lifetime, and suicide has become "nothing short of a pandemic of global proportions"[10]. It seems far deeper than a desperate cry for help or a fevered response to the growing, almost intolerable, stress and strain of modern life; it seems to have something to do with a still unknown, mysterious evolutionary imperative.

More and more people across the spectrum of gender, age, ethnicity and religion have come to believe that the only dignified way to cope with pain, grief, suffering, sorrow and even pedestrian disappointment is not by erasing the cause but by removing themselves from the very world that creates the 'cause'. Murder is not lagging all that far behind; our reluctance to kill — for revenge, profit, release from stress, pleasure, fun, or gain — has dramatically faded and we are ever inventing new 'rational reasons' to eliminate each other. What is shocking is not the numbers of those who kill themselves and/or kill others, but the utter ordinariness of the triggers and casualness of causes; it seems as if everything and anything man is capable of thinking, feeling and doing can result in one of the two or even both. Fundamentally they are seen, rationally and emotionally, as an 'honorable' option in problem-solving and conflict-resolution. The boundaries between murder and martyrdom, suicide and salvation are blurring, leaving us with no yardstick for any moral judgment.

Mass murder is getting justified as a 'just war' and mass suicide, which is what our assault on biodiversity amounts to, is legitimized as the 'price of progress.'

While much attention is focused on the politically or religiously motivated 'suicide terrorism', the more important point that the human mind itself has become a tool of terror, whose epiphany is self-destruction, as a way to cope with the inanities and inequities of modern life, is largely lost sight of. While we tend to think of terror as a tool of the 'terrorist' or of the State or something like blowing up a bus or a plane, the fact of the matter is that it is much closer home; indeed *we* are the home; almost everyone is a perpetrator and a victim. Terror is a weapon of the mind; the aim is dominance, power, and control, and there is hardly anyone who does not utilize them to the detriment of someone else. Someone or the other is terrified of us; and we are terrified of someone or the other. Our growing propensity to embrace death as a refuge from life's indignities and insecurities signifies not only a profound and lethal transformation in the internal psychological balance of the human persona, it raises the chilling question if we, in so doing, are somehow furthering a mysterious cosmic cause, a divine purpose. Could it be a way to maintain a kind of life-balance on earth? Clearly something so basic and causal to life — and creation — cannot 'just happen' without evolutionary implications.

What we do know, though, is that the human personality, perhaps more than ever before, is now driven by what goes on inside its head. The human mind, with a dimension of depth matchless in the universe, is the predominant force in the human consciousness as well as the epicenter of all the torment and turmoil in the world. It is a temperate habitat for some of our most virulent and violent passions, our darkest desires. Worse, too often, what we desire, far from being autonomous, is in the context of what another person desires of the same object. If two persons want something, the third wants, and the fourth, and so on; it then spreads like an infection. In that sense, desire is an imitation, an infection. It is a triangular equation — the subject, the object, and the desire to be. As René Girard noted, 'all desire is a desire to be'. That leads to conflict and confrontation, unleashing other desires.

While we talk of a multitude of freedoms and liberations, we ignore the most basic of them all: emancipation of the mind or rather, of consciousness from the grip of the mind. We talk of change but sidestep the most fundamental of all changes: that of consciousness. The expression 'sick and tired of life' is far more commonplace than being 'in love with life', regardless of age, race, religion, gender or culture. Human ambition has long struggled to make some objective sense of the human subject, not merely the sensory or thinking subject, but the feeling, living human persona. That struggle only deepened as man fashioned a culture, a society, and a way of life distinct from his fellow animals, a self-professed distinctness that has become a moral cover for inflicting soul-stirring cruelty on animals. As Chesterton said, the more we look at man as an animal, the less he will look like one. It is so ingrained now, that life as we know it is almost unthinkable if that distinction is erased. It is a reckoning that, some day, will come, for all mankind. At its deepest depth, the malaise of man stems from, in the words of the philosopher Owen Barfield (*Saving the Appearances: A Study in Idolatry*, 1965), our "inveterate habit of experiencing matter devoid of spirit, and consequently of conceiving spirit as less real, and finally as altogether unreal."[11] Bewildered by the 'real of the real' and the 'unreal of the unreal', that 'habit' has turned into a tumor of hate.

Stanford professor and author of *Science and Human Transformation* (1997), William Tiller wrote: "we have to recognize that there is a metastasized cancer in the body of man. If humankind is to survive, we have to deal with that metastasized cancer. We have to cut out the parts that need to be cut out, in a surgical way. We have to heal the parts that can't be cut out."[12] We cannot harbor hatred in our hearts and expect the world to exist in rhythmic harmony. As for our nexus with Nature, to paraphrase the Scottish poet Robert Burns (*To A Mouse*, 1786), man's dominion has broken Nature's social union, severely testing Nature's renowned resilience. We have forgotten that to be 'controlled', Nature must be obeyed, as pointed out by Francis Bacon, acclaimed as the 'father of science'. The price of 'defiant control' can be exacting. We cannot make crooked choices and hope that baneful consequences will pass us by in innocence. We cannot keep doing the same thing over and over again and just hope that the next time things will be different.

Topping the inventory of our angst is the problem of — and with — God. Our relationship with God, by far the most important of all, and the only one that is not inherently constrictive, is dysfunctional; all the things we do in the 'name of God' just do not add up; if any, they negate each other; a kind of a zero-sum game. He is on everyone's lips but in no one's heart; His utility, a perpetual parachute; our devotion, a cry of desperation. Globalization, it has been said, is good for the gods and there are more places of worship, for example in India, than schools or hospitals. Yet, most people feel 'let down' or 'forsaken' by God as if He is beholden and bound to us. Adding a new dimension to our search for God, science is looking for a 'God gene' (VMAT2) that predisposes us to believe in God, and a 'particle' in physics — what physicist Leon Lederman called the 'God particle' — which, so they tell us, transforms the intangible into the tangible and makes life possible.

While some are worried about the experiment going horribly awry, the more important question is how it might influence the great battle between good and evil. Not simply with the divine, our relationship with fellow humans too is in tatters. With all our 'culture' and structures of cohabitation we do not 'relate' to each other in any sense of synergy. We 'interpret' each other, not always by or of the person directly affected. Someone 'interprets' something — scripture, statute, law, language, word, even behavior — and someone else loses liberty and life, indicted and incarcerated, and is subjected to pain and suffering. Indeed much of the interpersonal strife and social and religious violence stems from intermediation and interpretation, from being 'processed' and 'packaged', made suitable for our ingestion and intelligence.

Our breathtaking diversity, the tapestry of our plurality, has become an orchestra out of tune, a debilitating drag on human ripening. We are unable to preserve specificity and at the same time, subordinate it to overriding unity. In the event, the fulfillment of every individual aspiration is chipping away at generic good, and the interests of the smaller unit — individual, family, community, nation — has come to overshadow that of the larger and bigger unit of humankind. Starved of any sense of significance, many people deem their lives as drudgery devoid of delight, feel abandoned and not wanted. Deep in their hearts they believe that, in the words of the Czech playwright Vaclav Havel, their lot is a 'diabolical trap set by destiny'. Maybe we too are like the mythical Greek King Sisyphus, condemned to an eternity of labor and turmoil for our unspecified but ubiquitous crimes against the gods! And it will possibly end only when we cleanse and transform ourselves inside out.

Almost everyone is discontented and disenchanted; as a reflex and rebound, everyone wants more of everything beyond what one can either use or consume; or even discard because, we fear, someone else might use it! Bitten by the bug of 'ownership' all the way from another person to another planet, possessing more than he needs, acquiring more than he can keep, coveting what another person has or might want, such are the symptoms of modern man's malaise. Even death is no cure; we want to leave behind memories, memorials and property for progeny. Everyone wants to grab the 'good things of life' without doing any good to anyone. Dangling between nihilism and narcissism, between the fluid and the fixed, between free will and fate, between the longing for certainties and the inevitability of change, man today is meandering, caught in the web of what Goethe called the 'maddening maze'.

As Oscar Wilde quipped, the only temptation we cannot resist is temptation. We want to be rescued without getting lost, liberated without surrendering and sharing without sacrifice. Muddled in our mind, we stand in our own shadow and wail why it is dark. We seem overpowered by our ravenous maw and restless groin, and nothing gives greater pleasure than satiating the two. In our confusion about our real identity and irreplaceable essence, unable to transcend from the plateau of the individual to the platform of the universal, we try to label all that we cannot conceive as 'mystic' and in so doing, as the Danish philosopher Soren Kierkegaard noted, we negate ourselves.

In the scriptural context, individual identity is a beguiling chimera and the only authenticity is divinity within every being and in everything. To borrow the words from a George Harrison lyric, we hide behind a wall of illusion; never glimpse the Truth; then it is far too late (*Within you, without you*, The Beatles, 1967). But we behave as if the only truth is physical, and divinity, at best, is effervescent but external, to be envisioned, not experienced.

And 'culture', which includes the sacred, the secular and the profane in human thought, the signature of our social identity, some pundits predict, will soon replace ideology and economics as the new battlefield of barbarity and bloodletting. But that, truthfully, should not be too upsetting; for, to paraphrase Anna Akhmatova 'it loves blood; the human appetite'. That 'appetite' will forever be a part of our lust for life and we do not have within us what it takes to quench it. But what is already clear is that the compass and coordinates that man has so far relied upon to navigate the ocean of earthly life — family, religion, country, tradition, and values — are no longer apt for the human condition to find its full utterance. The line between religious and sacrilegious is thinning and we seem to be, even against our will, sliding down the moral slope. But we, as individuals, behave as if we have nothing to do with what awaits the species, that we owe nothing because we got nothing; and in any case, we mutter to ourselves, 'what can *we* do?'

That nonchalance and insensitivity comes from another paradox of human life. Man is, in the idiom of the French Nobel writer Alexis Carrel, both 'unity' and 'multiplicity' and the apparent tension between the two dimensions torments life. While multiplicity, diversity, and duality are the order in the cosmos, the principles of uniformity and linear continuity have been the dominant human intellectual aspirations. While our mission on earth is to harmonize *dwanda* or dualism, we strive to eliminate one of the two. That creates all our problems, for, as the *Brihadaranyaka* Upanishad points out, it is only through duality that we can relate to or understand each other. We can live with turmoil and terror, mayhem, and massacres in the world, but not any convulsion that disturbs the tenor and temper of our daily lives, much less any radical revisions in the style and substance, the content and character of our prosaic existence. What matters to us is not eternity or the fate of the world; it is the time and place of our daily presence. While the nature of Nature is turbulence and creative chaos, we crave for the stability of a stone, a life without worry or work, a ripple-less river, a wave-less ocean. While conflict is endemic to life, instead of turning it into creative force, we try to erase it. Yet chance and happenstance, fate and fortune — not choice and calibration — envelop our daily lives. It is the inherent unpredictability of individual lives that mocks at us. Roman philosopher and poet Horace (*Odes, I.9.13*) wrote, *Quid sit futurum cras, fuge quaerere* — do not ask what tomorrow brings. Indeed much as we might like it, knowing the future could be terrible; if it is rosy we will be complacent and stop striving, and if it is bleak we will go to pieces and even stop working, thinking it is of no use in any case. We lead such charmed lives that if even a few of the myriad things that happened in our lives had not happened or happened differently, we would almost be a different people. We crave for comprehensive predictability and uneventful gradualism, and smooth progression through life, but we do know that everything can crumble by an unexpected event, an illness, a death, an accident.

The best one can do, as another Roman philosopher, Cicero, advised, is to hope for the best, plan for the worst, and endure whatever shall be.

The problem is not only the fickleness of the future. It is also that we really do not know how a particular human personality develops, or predict how any one of us will react to a particular_circumstance, provocation or seduction. Random happenings far removed from the immediacy of our lives — wars, famines, climatic changes, accidents — could turn our lives upside down. We want to 'choose' and 'control' everything in every circumstance, from what we eat to whom we mate, what we buy to how we die. The unexpected, the unintended, the unpredictable, the chaotic are *constants* in our lives. No matter how much we want to orchestrate events, too often the result seems to depend on essentially independent factors that exist outside the context of the process under way. If the result is favorable, we call it good fortune; and if it is unwelcome, it becomes ill luck. Fate seems to delight in thwarting our carefully crafted designs to lead lives of perfect order, tranquility, peace, and prosperity. We want to fool fortune but we end up, in Shakespeare's phrase, as a 'fortune's fool'. Fate, it has been said, is beyond the control of gods and goddesses; it is the raw power of Nature that controls the ebb and flow of cosmic energy. Some say it hides in the deep cosmos; and some insist that it is in the depths of our subconscious.

The fact of the matter is that we seem at the mercy of so many factors and forces, pulls and passions, compulsions and constraints, that we cannot recognize the difference between what we do and what we *have to* do, much less what we *could* and what we *ought to* do. As Edwin Arnold (*The Light of Asia*, 1879) hauntingly puts it, "we are the voices of the wandering wind; which moan for rest and rest can never find; Lo! as the wind is, so is mortal life; a moan, a sigh, a sob, a storm, a strife."[13] We want to go home, after losing our way on the moot of life, but we do not know where and what our home is, and end up like the child in Emily Brontë's *Wuthering Heights* (1847), peering through the window on a stormy night and crying "Let me in, let me in!". We do not know what accounts for time's unidirectional flow, and if there are truly any 'times' save the present 'time'.

In the *Katha* Upanishad, the Hindu God of Death Yama asks Nachiketa, the embodiment of the eternal seeker: "What are a billion years compared to eternity? Not even a glimmer. Why, then, do we scramble after such short-lived earthly goals, goals that even if attained, prove to be worthless since they vanish away so quickly?"[14] Why, indeed! Perhaps we scramble after such earthly goals because they are the only ones our senses can grasp, our mind can relate to, and because they give the *appearance* of giving 'pleasure'. *Vedanta* says that everything in life is merely appearance; the world we experience is not the same as the atomic, physical universe. It is the mind that causes this delusion. It has become almost impossible to perceive which is the more dominant force — our mind, or our sensory sensations, or something still unknown. As a result, we seem almost pathologically powerless to alter our behavior even when we know that such behavior can be catastrophic. While we can see fairly clearly the probable consequences of our actions, we seem incapable of injecting those factors into our daily decisions. Our inexplicable paralysis to act upon the growing menace of violence so visible, and the corrosive coarseness of our conscience make us wonder if man has incurred the Cassandra Curse: 'we simply will not believe anyone will believe us' and so we refuse to believe ourselves, or believe that we can change our behavior. So we hibernate but hope; drift but dream of glory and greatness.

To let fall a tear for humanity

Dreams and destiny have their own dynamics, but, to paraphrase Shakespeare, (*Henry VIII*) this is a testing time in the life of our species — a time that bears a weighty and serious brow, full of scenes to draw the eye to flow, to let fall a tear. As a lyric goes, 'a simple tear within itself is the key that holds the secret to our humanity'. But few among us can spare a 'tear' for humanity because we do not innately and effortlessly feel connected to the amorphous entity of humanity. Although in the deepest and lonely depths of our hearts, the ultimate mystery of our existence rankles, there are many who find no problem in believing that human species surely is doomed, but that somehow they themselves would be saved! In the myriad things that constitute the mosaic of life, the most important things, the ones that cause most misery, have roots so simple, so obvious, and so familiar that we pass them by with barely a glance. They escape our attention because they are too close or too deep; right in front of us and inside us; resulting in our losing our way between the casual and the primal, the immediate and the important, the event and the eventuality. We find it hard to realize that the earth is not the lifeless ground under our feet, open to endless exploitation, a bottomless sink for the industrial civilization. We are increasingly incapable of perceiving her as the Mother, who carries us on her back, who steadies us when we stumble, and forgives us for all the indignities we heap on her. Most people do not care what happens to earth's plant and other animal species; they do not even care about their own species. Unconcerned about the consequences, we are depleting our natural stocks — water, hydrocarbons, forests, fish, rivers, and arable land — without a thought to recycling or replenishing. It is becoming clearer as every day passes that a warped understanding of the biosphere, the global ecological system that integrates all forms of life on earth, has much to do with the perilous state of the world. If we continue to contaminate the bed we sleep on, one day we will choke on our own waste. As the American ecotheologian Thomas Berry puts it, we have some sort of moral sense about suicide, homicide and genocide, but not of *biocide*, the killing of life supporting systems and ravaging of the earth itself.

At its very epicenter, the point where the seismic rupture begins, the issue boils down to this solitary truth: all through the labyrinthine path of evolution and despite our strong social predisposition, we have not managed to acquire any enduring sense of what we might call *species-hood*, the sense that we have something vital at stake, above all else, in the well-being of another person. We hardly give any weight simply because the 'thing' we are dealing with is not an ant or animal or angel but one of our own kind, made up of the same body, blood, brain, and nervous system. We have never managed to truly believe that we have a shared destiny on a crowded planet, and that coming together is better than standing apart, that another person's misfortune can be of no profit to us.

Instead, what we have is 'victimhood': everyone, even a scamp, thinks that he is a quarry, a stoic sufferer. It is a state of mind in which we don the garb of a champion of the oppressed while trampling on the down-and-out, dissociate ourselves from any responsibility for what happens to us or done by us. We do not seem to be accountable to anyone, feeling morally right in whatever we do, and we expect unquestioned sympathy for all the wrongs, real or imaginary, done to us. There are many fringe benefits of victimhood; and in the contemporary culture, new rewards are continuously being discovered. There are many villains out there but the real 'villain' lurks inside us: to divert our own minds, we simply look for an external enemy. Man has always viewed himself both as a master and a martyr, a chosen being and a scapegoat, and the mix comes out in myriad ways in everyday life.

Our long trail of evolution seems to have loaded us with some very hoary and many unsavory predispositions and traits, a hangover of the struggle for the survival of the fittest; of our hunter-gatherer past when having those 'negatives' conferred a reproductive and combative advantage over other species. Some biologists and anthropologists speculate that humans may well have a 'rape gene' or a 'killer gene', with strong roots in evolution tucked away in some corner of our consciousness. That does not deter us from laying claim to constitutional 'perfection', which shows up in such expressions as man is 'almost perfect', 'near perfect', 'potentially perfect'. We also say that the human has limitless potential, leaving the question unanswered as how something perfect can still have so much unfulfilled potential. To borrow a phrase from the American philosopher Reinhold Niebuhr, our eternal 'pilgrimage to perfection' will go on until we learn to turn that pilgrimage inwards.

Life is a stream of 'disharmonies', capable of no perfect way; no ideal 'perfection' in organic life can exist; no 'perfect' dieting, no 'perfect' mating no 'perfect' bliss, no 'perfect' conduct or character — and no idyllic human society. A partial being cannot be perfect; an unfinished product cannot be a masterpiece. From the biological point of view, individually we are a series of involuntary 'experiments' on the part of an imperfect species towards an uncertain end. Neither scripture nor spirituality, or even science, can change that truth, even if man becomes 'immortal', which some scientists like Ray Kurzweil say is as close as twenty years! We have not found a way to connect man as an autonomous unit of life (born apart, living separately, and dying alone), and as mutually enriching members of a common species with an indissolubly shared destiny. One of the claims that we often make for our greatness as a species is our capacity to conceive and create what we call 'civilization' and there is no attribute we cherish more than 'being civilized'. It is innate to every 'civilization' to lose its vision, vitality and inner energy and fall into a state more sordid than that of the savages. The world today, borrowing a phrase from D.H. Lawrence, is like "Augean stables with metallic filth". Lest it be forgotten, monstrosities like Nazism, as Polish sociologist Zygmunt Bauman reminds us, was not caused by the suspension of civilization, but were products of civilization. He argues that civilization, instead of making us moral, overcomes morality. We often think of 'being moral' or a 'good person' in negative terms; *not* violating a rule, law, canon or a code of the state or scripture.

More fundamentally, the essence of morality or goodness ought to be how we act with regard to other living beings, what we do to lighten the load of another person; whether we are able, even momentarily, to bring back a smile on a somber face. We humans are bred to believe that civilization is what separates modern society from our primitive past, and 'being civilized' is the highest acme of being human. What we actually experience, and what we call 'civilization' is, in its bare bones, a life suffused with the three 'C's — comfort, convenience and control — in hot pursuit of the three 'P's — pleasure, profit, and power. Such is their corrosive effect and corrupting influence that, as the American astronomer Carl Sagan noted, it makes us "wonder whether civilizations like ours rush inevitably into self-destruction."[15]

We are 'civilized', but find it difficult to be spontaneously 'civil' to each other. The paradox is that a particular society might have all the outward trappings of civilization, with great achievements in fields such as the arts and architecture, but its people pursue moral decadence as the mark of being civilized. Rome was a great civilization, but the Romans — behaving in the belief that they were the elite of the world and that enjoying the 'good things of life' was their earned right — were far from 'civilized', in the true sense of the word. In fact that was why Rome, like almost all others, collapsed; and some historians are saying that our modern civilization is showing the same star-crossed symptoms of decadence and arrogance. Philosopher Adam Ferguson wrote that "not only the individual advances from infancy to manhood, but the species itself from rudeness to civilization."[16] If *not* being rude is the standard, it is anyone's surmise how many in the contemporary world are 'civilized'. If 'being civilized' is treating others with respect and, as Robert Frost wrote, acceptance of eccentricity to the point of doubtful sanity, then most of us are uncivilized. And if treating Nature with civility is the test, then the or even the primitive was clearly more civilized.

Without the slightest trepidation we assume that the modern man is the most civilized. The only 'evidence' for this plaint premise is that we have no *evidence* that other civilized forms, perhaps even more culturally and technological advanced than ours, ever existed. Evidence is elastic, expansive. And while there is widespread scientific acceptance that man came from a simian, there are many scholars and theosophists and occultists who say that there is a high probability that civilizations far greater than ours thrived in our ancient past, and that men then were not ape-like but 'god-like', both in body and spirit. That might explain why some, if not all, of the profoundest of insights, philosophies, and revelations that human genius has given birth to, were of hoary antiquity. They could not have been the imaginations or hallucinations of 'advanced apes' or brawny barbarians. With all our great achievements in the arts and the sciences, contemporary civilization almost seems chronically incapable of producing men and women of high imagination and soaring spirituality. It might be partly because our heroes and role models, the ones we admire and want to emulate, are men of muscle, women of bodily beauty, sportspersons and movie stars. Almost like a self-fulfilling prophecy, we lament that ours is an age of mediocrity, mechanization, and moral laxity. And such men prefer to go with the flow of the time.

That 'flow' that man is floating in is closely identified with the emergence of the machine as inseparably intertwined with human life. Man today is perhaps more 'mechanized' than 'civilized', and there is almost nothing man can any longer do now with bare hands — from cooking to cleansing, eating to entertainment, walking to 'making love'. That mechanization is not confined to gadgets and appliances for use by or as supplement to the human hand; it is far deeper and extensive. Even more disturbing, there are predictions that machines with human-like intelligence might even outnumber carbon-based life forms, and that eventually humankind and machinery will fuse into one, something similar to what futurist Ray Kurzweil in his book *The Age of Spiritual Machines* (1999) called a 'Spiritual Machine', although one wonders why he chose to call them 'spiritual' when they are the very antithesis of what we normally understand as spiritual. Even if we discount the 'spiritual' aspect, there is no doubt that advances in artificial intelligence will profoundly impact on human consciousness and blur the boundary between machine and man. The scientific air is already thick with talk of human chip implants to improve our memory by enabling us to search our own memories like any other computer search engine. Of all the uncertainties that we face, perhaps the greatest and the most baffling is how technology is going to affect human *nature*.

The tragedy is that, though technology has given us the infrastructure for a heterogeneous but harmonized humanity and a platform for transforming competitive, national societies into an enlightened planetary civilization — instant communications, intermixing of people — the reality is that more walls are being built between man and man, and that humankind is more fractured and fractious than ever before. Ensconced behind walls, we communicate with each other through the mediation of technology. Technology is also the medium for man and his desires — what we desire and how we get what we desire. The Upanishads tell us that desires are so thickly overlaid with dark clouds that they prevent us from seeing what they really are. Desires are our most primal motivator and mediator; they are our destiny. We cannot run away from them, we can only turn them around and make them agents of change. St. Augustine said that we wonder at the 'wonders of Nature' but pass by ourselves without even wondering about ourselves, the wonder of wonders.

Whether we are actually a 'wonder' in any positive sense is another matter. But that is only just one of the plethora of paradoxes, ironies, asymmetries, and contrasts that underlie the human condition. The paradox that has bedeviled human life most of all is that man is part of Nature and yet has demonstrated the ability to transcend Nature; but in so doing he has disturbed the equilibrium and balance of Nature. Another paradox is that he is ephemeral and finite, and yet a spark of the eternal and Infinite dwells in him, while he spends all his life unaware and unmindful of it. Man has long labored under the tension between the subjective (*I am*) and the objective (*it is*), and between being an autonomous individual and the reality of his desperate dependence. No one could be quite sure what any human being would do or would not at any given point of time or at different times. We have no clue as to what makes us behave the way we do. Evolution itself is paradoxical, so is life. But paradox is not necessarily negative or always inimical; it could be positive, a powerful engine of creativity and innovation. However, the way it has matured and impacts human life, it has turned into a mortal peril. It has been said by saints and philosophers alike that in creating man, God has given him the unique power to fashion himself into whatever he wants, power to degrade himself into the lowest forms of life, or rise up, with intellect and discriminating capacity, to the highest forms, beyond the realm of the human.

Another anomaly that mocks at human capacity for rational thought is mankind's eternal search for eternal life, while inventing every day new ways to shorten each other's lives. Much of his life is spent in erecting barriers to death, and at the same time man embraces death for as many reasons as his intellect can conceive. While man dreams of immortality — which he misconstrues as making the material physical body (or rather the body bolstered by machine) perpetual on earth and to transport it to other worlds — what he gets, as a verse in the Upanishads puts it, is 'death after death'. While all life is subject to decay and dissolution, he craves for illusory continuity. And all through life, he suffers in varying degrees of intensity until the dreaded hour strikes, none the wiser as to where he came from, why he has to die, and where he is heading to. In the Mahabharata (*Santi Parva*), it is said that there is only one foe of man, and not another; that foe is identifiable with ignorance. In ignorance man enters this world, in ignorance he exists, and in ignorance he exits. We are ignorant if birth is a blessing or a curse, if a baby is a better 'human' than an adult; and if death is deliverance or a prelude to punishment, and how best to use the interval; whether to make merry while the money lasts, or do penance for the sins of our species while the body is decaying. We know neither how to live and let live, nor how to die in dignity. Indeed we live as if we will never die, and die as if we never lived. We exult at the dawn of spring, unmindful of the fact that as the seasons smile our life ebbs.

At the core of our unrest and quest is self-definition; the yen for identity is timeless, and now, topical, it is both defining and destabilizing the ebb and flow of our life. Every color of collective identity— ethnicity, race, age, language, gender, and nationality — has become a 'bone of contention', a reason for rancor, a headwater of hate and a backwater of blood. So much blood has been spilt on earth through human actions for millenniums, to discern, to protect, and further one's place under the sun and one's particularity as a person and as a people, that it is a mystery why earth has not turned red and all crop beetroot. While Hitler was an extreme example, all of us are ruthless when it comes to *lebensraum*, 'living space, land and resources'. Distinctiveness has come to mean divisiveness. All life, and individual identity and personal worth and value have come to be negation, not being another person, not belonging to another faith or nation and so on. Negation can, in spiritual terms lead to the Upanishadic maxim *neti, neti* ('not this, not this') as a way to define the core of our soul, or it can become, as it has in the contemporary world, a springboard to selfishness.

We must draw a distinction between 'Non-Being' and '*not* being'. The former is a state of ontological differentiation between two beings; the latter is a state of assertion by exclusion, denial of any other identity. The Buddha said enlightenment is the ending of identification. It is in fact an echo of the central theme of an ancient spiritual text, *Ashtavakra Gita*, which some scholars think is as lofty and topical as the more famous Bhagavad Gita: If you detach the body and rest in intelligence you will at once be happy, peaceful, and free from bondage.[17] Some other translators use the word 'consciousness' instead of intelligence. An ancient Hindu text says that the *jiva* (individual soul) and *Shiva* (God) are one; when in bondage it is *jiva*, and *jiva* freed from bondage is *Shiva*. And when *Shiva* as *jiva* leaves the body, it becomes a *sava* (corpse).

Most of the time, we are a blend of all three, *jiva*, *Shiva*, and *sava*. What we do in daily life is fight the demons of different identities, personal, social, spiritual, obligatory, each at war with another, camouflaging our true essence, the *Shiva* inside, and draining all spiritual and psychic energy. We are all human collectively but, as the psychologist Carl Jung noted, each of us carries his own life-form — an indeterminable form which cannot be superseded by any other. The much-advertised process of 'globalization' has shrunk geography but widened the chasm between man and man, by making human interfacing optional to human existence. The evaporation of the historic delineations of territorial boundaries has not done anything to make the world a safer or a better place. The world is electronically interconnected, but humanity has never been more emotionally disconnected than at the morrow of this millennium.

Emotion, it has been said, has a vital spiritual function and is the language of the soul. Indeed, as Jung noted, emotion is the chief source of 'becoming conscious' and there can be no true transformation without an emotional undercurrent. Our muddled state of mind about our primary identity has also marginalized the most important human attribute, which philosophers like the Italian Renaissance mystic Giovanni Pico Della Mirandola have called the 'Dignity of Man'. While earlier our common interests were primary, now our private interests have become predominant. The best that we can internally mobilize towards another person is empathy, not a sense of sharing. That feeling of being separate has led to a feeling of superiority. That attitude over time has become a reflexive habit, a kind of cancerous response. It is not as though our identity of separateness is a modern phenomenon or a malaise of modernity. Our vision gets astigmatic and does not allow us to see the real as real, and the unreal as unreal. We think we live because we think we exist; we view the world as the actual because that is all what our senses can experience. But we 'experience' the experiences over and over, yet we become none the wiser or better. It defies logic; why, with our 'unique' reasoning and discriminatory capacity, we so often fail to build on our experiences.

The fact is that there is a fundamental disparity between the way we perceive the world, including our own experience in it, and the way things actually are. What is qualitatively different is that while earlier such a distorted vision of identity did not allow us to clearly see the spiritual path, it is now identified with existential nihilism. We prefer the cosmetic to content, appearance to essence, image to idea, and the symbol to that which it symbolizes. And, in moments of searing solitude, we echo Thomas Carlyle's plaintive cry (*Sartor Resartus*, 1831), "But whence? O Heaven, whither? Sense knows not; Faith knows not; only that it is through Mystery to Mystery, from God and to God."

Brooding on the Brink

And, compounding that wistful wail, our tangled and rancorous relation between faith and reason, belief and behavior has brought us to the edge of the abyss of annihilation. We lack the nerve to leap forward or lurch backwards. We are poised between a dying world and a world groping to be born. Sandwiched, appropriating the words of the father of science fiction H.G. Wells, a growing number feel that "there is no way out or round or through the impasse". In fact, such was Wells' sense of exasperation about the state of the human condition that, towards the end of his life, he wrote a book titled *Mind at the End of its Tether* (1945), in which he argued that it might not be such a bad idea if the human species were to be replaced by another species. Yet the great irony, and tragedy, is that, more than any generation before us, we, the bunch or cluster of humans of our time, command the resources for self-realization and species-upliftment. Man's very strengths and blessings — his ability to juxtapose and judge, extrapolate and analyze, put two and two together and make twenty-two, and his awareness of his past and the future — have, instead of erasing the sense of 'being separate' and the feeling of 'being different', become his terminal vulnerabilities.

The metaphor of a narrow abyss cleaving the face of the earth down to its core has long been used by theologians as well as philosophers and poets. John Milton wrote hauntingly in his classic poem *Paradise Lost* (1667) "O spirit… and with mighty wings outspread; Dove-like sat'st brooding on the vast abyss."[18] Man is afraid to leap forward and is fearful of going back, ceaselessly calling, shouting over shadows (and no one seems to care), he feels utterly helpless, afflicted with searing sorrow and ceaseless suffering. The problem is that the very things that give us joy also give us sorrow, the things that give us happiness also bring unhappiness. Man's fate resembles that of the rat on the wheel, the cheese always out of reach; man's fate is akin to that of a dreamer waking up and seeing on a stormy night a crying face on the window pane, kind of his own, only to wonder why. His realms of perception, appearance and manifestation seem ill-equipped to comprehend the true certitude of his predicament and pain, misery, and misfortune. Most people have enough empathy to sympathize with the misfortune of others, not enough fortitude to endure them own their own. All the sermons of the scriptures, words of wisdom, seem to be of no avail in empowering us through the passage of life.

We are alive on default mode, by the power of habit, waiting for the delivery of death. We must take risks we did not even dare to tread on before. The analogy of the abyss is also invoked by Nietzsche in describing the inherent dangers in the human quest for perfection. In his work *Thus Spake Zarathustra* (Prologue), he wrote that "man is a rope stretched between the beast and the *Overman* — a rope over an abyss". Nietzsche also wrote that "He who fights too long against dragons becomes a dragon himself"; and "if you gaze too long into the abyss, the abyss will gaze back into you". It is not a lone dragon but several that man is fighting: anger, malice, violence, money, lust, and greed, and in harboring them we are *becoming* them. Of them all, malice, the secret feeling of enjoying the other's misfortune, what the Germans call *schadenfreude*, is the ticking time bomb hidden in the human breast. A candle, it has been said, loses nothing of its light by lighting another candle; malice makes us put out our candle to keep our neighbor out of the glow. And unless we find a way to find the abyss and exorcize it, we will tumble into the abyss ourselves.

In pushing man to the edge, the dominance of economics in the melting pot of life has much to do. Economics, an inexact science in the eye of economists, has made man an insecure and unhappy being. Our economic behavior is but symptomatic of our overall behavior. In the present global financial crisis, what we must bear in mind is not merely an outcome of flawed macroeconomic management, but our inability to factor in the role played by emotions and psychology in economic decision-making, what John Maynard Keynes curiously called 'animal spirits', and not by the 'weighted average of quantitative benefits multiplied by quantitative probabilities'. Money is the *mania grandiose*, the overpowering passion of mankind. At this juncture, a prerequisite for *moksha* for man is liberation from money's hypnotic hold. To put it into perspective, without such liberation there cannot be any spiritual growth or transformation. Money is more than an addiction, more than a vice, more than an emotional comfort. It is one of the few, maybe the only thing that is trouble in whichever way you touch it: having, not having, having too much or too little.

If somehow money suddenly collapses or becomes worthless, it is hard to imagine if human society will hold. It is a huge stretch of hope if man could then go back to the pristine pre-money days and happily live forever thereafter, without the problems money has brought. Probably, he will be disoriented, not knowing how to spend a single minute or how to relate to another human. As of now, as Scottish historian Niall Ferguson puts it, money is 'not a thing' but the most valued 'relationship'. It is even claimed that money, more than technology, is what empowered man to surmount, in Edward Gibbon's words, 'the grossest barbarism.' The wheel has turned full circle, and today the money that matters is not what you can touch, feel or possess but the 'invisible' money; more precisely, it is not what we own but what we owe to others — the debt — that drives the world. Indebtedness creates and causes fear and erodes freedom. Indebtedness has always been a part of human culture and human history, and it can not only be economic or monetary, but also moral and spiritual. Nothing highlights morality — or rather the lack of it — more than our attitude towards money. Much of our muddled life is spent on 'making a living', which means making, maximizing, manipulating, and multiplying money.

Yet money has a legitimate place in human aspiration. It is how we earn, keep and spend money that makes the difference. In our obsession with earning, we are unable to keep our faith; in our deadening desire to amass wealth, we are undermining our integrity. Money is an essential part of life's balance sheet; in the myriad *givings* and *takings* of life, money is central. And since, as it is said, the only things we take beyond life are what we give in life, how we handle money is crucial not only to the quality of life but also to the shape of our afterlife.

Risks, change and transformation

Human nature is so complex and convoluted, multi-layered and multi-centered, that for long, debate has raged if humanity is better off through unfettered individual actions. The premise being that the very need for mutual survival, what Adam Smith called 'invisible hand', will compel peaceful exchange, and temper and self-correct any social excesses. Judging by the present state of the world, and the state of 'capitalism', it is now increasingly clear that the earth is too finite and fragile, and the collective needs of humankind are so interwoven that they cannot be left entirely to the natural impulses of human beings. Essentially, human life is subject to two colliding forces: constancy and change. Constancy comes in the form of repetitiveness; till death strikes, every day we do all the things necessary to be alive — eat, defecate, sleep; in that sense every day is a life by itself. Although we do not want to, we take 'risks' every day as part of the sheer act of living. Every minute, we make some choice or the other, and every choice has a consequence, and any choice can lead to uncertain and unwelcome outcomes. The Greek philosopher Herodotus said that great deeds are usually wrought at great risk, but we want great rewards *without* any risk.

Still, as a species, humanity has always lived under the shadow of some crisis or the other, from ambushing predatory animals, to epidemics and plagues, to genocides and world wars. These were deeply traumatic events that left scalding scars on human consciousness; but they were still in their impact only ripples, some tiny, some big in the ocean of life. Our perception of risks, the attendant lure of reward and fear of failure, and our cognitive processes to confront them have been shaped by the fact that all the risks we have had to face until recent times were of four kinds: routine, calculated, acceptable, and endurable. What we face now are risks of a different genre, so unlike anything that mankind has seen, that we are even incapable of apprehending these so-called 'existential risks', whose threats are so grave that even a tiny probability is unacceptable, and whose occurrence could cause our own early extinction or cripple all intelligent life on earth. The 'normal' extinction of a mammalian species on earth is believed to take about ten million years. *Homo sapiens* can therefore expect to last another nine million years[19], provided this 'hallowed' species does not act irresponsibly and self-destructively, provided it does not exercise its relatively new-found ability to manipulate the physical world towards a premature and apocalyptic end.

We are defenseless in our perception and preparedness because even our imagination cannot envision such risks, and our collective fear-response itself is ill-calibrated to that kind of peril. These risks are of a character for which the institutions we built, social norms we nurtured, and risk management tools we fashioned are ineffective, and indeed such instruments compound the very risks they are supposed to surmount. Let us also not forget that every risk offers an opportunity; they are two sides of the same coin. Existential risks offer evolutionary possibilities that might otherwise take much longer time to mature, or pose dangers that might well lead to our own premature passage. Cognizant that the world faces enormous risks that require concerted and coherent actions, the world is groping for ways to cope with them.

Consistent with our penchant to create an institution when we face any crisis, an independent organization called the *International Risk Governance Council* (IRGC) was established in 2003, whose objective is to help understand and manage emerging global risks. The fate of this too is likely to be no different from that of many others. Institutions are useful as they provide a process and a platform to address an issue but their efficacy and effectiveness depend on their *human* infrastructure. What is needed is a fundamental change in our mental and psychological faculties of risk perception, risk analysis, and risk aversion, so that every individual action contributes to meeting and mitigating the enormous challenges that humanity faces. Most of them, like climate change — perhaps the greatest crisis the world faces — are caused or aggravated by isolated human actions fuelled by different priorities, and their solution also lies in a basal change not only in what we do, but also how we do the ordinary things of life. There is enough evidence in human history, particularly in the past century, for us to recognize and take very seriously the fact that, as the Polish philosopher Leszek Kolakowski puts it, the Devil is part of our experience; it has found a cozy corner in our consciousness. And it does seem that the seed of the divine innate in us, designed to come to fruition and make man a god, is drying up, with the devil virtually standing unchallenged. And if evil exists in the world so that with the faculty of free will we can abjure it in favor of goodness, as Jewish mysticism hypothesized, we have belied that divine expectation by making evil our 'natural' choice.

But perhaps the greatest 'risk' humanity faces stems from a source embedded deep within: our consciousness and the way it has come to be. Although we are not conscious of it, our consciousness is the casualty of our culture and civilization. It is consciousness that makes us what and who we are, and differentiates us from other living beings. Almost everything we associate with human society — religion, education, recreation, money, market, the way we care for our very young and very old — is corruptive. Our 'way of life' has not found a way to stay connected with the divine within and still enable us to do our daily duties, the essence that is held in our scriptures and spiritualism. In practical terms, such a profoundly conscious approach, the essence of the scriptures and ancient wisdom, would mean putting the other person, his needs, his wants, and even his weaknesses, ahead of us, no matter what the circumstance — at once the easiest and the most difficult thing to do in real life.

Such is the stubborn strength of our mind-centered and malice-soaked consciousness that it has remained almost impervious to the preachings of the scriptures and the teachings of prophets like the Buddha, Christ, Mahavira, and Zoroaster. It is our consciousness that stands between them and us. Their very name evokes reverence in us but something holds us back from practicing what they exhorted us to do; and that is our consciousness. Periodically, we pay homage to them, and then, without even the slightest feeling of inconsistency or incompatibility, continue to plod on with our pettiness, perfidy, pride, vanity, malice, and malevolence; always trying to put someone else down with a disparaging word or a dismissive gesture, always trying to exploit every discomfiture to our selfish advantage, and leaving no stone unturned to throw stones at the weak and the vulnerable. What propels us is that very consciousness. The demon in us often shows up while dealing with the defenseless; we flaunt our manhood and valor against those who are dependent on us and who cannot retaliate; that demon is our mind-centered consciousness. Furthermore, we tend to think that we are responsible only for what we do, not for what we say. It is a trick that the mind plays on us. We must remember that whatever we say — in anger or in an inebriated state — is what is already inside us. The mouth is simply another gate and, as Publilius Syrus, the 1st century Latin writer of maxims had put it, speech is the 'mirror of the soul'; a projection of our personality. Words matter as much as deeds, if not more, because we are more garrulous than functional, and a wounding word is sharper than a physical blow. We are all snared with the words of our mouths, and our words can cut to the core of another person's self-esteem. The boneless tongue can be more deadly than the slithering snake. The word of man, as the English philosopher Thomas Hobbes noted, is too frail to be truthful but strong enough to be deadly. And as Louise Hay says, if we are to be responsible for our lives, we have got to be responsible for our mouths (*The Power Is Within You*, 1991). The toxic burden that the earth carries comes more from the noxious mouth than by the vicious hand. As a Yiddish saying goes, words should be weighed, not counted. If our mind is the invisible enemy, our mouth is the visible one.

Whether it is the hand or the mouth, words or deeds, the fountainhead is the mind. Whatever was the place of the mind in human consciousness in our prehistoric past, it has now assumed unchallenged ascendency. Despite occasional attempts to control it, it has steadfastly refused to yield its primacy and has 'successfully' fought off the forces of love, goodness, and compassion. As the American social philosopher William Thompson puts it, "for the first time in human evolution, the individual life is long enough and the cultural transformation swift enough for the individual mind to be a constituent player in the global transformation of human culture"[20] — and, one might add, of human destiny. The paradox is that it is the mind that has created the mess we want to get out of, and it is again the mind that is supposed to save us.

The enduring dilemma is that, as Albert Einstein cautioned us, the intelligence that caused the problem cannot solve it. For example, we assume that our intelligence, a mental capacity that encompasses many abilities, such as to reason, to plan, to solve problems, to think abstractly, to comprehend ideas, to use language, and to learn, evolved for our survival and for the exploitation of resources in the service of growing populations. But for that 'intelligence' we would not be where we are now. But that very intelligence is ill-suited to the living context in which man's foe is not another predatory species, or harsh Nature, but another man with the same kind of intelligence. Our material world is a mental world; our technological world is mental; our whole existence is mental. In short, our reason — which the Indian sage Sri Aurobindo called the 'Governor of Life' (*The Human Cycle*, 1949) — is the Rubicon that we must cross; but we cannot cross it because that very reason itself tells us that if we do cross it, we know not where to go. We want to rise like a Phoenix without burning ourselves and our nest. We are caught in a classic Catch-22 conundrum, a kind of 'double bind': what we must do, we cannot do, because, to do what we must, we have to do what we cannot do.

The 'inner world' of our consciousness is what shapes our beliefs and limits and leverages our experiences of life. Until we set this 'world' in order, our visions of a 'new world order', of a 'just human society' will remain as they have been all through the ages: utilitarian. Every day, we journey externally but not move even an inch in a whole lifetime on the 'inner journey'. A journey that, as the Upanishads describe, is from the phenomenal world of existential ignorance to spiritual Self-realization, or simply from the 'self' to the 'Self'. It is the same journey from the state of being 'unenlightened' to 'enlightened' in Western philosophy, symbolized in Plato's celebrated allegory of the cave, or the Myth of the Cave. The trouble is that the mind transforms or rather tarnishes everything it touches. Its sense of reality is highly circumscribed, like that of the humans in the 'cave', chained all their lives, facing a blank wall, seeing only projections on the wall of shadows of things. Scientists like Arthur Eddington say that we visualize theories about life and the Universe which are shaped in our own image and patterned after the forms of our own minds. But we are still not quite sure what the mind is in relation to our brain and consciousness, or of its origin or its real role; but the mind does seem to have acquired the avatar of a rogue elephant on the rampage.

For the record, let us recapitulate, how, for something so synonymous with man, the scriptures have described the mind: mischievous, monkey-like, feeble, fickle, frivolous, spiteful, wayward, wind-like, and so forth. In this conception, the mind is the storehouse of all the negative drives or thoughts. It has been said that every thought creates certain vibrations around us and becomes a prayer, and that every prayer is answered. If a thought is negative and gets answered as a prayer, then our prayers cancel each other's effects. The fact is that we have not managed to be either tidy or thoughtful in our thoughts, and our emotions rarely have compassion in the default mode. If malice is the most pernicious of human attributes, the mind is the mother of malice. And, for whatever reasons one could surmise, the mind seems to have reasoned out its options and come to the conclusion that if being nasty gets all the nice things, why be nice at all? If being rude and crude makes another person obey your command, why take the trouble to be civil? If humiliating another person takes you on a high, why be humble? If insulting someone makes you feel great about yourself, why fight that temptation? If violence (which is not necessarily or only physical harm) is a shortcut to success and survival, why tread the arduous path of persuasion and peace? And if someone stands between me and my want, the mind reasons, what is wrong in removing the obstacle, whatever be the means? Our mind wants to succeed in every circumstance; in effect to be a 'complete power' beyond all imagination. The irony is that we fear our inadequacies; what we should fear is our *power*.

In the Hindu scripture Srimad Bhagavad Gita, it is written that our senses and their gods are under the control of the mind, described as the invincible enemy of an irresistible force, which sets the wheel of *samsara* (the living world) in motion, and that anyone who brings the mind under control is the 'God of gods'.[21] From antiquity to modernity, we have been at it, to turn ourselves into such 'Gods'. Apart from the fact that much of human interfacing is to impose one's will on another's mind, mind-control is now the ultimate tool of conquest and terror. The fear of one's own mind being broken down and then reshaped to someone else's specification and requirement haunts many people. It is the absolute invasion of privacy; a process through which one seeks to control not only how another person acts but how he thinks and feels. Increasingly it is the favorite of tyrants, cult leaders and state surveillance agencies and 'secret services'.

In a more subtle sense, such mind-control is the objective and thrust of the information, communication, and entertainment infrastructure that underpins modern life. While what man needs is cathartic cleansing and consciousness change, what he is aiming at is 'brainwashing'. Although the term is of recent vintage (1950), coined by the American journalist Edward Hunter (from the Chinese *hsi nao*, literally 'wash brain'), the attempt itself is timeless. In fact, it is what much of human interfacing is all about, to externally subvert and undermine the autonomy of another individual's own thinking and choices, to bend the other's will to our own at its very source — the mind — through persuasion, manipulation or coercion. Force, intimidation and coercion will always have their attraction to those who have the means to bring them to bear. Their use in human affairs is timeless, but what has made this a mortal danger to mankind is the tool of *technology*. We are told that the technology is already out there with which one can hack straight into our brain, to confine us to an electromagnetic field that cocoons and conditions our every thought, to, in effect, erase our life's memories and substitute them with a new, false set...

We have learnt by now that it is foolhardy to dismiss such predictions as science-fiction. In fact, the greater danger perhaps is not what such actions seek to do to us, or with us, but what unexpectedly could emerge and transform us into beings that even ardent technophiles would not want to be. One of the lessons of human history is that the impact of any kind of knowledge depends on who the knower is. The same knowledge could yield different results if applied by different people. Piety, purity, or the lack of them, has a vital bearing on the delivery. And man has unfailingly shown that he misinterprets or misuses every kind of knowledge or power he has access to. The scriptures are a case in point; the ease and dexterity with which we make a mockery of them is appalling; and our unquenchable thirst for scientific power will fare no better with the kind of consciousness we have. That over one-third of mankind is still denied the basic needs of a dignified life is a stark reminder of our ability to misuse or misdirect every kind of power. That we keep on amassing weapons of mass destruction, nuclear and biological, capable of killing us many times over is another.

Knowledge development, according to evolutionary epistemology, is supposed to be the direct extension of evolutionary development, but somewhere down the line they got disconnected. What evolution has made us to be was not what Nature intended; nor what we want to be. We have focused on knowledge, not the knower. Innate in each of us is an embryonic empathy that struggles to blossom from the deepest depths of our being but the wages of evolution weigh it down. In truth, notwithstanding our claims of having mastered the universe and mapped the genome and unlocked the secrets of life, we have not made much, if any, headway in the four fundamental directions of knowledge — knowledge of self, knowledge of God, knowledge of the world as it really is, and knowledge of afterlife. There has always been tension between our knowledge of how to get the best out of life and a good afterlife. But the knowledge experts reassure us that we are in the throes of a 'knowledge value revolution', of a post-modern knowledge society, which will usher in a glorious future for mankind, and make the world a better place.

The spiritual dimension of our 'being', which the scriptures and the saints say is our true essence, is twisted so much in practice that it is hard to distinguish a truly spiritual seeker and a crafty charlatan. There are more 'brands' of spiritualism than perhaps of soaps in a supermarket, and the 'consumer' is clueless about how to separate the fake from the real. In the Mahabharata, while describing the ongoing *Kali Yuga*, the Dark Age, it was presciently written that men of our age will have the capacity "to fool the world that man's insatiable appetite for wealth and power was really a spiritual quest."[22] The Dalai Lama says that the essence of spiritualism is in our attitude towards 'others'. If we are callous, condescending and casual to their distress, then we are not spiritual. Our fuzziness about spirituality extends to other critical areas like love and hate, which have always shared an uneasy relationship and now seem seamless. For any of that to truly and substantially change, we need systemic transformation, a complete change in perspective, goals, and priorities. In the Mahabharata (*Santi Parva; Section IX*), King Yudhisthira, remorseful that he was instrumental in unknowingly slaying his own elder brother Karna in the battle at Kurukshetra, tells his younger brother Arjuna (who was actually the killer), that he would go off into the forests divesting himself of desire and wrath, and turning his gaze inwards and casting off pride of soul and body. In that single sentence, Yudhisthira expresses the thrust of the direction of the desirable human transformation — to control, if not abjure, desire, wrath, and pride, and to 'gaze inwards'. The phrase 'transformation', more often 'change', is one of the most frequently used expressions in human communication. The irony is that we still behave with the intent that, as the French saying goes, '*plus ça change, plus c'est la même chose*' (the more things change, the more they are the same). After all, we are dealing with humans and human nature, and these are hard nuts to crack. Like much else in life, we want to 'control' change too; apply it selectively on our own terms. Even time we want to be able to pass selectively. What Einstein said about relativity — when you are with a pretty girl, an hour seems like a minute, and when you sit on a hot stove for a minute it is longer than an hour — applies equally to all life. We want to bend time, space, and fortune to our resolve randomly and relatively. We want choice over what we want to change and what should be stable. We dream of soaring to new heights, but are addicted to the comfort of the ground.

The underlying premise of human transformation is that man has not attained his full potential, and that, through a still indeterminate process, man can become a radically different — and better — being than he is, and do things he only dreams of doing. On the other hand, the transformation that scriptures like the Upanishads envisaged is the *inner* transformation, in the midst of outward conformity and continuity. A good chunk of our life is spent tiptoeing through the minefield of sensual, moral, monetary, and ethical temptations and trespasses, always struggling to hold ourselves back from doing what we want to do, fearful of committing a crime or a sin. For only we, humans can commit either of them. We hesitate, not because they are bad but for fear of the aftermath. Animals cannot because their intent is innocence. For example, animals kill for food and survival; man murders for game, gain, and power. Wisdom is not only how knowledge is used, but also knowledge not used with the power to use. Perhaps the greatest of all temptations is to keep shut some doors that science and technology open for us. The kind of transformation currently underway is technological, focused on the physical, raising profound questions about its sustainability and implications. While there is little doubt about the potential power of science, the question is: can man be trusted to marshal it for the common good? Chances are that unless we latch on to it for 'moral progress' — shift the focus from what science *could* do, to what it should and ought to do — it might lead to making man a greater menace than he already is. In spiritual terms, transformation means awakening, awareness, growth, and renewal; indeed it is the ultimate evolutionary step that the spirit can take; the birthright and basic duty of every living creature. In this view, the meaning and mission of life itself is transformation; it is to do God's work on earth, which, in the contemporary context, is to see that the ability of the earth to sustain human life is not destroyed by human conduct, and to treat every person we encounter as someone whom God wants to help through us. Put another way, without conscious effort to overcome the weaknesses inherent in the 'animal inside man', man is no different from other animals; if at all, he is far worse. Humans, it is said, are a unique kind of amphibians — half spirit and half animal. As spirits, they belong to the eternal world, but as animals, they inhabit the earth. Spiritual progress is to transcend the animal half. This offers an opportunity to become — or evolve into — someone radically different between birth and death. It means that man alone has in him what it takes to transcend his lineage, environment, and consciousness, and to become a Christ or a Buddha — but also to become a Ted Bundy or a Charles Manson. A Sufi poet noted that Nature has taken a million years to make man, but we have only a lifetime to become more than man. Of all the generations, at least over the past ten thousand years, our generation, and the one to come after us, have the uncommon opportunity to be the orchestrator of such alchemy of the human condition. For what has always been on the fringes of human endeavor — the preserve of saints and sages — is today moving into the mainstream of human aspiration. Unable to cope with the modern-day strains and stress-related problems, transformation is being sought as a solution to life's problems and as a tool for personal development at the expense of psychological, much less spiritual, development. Humans have always dreamed of states of existence different from the ones that they are in, in their everyday lives; they yearn to become the best they could be. We have the rare capacity to conceptualize our existence independent of any external or transcendental authority, and thus to transform the attendant conditions in full cognizance of the historical potential and evolutionary implications of such a transformation. How we pursue transformation, consciously or subconsciously, physically or spiritually, intellectually or intuitively, are the questions that apply to every individual.

Behind any significant, not symbolic, transformation there has to be deep disaffection, if not disgust, with the status quo. The gut-wrenching feeling of dissatisfaction with our mental state and physical constraints has been the starting point and the main motivating factor for sacred as well as secular scholasticism. Transformation, most thinkers, including James Redfield, author of *The Celestine Prophecy* (1993), consensually agree, begins with an overpowering restlessness, a sense of gnawing discontent. If restlessness can be converted into a quest, and if that quest becomes an inward journey, it can lead to a moment of blinding insight, a riveting revelation. It can pave the way to what the Upanishads call self-realization, to that split-second parting of the mind's veil of cosmic ignorance, which was what the Buddha experienced in his transformation. From ancient mythologies to modern pop culture, humans have created myriad images of transformations of the body and mind into apparitions that allow them to interact with the world. In practical terms, when people say that they are for change, as American poet Maya Angelou puts it, they mean *exchange* — exchange of our misery for another's good fortune. Change, as the cliché goes, is the only constant in Creation and pervades all shapes and phases of life. It can be fast or slow; or infect like a pandemic. Change is at once a truism and true, a platitude and profound, self-evident and elusive. It can be straight or serpentine, casual or cataclysmic, but it is inexorable. It is synonymous with surprise, often the unwelcome kind, the result of multiple small changes that accumulate and, at some ungodly hour, burst out when we are least on guard.

At the general level, opinions differ about whether the so-called human condition, which broadly encompasses all the experience of being alive as human, has changed or requires change. Our ambivalence about change is a huge complicating factor in the design of our future. While on the one hand we cherish the *status quo*, on the other hand, we routinely adapt to change perhaps more rapidly than any other species. According to Fyodor Dostoevsky, the human is the creature that can adapt to anything. Our reflexive adaptability helps us to survive; but it also makes us prone to accept injustice and exploitation. Change of any lasting kind is inherently unsettling and entails suffering and sacrifice that is not evenly spread or shared. And it often brings conflict and tension, not only between different socioeconomic groups but also between generations. From a species perspective, the fact of the matter is that the human *way* of life is changing the very premise of human life. But that is happening inadvertently, without an awareness of who or what we are. The Indian philosopher and spiritual guru Jiddu Krishnamurti said that the key to transformation is to understand who we are and through that understanding undergo transformation. Sri Aurobindo said that transformation need not only be moving from matter to spirit, but also spirit moving into matter, which is to evolve into a higher species. The classic dilemma is, whether we should 'let it happen' or 'make it happen'; to sail with the current or against the wind — in practical terms, should one be a 'passive observer' or 'an active partner'. In truth, man never had the luxury of benign inaction; and if ever, it is long passé. Man, more than ever before, is a principal player, if not a choreographer, in the epic play of his own transformation. But, the trouble is we are actually doing the worst we possibly can: by not 'letting it happen' (letting Nature deal with us), and 'making it happen' in the wrong way. At once enfeebled and emboldened by technology, which is now primarily driven by its own momentum, man now can do things not intended in his origin; in that sense, he is changing the world without inducing in himself the kind of changes that are necessary to manage that change. As Fritz Schumacher (*Small is Beautiful*, 1973) noted, while Nature is self-balancing, self-adjusting, and self-cleansing, technology is not.

With all its self-sustaining power, the march of technology would still have been manageable. It is the virtual merger of prehistoric technology (which is as old as man) with modern science (which is barely three or four centuries old) that has brought forward the peril. The fusion of science with technology has telescoped the time lag between invention and application, fundamentally altering every event and experience from the womb to the tomb. And indeed even the role of the womb; it is said that in the past few decades over 300,000 babies have been conceived *in vitro*, outside the mother's womb.[23] As for the tomb, quite apart from its growing price tag, we would want to put it away for good if we only could, and, like in the fairy tale, live forever. The virtuosity of modern technology has also, as noted by Kierkegaard, created masks behind which humans hide from one another. Technology gives man the fantasy of invincibility and in that state, he imagines himself to be the master of manifest destiny, the future a chunk of virgin clay in a sculptor's hands. We are now in the throes of four concurrent revolutions — computer, biotechnology, nanotechnology, and quantum mechanics — each of which is powerful enough to turn the world topsy-turvy. When it comes to science-driven technology, we do not know how to harness it without becoming a 'horse', how to use a tool without becoming its tool. Karl Marx once wrote that the production of too many useful things renders too many people useless, and those 'useless' people can use those 'useful things' for destructive purposes. His vision of 'communism' might be in tatters, but his perception of human nature endures.

Equally troublesome is the historicity that technology has altered the very ambience in which human character incubates through adolescence, which is a critical twilight zone between childhood and adulthood when major physical, biological, psychological, and mental changes occur. Today's adolescents, psychologist Daniel Goleman tells us, are "unintended victims of economic and technological progress" and "spend more time than ever in human history alone, staring at a video monitor."[24] In future, the effect of technology-suffused human life could be to change, as a part of natural selection, the very genetic makeup of the human organism, putting our own genetic future into our hands. As if that is not scary enough, scientists like Freeman Dyson (*Our Biotech Future*; NYRB; 19 July 2007) are saying that the 'Darwinian interlude' that lasted three billion years might be over, and that the earth could be back to horizontal transfer of genes, blurring the boundaries between species. In what we might call pre-ancient times, we are told, horizontal gene transfer — the sharing of genes between unrelated species — was prevalent and separate species did not exist. It means that sometime in the future, the inhabitants of earth might be hybrids of different species, half man half dog, for instance. While that contingency is clearly a long while away, it is being predicted that in the very near term, say in the next thirty years, "newborn children could have children, and 100-year-olds could have children."[25] What a prospect! With religious knowledge not making any new advances, science is replacing religion as the primary human response to the trauma of meaningless life and pointless death. As a rebound, we want to make God mortal and man immortal! On the other hand, there are those who say that in that very twisted quest we could turn out to be a clone of Jonathan Swift's *Struldbrugs*, who do not die but continue aging, and who are legally as 'good as dead' as soon as they complete eighty years. The real risk is that in our thirst for the superhuman, we might end up as subhuman, or may be more 'modern man' than we would like to be.

But we must first shed the shibboleths that shroud our vision of ourselves, the illusion of our solitary splendor and the inevitability of our indispensability. Blinded by our vanity, we are like Hans Christian Andersen's emperor, having 'nothing on at all' but smugly feeling fully clothed. With every passing day, both our 'uniqueness' and indispensability are crumbling. Perhaps the only thing that is truly unique about us is that we cook our food, which, in fact some evolutionary biologists say, is what spurred the evolution from ape to man! Once and for all we must shed our claim of exclusivity, the illusion of human *exceptionalism*, that we are divinely favored over all others. That does not negate the doctrine of inherent divinity, that everything created is a personalized expression or extension of the Creator; it is about how we externalize it; it is about how we treat the 'other divinity'.

Many other creatures have sharper sense organs than we have, and seem to coexist more peacefully than we do. As a gross body, we are no 'big deal' either. Big deal or no deal, it is the body that beguiles us, bothers us. It is the body that grows; from an average weight of about 4 kg to anywhere around 120 kg; from a length of about 50 cm to anywhere between 150 cm to 210 cm. But in its very growth, there is also the regression that we call ageing. We do not know why we cannot 'grow' young, but that is when trouble starts and the body, the true love of our life, loses its luster and we even start loathing it. The uncertainty of the known holds us back to the body. But something is changing. Man is finding causes and reasons to put something else — religion, revenge, relief from pain or from the pressures of being 'successful' — ahead of clinging to the body. There are other animals beside the human on earth whose physical frame is larger, heavier, stronger and even more beautiful, maybe even smarter. When it comes to questions of life and death, they do not seem to be as tormented as we humans.

In broad biological terms, we are bipedal primates that belong to the mammalian species, *Homo sapiens*, and the human of today, of about 150,000 years vintage, is termed *Homo sapiens*. By the time the human reaches adulthood, the body will consist of 100 trillion cells, the basic unit of life, 206 bones, 600 muscles, and 22 internal organs. What distinguishes man from other animals is the brain that is capable of abstract reasoning, thinking and deduction, the ability to make the whole more than the sum of its parts. Sometimes man is also called a 'Machiavellian primate', "referring to our ability to 'read minds' in order to predict other peoples' behavior and outsmart them."[26] We are also Machiavellian in another sense, in our tireless effort to prevail over another person regardless of means or morality. That one-upmanship, the compulsive urge to pull someone down and get on top, is wholly human. The belief that animals *cannot* do what we *can*, that they are incapable of thinking rationally, to feel pain, to plan, to weigh options, and sacrifice, has been at the core of our moral calculus. New research is demonstrating that the 'moral intelligence' difference between humans and other animals is one of degree, rather than kind. The recent book *Wild Justice* (2009) by Marc Bekoff and Jessica Pierce elaborates this point. It is now being said that there is a high probability that even that the premise that the human is the only rational animal may not be true, and that, at the least, some primates like the chimpanzees could have "human qualities including the ability to feel fear and happiness, create tools, use languages, remember the past, and plan for the future."[27] But then, that rationale misses a central point. It assumes that if we are somehow convinced that if only we can be sure that an animal feels pain, we will desist from inflicting it. It is not true with animals; as it is not with other humans. Hurting someone — man or beast — has never been much of a deterrent, least of all at this time of moral relativism. The worst features of human behavior have nothing to do with our animal roots; they are wholly human. Zoologists like Desmond Morris (*The Human Zoo*, 1969) suggest that we are more 'wild' in our urban environment than wild animals in the jungle, and that the phrase 'human zoo' is more appropriate than 'concrete jungle'. Nothing any animal has done to another animal in the jungle can be compared with what man has done to another man in the civilized world. Some like Paul Wapner even argue that we would be better off if we 'cultivate wildness' in our cities, homes and within our own selves as way to live in harmony with Nature.

The Three 'I's of the Human Condition

Whether living in a human zoo or in a warped world, what we most often manifest in life, more than love or hate or faith, are the toxic triad of indifference, intolerance, and injustice. While we all want, at a certain level of awareness, to be good, decent, and caring, what we actualize in the vortex of daily life are these three. Of them, indifference seems relatively benign but it is the one that is most deleterious. That is because our mind does not let indifference come in the way of our feeling good about ourselves: either it is the suffering of a neighbor, or the travails of the 'bottom billion', to borrow a phrase from Paul Collier. The ever-escalating horrors we see in the world are but a reflection of the growing number of 'good' indifferent people. Bernard Shaw called it the essence of inhumanity. Manifested as an unfeeling passivity, apathetic ataraxia in the face of need or suffering of another person, few are guiltless. As the Nobel laureate, author, and Holocaust survivor Elie Wiesel said, indifference is tempting, even seductive, the all-embracing opposite of every human value that pervades the human universe and reduces the other to an abstraction. Indifference is more than not extending a helping hand to those in distress; it is a state of non-existence, virtual non-being. The worst of people's trials and troubles do not in the least affect the tenor and tempo, the pulse and beat of our languid lives. Ignorance is bliss but knowledge does not impel us to pause. The moral of our mindset is that nothing is sinful that which we do not know; the narrower the arc of our 'knowledge', the less accountable we are.

The second 'leg' of the triad is intolerance, which is but an acute extension of indifference. Even tolerance is an extension of indifference. The French philosopher Voltaire answers his own question "What is tolerance?" by saying that "it is the consequence of humanity. We are all formed of frailty and error; let us pardon reciprocally each other's folly — that is the first law of nature."[28] Intolerance has also been described as an expression of violence. Bernard Shaw said that all improvement in human affairs is grounded on tolerance. To tolerate means to bear or to endure, as it were, a lesser nuisance; acceptance comes from the recognition that there are no absolutes in life and every one is a speck of the divine. Intolerance manifests in numerous contexts — social, economic, religious. Since no two things are entirely equal in life, the scope for intolerance exists in almost every relationship. Intolerance leads to the loss of discriminatory capacity and ultimately to violence. It is the chief source of negative energy on earth. While we routinely — and stridently — proclaim that creativity comes from the clash of opinions, what we truly like is, as the phrase goes, to embed ourselves in 'the reassuring womb of an echo chamber'. The first step to combat intolerance, as the Austrian philosopher Karl Popper puts it, is to "claim, in the name of tolerance, the right not to tolerate the intolerant".[29] And it has to be addressed from many fronts, starting with education from the earliest phase. Today, by the time a child comes out of the kindergarten, intolerance would already have taken root in him; what is instilled in a child's mind is that the burden of life is to compete, to prevail, to be a winner, and that mindset inevitably produces intolerance.

The third leg of toxicity that consumes much of life is injustice, which is often the visible face of intolerance. For Alexander Hamilton, the first duty of society is justice; and for Benjamin Disraeli, justice is truth in action. On both counts, human society has failed. Much of our life is spent in the shadow of what William Lane, an Australian social reformer characterized in his work *Creed of Humanity* (1890) as 'the savage brutal competition which drives us to tear each other's flesh', and which makes man an embodiment of merciless malevolence. Competition can be constructive or destructive and the latter seems more suited to the human mind. Competition, like conflict, is inherent in the living world, but it is only in the case of the human that it comes in the way of coexistence and cooperation. Only humans have not fathomed a way because we alone do not know what 'enough' is. In the Mahabharata, it is written that "contentment is the highest heaven; contentment is the highest bliss. There is nothing nobler than contentment."[30] That is one thing that eludes the human mind, while discontentment manifests in many ways.

The malevolent mix in the morass of life manifests itself in many ways, most of all as anger. Modern man is, above all, an angry creature. Anger excludes none and afflicts everyone — young and old, rich and poor, male and female. Logically, since the historic human is now living longer, healthier and more prosperous (at least some sections of humanity) than ever before, that should have made mankind happier and harmonious. But what we have is the opposite. Anger comes often from fear, and it was designed to help during times of mortal danger. But the triggers have changed, have been trivialized and the anger response has remained and got entrenched. Sometimes, we are even angry that we have to share our living space with other creatures. Perhaps, the explanation is that there is some chemistry to anger, and our growing intolerance, irritability, and rage perhaps is fuelled by our ingesting, inhaling, and imbibing mindboggling varieties of chemicals in our daily life. Almost everything we put into our body and brain is toxic. Chemicals are affecting — and infecting — not only our external environment but also our internal balance. The smallest things, arising out of unfulfilled desire and disobeyed demands tend to throw us off balance into frenzied fury and violent temper. We are in such a state of human hostility, that any denial of a demand can become a death sentence, and a rebuff or reprimand can lead to an acid attack and, if one can grab a gun, to mass murder. Other triggers are the coexistence of obscene opulence and dehumanizing poverty, and displacements of discriminated populations and enforced abdication of homes and homeland.

The toxic effects of anger have long been recognized. In Buddhism, anger is the foremost obstacle to *bodhichitta* — enlightenment of the being. The Buddha told one of his disciples, "Manjushri, what we call anger destroys all of the virtue accumulated in one hundred kalpas [periodic manifestations and dissolutions of universes that go on eternally]."[31] In the Bible, it is said "But now ye also put off all these: anger, wrath, malice, blasphemy, filthy communication, out of your mouth." (*Colossians, 3:8*) The Prophet Muhammad said "do not be angry and furious."[32] The Buddha even said "you will not be punished for your anger; you will be punished *by* your anger."[33] In the Bhagavad Gita, Lord Krishna says that the three gates of hell are anger, lust, and avarice, and further singles out anger and says "From anger proceedeth delusion; from delusion, confused memory; from confused memory, the destruction of *buddhi* (reason); from destruction of *buddhi*, man perishes".

According to the theory of *karma*, if you generate an intense karma through anger, you will delay experiencing the results of your virtue simply because the intensity of your anger is greater than the intensity of your virtue. The sage Narada, while urging the rishi Valmiki to write the epic *Ramayana*, describes the qualities of Lord Rama, and mentions *krodh-jeet*, the conquest of anger, as one of them. Such is its hold over human frailty, that anger is included as one of the seven deadly sins — the cardinal sins — in early Christianity. Yet none of this has made any dent in the armor of our anger. Anger seems to serve several purposes: it offers us an alibi, it releases our pent-up emotions and frustrations; it gives a sense of control; it makes us feel good, and superior to the recipient of our anger. We give vent to our anger at home, on the street, at work, at play and even in a place of worship. It is a passion that causes more harm to the one who exhibits it than to the one who receives it. And anger is not always an aberration or a wayward emotion; it is also a kind of 'lie-detector test'. Often, it is through anger that what is within us is blurted out, and our raw cogitation and feelings come out spontaneously. The words that we utter when we are angry are not, as we like to think, what we do not mean, but what, deep inside ourselves, we want them to mean.

Chigyogoisui — Unity of Knowledge and Action

The 'human way of life' is marked by man's almost insatiable thirst *to know*, which is to infer more than what appears to be, a trait that distinguishes him from his fellow animals. It was because we were able to go beyond the limit of 'need to know' that we have been able to fashion a way of life so different from any other. At the same time we are paralyzed by our inability to act with the knowledge we have. In scriptures like the Quran, it is said that one of the manifestations of God is as a conveyor of knowledge. But it is also said that no one can live without action, *karma* in Sanskrit. How to harmonize knowledge and action and devotion — *jnana, karma* and *bhakti* — is one of the main messages of the Bhagavad Gita. The Upanishads say that a life of bare knowledge or of bare activity are alike, and are fraught with evil. How to synthesize and harmonize them is the practical question. Adding to the quandary, the Advaita Vedanta differentiates five kinds of knowledge: *prattaksa* (gained by the senses); *anumana* (gained by inference); *upamana* (gained by analogy); *arthapati* (gained by superimposition of known knowledge on apparent knowledge); and *agama* (gained from sacred texts like the *Vedas*). The highest knowledge is Self-knowledge, what the Upanishads call 'Self-realization'. The human faculties of observation, deliberation, and discrimination, *viveka* in Sanskrit, have been crucial for human survival. They are needed because everything in life is 'mixed-up' and we need to 'discriminate' and decide. But they have fallen short of being able to discriminate the ephemeral from the permanent, the perishable from the imperishable, the pleasurable (*preyas* in Sanskrit) from the beneficial (*sreyas*). We rely on our intellect (*buddhi*) to do so, opening a wide crack between knowledge and wise action. Man's struggle to comprehend, so to speak, the 'meaning of his meaning', the purpose of his presence, his relation to the cosmos, and to move from the shadow of death to the sanctuary of immortality, has over time crystallized as the three strands of religion, philosophy, and science — or the spiritual, metaphysical, and material. And man's almost pathological paralysis to harmonize the 'triad of thought' has greatly hampered human endeavor to find a way to mold into a better being. And religion, or rather the way it impacts, long identified with the best of human behavior, looms large in that respect, fast becoming a central issue of our time. Perhaps, when the dismal tale of the premature passage of the human species is written, it might well record that the most lethal — and tragic — aspect of human life has been our star-crossed equation with what we claim to be God's own direct word: religion. It has acquired what physicist Steven Weinberg calls 'deadly certitude' that makes a zealot truly believe that cold-blooded killing is doing God's work. Not only does it claim monopoly with God, our sense of morality and even our wanting to be 'good' is intertwined with religion.

What we do and how we do as religious practice has societal and planetary implications. Further, as Robert Wright argues, religion too, like an organism, changes in response to changing social conditions in the real world (*The Evolution of God*, 2009). Religion is no longer a means to 'true worship of true God', or to tame our passions or cleanse and transform ourselves through prayer and piety. Religious fervor has become a kind of frenzy, a major source of dissension and discord in human affairs and seems to stoke our darkest desires. Man seems ready to set aside every other identity, and willing to sacrifice every other relationship, rationale, norm or value or code of conduct, to respond to his religious impulse, which is increasingly being perceived as fighting an implied threat from another religion.

It is ironic that the murderous ire of religious righteousness is not directed against atheists who openly ridicule or denounce God, but against those whose faith in and devotion for God is no less but who say that their vision of divinity differs. Prayer, which is supposed to make the one who prays a better being, has become a passport to conduct that violates every scriptural injunction. Like much else with man, it has opened a chasm between precept and practice. Every religion prescribes a certain personal and communal code of conduct. Islam, for example, claims to be the divinely inspired complete way of life. One of the *mahavakya*s in Hinduism proclaims not virtual but actual divinity of every human being. The risk lies in their misinterpretation and selective adaptation, which can easily slip into reckless religious bigotry, obliterating or obscuring the divine and unleashing the devil inside. If, as some researchers say, there is in all of us a genetic urge to worship, called God-gene or God-particle, then it has, mixed with malice, mutated.

Instead of acting as a balm on frayed nerves, religious thought is adding 'holy' fuel to the human fire, and religious anger is now a major springboard for violence, aggression, and mayhem on earth. We are face to face with what

Sri Aurobindo called "Ignorant human confusion of religion with a particular creed, sect, cult, religious society or church", and as a consequence, we have to accept the bitter truth about "the historic insufficiency of religion as a guide and control of human society."[34] These are prophetic words and the world today is a testimony to Sri Aurobindo's prescience. The spirit of true religion — piety and purity, compassion and oneness of all — is compromised by self-righteousness and the driving desire for competitive gain. Some skeptics go to the extent of saying that it has offered to man the perfect pretext for the dance of the devil on earth, a 'sacred' cover for our awful behavior.

The question as to how this kind of religious fervor will mature and come to fruition in the decades to come might depend to a large extent on the history of this troubled century. While for long, it was expected that the clash between 'godly' religion and 'godless' science would be the major source of global instability, it is the fight between different religions that is at the root of much of the violence in the world. The fact is that the supposed clash of faith and reason has never evoked the kind of raw wrath and dark emotions that inter-religious conflict ignites, when a zealot believes that his religion is 'in danger'. The dilemma we face is that we cannot live with the way religion shapes our lives, nor can we do without it. And we seem powerless to make any religious difference to either pursuit.

But if we think that we can escape the grip of religion and embrace science, the truth is that science fares no better as a force of stability in human affairs. The problem is that empirical science validates itself by claiming that its assertions are based on measurements of physical reality, which is far from vindicated. Furthermore, it has ignored the moral difference between what we could do and what we ought to do, and that some doors are best left unopened, and, if opened, one should not cross the threshold. Without a spiritual dimension or self-abnegation, scientific practice in its barest essence, is trying to liberate man from his biological base, the consequences of which could be such that human intelligence is incapable of even imagining. It could make the human ego — the one that separates the 'I' from 'we', and the 'we' from 'God' — stronger, not weaker, and our sense of individual identity more entrenched and hedonistic.

The human species has been wondrously creative but, tragically, our creativity about things has always been at the expense of the deeper knowledge about the basics of life. We seem fated to strive for liberation without knowing the source of our bondage. Furthermore, even what we need to *know* to be 'competitively successful' in life has become so vast and demanding, that there is little urge or energy left to know, knowing which, as the Upanishads say, nothing else need be known. Every calling, every avocation — of a doctor or lawyer or a housewife — is all-devouring, shutting out all other windows of the world, transforming every one into a 'specialist', if not a 'super-specialist'. Knowledge itself has fractured our personality. The Vedas proclaim that all knowledge is in each of us and the 'knower' within awakens and brings it to the front of knowledge. They also say that a life of either bare contemplation or of bare action alike is fraught with evil. The Japanese use a phrase called *chigyogoisui,* meaning 'unity of knowledge and action'. Just as a bird cannot fly with only one wing, knowledge becomes meaningful only if it is combined with rightful action. Human intellect has a tendency to rapidly absorb and adapt the wrong kind of knowledge for destructive purposes, and becomes lethargic, if not paralyzed, when it comes to the right kind or constructive knowledge.

The American author Edgar Allan Poe, dubbed as the master of the macabre, wrote that human creativity will have no appreciable effect upon humanity, and that "man is now more active — not more happy, nor more wise than he was 6,000 years ago."[35] Poe also wrote that "there are moments when, even to the sober eye of Reason, the world of our sad Humanity may assume the semblance of a Hell."[36] Aldous Huxley even wondered if our world is another planet's hell. The one difference could be that our world is full of gadgets, avowedly to make our lives better, but in fact are perhaps meant to enfeeble us, a sort of punishment for sins on the home planet. At least, Yama, the Lord of Death and Hell, will not turn God into another gadget, as we have done, a ubiquitous bell-boy at man's beck and call. When that 'boy' does not respond promptly to every jingling of the bell, we chastise him for not 'doing his duty'. Many things that man wants might be denied to him, but what is not taken away is the power of choice in the direst of circumstances. Viktor Frankl, recalling those fellow inmates of Nazi concentration camps who gave away their last piece of bread to others, wrote in his classic book *Man's Search for Meaning* (1946) that "they may have been few in number, but they offer sufficient proof that everything can be taken from a man but one thing: the last of the human freedoms — to choose one's attitude in any given set of circumstances, to choose one's own way."[37]

Whether or not we know the *meaning* of it, one of the most common phrases associated with life is 'meaninglessness', or 'absurd' as Albert Camus termed it. In one sense, it is a state of the mind; and in another, of the moment. A good meal can give meaningfulness to life and a bad stomach, meaninglessness; a bereavement can make life look absurd, and a birth can make it fulfilling. In fact, it is the apparent 'meaninglessness' that gives practical meaning to life; for if there is 'meaning' that we can effortlessly fathom, then there is no search, no 'inner trail' and no 'inner reward' — and no good or God. In our 'meaninglessness', many turn to God and, as Pope Benedict XIV put it, if God is laid aside, then all our hopes, big and small, rest on nothing. Meaningful or meaningless, belief and behavior are disconnected. We see this disharmony and dislocation throughout the behavior processes of mankind, in political, economic, and social and religious disorders.

We may believe in many things, but when it comes to 'doing', we are governed primarily by the perception of self-interest and of self-righteousness. It springs from the instinctive sense that what we are doing is good for us and therefore must be good for everyone else. We do not know whether we should be thankful or regretful that all our beliefs do not become deeds. And we do not know why certain beliefs become behavior and others do not, and why certain people's behavior is so bizarre. It seems to have little to do with nature or nurture, upbringing or ambience. The psychologist Carl Jung said that the important thing is *to know* or *not to know*, not *to believe* or *not to believe*. But if 'knowing' does not become action or becomes wrong action, then perhaps ignorance is bliss.

But with the bunch of beliefs we harbor we want to 'govern' God. In today's world, the phrase 'God-fearing' is taking a wholly new and menacing meaning: the tables are turned and God must fear us, based on what we are doing to His other creations and to His credibility, calling Him redundant and toothless. We want to 'create' tomorrow's God, tailored to our precise specifics. And despite the fact that much of mankind formally affirms its abiding faith in God, there are more 'devout' people than decent people, more 'conscientious' people than compassionate people, even more 'god-men' than godly men in the world. As a result, our passionate personality has eclipsed our compassionate companion.

To lead a wholesome life, man needs both passion and compassion in the right mix, and each has a place and a time to manifest. But the key to human transformation is to make compassion a reflexive reaction, not a labored or reciprocal response; and passion should reinforce compassion. We must distinguish also the difference between co-dependence, which is largely based on reciprocity, and compassion, which is an unconditional commitment, and whose reward is in itself, a kind of self-enrichment. Passion or compassion, it is what we generally refer to as culture — broadly defined as the full range of learned human behavioral patterns — that colors almost everything we perceive, think, and do. And to change human condition, we must change human culture. Some see the current planetary crisis as a transition within the larger perspective of human social evolution.

It is also now being hypothesized that the process of natural selection can act on human culture as well as on our genes, and that the cultural traits affecting survival and reproduction evolve at a different rate than other cultural attributes. We now read about 'cultural engineering', which really is manipulation of the thought processes of the individual to not-so-'freely' choose what someone else 'freely' wishes us to choose. Our culture and consciousness are so far removed from genuine and authentic compassion, that a radical redesigning of the human culture becomes indispensable. The seeds of compassion must be sown in consciousness in the cradle. It has been said that by the time a child reaches the fifth year, almost up to 80 percent of its brain is developed, and much of the predispositions and its basic character and values are molded. Bahá'u'lláh, the Persian founder of the Bahá'í Faith, taught that each human being is "a mine rich in gems", unknown even to the owner, let alone to others, and inexhaustible in its affluence. Life in this world, according to him, is like the life of a child in the womb of its mother: the moral, intellectual, and spiritual powers that a human being develops here, with the help of God, will be the '*limbs*' and '*organs*' needed for the soul's progress in the worlds beyond this world. Paradoxically, we are prepared to do anything for our children, even give our lives, but do little about the environment in which they grow their 'limbs' and 'organs' in the world. Consciously or subconsciously, in the name of upbringing, we try to make them our own mirror images, which means that the future generation inherits the same mindset as ours, and more likely an even more corrupted consciousness.

Neither culture nor civilization has made any difference to the central realities of life. For many people, indeed for the vast majority, suffering and sorrow, bereavement and grief appear to underlie much of mundane life. Pain or suffering is one of the most studied subjects, embracing a wide range of disciplines and fields. Much of the thrust of the scriptures and of the teachings of prophets and mystics and sages are about how to deal with suffering.

A new academic discipline on the study of infliction of suffering, called *panetics* has come into being, and an International Society for Panetics was founded in 1991. But the end, or even the beginning of the end, is nowhere in sight; indeed, the more one tries to shed suffering the more it sticks. And modern man seems more susceptible to suffering, and it is the root of the turmoil and terror in the world. Most people spend enormous energy to avoid suffering in their own lives and in the lives of those they cherish. We tend to view God's goodness from the prism of our own suffering. We spiritually suffer, primarily because we are unable to share our prosperity and others' adversity, our hopes and others' pain. Sharing is the antidote for suffering. In other words, it is sharing, or rather, *not* sharing, that is the 'trouble'; not suffering. In his book *The Search for the Miraculous* (1947), the Russian philosopher P.D. Ouspensky says that without sacrifice nothing can be achieved in life, and that a man will give up anything but not suffering.

But, some say the ways to mitigate and manage suffering are as commonplace as suffering itself, if only we do not try to avoid it like the plague. The deaf-blind American author Helen Keller said that "the world is full of suffering; it is also full of overcoming it."[38] The way to overcome suffering is also very simple: not to impose suffering on others. And even more, alleviate a tiny fraction of the other's agony, for the pleasure that that person gets, more than matches our suffering. Many saints have brought on themselves others' suffering. We pray to God to relieve us of our grief but, it has also been said, grief itself is a gift of God; it cleanses and purifies, and allows us to feel the pain of others.

Loaded with pain and suffering, life seems pointless, but we cannot also see any 'point' beyond life, and therefore we 'linger', for lack of a 'known choice'. The problem is that the three dimensions of human life — physical, intellectual, and spiritual — run on parallel tracks, very often, in most lives, without any intersections; and the physical runs ahead of the intellectual, and the intellectual ahead of the spiritual. The same signature, intelligence, that allows us to plan, hope, imagine, give substance to God, and to hypothesize, to work, worry, and worship, and anticipate outcomes, has become the stumbling block to real change. And it has failed to bring about both conceptual and operational rapprochement and reconciliation within the triad of human knowledge — religion (revealed) philosophy (speculative), and science (deductive). Each claims exclusive legitimacy and, like a jealous spouse, brooks no erosion of its monopoly.

The other '*triad*' that underlies all human action — perception, analysis, response, whose locus is the brain —, has rarely led man to the right choices in life. The problem is that we identify 'intelligence' with IQ (intellectual intelligence), which is really our cerebral power to acquire, apply, and absorb knowledge, while sidelining our EQ (emotional intelligence) and SQ (spiritual intelligence). The SQ is a concept pioneered by authors Danah Zohar and Ian Marshall in their book *SQ - Spiritual Intelligence: the Ultimate Intelligence* (2004). The neglect of EQ, and even more, of SQ has led to the distortion of human personality, priorities, and predispositions. It has made us confuse *the* world we see, the 'world' we are within, as the world as it is, and we have lost our internal moorings, and the natural attributes of EQ and SQ have slipped into comatose slumber. What comes out is what is within. If we hate someone it means there is hate inside us. Indeed, we cannot even observe externally that which we are incapable of conceiving internally. While what we need is congruence and confluence, what we have is (despite some recent attempts to induce greater harmony between all branches of knowledge) conflict and confusion. Underlying all this restlessness and angst is the basic question: is the human form of life designed and entitled to know all? Is the knowledge we want to know, present but hidden in Nature, waiting to be fathomed and discovered, as scientists like Stephen Hawking and Steven Weinberg contend? Or is it, as scientists like Freeman Dyson argue, some of the secrets of Nature might well be beyond mathematical formulas, beyond the natural capacity of the human mind? Will we be forever, as Isaac Newton wrote towards the end of his life, be consigned to the fate of a boy finding a 'smoother pebble' or a 'prettier shell' on the seashore, while the great ocean of Truth lay undiscovered?

Malaise of Modern Man

We might not be privy to the ways and wiles of Nature. What we well know, at the practical level, is that the sinister shadow of evil — lurking in the dark recesses of our consciousness and waiting for a vulnerable moment to emerge — is now unbridled, no longer content to be the lukewarm absence of the good, or the occasional subversion of virtue. It is not contingent or an ugly aberration; we are not even sure which 'virtue' leads to virtuous conduct. Why evil men do what they do has been the matter of long-standing philosophical debate: is it out of ignorance that they do what they do (as Socrates believed), or do evil men do what they do while knowing fully well what is morally right? The fact is that most people *do* know; in fact, they do evil not because it is 'good', but because they *think* it is 'good' for them — it makes them rich or powerful, or gives the means of pleasure. While what attracts an individual to evil is multilayered and complex, the fact is that in the modern world, evil is so alive and stark, monstrous and mundane, that everyday life is nearly unimaginable without coming face to face with it. And often, far too often for our comfort, that face is our own in the mirror, the projection of our own personality. Human evil has an ancient pedigree. In the Bible (*Genesis, 6.5*) it is said: The Lord observed the extent of human wickedness on earth, and He saw that everything they thought or imagined was consistently and totally evil. It has grown from banal to brazen, from moral turpitude to mindless terror. It has its own sturdy legs to straddle upon, unapologetic and proud, even boastful — almost a human calling, a whole new discipline, independent of the person, cause, and event. Some even choose to be evil for its own sadistic sake, without any direct link to any expected advantage — it seems so much more 'fun' than any other 'game'. Menacingly, its dark shadow crashes into every corner, conversation, and conclave, every place of work or worship. While we look for it in some dastardly deed or deviant act, the melancholy truth is that evil is embedded in myriad ways in 'normal', if not respectable, life. The connecting thread is the impulse to cause pain, misery, and distress to another person, or even kill or main him, which could be as casual as avenging an insult to 'God', or in self-righteousness against a deliberate slight or dismissive gesture.

And what has been called the 'unremarkable face of unspeakable evil' is not confined to the criminal realm or to the minds of men like Caligula, Genghis Khan, Hitler, Stalin, Mao or Pol Pot; nor is it necessarily unlawful. Although a common phrase, there is no such thing as inhumanness where evil is concerned. We are all human, even if we or some of us do horrible things. The mind of a monster — or a Mahatma — has defied all our attempts to unravel. Judging from the way the world reacted and acted to symbols of horror, from Auschwitz to Armenia, from Bosnia to Darfur, it is hard to 'rationally' imagine what it takes to rouse the moral outrage of humankind or to ensure that such horrors do not recur. Equally, it is hard to even speculate what is the nadir below which man will not descend in depravity. Evil-doers do not just commit acts that do grievous harm to others; they even choose to behave subsequently in a manner that deliberately aggravates the harm. Faith or belief has never been a barrier or impervious screen to evil. While we bemoan evil and condemn evil people, the bitter truth is that most of the evil in the world is caused by people who believe they are good people. The evil they yield does not negate their 'goodness'.

While evil is the visible face of what ails man, the mainspring of what ails man is rooted in his instinctive sense of superiority, if not sacredness, called anthropocentrism, blamed by environmentalists as being at the root of the ecological crisis. Too often, our view of what is good for the universe is what is good for us; what is virtue is what is valuable to the human race; indeed, history itself is a history of our own kind, always man at the epicenter. And at the end, man always sees himself as the master, mover and shaker, the valorous, victor or victim, utterly oblivious to his cosmic insignificance. Our 'history' is but a chronicle of barbarity that has nothing to do with beasts. The so-called *anthropic principle* proposes that 'the universe must have those properties which allow life to develop within it at some stage in its evolution', which could imply that our universe has been 'fine tuned' by an intelligence external to human life. In short, this view holds that the cosmos is old enough and big enough to have already evolved a carbon-based formula of life. The building blocks of life, it suggests, are not produced on earth but in the cosmos, in the stars, underlining the interconnectivity of the universe.

The other view posits that mankind is an insignificant or fortuitous accident lost in the immensity of the cosmos or, in the words of physicist Steven Weinberg, a farcical event in the chain of accidents. The earth itself is a blue dot in the Milky Way; our sun just one among millions of other suns of a small galaxy, which, again, is just one among hundreds of millions of them. We think of ourselves as natives of the earth but some scientists even say that we might actually be extraterrestrials and that life actually came from some other planet. Even if we assume that 'intelligent' life is confined to this planet, the sweep of the history of life on earth is far grander and greater than that of the rise of man as a pre-eminent species on Earth. The cosmic eye has seen meteorites the size of Manhattan hitting the earth, continental drifts and breakups, dramatic changes in climate, the opening and closing of corridors of intercontinental migration, and the wholesale extinction of species, some of which were far more resilient and stronger, though not brainier, than man. Our faculties of conscious awareness, thinking, information analysis and application and prioritization have been so myopic that we have repeatedly refused to heed the warnings of looming nonlinearities and the telltale rumblings. But the far greater and more imminent threat to both earth and man at this juncture may not be a menacing meteorite, or even convulsive climate change, but malice in the mind; it may not be a continental drift but technology run amok; it may not be an invasion from Mars but the corrosion stemming from within man's consciousness.

There is a growing disconnection between our cognitive ability and social conduct, knowing and doing, precept and practice. The gap between ignorance and awareness is easier to fill than the gap that yawns between what we know and what we do. It is now widely accepted that we are governed not by a single seamless brain but by several parts of the brain — or even several 'brains' — which are both interconnected as well as autonomous, and the interplay of these entities determines our behavior. Therefore, like the universe which is now being termed *multiverse*, our brain too is not a 'uni-brain' but a 'multi-brain'. The part of the brain that deals with acquiring and storing knowledge seems to be poorly connected with those parts that relate to action. It is a congenital deficiency of the human species, and with the knowledge revolution — or more accurately the information revolution — that is sweeping the world, that 'deficiency' has become a serious drag on human betterment. Modern science claims to have created a 'global brain' but it has no say in how that 'brain' functions. If its working remains as disorderly as our personal brain, it could turn into a 'global drain.' The booming belief in God has had little bearing on our 'global brain'; if any, it seems to embolden our individual brains to be more callous and cruel. And secularism, which is considered to be synonymous with 'being progressive', has come to erode much of the traditional territory of the sacred.

God and Good Men

In both secular and sacred thought, we have a far better idea about evil and evil-doers than, ironically, of goodness and good men. Someone, probably English crime writer P.D. James, remarked that we would be better off if we learnt to behave like 'good animals' and less like 'gods'. Since, according to science we are essentially 'animals' — the human animal — what remains to be learnt is 'goodness'. Most people want to be 'good' and also be 'good at', but the world of 'goodness' is such a maze that they often lose their way. Wanting to be 'good' we often end up doing 'bad'. The irony is that we claim we will do anything to be good except doing good to someone else. Still, such is our longing for 'good' that if only someone can make a 'goodness pill' the sales of it will break all precedents. Its attraction lies not only in that we do not have to rack our brains wondering what is good and what is bad but, even more, it bridges the yawning chasm of our lives — knowing what is the right thing to do and not being able to do that. Since no such pill yet exists, we have to struggle with questions of theology, moral philosophy, and practical life. Is goodness synonymous with being virtuous? Should we be good for 'goodness sake', or for God, or for our own self-respect? Is it personal rectitude or public morality? Is it what we do or how we do? What is the litmus test? In raising such questions, we assume that in the human world there is a sharp line between 'good people' and 'bad people', and 'good things' and 'bad things'. And that if we *do* 'bad' we *are* 'bad', and if we *do* 'good' we *are* 'good'. In reality, we often find that we can do 'bad' deeds and remain 'good' men, and do 'good' deeds and not necessarily be 'good' men. An assumption is that to be 'good' or to do 'good' we must do something heroic and extraordinary, and sacrifice something. Too often we downplay the power of unlabored affection, a tender touch, a toothy smile, a kind word, a listening ear, an honest compliment, or the smallest act of caring, all of which have the potential to turn a life around, and are the true signatures of goodness. And too often we look for grand gestures like generosity and charity. We tend to think it is okay to give a withering look if we can follow it up with an act of kindness like giving alms. And we behave as if we have a 'right to be rude' if the other person happens to be a subordinate or a dependent.

We cannot think about goodness for two minutes without the thought of God cropping up. The question is not about goodness of God — that we just assume — but about God's role in ensuring our goodness. Does God really like good men or is it that because they are good, He wants to test how good they really are? And how does He judge goodness? It is a part of anthropocentrism to believe that God's job is to keep us good, and that if we fall prey to evil, He has implicitly failed or forsaken us? And when we are at a dead end, we turn to the question of all questions — what is the *matter* with God? The pervasive indignity, injustice, and cruelty in the world have led many observers to ask why God allows the 'innocent' to suffer and the 'evil' to triumph. In the Karma theory, it may be noted, the 'innocent' may be the 'evil' ones in another life and their suffering a way to pay for their *papa* or sins. When one unspeakable horror is brazenly followed by another, more unspeakable or unthinkable horror, without let up or hindrance — Holocaust, Gulag, Rwanda, Bosnia, Darfur — the troubling thought does cross our minds if such things on such scale, particularly those triggered by religious rivalry, could happen without some sort of divine imprimatur.

Or is man a creature whose evolution has gone so awfully awry that even God cannot set it right? Some say Hitler's Holocaust or Stalin's Gulags happened on earth, not because of human viciousness but because of what has been dubbed, in the words of Martin Buber (1952), as "eclipse of the light of heaven, eclipse of God."[39] It is not just that modern men, due to their absorption in technology and material progress, have become incapable of hearing God's voice. The timeless question is why does God allow 'good men' to fail in life and fall in sin? Human history, mythology, and sacred texts are full of gods, 'good men', spiritual leaders and many others who succumbed to temptation. In the Bible, David, dear to God, committed adultery with another man's wife, got her pregnant, then had her husband murdered to cover up the affair.

Man is frail in flesh, mind, and spirit. Why does not God make us stronger and impervious to temptation? God Himself might have chosen, looking at what man has wrought on earth, to stay still and silent in our age and time. The Hindus however explain this as the inevitable symptoms of the Kali Yuga. According to the Hindu concept of cyclical time, we are living in the evil age of Kali Yuga, which is said to have started more than 3,000 years ago, and expected to last another 432,000 earth years. It was at the beginning of the Kali Yuga that King Yudhistira, in the great epic Mahabharata, who asked the immortal sage Markandeya, "When morality and virtue come to an end, what will remain?"[40] We know what 'remains', now and here, but why must it be that way? Are we required to be 'bad' simply because we are born in this *yuga*? Who benefits from human misery? Is everyone born in this age of hardened sinners doing their final 'time' on this hell of a planet? What cosmic cause is served if we are forced to do things we do not want to do, but are unable not to do? Bereft of any answers suitable to our intellectual intelligence, we again turn to God, but He remains an inscrutable Sphinx. It raises the question, in the words of one of the characters in Cormac McCarthy's novel *Blood Meridian* (1985) "If God meant to interfere in the degeneracy of mankind, would he not have done so by now?"[41] In other words, does our decadence have a divine sanction? Some theologians skirt around the torment and argue that God's designs are not for us to discern, that He is not answerable to anyone, nor is He in any kind of moral bondage to man. Some say that events like the Holocaust and the Gulag are God's punishments, but does it mean that people like Hitler and Stalin were God's chosen people? and that they and their henchmen were, so to speak, 'doing God's work'?

If God is faultless and horrific things keep happening, and the 'evil'-doers seem to go scot free, then how does one make sense of it all? The answer is startlingly simple — just extend the time frame beyond birth and death. One must look at life as a continuum that stretches over multiple lives in myriad motifs, in each of which we carry forward both the good and the bad we do, and what we call 'quality of life' and suffering are but a reflection of these actions; a sort of perpetual collection of dues and payback of debts; and in so doing, we again continue to do both good and bad things, and the cycle continues. Our spouses, children, kinsmen — indeed every arrangement of human relationship — act as agents of happiness or the reverse, depending upon one's past acts.

Only in the human condition does a single person, or at most a handful, can make a difference between clinging to life and embracing death. The Bible gives a good deal of attention to the reality of suffering. It does not regard it as an illusion as some religions and sects do, nor deal with it superficially. One of its larger books, the Book of Job, is given solely to this question. In orthodox Christianity, there is no salvation sans suffering. While all religions deal with suffering, it is the Hindu and Buddhist karma theory that, on the face of it, appears to be the most plausible explanation for all that seems so incomprehensible, unfair, and unjust in life. It is also the one that 'explains' why our fates and fortunes fluctuate so widely. In the karmic perspective, it is through suffering that one transforms oneself — the more intense the suffering, the faster the transformation, a kind of fast-track penance or payback for previous *papas* or sins. In the Mahabharata (*Anushasana Parva*), it is said that as light and shadow are related to each other, so are men related to karma through their own actions. And every action could be a springboard for suffering. Maybe, it is because of that that we seem to be almost unconsciously, or at a deeper level of consciousness, in search of suffering and are afraid to 'sacrifice' suffering. But that does not allow us to let off God from our troubles, frustrations, and failures of life.

Invoking divine 'callousness' as the cause, some revolutionary 'thinkers' like Neale Donald Walsch assert that "the God in whom you believe *isn't real*. The God in whom you believe is *made up*. It is a God you *created* out of *thin air*, having *nothing to do with Ultimate Reality*" and that, in any case God was, "never able to create a just society or a joyful harmonious civilization, to say nothing of a peaceful world."[42] If God were to do all that, what is man supposed to do — exploit and kill, and find fault with God for not stopping us from doing that! According to this line of logic, God is not only the Creator but also a 'Capricious Director' of the world and we are all hopeless puppets dancing to his whimsical tunes. The basic premise that prompted the doctrine of the ineffectiveness or indifference of God is reflected in the comment of Arthur Koestler, the author of works like *Darkness at Noon* (1840): "God seems to have let the receiver off the hook, and time is running out."[43] Or maybe He is calling, and man has left the receiver off the hook, or maybe the phone is ringing but the strident sounds, the maddening echoes of our civilization do not let us hear Him! In any case, how can we be sure that a 'New God' will fare any better? In fact, what we must worry about is not 'tomorrow's God' but about 'tomorrow's man' and what that means to the world.

Narcissism and Nihilism

If 'today's man' is a harbinger, if he is a sign of things to come, then the world will become a more perilous place. Modern or post-modern man is constantly drawn towards two conflicting determinants, two extreme responses to reality: he is in love with himself; and he is compulsively self-destructive. We love and loath ourselves at the same time; suffused with both self-absorption and low self-esteem. Our narcissist personality is so precariously poised that we cannot tolerate even a hint of criticism and disagreement. Most narcissists are paranoid and view themselves as 'victims'. Narcissism, someone said, is 'conspicuous nihilism'. If man continues along the same behavioral path, tomorrow's man will be a more paradoxical and perilous being, putting both the species and the earth at greater risk. Although we can feel the tremors in our bones and watch the birds flying in haste and beasts running in panic sensing mortal danger, we ignore the ominous signs of where man seems headed. We choose to turn the Nelson's Eye and pretend not to see the darkening clouds of what man has wrought on earth, what he has done to his own innate integrity. Like Janus, the Roman God of gates and doorways, we present two faces, one to look at ourselves and the other for the 'others', one face that shows our noble profile, and the other our meanness and cruelty. We seem to have lost our moorings and are not quite sure if life is inherently amoral and absurd and not worth all this bluster and bother.

The very instinct for 'survival', supposedly hardwired into all living beings, that is supposed to predispose us to fear death and abhor annihilation, the primary force behind evolutionary adaptation and conditioning, is no longer so sacrosanct or sharp. We still retain the cave man's survival reflexes, but it is not an absolute; other things, sometimes seemingly trivial and trite, can now override that instinct. As a result, man has become narcissistic and nihilistic, at once self-absorbed and self-destructive, a toxic brew that scalds everything it touches. In the garb of faith and passion, religion and revenge, life and death have become seamless; one can no longer easily identify which is the dominant passion at any given time and situation. We long for peace of mind but our lives are broken into a plurality of pieces; we dream of becoming better but we are bitter at our deepest core. We have, amongst us, many pious people who fervently believe that the shortest route to Paradise is through a bomb blast, no matter who happens to be its victim, even one's own mother. Wrath and revenge dominate the human mind. An ancient proverb, sometimes attributed to the Roman philosopher Euripides, says that those whom the gods want to destroy, they first make mad. That state comes ominously close to the current state of the human mind. 'Madness' comes uppermost to the mind when one looks at the contemporary scene.

If all this angst is the view through an earthly microscope, how would the vision be through a telescope from the skies? The first thing that any ET (extraterrestrial) out there will notice is our chronic or congenital inability, at some tangible level of our self-awareness, to recognize that we share a common fate on a crowded planet that is losing its life-supporting potential, consequent to human behavior. Indeed researchers like John Mack, the Pulitzer Prize winning author who investigated alien encounters and human abductions, say that the principal reason why aliens visit earth is to warn us that our cavalier tree-cutting, water-polluting, trash-dumping habits will have dire consequences if we do not change our ways.[44] But we behave as if we are under some kind of a spell and refuse to hear or heed such warnings. The world's fundamental misfortune, according to Soren Kierkegaard "is the fact that with each great discovery... the human race is enveloped... in a miasma of thoughts, emotions, moods, even conclusions and intentions, which are nobody's, which belong to none and yet to all."[45]

We proclaim ourselves as 'rational' beings, capable of reasoned analysis and thinking through, but we behave in the most irrational and irresponsible way, even when it comes to issues pertaining to life and death. We have not learnt how to make 'rational decisions' that involve extreme risks, how to reach a 'common good' based on 'shared sacrifice'. Every act — even an impulse — is tantamount to making a decision, an outcome of mental processes leading to the selection of a course of action among several alternatives. Which means that for us to make any radical shift in the way we make choices and decisions, we must alter the dynamic and direction of our 'rational capacity', the principal faculty with which we navigate through life. We have to change what we consider as the desirable outcome of any event, situation or crisis. 'Rational' man may be, but that has not helped him to make sense of his own life. In the Hindu scripture *Janaka Gita*, this practical point is rammed home through rhetorical questions: 'In whatever objects faith was placed and the heart was set with love, all those have perished even while being seen. What then is good here on earth?' and 'In childhood, one is under the sway of ignorance. In youth, he is overpowered by women. The rest of his life is absorbed by worries of the family. What can this fool do at any time?'[46] Not much or nothing, in so far as his life is concerned. But in relation to life in general, man counts a great deal. But the root of the matter is, as Alexis Carrel puts it, "Most of the questions put to themselves by those who study human beings remain without answer. Immense regions of our inner world are still unknown."[47]

Vedanta says that the external world — the universe, the stars, the galaxies as well as our physical body — is mortal, and the inner world is immortal. The journey towards immortality has to be within; it is not to become a cyborg, with nanobots replacing internal organs, as scientists predict will be the wave or 'way' of the future, but to become primarily a spiritual being. When the shackled programmed consciousness finally opens up to the infinity of the mystery that has been hushed up until then, 'a person often finds himself drowning in limitless implausibility', to borrow the words of Jack Haas (*The Way of Wonder: A Return to the Mystery of Ourselves*, 2002). For, when the consciousness is finally distanced from all its previous assumptions, associations, ideas, and beliefs, it suddenly stands upon the brink of the chilling chasm. It is at this edge that some sink, some swim, some fall to perdition, and some learn to fly, not to the skies, but within. Barred from access to the universe within, most men meander aimlessly till death delivers deliverance.

The Way Forward — the Way Inward

'The way inward' — *that* is the greatest mystery, the tantalizing secret. Why is the meaning of our being so hidden? What divine purpose does it serve to keep us away from our own core? Why are we hypnotized into thinking that we are what we are not? We are supposed to be the only creatures who can *imagine*, but that has not helped us much in imaging who we are and what is the life-force that propels us. Some say that man is yet to be; as of now a possibility, a potentiality. Some others say that man is a relic, that he is living a posthumous existence. He daily discovers new planets like the earth, new galaxies and nascent stars, but cannot cross the frontier of his own skin. In a spiritual sense, both — the external and internal — are replicas of each other but we are somehow blinded in our vision of the inner world. The outer world is the phenomenal world, the world of mind and matter, of other people and the living environment. It is the world of action and reaction, belief and behavior. The 'inner world' or 'inner space' is the world of spirit, of our psyches, conscious and subconscious; beyond reason, beyond mind, beyond the reach of the five senses that are externally directed. The 'inner space' is where we make our choices and decisions. And for stability, peace, and harmony in the outer world, we need the same in the inner world. So, in order to access that 'innerscape' we must somehow find a way around or through our egotistical, self-righteous behavior, which views life as a game in which one man's gain or loss is balanced by the losses or gains of another. Whether it is the energy crisis or global warming, the 'problem' of population or looming 'water wars', the clash of religions or nuclear or biological terror, it all comes down to our perception of our place and role in the human community, and to our smug sense that none of them have any bearing on our personal lives, or strong enough to warrant any compromises with our cocoon of comfort. It is not a question of '*who* is right'; it is one of '*what* is right' and how to do the good we want to do. For that, we must move inwards, embark on a voyage within. The final frontier is the deepest depth within. The ultimate conquest is the conquest of the six enemies within man's own consciousness: *kama* (lust), *krodha* (anger), *lobha* (avarice), *moha* (delusion), *mada* (pride), and *matsarya* (malice). No spiritual progress is possible without their containment. It is the inner *jihad* that everyone has to wage. For 'good governance' in the external world we must strive for what Margery Kempe, the English mystic, called 'spiritual self-governance'. The Buddha said that it is foolish to guard against misfortune from the external world if we leave the inner mind uncontrolled. What the human race needs is to fundamentally alter the processes that precede and propel and then burst out as behavior in the outer world. It means that we must bring to bear a new focus and a new balance deep inside the core of our consciousness. It means that we must take conscious charge of our spiritual evolution. Though our reflexive consciousness is ripe enough, the challenges we face are grave enough to impel us to do that.

We must realize that for us to manage change wisely, we need to change the forces that presently direct the 'change' in human life; we have to change the conductor as well as the orchestra. To change what we see, we must change *how* we see. The 'world,' for all practical purposes, in the words of Madame Blavatsky, is nothing but an individual 'living in his personal nature.' Every individual is both the irreducible minimum and the entirety of life. The change we need at this juncture has to be both 'vertical' (individually), and 'horizontal' (as a species). It has to be a shift not only in the way we comprehend the external world; it must go beyond or beneath that, a shift in the 'way we comprehend the way we comprehend', and in the way we 'relate with our relationships' and in our sense of priorities. Change cannot be always and wholly endogenous or *in situ*; we must create the necessary context, conditions, and the potential. We have been chanting the mantra of change or challenge for centuries without being clear of what it entails and its prerequisites. Change must be seen both as a process and as a means to human betterment, and to uplift the species to a higher level of consciousness. The transformation we must seek and strive towards ought to be, as sages like Sri Aurobindo have envisioned, to evolve ourselves into a *de facto* new species, a higher mode of life; to struggle to see, as the Bhagavad Gita exhorts, ourselves in all and all in ourselves; not so much to remake the world into an El Dorado but to remake ourselves into better beings, not to slay the demons of the nether world, but to exorcize those that lurk within and nibble at our soul.

If there is one message from our past, it is that individuals matter, but a stray sprinkling of disconnected deeds will not do; we must convert the gentle breeze from good men into a benign gale that sweeps across all hurdles, like a rising tide that lifts all boats. The critical point for species-scale change will come when the momentum for change becomes unstoppable and irreversible even by the original agents of that change, when a 'critical mass' of small changes tip the balance of a whole new way of life, what Malcolm Gladwell calls the 'tipping point'. It is the smallest number of awakened human beings whose collective conduct can initiate a significant shift in global consciousness. At some unspecified point, a single individual can make a collective difference. We must behave as if we are that one extra person who can tip the scales and turn individual motivation into a mass movement. This concept is sometimes referred to as 'memes', ideas that are spread by the behavior that they incubate in their hosts and become 'social or ethical epidemics'. We do know, but not how, a trivial incident or a tiny defiance or a small disquiet in some nondescript corner can become a global phenomenon and a universal norm. The process through which it spreads is unclear, but it can be both horizontal and vertical, encapsulated in a single generation. It has happened, though seldom, when a random idea or a strange habit suddenly acquires the characteristic of a pandemic disease and human behavior dramatically changes, driven by an invisible catalyst. Right now, we need that kind of 'positive pathogen', if you will, a 'white plague', a 'spiritual smallpox', that invades and infects humanity and breaks through the false sense of immunity we feel from the fate of the world. In the words of the theosophist and author Gottfried de Purucker (*Man in Evolution*, 1941), we must let the spiritual being play on the physical body as the master musician plays on a wondrous lute or harp.

The master key to unravel mankind's misery is to strive towards an altogether new insight into 'intelligence'. First, it is not a human monopoly;

every harp of the orchestra of life on earth, including plants and trees have it, which is not necessarily inferior to the human. Second, it is not also the monopoly of the brain or the mind; it is in every cell in our body. Third, the human heart is a tremendous storehouse of cells with memory, energy, and intelligence. Fourth, we must find a way to harness the other two intelligences, the emotional and spiritual. The *Brihadaranyaka* Upanishad talks of the heart as 'the source of all things', the way to feel stillness. For reasons still unclear, the equilibrium between the two independent but intertwined sources of human cognitive capacity — mind and heart — got distorted, with one of them, the mind, becoming the monarch, and turning the heart simply into a powerful 'double' pump that backstops life, fundamentally changing the human personality and predispositions. While the mind became synonymous with the practical world of strength, logic, reason, and success, the heart came to be often associated with weakness, emotion, sentiment, compassion, and love. Frontier research is reinforcing ancient intuitive wisdom that the human heart is far more than what modern medicine has 'discovered', and that it is actually the key for the human to evolve any further. As Gary Zukav (*The Seat of the Soul*, 1989) says, we cannot find our soul with our mind; we must harness our heart.

We are like the fisherman in Oscar Wilde's beautiful story *The Fisherman and His Soul* (1891), a story about the power of love, described as better than wisdom and more precious than riches, and fairer than the feet of the daughters of men. The fisherman, rebuffed by the priest, goes to the marketplace to sell his soul to wed the mermaid, and says "Of what use is my soul to me? I cannot see it. I may not touch it. I do not know it". The merchants scoff and say, signaling the state of present-day man's mind, "Of what use is a man's soul to us?" and "Sell us thy body for a slave". For most of us our body is our identity, more real, and useful than the soul. We too long for 'love' but marginalize that which is the fountainhead of love: the heart. Tellingly, the Soul, in the same story, having been cast away without the heart, tells the fisherman that without the heart it learnt to do all the bad things and to 'love' them.

Elaine Matthews (*Heartbeat of Intelligence*, 2002) says that "as a species we have forgotten how to love. But love alone is not the key. The key is knowledge of heart intelligence."[48] Love, flowing from the heart, can also act as a bridge between the head and the heart. The ancient Chinese philosopher and founder of Taoism, Lao Tzu, wrote that "Love is of all passions the strongest, for it attacks simultaneously the head, the heart and the senses."[49] The Upanishads describe the heart as a 'cave' or a 'lotus' inside our consciousness, and as the favored abode of God. The blossoming of the 'lotus' is a metaphor often used in spiritual parlance. The lotus rises up from the mud of the swamp, grows through the murky waters, and blossoms into a pure white flower. The message from this is that we too can rise from the world of sin and senses, and attain spiritual illumination. The sage Ramakrishna Paramahamsa said 'Bring your own lotus to blossom; the bees will come of themselves'.

In his book *Consilience* (1998), Edward Wilson says that "in the quest for ultimate meaning, the transcendentalist route is much easier to follow. That is why, even as empiricism is winning the mind, transcendentalism continues to win the heart."[50] It does not mean sidelining the brain or suffocating the mind; it means that the brain—mind has to learn to work in harmony with the heart. Many are the instances in history when the non-physical dimension of the heart has guided men, at times of great peril and darkness. The Peruvian spiritual author, Carlos Castaneda said that while choosing any path, choose the one with a heart. And Jesus said that those that are pure in heart will see God. The unraveling of the Ultimate Truth, the truth behind appearances that blur our vision, is possible only through deep contemplation in the heart. John Stuart Mill, the British philosopher and essayist, acclaimed as one of the brainiest men of modern times with an IQ of 200, hit the nail on the head, when he said "No great improvements in the lot of mankind are possible until a great change takes place in the fundamental constitution of their modes of thought."[51] To induce and orchestrate such a change, man needs both the cold reasoning and craftiness of the mind and the clemency and compassion of the heart. For some time, the mark of human excellence has been measured by the IQ (intelligence quotient); in the mid-1990s, psychologists like Daniel Goleman discovered the EQ (emotional quotient), with emphasis on feelings as the measure of human wholesomeness; and now, at the turn of the 21st century, it is the SQ (spiritual quotient), which is being extolled as the new dimension of human aspiration and intelligence. SQ, it is said, will enable inquiry into questions such as 'Who am I?', 'Why am I here?' and 'Whither am I headed?' It could metamorphose our personality and make us more 'naturally' compassionate.

The German atheist philosopher Schopenhauer said that universal compassion is the only guarantee of morality, and for that we must touch and tap the human heart. As the Indian mystic Osho puts it, "this is one of the mysteries: that the mind can speak, and knows nothing; and the heart knows everything, but cannot speak."[52] According to him, the center of human personality has shifted first from the navel to the heart and then to the brain, with disastrous consequences. He says that, "In Patanjali's [the author of the famed *Yoga sutras*] days, the center of the human personality was not the brain; it was the heart. And before that, it was not even the heart. It was still lower, near the navel. The center has gone even further from the navel. Now, the center is the brain"[53] Osho says that "a catharsis is needed because the heart is so suppressed, due to your brain which has taken over so much of your being that it dominates you. You have never laughed heartily; never done anything heartily. The brain always comes in to systematize; and the heart is suppressed."[54] And that "If the heart is unburdened, then the center of consciousness is pushed still lower; it comes to the navel. The navel is the source of vitality, the seed source from which everything else comes."[55] He concludes that "consciousness must be pushed down to the source, to the roots. Only then is there the possibility of transformation. The ultimate cannot be known through the brain because when you are functioning through the brain, you are in conflict with the roots."[56] The psychologist Carl Jung said that 'there is an extraordinary distance from the head to the heart, a distance of ten, twenty, thirty years or a whole lifetime'.[57] If man could move the center of his being back to the heart, if not the navel, then his whole personality will change and his whole attitude and frame of reference to the universe and towards his fellow travelers, other humans, will be as different as light from darkness.

The physical distance in the body, between the brain and the navel, is less than a foot but the spiritual space is an eon. The aim should be to first reach the intermediate halt, the heart, as the fulcrum of consciousness. Only then can we differentiate between the surreal and the real, the unknown and unreal, non-existence and existence, solitude and loneliness, and emptiness and nothingness. Most people feel that their lives are empty, and that feeling comes because they perceive themselves as a being in entirety, and view the universe from the prism of their pleasure. Emptiness leads to alienation, alienation to anger, and anger to hate and violence. It is this sense of emptiness that dwarfs and distorts life, and one must come to grips with it. But it is not 'emptiness' that is the problem; it is that our thoughts are of the wrong kind. It is the corrupt mind that causes misery; not an 'empty' mind. One of the most enchanting doctrines in Buddhism that deals with such issues is called *sunyata* in Sanskrit, or *kong* in Chinese. The Buddhist philosopher Nagarjuna once said "For him to whom emptiness is clear, everything becomes clear; for him to whom emptiness is not clear, nothing becomes clear". It is also elaborated in the Sikh scripture *Aad Guru Granth Sahib*. The doctrine of the void is a method of rejecting all attachments because things have no 'self'. 'Void' is not vacant. This positive concept of 'void' is often compared with the emptiness inside a vase or the music that comes from the emptiness of a drum. It is a state in which all polarity, all subject–object differentiation has ceased to exist. But in Mahayana Buddhism, in the *sunyavadah* doctrine, this is a positive concept. It posits that form is emptiness and emptiness is form, which signifies the absence of absoluteness of existence of anything. Once we recognize that all of us are at once autonomous and interwoven, a part and whole in the mosaic of creation, and that there can be no isolated transcendence, the essence and direction of spiritual transformation becomes clear.

Such a state or kind of consciousness is best described in the *Isha* Upanishad, in the famous peace invocation "*Om purnamadah purnamidam purnaat purnamudachyate, purnasya purnamadaya purnamev-aavashishyate.*"[58] It is a crisp and profound verse, consisting of just one noun, two pronouns, three verbs and a particle for emphasis. It is roughly translated as: "That (pure consciousness, the Supreme Reality) is whole; this (the manifest universe of matter; of names and forms being illusions) is whole. This whole is projected from that whole. 'That' is the all encompassing, all-devouring Macrocosm, and 'This' is the infinitely diffused microcosm. When 'This' whole is taken away from That or merges with the whole, all that remains again is the whole. Although the Sanskrit word, the noun, *purnat* is loosely translated as 'whole' or sometimes as 'completely filled', 'infinite' or 'perfectly perfect', the import and essence is far more subtle. 'Fullness' can indicate a state of satiation and the word 'Completeness' can denote a state arrived through the path of the 'Sum of the parts'.

It is perhaps best described as a sublime state of sublime realization when the ultimate limitation, the individuality through which we limit the world, drops off from the consciousness; much like a snake sheds its skin. It is a state when the sense of limitation, as "Individuality" drops off, as a superfluous antiquity from one's consciousness. In stating that '*aham*' and '*idam*', 'this' and 'that' each are *poornam* (whole or complete), it is reminding us that though the two might appear *bheda* or different, they are in fact identical. Another analogy is that form is a wave invented by the ocean of consciousness to understand its own formlessness. What is eternal is the ocean, but without waves it is incoherent. The paradox is that what is eternal is formlessness, but without form it is expressionless.

What we consider in life to be important, the Upanishads never tire of reminding us, are the impermanent, ephemeral, and illusory, that the idea of the external is what limits us, that the Universe is within, the Creator and the created are the same, and that we are endowed with all the attributes of the Infinite. From the soaring perspective of the Upanishads, it is in the smallest particle of matter that the entire cosmos is reflected, and there is ultimately no unbridgeable gulf between the individual and the cosmos, *jiva* and *Ishvara*, microcosm and macrocosm, *pindanda* (world of the body) and *brahmanda* (world of cosmos). In short, we long to be that which we already are. It was a perspective that was later embraced by many philosophers like Leibnitz who proposed that the ultimate elements of the universe were individual beings that he called monads.

The ancient rishis of India and the saints and sages in our own time have demonstrated the ability to see the same patterns from the largest to the smallest scale, and intuitively recognized their interdependence and interchangeability. In one word, they were able to draw upon or invoke 'heart-centered' consciousness. At a point of time when human consciousness is called on to take an entirely new dimension, to effect a real transition, a seed surviving from the past is needed to shelter the tender germ of the future.

What could that seed be? It cannot be the body or its sense organs or the mind; it could only be the heart. The seeds pregnant with all possibilities, the germs of all genres of life, have each one of us already inside them. And each one of us must give birth to a new sprout, a new species, the 'nobler man', the 'Infant Buddha'.

The question is not if we will be transformed. Transformation is a continuum, universal and pervasive. At one level, 'being alive' is *being* transformed. The passage from one phase to another phase — from infancy to adolescence, from adolescence to youth, from youth to old age, and finally to death — is transformation. At another, more profound, level, it is transformation that virtually alters everything that we have come to associate with 'being human', everything we call the human way of life, that lets us look at another life as an extension of our own. Some call the future human species *Homo noeticus* ('Enlightened Next'), which physically resembles *Homo sapiens* but has a "marked increase in consciousness." The scriptural transformation is spiritual, which is to transform the deepest aspects of the human spirit through self-knowledge and divine grace so that every thought, word and deed becomes a ripple in the universe of consciousness. Mainstream science, for long, has ignored the psychic and spiritual dimensions, focusing on only the physical.

Racking our brains, thinking about all these matters, we feel weary, exhausted and the mind tells us to 'forget all this; savor the pleasure of the moment and get on and go along'. But something else whispers in the void, that is why we are human. Whenever we want to be the human future, the 'question' of God comes up. Does He *really* want us to be any different from what we are and what divine purpose does our decadence serve? How do we go forward and inward? Drawing upon Nature as the reservoir of all knowledge and the living world as the source of inspiration, there are essentially three parallels that point to the way of our probable future. First, the scientific way is to give man the choice to be a virtual immortal superman and transform the species into a *superorganism*, much like the 'social insects' like the ants and the bees. In spiritual terms, the soaring Upanishadic maxim of seeing the Self in all and all in the Self, comes close, in practice, to the idea of the human society turning into an ant colony. But the means are different. While the mandarins of science bank upon communication technologies like the World Wide Web and transcontinental travel, the spiritual hopeful draws upon divine devotion and intuitive intelligence. The second, the lemming way, refers to the Arctic rodents that, as the legend goes, commit mass suicide or tumble over the cliff, impelled by the pressures and pulls of their life. The third is the way of the caterpillar that becomes the beauteous butterfly. All three are possible archetypes; we possess the minimum elements needed; which way we go is a matter of moot. Clearly, the butterfly is most appealing, the rodent the least; and the ant seems so far removed from our present personality. The caterpillar ceases to be the creepy creature and soars into the sky as a Monarch butterfly. Likewise, we want to remain the same 'crafty' creature and still become a glistening, if greedy, 'god'.

In any scenario, what we need for real change is a minimum mass of humans who are prepared to turn their gaze inwards and since we do not know the nebulous number, everyone should behave as if he is that one person who would tilt the scales. Whether we do a 'butterfly' or go over the cliff like the legendary lemming depends on the myriad choices of daily life, which, in turn, depends on the character of our consciousness. Whichever way it is, it does seem that this generation of humans has the unique opportunity denied to all previous generations, to take humanity to a higher stratum of consciousness or accelerate its extinction. Scenarists like the eminent Australian microbiologist Frank Fenner are predicting that the 'end' could be within the next hundred years, kindled by overpopulation and 'unbridled consumption'. One should perhaps change the order and put our insatiable appetite for consumption (which reflects as an assault on Nature and leads to global warming and climate change) ahead of the 'problem of population'. It is human avarice and malice that is the 'mother' of all problems, not the number of humans alive on earth at any given point. Grim and gloomy as the future might seem, the history of the human race shows that, given the proper context and state of consciousness, man is capable of surprising — and surpassing — himself. At this point in time, that surpassing has to be to overpower malice in his mind and make compassion compulsive. And our heart should come center stage. For, as the French playwright Jean Racine wrote, "A noble heart cannot suspect in others the pettiness and malice that it has never felt". If we cannot suspect we cannot see, and what we cannot see we cannot act upon. Although their numbers are meager and might constitute only a tiny fraction of mankind, there are apparently enough humans on earth who genuinely want to embark upon the path of compassion and self-discovery. According to occult belief, just as animal consciousness evolved into human consciousness, human consciousness must eventually progress towards God-consciousness and enter a spiritual kingdom with powers and knowledge undreamt of. The only route for human betterment — at this juncture, even for sheer survival — is to move up on the spiral of consciousness and transform the very 'nature of human reality', which then will empower us to see and relate with the Outer reality differently. An ancient Buddhist philosopher Vasubandhu wrote that "pure consciousness transforms itself..." (Trimsatika). To make it 'pure' we must cleanse it of mind-dominance. That is the most formidable challenge man has ever faced — and failed. We need a new catalyst, a new trigger, which so far neither religion nor science was able to provide. Recent advances in the body of our knowledge like quantum physics concerning the interplay of consciousness and the physical world, indicate that instantaneous changes in widely separated systems can occur. That in a mysterious manner the separated particles remain in constant contact offers new hope that science and spirituality can join forces in consciousness-change and in furthering the cause of the '*manava dharma*', the righteous duty of all humankind on earth. It could mean that the idea of oneness or *poornam* envelopes atoms and humans alike. And that, coupled with the re-energizing of heart intelligence, could jump-start human transformation.

2

Human Condition — Paradox to Peril

The Human in the Universe

'Being human' — that is the magic mantra we chant to justify our condescension and cruelty over everyone else as far as we can see with the naked eye or telescope or microscope. That is what defines — and confines— our earthly existence. But 'being human' is also not being satisfied with 'being human'. As Albert Camus quipped, man is the only being that refuses to be what he is. And that is at once the promise and peril of man. The promise is that that 'refusal' can lead to self-analysis and salvation. The peril is that, unless guided properly, it can, in the words of D.H. Lawrence, make man 'the only animal in the world to fear'. The reason promise can so easily slip into peril is because we really do not know who we really are or ought to be. In the words of the Persian poet and philosopher Jalal ad-Din Rumi (*The Essential Rumi*, 1996), we wonder 'Where did I come from? What am I supposed to be doing? Who is it in my ear who hears my voice? Who says words with my mouth? Who looks out with my eyes? What is the soul?' Man has long wondered how and where he belongs in the grand scheme of the cosmos. Astronomers tell us that the earth is a tiny blue dot in the Milky Way, and our sun is just one among millions of other suns in our small galaxy, which is just one among hundreds of millions of galaxies in the universe where new suns and planets are constantly being formed. Would there be any point in having a universe if we humans were not here to observe it? When American historian Harry Elmer Barnes asserted that "Astronomically speaking, man is insignificant," George Coe, professor of religious education, replied,

"Astronomically speaking, man is the astronomer." Significant or insignificant we might be in the universe, there is no denying that our lives are interwoven with the universe. As French astrophysicist Michael Casse reminds us, "When we drink a drop of water, we drink the Universe, because a molecule of water, the H_2O, gathers in itself the hydrogen — a vestige of the initial explosion, the Big Bang — and the oxygen, produced in the furnace of the stars and exhaled by them". The particles that were composed at the beginning of the Universe, the atoms that were forged in the stars, the molecules that were constituted on earth or in another place… all that is also inside us". At the existential level, we still debate what 'being' is, and if 'non-being' is not 'being'; and if what we call 'living' is real or simply a 'dream within a dream'. Capturing our quandary, Shakespeare exclaimed in *Hamlet* 'To be or not to be'; and the French surrealist A. Rimbaud — who, in his teens, was dubbed by Victor Hugo as 'infant Shakespeare' — pronounced 'I am someone else'. The Greek playwright G. Xenopoulos (*The Secret of Countess Valerena*, 1904) satirized the problem with the words "If I wasn't the one I am, who would you like me to be?"[1]. Whenever we think of 'getting' something or 'becoming' someone else, it always implies that what there is right now is somehow deviant or deficit, that "there is in 'me' something missing, and I have got to get some kind of experience or some kind of quality that is going to make me fulsome, and then, once I get it, it is going to be mine and I can keep it." The trouble is that most of us want to be someone else, but we cannot make up our minds *who* that someone ought to be, because we really want to be a 'super-being', indestructible and impervious to age and death, to 'time and tide'. That sets up the stage for our assault on Nature and approach to God. And we want to know if we are a lumpen mass living — as Karl Marx described the toiling peasants of France — like 'potatoes in a sack', or if we are divine beings with an ordained place in the universe? ***We*** may quibble and debate about what 'life' is but more practically, the question is: when interdependence of life on earth is so obvious, why do we experience ourselves, our thoughts, our feelings, our desires as something separate and stand-alone from the rest?

Spiritually, that quest for our essential identity is also the quest for God, and is symbolized by the Vedantic question 'Who am I?' That disarmingly simple but causal question, made famous by the 20th century saint of southern India, Ramana Maharshi, in the Tamil language as *Nan yar*, has come to capture the quintessence of man's spiritual aspiration. Ramana Maharshi said that that very query or thought will destroy all other thoughts and, like the stick used for stirring the burning fire, will itself be burnt, leading to self-realization. The British philosopher Derek Parfit (*Reasons and Persons*, 1984), who specializes on issues of individual identity, rationality, and ethics, put it starkly when he wrote that we are not what we believe ourselves to be, that actions and experiences are interconnected but ownerless. And that a human life comprises of a bundle of enmeshed mental states rolling like tumbleweed down the days and years, but with no one (nothing) at the center. All human knowledge, all human endeavors, the 'spur that makes man struggle with destiny' (Donald G. Mitchell), has been to overcome that which evolution has made us to be or accidentally pushed us into, biologically, psychologically or spiritually. We are the only species that is not content to be what it appears to be, that does not accept the state of its being, the condition of its existence. Man is also the one who is aware, at some level or depth, that he is more than what he has become. And that he is special, unique, indispensible and yet limited both by his body and mind. The cumulative effect of all these diverse forces, pulls, and pressures, has created a huge imbalance and dis-equilibrium that is at the epicenter of the turmoil in the human world. And the heart of man's predicament is his ignorance about his core identity as a living organism on earth, and about what his mission and mandate on this crowded planet is. As theosophist and occult master George Gurdjieff noted, 'identification' is one of our most terrible foes, and man is always in a state of identification; only the object of identification changes. Identity is both a tag and a gag. But if we do not know who we are, how can we 'become' what we want to be? How then can we have a goal or a destination or know our destiny or direct our effort? Without clarity about the starting point how can we reach the finishing line?

That ambiguity and perplexity has led to our obsession with '*I*', animosity with '*Others*' and ambivalence about '*We*'. These are the most commonly used personal pronouns that occupy commanding heights in all human interactions. By the way we use these words, we understand and deal with our lives and the world at large. The word 'we' refers to something that concerns us as a group, a community, or a society. But behind the generic 'we' there is the 'I', and it makes or breaks the 'we'. For any serious spiritual search or inner change, one has to inquire into this ubiquitous 'I' behind the collective 'we' and 'they' or the 'others'. Unless we have a reasonably clear comprehension of the distinction and distances between '*I*', '*We*', and '*Others*', we cannot make any tangible spiritual progress; nor can we truly coexist and complement each other. More so because, according to some developmental psychologists, the sense of separateness is not innate and a newborn does not have it until the age of three. Indeed, the primary reason why humans, on the one hand, plunder and poison the environment that sustains their life, and on the other hand, exploit, demean and deny dignity to fellow-men is one and the same — the denial of the same rights and respect (which they hold dear to themselves) to '*Others*', who are often considered as a conglomerate comprising nonhuman forms of life, other species, other races, religions, nations, classes, and communities of all kinds. And unless we know what separates — an ocean or a valley, mountain or a meadow — how can we build a bridge across? Unless we know or understand the differences that define us — what is '***me***' and who are '***you***'— we can neither understand the mystery of the self and the lever of the cosmos, nor make diversity bind us, or keep our faith in each other. Unless we try not to annihilate the distance or change another person in our reckoning and change ourselves and accept 'others' as they are, the wondrous diversity of Nature will be a crippling burden in the voyage of life. In secular tradition, the cultivation of a personal identity is considered to be an appropriate value base in dealing with the uncertainties of life and to provide a sense of coherence and direction to our intellect and effort. That 'value base' is something to identify with, and all the things we have tried — relationships, religion, race, nationalism, society — have largely led us astray. One must draw a sharp line between 'I-centeredness' (or self-centeredness), and selfishness. While the former inquiry is a tool for introspection and self-abnegation, the latter is the external symbol of egotism, the main hurdle to spiritual growth, and the one that stands between man and God. Our essential affinity with divinity is what all scriptures affirm. The Hebrew Bible says 'Thus saith the Lord: Ye are gods and children of the Most High' (Psalm, 82:6). If we feel bereft of the gods, it is because we have forgotten our true identity. Are we then gods in eclipse, veiled by the divine *maya*? Or 'civilized brutes with hidden fangs'? Or simply simpletons, with an oversized ego, who do not even know what is good for them?

Only next to 'being human' is the phrase '*human way of life*' the most commonly used expression. It is at once a euphemistic cover-up, an explanation, and an excuse for brazen human behavior. It means that with the 'human way' everything can be extinguished; anything 'human' supersedes everything non-human. Psychologists and scientists have long struggled to explain human behavior. One school of thought is that our common ancestry makes any difference between other animals and humans only quantitative, a question of degree, not kind. Some have tried to cast it in purely mechanistic and deterministic terms. Some others have argued that non-humanistic processes of thought and knowledge cannot be equated with those of the human, that they cannot be explained, in the words of the American 'intellectual historian' Arthur Lovejoy, 'in terms of molecular displacements taking place under the skin'. The truth of the matter is that every behavior in any space and time is unto itself. Every human or every animal does not behave the same way. Even individually we do not 'behave' the same way all the time, and in every circumstance and relationship. And we cannot even predict how any of us will 'behave' in the face of a certain temptation or provocation. But all life, human or otherwise, in its essence is the same — a process of inexorable decay; even death is a 'rigid cold decay'. We equate decay with decadence and instead of using the inevitable as an opportunity to 'grow', we treat it as an implacable foe. The human too is an animal, but human life differs dramatically from 'other' animal life. How that 'difference' makes a difference to the rest of life on earth and to the one that sustains life, Nature, is the question. Scientists tell us that the evolution of life on earth is not always through natural selection and survival of the fittest, that it is not necessarily and always 'progressive', or that it is not predictable and dotted with contingent and fortuitous events. In that perspective, where do we fit? Clearly, life did not manifest in the human composite just a geologic second ago, because evolutionary theory predicts that such an outcome is based on themes of progress and increasing neural complexity. According to this line of logic, humans arose, rather, as a fortuitous and contingent outcome of thousands of linked events — in Edgar Cayce's words, "from time to time, time to time, here a little, there a little, line upon line and line and line upon line" — any one of which could have occurred differently and sent history on an alternative pathway that would not have led to the advent of consciousness. There could have been hundreds, if not thousands, of eventualities that need not have led to the arrival of the human on earth. The broad scriptural wisdom is that the human manifest of life is very rare, that it comes after many, many millions of births, after many, many millions of years of rotation through different species of life. We have changed countless dresses as aquatic animals, perhaps as many fishes and aquatic animals as there are in all the seas, then we changed bodies as creepers, plants and trees for many, many years. Then we changed our bodies in insect life, reptile life, and then we changed our bodies in hundreds of thousands of beasts before 'becoming human'. The purpose of human life, in this view, is God-realization. If intended as the launch pad for divine lift-off, the reality is that, despite millenniums of the continuum of life and thousands of succeeding generations, we remain firmly grounded, if not going underground.

Throughout history, the search for individual identity has been a focus of many great cultures and civilizations. We are groping to 'know' the essence or attribute (or set of attributes) that make us fundamentally what we are, and without which we lose our irreducible identity as a particular reflection of life on earth. It is through identity that we seek authenticity; without it we feel illegitimate. Our thirst for identity runs parallel with our need to form relationships of different sorts and intensity with other humans. All relationships are now under tremendous stress because we feel increasingly rootless and worthless, and we are unable to harmonize different parts with the whole; each thinks or behaves as if it is the whole and looks at other parts, at best, as irritants. By intent every relationship entails erosion of individual identity and autonomy and that creates problems. If relationships are to be enriching, not enfeebling, they must reflect and enhance who we really are, beyond any limited image of ourselves fathered by family, society, or our own minds. They need to be germinated on the whole of who we are, rather than on any single form, function, relationship or even feeling. This presents a tremendous challenge, for it means undertaking a journey in search of our deepest nature. Our nexus with someone we love can in fact be one of the best vehicles for that journey. When we view it this way, intimacy, or any connection with any other person, becomes an unfolding process of personal and spiritual development. Bika Reed, in her book on ancient Egyptian texts on spirituality, *The Field of Transformations: A Quest for the Immortal Essence of Human Awareness* (1986), writes that in the spiral of continuous self-creation, the inconceivable 'I' is the essence of life. It is based on the premise that, to paraphrase the Swiss psychologist Carl Jung, the very purpose of human life is to kindle a light of meaning in the darkness of mere *being.* But we pass through our life without the slightest awareness that everything we believe to be true is merely an opinion, an explanation, an excuse, or a misinterpretation; that we have swindled the grandiosity of being by conceptualizing within the context of limitedness; that we have persisted in the shallows of interpretation and shadows of learning, only because of an addictive vertigo of the heights of the unknown.

Caught in the coils of the things we need to do, physical, biological, material, we are forgetful of the whole of what we ought to be — to become fully 'human' we have to work our way to that whole. One of the theological, theoretical — and existential — aspects of life is how to harmonize the particularity of everyday life with the Advaitic (and Buddhist) insight that everything in life is void of any absolute identity or permanence. Everything is relative and transient but we have to act as if they are absolute and eternal. The great Buddhist scholar Nagarjuna wrote that *nirvana* (liberation) is simply *samsara* (worldly life) rightly experienced in the light of a proper understanding of the emptiness of all things. Everything is instantly autonomous, yet mutually dependent; all things are in a state of permanent flux, inducing and undergoing transformations every minute and all around. Every individual is an example of the entirety of the human species. He is unique with his own peculiarities and is also a sample and specimen of humanity. Our ambivalence and fuzziness about our essential identity — our own and that of the world — is the root cause of suffering, and it arises from our tendency to think that all objects exist in the world as they appear to our perception, as independent entities. Although views might vary about what one should attempt to identify oneself with, without identity there is no action, and without action there is no creation. The Upanishads say that if we can see the 'self' (relative to self-identity) in the Self that is relative to *Atman/Brahman* (which is tantamount to perceiving the cause in the effect and the Creator in the creation), then we can relieve ourselves from the sorrow and suffering of *samsara*, the world of matter and mind. Man will then be able to subdue and pass over all evil, so that evil will not subdue and pass over him. The basic problem is that the modes of human cognition applicable to 'things', including ourselves, fail us when we raise the question of the essence of our integral identity, and the paradoxical promise innate to the human condition turns into mortal peril. Erich Fromm called man an anomaly, a freak of the universe, a creature set apart while being a part. A new theory is that we are all aliens sharing a cosmic ancestry, that human life started from outside our present planet, and was then brought here by a comet. We are not quite sure what it all amounts to. No one can be quite sure about other species but man, although immersed in the minutiae of mundane life, is a virtual hostage of his sense organs; eyes, ears, mouth, nose, and skin. Our knowledge of the outside depends on our physiological methods of perception, which are filtered through the five external openings. We rely exclusively on our senses to react, relate and comprehend, and yet if there is one lesson of life, it is that our eyes can lie, our ears can misinterpret, our skin is a captive of comfort and our mouth can be a menace. Nothing is as it smells or feels like. Expressions like 'I saw with my *own* eyes' or 'I heard it *myself*' to signify the truth might not always be what we believe it to be.

The complexity and the criticality of our true identity is such that the refrain '*know thyself*' has been the clarion call from the Vedas to the Delphic Oracle, as a way not only to comprehend the meaning of our being, not only to be wise, as Socrates tirelessly preached, but also as a means to know or realize God. The Prophet Muhammad said that he who knows himself knows the Lord. But in one sense, the point of departure, so to speak, for knowing ourselves is to know that we know nothing; or even, as the Firesign Theatre album intones, '*Everything you know is wrong*'. And *that* 'knowledge' or rather the absence of it, becomes the launch pad for understanding our true identity, which is inseparable from the greater identity. In its most elemental import, our sense of individual identity is dependent on our perception of who the rest of the humanity is, and on our perception of the one who is the only 'knower'. Compounding the confusion about the essence of our identity, we are circumscribed in 'real' life by a web of often conflicting identities as a parent, a child, a relative, a friend, a citizen, a worker, etc., and much of life-energy is used up in reconciling the responsibilities of these identities. Hovering over them all, and connected to our search for meaning, is our divine identity, which, the scriptures say, is our inherent identity. But such is the sway of scientific technology today that our 'digital' identity is obscuring our 'divine' identity.

Whether it is 'divine' or 'digital', or 'demonic', whether we are human beings having a spiritual experience or spiritual beings having a physical experience, what or whom we call 'Others' and our connectivity with that phenomenon constitutes inter-subjectivity and objectivity in the human world. We are *that* which we are *not*, or appear to be not — '*neti, neti*' (not this, not this) as the Upanishads pronounce in relation to the *Atman,* the soul. In short, we have to eliminate the limitation of 'Others' to define and give value to our own lives. It gives us an opportunity to go beyond our own selfish selves, to put others' happiness ahead of our own. We are 'double-faced' about autonomy too. While most people cherish their autonomous living space, they have no qualms about appropriating or encroaching on the autonomy of others, and there are some who find comfort in the abdication of their own autonomy for survival or material gain. What Erich Fromm called 'individualized man' has not found a way to foster a spontaneous sense of solidarity with the mass of mankind. In the human world, 'each one of' is made up of 'parts' of other humans, and the interplay of these parts contributes to personal identity. In practice, however, we do not care much about 'other' human beings if they are not connected through another intermediary like family, religion, race, and country, much less try to acquire objective knowledge of what they truly want and need. Indeed, we often show scant consideration, utmost callousness and morbid cruelty towards them, and the best of us show no guilt or remorse, or fear divine disapproval. And we feel morally justified because they are not one of 'us'. The gulf between '*us*' and '*them*' is at the root of many wars and atrocities throughout history. We do not find it morally offensive to torture 'them' to keep ourselves 'safe'. The context in which a man who considers himself to be 'upright' and 'honest' will not commit or condone terrible things to other people is entirely debatable; it all depends on what is apparently at stake. As the famous Milgram Experiment' showed, during the trial of German Nazi criminals of the Second World War, most people can — in the name of 'obedience to authority' — become agents in a terribly destructive program or process, despite violating their deepest moral beliefs; in reality, they were 'saving their skins' or 'being plain patriotic'. The perpetrators were 'human' too and, as the 20th century Swiss-German philosopher Frithjof Schuon said "everything that is human is ours" — no exceptions, no 'but' or 'if' or 'however' or 'nevertheless'. The litany of human cruelty is so timeless that the mention of any single instance — genocide, methodical torture, organized rape, maiming of children for begging, or extraction of internal organs from persons who are still alive for sale — as the 'most horrific' would, so to speak, be 'unfair' to the others. Somewhere along the evolutionary path, callousness and cruelty got ingrained in our consciousness, and there are some like Friedrich Nietzsche who think that it is irretrievably locked together with many admirable human attributes and achievements. In other words, 'no cruelty, no creativity'— some sort of evolutionary 'package deal', the price humanity is paying for the transformation of man from a prey to a predator.

We have not found a way to appease our urge to 'belong' without eroding our essential identity, or to be socially 'useful' without chipping away at our innate integrity, the priceless ability to keep what is one's own, untarnished by any alien intrusion. In the modern world, that is what is at great risk, one's innate integrity. Integrity is more than honesty or even truthfulness; it is an inner sense of 'wholeness'; to be able to behave according to our beliefs, values, and principles. Truthfulness is telling the truth to others; integrity is telling the truth to one's own self. It has nothing to do with rules or law; it does not involve accountability to any external entity. It is the test of character. Too often our actions are expedient, necessary to avoid the consequences. Abraham Lincoln said that he had 'no policy'; he just tried to do his best each and every day. That 'best' was determined by his inner being, or inner voice, as Mahatma Gandhi called it. As the world shrinks into a 'global village' (a metaphor for global electronic connectivity coined by Marshall McLuhan) that village has come to be neither global in its reach — vast areas and populations of over a billion are left out — nor endowed with the coherence of a classical village. The greater reality is global divide in multiple ways. And as cultures both converge and clash, identity in diversity is becoming at once fluid and fixed, narrow and multifaceted, increasingly a fractious fault-line in human affairs. Historians like Samuel Huntington have talked of the impending 'clash of civilizations', that the future global order — and conflict — will be defined, not by ideology or economic divide, but by subjective cultural identity, which includes factors like language, religion, history, traditions. There are others like the Indian Nobel laureate Amartya Sen, who demur and posit that identity is too multifaceted to be defined by any single factor, and what Sen calls 'choiceless singularity of human identity' could make the world more explosive.

Quite apart from the debate about the probable flammable factors for future wars, there is also growing hunger for a 'meaningful life' without necessarily knowing the 'meaning of life'. The mix of the two becomes a searing craving for a 'meaningful identity', which often becomes a monster of vitriolic nationalism, ravenous religiosity, or ethnic savagery. A growing number of people feel that if we cannot read the preface to birth and the postscript to death, why bother about what happens in between. Some predict that identity in its multiple manifests — personal, psychological, cultural, social and religious, ethnic — will be the defining issue of this century. That is because we do not harmonize; we negate the other identity. It means we will eliminate or emaciate each other in asserting one or the other of these identities.

Harmonizing Personal and Collective Identity

Our perplexity about our personal primary allegiance is but a reflection of our confusion about our collective identity. From the perspective of the individual, the collective identity is a part of his or her personal identity. Sometimes, the sense of belonging to a particular group will be so strong that it will overwhelm other aspects of the person's personal identity. At other times the individual interest dwarfs the collective identity. To harmonize the individual and collective identities, we should first come to terms with our existential identity as a species and the particular essential characteristics that every unit of the entity must possess. Are we simply a 'special animal' — 'made-over ape', as some call him — with a complex biochemical mechanism and with some rather rare abilities, some remarkable 'extras', derived from harnessing bipedalism, longer life span, and a bigger brain better than that of any other being? Or are we a special being created or evolved for furthering an altogether different cosmic cause? If it is the latter, why is it shrouded in such mystery? If we too are animals, does it also include the mind, beside the body? The practical shape and setup of our angst for knowing who we are and what we should do is hard to visualize. As individuals, the challenge is even more daunting because some are able to fuse or harmonize the different 'identities' like nationality, ethnicity, religion, language with relative ease, while others are torn asunder and turn violent. Human personality cannot be understood unless we look at man in totality, which includes his drive to know the meaning of his very being. The meaning of mankind, the 'proper study' in Alexander Pope's words, is *Man*, and the meaning of man is the measure of man, which is to discern the drives, forces and dialectics of human actions and reactions. And the meaning of man can only be measured in the milieu of the cosmos. According to ancient Indian philosophy, both the individual and the universe are composed of *panchabhutas*, or the five primary elements — *prithvi* (earth), *apa* or *jala* (water), *tejas* or *agni* (fire), *vayu* (air), and *akasha* (ether). These elements are kept in a certain balance in the universe and in the body. Any radical variation in this balance results in natural disasters, and diseases in the body. In death, the five elements of the individual body unite with those of the cosmic body. The purpose of human birth is indeed to dissolve or merge or unite our identity as finite (and mortal) individuals with the infinity of the universe. The impediment is our ego, which manifests as our identity, and all spiritual practices are designed to overcome this obstacle.

Pleasure and Pain

Man has been called everything, from a moron to a Mahatma, malicious to a meaning-seeking animal, but the connecting thread in modern life is a gnawing sense of meaninglessness, and to escape that abyss man plunges into the pursuit of what we casually call 'pleasure'. In the pursuit of pleasure he often encounters 'pain' and to escape from pain he seeks more pleasure from more sources. So, what is the essential character of pleasure? Is it yet another hangover from the cave days that, at best, should be ignored? Is it the 'ultimate object of all endeavor' or a Satanic temptation? Or a simple stimulation of the senses, something as simple as living, the creation of a neural miracle that makes life worthwhile? Whatever it is, we somehow *know* it — we can smell it, taste it and feel it in our bones — and we want it in abundance, by hook or by crook, through drugs or through divine grace. And it has come to delineate what in the modern vocabulary is described as the 'quality of life', which really means plenty of everything and enjoyment, often at the expense of other people and Nature. And the pursuit of what we call 'happiness' in good measure hinges on it. The opposite or even the absence of pleasure, we presume, is pain, which is an unpleasant sensation that causes discomfort, distress, hurt, suffering, and agony. Pain is the central fact of life; the one thing we viscerally want to avoid and run away from. Elaine Scarry in her book *The Body in Pain* (1987), notes that pain is such a radically subjective, inexpressible, and incommunicable experience that it cannot be either denied or confirmed. Most people experience some kind of pain — physical, mental, and psychological — for much of their lives, and all life is a tireless attempt to avoid, escape, and alleviate pain. We instinctively identify sensuality and indulgence with pleasure, and deprivation or getting hurt or restraint, with pain. Our embrace of pleasure and abstinence from pain frames our daily struggle and earthly existence — not only ours but even that of animals; there is growing evidence that animals too can (and do) experience the same emotions, chipping away at one more of our citadels of 'uniqueness'. Although we abhor pain, some say that one of the things that angels envy in us humans is our ability to experience pain! Perhaps it is because only through pain can we know joy. Often, what gives immediate pleasure can cause long-term pain, and vice versa. Furthermore, not all pleasures or pains are the same, there could be 'good' pains and 'bad' pleasures, and our inability to grasp the sources of true pleasure and true pain is the cause of much of our unhappiness. In one sense, our control of life depends on our ability to use pain/pleasure, instead of having *them* use us. The scriptures say that to accept and treat both pain and pleasure with equanimity is the hallmark of a wise man, a *sthithapragna*, as such a person is called in the Bhagavad Gita.

The Vedas proclaim that 'separation is death; union with self is life'; and that "*Ekatma sarvabhoota antaratma*" (the one *Atman* is present in all beings). "*Tarati sokam atmavith*" (the knower of the Self overcomes sorrow), say the Upanishads. It is important to note the distinction between the 'self' as relating to one's own self and the Vedantic 'Self'. The Western concept of self-knowledge is symbolized by the ancient Greek aphorism inscribed in the pronaos (forecourt) of the Temple of Apollo at Delphi: *know thyself*, which primarily is a search for truth, an intellectual process of knowing the meaning of man and of life. The Self-knowledge as described in the Vedas and Upanishads is a much broader theological concept and covers the relationship between man, self, and God. It is to intuitively know or rather 'realize' that there is no difference between the *jivatman* (the individual self), and the *paramatman* (the universal Self). The *Mundaka* Upanishad gives a sharp description of the individual self and the universal Self using the analogy of two birds of golden plumage perched on top of the same tree, which is the body (and by extension the universe), the former tasting the sweet and bitter fruits of the tree and the later calmly observing. The individual self, deluded by forgetfulness of his identity with the divine Self, bewildered by his ego, grieves and is sad. But when he recognizes the Supreme as his own true Self, and beholds His glory, he grieves no more. The implication is that we feel as if we are drowned, submerged, in the deadly ocean of *samsara*, in the continuum of birth, death, pain, and confusion. Adi Shankara points out that the individual is overwhelmed with confusion because it cannot understand what is really happening to it, and why. Just like a piece of driftwood on the swirling sea, the individual is lifted up and down, thrown onto the shore and then pulled back into the sea. Experiencing within its own being the presence of God — and thereby realizing that glory as his own — the individual becomes liberated from suffering and sorrow. Such knowledge erases the sense of separateness. It is consciousness that is the key to personal identity. We are the same person only to the extent that we are conscious of our past thoughts and actions, in the same way as we are conscious of our present thoughts and actions.

At a practical level, we have not discovered a moral *modus vivendi* to reconcile and harmonize life on three planes: (1) the complex of 'needs, wants and desires' that characterize the 'I' of one person with those of another 'I' of another person; (2) the reality that the birth, travails and death of one person are organically related to those of another person; and (3) the autonomy of human behavior with the cosmic maxim that the tiniest act, maybe even a stray thought, of every person has a collective ripple effect on human evolution. What binds us, above all, is ignorance centered somewhere about which we are utterly ignorant. Everything in Nature seems to limit us, like the law of gravity, like the organic nature of our being, and the wheel of birth, life and death, what is called the *samsara-chakra* in Sanskrit. Mired in ignorance about our true essence and subjected to forces over which we have absolutely no control, we meander meaninglessly in the pursuit of the phantoms of pleasure, profit, and power. We are pitch-forked into what we call life, or somnambulism as Thomas Carlyle called it, without our permission or previous experience, and we die without knowing about what is going to come next. We are all aware that death, defined as irreversible damage to the chemistry of life, like reproduction and metabolism, is an essential feature of life. The subconscious in man has not only an instinct for life but also an abhorrence of death, and for reasons we do not know, the dread of death is weakening in the face of the rigors of modern living and a heartless society. Battered and bruised, deprived of any hope of a future of their own making, death has come to be for many the 'only victory in life'. Vedanta, in a flash of intuitive brilliance, says that the way forward is the way *within*, that in knowing oneself, one gets to know who the 'others' are; and in knowing who or what we are *not*, we will also know the oneness of all. The 'I'-thought is the first to arise in the mind, and if this question is tirelessly pursued, all other thoughts will be extinguished, and finally the I-thought itself will meet the same fate, opening the door to self-dissolution and awakening of the non-dual Self. In the Upanishads, the essence of identity is approached through what we might call a 'sculptor's chisel': just as a sculpture emerges as one chips away at a stone, so does our true essence get revealed by eliminating what it is not: "I am *not* the five senses"; "I am *not* the sense-organs"; "I am *not* the gross body"; "I am *not* the mind" ... "I am '*neti, neti*' (*not* this, *not* this)". By exhausting everything, one is left with Nothing or Everything, the all-pervasive but visually invisible *Brahman*, the existence — consciousness — bliss, as Indian lore has it. In the sense in which Ramana Maharshi expounded his philosophy, it is a step forward in the Advaita philosophic thought of non-dualism — it is no longer a question of the union or unity of the I-persona and God: there is no 'I' at all; everything and everyone, from the spider to snake to ape to man, they are all wholly and nothing but God; pure God. In other words, it is a giant leap beyond the Upanishadic maxim '*Aham brahmasmi*' (I am *Brahman* or God). If there is no 'I', there can only be God. For man, more so for the modern man, to reach that certain shore of genuine experience of self-knowledge, which can reveal to him the true meaning of his existence, has been an uphill, almost impossible task. Thwarted in his thirst, mired in desolate despair, expectation turning into exasperation, liberation is dangling before man as a release from the burden of the body, to escape from the tedium of life. Man's agony comes from realizing that our carnal flesh refuses to respond to the requirements of divine dictum or the Law of Nature. Those things which we often despise, we find ourselves doing. Those things which we desire, we fail to do. As Paul describes his frustration in the Bible, with his mind he desires to serve God. He agrees with the Law of God and rejoices in it. He wants to do what is right, but his body will not respond. He watches, almost as a third party, as sin sends a signal to his body and as his body responds, he wails: "Wretched man that I am! Who will set me free from the body of this death?" (*Romans 7:24*). To borrow the words from a Michael Jackson lyric, for many who see a rainbow all in black and feel a bad taste in the mouth through bitter tears, merging with God has come to mean all-round annihilation.

Man — A Mixed Blessing

From the first breath of the new born to the last breath before death, everything we do is grounded in the belief that we are the finest, the best, and the brightest on earth. While we are too close to action and too subjective as central characters in the terrestrial play, it is fair to presume that the presence or existence of the human 'habitation' on earth has been a mixed blessing. We never consider ourselves as 'co-habitants', but as the sole-habitants of the earth, if not the sovereign ones. In objective terms and in the context of what we are equipped with by Nature, we have never been able to fulfill our premise or measure up to our full potential. It was not widely off the mark when the American music band *Death* said, in the lyrics of their composition *In Human Form* (1993), that [the human form is] "an atrocity laced with greed; filled with evil intentions, ready to attack; dark emotions run through its veins; this creature in human form is out of control". But that dismal 'vision' is based on behavior. Whatever was our origin, however we are made, and whatever brought us to the present pass, it is open to question if the earth would not have been better off had man never materialized. The scriptures, on the other hand, view the human form as a vehicle to transport the inhabitant to the realm of the divine. Science says a human being is the finest form there is — or could be — on this planet. The scriptures and science might be united in extolling the human as the pinnacle of the pyramid of life on earth, but there are vital differences in their views of life. While our ancient wisdom preaches the oneness of all life, moral conduct, spiritual growth, and God's grace as necessary in life, science says that the goal of human life is to sip the cup of life to the last drop, bolster the body, boost brainpower, yet remain human and be alive perpetually. According to science, there is nothing much left for man beyond the basics, biology, survival and reproduction, and eventually, as Bertrand Russell puts it, all the genius of Man and his achievements since his advent on earth are doomed to be buried beneath the debris of a universe in ruins. But that has not yet happened, nor has it deterred science from trying to make man, more precisely the body, immortal and impregnable. It is this epic battle that man is waging now. The human body is remarkably well designed, exquisitely engineered. In the words of the Italian Renaissance philosopher Pico della Mirandola, there is nothing to be seen more wonderful than the image of man. Michelangelo's 'David' and Leonardo da Vinci's 'Mona Lisa' reflect this image. But it is not the last word; and it is a perplexing paradox. The human is at once versatile and vulnerable; formidable and fragile, highly adaptive but liable to collapse anytime and become an easy prey. There is a Turkish proverb that says, "Man is harder than iron, stronger than stone, and more fragile than a rose". Most of our organs have a great deal of extra capacity or reserve: They can still function adequately even when damaged. But every single part or process, from the skin to the heart to the digestive system and the nervous system, is prone to disease or crippling disorder.

Despite great advances in epidemiology, we still do not know — or know very little — of the relation between what we eat, drink, and breathe, and where we live, on the one hand, and our susceptibility to a certain disease, on the other hand; and why, in an identical environment, different people are differently susceptible. The human organism is not impervious or immune to germs, including parasites, bacteria, and viruses. In fact, we live in a world of germs and they are everywhere, in the air, food, water, plants, animals — and even inside us. Most of them are harmless, even beneficial, but some can cripple and kill. Despite the tremendous progress made by medicine to combat these foes, disease always seems to stay a step ahead. Of all the things that cause us pain and suffering, sometimes excruciating and unendurable, disease and disability are the foremost. They can rob a man of his dignity and desire for life, underscore both the power and the fragility of the human condition. Even saints were not immune to disease and death as was the case with Therese of Lisieux and Bernadette Soubirous, who suffered serious illnesses in their short lives. The Indian rishis, Ramana Maharshi and Ramakrishna Paramahamsa agonizingly suffered due to cancer and succumbed to it. It is this very human body that finally falters and fails and many great lives came to an abrupt end, not for want of will, but because of the inability of the body to endure. The history of humanity would have been different had such people's bodies kept pace with their will. The length of life itself is measured by the durability of the body. What is the role and purpose of the body in its present journey on earth and in our spiritual quest to the final destination? We get mixed or conflicting messages from the scriptures. On the one hand, the human body is extolled as the very abode of God and as the vehicle for God-realization and, on the other hand, the illusion of body-identification is the root of all evil and the main obstacle to spiritual progress, the 'limiting adjunct to the *Atman*'. In one ancient Hindu text, the *Uttara Gita*, which is a part of *Brahmanda Purana*, it is written that the body is extremely impure and cannot be purified, while the Self (*Atman*) is ever pure and does not need purification.[2] And again, on the one hand, we are asked not to run away from our worldly responsibilities and are told that renunciation is not abdication and, on the other hand, we read in the Upanishads that 'unless a man feels disgusted with the worlds to which his actions may bring him, and unless he believes firmly that the world beyond the reach of his actions can never be obtained by any actions however good, man cannot obtain *moksha* or mortal liberation.'[3] The *Kathopanishad* says "The human body is the only chance where a person could receive liberation from the eternal bondage and the inflictions of *maya*. If you do not realize God before death overtakes you, it would be the greatest desire of your life and you will be suffering for uncountable lifetimes by taking birth in various species."[4] A Hindu scripture says '*manav shareer ko tarsey dev*'; meaning that gods (angelic beings) yearn for the human body. The Sikh scripture Gurbani, strikes the same note and says that human birth is a precious jewel and even the demi-gods long for this human body; among all the living species, only human beings are the most fit to be instructed about the nature of truth or the essence of divinity. It is because, while the gods may enjoy many enviable attributes, they cannot, as only humans can, make the final leap to God. It is an article of sublime faith in Hinduism that the real and sole purpose of human life is the realization of the Self or God and that the way to this realization is the only true religion. But as ages passed, this insight got superseded or superimposed by worldly desires. The Self, the self, and the senses all got mixed up. But the sacredness of the human body was never off the radar of human thought and belief.

The Indian spiritual teacher Swami Vivekananda who shook the World Parliament of Religions (1893), in Chicago, USA, with his imposing presence and eloquent mastery of Indian philosophy, said "The moment I have realized God sitting in the temple of every human body, the moment I stand in reverence before every human being and see God in him, that moment I am free from bondage, everything that binds vanishes, and I am free."[5] While this is the mainstream view, Ramana Maharshi says "It is not true that birth as a man is necessarily the highest, and that one must attain realization only from being a man. Even an animal can attain Self-realization."[6] All are the creations of God and while various vignettes of life have different traits, to say that one particular creature is superior and only that creature can reach God sounds illogical. But all scriptures do not share this view. The Bible says that God made all animals that walk on the earth (the sixth day), on the same day. He created man separately in His own image with the intent that man would have dominion over every other living thing on Earth (*Genesis, 1:26-28*). The Apostle Paul stated clearly that man is not an animal when he wrote "All flesh is not the same flesh: but there is one kind of flesh of men, another flesh of beasts, another of fishes, and another of birds" (*1 Corinthians, 15:39*).

Another important question that often crops up in theology is what we might call the connectivity of human destiny. Do we all inhabit separate bodies, live separately, die separately and any interfacing in between is only a social, not spiritual need? Are we responsible for our own behavior or also for that of others with whom we get connected? Does every man pay for his own sins and reap the fruits of what he sows, or is there a collective spin-off, good and bad? In karmic terms, if *karma* is strictly individual, one pays or gets rewarded for one's actions through bad or good karma, carried over from birth to birth; or, if one's actions have any bearing on other's lives, at the level of family, community or country, they do result in a collective spin-off. El Morya, one of the founders of theosophy and *Agni Yoga*, who lived in the late 1800s, wrote thus "There are many combinations of personal, family, and national *karma*. One may ask if it is possible that an injustice committed against one person could affect a whole country. Indeed it can, especially since many who are involved with one another reincarnate in the same country. People acknowledge that physical characteristics are transmitted through generations; it is regrettable that they are not aware that karmic traits can also be transmitted."[7] In other words, every individual deed has a species spin-off; it primarily affects that individual but also has a bearing on the lives of those around, the family, group or community, and on the whole of humanity. In varying degrees, every relationship in the world is an interplay of individual *karmas*; the more intimate a relationship, the more intertwined are the *karmas*. Personal *karma*, group *karma* and cosmic *karma* are combined. What the world is today, is the cumulative fallout of the collective *karma* of all the generations that have come and gone since the time of the first man. And more topically, every thought, word, and act of every individual is an input into the makeup of future generations. We are responsible for what we think because only at that level we exercise real choice. Reincarnation is not simply an endless succession of transmigrations from one body to another on this planet. There are also several worlds and more planes of existence than what we call life on earth. Together they constitute a complex web and constantly impact each other. Many things baffling in life such as the apparent triumph of evil and suffering of the virtuous, and questions such as why some people seem to have all the luck all the time become explainable, if not explained.

While life's journey might take us from planet to planet and from one form to another, on this planet at least the vehicle of experience remains the body. But the body is not all, or only what we see in the mirror. According to Hindu traditional belief, the body consists of five primary elements called the *mahabhutas*: earth, fire, water, air, and ether. And we are not a single 'body' but five, called the *koshas*, or sheaths. The *Annamaya kosha* covers the gross or physical body, the *Pranamaya*, *Manomaya* and *Vijnanmaya koshas* cover breath, mind, and intellect respectively. The highest, *Anandmaya kosha* is the sheath of bliss.[8] The Bible says that the body is the temple of the Holy Spirit within us, which is co-equal with God. Then again, the scriptures somewhat downgrade the body as a vehicle prone to sin and selfishness; and we are also exhorted to shed our body-consciousness and identification. These two visions — inherent holiness and captive of sinful senses — are so conflicting that human consciousness has not found a *modus operandi* of reconciliation. Since the 'holy' way is too complex and hazy, we tend to follow the sensual path, which does not require any effort. And that is trouble. The way we should view and relate to our body, and how we should steer its evolution, is an important issue in the context of transformation. Contrary to the conventional view that the human evolution has pretty much run its course, new research and findings indicate that we are still evolving. Some 700 regions of the human genome have been reshaped by natural selection during the past 5,000 to 15,000 years.[9] And this discovery has enormous implications for the future. It is important because evolution is adaption to the environment, and the future man might genetically reflect the technological and gadget-suffused environment. Our domestication of high technology including biotechnology, that some experts predict will soon happen, could get under our skin; what is external now could be integral and internal in the future. How exactly we cannot tell, but how we live now will affect not only the lives, but also the bodies of future generations. Often, our body is the only visible reality, the only tangible experience. But that body too is not constant even during one's lifetime. In youth, it is our pride and joy, and in old age a drag, an embarrassment and even ridicule till death puts an end to its misery. The Buddhist scripture *Dhammapada* describes old age (*jaravagga* in Pali) in such terms as 'thoroughly worn out', 'putrid mass breaking up', 'a nest of diseases, perishable', 'ending in death'. Every day becomes a struggle to cope with its vulnerabilities and infirmities; its weight is the measure of our worth and health; its curves and contours, the symbol of self-esteem. Our battle with the body is what preoccupies most lives; it consumes much of our thinking space and absorbs much of our ingenuity. Nothing, not even death, is more dreaded in life than old age itself, which symbolizes just waiting for death, seeing death all around, and in the meantime being subjected to debility, decay, and disease. It is all very well to say that age is an issue of mind over matter, and if you do not mind it does not matter; but it matters because in ageing, man loses both his identity and dignity, and some kind of pain — physical or mental — becomes a constant. Science is now focusing on this and is promising that it will soon drastically curtail the duration of, if not eliminate, old age by extending youth and warding off death. Even if science succeeds in that attempt, the body still remains vulnerable to physical destruction.

The Rope and the Snake

Whether it is the ravages of ageing or the dread of death, or even attachment to material things, they all come from our inability to sift and separate, distinguish and differentiate what Vedanta calls 'real' from the 'unreal', apparent from the actual. In most things we do, we just seem unable to see what needs to be seen, know what needs to be known or get things done in the right way at the right time. We cannot make up our minds, with all our powers of differentiation and discrimination, whether we are different or not different from the Ultimate Reality. Some say we are identical; some, that we are separate; and some others, that we are both identical and separate, different and non-different. If we are confused at such a fundamental level, then everything gets mixed up and life gets — or appears to get — drained of any meaning. That is why much of Vedanta grapples with this question. The doctrines of *maya* and *avidya*, for example, are meant to remove the cobwebs and mist that cloud our vision and comprehension. And despite all Vedantic explanation and illumination, man remains mired in his mind. Compounding the problem, we are also not clear where we are now poised in the grand scheme of Nature, on the canvas of the Cosmos. Many great thinkers have speculated that the human is not the last rung on the evolutionary ladder, not the ultimate product, and that it can — and should — evolve spiritually into a new species, a *de facto* divine life on earth, as different from man as man is from animal. For that, he must transcend the limitations of his body and mind, a body that is "more luminous and flexible and adaptable, entirely conscious and harmonious."[10] Sri Aurobindo called that life "supramental existence". With the body and mind acting as impregnable barriers to all labor to touch his own soul, man has turned headlong into hedonist hubris and material prosperity. None of them are sought in their own right or for their own worth, but in comparison and competition to others. Our desires, even our devotion to God, are comparative, competitive — and even confrontational. We want to please — or appease — God 'more' than others to obtain earthly advantage. The legendary Hebrew King Solomon, known for his enormous wealth, power, and wisdom, wondered, towards the end of his life, how we should spend our brief time on earth and, after having ruled out the paths of pleasure, knowledge, wealth, and power, he said "Be happy and do good as long as you live. Whatever you do, do it with all the might you have, you never know when life might end" and "God will bring every deed into judgment including every hidden thing, whether it is good or evil."[11] More than 3,000 years since, and after the rise and fall of many empires and civilizations, that wisdom stands true. The bitter truth is that the world has never been short of wise men or words of wisdom, but it stands soaked from crust to core all through history with the toil and tears of the helpless and hopeless.

Human passions have always been stronger than the ability of human social personality to cope with them, and increasingly, they are in conflict with human priorities. Psychologists have long debated what constitutes 'personality' and why it differs so radically from individual to individual, even among siblings. Moreover, if we think we are stuck with our personalities, and there appears a possibility of changing them, the question remains: how and to what extent? The paradox is that while genetic inheritance of personality is an important factor, at least partially, some psychologists like Daniel Nettle (*Personality: What Makes You the Way You Are*, 2007), maintain that parenting cannot have any measurable impact on a child's personality, and also that while our basic personalities do not change significantly after childhood, our behavior can. The question is, if genes cannot wholly account for the cluster of traits that add up to our personality, and if parenting is only a marginal input, then what 'makes up man' and the way an individual acts and reacts? The answer to that question takes us to theological theories like predetermination, fate, and *karma*. The goal of human life has been viewed scripturally as a process of personal development and liberation. At the same time, all religions emphasize that when it comes down to a choice between individual rights and even life and social good, one must choose according to the larger interest. Religions preach belief, virtuous conduct and piety, *taqwa* in Islam, as guiding principles, and together constitute a social ethical code of conduct. Man's planetary responsibility as *khalifah*, a vice-regent, is another important aspect particularly in the present context. Despite all that, there has always been a clash between our personal priorities and the common good. Even spirituality, contrary to its premise, has been deemed as self-development divorced from social responsibility. Although long viewed as a bridge between different religions and between science and religion, spiritual quest has become an expression of existential restlessness, a desperate cry for help, an escape from all moral ambivalence. It is so identified with religion that many who practice the essence of spirituality loathe to be called 'spiritual'. They do not see any need for any label; they are content to lead a life of service, simplicity, and compassion for the weak and vulnerable. But, for the so-called Generation X, like much else in modern life, spirituality too has become selective and another 'virtual', distinct from the real or actual. We choose what suits us and set aside what our senses do not like. There has always been a clash between what man can do and what he ought to do, and that gap has become wider than ever before. Our intellect, emotions, and feelings are increasingly at odds with the collective imperative. As a result, 'we sail in fragile vessels across a raging sea of uncertainty', terrified that the next tsunami might topple the 'vessel'. Whether we are beguiled by *maya* or the mind, we live in a world vastly varied from the one we think we live in, or the world we ought to be living in. We are caught in the black hole between the real and the unreal, what we experience and what that is.

That brings up one of the most profound theological, metaphysical, and philosophic questions: what really is the character of human experience? Since time immemorial, the question that tormented the minds of spiritualists, scholars and philosophers was about the true nature of our existence, the reality of the things and the objects of the world that we so painfully experience. What is real and what is unreal, actual and virtual, and how does one differentiate? After a lot of introspection and striving, they came to a conclusion that what is real should be 'permanent', 'eternal' and 'unchangeable'. Since everything in this world is changeable, transitory, and momentary, it cannot be 'real' in the true sense of the term. And if everything is unreal, can there be anything really 'real'? Is it a matter of 'knowing' or 'not knowing' that is a question of the limits of human comprehension? Or is it far deeper, that there isn't anything real in creation? A famous prayer, sometimes called the *Abhyaaroha mantra*, in the *Brihadaranyaka* Upanishad begins with '*Asato ma sad gamaya*', meaning 'Lead Thou me, from the Unreal to the Real'. The problem is that we confuse the unreal with non-existence; the universe is not unreal, but our perception of it is; the illusion is real. Vedanta says that all our miseries come from our mistaking the vain appearance for the real, which is *Brahman* or God. Many analogies are offered to make the distinction intelligible to a lay mind. One of the most famous is the often-quoted example in the Upanishads, that of the 'rope and serpent', or *rajju - sarpa - bhranti* as it is called in Sanskrit. This analogy is employed to explain the delusion of daily life. It roughly means that in dim light where things cannot be perceived clearly (*agnana, avidya* or *maya*) even a piece of rope (*rajju*) can be mistaken to be a snake (*sarpa*), and one can actually experience all the emotions (fear, anxiety, etc.) associated with a snake. However, when bright light (*gnana*) is brought to bear, one will then see the rope clearly and all emotions associated with the non-existing snake will at once dissolve. The message is that the pangs of sorrow or the allure of happiness associated with worldly pleasures are because of our state of existential ignorance or the product of *maya*. But when one is exposed to knowledge of the real and the unreal, the *samsarika* delusions disappear and one will be able to perceive the real. The analogy assumes that the actuality is the rope and the illusion is the snake. But what if it is really a snake, which the world actually resembles, and the illusion the harmless rope? In one sense, it hardly matters; and in another it means everything. In his masterpiece *Vivekachudamani*, the great Adi Shankara says that one who is overpowered by ignorance mistakes a thing for what it is not; it is the absence of discrimination that causes one to mistake a snake for a rope, and great dangers overtake him when he seizes it through that wrong notion. Hence it is the mistaking of transitory things as real that constitutes bondage. *Adi Shankara also says that only t*he man who discriminates between the real and the unreal, whose mind is turned away from the unreal, who possesses calmness and the allied virtues, and who is longing for liberation, is qualified to enquire after *Brahman*. Ramana Maharshi uses this allegory and says that the realization of the Self which is the substratum of human life will not be known unless the belief that the world is real is removed.

But the point is that, so long as we live in this world it is hard not to believe, even less to behave, that life is not real; it almost seems an insult to our intelligence. One would be tempted to say that if all that we experience in life — its triumphs and tragedies, ecstasy and suffering, highs and lows — are not real, then it does not really matter what is 'real'. Vedantists try to get over the apparent impasse and say that the unreal is not the world per se but that the way it appears to be to our senses is not real. Does it mean that the earth is not what it seems? That man is not what he pretends to be? That a tragedy is a triumph and vice versa? That pain is pleasure and death is life? Then again, the concepts of absoluteness and relativeness and the dream state are introduced to explain the paradox. It means that even the real or unreal are not absolute; it is like the reality of what we see in the dream state. Whether it is mistaking a rope for a snake, or a snake for a rope, the villain is 'dim light', which induces the false inference and the consequent fear and loss of the power of discrimination. That, in turn, is caused by our exclusive reliance on the six sensory organs — eye, ear, nose, tongue, body, and mind. The sense-organs, particularly the mind, dominate our consciousness and unless that 'domination' is greatly dimished, the 'dim light' cannot be brightened enough to differentiate the perceived and the actual. It is the filter of clouded consciousness that causes the confusion and suffering and misery.

Throughout history, from Babylon to Greece, India and China to Europe, the eternal symbol of the snake has been a constant in myth and mythology, culture and fable. Snakes were regularly regarded as guardians of the Underworld, or as messengers between the Upper and Lower worlds because they lived in cracks and holes in the ground. The Gorgons of Greek myth were snake-women (a common hybrid) whose gaze would turn flesh into stone. The Hindu God *Vishnu*, one of the *Trimoorthis*, is often portrayed as perched on *Shesha*, the giant multi-headed serpent. And in the epics Ramayana and Mahabharata, Shesha incarnates as Lakshmana and Balarama respectively, the brothers of Rama and Krishna (who are the incarnations of Vishnu). The Hindu God Subramanyaswami is worshipped in the shape of a serpent. Practically every god has an animal as a companion-vehicle: Ganesha has a mouse or rat; Vishnu has the giant eagle, *Garuda*; Shiva has the bull, *Nandi*, etc. The symbolism is meant to convey the message that the difference between gods and animals is not that wide. In many tribal cultures, snakes are viewed as highly spiritual beings. John Milton wrote in *Paradise Lost* about the infernal serpent that, with guile, envy, and revenge, deceives the mother of mankind. *Nagalok*, the snake-people, are supposed to exist under the earth. Contrary to the modern view of the serpent as slimy and treacherous, the snake is also associated strangely with wisdom because it ponders before it strikes, and it is able to revolve its head without moving its body and thus can see in all directions. It is a fascinating transforming process. In the Tantric Yoga, *Kundalini*, 'the coiled one' is the invisible storehouse of energy that yogis believe resides at the base of our spine, coiled just like a snake in the equally invisible energy center (*chakra*) called '*Muladhar*', close to the coccyx. The unleashing of the immense power of the coiled serpent is the aim of many yogis and aspirants. One of the snake's most noticeable characteristics is the regular shedding of its outer skin including its eyecap as it grows. Once the skin is shed, the old inner layer becomes the new outer layer, and a new inner layer of skin begins to develop. It is a metaphor for how we shed old ways and habits as we grow into higher spiritual energy, symbolizing the process of death and rebirth. That the Upanishads, so rich with stories and symbols, chose this analogy to make such a seminal point is worthy of note. The snake evokes many emotions, sacred and slimy, awe and fear, beauty and ferocity; in this instance, it is used to illustrate the doctrine of superimposition, how an illusion becomes a reality.

We may use different analogies and myths to describe the innate secret power within, but the fact is that only a few people are able to see more than the immediate and realize how their lives are entangled with those of others. Even they fail to relate their actions or inactions to the fate of the species. The irony is that we value everything by comparison with others but we give little value to human connectivity. All life is but a ritual, biologically or socially required. Biology we are born with, and being social is what is needed to share the same earthy existence. Most creatures are 'social' in varying degrees, and man, in particular, has always been a social animal. Even our earliest ancestors, even with smaller brains than ours, had to be 'social' for sheer survival in the face of predatory animals and drastic climate shifts. But that has not made human society harmonious; we crave for company but also, even more for control. Perhaps in no other species is this one-to-one relationship as troubled and tenuous as in humans. With all our much-hyped powers of perception and seeing the big picture, we are somehow paralyzed from recognizing that, although our features and attributes may be different, we are but bits and pieces of a bigger whole. Our very cognitive process is a captive of the cycle of cause and effect, work and reward, and action and reciprocity. The doctrine of reciprocity has two facets: at one level, it is giving back what we receive; at another level, it is *not* doing to others that which we do not want others to do to us. The latter is one of the unifying principles in all religions, often called 'the golden rule'. When an emperor asked Confucius what should serve as a principle of conduct for life, he replied '*shu*' — reciprocity. How deterministic is the doctrine of causality — or reciprocity — is debatable. The human mind views every circumstance and cause as a way to fulfill a desire. A famous verse in the Upanishads says 'You are what your deep, driving desire is; as your deep driving desire is, so is your will; as your will is, so is your deed; as your deed is, so is your destiny'. In Buddhism, desire, with action consequent upon desire, is the cause of rebirth, and *nirvana* is the cessation of rebirth. Deliverance from desire is the deliverance from the cycle of birth and death. Desire itself is not bad; it is selfish desire or malice that is bad.

At the root of desire is thought, and thought, as the scriptures say, is the most potent power in the cosmos. Every thought, positive or negative, seeks similar thoughts in the universe and coalesces into a formidable source of energy. A single stray thought of a single Paleolithic man might have had an influence in shaping man as he is today. A wise man once said "Watch your thoughts, for they become words. Watch your words, for they become actions. Watch your actions, for they become habits. Watch your habits, for they become character. Watch your character, for it becomes your destiny." Whether or not language is the exclusive mode of communication of humans, it has significantly shaped human personality. It has two dimensions: talking and listening. Between the two, it is talking that is the preferred mode. Many scriptures and spiritualists emphasize the virtues of what in Buddhism is called 'the art of deep listening' as a way to overcome pain and suffering. It enables us to let go of any beliefs we have about the other person, and of our prejudices and past memories of him or her that inhibit our reaching out. Habit, which is defined as an acquired pattern of behavior that often occurs automatically, is pervasive in nature. As the American psychologist and philosopher William James says, "when we look at living creatures from an outward point of view, one of the first things that strike us is that they are bundles of habits"[12]. Habit shapes not only behavior but even conditions our nervous system and mode of thinking and because it is a 'reflex discharge' as James puts it, habit can greatly influence how we relate to another person. Everything in life — indeed life itself — is a habit; our daily chores are a habit; insulting can be a habit; so is 'being insulted'; exploitation and being exploited become a habit. Habit, over a period of time transforms into addiction. We cannot then help being nasty or cruel if we acquire that 'habit', and it becomes such a part of life that we cannot do without it, whether it is finding fault with, or humiliating or exploiting someone. It then becomes, as it were, our second nature. But then habit also offers hope; if only we can make 'being kind and caring' a habit, then we do not have to struggle to be good every day; it could become our 'reflexive response' to every provocation and temptation.

Dwanda-atheetha and the Principle of Polarity

The illusion of the rope being a snake or vice versa leads us to another, even grander, illusion of the 'pair of opposites'. In Nature, according to the Principle of Polarity, everything is dual; everything has its pair of opposites: like and unlike, love and hate. Opposites are identical in essence, but different in degree; extremes meet in a melting pot. *Dwanda* or duality is not some metaphysical or mystical mumbo jumbo. It is practical and pervasive in mundane life. We live in a world of duality — male and female, two chromosomes, two cerebral hemispheres, light and darkness, heat and cold, love and hate, good and bad, pleasure and pain, victory and defeat, profit and loss, happiness and misery, prosperity and poverty, life and death, etc. We recognize one of any two only if the other is also present. The ultimate state of consciousness is what Vedanta calls *dwanda-atheetha*, which is to go beyond the 'pairs of opposites'. The Principle of Polarity embodies the axiom that all manifested things have two sides — or two aspects or two poles — with manifold degrees between the two extremes. The bedrock of creation is that *everything* is dual: everything has poles; everything has its opposite; thesis and anti-thesis are identical in nature but different in degree; extremes meet; all truths are but half-truths; all paradoxes are appearances. Spirit and matter are but two poles, and a major goal in spiritual life is to experience the 'harmony of opposites', which really is to treat the pair as one, or that 'the all' and 'the many' are One. Jalal ad-Din Rumi said that God creates the 'pair' so that we have two wings to fly, not one. There is no 'natural' equality or absoluteness in Nature, and that leads to relativity and contrariety, and gives the fallacious feeling that we can choose one and shut out the other. Yet, there is an underlying unity between the two contrasts. It is how we achieve that harmony that makes the difference between drudgery and dedication, misery and ecstasy. We call one end of the moral scale good and the other bad, or evil. A thing is 'less good' or 'more good', the "more" or "less" being regulated by the position on the scale.

The philosophy of the 'unity of opposites' has a long pedigree and has been the focus of a good chunk of scriptural and philosophic inquiry. The Jewish Kabbalah describes the Infinite God' as a 'unity of opposites', one that harmonizes within itself even those aspects of the cosmos that are antithetical to each other. The *Chandogya* Upanishad (7.24.1) says that the Infinite is immortal while the Finite is mortal. The Ultimate is non-dual, and any presence or awareness of duality makes the awareness finite. The Infinite is the fullest expression and manifestation of the Absolute Reality, *Brahman*. The doctrine of *coincidentia oppositorum*, the interpenetration, interdependence, and unification of opposites, has for long been one of the principal manifests of mystical (as opposed to empirical and philosophical) thought. Mystical experiences can only be understood in terms that violate the 'principle of non-contradiction', which is at once of unification and going beyond both, *dwanda-atheetha* as it is called in Sanskrit. The premise is that presumed polarities in thought do not exclude one another but are actually necessary conditions for the assertion of their opposites. Not only mystics but even some scientists like the physicist Neils Bohr commented that superficial truths are those whose opposites are false, but that "deep truths" are such that their opposites are actually apparent contradictories. The Bhagavad Gita describes a *karma yogi*, among other things, as a person unmoved by pairs of opposites. Lord Krishna also says, while delineating Himself, that He is the compound called *dwanda* among all compounds. One of the essential attributes of a *jivanmukta*, the enlightened one who attains liberation while still remaining in the human body, is to transcend *dwanda* and to be in a state of non-duality. The word 'yoga' comes from the Sanskrit word *yuj*, meaning to join or unite. It is the union of all aspects of the individual: body, mind, and soul. Hence, yoga reunites all opposites — mind and body, stillness and movement, masculine and feminine — in order to bring about reconciliation between them. Chinese sages called this dynamic interplay of two extremes *yin* and *yang* — positive and negative — and have extended this principle to the function of daily life. The pre-Socratic Greek philosopher Heraclitus, among others, propounded this as a way to make sense of the phenomenal world. Such insight into the unity of things is itself a kind of transcendence, and is found in various mystical traditions. The idea occurs in the traditions of German mysticism and Buddhism, among others.

Perfection means to be complete, being so good that nothing else could be better. The opposite of perfection is imperfection, which is the condition of every living creature. Anger is an impairment to perfection ; malice is an impairment; greed is an impairment; obscene wealth is an impairment; leaving someone in distress is an impairment. We often confuse perfection with excellence by which we really mean efficiency, which is really to produce maximal returns with minimal effort. In one sense, there is perfection in the imperfection of the human being; and we should focus not on the perfection *per se*, but on managing the mediocrities in as perfect a manner as possible; not try to do extraordinary things but do ordinary things extraordinarily. The great, 'almost divine' Italian artist Michelangelo said that "the true work of art is but a shadow of divine perfection." In either sense of completeness or flawlessness, the human being is far from perfect. Our imperfection is not only physical and organic; it is equally, perhaps even more, mental and moral. Our bodies are good enough for us to exist as earthly beings. Even if we become bionic and have the strength of a superman and the agility of a cheetah, it would not make a difference to our imperfection. Even if we attain physical immortality (as science is trying to do through genetic mutations), we would still remain an unfinished product. Our minds and moral norms are not good enough for realizing our full potential and to share earthly space with other human beings or other life forms. It is really not very productive to debate whether morality is innate, or if it is simply a legal inconvenience or 'social lubricant' or religious rigmarole. The fact is even a monster wants to be 'moral'. Zygmunt Bauman says that we innately have what is called 'animal pity', which we feel when we see others suffering. If that were true, there is little doubt then that it has been smothered by the 'human culture', which we have so zealously nurtured over millenniums. What the mind has done is to make human culture so elastic and so specific that it lets us get away with the feeling that we are 'moral' while doing immoral things. Every human relationship and institution has created its own moral standard. Marriage has its own morality; so has market and so has property. And today, it seems that society's morality cannot keep up with technology. Indeed, that technology has eroded the moral dimension of every human institution from marriage to family to nationality, inappropriate to the technology-conditioned human personality. Yet, given the context of human life and the need for intensive human interfacing, without the restraint of morality — whatever may be its source or color — the full fury of human senses would tear us apart.

We should not blink or shy away from the fact that it is the 'fear' of society, of God, or of Hell that keeps us from succumbing to the allure of evil. We do not fear what it takes to be evil; we fear what might happen after evil is done. Swami Vivekananda said that if the law does not restrain us, we will all rob our neighbors' houses. Anonymity has its value but it is proximity that clouds our lives. The French philosopher of social sciences Rene Girard says that sometimes the most suitable victim is the neighbor. That is because the most tangible face of the opposite of the 'I', the '*Other*', is the neighbor. That was why Jesus put the commandment 'Love thy neighbor as yourself' next only to love of God. 'Neighbor' here is not only the one living next door; it is all of humanity, which is but the creation of God. One cannot love God without loving His closest likeness. It simply means respecting others and treating their needs and desires as highly as we treat our own. Every great spiritual teacher has said that one cannot love God while being nasty to a fellow human, indeed to all life. Evolution, culture, civilization, mind, heart, scripture or science, they all trickle down to one single thing: how do we treat and relate to others. When all is said and done, the bottom line is behavior and the true test of character is conduct. And we are also not quite sure what 'being moral' ought to be in terms of practical behavior. Perhaps one of the most cogent expositions on 'goodness' is contained in the Buddhist discourse *Metta Sutta*, also called the *Suta of Loving Kindness*. It contains, among other things, the following aphorisms. It begins with the words, "This is what should be done by one who is skilled in goodness and who knows the path of peace", and the word 'skilled' gives the impression that goodness can be inculcated and cultivated. The 'good' are those who are "able and upright"; and "straight forward and gentle in speech; humble and not conceited; contented and easily satisfied; unburdened with duties and frugal in their ways; contented and calm; and wise and skilful; not proud and demanding in nature." The discourse further exhorts: "Let them not do the slightest thing that the wise would later reprove. Let none deceive another, or despise any living being in any state. Let none through anger or ill will wish harm upon another. Even as a mother protects her child, her only child, so with a boundless heart should one cherish all living beings". The discourse ends with "the pure-hearted one, having clarity of vision, being freed from all sense-desires, is not born again in this world."[13]

Apart from 'goodness', humans suffer from a psychosis of 'greatness'. We talk of great men, great works, great civilizations and countries as the highest realm of human creativity. We use terms like greatness, genius, giftedness, charisma, goodness, godliness, icon and heroism without clear boundaries. All of them have meaning in relation to the opposite. Someone is great because the rest are deemed ordinary; someone is godly in comparison to the garden-type mortals, and someone is heroic when he performs an extraordinary act of courage or chivalry or magnanimity. While no two lives are equal, both in terms of their content and their legacy, and no life is too insignificant to make some difference to other's lives, the fact also is that some men have changed the tide of history by their very presence on earth, and some others have left a trail of misery and destruction. Loosely speaking, *great men* are those who leave their indelible, not necessarily positive, imprints on history; *genius* is one who through his cerebral strength creates something of timeless value or beauty or one with an IQ level higher than 140; *giftedness* is an intellectual, artistic or creative ability higher than the average; *charisma* is what one exudes that makes one person follow another even against his will; *goodness* is what is decent in man; *godliness* is the outward manifestation of the divine within; *icon* is one who is larger than life and whom we admire uncritically; *heroism* is an act of bravery beyond the call of duty or the bounds of self-preservation. Thomas Carlyle said that the history of what man has accomplished in this world is essentially the history of great men who have worked here. Shakespeare famously wrote that "some are born great; some achieve greatness, and some have greatness thrust upon them". On the question whether great men shape society (as Carlyle postulated) or society makes great men (as Herbert Spencer argued), we cannot come to any definitive conclusion; the safest solution is to opt for a mix of both. Some people show greatness by their mere existence and example; some simply by a seminal idea; some by their oratory eloquence; some by their writing or visual representation; some by capturing or controlling the levers of governance; and some through the barrel of a gun. And then the question is: what motivates or inspires a hero or a great man — personal gain or social purpose? On this too, opinions vary. The German philosopher Georg Hegel, for example, argued that a great man might be motivated by personal benefit and yet be serving a public purpose. Then again, all great men do not necessarily achieve 'greatness'. Many a 'great man' has lived and died anonymously. Chance, fate or luck or destiny plays a dominant role, whichever way one would wish to characterize the phenomenon. Increasingly, in the face of the ineluctable forces that are patently beyond any semblance of human control, the deeds of 'great men' seem to wither into transience, and they are shown up as all too human or nothing but human. And, in terms of the moral calculus, the Greek scholar Athenaeus wrote that goodness does not consist in greatness, but greatness consists in goodness. Samuel Johnson said that nothing is truly great which is not right.

Whatever might be the perils or subtleties of 'greatness', there is hardly anyone who does not dream of being or becoming 'great'. Some want to be great to wield power; some want to attain fame and fortune; some want to attract social esteem and recognition; some want to do 'good'; some just want to 'feel good'. At the same time, we often lament that the world of today is a world of mechanization and mediocrity, starved of great men and great leaders. Greatness is necessarily not goodness; in fact, more often than not, most great men, save prophets and saints, were morally flawed men, as Paul Johnson's book *Intellectuals* (1988), so scathingly shows. Someone said that it is the prerogative of great men to have great defects. The closer we get to great men, the clearer it dawns on us that they too are ordinary men. A deep disconnection often exists between public profundity and private profanity in the minds of many great men. Their soaring intellect and lofty idealism has often been powerless to withstand the temptation to take unfair advantage of the dependent and the defenseless. The general human propensity to mouth piety and platitudes, but act with malice and meanness does not spare even great men. That raises the central question 'what is the litmus test for greatness?' Is it 'being good', or is it something that is independent of one's personal behavior? Or is it the way one alleviates the other's pain and suffering? By normal standards of behavior, Hitler could be considered as having 'done the right thing' after all, as he married his mistress Eva Braun as a 'moral gesture' minutes before they committed suicide. He was a 'good' man in that relationship and in that instant. But he was evil personified in his public life. And then there are others who are publicly prudish and privately licentious. 'Great' men can be the catalysts of change or manipulators of minds. In either case, their legacy and impact lasts long after their death. It is also important to note that for great men to become great and for charismatic leaders to showcase their charisma, there has to be some sort of grave political, economic, social or spiritual context, wherein their potential followers or admirers find such leadership to be their sole hope, which is tantamount to suspending or abdicating their freedom and free will. In fact our relationship with great men highlights our ambivalent equation with freedom and free will. On the one hand, we value our freedom, but on the other hand, we crave for the authority of something or someone strong in whose name or cause we are willing to surrender that very freedom. Often, what we hesitate to give God we give to these men — total trust. And we let them — total strangers — exercise more control over our thoughts, feelings, and emotions than those whom we know and 'love'. Erich Fromm divides freedom into '*freedom from*' (the process of becoming emancipated from the restrictions placed on humanity by other people or institutions), and '*freedom to*' (the use of freedom to behave in ways that are constructive and respond to the genuine needs and wants of the free individual/society by creating a new system of social order).

In other words, what we are really comfortable with is not freedom to choose and to act with free will but to '*escape from*' freedom, which is to escape from one's own self and to find comfort and security in the suffocating strength of another person. Deep in the human psyche lurks a desire to be subjected to authoritarianism, a desire to be absolved from the burden of decision-making. And in surrendering to a 'superior power', be it great men or God, we feel lofty, lifted and elated, freed from guilt for our foibles, and we surrender our right to know what is right and wrong. There is something in the human psyche that impels us to credit other human beings with sainthood or even godhood, and to willingly elevate the fallible to the status of infallibility, and to assume that another mind should be given headship over our mind. That enables great men to make you do things, for good or bad, that you would not otherwise think of doing or actually do. Generally, it was believed that charisma is something that you have or you do not have. Now, scientists say they have found the secret to this magical quality and that it can be learnt. And that charisma is, in a way, infectious. It is said that when you see someone else who is charismatic, you tend to mimic their mannerisms and their facial expressions without realizing it — and maybe also mimic their mental attributes, which offer both promise and peril. Promise lies in a few men motivating and inspiring many others to do things they would not otherwise do for the good of the world; and there is peril, too, because these very men can, with equal ease, make us do horrible things. History has recorded for us that truly great men were in fact semi-divine like Jesus, the Buddha and Muhammad, and to grow to such a status, or to even come close, a spiritual foundation is necessary. Another ingredient is personal purity and transparent integrity. Emerson said that "if two or three persons should come with a high spiritual aim and with great powers, the world would fall into their hands like a ripe peach."[14] Well, the fact that it has not quite happened that way does not negate the message. But it does signify how far down the moral slope the world has slipped.

The issue of what constitutes greatness, hitherto a scholarly question, now becomes practical, as science is promising to re-engineer the human persona through genetic manipulation, which raises the possibility of made-to-order greatness. Scientists claim to have identified genes like the spiritual gene, god-gene, etc. Would it be possible to implant 'greatness', and also goodness into the 'make-up' of posthuman man? We must bear in mind that greatness, like every other human attribute is a means to an end. That end is to contribute to the good of the world. Great men may mould history, but it is *good* men who, as Emerson puts it, make the earth wholesome. Goodness may be anonymous, but it does not go in vain; it is like fragrance; you can smell it, not see it; it lingers long after the flower withers. Like evil, goodness is not only an act but also a word and a thought. A kind word goes a long way. We commit more sins through 'word of mouth' than by direct deed. Perhaps, of all the organs in the human body, it is the mouth that is the most vital — and lethal. It is not only the primary point to ingest the food needed to keep us alive, but it is also the primary point of interaction with the external world. It is one of the very few organs with which we can exercise volitional choice — keep it open or shut; but more good happens when it is shut. Human history would have been so different — and better — if only man knew how to use his mouth wisely. But even the mouth is only a mouthpiece. The master is the *mind.*

A Thinking Pigmy

The operational arm of the mind is what we call 'intellect' or 'intelligence'. It is 'intelligence', the ability to draw inferences from what we perceive of the world around us, from abstract ideas and concepts and experiences, from our reasoning powers, that distinguishes us from fellow-animals. While it has helped us arrive and overcome some of the limitations of Nature, what is surprising is that intelligence has blinded us from doing what is truly good for us; it has accentuated inherent differences and has fashioned a culture and civilization which threaten the very survival of 'intelligent' life on earth. Our intelligence seems sufficient most times to know what is right, but not to empower and enable us to do right. And most of us do not use intelligence intelligently. The human race has now reached a stage where we need to revisit what that 'intelligence' has come to mean, and what price humanity has paid for letting it be the dominant force in human affairs. The irony is that although 'intelligence', which comes from a Latin verb '*intellegere*', meaning 'to understand', we hardly understand anything worth understanding. We must revisit, at this juncture in the evolution of human consciousness, our reverence for reason, addiction to deductive empiricism, veneration for linear thinking, and skepticism of mysticism. One of the basic assumptions of 'being intelligent' is that we can separate facts from fear, and, given that knowledge, be rational and do the right thing — in other words, make us better persons. But in practice, our intelligence is a tool to prevail over others; and when we do not always succeed, it fans the flames of fear. Modern man has more fears that harass and haunt him than ever before, above all the fear of his fellow men and what they might do. Bertrand Russell said that conquering fear is the beginning of wisdom. The British spiritual writer Rodney Collin said that fear is the most powerful projection and a terrible force in the world, and that it is fear that is behind all the irrationality and chaotic emotions that dog mankind.[15] Fear is the lever that moves much of life. It is the principal trigger for insecurity, aggression, and war. There is also a collective fear, which Bertrand Russell said breeds a herd instinct and leads to ferocity towards those outside the herd. But can Nature really afford a truly fearless man? It is fear that holds us back from crime and sin, and all fear is not all bad. Perhaps, the most formidable obstacle to human happiness, progress and transformation is our smug self-righteousness, our chronic, almost pathological ability to find everything wrong with others and nothing in ourselves, the mindset to make an exception of oneself, which has been called the greatest of all sins and the root of all evil. It should be sharply distinguished from self-esteem or self-respect. Jesus said that we notice the mole in our brother's eye and ignore the blemish in our own eye. From any reckoning, this ought to be a time for serious stock-taking, a time to step aside and look inside, both as an individual and as a species. As Thomas Berry says, "we are not simply in another period of historical change or cultural modification such as these have taken place in past centuries in the human order. What is happening now is of a geological and biological order of magnitude. We are upsetting the entire earth system that, over some billions of years and through an endless sequence of groping, of trials and errors, has produced such a magnificent array of life forms, forms capable of seasonal self-renewal over vast periods of time."[16]

Man today, bristling with brittleness in body and mind, shorn of his spiritual essence and captive of what we might call 'militant rationality', is dreaming of immortality when his very reason for being, his very 'be all and end all', as Shakespeare puts it, is getting eroded. Modern man, called *Homo sapien sapiens*, is a relatively new phenomenon on the evolutionary scale, so new that it is almost a new form of life on earth. By his extreme dependency on technology, contemporary human has essentially become a terminally dependent being; and by living separately from the natural world, he has forfeited the love of Mother Earth; and by acquiring power that he is not equipped to handle wisely, he threatens his own existence. So, in a way, all traditional methods of 'treatment' have become inadequate. The whole human habitat is artificial now: the air, the water, society, and man's living conditions. Nothing is 'as-is-where-is' or natural any more. Everything is processed, polluted, and peddled. We pride ourselves for our capacity for calibrated and careful thought but we are in fact, a 'thinking pigmy' as Colin Wilson puts it in his book, *The Outsider* (1956). He wrote that "All men and women have these dangerous, unnamable impulses, yet they keep up a pretense, to themselves, to others; their respectability, their philosophy, their religion, are all attempts to gloss over, to make look civilized and rational something that is savage, unorganized, irrational."[17] Most men are marginal men, fixated on the edges of life, not fully alive and not yet dead, paralyzed by personal preoccupations and terminally drained by the 'trivialities of everyday life', by the adjustments, and compromises, needed to share the same with other humans. At the very crux of human existence, everyone is the same, exalted or debased, self-absorbed being. Man acts sometimes as if he is immortal and at other times, as if there is no tomorrow. The terrible tragedy of man is that although he has been called a 'social animal' by philosophers like John Locke, yet he cannot stand another man's company for too long. Human personalities clash almost seamlessly, and yet what man has and aspires to have, has value relative to what others have or want to have, or do not have. In other words, modern man wants competition without competitors, a kind of 'absolute relativity'. If there were no one else around, man would either be insane or be a saint. He is wrapped in self-righteousness beyond the needs of self-belief and in self-pity; together, they rob him of one of the essential 'abilities' of the human condition: a sense of shame and guilt. He has an appetite only for greed, not guilt. And a man wholly devoid of guilt is more menacing than a man-eater. A guiltless person has to be a near-perfect being, and man is the epitome of imperfection.

Torture and terror, at the core of which is calculated and deliberate infliction of pain, are embedded in our history, and all civilizations that practiced them were privy in some way or the other. Torture and terror are both very old and very widespread. Man has used every available tool and technique for torture, just like insects such as bees, wasps, sheep ticks and assassin bugs (which first stab their prey and then inject a toxin that dissolves the tissue). To be terrified of somebody, you do not have to be tortured, at least in the physical sense. Today, we have a new category of sacred nihilists — the terrorists — who live in a state of absolute certitude that nothing is a crime or a sin in the cause of their conviction. On the other hand, once labeled as such, that person virtually ceases to be 'human' in the eye of the state and society, and unspeakable indignities and horrors are committed on their bodies to make them 'confess' and betray their collaborators. Assuming the cause to be good, it is based on the moral premise that to do evil today is ethically in order if we have some basis to hope that in the future, at the end of a long chain of causation and chance, something good will emerge. Just as war is considered a 'preferred moral choice' by many 'honorable' people, torture too is justified, a 'necessary nuisance'. It finally comes down to numbers; that inhumanity is justified if those who suffer are fewer than those whose suffering it is supposed to preempt.

Almost every State indulges in torture as a means of intrusive interrogation and coercive confession, which, as Elaine Scarry in her work *The Body in Pain* (1985) explains, is to deconstruct the victim by separating the voice from the body, the person from his knowledge; to make the voice, disoriented by pain, speak as the torturer wishes. Pedestrian torture play makes us *not* to say what we *want* to say, or to refrain from doing things that we want to do, and to accept humiliation. Silence and conformity seem preferable or less painful than the consequences of resistance. The triggers for torture are many, ranging from 'just fun' to seeking 'truth', to protect the innocent, to abort evil, etc. But that, in a macabre sense, is the tangible or 'organized' torture, which is but the tip of the iceberg. Scholars have long debated what conditions and social contexts are more conducive to terror and torture, what kind of governance and legal system is likely to eliminate or greatly minimize them. Some even apprehend that terror and torture will be on the 'agenda of the future' and that "it is always possible to argue that contextual indicatives require terrorism and torture; it is always possible to say that praxis demands setting universalistic ethics aside; it is always possible to say that 'our' experience overrides any cross-historical or cross-cultural principles."[18] The debate can go on but the fact of the matter is that 'when push comes to shove', few will hold back on the ground that torture is a moral transgression or violation of 'human rights'. That is part of being the beast we are. The ugly reality is that most people live in fear, if not 'terror', of someone (a spouse or a boss) or of something (like losing a job or of dying) or of what lurks in the dark corners of their conscience. To terrorize somebody or to accept being terrorized is not very difficult; the mind quickly adjusts to both situations and soon both become a habit. Terror is a way to exercise power, to control, which is one of the deepest and darkest human drives on par perhaps with sexuality.

Power, Passion and Love

The lust to exercise power is one of the basic human passions, and philosophers from Plato forward have agonized over its character and content. Why do we so compulsively want to dominate another person? Is it because we control so little of our own lives — our DNA structure, our parentage, the length of our life, even how we behave — that, as a kind of an inverse reflex, we want to control someone else? Or is it simply a symbol of our struggle for survival? Or does that have a deeper source: simply to be true to our nature? Whatever be the dynamic, power has been the dominant determinant throughout human antiquity and history. It was the lure of power — to become God — that enticed Eve to eat the fruit of the forbidden tree and fall prey to the wiles of the snake. In its essence, it is the desire to bend another person's will to our advantage, to rearrange reality, as it were, to be in congruence with our taste and temper. Simply put, we want power because we want to control. We want to control everything that we see and touch — other people, events, our neighborhood, Nature, God — everything other than our own selves. We want to control because we want to prevail, and we want to prevail because 'to prevail' over another person is one of the dominant human characteristics. Since everyone wants the same thing and wants to be, in Nietzsche's words, master over all space, it leads to confrontation and conflict. Human endeavor has always pursued two contrasting objectives: justice and power. The balance between the two defines, to a large extent, the quality of the human condition. For, justice without power is impotent, and power without justice is tyranny. The need for justice stems directly from the inequity inherent in human nature. Man cannot be trusted to be left alone with his raw passions, priorities and predispositions, without posing a threat to another man. Man is a passionate being and is capable of experiencing strong emotions, compelling feelings, enthusiasm, or scorching desire for something or someone. Well directed, passion can be a powerful positive force; without being passionate, man can achieve precious little. But wrongly directed, it can be an awesome destructive power. How, why and when passion turns deadly is a question for psychologists and scientists. What we call 'culture' and 'civilization' are, as Aldous Huxley noted, arrangements to domesticate our passions and 'set them to do useful work'. Which means, the world is better off with man 'in a cage', or tied to a rope, the only question being the length of the rope. Since the people who 'set us to do' are also humans with passions, we end up carrying out actions triggered by the passions of powerful people.

Unlike animals, we cannot easily share living space. To cater to the needs of the needy and the wants of the vulnerable, we need social justice. To channel individual power we need a common or collective power. But we have not found any natural order or human habitat that ensures justice even while letting every man be his own master. In that sense, there has never been a 'just society' in human history; and no 'ism' — communism or socialism or capitalism or any kind of kingdom — has delivered the right mix of power and justice. And that makes power an imperative for greed and glory alike. Our modern Machiavellian world is nothing but a cauldron of craving for power. Power can be positive or negative, having regard to the nature of action (to induce or resist), to the type of action (violent or pacific) and to the intended outcome (to do good or to harm). Power can be physical, psychological, mental, moral or spiritual. Some kind of power is pervasive and is implicit in every human interaction. How we wield power is a true test of character. The way power is exercised depends not only on the nature of our own power, but also on the nature of powerlessness of the other person. Our irritation is often focused on the helpless; our insults on those whose position prevents them from insulting us back; and our anger directed at those who feel acceptance is less troublesome than retaliation. The test of character, Lincoln said, is not adversity, but the exercise of power. Power is of various kinds — spiritual, intellectual, artistic, political or social — but in any form it boils down to one thing; the ability to influence events and to dominate the lives of other people. We all have some power; no one — not even a beggar — is powerless. Powerlessness does not always mean *not* having power; it is a question of will; it is also being restrained (or not letting be restrained) from exercising the power; and the restraint is the fear of 'what might happen'. Whatever power one has, if one demurs from using it for whatever reason, he becomes powerless, if not helpless. Often, we paralyze ourselves, feeling or thinking that exercising power entails more effort and higher cost than submission. No one, not even a child or a slave, is wholly without power. Stillness is power; silence is power. Often times, we become powerless because we cannot countenance the consequences of exercising power. We all experience this phenomenon, at some point or the other, in life; it has a bearing on who the other person is. Parents have power; children have it; spouses have it; friends have it; enemies have it; scientists have it; the State has it in abundance; and citizens have it. If true character is what we do when we *think* no one is watching us, real power is how we treat an other person who is in an unequal situation. The true test of character is not how we behave when we are powerless, but how we use power and how it affects other people.

Power and passion, or rather the way they are channeled, are also changing social values. In a world that scoffs at 'softness' and worships 'strength', such acts as lying, cheating, deviousness, and deception no longer elicit social reproach; they are just a part of what it takes to survive in today's world. And those who do not want to pay that price are choosing to quit, leaving behind a note that they are not mentally fit for this world. Why is falsity so ingrained in us? Are we 'natural-born' liars? While deception is not confined to humans and many animals resort to it to outwit a predator or a prey, human culture has made it a defining signature, the calling card of the human way of life. David Smith (*Why We Lie*, 2004) proposes that "we evolved with our conscious mind aware of only a fraction of what we think and feel, and that this occurred because we cannot lie without giving away clues that might give us away — the evolutionary answer to this dilemma is that our mind lies to our conscious selves, in order that we can, with all sincerity, lie to others."[19] We lie because we have so much to hide. As Denise Breton and Christopher Largent say in their book *The Paradigm Conspiracy* (1996), shackled with secrets we interact with each other, not heart to heart but lie to lie. And 'lying', which is not only being untruthful but also not acting on what we know, becomes comforting, a way not to face up to the inconvenient and the unpleasant. While deception developed as an evolutionary need, it remained entrenched within, because the mind, rather the unconscious mind, found it a convenient tool to prevent us from knowing the 'real reality' and to perpetuate its hold. Scriptures and saints, philosophers and pundits have exhorted mankind to cultivate what Vietnamese Zen master Thich Nhat Hanh calls the 'mind of love', which, he says, lies buried deep in our consciousness under many layers of forgetfulness and suffering — and one might add culture of combativeness and civilization of comfort and control. Love is a gift, of one's own self, the divine side of the 'noble savage', the 'civilized brute'. In Greek, 'love' is expressed in five distinct words: *epithumia* (desire–attraction), *eros* (longing–romance), *storge* (belonging–affection), *phile* (cherishing–friendship), and *agape* (selfless giving–Christian love). Of these, what seem to be uppermost are attraction and longing, and what have gone into recess are true friendship and selfless giving. And man's proprietary instinct, the sense of 'owning', has overwhelmed love.

The story of 'love', of its negative 'transformation', symbolizes the story — and tragedy — of man. Why, and how, has love gone bad, or mad, that is the question. As perhaps nothing else, love is the one emotion that can catapult man to the Everest of heights, but can also push him down into the darkest of depths. We need to narrow the gap between what we are capable of bestowing upon one person — the one we love or are in love with — and our attitude towards the rest of the humanity. What we are capable of is something like what Catherine said about Heathcliff in *Wuthering Heights* (1847): "If all else perished, and he remained, I should still continue to be; and if all else remained, and he were annihilated, the universe would turn to a mighty stranger: I should not seem a part of it". Leaving nothing to chance she says "I *am* Heathcliff! He's always, always in my mind: not as a pleasure, any more than I am always a pleasure to myself, but as my own being". It is another matter that she chose not to marry to love and save him! Like Catherine, so many choose life over love, and mind over heart. While unrequited love has always been a scorching feeling, it evokes savagery today. While non-romantic, interpersonal love has always been a strong social bond, it is now conditioned by race, religion, and riches. We may sing 'love is all we need' but that cry gets no echo. Swami Vivekananda's panacea "one burning love, selfless"[20] is what the world needs. In its absence, much of mankind is a wasteland and what we call 'love' is 'hyphenated' love: romantic-love, marital-love, parental-love, fraternal-love, patriotic-love, etc. We love the bond that connects, not the person. In the *Brihadaranyaka* Upanishad, the sage Yajnavalkya tells his wife Maitreyi that everything in the world is the love of the Self, not of the husband or wife or son or anything else. The Self here refers to the eternal *Atman*, the Self that Lord Krishna referred to when he said "I am the Self, seated in the hearts of all beings",[21] not the transient body. It is essential for our spiritual journey to get some clarity on this point. What goes by in the name of love, interpersonal or impersonal, does not deter anything abominable anymore — murder, maiming or massacre; they are all explained away, if not justified, for the sake of love, in the name of love, and at the altar of love. The paradox lies in the fact that love, which has been glorified by scriptures and saints as the natural condition of man, is marked by an inability on our part to make it spontaneous to our way of life. On the other hand, judging by what goes on in the world, man loves to hate. And when man is 'in love', he is capable of superhuman sacrifice or subhuman savagery. The impulse to control, the push for possession, the rage for ownership, permeates love too. Just as we want to squeeze profit out of every possession, sacred or profane, we also want our love to be profitable, good, bad, or ugly. It is almost as if the human mind has come to the conclusion that to survive and to 'progress', love and what it entails — sacrifice, caring, compassion — are no longer appropriate; perhaps passé. Being loved is the most sought after state but that is one thing most people feel deprived of. Love is at best reciprocal, often an exchange, part of a package. One cannot anymore be sure whether to fear or favor someone who 'loves' you; at least, one can be sure of what to expect of hate.

Love can turn into hatred (failed love marriages) and hatred into 'love' (love of the captive towards their captors). Some like to put it differently: it is not that love becomes hate, but love leaves, and hate steps in, or the other way around. And it is possible to exhibit both towards the same person, albeit at different times and contexts. Man is capable of killing the very person he saves. Some, like the essayist William Hazlitt, said that hate, more than love, is a virtue, even a divine attribute, and that "love turns, with a little indulgence, to indifference or disgust; hatred alone is immortal."[22] It all depends on what or whom or why we 'hate'. One thing is clear though: hatred in itself is a deeply and dangerously seductive thing which can more easily lead one into paths of self-destruction.

But there is lingering hope that humanity will be able to make 'selfless love' its primary impulse (not its habit of hatred), without the need for an epic struggle. Hope, also called *elpis* in Greek mythology, is a wonderful thing; it is, in Christian theology, one of the three virtues (faith, hope, and charity). But not everyone agrees. Nietzsche, for example, wrote that it is the most evil of all evils since it prolongs man's torment. Martin Luther King Jr. talked of finite disappointment and infinite hope. One can cultivate the 'habit of hope' and when that happens, life itself becomes hopeful. And hopeful people are usually positive people, and they exude love. With good fortune, we may still meet people, in whom this sublime energy, love, shines strongly, allowing us all to bask in its luminous light. The great saints and *bodhisattvas* completely emptied themselves of ego and transmitted such love. But their love, unlike ours, is unconditional and all embracing. Self-serving motives, self-righteousness, attachment, expectation of something in return, grabbing, egocentric attachment, being conditional, partial-heartedness, none of these have any place in love and, in practice, they completely block the artery of love. Placing ourselves first and at the center forecloses the possibility of feeling the thrill of love. But in a travesty befitting our time, the term 'love' is perhaps the most used, but what we actually do with that love is a travesty of what it ought to be.

We are lost somewhere in the melting pot of sacredness, sex, sin, love, marriage, monogamy, fidelity, pleasure, guilt, shame, religion, etc. For too many people, sex is something to satiate or a skill or a resource to be harnessed for survival or for worldly advancement. For them, sexuality is reduced to sex based on pleasure, hedonism, and permissiveness. Sexual relations then become short-lived, anonymous, and promiscuous — ones in which the partners can be interchanged to enhance the inventory of their experiences; their connection is confined to the satisfaction of their sexual appetites. The subject becomes only an object of pleasure. In times of war, sexuality also becomes a means to geopolitical ends. We have not really made up our minds about such carnal relationships — what such a relationship is intended to be in Nature, and what we ought to do with it to ensure a bright posthuman future. As things stand now, we are heading for a future in which sex for anything other than pure pleasure would be deemed anti-social. Women will be, it is claimed, liberated from being 'necessary, vulnerable vessels for the next generation'. In the epic poem *Paradise Lost* (1667), Milton wrote of Satan spying on the endearments of Adam and Eve, not yet fallen, and of seeing 'undelighted all delight'. Milton saw pure sex as a paradisal source of delight. That delight has become a prescription for pain, across all perquisites of success in life. Worse, the adage "Everything is fair in love and war", is a guiding principle in one's 'love' life. We cannot remove sex from all love, but love is as important for living as sex is for procreation. We cannot ignore the facts that while our spirit or soul is gender-neutral, our bodies are not; that turns creative energy into stress and tension. The tension comes from the paradox that while we exist in a sexed body, deep inside we are asexual. There is a theory that for a long time there was only one gender that later split into two, and since then it has been an endless attempt to become whole again. Since we cannot unite the two physically or erase our gender-specificity, we must do so energetically or spiritually, what has been called 'spiritual orgasm'. The problem is that while we are trying to reconcile the tension within our own sexed nature, we also find ourselves living in a culture that accentuates sexual tension. Although biologically and spiritually no one is wholly male or female, being one — and not the other — becomes our overarching identity and obscures everything else, even our relationship with God, putting a drag on our spiritual progress. Uncontrollable or unresolved, sexual drive is swimming around in our subconscious, trying to find fulfillment in the physical world. The key is to merge that drive with love so that it is freed both from levity and guilt. The Indian mystic and 'guru' Osho says that "The proportion of your love is the proportion of your being".[23] What we fail to recognize is that love is not an option but an imperative; it is not just what we intensely, even 'unbearably' feel towards someone else; it is vital for our own fullness. For love, we are not only giving but also growing; indeed it is through 'giving' that one 'grows'. But much of what is proffered as love is at best reciprocity, often grabbing, not giving. Love and hate are generally considered incompatible, if not mutually exclusive; where there is love, there can be no hate, so it is said. We can no longer take comfort in that cover. Hate is the shadow of love; hate and love coexist, even criss-cross and merge. What lies in a 'loving' relationship is a *quid pro quo*, duty, obligation, often retaliation when it is unreturned. Love is when you do not *have* to love, when and where there is no expectation. For hate to turn into love it takes a while, but love can turn into hate in a very short time. Love can turn into hate not only when it is unrequited but also by the coarseness of prolonged physical intimacy; indeed, one could even kill the one loved, not for any gross 'betrayal' but also because of the common pressures of cohabitation, as we read so often in the 'news'. For love, we need respect. Because familiarity breeds condescension, if not contempt, man has not found a way to manage either intimacy or isolation;

either of which can lead to suicide or homicide. The intensity of passion or the pain of isolation simply changes color and character. And hate could turn into love *à la* 'the Stockholm Syndrome'.

Human social life is a whirling web of relationships, in each of which one is required to share living or emotional space with other humans, with all the attendant ego clashes and adjustments. The duties and responsibilities entailed in each relationship are not always consistent with those of others, and that creates discord and tension, and we do not have the wisdom to harmonize them. Our union here with wives, husbands, kith and kin, and friends is like that of travelers at a roadside inn. In fact, just as the universe is really *multiverse*, as astronomers proclaim, we are all multi-beings, each being specific to a relationship. Without the authenticity of a relationship, we remain virtual non-beings. Even in a single relationship, the dynamics can dramatically change, and the 'balance of power' can shift, and the connecting thread can oscillate from caring to cruelty, from harmony to hatred. Prolonged intimacy between two humans has a very ambivalent effect on the human condition. In intimate relationships, we have no cover of culture and we transgress boundaries, permissible and impermissible, those that normally contain and channel human passions. It could either fuse two souls or rob their respect. It is in the context of such relationships that both the individuals' strengths and faults, and raw vulnerabilities and innate virtues can be highlighted, stripping them of the cover of civility and of the sanitization of culture. One of Dostoevsky's characters in his novel *The Brothers Karamazov* exposes the paradoxical nature of the human condition and says "I love mankind but I am amazed at myself: the more I love mankind in general, the less I love people in particular, that is, individually, as separate persons". And then, he goes on to say "… I am incapable of living in the same room with anyone for even two days". It is that chasm that we should bridge, between the abstract and the actual, between the impersonal and the intimate. Human society may never resemble the mythical Tibetan kingdom of *Shambhala,* the perfect place of peace and tranquility and happiness, in which all citizens are able to transmute aggression into love. The fact is, as Dostoevsky says, "Until one has indeed become brother of all, there will be no brotherhood. No science or self-interest will ever enable people to share their property and their rights among themselves without offense. Each will always think his share too small, and they will keep murmuring, they will envy and destroy one another". But what we can — and must — do is to insure that hate does not become an all-embracing or all-consuming passion within and distort the core human personality.

Moral Foundation of Mankind

For most people, though, the relentless daily grind, the sheer wear and tear of worldly existence ebbs away all passion and sensitivity. 'Life' for them is more a scream of pain than a song of pleasure, more a test of endurance than of enjoyment. That makes us a 'soft species', and in the natural world, only the strong and the resilient survive. But we are also a species armed to the teeth with horrendous weapons. Our addiction to comfort, convenience, control, and technological quick-fixes has so enfeebled the human organism that it has become an easy prey today to every passing vulture or virus. With the dramatic discoveries in genetic technology, we are told that it is not improbable that a tyrant, a fanatic or a desperate man can create a 'doomsday' virus with 100 percent mortality. The human species has not, since its advent on earth, devised a way to manage and reconcile interpersonal interests without conflict and violence. Nor has it discovered or innovated the way to 'god governance'. In fact, based on our track record, it does seem the human being is simply ungovernable. The successive *modus operandi* of governance have progressively made it worse, not better, raising the question if the human, with the kind of psychological personality he has developed, is simply ungovernable. The latest paradigm of human governance, the Nation-State, is perhaps the most ill-suited for conflict resolution, which has become the most pressing need of the hour. It is the worst form of governance because it is centralized; it is top down and distant. And 'nationalism', its ideological offspring, a sentiment or a form of culture, has been, for the past four centuries, the dominant political principle; and it has been responsible for more bloodshed than perhaps any other ideology in human history. Erich Fromm called it our form of incest, our idolatry, our insanity, and Einstein called it infantile disease, the measles of mankind. Along with the Nation-State and nationalism, another beguiling but corrosive concept has come into being, the 'national interest', which, it is implicitly accepted, overrides any universal principle or precept, and whose pursuance, whatever it entails, is the highest duty not only of the State but also its citizens. We judge all events, local to international, from a 'national' perspective, not a human or religious or moral perspective. A billion people deprived of the basic needs of daily food, drinking water, and stable shelter due to mass poverty is a failure of governance at all levels. So is the case with global warming and climate change, and the 'once-in-a-generation' natural disasters, which, it is said, devastate seven times more people than a war.[24] In fact, archeologist David Keys posits that a global catastrophe was triggered by a single event, a volcanic eruption, in about 535 CE resulting in prolonged (up to three years) bad weather worldwide. The first calamity to follow the catastrophe was drought in some places, and massive floods, followed by famine worldwide and plague in certain parts of the world. That scenario looks eerily contemporary, if we replace the volcanic lava by melting glaciers and warming oceans. But we are paralyzed by doubt and passivity; we just hope such things will not reach us if it is really that bad. Constructed as we are, with the consciousness we have, the way things inside us churn, we are simply incapable of acting any other way.

Either as individuals or as communities or countries, we are just unable to put the larger interest ahead of the narrower interest. Our idea of moral imagination or indignation places no value or virtue in sacrificing a bit of the certain present for the uncertain future. Deep inside, we feel that we owe as much or as little to those who are yet to be born as to those who are already dead. We are so smug in the cocoon of comfort and convenience that we are prepared to trade everything — even our future — for the perpetuation of that comfort and convenience. For, we simply cannot believe — indeed we are incapable of experiencing any such belief— that anything can really endanger the future, least of all the fruits of our (and our forefathers') struggle: our lifestyle.

The primary reason why nationalism and national interest have been so devastating is because it is implied and intellectually assumed that they are outside the rigor of morality, and all values and principles we hold dear as individuals do not apply when nationalism and national interest are invoked. As human innovations that draw power from human beings and are meant for human benefit, they cannot be immune from the normal human moral discipline. For, as Einstein wrote, "the most important human endeavor is striving for morality in our actions. Our inner balance and even our very existence depend on it. Only morality in our actions can give beauty and dignity to our lives."[25] We cannot expect to bring back the moral imperative into our lives if we leave out our collective personality. Our moral duplicity with the State highlights a bigger problem. Our sense of morality, like our sense organs, is externally focused: *we* are moral and good; it is *they* who are not. Robert Stevenson captured our moral sophistry well when wrote that there is so much good in the worst of us, and so much bad in the rest of us, that it behooves all of us not to talk about the rest of us. The real problem with 'being bad' is not totally being bad, that is bad enough; it is *not feeling* bad by being bad and doing bad things. Long after the provocation or temptation, we feel no remorse or regret, shame or guilt; we lack the courage to admit even to our own conscience that we were wrong. All this is not just a question of individual ethics or personal fate. It leaves an imprint on our collective consciousness. Just as humans are changing the environment, and that environment in turn is fuelling human evolution, we can, by cultivating a compassionate consciousness and by creating a more moral milieu of living, change the direction of human evolution. Again and again, the spiritual journey hits the same roadblock: the gap and disconnection between what we know and what we do, what we profess and what we practice, what we can and what we ought to.

Many ancient prophecies have become fulfilled now and make interesting reading. The Mayans, whose Central American civilization, reputed as the most advanced in relation to time-space knowledge, prophesied that beginning from the year 1999, we will have 13 years to realize the changes in our conscious attitude to stray from the path of self-destruction and instead move on to a path that opens our consciousness to integrate us with all that exists.[26] The Mayans believed that, having known the end of their cycle, mankind would prepare for what is to come in the future and it is because of this that they would have preserved the dominant species; the human race. According to them, "coming changes will permit us to make a quantum leap forward in the evolution of our consciousness to create a new civilization that would manifest great harmony and compassion to all humankind."[27] And "seven years after the start of Katun, which is to say the year 1999, we would enter a time of darkness which would force us to confront our own conduct". For the Mayans, "this is the time when mankind will enter '*The Sacred Hall of Mirrors*', where we will look at ourselves and analyze our behaviors with ourselves, with others, with Nature and with the planet in which we live. A time in which all of humanity, by individual conscious decisions, decides to change and eliminate fear and lack of respect from all of our relationships."[28]

The Mayans were dead right about the target and the direction; perhaps not about the date. We need to look at ourselves and analyze our behavior, eliminate fear and restore respect, and the goal ought to be a quantum leap in the evolution of our consciousness. The external manifestation of our consciousness is our behavior, which is really how we externally project our desires, passions and emotions that affect the lives of other people. There are two diametrically different paradigms of 'behavior' in human life: the behavior of others and our own behavior. Often, what we consider as obnoxious in the behavior of others, we are oblivious of it in our own selves; though we criticize the conduct that is repugnant in others, we fail to see it in our own conduct. Goethe said that behavior is the mirror in which everyone shows their image but do not see it themselves. The vehicle for behavior is the body; and the *sarathi*, the one at the controls, is the consciousness. Consciousness is what we are inside; behavior is what we are outside. And behavior has a huge bearing on how the human body will evolve in the future. As a matter of fact, human physiognomy has changed over evolution, a change that, significantly, has taken hardly one ten-thousandth of the total time span of life on earth. Primitive man was marked by a flattened skull of relatively small cranial capacity, a retreating forehead and chin, heavy, massive jaws, and a short, thick neck. Modern man, by contrast, has a typically near-vertical forehead, a domed occipital lobe, relatively large cranial capacity, a slender neck, jaws of reduced size, and a marked eminence of chin. This 'transformation' was the result of how the body and its faculties were harnessed for dedicated purposes. And that will happen in the future too. But science is focusing on reengineering the human body, leaving human behavior to human culture. Plastic surgery, prosthetics, robotics, electronic and digitized vocal chords, implants for hearing, chemicals to adjust and fine-tune brain functioning, genetics, and cloning organs are the current ways to augment and upgrade our physique.

At the same time we are soaking our body with a scary cocktail of chemicals. It is utterly amazing and shocking how resigned and reconciled we are about the poison we put into our bodies — 'pollution in people' — through chemicals in the food we eat, in the air we breathe and in the water we drink. Someone said that the human cadaver is so full of toxic chemicals that animals would not touch human meat. How thisgrowing menace of chemicals in our life will play out is uncertain. For example, if sex continues to be the obsessive passion for the brain and the body, independent of procreation, and if it continues to distort Nature's priorities, then Nature itself, as a defensive measure, might change the very act of sex to bring it back within the bounds of the original intent. What role computerization will play in human evolution is anybody's guess. One view is that computers offer one way towards overcoming the speed and capacity limitations of the human mind. It is assumed that a mental task reducible to a set of written rules can be reduced to a computer program, which leads to the euphoric expectation that practically any task the mind performs can be analyzed in detail and programmed. The virtuosity and speed of computers is galloping at a breathtaking speed. Computers with television cameras are learning to recognize faces and common objects by sight. Adding mechanized appendages to a computer empowers it to grasp, recognize, and manipulate objects, and to move through a cluttered environment. Some predict that soon, we will have computers with superhuman mental powers with superhuman speed. Even if we discount the hyperbole, the fact remains that computers and the Internet have fundamentally altered the way the human mind was used before. It is idle to think that it will not have any effect on the evolution of the species. Some keen observers of the human condition apprehend that, for example, if the majority of mankind wears spectacles, all children born maybe hundred years from now might be short-sighted at birth, as a mark of adapting to the living environment. And if we use computers and calculators more than the brain, then the future human brain will provide for that even at birth. The bottom line is that even if computers can substitute the current mental tasks, it is still the human mind which will decide *what* to do, with and to what capacity, and that will not change the way humans use the tools they have.

The basic tenet is that every trivial thought we entertain, and every menial act we do (or do not), will have a say in the mental and physical make-up of future generations. Mind-incubated malice, the withering will to wish ill of others sans self-gain, has come to infect a major part of human consciousness and that has made the human condition coarse and corrosive, divisive and destructive. The missing link, the fatal insufficiency, in the human condition is harmony, which Nature has in abundance. We often confuse equality with harmony. Indeed, if there is equality, there is no need for harmony. Nothing is more unnatural than equality; the challenge is to induce equity in inequality and harmony in heterogeneity. In trying to remove inequality that is intrinsic in Nature, we end up creating more inequity. Marcus Aurelius said, "He who lives in harmony with himself lives in harmony with the Universe."[29] The disharmony at the deepest layers of our being manifests externally in multiple ways, from broken homes to the clash of faiths, ethnic cleansing, virulent nationalism, religious zealotry, nuclear terror, and road rage. Few are satisfied with their own good; many want others to bite the dust. We are all prisoners of passions which are increasingly projected as prejudices. The end result is the warping and corruption of the myriad, often moral, choices that our transient lives entail. At the same time, we are also reassured that many behavioral tendencies could also be genetically fixed with the discoveries of specific genes that predispose a particular person in a certain direction. For instance, scientists say that they have discovered what they call a 'divorce gene', which means that in certain individuals, any stress in an intimate relationship might prompt them towards separation rather than reconciliation. Human behavior and responses to situations and experiences are far too complex and, according to some religions, the roots go back to the time even before birth. While, as the popular song *Que sera sera* goes, 'whatever will be, will be', and divisiveness and hatred, not compassion and love, have come to be the pervasive passions in the human way of life. Feelings of visceral dislike, a desire to annihilate the source of our unhappiness, or deeply felt loathing for something or someone, seem to occupy a lot of our psychic space. In addition, there are many who suffer from self-hatred, partly as a result of low self-esteem. This could be a hangover of our prehistoric or primal past in which survival depended on suspicion, and which became an instinct and got embedded in the brain, as a kind of protective programming. That instinct of distrust manifests as hatred when combined with other factors like insecurity, jealousy, and malice. The way to combat hatred is to cultivate love and compassion. At this point, it really does not matter if man is a '*Noble Savage*' or a '*Civilized Brute*' and we cannot be even sure who is being unfair to whom — man or beast. Edgar Allan Poe, in his book *The Black Cat* (1843), was merciless in writing that "there is something in the unselfish and self-sacrificing love of a brute, which goes directly to the heart of him who has had frequent occasion to test the paltry friendship and gossamer fidelity of mere Man."[30]

Knowledge, Ignorance and Illusion

We just want to *know*; no *ifs* or *buts*; either in daily life or in matters of greater import. That yen for knowing — to know why the stars shine, as Bertrand Russell phrased it, has been the primary driving force in every human adventure. Being curious might have killed the proverbial cat but man has come out clearly better off. Being nosy, wanting to know that we need not — and even should not — know, the human species has achieved much. To the extent that we can discern patterns and create cause/effect relationships, our unquenchable thirst to know enables us to better predict and manipulate the future. This trait had made us better hunters, to design and build tools, to control fire, and to develop agriculture. But it has also entailed a heavy price, starting right from his Biblical banishment from Paradise. While the differences between terms like data, information, knowledge, and wisdom are the stuff of punditry, it is 'wisdom' that man has long longed for. The great Greek mathematician and philosopher Pythagoras, when asked what he did, reportedly answered that he was simply a lover (*philo*) of wisdom (*sophia*). But anyone can tell that 'what we *do* know' about the true fundamentals is very little: what life itself is and ought to be; why one human is alive and another dead, not vice versa; and what awaits us thereafter. Is this all some somnambulistic sleep walking, a dream within a dream? Our knowledge is mostly about 'what'; very little of 'how'; and almost none of 'why'. The real knowledge that we do not have is the 'way we know what we know'; that is how — or why — we think we know, and the certainty that comes with it. And from certainty, an emotional state which some psychologists call our 'certainty-bias', comes intolerance and vanity. Voltaire said that doubt is not a pleasant condition, but certainty is absurd. Doubt is unpleasant because we just do not know what to do, and that is deemed an affront to human intelligence; certainty is absurd because we know we cannot be certain of anything, and anything might happen to anyone, anytime.

Don Miguel Ruiz, the Mexican spiritual author of *The Voice of Knowledge* (2004) says that "so much of the knowledge in our minds is based on lies and superstitions that come from thousands of years ago. Humans create stories long before we are born, and we inherit those stories, we adopt them, and we live in those stories."[31] The Irish poet T.S. Eliot wrote, "Where is the life we have lost in living? Where is the wisdom we have lost in knowledge? Where is the knowledge we have lost in information?"[32]

It might sound outrageous, but some say the kind of 'knowledge' that most people hanker after is worse than 'uncorrupted' or innocent ignorance. The Upanishads tells us that "into blind darkness enter they who worship ignorance; into darkness greater than that enter they who delight in knowledge."[33] The Upanishads divide knowledge into higher and lower knowledge; *paravidya*, the higher knowledge, is the knowledge of the Self, the all-pervading force that is both inside and outside, everywhere and nowhere; *aparavidya*, the lower knowledge, is all the rest, in a breathtaking candor, including the knowledge of the Vedas itself. There is an arresting story in Hindu mythology about the great rishi Narada. Feeling restless, Narada, the most celebrated of all sages, immortal and ever present, approaches another great rishi Sanathkumara and asks him to relieve him of his deep distress. Sanathkumara asks him to show what he does know and Narada enumerates his encyclopedic knowledge of all the sacred texts, and then says that what he knows is 'only words', not the knowledge of the Self, and because of that, he is afflicted with sorrow. It must be borne in mind that the 'Self' referred to here is different from the self in selfishness and self-righteousness. The Self in the present context is the Self of Self-realization or God-realization, at once the *Atman* and the *Paramatman*, the individual soul and the Supreme Soul. In the *Brihadaranyaka* Upanishad, the sage Yajnavalkya explains the ambit and the nature of the Self, to his wife Maitreyi. He tells her that the body is the abode of the Self, but that the Self itself is immortal, and that the Self is everything (the Infinite). In a famous passage, he says that it is only for the sake of *that* Self that everyone and everything in the world is dear and loved — husband, wife, children, wealth, etc; the Self, in its true nature, is one with the Supreme Self. Yajnavalkya further clarifies: "Verily, my dear Maitreyi, it is the Self that should be realized — should be heard, reflected on, and meditated upon. By the realization of the Self, my dear, through hearing, reflection and meditation, all this is known". According to this line of thought, the Self is the totality, the sum and substance of everything, the sole source, the origin and destination of the universe, the point of convergence of all reality. And the knowledge of the Self is the highest spiritual knowledge. The way to God and the quest for the Self is the purpose of human life; the highest state of consciousness. In practical life, we identify ourselves with the abode, not the indweller, and that, the scriptures say, is the root of the suffering and misery of life.

That ignorance, or illusion that obscures our vision, Vedanta calls *avidya* or *maya* (both are similar but not identical), which is again a part of the play of the divine. Vedanta states that *maya* shields the Truth or *Brahman* from the Self or *Atman*. The doctrine of *maya*, commonly attributed to Adi Shankara, but which actually has its roots in the Upanishads, is an important theological and metaphysical explanation to many baffling things in life, such as the source of suffering and why we are so incapable of comprehending, and remain oblivious of our true divine identity. It is a profound, subtle, almost mystical concept. The *Shvetashvatara* Upanishad clarifies: "Know Nature to be *Maya* and the great God to be the Lord of *Maya*". It cannot be comprehended through ordinary intellect or linear thinking. To understand, one must rise above that which we are trying to understand. Swami Vivekananda said "in *maya* we are born, in *maya* we exist and in *maya* we die". *Maya*, which literally means 'that which is not', proposes that the world of experience is merely an appearance in the background of the *Brahman*. It is *maya* that holds us captive to *dwanda* or duality; it is *maya* that obscures and obfuscates divinity. It is *maya* that distorts our inherent essence and also the one that mediates the relationship of the phenomenal world and the Supreme Force. Although it is now accepted as a key element of the Advaita philosophy, it was not unchallenged. Another great *acharya* or teacher, Ramanuja, who advocated the theory of *Vishishtadvaita,* raised questions such as: Is *maya* real or unreal? If real, how can it be only an appearance? If unreal, how can it be an *upadhi* or limitation on the indefinable and illimitable *Brahman*? If *maya* is another manifestation of the *Brahman*, what is the purpose in making the veil of ignorance so impenetrable? It would be highly erroneous to look at such questions as contradictions. They constitute an evolution of the basic idiom of Shankara, which, as we noted, emanates from the Upanishads. The real confusion comes from the assumption that *maya* means that the world itself is an illusion. What is implied, is that the world we see and live in is only 'relatively' real, not absolutely real; the illusion is the appearance, filtered through the mind, of it being distinct and separate from the *Brahman*. The underlying idea and the basic message is that the creator and the creation, the living world and the Almighty are not different, if not one and the same. Such understanding is supposed to lead to view all life as sanctified by a divine presence, as sacred, and should be treated no differently from God.

Just as there are different kinds of knowledge, there are also different kinds of ignorance. One way of categorization is *ordinary* ignorance (for example, not knowing tomorrow's weather), *willful* ignorance (knowing which creates more problems, and we therefore avoid that knowledge), and lastly, what some experts call '*higher* ignorance' (the more we try to know about a particular matter, the more we realize how 'we can never know enough about it').[34] The third kind of ignorance is what impels us to ponder over and fathom if we are just another species on earth or the exalted one; whatever, we are still bound by the boundary of an earthly life and by the state or level of our consciousness. Another related issue is the nexus between ignorance, knowledge, striving, craving and belief. Ignorance, as the adage goes, may be bliss because then you do not have to make choices. Knowledge, unless it is of the right kind, can become a burden and distort the choices. Striving is necessary just to live and the quality of that striving, carnal or spiritual, can make a difference to the content of life. It is craving that the scriptures condemn and that increases suffering, a maxim that is at the core of Buddhism. Craving is obsessive desire, the more you get the more you want. As for 'belief', everyone has to believe in something or the other; believing is not the same as 'believing in belief'. Belief is a structure, a system and is presumed to be without 'proof', and in the modern mind, proof is 'truth'. At the same time, there are many sworn 'rationalists' and scientists who admit that they believe in things beyond proof. The human mind confuses belief with belonging, and belonging with bonding; when you 'belong' to someone or something — religion, ideology, nation — exclusivity and monopoly come to the fore. The way to make religion more 'humane' is to rid it of its exclusivist monopoly, that if one owes allegiance to one religion, he or she is automatically excluded from the faith of another religion. We have not learnt how to bond with fellow humans without belonging. Belief coupled with belonging becomes a dogma, a creed, and breeds a mindset of intolerance and 'otherness'. Bonding is solidarity, a sense of sharedness. Non-belonging is detachment, the central message given in scriptures like the Bhagavad Gita. Detachment enables you to do your personal righteous duty to fulfill your innate potential.

We must acknowledge that, although we are an integral part of Nature, we live not in the natural world, but in a man-made (or more accurately, brain-made) world. The tool of the brain is technology. The advent or onslaught of the 'Information Revolution' powered by miniaturized computerization, has dramatically altered the boundaries of life and liberated us from the bounds of the body. We can virtually be anywhere and experience every experience without actually being there, or being a subject of that sensation. The world is now called 'flat', and technologies like the Internet have drastically altered the rules and norms that have governed and circumscribed human interfacing for centuries. Information is exploding at such blinding pace that we face a huge problem of how to adjust our lives in this new landscape. Some see it as an opening to a Utopia, the human race finally functioning as interconnected parts of a 'superorganism'. Such a scenario seems to ignore that which truly separates us from other creatures, and the fact also is that information technology itself is not nascent but ancient. As Robert Darnton, the American cultural historian puts it, we have had "four fundamental changes in information technology since humans learned to speak": The first was *learning to write* around 4,000 BCE, which has been described as "the most important technological breakthrough in the history of humanity."[35] It opened the way to the advent of books as a force in human affairs. The second was when the scroll was replaced by the codex, *books with pages* that one turned, and the page emerged as a unit of perception. The third was when the *invention of printing* with movable type transformed the codex in the 1450s. The fourth was the great change brought about, sometime in the 1980s, by *electronic communication* through technologies like the Internet and the Web. Much of what was deemed, in fact, is now considered as inaccurate. The latest fundamental change is still unfolding, which is being called the dawn of the Information Age and so forth. The now-ubiquitous *Blog*, a contraction of the term *Web Log*, is a website through which individuals can 'stay in touch, with like-minded people'. More than a million blogs, according to one estimate, have cropped up in the last few years. While telephone, as someone said, took 'the voice out of the flesh', the cell phone has destroyed distance and reordered the dynamics of human relationships. For the first time in history, the relations between intimate partners lack clear guidelines, supportive family networks, a religious context, and a compelling social meaning. Technology has changed the dynamics of human equations. It has become the main mediator between human beings. What was once considered to be appropriate in human interfacing and as a way of showing affection and love, is now substituted by the sound of voice emanating from a machine. A mother's hug is replaced by cell-phonic talk. All this goes by the name of communications revolution, but as Soren Kierkegaard pointed out, all true communication is personal. In the very impersonal character of technological communications, some find virtue and validity. In the face-to-face interfacing, one is revealed by uncontrolled immediacy, and how we are and what we are becomes more important than what we have to say. But in mediums like the Internet, one can communicate what one wants to regardless of appearances and atmospherics. There are concerns about the emergence of one more divide — the digital one, and about its effects on human health. "Each change in technology has transformed the information landscape, and the speed-up has continued at such a rate as to seem both unstoppable and incomprehensible."[36]

'Being knowledgeable' was long considered as being intelligent. And the source of intelligence is the brain. Whatever the nuances are, the question is how all the information-cum-knowledge that we have impacts the human personality. As the American management 'guru' Peter Drucker puts it "So far, for 50 years, the information revolution has centered on data — their collection, storage, transmission, analysis, and presentation. It has focused on the 'T' in IT. The next information revolution asks: What is the *meaning* of information, and what is its *purpose* ?"[37] The main existential problem of man has long been how to interact with another man, and that necessity is rapidly diminishing. When it comes to seeking answers to the fundamentals of life, the scriptures say that intellect or knowledge is of little use. But it is intellect and knowledge that we worship even as a way of life, and as a means to 'happiness', the mind-molded knowledge is of little use. As Bertrand Russell wrote in his essay *Impact of Science on Society* (1952), "unless man increases in wisdom as much as in knowledge, increase of knowledge will only be increase of sorrow."[38] No one seriously questions that statement, but the trouble is our intelligence cannot functionally differentiate knowledge from wisdom. Albert Einstein wrote in his book *Out of My Later Years* (1993), that 'we should take care not to make the intellect our God; it has of course powerful muscles, but no personality.' Indeed, there is an emerging branch of knowledge that the main, if not the sole, problem that hampers human harmony and further evolution is our intellect which we commonly identify with intelligence. Mahatma Gandhi said: "The human intellect delights in inventing specious arguments in order to support injustice itself."[39] It is ingenious in making the illogical appear logical, cruelty as consideration, rudeness as necessity, and bad beh-avior as just response. The *Kathopanishad* compared the uncontrolled mind to the vicious horses of a chariot. The mind is a master at offering explanations and excuses for all acts of commission and omission, constantly offering excuses and making us feel 'good' about ourselves. It is not injustice alone that is justified, but also intolerance, cruelty, exploitation, genocide, slavery, tyranny, and oppression. Some form of systematic exploitation of labor — physical or sexual, being held against their will, being treated as the 'property' of another person, being deprived of the right to refuse to work or the right to leave, or to receive due compensation as a return for labor — has existed (and still exists) across cultures and civilizations and throughout history. That many great men like Thomas Jefferson felt no pangs of conscience in supporting and practicing slavery for life is symptomatic of the human mind. It was reported that by the year 1860 almost four million slaves were held by a population of just 15 million in the United States. And many of the 'slave-owners' could have been 'decent', 'god-fearing' human beings. Deliberately or subconsciously, we ignore the true nature of our actions through the three stratagems of evasion, explanation, and excuse. In the womb of the cosmos, it is thought that truly matters. The Irish poet T.S. Eliot wrote "Wait without thought; for you are not ready for thought: so the darkness shall be the light and the stillness, the dancing."[40] But, for the mind, to be without thought is death; in darkness, we harbor dark desires and in stillness we scheme. For a candle to be useful in the darkness, it must be lit. Mired as we are in the physical world, we expand our life in the immediacy of instant gratification, ignoring the spiritual demands made on us. Devoid, or deprived, of Self-knowledge, we do not even try to better ourselves. Instead, we insidiously denude each other's dignity. 'Dignity' is a precious human right and as the Roman philosopher Marcus Aurelius noted, there is a proper dignity and proportion to be observed in the performance of every act of life. And everyone is entitled to, allowed and enabled to live in dignity. And since we often deny it to others, as the Anglo-Jewish writer and the 'activist for the oppressed' Israel Zangwill said,[41] our decision-making and our choices become skewed. The intellect that drives our lives, as Vedanta tells us, cannot distinguish appearance from reality, illusion from image. The conundrum is that the mind-driven intellect alone is not good enough to orchestrate human life, though we have come to depend upon it completely. Isolation, in fact, can be deceptively dangerous. As Lewis Mumford, the American writer and historian of science and technology wrote, "one of the functions of intelligence is to take account of the dangers that come from trusting solely on intelligence"[42] Well, it has not happened, and that makes up the story of our species and the challenge of our time. The challenge is to actualize that kind of intelligence rather than the one we have.

The Self and the Razor's Edge

Man has long speculated about his innate nature and wondered about his true relationship with God, and about what happens after his body crumbles and dissolves into dust. From Nachiketa of the *Katha* Upanishad to Larry Darrel in Somerset Maugham's novel *The Razor's Edge* (1944), many have wrestled with these issues. Incidentally, the title of Maugham's book comes from a verse in the Katha Upanishad "Get up! Wake up! Seek the guidance of an illumined teacher and realize the Self. Sharp like a razor's edge, the sages say, is the path, difficult to traverse."[43] Larry, for example, ruminates: "I want to make up my mind whether God is or God is not. I want to find out why evil exists, I want to know if I have an immortal soul or whether when I die, it is the end."[44] We still do not know; probably never will, possibly because there are no answers, not even in Nature. Even the Buddha, who saw and perceived everything that human consciousness is capable of — and maybe even more —, chose not to answer questions concerning God. One gets a 'gut feeling' that we are passing through or passing into, or that something or someone is pushing us into an 'unknown unknown', as distinct from a 'known unknown' like death. The French Nobel Prize winning author Alexis Carrel wrote, "Mankind has made a gigantic effort to know itself. Although we possess the treasure of the observations accumulated by the scientists, the philosophers, the poets, and the great mystics of all times, we have grasped only certain aspects of ourselves. We do not apprehend man as a whole. We know him as composed of distinct parts. And even these parts are created by our methods. Each one of us is made up of a procession of phantoms, in the midst of which strides an unknowable reality."[45] In its wanderings as an 'unknowable reality', the ship of mankind has entered virgin waters; the compass we have is malfunctioning and we see no dawn on the horizon. It is not the fate of the living, much less of the dead, that troubles many sensitive people like American cosmologist Brian Swimme, who says that he is haunted and terrified by what 'the unborn' are going to see when their time comes, say in a thousand years or so. Thousand years is too long even to be 'terrified'; there are many who think that humans have a 'window of opportunity' for a century or two at best.

Yet, we must continue to believe that there is a future, and that we do have some say in shaping it. As Soto Zen priest Shunryu Suzuki wrote, "As long as we have some definite idea about, or some hope in the future, we cannot really be serious with the moment that exists right now."[46] And unless we are seriously aware of where we are, what we are and what we want to be, we cannot make any difference. And unless one attempts to make some difference, life is not worth a bother. The next minute is as near or distant as the next millennium; and we can make a difference to the minute, but in so doing, we can change the millennium too. The future, because it is the future, might not fit neatly into our palm to be manipulated, but it might not also slip out altogether. The old adage 'hope for the best and prepare for the worst' is still the only way to get on with life. In fact, there can be no hope without despair and suffering; indeed, it is only when these seem intractable that we turn to hope. We turn to hope because we cannot accept that something we want is denied, and that something we crave for remains beyond our clutch. We feel entitled to fulfill our desires and dreams, and when the ground reality shows that the high probability is that they will elude our reach, we turn to hope and God. In Greek mythology, when Pandora opened her box, she let out all the evils except hope. Apparently, hope was first considered to be as vicious as all other evils. But on realizing that humanity without hope would be dysfunctional, Pandora revisited her box and let out hope too. In fact, some philosophers like Nietzsche have argued that it was a ruse played by the gods to make man suffer endlessly without escape; if hope was not given to him, they were afraid that man would call it quits and upset their cosmic play. It now seems that modern man has become wise to the ruse and that is why more and more people are choosing suicide, overcoming the obstacle of hope when their life, in their view, becomes not worth living. Many hover between 'hopelessly hopeful' and 'hopefully hopeless' conditions, never knowing how to balance, in the words of Martin Luther King Jr., "finite disappointment and infinite hope."

In terms of 'conscious compassion', the human, as he is currently perched, is perhaps at the very bottom of the ladder. Evil — the more monstrous the better — fascinates, indeed transfixes his attention. We fight dullness with vulgarity, boredom with prurience. We seem to be nonchalantly living up to Hannah Arendt's haunting phrase 'banality of evil' to the extent that we have 'normalized the unthinkable'; the horrendous has become the honored. There is a growing breed of men who embrace the gospel of nihilism, who think that they can become 'overmen' by transcending both good and evil by turning away from both; in that attempt they become easy picking for evil. It is hard even for us to know for a fact how much of our inside is immaculately pure and how much is 'filthy right down to the guts'. Nietzsche is most often associated with nihilism. In *Will to Power* (notes 1883–1888), he writes, "Every belief, every considering something true, is necessarily false because there is simply no true world."[47] For Nietzsche, there is no objective order or structure in the world except what we give it. The French philosopher Albert Camus wrote in his essay *The Rebel* (1951) how metaphysical collapse often ends in total negation and the victory of nihilism, characterized by profound hatred, pathological destruction, and incalculable death, which is pretty much what the world is today. He also wrote that the 'rebel' can never find peace; he knows what is good and, despite himself, does evil, which is pretty much what man is today.

The underlying reality of life is the body; it is the object and the subject, entity and experience, the medium through which we relate to the world outside. However much we might convince ourselves that we are not just physical bodies, we cannot disconnect ourselves from the sense that the reality is just three: that we are inside the body, and that there is a world outside, and that there is a Supreme Force. To relate to the last two we need the first. The much-venerated-yet-despised body is essential to reach our full potential; yet it is the limitation that weighs us down. Unless we get a grip over our bodies, we can do nothing worthwhile in life. If the Self — which is both inside and outside, everywhere and nowhere — is the Primal Force, the *moola karana* in Sanskrit, then how does one connect and bridge with it? The inquiry about the Self or the Supreme Soul is the thrust of the Upanishads. In the *Katha* Upanishad, Yama, the very God of Death says that the Self is subtler than the subtlest and beyond all logic, that it is both immortal and indwelling and that "Bodies are said to die, but That which possesses the body is eternal."[48] In a famous verse, the Upanishad compares the body to a chariot, the self to the owner of the chariot, the *Atman* or the individual soul to the charioteer, the mind to the reins, and the senses to the steeds. Our inability to differentiate the self from the body, the real from the unreal, is said to be the principal cause of the malaise that afflicts mankind.

That inability affects all aspects of life. Despite what scriptural axioms and religious tenets preach and prescribe, man has not been able to shift the spotlight from the stars to the soul, from craving to striving, from the struggle for sheer survival in an unfriendly world to the search for meaning beyond survival. There is a gnawing feeling that the two guiding stars of human history — religion and science— have had little bearing on the quality of the human condition. Religions, as Swami Vivekananda said, have become "lifeless mockeries."[49] We live in a twisted world of galloping religiosity and accelerating evil. Some thoughtful people are saying that the human world is in a state of "desperate ferment of faith", of "holy restlessness" and in a "second Age of Faith."[50] What 'being religious' has come to mean is, in fact, having a perverse effect on those who are truly religious. In these troubled times, many people traditionally would have liked to turn to religion for solace and guidance, but what they see is that much of that very turbulence and terror is inspired by one or another religion. The scriptures also indulge in a kind of 'double-speak' about the role of reason in the quest for meaning. On the one hand, they say that man must go beyond the bounds of reason, logic, deduction and deliberation, to know the answers to the essential questions of life. But on the other hand, they also say that, as the Buddha said on his death bed, "be a lamp unto yourself", and that no one's word, not even a prophet's, nor the words of any holy text, should be taken on faith as the Truth unless it satisfies our intellect, reason, and empirical testing. Theologians and pundits might explain the apparent contradiction, but it still further confuses the already bruised minds. When they want to take refuge under the wings of the other primary source of search for truth, science, what they discover is that much of science and its cousin technology have become an enfeebling search for comfort, convenience, and empowerment for mass murder with minimal effort. What modern technology has done is to make the manifestation of man's primal instincts of faith, fear, anger, rage, revenge and retribution more destructive, definitive and deadly. Murder is simply the 'natural' — and logical — culmination of human dissent and articulate individuality. Any minor or mundane human conflict or uncontrolled human passion and unfulfilled desire can now reach its climax in a killing — and with telling effect in terms of numbers; with one weapon, the human homicidal power multiplies manifold.

Other than sex, most other human desires arise from money. In the world of money, there is little room for 'losers'. The weak, the dispossessed, the disadvantaged, and the marginalized lose out in the competitive culture of the free market. With growth and profits as the driving forces, it spawns conflict, impoverishment, and predatory exploitation of natural resources.

With over a billion people starving or malnourished any discussions on matters of spiritual growth with them sounds hollow, if not hypocritical. Put simply and starkly, the continued human presence on earth is becoming a threat to continuance of life on earth. The state of man today is close to what the *Shvetashvatara* Upanishad described a long while ago: "Men may succeed in rolling up space like a piece of leather, yet they will not experience the end of their sorrows without realizing the luminous divine (truth within them)."[51] Most lives today are robotic lives, responding to bodily needs, often unloved and unwanted, drifting from one 'comfort' to another, devoid of joy or élan or purpose. They live because they know nothing else. So much effort for so little gain is the sum of many lives. Heart-centered intuition, which guided man for more than three-fourths of his existence on earth, has gone into recess, and mind-centered intelligence has taken over. The assumption is that 'intuition' has remained pristine, but it may also be that intuition too has been defiled. Our spontaneity may have gone sour; we might not be able to count on our 'gut instinct' or heart-felt emotion to distinguish between right and wrong. As Stephen Bernhardt says, 'human beings no longer live in a natural environment; their environment is now a result of their own intellect.' According to Carlos Castaneda, while making choices in life we should choose the path of the heart. The intellect is a critical faculty, but it is severely conditioned, if not impaired in the search for meaning. Indeed, the mind itself is unable to harmonize its own inherent cognitive capabilities with those of the machine. Our mind-centered intellect has prevailed over the world outside and over every other living creature on earth, but has remained easy prey to our own prowling passions. Man is now a virtual hostage to his own mind. Everything 'human' is in a 'state of denial', as Jeremy Griffith terms it, or in disarray, drifting from birth to death, bereft of any intelligible purpose. 'Being alive' for most people is being in pain of some kind or the other, physical, psychological, or mental. Human consciousness itself is intellectually trapped and spiritually emaciated. It is driven by the mind, and the mind offers self-righteous reasoning to rationalize our every act of commission and omission, of bigotry and cruelty. Shame and remorse, among the basic requirements of human life, are in a state of exile. We may say that the world is corrupt, that mankind is crumbling, but we never question our own impeccable credentials as 'good', if not 'god-fearing' human beings. What the human needs most of all is reconciliation in his way of life, in the world of relationships; most of all within his own self. Man has acquired and accumulated knowledge to an awesome degree, but lost his wisdom somewhere in the sensory woods. And knowledge without wisdom is, as the scriptures say, the perfect recipe for ruin.

Such is the spell of egotism, which Thomas Carlyle called 'the source and summary of all faults and miseries', that everyone is for wisdom, and everyone thinks they alone are wise and others are 'otherwise'. Everyone condemns egotism but puts it squarely in someone else's court. Egotism has been called Nature's compensation for mediocrity; the main impediment to true greatness, lasting happiness, and to transformation. All religions condemn egotism, but it is necessary for any true achievement; all great men were egotistic but they directed it to the right goals.

All human endeavors are to control and conquer time, distance, disease, death, and most often, at the practical level, another human. The desire to control is a basic desire. We want to be 'in control' of our lives, our body, our mind — and everything of others. At this juncture, man is at once the predator and prey, the hunter and quarry; the defiler and defiled; the exploiter and the exploited. We perpetually bounce back and forth, and none of us can be sure, like Shylock in Shakespeare's *Merchant of Venice* (1597), if, in the final analysis, we are the victims or the villains.

Despite his obvious vulnerabilities, man suffers from an illusion of invincibility and paranoia of persecution. The irony is that as a species, man is the conqueror; but as an individual, he perceives himself as the vanquished. As a species, man has made the world his own; but as an individual, he is a virtual slave of the system he has installed in his own world. The physical world is just another layer of knowledge; in reality, everyone lives in a unique mental world of one's own creation. Often, man is not conscious of what he is and what he is doing. As Brian Swimme says, "we refuse to grieve (for our ethical trespasses)" and we "are afraid that if we begin to grieve, we will become so overwhelmed, we'll become catatonic and useless."[52] We cannot tell how long the *Homo* genre of life is programmed to endure on earth and who will then take over the reins of governance of the planet after we are gone. But it does appear that if the human species had not existed, Mother Earth would not have been any worse-off. And even worse, when we finally depart, it would take a long time for the planet to recover from the havoc inflicted on it by us humans.

Whenever we are carried away by our grandeur and glory, it would be useful to place the human in perspective on the grand canvas of the cosmos, where distance is measured in millions of light-years. There are billions of suns in our 'local' Milky Way galaxy, and billions of such galaxies tearing across the unimaginably vast expanse of space. On the other side, the microcosmic universe of the molecule, the atom, and the quark is equally staggering. Each breath we take contains a trillion atoms, and each atom is a complex universe by itself. Further, man's claim for terrestrial hegemony and legitimacy, let alone eternity, is fast wearing thin. His self-proclaimed privileged position as the most rational, intelligent, and enlightened species on earth can no longer stand any test of logic or intelligence. Bertrand Russell wryly remarked that he was searching all his life for evidence to support the premise that man is a rational animal. That very 'logic of rationality' points to a contrary conclusion: that man is not only the most complex but also the most irrational being on earth, and that perhaps, man might even be, in the words of the English dramatist W.S. Gilbert, 'Nature's sole mistake.'

Human Depravity

Poised as we are, we are uncertain as to whom or what we should turn to as a guide: scriptures or science, intuition or intellect, God or gadgets. We must remember that today much of even non-violence is in the shadow of violence. It is negative in the sense that our non-violence is based on the fear of another's violence. Violent responses are often our natural instinctive responses. We cannot wholly wish away or slyly sidestep human violence that is often laced with malice. We have to accept the reality of its deep roots in the human psyche. Today, violence is the weapon of the strong and of the weak; of the oppressed and of the oppressor, and the preferred way to get along in the world. It has become commonplace to convince oneself that there is no escape from violence if one does not want to be a perpetual loser, that 'might is right'. Further the violence we are bothered about is what touches us personally; the rest is 'news' that titillates our attention, a secret sense of relief that we are not the victims and, even worse, someone else is. Violence is part of life; birth is violence, so is death. The animal world is not without its share of violence and cruelty. The irresistible instinct for survival plays a leading part in the perpetuation of violence among beasts too. But man alone kills for power, pleasure, and profit. In *The Brothers Karamazov* (1880), Dostoevsky asserts that no animal could ever be as cruel as man, so artfully, and so artistically cruel; we may add, on the morrow of the 21st century, 'so scientifically and so technologically' efficient. Man's violence directed at his own kind, as well as towards other species defies description, even reason. Like the origin of evil, the basis of the streak of the virulent in the human species, often tinged with wanton cruelty, is still a mystery. By violence, we often implicitly mean a dastardly act of murder, rape, or war. These are extreme and heinous, but human violence is far more subtle and pervasive: injustice is violence; ingratitude is violence; indifference is violence. The attraction to abuse the powerless, the lure to ridicule the defenseless, seems to act like a drug on the human personality. It is as if we are programmed never to let go an opportunity to humiliate or hurt another person if we know we can get away with it. Language and choice of words have a tremendous impact: it could be scooting or scalding, they convey what we think of ourselves and of each other. In some cases, violence stems from childhood deprivation, resulting in more violence in adulthood. Sometimes, human violence is a survival response to violence in nature. Some posit that it is 'learned behavior'; others say that it is an infectious disease endemic to certain environments and communities. Over the last decade or so, there are stories about genetic explanations for violence, about genes for such traits as 'ruthlessness' and 'murder'. Genes may have something to do with the propensity for violence, as they do for other character traits. Several well-regarded scientists including anthropologist

Richard Wrangham and psychologist Steven Pinker have emphasized the evolutionary and genetic factors that trigger a person's consistent engagement in violence, despite cultural differences. But depravity need not spring from deprivation. The true nature of human 'depravity', whether we are basically good or evil, is an important theological concept. Whether depravity and sin are at the edge or center of our being is debatable. The 'doctrine of total depravity', which we are told is different from utter depravity, is a central tenet of Christianity, that humans live in 'captivity to the law of sin'. It posits that because of the *Fall*, all humans are 'enslaved in the service of sin' and that 'man cannot be justified before God by his own works'. Whether we are 'totally' or 'utterly' or 'partially' corrupted, the question is: are we in such a state that we cannot be saved without the special and direct divine intervention?

In the Hindu concept of cyclical (not linear) time, creation is now poised in the age of the *Kali Yuga*, at the end of which all creation will be destroyed, and then the world will go back to the beginning of the Age of Truth, *Sathya Yuga*. In the new cycle, the *Sathya Yuga* will be followed again by the *Treta, Dwapara* and *Kali Yugas*. What we witness in the world, closely, indeed eerily, corresponds with the predictions for the *Kali Yuga*. The Hindu epics like the Mahabharatha and Srimad Bhagavatham contain graphic descriptions of the degraded human condition in the *Kali Yuga*: this *yuga* will be "wedded to avarice and wrath and ignorance and lust, the right hand will deceive the left, and the left and the right will entertain animosities towards each other, desiring to take the other's life."[53] In Srimad Bhagavatham, the sage Suka describes to King Parikshit the unfolding of the Age of Evil, *Kali Yuga*: "Thenceforth, day after day, by force of the all-powerful time, O king, righteousness, veracity, purity (of mind and body), forgiveness, compassion, length of life, bodily strength and keenness of memory will decline. In the *Kali* age, wealth alone will be the criterion of pedigree, morality and merit. Again, might will be the only factor determining righteousness and fairness. Personal liking will be the deciding factor in making the choice of a partner in life, and trickery alone will be the motive force in business dealings. Capability of affording sexual delight will be the (only) criterion of masculine or feminine excellence, and the sacred thread will be the only mark of Brahmanhood."[54] And "filling one's belly will be the (only) end of human pursuit and audacity of speech will be the only criterion of veracity. Skill will consist in supporting one's family; virtuous deeds will be performed (only) with the object of gaining fame; and... in this way, the terrestrial globe will be overrun by wicked people..."[55]

The scriptures vividly describe the 'end of the world' scenario and what then will happen to the human species. The two common features are that the world as we know it will end, but the faithful will be saved. Most Western *monotheistic* religions have doctrines claiming that the 'chosen' or 'worthy' members of the one true religion will be 'spared' or 'delivered' from the coming judgment and wrath of God. They will be ushered into paradise either before, during, or afterwards, depending upon the end-time scenario to which they hold.[56] Although every religion predicts the end of the world and the moral debauchery of mankind, according to some it will not be the first time. The Jewish Torah, for example, records a fateful moment in human history when mankind was truly on the brink of annihilation. It reads, "and God saw the Earth, and behold it was corrupted, for all flesh had corrupted its way upon the earth. And "God said to Noah, 'the end of all flesh has come before Me, for the Earth is filled with robbery… and behold, I am about to destroy them'."[57] It is almost universally acknowledged that corruption, in its broadest sense, is insidiously sapping the vital energy of our species, and robbery — in its widest sense of taking more than one's due from another person, or from society or from Nature — has become endemic to the human condition. What is corrupted at this juncture in the life of the human species is consciousness itself, and almost everyone is guilty of 'robbery', in its Biblical sense. The dark doings of the *Kali Yuga*, foretold so vividly and unerringly, are already apparent. The world seems single-minded in its devotion to 'normalizing the unthinkable' and the horrific is becoming commonplace. Unconditional, nonreciprocal, selfless love is the first casualty of this Age. No word is more abused, misused, and misapplied than 'love', which has dried up in almost every relationship. What is more regrettable is not really the 'death' of love but of compassion. Our passions, not compassion, rule us. We need both passion and compassion for a wholesome life. As Honoré de Balzac said, all humanity is passion and without it all human endeavor will be ineffectual. And compassion is not mere kindness but, at a more fundamental level, as Thomas Morton said, is the keen awareness of the interdependence of all living beings. We must be passionate about compassion and inject our compassion into our passions. But what we tend to do is isolate the two and give free reign to our sensory passions.

The past hundred years, in particular, have triggered changes whose ambit and depth have few parallels, if any, in recorded history. Modern human beings have almost become a new 'sub-species', whose mode of living and thinking scarcely resemble that of even two generations ago. Man has become at once the most creative and destructive being on the planet, capable of giving and taking life with equal poise, virtually replicating, if not replacing Nature. In so doing, he has lost control over his imagination, and the boundary between what he can do and what he is capable of destroying has become blurred. Each day brings new and more horrific horrors, as if the perpetrators, no different from any one of us, are in some kind of a macabre competition. The lethal baggage is not only mass murder, torture and mutilation; it is creating a murderous mindset for the generations to come. The horrifying fact is not only that more than two million children have been killed in combat in the last decade, at the rate of some 500 per day[58], but that they are also the killers. Peter Singer in his book *Children at War* (2005), notes that child soldiers, some not older than six years, are to be found in three-quarters of the current fifty or so conflicts. He reveals that in the Sierra Leone's Revolutionary United Front, 80 percent of the fighters were aged between seven and fourteen. It is pointed out that "not only have conflicts fought by children become easier to start, harder to end, messier, and with greater loss of life, but they are creating a brutalized and disaffected generation who are growing up knowing nothing but violence."[59] Many of them do not know life without a gun, and some "sit and look at running water and just see blood, of course, if and when, they see any running water."[60] This is one horror even the prophets of *Kali Yuga* did not and could not envision: mothers killing their children as a trade-off for sex, or children killing their fathers for 'suicide' compensation or to inherit their father's job; or teenagers getting rid of their new born by dropping them down the garbage chute. For some parents, in a terrible commentary of modern life, the fear of leaving their children alive in today's world has become more terrifying than the awful act of murdering them in cold blood — in their mind, it is an act of concern, compassion, and cascading love, not cruelty or callousness. They may all appear isolated (even reckless acts of some twisted or tortured minds), but they are still the acts of full-grown human beings, and what they do symbolizes the banal barbarity that the human culture is capable of. With the adult mind conquered or corrupted by evil, with child warriors growing into positions of prominence in society, and with technology offering an endless supply of easier ways of killing, the world yet to come looks truly terrifying. It is utterly mystifying how, among the millions of species on earth, it is the human — so well-tooled, so blessed, and with such reasoning power and so sharpened in the skills of survival — who has turned to be so vicious and violent. And this, especially when he does not *need* to be so for survival or for supremacy.

Evolution and Culture

Perhaps, of all the attributes of which we are very proud of, none is greater than 'culture', a ubiquitous word, which in broad anthropological terms covers "the full range of learned human behavior patterns."[61] That is 'human culture', the generic way man has organized his life and the way he relates to the universe. It is the sum total of all that man has experienced ever since his brain developed to the present dimension some 200,000 odd years ago, an experience that includes a motley mix, from tool-making to advanced technology, from sexual modes to social interfacing, from the way we make and eat food to the way we amuse and entertain ourselves. It is what we do in the name of 'culture' and its twin brother, 'civilization' that is causing the present planetary crisis. And we must remember that the way we address the problems that confront the world will affect not only our lives and the lives of our children and grandchildren, but also possibly heavily influence the direction of human evolution. What is needed for any meaningful human betterment is nothing less than the transformation of human cultures, values, and priorities, from the individual to the society. We should nurture what has been called a 'natural longing' to show respect and gratitude to those who deserve it, and repentance and reparation to those who wrong us. All religions extol the virtues of heart-felt repentance; it cleanses every sin and opens the way to God. Ingratitude is one of the five great sins in Hinduism, and repentance is the second principle in the gospel of Christianity. Without gratitude and repentance, no radical change is possible in the content of the human condition. While we have attained virtual suzerainty on earth, we are "cut off from an intimate life-enhancing connection with the natural world, and we are undermining our biological support systems at an alarming rate."[62] And that 'cut off' has also led to the paradox of great intellectual and scientific activity that has bestowed meaning and satisfaction, creativity and spirituality, on humans. The English antropologist Edward Tylor (*Primitive Culture*, 1871) defines culture as "that complex whole which includes knowledge, belief, art, law, morals, custom, and any other capabilities and habits acquired by man as a member of society."[63] In fact, a sizable part of human evolution has not been biological or neurological, but *cultural*, or as some would say, bio-cultural. It was culture, which included his tool-making capacity that allowed early man to subjugate and survive his predators. Culture affected the direction of human evolution by creating non-biological solutions to environmental challenges, thus potentially reducing the need to evolve genetic responses to the challenges. Some thinkers like the French biologist Jacques Monod say that evolution is a "series of chance events governed by necessity."[64] Others like Motoro Kimura say that it is "a series of coincidences triggered off by coincidences."[65] Some others say that it is "a sort of rectilinear predetermined process generated by a directing principle."[66] And they raise a doubt whether evolution is only horizontal, refining and improving the existing condition, or it is also vertical, moving towards qualitatively superior forms of life. In other words, is the next stage of evolution, the posthuman future, going to throw up an 'improved man,' maybe devoid of malice and aided by machine, or can the human really evolve as a different genre and genus — a higher step in the ladder of life?

It was the adoption of farming that facilitated a break for man from the evolutionary path of animals, by generating what economists call a 'social surplus.' There are important milestones in human evolution, from standing erect to the design and development of tools, to the injection of science into technology which then became the most transformational event in evolution. Dwarfing all these is the acquisition or development of the mind by man. We will never be able to put a precise date in the last two million years, but whenever it was, or whatever was the process or trigger, it was the most decisive development since life started showing up on earth some six billion years ago. In Christianity, Adam was the 'first fully conscious, intelligent human' and it was his intelligence that was the cause of his fall and the foundation of the human condition. It was his mind that was seduced by the 'logic of Satan' that, contrary to what God told Adam and Eve, by eating the fruit of the forbidden tree of knowledge, man 'could be like God, knowing good and evil'. One wonders why knowing good and evil, which we normally consider a virtue, earned such terrible divine wrath and banishment. One 'explanation' is that by eating the fruit from the Tree of Knowledge, they became aware of themselves as being separate from Nature while still being part of it, which was why they felt "naked" and "ashamed": they had evolved into human beings, conscious of themselves, their own mortality, and their powerlessness before the forces of Nature, and no longer united with the universe as they were in their instinctive, pre-human existence. It was, in John Milton's phrase, the 'mortal taste' of the forbidden fruit that brought death to the world! Milton also wrote "It was from out the rind of one apple tasted, that the knowledge of good and evil, as two twins cleaving together, leaped forth into the world."[67]

The scriptural hypothesis is that man is at the pinnacle of creation, at least thus far. That full potential though is still veiled, and the purpose of life is to peel away the veils. In Vedanta, that veil is called *maya*, which itself is a manifestation of God, a kind of divine deception. Why God makes man potentially perfect and creates a barrier to his perfection is a theological question akin to that of why God creates or tolerates evil and the suffering of the innocents. Is creation some kind of a divine ploy or a hobby, as Greek mythology suggests? Or is it some kind of a trade-off for freedom and free will? According to another view, all that we find in the world is impermanent, and an imperfect representation, a fractured expression of the Perfect Being. In other words, human imperfection mirrors the imperfection of creation itself. If we are aware that everything in the world is both impermanent and imperfect, we would be able to savor the present. The philosopher Heraclitus said that one cannot bathe twice in the same river. The metaphor of river is often applied to life. Life flows, like a river, sometimes languidly in summer, sometimes like a swirling torrent in the monsoon, sometimes fertilizing, sometimes eroding, sometimes enriching, sometimes destroying; but it always makes a difference. And because everything in life is in motion and is both flawed and in flux, there is hope for betterment. Because, every condition is conditioned, there is scope for human effort. If everything is fixed and perfect, life becomes meaningless. In Zen philosophy, it is said that the most precious thing in life is uncertainty. Another school of thought believes that man is, by design, left unfinished, but with a thinking mind and a feeling heart, each with the capacity for remembrance, while the 'finishing' itself is left to man. That is the greatest challenge, the opportunity and the 'vote of confidence' in man, God's own prerogative being given to man. Even among evolutionists, there are differences regarding the inter-relationship of the individual organism and the species in evolution. Darwinism gave primacy to genetic mutations within the individual organism, but what has come to be called 'big-sociology', gives importance to the way an entire species is transformed, based on the principle that mutation is incorporated into a species systematically, not randomly, through natural selection. Some say that since species-evolution is not a steady and single climb, at any stage, humans at different stages of evolution can exist, just as chimpanzees are still around along with man. It is also being 'scientifically' speculated that a good chunk of humanity, particularly people living in affluent societies are no longer governed by the principles of natural selection and genetic mutation, virtually bringing evolution to a halt. Future generations, at least in these parts might not be any different from the present generation; if any, they might well regress, as they no longer have to fight just to stay alive, and their comfort and convenience might enfeeble them and take a heavy toll. The very expectation of long and healthy life and immunity from diseases might work against the evolutionary tool of natural selection. Inferentially, it means the hope for human evolution rests on the impoverished people, who are now vulnerable to debilitating diseases living in the so-called Third World. Does it also mean that for the 'good' of humanity, they should continue to stay in the same condition of despair, deprivation and destitution! If so, should humanity be prepared to pay the price?

The discovery (in 2003) of the fossil remains of a tiny human-like species, on the Indonesian island of Flores (near Java), gives some credence to the theory that more than one 'human' species could have cohabited almost at the same time on earth. From these finds, it is being inferred that the ascent of man is not an evolutionary inevitability; descent is also possible, or at least there could exist around the same time more than one kind of 'human'. In fact, many paleontologists believe that anatomically modern humans might well have coexisted on earth with at least two other closely related kinds: Neanderthals, *Homo erectus* and dwarfed hominids. The Javanese dwarf, called *Homo floresiensis,* is really a miniature man, about a meter tall with "a brain not much bigger than an ape's."[68] The inference scientists draw is jolting: this species, a mini human species, flourished as late as about 13,000 years ago, long after the *Homo sapiens* became the dominant species on earth, and possibly co-existed contemporaneously. That raises the strong possibility that, as the journal *Scientific American* puts it: "With *Homo sapiens* arriving in eastern Asia 35,000 years ago, and relic populations of *Homo erectus* possibly persisting on nearby Java, three human species may have co-existed in this region not so long ago."[69] The Java discovery raises the question if there could be circumstances which could trigger the advent of another 'spin-off' human species, and opens the matter of brain size and intelligence. The question is how could a brain, the size of a grapefruit, have engineered cognitive capacities comparable to those of the modern man? A simple answer may not satisfy our brain-dominated consciousness: they *did not* derive their intelligence principally or exclusively from the brain. What propelled them was 'heart intelligence', which is connected to but quite independent of the brain. This recent discovery is turning upside down our theory of collective cognitive development.

If it is probable that two strains of humans could co-exist, there could have been, in human history, a third strain — the 'superhuman species', existing simultaneously or before the advent of modern man, as occultists like Blavatsky long ago speculated. It was even said that the first few generations of humans might have had three eyes and four arms! It is an intriguing thought that maybe, just maybe, some still do have such extraordinary features, in some still undiscovered island, or in Shangri-La or Shambhala high up in the Himalayas! And maybe they exist on another planet. All this might seem speculative fantasies, but they underscore how little we know of our past and about 'out there'. More importantly, they cast a new light over the future course of evolution. Clearly, a thorough and simultaneous transformation in a species as diversified and disparate and self-centered as the *Homo sapiens* is a near impossibility without its total annihilation first. Is it then conceivable that a section of *Homo sapiens* could evolve into a 'higher species' — hopefully not the mental 'God-Man' of Mark Hamilton, but one with a more compassionate consciousness, an essentially spiritual being — while the rest stay the course and eventually become extinct, possibly by their own hand, or because they were unable to adapt to the changing environment, or because they stopped evolving as the critical factors necessary for evolution were absent?

It is this disconnection between 'perceiving and thinking', or between intelligence and intuition, or, as some like to put it, between the right and left brains, and between the heart and the brain/mind, and the consequent dominance of brain-based thinking and intelligence that has fueled the historic human civilization. We separate ourselves from our prehistoric predecessors, the so-called barbarians, by our concept of 'civilization.' That assumption bears some reflection. Civilization is the state of society in which its constituents, the human individuals, are able to satisfy their basic needs like warmth, food, shelter, and sex with very little effort, and feel so secure that they could do other things pertinent to the development of their mind and spirit. The assumption is that once people acquire a certain control over their material needs, they will divert their 'surplus' labor, time and energy, not for the purpose of furthering material aggrandizement, but for the pursuit of higher values and goals. In actuality, what has happened is that once man mastered his material life he has not stopped there but pursued the same goals that our 'barbarian' ancestors did. In the main, though, man no longer lives in the milieu of Nature but in a 'soul-less civilization', and he is dangerously dependent on technology, or as some call *techno science*, which could determine the drift of evolution. Evolutionists talk of 'moving target selection', 'arms race' and 'escalating spiral', to indicate that animals develop features necessary for survival, but the predators also develop the features necessary to catch and kill their prey for their own survival, and sometimes the spiral gathers inexorable momentum, spins out of control, and a species become extinct.

We assiduously nurture the unassailable conviction that 'we are the best that there can be'. We are also taught to believe that primitive or prehistoric man, was an 'automatically reacting, unconscious' being, who lived by 'blind beliefs,' and led a robotic life, unaffected by reasoning. This premise has long been questioned by those who were on the fringe of organized belief systems. They argue that the human beings of earlier ages were not only physical giants but also that those civilizations were more 'civilized' in the sense of living in harmony with Nature and in resolving inter-personal conflicts. One pointer could be the epics of those ages like the Ramayana and the Mahabharata of India. Such epics are not only stories but also snapshots of that time. Often, the literature and crafts and arts of the times offer a peek into the state of the society of that time. The Egyptian pyramids, the frescoes of Ajanta in India, the Kailasantha temple of the Ellora Caves (carved out of a single rock that covers an area double the size of the Parthenon in Athens), the Temple of Delphi, the Nazca Lines in Peru, all speak of what the 'primitive people' were capable of. These people showed not only astonishing technical capacity but also awesome tenacity and commitment of a whole society over several generations, as many of these structures and art took centuries to finish. Human creativity cannot but depict contemporary lives and morals.

Acceptance and Tolerance

In whatever way biologists might define the attributes of an 'intelligent primate', in practical terms, a tribe of such primates is a conglomeration of disparate and autonomous individuals, capable not only of social living and interbreeding but also of finding harmony in diversity and common ground for common good. Acceptance and tolerance are necessary qualities for coexistence and cooperation. It is one litmus test that the humankind has woefully and wholesomely has not measured up to. Maybe one could even say that it is the 'hallmark' of our culture. We have not really learnt what and when to accept, and when and what to tolerate. Sometimes we like the *status quo*, and sometimes we do not; sometimes we want to change, and sometimes we resist change. We tolerate things we should not tolerate, and are intolerant when we should be tolerant. In fact, all of human history and its attendant atrocities and horrors are but extensions of endemic non-acceptance and intolerance. The problem is not about doing what one wishes to do, but asking *others* to do what one wishes to do. There is nothing wrong with competition *per se*; it forces us to excel. We must distinguish between unity, which is desirable, indeed imperative, and uniformity, which is destructive. Another characteristic of the human mind is the pathological desire to possess: we want to possess everything we see, like, and touch — whether it is property or a person, a gadget or a garden — which incubates friction since someone else might want it even more. We are intolerant of sharing. When our time is finally up and our successor species has to write an epitaph on the tombstone of its predecessor race, it might well inscribe intolerance as the main cause of our premature passage. Whatever might be the immediate cause, intolerance is playing a major role in creating the conditions and in setting up the scenario. Practically, in every crisis that humanity has faced, intolerance has been the driving force. The classic silent-era film *Intolerance: Love's Struggle Through the Ages* (1916), chronicles mankind's intolerance during four different periods in human history like the Fall of Babylon; the crucifixion of Christ; the French Renaissance, the failure of the Edict of Toleration, and the resultant massacre; and modern America. One could add many more, triggered by cultural, economic, racial, and religious causes. In effect, intolerance in human affairs has been constant, continuous and universal, affecting individuals as much as communities, societies, and nations. The well-known British historian Paul Johnson says in his *Modern Times* (1983): "The study of history suggests that the sum total of intolerance in society does not vary much. What changes is the object against which it is directed..."[70] Intolerance has been called "the most socially acceptable form of egotism."[71] It is the ugly outgrowth of the '*I*'-ness that defines the human personality. The most visible face of the ego is intolerance. Our intelligence often manifests as strong opinions, beliefs and prejudices, but it gives no room for others to have the same. We search for information, not as an input to making choices, but to reinforce our prejudices. Emerson said "People seem not to see that their opinion of the world is also a confession of character."[72] The fact is that truth or reality can rarely be seen from the prism of a lone person. And self-belief is not inimical to acceptance; it is self-righteousness. Intolerance is the reflex of an insecure person; according to British the occultist and writer Aleister Crowley, "Intolerance is evidence of impotence."[73] Most people are intolerant in some way or the other but it is more in the mind, and remains passive. And it is not always negative: intolerance in the face of intolerance is good; intolerance to fight inequity and injustice is necessary. But most people show, not the 'good' intolerance but 'bad' intolerance. 'Aggressive intolerance' of all sorts — personal, professional, political, racial, ethnic, religious — has taken a firm root at the deepest level of our consciousness, and few, if any, are untouched by it. It is mainly responsible for much of what is wrong with the world today. And it, more than any other factor, bears a huge chunk of responsibility for the breakdown of all kinds of relationships as well as for the wrath, discrimination, violence and hatred that are suffocating the world today. We use double-standards to judge ourselves and others, oblivious to the foibles in us which we find and magnify in others. As the American 'self-help' guru Wayne Dyer (*Your Erroneous Zones*, 1976) says, when you judge another person you are defining him. The workbook of

A Course in Miracles (published by the Foundation for Inner Peace), a book that Wikipedia describes as a "self-study curriculum (spiritual in nature) that sets forth an absolute non-dualistic metaphysics yet integrates (its definition of the principle of) forgiveness emphasizing its practical application in daily living" says "Today I will judge nothing that occurs". Anyone who has ever tried to put that into practice, knows how almost impossible it is to keep that promise. What is it about judgment that makes it so hard to let go of? "It is curious", Jesus says, "that an ability so debilitating would be so deeply cherished."[74] We feel compelled to pronounce our judgment and to correct the errors of the world around us, an onerous, even distasteful task that drains our energy. Yet, ironically we *do* cherish it. We constantly choose to judge, and we find the idea of giving up judgment to be beyond ordinary human effort.

Whether it is evolutionary or environmental, innate or imbibed, we are all imperfect, but we have eyes only for the faults of others. We do not accept life; we do not accept ourselves; we do not accept others. We live in a state of denial, resistance, and rejection. What most people yearn for is acceptance and a feeling of being wanted, just to be missed. We are overly indulgent towards intolerance, and impatient with diversity and difference of opinions. The Italian poet and philosopher Giacomo Leopardi, said: "No human trait deserves less tolerance in everyday life, and gets less, than intolerance."[75] Acceptance is not condoning sin or ignoring injustice; it is simply to desist from compelling others to lead their lives in a particular way; it is to desist from judging others because no norm is foolproof if solely based on human intelligence, which is inherently imperfect. In the highest sense, acceptance is love, and intolerance is a manifestation of hate, and exploitation is the opposite of compassion. It stems from a culture that worships the winner and ridicules the loser, a culture that considers tolerance and success as incompatible. In common parlance, success often is another name for short-cut, a quick way to achieving an objective regardless of all scruples. Does it all mean that success and morality and spirituality are incompatible and irreconcilable? At first glance that does appear to be so, but a deeper look belies the premise. It depends on how we delineate the boundaries. There is an emerging new breed of 'success seekers' who believe that success can be sharing too, and not necessarily unscrupulous, who put people ahead of profit, personal fulfillment before material gain. But such seekers are too miniscule in number to tilt the social scales, or to make a difference to the human moral balance sheet.

Civilization and Chemicalization

As a result of our obsession with 'success' in conjunction with another ubiquitous word 'progress', man no longer lives in the natural order. In that order, fruits ripen in their own time and in general, things mature in consonance with natural laws, and as a part of and as an input to the larger cause of life on earth. Human culture has sought to change that — to improve upon what Nature offers as food and medicine and to want a menu of choices more than what is naturally available. The main facilitators of that gratification are synthetic chemicals, and between them and toxicity there is only a thin line. We are told that more than 100,000 chemicals are already in the marketplace, and that about 1,000 new ones are being introduced every year. We have been made to believe that through chemicals, we can lead better lives, and that manufactured chemicals are no different from naturally occurring products. The path of 'progress' that modern man has embarked upon, which requires industrialization and processing of everything that Nature offers, has led to the 'chemicalization' of everything that goes into our body. As a result, we live in a 'chemicalized' milieu, the impact of which, scientists tell us, is "changing both the social and mating behaviors of a raft of species,"[76] through what are called 'endocrine disruptors', which "potentially pose far greater threat to survival than, for example, falling sperm counts caused by higher chemical concentrations."[77] In what we may call chemically afflicted societies, and increasingly universally, many people are plagued by mysterious neurological disorders that rarely, if ever, existed just a century ago. We have disorders with all kinds of complex sounding names like Amyotrophic lateral sclerosis (ALS), Lou Gehrig's disease, fibromyalgia and Alzheimer's disease, and so on. Many things we use to improve our 'quality of life' are loaded with chemicals, about which we know nothing, not to speak of their effect. Our body tissues themselves have become toxic because of our quality of life. One expert on toxins in food wrote that we are so contaminated that, had we been cannibals, our meat would be banned from human consumption. We are often reassured by the authorities and by the chemical industry with phrases such as 'no direct evidence', or with the argument that at 'low' levels those chemicals are either safe or pose 'low risk'. That may be the truth, but it is not the 'whole truth'. Each of the chemicals in question might qualify for such descriptions at that level in isolation, but together and with thousands of other chemicals we are exposed to every day in our civilized world and in urban settings, their cumulative effect might no longer be 'low risk', particularly for children. It could affect not only their health but also their behavior. Then there is a phenomenon called 'body burden', which is the effect of these cumulative chemicals inside the human body. Randall Fitzgerald, author of the book *The Hundred-Year Lie* (2006), on the prevalence of toxic chemicals says, "The problem here is that our bodies do not recognize these synthetic chemicals, most of which have been invented, patented and produced since World War II. Our livers, which are the main detoxifying organs of our bodies, do not recognize these synthetic chemicals, and as a result, do not metabolize them. Instead, the chemicals are either pushed off into the far reaches of the liver, to be stored, or sent into body fat and body organs to be stored. As these toxins accumulate, they begin to interact with each other."[78] Fitzgerald says that we do not know the synergic effects of two or more chemicals in the human body and that chemical combination could increase toxicity and cause neurological damage. He warns us that we are becoming a mutant species, and cites the example of the fish and amphibian species in the lakes and in swamps becoming hermaphrodite and developing both male and female sex organs as a result of the toxic chemicals dumped into those water bodies. Fitzgerald adds that every day, we play what he calls a game of biological Russian roulette with our bodies, based on our food, medicine and environmental choices. Furthermore, there is now emerging evidence that chemicals in the environment can influence animal behavior drastically — can humans escape it? Maybe much of the malice and the violence in human behavior is chemically induced. We talk about 'substance abuse' and 'drug dependence' of the youth in affluent countries but not about our 'chemical dependence', which perhaps is at the root of all those dependences. We worry about 'cold-causing viruses' but are oblivious to the surge in human violence possibly influenced by the chemicals that we imbibe through our food, water and the air. Chemical pollution is far more deadly than atmospheric pollution, and it is possibly altering the processes that determine human personality and behavior. Man is addicted to chemicals because they offer what the human mind wants: comfort, convenience, instant gratification, and short-term security. In the long run, the combination of chemically weakened human bodies and toxic habitat could threaten human survival more than the specter of nuclear holocaust. In fact, some scientists say that one of the emerging frontiers of research is to find a way to keep the human alive and healthy in a much more toxic world. But as someone said, we are actually not living longer but 'dying longer', kept alive longer through technology.

Unmindful of all these portents, man is waging a war on the very source that provides his life-supporting infrastructure. Human civilization is increasingly becoming noxious to Nature. Instead of being caretakers and custodians, we have become predators and exploiters. On the other hand, those who advocate the cause of Nature seem to imply that man must suffer so that Nature remains pristine. In the words of Peter Schwartz, "Human beings survive by reshaping nature to fulfill their needs. Every single step taken to advance beyond the cave — every rock fashioned into a tool, every square foot of barren earth made into productive cropland, every drop of crude petroleum transformed into fuel for cars and planes — constitutes an improvement in human life, achieved by altering our natural environment. The environmentalists' demand that Nature be protected against human 'encroachments' means, therefore, that man must be sacrificed in order to preserve Nature."[79] 'Conquest of Nature' is considered as the telltale sign of human civilization. But every power won over Nature, as the Irish essayist C.S. Lewis (*The Abolition of Man*, 1843) says, is a power over man as well; it could be directed against himself — a kind of a returning boomerang. It is true that man has come this far by harnessing Nature. The difference between the attitudes of pre-modern man and modern man is a state of mind, the desire to tap the magnanimity and munificence of Nature, and the thought of being a conqueror. It is the difference between a baby suckling at the mother's breast and a rapist ravaging the same breast. The home of human 'civilization', it is useful to remind ourselves, is Planet Earth. It is on the soil and sweat of the Earth that man created the infrastructure for his way of life, by harnessing its resources to cater to his comfort and convenience. Now, some scientists say that we are in serious '*erotological overshoot*', that we might run out of both room and resources on earth as early as 2050,[80] and that thankfully, we are now poised on the brink of an interplanetary civilization. But, let us come down to earth and remind ourselves that we have not created even a planetary civilization that treats the Earth as a holistic entity, and humanity as a coherent community. Alfred North Whitehead wrote that "Civilization is the victory of persuasion over force."[81] On that account alone, what man has created never was 'civilization'. It is fear and force that have been the driving forces in human society from the earliest to modern times, more so now than ever before. The noted historian Arnold Toynbee wrote "to be able to fill leisure intelligently is the last product of civilization."[82] We have failed that test too. Technology has created a lot of leisure, at least in some parts of the human world, but our civilization has not found a way to fill that leisure wisely. If anything, it has fuelled avarice and violence. Furthermore, the current civilization is based on ownership and is built on fragmentation and fracturing of the earth; not only nation-states but even individuals behave as if they own a bit of the earth. Once you buy it, you can do what you want with it, subject only to the law of the land, not the law of Nature. The key concept is 'to afford', which means having enough money, preferably legitimate, by which you can acquire and use or misuse anything regardless of its effect on the planet. The Latin writer of maxims Publilius Syrus said that "we are born princes and the civilizing process makes us frogs."[83] C.P. Snow (*Two Cultures*, 1959) said that "civilization is hideously fragile...there's not much between us and the horrors underneath, just about a coat of varnish."[84] Few people would stand up to the test of what we would or would not do if we knew we will be found out; fear is the fulcrum of human morality, of the law, of consequences, maybe even of God. Fear leads to intolerance; to aggression. Emerson predicted that the human race is likely to 'die of civilization'. Because civilization, as Aldous Huxley, one of the most perceptive of social scientists and the author of *Brave New World* (1932) said, is designed to domesticate human passions and set them to do useful work, the practical effect of which is a platform of material comfort, satiation of escalating wants, planned obsolescence, permanent playfulness and titillating entertainment, onslaught on nature and spiritual vacuity. We no longer wholly own our own attention and have forgotten how to be truly engaged. The means are science and technology, brain and brawn. The human mind is drawn more towards entertainment than enlightenment. As a chronicle of Hollywood history puts it "mankind has always recognized the importance of entertainment and its value in rebuilding the bodies and souls of human beings."[85] Indeed human mind seems incapable of entertaining any thought or topic seriously without some entertainment, is unable to focus on anything without sensory pleasure. Modern man wants everything as entertainment; he wants to be 'amused'; it is more than a diversion or a means of spending leisure; it frames our life. It may be because life is so 'somber' and devoid of joy; being entertained lets us forget our sorrows, at least momentarily. As someone wryly remarked, it is moot if entertainment is killing our children, or or if killing children is entertaining the adults. The lines are blurred now between mass media, news, propaganda, information, entertainment, economy, exhilaration, industry, fantasy and morality. At any point, we cannot be sure which of them is dominant. And it shapes our life, and as the preponderant part of our living environment, it will have a huge bearing on the future human evolution. Anthony Robbins, the American self-help guru and writer says that "we aren't in an information age; we are in an entertainment age."[86] It reflects both the stagnation and the shallowness of our mass culture. The celebrated 'political theorist' and Nazi refugee Hannah Arendt wrote, "Culture relates to objects and is a phenomenon of the world; entertainment relates to people and is a phenomenon of life."[87] We are increasingly encircled and influenced by images: photography and cinema, but even more television, video and computers. Visual images are becoming so powerful that this surge in visual imagery has become "virtual reality". This, in turn, leads to manipulation of information and images portraying news. We tend to believe what we 'see' rather than what we hear or even read, but most people do not know how to "read" visual images, and this leads to misinterpretation and to simplistic identification with reality. It is a potent weapon for advertisement, which someone described as making us do what we do not want to do, and buy things we do not need. And it leads to wanton waste and addictive profligacy.

Consumerism and its Critics

Our consumerist culture is perhaps the most wasteful user and the most inefficient manager of natural resources, land, and water. Our profligacy and callousness is mind-blogging; we take these resources for granted as we do the air we breathe. It is based on the premise that waste is an inherent part of the process of 'progress' through which we get the things we want for good life and pleasure, the way to individual self-fulfillment. We routinely 'use' and 'use up', 'consume' and 'contaminate' the natural world. It is an ironic coincidence that 'consumption' in medicine was the popular name for tuberculosis (TB), and consumerism and TB carry the same connotation — using up, wasting, withering away, and destruction, in one case the body, and in the other, Nature. Misuse can be direct or indirect, excess use or wrong use, and it covers aspects like depletion of forests and freshwater resources. Although the world is worried about oil supplies, there are many who predict that 'water wars' will be the wars of the future. United Nations (UN) figures suggest that there are around 300 potential conflicts over water around the world, arising from squabbles over river borders and the drawing of water from shared lakes and aquifers. And according to the World Health Organization (WHO), "around one-sixth of the 6.1 billion people in the world lack access to improved sources of water, while 40 percent are without access to improved sanitation services,"[88]. Declining glacial freshwater flows in areas like the Tibetan plateau are said to affect about 500 million people in Asia and 250 million in China. As demand for water hits the limits of finite supply, potential conflicts are brewing between nations that share transboundary freshwater reserves. More than 50 countries in five continents might soon be caught up in water disputes unless they move quickly to establish agreements on how to share reservoirs, rivers, and underground water aquifers.

The moral behavior of man cannot measurably improve unless new rules and dialectics are brought to bear on the dynamics and social norms that govern economic theory and practice. Man's overbearing obsession with consumerism has to be done away with. As the lives of the super rich show, there are no limits to human extravagance or rapacity. It is the runaway consumption that is destroying the infrastructure for life on earth. We have to redefine economic morality. We must disconnect personal happiness from conspicuous consumption, and 'feel-good' feeling from the purchase of material possessions. Frugality has to become morality and respectable, if not hip. The moral distinction between needs and wants has to be restored. The almost obsessive focus on the economic side to the exclusion of other factors, perhaps more important pursuits, has introduced a major fracture in human life and has divided most of mankind into two antagonistic camps: the rich and the super rich, and as the American author Scott Fitzgerald (*The Great Gatsby*, 1925) famously said, "the rich are different from you and me."[89] He explained how: "They think, deep in their hearts, that they are better than we are because we had to discover the compensations and refuges of life for ourselves. Even when they enter deep into our world or sink below us, they still think that they are better than we are. They are different."[90] And Ernest Hemingway quipped "Yes, they have more money."[91] They have more because others have less money; it is both absolute and comparative. While the evils of contemporary consumerism (which is but a function of our way of life) cannot be denied, one must not also overlook the fact that 'consumption' (which is the purchase and usage of consumer goods) is necessary for lifting the lives of over a billion people from the trap of extreme poverty. The 'consumption' disparity is telling. It is reported that the richest 20 percent of the global population accounted for 75 percent of the total private consumption in the year 2005, and the poorest fifth just 1.5 percent. Aldous Huxley wrote that "the peace of the world has frequently been endangered in order that they (the rich and the powerful) might grow a little richer."[92] Despite the tiresome and hypocritical campaigns to 'eradicate the scourge of poverty,' the divide between the dirty rich and the dirt poor, obscene opulence and grinding poverty, has never been sharper or wider than now. Often, abject poverty has been depicted variously as an economic issue, a social stigma, a political irritant, and a strategic time bomb. But in its barest essence, it is a moral affront. Poverty degrades man of dignity, the most basic of all human rights, and its persistence robs the other rights of any semblance of moral legitimacy. Obsessive concern about wealth or rather the lack of it, prevents the *all round* development of the human personality, and the poor and the rich alike lose their sensitivity and humaneness. Poverty and deliberate deprivation of the basic needs have a ripple effect and degrade the human condition. For a human being to bloom to his full potential and become a kinder and gentler being, he must nail down economics or wealth into its proper place and not let it completely control all levers of human life. Our patterns and models of consumption are so much a part of our lives, that to change them would require a massive cultural catharsis, not to mention traumatic economic dislocation. In one word, we must rethink what we associate with what we call 'progress'.

'Progress' in the words of Christopher Lasch, "rests on the belief that human wants are insatiable, that new wants appear as soon as the old ones are satisfied. And that steadily rising levels of comfort will lead to an indefinite expansion of the productive forces required to satisfy the revolution of rising expectations."[93] Lasch begins his thought-provoking book, *The True and Only Heaven: Progress and Its Critics* (1991), with a very pointed and pertinent question that touches the very core of the issue: "how does it happen that serious people continue to believe in progress, in the face of massive evidence that might have been expected to refute the idea of progress once and for all?"[94] It is like the question 'why does man choose the path of evil when righteousness gets him everything he aspires for?' There is no easy answer. A possible explanation is that it is wholly rational, from the perspective to own, to possess, to accumulate, and to have something that others do not or cannot have. The fact is that "the dialectic of 'progress', however, which has the potential to end all suffering and misery in the human and non-human world, may also have the ability to usher in a new stone age on the wings of technology."[95]

The meteoric rise of the economic and material aspects of man has virtually snuffed out his spiritual faculty and contributed to the ever-mounting immorality in the world. Man is now accustomed to consistent economic growth, rising living standards and steady supply of 'affordable' consumer goods. It has necessitated the diversion and use of enormous social resources and human time and energy, inevitably at the cost of non-material pursuits. In the process, it has distorted human priorities and personality. The conventional wisdom holds that economics is holy; progress has gathered all the trappings of a religion, affluence is the passport to social esteem, greed is good, and the poor are a thorn in the flesh, at best a prick at the conscience — they are paying for their past sins or are plain lazy. Excessive focus on economic progress, which is another facet of 'fundamentalism' or 'extremism', has stoked the embers of evil in man. Conspicuous consumption, obscene opulence, callous inequity, wanton wealth and degrading poverty have become the hallmarks of the present society. And most wars have economic underpinnings. A major intellectual — and spiritual challenge — is to get away from this 'growth' model. In a recent book (*Eaarth: Making a Life on a Tough New Planet*) environmentalist Bill McKibben argues that earth, which he calls *Eaarth,* can no longer support the economic growth model that has driven the world for 200 years, which is based on the premise that more is better and that the answer to any problem is another burst of economic expansion.

But we must remember that man's economic personality is an extension of his aggressive and avaricious personality. Waging war has become a habit; getting what he wants has become compulsive; disregard for means has become pathological; man has extended all these traits towards Nature. Some say that the real and perhaps the most decisive 'world war' ever is the one we are waging on Nature. This 'war' has led, among other things, to such a wide range of potentially catastrophic consequences that it is hard even to enumerate them: climate change and global warming; desertification; pollution of the biosphere; endangered biodiversity and species loss; and global water crisis. It is estimated that two billion people will face water shortages in 2025 — three billion, in all likelihood, by 2050. While water is illustrative, the larger issue is the balance between human activity and ecological sustainability, between inevitable depletion of natural resources and their conservation, renewal and regeneration.

The world does not have, in the absence of any global authority, the mechanism or means to settle intra-state and interstate problems and disputes, anything that requires a holistic view of the world. But at its core, the issue boils down to the human understanding of life and man's inability to instinctively grasp what is truly in his own interest. The world mirrors the triumph of the narrow over the larger interest — individual over family, family over the community, nation over the global community. When choices are to be made, it is the preeminence of the exclusive over the inclusive, a the part over the whole. This is contrary to the doctrine of *dharma*, which specifically says that where there is a conflict or choice between the *dharmas* enjoined upon individual groups and society and humanity, we must choose that which is in the interest of the larger or the greater number. It even condones narrower *adharma* for the larger good. We must learn that in complex systems we cannot do only one thing and that the impact of our decisions may surface in unexpected places. While dealing with terrestrial issues, at least in the short term, there is no gain without pain, and the question is, how does one apportion or ration the pain and sacrifice among nations and individuals? The trouble is that we seem to have got it all wrong about what 'sacrifice' is meant to be. We view sacrifice as something we give or give up, some pain or loss we voluntarily endure for the sake of someone else. Etymologically, the word sacrifice means 'to make sacred' or to be sanctified; through sacrifice, one burns out and purges oneself of sins. In Sanskrit, both the doctrines of *yagna* and *tyaga* denote sacrifice; while the first refers to a ritual sacrifice, which is complemented and completed by the latter, which refers to offerings at the existential level. Blood sacrifice, which is intentional killing, as a high human ideal for the common good of society, is extolled in most religious traditions, involving the sacrifice of animals or even one's own kin. It has been said that any inquiry into sacrifice is in fact a theory of religion in miniature, that sacrificial activity lies at the very roots of a true religion, and that understanding sacrifice is essential to understanding the religious impulse in human beings. In the Christian religion, it was by shedding his blood that Jesus sacrificed for humanity. The Bible says that "Whoever sheds the blood of man, by man shall his blood be shed, for God made man in His own image" (*Genesis, 9:6*). In the ancient Vedic thought, the act of creation itself emanated out of *yagna*, the rite of sacrifice. In the famous *Purusha Sukta,* the *Purusha*, the Supreme God, consumes himself in the act of creation, to create all the worlds and all life. The father–son motif of sacrifice is common to the three Abrahamic religions; it is also the source, albeit differently, of the *Katha* Upanishad. The ultimate offering is the most precious gift of God: life, one's own as well as of the 'others'.

Comparison, Competition and Convergence

That brings up one of the most baffling of human traits. It is the compulsive habit to constantly compare and differentiate oneself from the 'others' and to feel better because of such comparison. It involves not only other humans but also other species. It is hard to tell if it is a matter of insecurity or superiority, catholicity or arrogance. In isolation we are all selfless; when our actions have no affect on others, we are magnanimous. Our ego shows up only in company. Our arrogance is toothless if there is no one to direct it towards. Our comparison is competitive, and competition comparative. Without some sort of comparison, mental or physical, we do precious little either as an act of altruism or selfishness. Control is another extreme way of comparison, and selfishness is not doing what one wishes to do, derived from the dictates of our conscience, but in expecting others to do what we wish them to do. Our knowledge is comparative; our education is competitive; our prosperity is comparative and competitive (we want more); so is our misery and suffering (we do not want it). Everyone thinks that their misery is the most miserable and their suffering the most intolerable. Our sense of worth of anything is nothing if it is worthless for anyone else. The Irish dramatist, Oscar Wilde, famous for his often cutting witticisms, said, perhaps a bit too cynically but not without a grain of accuracy, that "there are many things that we would throw away if we were not afraid that others might pick them up."[96] We do not know which evolutionary offshoot it was, man does not seem to find any worth, but only void in his own persona; it is only conjunction that appears to give substance to life; either we are better or worse; if neither, we are nothing. From comparison comes competition, and from competition comes conflict.

In Nature, nothing is absolute or equal, and that propels comparison and competition but not coexistence, it propels conflict but not harmony. Another facet of comparison or competition is imitation. Our desires arise from observing what others have. Aware of an absence within ourselves, we look to others to teach us what to value and who to be. And we desire to appropriate the other's possessions, loves and their very being to fill the void within; and it leads to frustration, rivalry, anger, and violence. That void is increasingly manifesting as comparison with regard to other fellow animals. While comparison with other humans can get contentious, with other species it seems relatively less risky — they cannot argue and contest. With regard to other species, the body of knowledge drawn from the scriptures and science is complex and confusing. One stream of thought — primarily religious — says that we are so unique that we are not 'animal' in any sense. Most major religions say that God directly and specially created humans, essentially and potentially both as sexual and spiritual beings. The Bible says that God created man in His own image and endowed him with the power to virtually mimic him. That particular maxim or rather license seems to have shaped our attitude and legitimized our casual, if not cruel disposition towards animals.

For long, it was the mainstream view that the human system of organizing knowledge is so distinct that human future development may not be controlled by the same principles as other animals. We differ in the use of advanced technology, use of controlled energy, use of clothes, use of sense-enhancements like glasses, telescopes or microscopes, advanced social organization, and advanced language. As science acquired more probing tools and techniques, much of the presumed uniqueness has withered. The last citadel of man is also crumbling, that is, man's ability to 'think'. Quite apart from the fact that we are not quite sure what 'thinking' really connotes, nor how that faculty might manifest differently in other creatures, researchers now even admit that other creatures may also *think*; only they do not — well, whatever it means — know that they think! And we deem it as an intolerable insult to be compared with lowly animals, least of all with irksome insects like ants. Apart from the fact that ants are far more antiquated than we are (1,000 million years), far more diversified (14,000 species and still counting), far more dispersed (every habitable habitat), and that they will certainly out-last us, some scholars and entomologists even call the ant a 'super organism' and ant civilization, 'the superior civilization'. Christine Kenneally writes, "In an advanced ant city, thousands of individuals work closely together to create a functioning colony in which there is a balance of cooperation and conflict. Some ant societies feature spectacular architecture and climate control. The most remarkable ant species have agriculture: they farm fungus and even domesticate other insects as livestock. In fact, at its height, ant civilization is remarkably like ours. A key contrast is that their society emerges from the hard-wired decision-making of thousands of efficient little biological robots, whereas ours is, at least partly, conscious and intentional. Despite this seemingly massive difference, it appears you can go a long way without a mind".[97] Tim Flannery writes, "Parallels between the ants and ourselves are striking for the light they shed on the nature of everyday human experiences. Some ants get forced into low-status jobs and are prevented from becoming upwardly mobile by other members of the colony. Garbage dump workers, for example, are confined to their humble and dangerous task of removing rubbish from the nest by other ants who respond aggressively to the odors that linger on the garbage workers' bodies".[98] Ants seem to have fused into a 'superorganism' and built a 'superior civilization' drawing on their instincts, not intelligence, drawing on their reflexes, not reason. The astonishing complexity of an ant colony and the way the ants, as members of the colony, seem to manage and take decisions stands in sharp contrast to the way we manage the human 'colony'.

Philosophers too have taken a crack at describing how peerless we are in creation. The German philosopher Schopenhauer, for example, said that "apart from man, no being wonders at its own existence".[99] We ought to but rarely do. St. Augustine aptly said that we wonder at many things but pass by ourselves without wondering. Sri Aurobindo said that man alone lives in three modes of time, the past, present, and future simultaneously. His disciple Satprem said that we are unique because we, of all things, make mistakes whereas animals do not since they live instantly and intuitively. The more pertinent point is how all these attributes have impacted human personality and behavior in relation to those that do not supposedly have such attributes.

Yet our self-assumed but scripturally sanctioned singularity is at the center of human thought. That is also the basis of our morality and even spirituality. For example, in the Ramayana, when prince Rama kills Vali, the king of monkeys, while hiding behind a tree, and Vali questions the ethics of that act, Rama, himself the direct incarnation of God Vishnu, dismisses the point by saying that hunting an animal is the right of humans, particularly of the royalty. In the Bible and Quran, of course, God specifically anointed man as the lord of all other species. Man has forgotten the difference between a trustee and a tyrant. We have forgotten that to be a steward is to tend, to care, to protect, not to turn other species into trophies and guinea pigs. So, what really separates humans from other primates?

Genetically, though there is not much, the difference between chimps and us is said to be no more than 2 percent, probably only 1 percent. According to a recent study, "nearly 99 percent alike in genetic makeup, chimpanzees and humans might be even more similar were it not for what researchers call 'lifestyle' changes in the 6 million years that separate us from a common ancestor."[100]

A more recent scientific speculation is referred to as 'gene regulation': "Since most primates share at least 90 percent of the same genetic sequences, it is in the ways by which genes are activated, regulated, the patterns of their expression and ultimately how and when they play out throughout development, that drive forward most differences we see in primates."[101]

Our intellect, a product of our brain, is not what puts us in a distinctive category; other creatures also have a brain and some rudimentary discriminating capacity necessary for survival and sex. Finding that many things once viewed as exclusive to humans like culture, mind, reading, tool use, morality, emotions, personality are no longer *only* human, we clutch at things like, in the words of anthropologist Ian Tattersall, "the fundamental human urge to adorn and elaborate."[102] There might be very few 'only human' capabilities, but in those 'common areas' humans certainly are special in the dexterity and ingenuity in their use. But perhaps it is not our strengths but our foibles and emotions, which have no discernible biological objective, that propel our purposes, desires, and passions, values and wants, which distinguish us from other species. What constitutes 'humanness' could be our experience of emotions like being in love and being able to jump into a river to save a drowning dog, and in the next minute, cut someone else's throat because that person rammed our car on the road. It may be an uncomfortable thought, but it could be that our negative traits like malice and murder are our unmistakable signatures. Finally, the impregnable barrier between other species and us is said to be our innate potential for God-realization that even angels are supposed to envy. Well, maybe yes; then again, maybe not. The scriptures say so, and our intellect is not capable of questioning them. But, as God's creations and children, how do we know that other species do not have their own ways to realize God? Swami Vivekananda, foremost among modern-day spiritualists, remarked that if a goat were to visualize God it would be as a goat — and perhaps the same would be the case if it were a dog. God Himself declared He will appear in the form, shape and size that His devotee aspires to. Incidentally, God actually did incarnate as an animal; the ten avatars of Lord Vishnu, according to Hindu scriptures, included the incarnations as *matsya* (fish), *koorma* (tortoise), and *varaha* (boar). That particular manifestation was what was needed to save the world at that time. God did not think it was any different from his subsequent avatars, one of which was *Narasimha*, the half man and half lion, which again was needed to slay the demon king Hiranyakasipu. While God did not hesitate to identify himself with an animal, humans hesitate, based on the belief that we are inherently incomparable. Animals seem to be 'superior' in another respect. For example, it has often been said that "animals have a talent for bypassing the mind and going straight to the heart."[103] And heart is a favorite habitat for God. Who knows, maybe other species, the lowly animals, may have more intuitive knowledge and divine interfacing than 'mighty' man.

There is another kind of impending 'singularity' that is being predicted — technological. When that happens, humans as they exist today will cease to be the top species on the planet, and the most intelligent. Computers will be many times smarter than men; we will be like children to them, and they, like gods to us. Eventually, computers will advance to the point where there is no difference between them and our current conception of an all-knowing and all-powerful God. Some evolutionary psychologists believe that, at this point in the life of life on planet Earth, natural evolution and natural selection are no longer in operation. As Harvard professor Steven Pinker puts it, "People, including me, would rather believe that significant human biological evolution stopped between 50,000 and 100,000 years ago, before the races diverged, which would ensure that racial and ethnic groups are biologically equivalent."[104] Many think that in the future, artificial breeding and genetic engineering could have more say than natural selection. The mutations that are affecting the human condition now are, on the face of it, culture-centric and lately cyber-centric. This is the theme that is expanded in the book, *Shattered Self: the End of Natural Evolution* (2001), by Pierre Baldi. While that view has been widely shared, there are new trends that seem to dilute that premise. Recent news reports have flashed headlines of speedy human evolution with the implication that instead of becoming more alike, humans are becoming more different. It is reported that a comparison of the genomes of several different people groups showed that many genes appear to have recent mutations, and that the rate of mutation has sharply increased over the last 10,000 years.[105] Does that, if further corroborated, have a message for the future? Is it possible that some humans could evolve into posthuman beings while the rest become posthumous? But one could also say that culture itself could have triggered such mutations. The field of cultural evolution is controversial because not all historians, social scientists or even biologists agree that cultural change can be understood in an evolutionary context. Some say that human beliefs and behaviors are too unpredictable, as it is also claimed that cultural revolution "has an arrow and a direction: towards greater complexity; towards higher civilization."[106] There are others, though, like the economist Robert Fogel, who argues that the human species, during the past 300 years has undergone what he calls a "technophysio evolution" which is biological but not genetic, rapid, culturally transmitted, and not very stable, which has enabled the species to increase its average body size by over 50 percent and longevity by more than 100 percent since the year 1800, and to greatly increase the robustness and capacity of vital organ systems. He predicts a rosy future when the trends would continue and even accelerate, offering man large space and 'discretionary time' for pursuit of issues like "life's meaning and other matters of self-realization."[107] Partially plausible it may be, but such analysis suffers from serious blemishes. First, the data and analysis are confined to a small part of the world, primarily the United States, and ignores the developing world, which has more than two-thirds of the world population. An unconscionably large number of human beings are hungry, malnourished, and susceptible to every passing infection; their bodies are shriveled and their brains paralyzed. Second, Fogel does not take cognizance of the effect of the processed and chemicalized food we eat and the toxic air we breathe, of our crippling and addictive dependence on 'add-ons' and appliances on the human body. Just as we cannot isolate the future from the present, our way of life and the context we create for living cannot be separated from the way human race will evolve in the future.

Along with his enfeebled condition, man's relationship with other species and with Nature will increasingly play a major part in human future. We are not, and never were, alone on earth, and as a fragment of the totality of life we cannot, simply put, survive as a species without the rest of life on earth. The human species is, even if it is the most potent and powerful, one of many millions of manifestations of life on earth, many of which existed long before man appeared and probably, but for man, will continue long after he is gone. Predator and prey, wildlife and vegetation, play interconnected roles in preserving and sustaining life. No one has a clear idea about how many species existed and became extinct since life began on earth. Scientists have formally identified and named about 17 million species, but the number is yet to be discovered and it may range anywhere between 5 million to 100 million, of which about 30 million would be insects alone. Every species will become extinct at an appointed time, and humans are no exception. Some species like the humans may have the power, but not the mandate, to cause the extinction of another. Human behavior, more than any other factor, is now the greatest threat to life on earth and to the ecosystem of the earth. A recent research finding is one of those 'stories' we read and quickly pass on to more arresting items (like a triple murder, for example): namely, that man is responsible for the biggest extinction of wildlife since the extinction of the dinosaurs, with a 35 percent decrease in biodiversity over the past 35 years.[108] Shorn of the scientific sophistry, it really means that man has murdered more than one-fourth of all other living creatures on earth in about half the life span of an affluent human being. There are those, the never-say-die optimists, who reassuringly say that death and extinction are part of nature, that 90 percent of all those species that ever lived are dead species, and that it is the way to make room for other life. In simpler terms, if we kill other species, it is no big deal; and if we kill ourselves, even lesser. There is nothing but death in Nature, and reaching the milestone of death is only a matter of time and effort. This is but one example of the nihilistic bent in the human way of life. What comes to mind is the question that recurs over and over again in any study of the human condition: why, with so much loaded in man's favor in the cosmos, and being able — alone he claims — to learn from his mistakes and to anticipate the consequences of his actions, is man's behavior so comprehensively irrational, so conspicuously irresponsible, so palpably against his own selfish self-interest?

3

Of Human Baggage and Bondage

Bondage and Liberation

The state of the human world reflects the state of a 'bonded being' bearing the baggage of a beast, bound by being human and aspiring to be a god. The duality or *dwanda* of 'bondage' and 'liberation' defines both the human condition and human aspiration. While we are not certain which is our natural condition — bondage or liberation — we, like Philip Carey of Somerset Maugham's *Of Human Bondage* (1915), expend much of our life to find 'some guide by which we could rule our conduct'. Not 'finding', we struggle to make sense by trial and error; we seek and search, twist and turn, and often find ourselves alone and adrift. And the more we strive and strain to free our spirit, the tighter the shackles become. Most people feel that they are entrapped in a cage, caught in a world not of their making, and carry a weight not of their choice and beyond bearing. And liberation — by whatever name it is called, *moksha* or *nirvana* or salvation — for them, is simply to be free (it does not matter *how*) from the pressures, pitfalls, perils, and frustrations of living with fellow men, and from pain and suffering. As for the weight they carry on their beaten backs, it is not only the weight of their own lives but the sum of over a million years of struggle for survival, to be 'civilized'. Whichever or whatever it might be, all human endeavor, spiritual or scientific, is to find a way to lighten that load, and even change the nature of the load. Because, while it makes no difference to a beast if it is burdened with sacred texts or scum, it makes — rather *should* make — a difference to man.

We want to escape, we want to be free, we want liberty, we long to lead our lives without pitfalls and pinpricks, we want deliverance — but we have no idea who or what is holding us back. The troubling thought that arises in this confusion is: have we got it all wrong, mistaking one for the other, and messing up our lives? The truth is that we want to overcome that which we do not know, and to achieve something we have no clue of. We have no inkling of how much of our 'bondage' is inborn, and how much of our 'baggage' is acquired; we are not even aware of their link to the motivating drives of human conduct. Nor do we know much about the mechanics of belief and behavior, and about the dynamics of the dispositions and deportment that shape our lives. Is the baggage 'culture' or civilization, or both, or is it really evolution? Is it religion or is it science that is the crushing pack on our back? Or are they all — baggage, bondage, and liberation — simply states of the fickle mind? Or are they byproducts of belief systems, the epicenter of which is the '*I*' thought? We will probably never know, or know in a manner that stands the test of our intellect; but we 'being human' all that ambivalence and ambiguity only spurs us to speculate, search, seek, and agonize. That seeking and the frustration of not 'finding' affects our behavior.

The scriptures deal with the subject from a loftier and larger perspective. The Upanishads say that ignorance of the Self (or *Atman* or *Brahman*) is the root of the bondage, and the knowledge of the Self is the final liberation. The birth and the death of an individual, the process of reincarnation, the urge for action propelled by desires and the compulsion to contain the consciousness within the four walls of one's own body — all these, according to the *Chandogya* Upanishad, are manifests of the bondage of the individual soul. Life is a prison-house, as it were, because of a very complicated type of nescience, or ignorance that envelops our mind-dominated consciousness. According to the Chandogya Upanishad, the first requisite for liberation is dispassion, an aversion to everything ephemeral or transitory, the outward symbol of which is the body. Smug sensory satisfaction and spiritual growth are antithetical. From this premise, the Upanishad goes on to say that every attachment is a type of bondage, and in the world of ceaseless action, liberation is the release from the fetters of desire and attachment, which is not passivity or empirical inactivity but detachment from the fruits of attachment. In the ancient Indian text, *Ashtavakra Gita*, it is said that bondage is when the mind longs for something, grieves for something, rejects something, clings on to something, is elated about something and dejected about something; and liberation is being detached from all those *somethings*. In this perspective, liberation relates to a panoply of 'bondages' rooted in our mind: from the cycle of birth, from suffering, and above all from our identification of ourselves with the physical body, the *Annamaya-kosha* as it is called in Sanskrit. Spiritual seekers have tried to attain liberation through the practices prescribed in the scriptures; and the modern-day messiahs have tried to attain it by using *reason* as the sole guide and *scientific method* as a road map. For a truly spiritual person, duality is bondage, and non-duality (which is described as 'one without a second') is liberation. In the Hindu scripture *Yoga Vasistha*, it is said that there is neither bondage nor liberation but only pure consciousness, which is another way of describing non-duality. The ultimate, final liberation is from the desire for liberation itself; the longing for liberation and to leave this earth forever, is yet another bondage. For a Vedantist, once we recognize that we are neither the doer nor the enjoyer or the sufferer but an instrument of God, liberation itself loses its luster. The fact is that our consciousness, and everything in the realm of thought, are completely conditioned, be it morality or God, bondage or liberation. Despite our longing for liberty and a life of freedom, it is in 'bondage' that we live and die; what we should strive for is not liberation but the *right kind* of bondage. Liberation might set us free, but in bondage, one could set *others* free or help lessen their burdens. Once a person takes birth, the life of that individual is constrained and carries a cross of some sort. But every chain or every cross is not necessarily bad — it is a matter of perception. Without any chain or a cross, a person would be like a feather that gets blown all over. A chain can be an anchor and a cross can be cleansing. What is only open to us is to experience and inculcate the 'right climate of conditioning' that lets our life not go in vain on this earth at this time. It has been said that one of the Buddhas, the Amitabha Buddha, refused *nirvana* or enlightenment for himself unless he was given the ability to bestow the same bliss on those who sought his refuge.

Impure consciousness, the one we have, is bondage we should seek liberation from, and the baggage we want to be unburdened from is the weight of evolution. In the state of existence we are in, these are all, like much else in life, selective states of mind; a sage or a *yogi* is free even in a prison, and a 'free' man can feel captive in the midst of his freedom. And more conformity is required in the 'free' world. In whatever state or condition one is in or aims at, the effort has to be liberation from the bondage of the ego, to rid oneself of the mental impurities and to be able to see things as they are (not as they seem to be), what is called *vipassana* in Buddhist thought.

In practical life, the combination — or intersection — of 'bondage' and 'baggage' externally reflects as behavior, which is the code word for the way we interact with the outside world. Human behavior is so often bizarre, so much outside the realm of 'reasonable probability', that it raises a more fundamental question — is man born free as an integral part of the natural milieu but become bound by his culture, crippling his innate potential for goodness? or is he 'naturally' too dangerous an animal to be let loose? The simple question — why certain people act and react the way they do and certain others do not, or why the same person behaves differently at different times — has baffled the best of minds. The answer lies in the three states: knowledge, ignorance, and illusion (*jnana*, *ajnana*, and *maya*, in Sanskrit). Put differently, when we *know* what to do; when we *do not know*; and when we *think we know.* These three states envelop and circumscribe our lives and become behavior. And by observing and decoding human behavior, we can gain the knowledge necessary to understand ourselves and others. We can learn how to show empathy and compassion towards fellow humans in distress. And we acquire the skills to influence and modify or moderate the behavior of 'friends and foes' alike for common good. Human behavior, at one level, is the result of attempts to satisfy certain needs. Some of these needs may be simple to understand and easy to identify, such as the need for food and water. There are also complex needs, such as the need for respect and acceptance, the need for survival, esteem, security, social bonding, self-fulfillment. At a deeper level, human behavior constitutes the visible face of the invisible within: *human consciousness.* It is the mirror that reflects our true nature.

One of the most baffling philosophical but also pragmatic questions is, *what really is 'being human'*? While there are several explanations, some labored, some facile, in broad terms it is what we do and how we do on earth, both as individuals and as a species. 'To behave' is a socially expected attribute; we say 'behave yourself', both as an advice and as an admonition. Although much is made out about 'being human' as the ultimate state of earthly existence, the real 'uniqueness' is about 'being an *individual*'. With so much in common, having more or less the same body, brain, and living environment, how can humans behave so divergently? Our behavior is more diversified than our bodies; our conduct more baffling than our appearances. No two siblings, not even identical twins, are really identical in their behavior. Research shows that twins do not turn out more alike if they are raised together than if they are raised apart. Nor do adoptive siblings. Each of us, even identical twins, is thus a *unique* individual, wholly human but different from all other humans. As one science report put it, "One twin might get cancer while the other is not susceptible, for example. Many identical twins clearly behave differently as they grow older, and some even grow to look less alike."[1] The fact is, humans have more in common physically, despite the variations in size, color, and race. The cells of everybody, who are alive today, regardless of where or how they live, contain the same 100,000 or so genes. Collectively known as 'the human genome,' these genes contain all the information that makes us appear and function as humans rather than as members of some other species. But there are others who question this mainstream view that genes contain the codes that control life. For example, the British research scientist Susan Greenfield in her book *The Private Life of the Brain* (2000), says, "the reductionist genetic train of thought fuels the currently highly fashionable concept of a gene for this or that."[2] According to her, "(1) emotion is the most basic form of consciousness; (2) minds develop as brains do, both as a species and as an individual starts to escape genetic programming in favor of personal experience-based learning; (3) the more you have of (1), at any moment, then the less you have of (2), and vice versa. The more the mind predominates over raw emotion, the deeper the consciousness"[3].

In his book *Why We Do It: Rethinking Sex and the Selfish Gene* (2004), the American paleontologist Niles Eldredge presents a major refutation of the almighty status of genes in evolution and human behavior and says, "genes have been the dominant metaphor underlying explanations of all manner of human behavior, from the most basic and animalistic, like sex, up to an including such esoteric as the practice of religion, the enjoyment of music, and the codification of laws and moral strictures... The media are besotted with genes... genes have for over half a century easily eclipsed the outside natural world as the primary driving force of evolution in the minds of many evolutionary biologists."[4]

It is in the manifestation of the mind that differences are more glaring than in the anatomy or physiognomy of human beings. The differences show up as irrational, even bizarre behavior that fits no pattern and defies every logic, even self interest. In Hinduism, it is said that *karma* works through the mind — *buddhi karmaanusey* — and makes us do things we are supposed to do, to redeem our *prarabdha karma* (the part of one's past karma, which is to bear fruit in the future). But in so doing we also acquire new karmic bondage. Language, perhaps the most advanced human attribute, is also a divider. It is said that "using language as a criterion, there are over 5,000 distinct human populations in the world..."[5]. Everyone's destiny is distinct, and why one sails through life with ease and why another, who is similarly nurtured and placed, faces stormy weather, no one can tell. Equally inexplicable is the behavior which is as disparate, diverse, and multilayered as the human race. Why certain people acquire certain personalities and their lives follow a certain course, as opposed to some others who follow a different path, is a question that defies any rational explanation. The manner in which we 'behave' depends on the subject and the context; and embraces a wide variety of circumstances such as personal, professional, social, sexual, and so forth. It is almost as if our consciousness assumes different 'avatars' while dealing with different human beings or even with the same person in different settings. One could be abominable or endearing, compassionate or cruel, caring or indifferent. The same human being is capable of different personality transformations in different settings, almost as if he manifests himself as different individuals. If what matters in the final analysis is behavior, then we seem to have no credible clues to its brittleness. To say that a person 'means well', is of little value, and has no meaning, unless that person acts righteously. In actuality, what we 'mean' is what we do, with or without our connivance. The adage, 'the road to hell is paved with good intentions' is apt. And that includes not only our conduct towards each other, but also towards the earth, and toward our cousins on earth. Behavior is not only what we physically do but also how we use the gift of language and the basic building block — *thought*. 'Bad' behavior is not only a stab in the back or a slap on the face, but also a stinging word or a cutting phrase; and 'good' behavior can be a silent hug or a soothing syntax. It is how we connect, or rather do not connect, to each other that has made mankind so fractious and fearful. It is our collective behavior that has led life on earth to the present perilous pass. We behave like a species impatient to meet its doom. The psychologist Havelock Ellis said, "The sun, the moon and the stars would have disappeared long ago… had they happened to be within the reach of predatory human hands."[6] Without the benevolence of Nature, without the earth's bounty, we cannot live for a second; without biodiversity, which includes millions of other species, human life is unsustainable. Many things are inexplicable in human behavior; this dependence on Nature and on our co-species is one of them. What is our true nature? What is normal and what is abnormal? What is the set of characteristics that is natural and necessary to be human? Does it emphasize freedom or bondage, license or liberation? Sages like Ramana Maharshi say that liberation is our real nature and the fact that we yearn for liberation shows that freedom from all bondage is innate in us. He said "One believes that there is bondage and therefore seeks liberation. But the fact is that there is no bondage but only liberation. Why call it by a name and seek it?".

Rousseau famously said, in the opening line of his work *The Social Contract* (1792), that "man was born free, and he is everywhere in chains". We do not know exactly what Rousseau meant, but his words probably refer to the corrupting influence of culture on our 'natural goodness'; and that God did not create society with all its inequities, but man did. To be 'born free' also implies that we are all born in equality. Both the assumptions are at best half truths. We may dream of freedom and equality, but the reality is that in bondage and in inequality we are born, and in bondage and in inequality we live, and there is no freedom or equality in what happens after we die. Nothing is equal in the death of a baby within twenty-four hours after it is born, and a person who lives for eighty years (400,000 babies die in a year, half of them in India alone, according to the charitable organization, *Save the Child*). Man has not found a way to harmonize individual freedom and common good, and when he did attempt to do so, he tended to compromise on freedom. We have not achieved the 'social compact' that Rousseau envisioned. But bondage, like its opposite, freedom, is neutral; it is not necessarily good or bad; it hinges on how the mind perceives it and reacts to it. Bondage means acceptance and restraint, and they are not always bad. Every relationship is a kind of bondage; it inherently limits even a modicum of freedom. It is non-acceptance and disobedience that causes trouble. It is disobedience, of God, that, according to the Bible, sent man out of Paradise and created sin. It is our disregard of the laws of Nature that has created the environmental crisis. The often used expression 'security of the slave', to denote a false sense of security, is not always negative; it depends on who the master is, and what kind of slavery it is. We are all 'slaves' of some sort or the other, slave to a habit, good or bad; or slave to someone we love or hate. The scriptures urge us to surrender to God or a 'guru' and in that sublime state, to suspend all judgment. This is what happens in the temporal bondage too. But Rousseau was dead right when he said, "One man thinks himself the master of others, but remains more of a slave than they". Indeed no one is a master or a slave for nothing, no one deserves either state; and that 'something' has little or nothing to do with what we are in this life. It is part of a continuum. The premise of culture is that man cannot be left to his appetites and desires, and neither Nature nor man trust an other man without chains. Basically what chains us or binds us is the mind, as Vedanta repeatedly says. A slave may be freer than the master, and a mother can be more in chains than the just-born — it is all a state of mind. The real bondage is our ego and the baggage is the byproduct of evolution, the foul fallout of our fight for survival over millions of years. We must recognize the awesome truth, as Laura van Dernoot Lipsky reminded us, that the kind of human activity which enabled us to survive is what is destroying us today.

Human Activity and its Toxic Fallout

The scriptures say that once the world comes to an end with death, darkness, and decadence, like a bad dream, mankind — or rather whatever or whoever remains, the truly faithful and virtuous — will enjoy thousands of years of beatitude, prosperity, and rectitude. The Hindu scriptures say that at the close of the *Kali Yuga*, God will incarnate with the name Kalki (the tenth avatar) in the house of the high-souled Vishnuyasha, the foremost Brahmin (one who is most virtuous) in the village of Shambhala, the exact location of which is hazy, but is generally believed to be somewhere in Tibet. Lord Kalki will be the king of kings riding on the fleet-footed horse Devadatta. He will traverse the globe on that swift horse and, with his sword, he will exterminate tens of millions of evil men and restore *dharma* and usher in a new *yuga*. Some say that the next divine incarnation, the savior of the world, would be a female. In the book *The Mystery of the Ages* (1887) by Marie, Countess of Caithness, the following prediction appears: "It was generally considered, at the turn of the next century, that the next Divine incarnation was about to come to earth and would be female, the advent of divine wisdom, or Theo-Sophia, and that the present age would be the age of making known all that which has been kept secret from the beginning."[7] Whether it is to be a masculine or a feminine avatar, his or her descent, it was foretold, will herald the beginning of another *Krita* or *Satya Yuga*, the Golden Age. As the great physicist Niels Bohr quipped: predictions are hard to make, especially about the future! But since, in Nature, change is the only constant and since everything comes back to where it begins, it would be 'logical' to hope that things, after getting worse, will become better and better till they become the best. For now, we must reckon with the present.

At the root of the turbulence and turmoil in the world is our choice to ignore the fact that in the grand scheme of Nature, the mighty man too is a biological being tightly dependent on the natural world, and he cannot be immune to the havoc he is afflicting on the natural ecosystems. As the American author Henry Thoreau of the classic *Walden* (1854), reminded us, "Nature is full of genius, full of divinity; so that not a snowflake escapes its fashioning hand."[8] That 'hand' can also take care of any human vagaries and vanities too. Bolstered, as it were, by Biblical and Quranic imprimatur, inebriated by the power and virtuosity of technology and seduced by visions of a 'good life', and perpetual 'progress', man is waging an undeclared 'war' on Nature, putting at peril the very biosphere that makes life possible on earth. Human activity is literally exterminating hundreds of species every day, which is euphemistically called loss of biodiversity. Eminent scientist E.O. Wilson says, "When we debase the global environment and extinguish the variety of life, we are dismantling a support system that is too complex to understand, let alone replace, in the foreseeable future."[9] Such a hypothesis is hotly and viciously denied by many other scientists. Those whose mantra is economic growth — prescribing it as a panacea for all human ills — characterize environmentalism as 'anti-human', based on the 'fear of change' and on the "fear of the outcome of human action."[10] They offer as proof the environmentalists' "stand for animal rights and their opposition to animal use in medical research."[11] In their extreme anthropocentric view, animals are solely meant to be hunted or eaten, and any cruelty, banal or bloodcurdling, is morally permissible if it is intended for human benefit. The anti-environmentalists even contend that laws such as the Endangered Species Act have proven to be a great hindrance to economic growth, and that the Kyoto Protocol, a UN treaty that seeks to impose limits on greenhouse emissions, is 'tantamount to murder'.[12] A 'concerned citizen' is completely confounded when he hears and reads such conflicting statements coming from 'eminent' people and 'reputed' scientists.

Strangely and sadly, those who claim that Earth and Nature come first, and those who contend that man comes first, claim that their findings come from the same 'facts'. Indeed, the sterile 'debate' about environmentalism is symptomatic of what afflicts the human condition. It shows that human intellect and intelligence can believe in anything it wants to, and is quite capable of finding the 'facts' that are necessary to substantiate its 'belief'. All this only goes to show that both 'beliefs' and 'facts' are subjective and contextual, and that the human mind is quite capable of creating them at will. We must remember that there are always inevitable subjective aspects to objective information; even the most 'proved' facts do not necessarily exist, neither in the external world nor in our minds. One of the qualities that humans do not have is consistency; we are selective in everything we think, say, and do. We are selectively compassionate and callous, kind and cruel, pious and profane, and we find no irony or inconsistency in that. And it highlights the perils of human reasoning, and analytical and deductive capacities. In such matters, science can be of little help; we have to decide by our 'gut feeling' and 'good sense.' Whether one subscribes to 'exceptionalism' or 'environmentalism', it is foolish and suicidal to ignore the implications of human conduct on earth. Really, the core issue that is hardly debated is the rightful place of man in the natural order, his rights and responsibilities commensurate with the package of faculties that Nature has bestowed upon him.

Man may or may not be "the culmination of this grand experiment of Nature that we call life",[13] or, as Vivekananda said, "man alone reaches the perfection of which gods themselves are ignorant".[14] But what we do know is that human society has been unable to fashion a way to live our individual lives as members of a larger community of humanity, and to manage inequality (which is inherent in Nature and more pronounced in the human species) with equality. Our society has not been able to permit the privileged to retain their power while allowing the handicapped to grow out of their handicap. Nor has it been able to let the strong remain strong while helping the weak retain their dignity. Man cannot be trusted to be left in his natural milieu, to simply live unhindered and not become a 'risk factor' to another person. Mahatma Gandhi, with his usual directness and simplicity of expression, captured the essence of human governance when he said that 'it is man's privilege to be independent, it is equally his duty to be interdependent'. The bridge between dependence and interdependence is governance. To ensure the larger and longer good in human society we need governance; to modulate and manage individual ambitions in the context of the collective good, we need governance. There is one idea that has inspired generation after generation of humans but which has always remained, save perhaps in mythical times, a step-ahead of its realization: *justness*. Justness is more than justice, more than 'law and order', and more than security and stability. While justice is a function of the law, justness is beyond the law; one can be lawful and yet be unjust. One could dispense justice and yet deny justness. Justness, in short, is a state of harmony, of synergy.

Man has self-awareness but lacks self-knowledge. He has become knowledgeable without knowing; he believes without belief. Other species may lack both knowledge and belief, but they intuitively perform their assigned tasks on earth, and in their very existence, they serve the cause of creation. It is only in the case of man, admittedly the most exalted of all life on earth, that the purpose is unknown to him. By any reckoning, we are living in an extraordinary moment in the history of human knowledge, and entrenched ideas about man, matter and Nature have been overturned with breathtaking virtuosity and velocity. But what the human intelligence will never *know*, what man is intended not to know, and what he knows or is allowed to know, is still the 'tip of the iceberg'. There are certain things that are '*known* unknowns' like death, and '*unknown* unknowns' like God, and the difference between the two is immense. Let us not forget that in the Bible it was man's attempt to *know* more than he was allowed to that led to his fall from Paradise. Through science, man is attempting to cross that cosmic barrier once again, and how Nature/God will react one can only surmise. Sometimes, ignorance is bliss and knowledge a burden. In life, some barriers are not to be crossed and some battles ought not to be won, and some answers are best left unearthed. On the other hand, it is man's ignorance of his true essence that is at the root of his malaise. That has been the centerpiece of all scriptural and spiritual quests, and increasingly, of late, the area of scientific pursuit too. The tangential question is as follows: if everything in Nature, even ignorance, is need-based, what role does human ignorance play in furthering Nature's agenda? Perhaps Nature knows something about us that we do not. It is man's non-comprehension of his meaning and essence that has made him such a suicidal and a destructive being.

Just as the death of one species gives birth to another species, new knowledge — while it solves or appears to solve some issues — brings in new mysteries. For example, our knowledge of our place in the cosmos itself is ever changing, chipping away at our insularity and claims of cosmic singularity. Scientists now say that the ordinary matter and energy that we know of constitute only 5 percent of the universe's total mass and energy, while 'dark matter' and 'dark energy' make up the unknown remainder. 'Advanced civilizations' in our galaxy are estimated to number 10,000 to nearly one million. Everything comes from and is a part of everything else. Even for a plant, soil and seed are needed. What baffles our intelligence is dubbed as an accident, a coincidence or synchronicity, or the way of fickle fate. Our intelligence is immense but also limited; we are not even aware, or we simply pretend to be unaware, that there are boundaries for everything in Nature. Astrophysicist Jayant Narlikar zeros in on the crux of the matter when he refers to the "inadequacy of the human mind to understand the universe in its entirety."[15] We have lost one of the essential requisites for spiritual growth, what is called *upasana* in Sanskrit, roughly translated as meditative contemplation. The irony is that, with all its inherent limitations, we have more knowledge of the beehive than of the dynamics of human behavior. We know more about the starry skies than of our own selves, despite repeated scriptural and Delphic exhortations 'to know thyself'. It has been said that 'He who knows himself knows God', and the Qu'ran says, 'We will show them our signs in the world and *in themselves*, that the truth may be manifest to them.' The Upanishads say that the knowledge of the Self is the highest knowledge, higher than the knowledge of the Vedas. Gandhi (*My Religion*, 1959) said, "There exists only one truth in the world and that is the knowledge of self. He, who knows himself, knows God and all others. He who does not know himself does not know anything. In this world there exists one force, one freedom and one justice, and that force is that of ruling over oneself. In this world, there exists only one virtue, and that is the virtue of liking others as much as one likes oneself. In other words, we should look upon others as we look upon ourselves. All other questions are imaginary and non-existing."[16] There are two things that are irrefutable in human existence: (1) what any human can do, good and bad, everyone else also can do; and (2) we can only offer what we have, and cannot see something in others that is not inside us. In other words, we cannot see evil in others if we do not have evil in our own selves. To the modern man, knowledge of the Self is no more than the knowledge of one's body and biology. In the spiritual context, however, it is the quest to answer questions such as 'who am I?', 'whence have I come?', 'where do I go after death?', and 'what is the true nature of reality?' At this point in human evolution, we are in a state of "knowing the world and forgetting oneself."[17] That is the fateful paradox that has become the hallmark of human intelligence.

Every species eventually becomes extinct, paving the way to the birth of another, either emanating from it or independent of it; in a way, in its extinction, it preserves that mysterious thing we call 'Life'. Just as in the human, different species have different life spans. We could well have become extinct several times by now, and no one can predict for how long we would be around. We cannot even be sure — if we do not hasten our doom as we are determined to do now — how much more time we have as a species. Some say that man has been around for approximately two billion years and could well survive for billions of years more, if the logic of the advent and extinction of species were to apply to us. We must also remember that man came pretty close to extinction once, with the human population barely numbering 10,000, and the fact that we scraped through a crisis like that was probably due to what Stephen Hawking called the Mind of God, not due to a magic wand or serendipity. Purely based on record and rationale, we ought to have given way to a more 'humane' species long ago. We are not quite sure when. Within the next two hundred or two thousand years, the species *Homo sapiens* may undergo one more evolution. Natural selection is supposed to make organisms fit for their environment, but there could be some exceptions. The reason, scientists say, is that "the environment in which particular species live are themselves changing, and relative to the organisms, are usually getting worse."[18] In other words, 'the human organism is not able to cope with the human behavior, which is getting worse. We do not and cannot know if we would be able to evolve into the stage of final evolution, the highest life form on earth'. Or if, in the attempt to attain that state, we will violate the laws of Nature to such an extent that we would destroy ourselves. Are the tremors and rumblings we hear with ever-growing intensity and frequency the echoes of the death dance of a dying species? Or are they the inevitable tribulations of a chaotic passage into the next tier of evolution? The fact is that man cannot stay much longer as he is. He has the opportunity that comes perhaps once in the lifetime of a species to turn transition into transcendence. Man is not what he 'thinks' himself to be; and no man is what he projects himself to be. Man *must* and *will* change, sooner than we think, with his cooperation or against his will. Change could be straight or serpentine, incremental or cataclysmic.

Man is tampering with the equilibrium of Nature, poisoning the atmosphere, and triggering and compressing into the span of a single lifetime a change that normally takes place in a geological time-frame. Despite millenniums of intelligence and endeavor, man has not found a way to manage the constraints of conflict inherent in his condition. Even if we do not really know what the essence of life is, we must start to live, not linger in nothingness. We have not found a way to being truly social beings, perpetrators as we are of endless conflicts involving individual aspirations, ethical demands, and social concerns. Given his obsession with minimizing if not eliminating effort, man has become the most dependent creature on earth. Without the prop of tools and technology, man is truly and totally helpless. It is slowly sinking into our psyche that war and violence, terror and torture are not malevolent aberrations or primitive irrational urges, but that they are "the near-inevitable outcome of the dynamics of self-interested, rational social organisms."[19] We tend to think that violence is anti-social, illegal, the work of the mad, malevolent, and marginalized. The reality is that much of the violence in the world is 'lawful'; indeed law sans violence is unthinkable as much as law only with violence, which becomes tyranny. In fact the State enjoys monopoly in the exercise of violence. Every institution created to manage human affairs, from the family to the sovereign State, has proved to be either inadequate or inappropriate. The human decision-making processes and capacities have singularly failed either to articulate or safeguard the irreducible human interests; what is good for the species is often not good for an individual. Above all, somewhere along the long path of evolution, we have lost our sense of a species, making man the only mortal enemy of man. And our defining difference, spirituality, is left behind with the scriptures. We are so much exposed to competition, conflict, aggression, and violence that the human condition and the mind itself are 'militarized.' At this moment in the history of life on earth, the grim reality is that what we call human culture, and the way man organizes his life and conducts himself in relation to 'others', have become a cause for grave cosmic concern.

The underlying premise is (1) that the human being is special and unique, and man's fate is a 'make or break' matter for Nature; and (2) that any impending human extinction is a catastrophe to be avoided at all costs. Both reflect an exclusive human perspective. It never occurs to us that perhaps we are just like any other creature that walks or crawls on earth, a mix of mind and matter, dust and DNA, carbon and consciousness. We might well have some special attributes, though the meaning of 'special' to us is rather flexible, but that does not necessarily make us indispensable. But the prevailing mindset is that we are unique and blessed, and therefore we ought to be eternal, and anything less is a colossal cosmic calamity! We know not what awaits man in the womb of time and therefore we should do whatever we can in our allotted time to further the glory of creation. In Sanskrit, it is interesting that the word *kaala* means both Time and Death. In the great Indian epic Mahabharata, it is said that Time is cooking all living beings in the giant cauldron of cosmic delusion — with the sun as the fire, day and night as the fuel, and months and seasons as the ladle to stir the brew. In a similar vein, Roman philosopher Marcus Aurelius said, "Time is a flood, an impetuous torrent which drags with it all that is born. A thing has scarcely appeared when it is carried away; another has already passed; and this other will soon fall into the gulf."[20] The human species too gets cooked and falls into the 'gulf'. The question is not how soon or far, but what imprints it will leave, on the sands of Time. And when the time comes, would man leave behind the earth and the universe in better shape or worse?

Lives of Quiet Desperation

Despite millions of years of evolution, millenniums of culture and centuries of civilization, we have failed the basic test of an enlightened, egalitarian community, namely, being able to interact with another human being without trying to denude his dignity and without trying to exploit him. And yet everyone in our present society, even the exploiter, the oppressor, or the tyrant, feels he is some kind of a 'fortune's fool', a puppet, a cat's paw, and feels others are taking unfair advantage of him. Human society has long agonized over where the 'problem' lay. Some have argued that the problem is with the innate human nature, and that once we 'fix it', all the problems of the world will wither away. And there have been others who posited that the crux of the matter is the structure of society and once that is set right — made more just, more egalitarian, less divided, fair — all problems that bother humanity would vanish. The English author John Wilmot, in his poem *A Satire Against Reason and Mankind*, called man "that vain animal who is so proud of being rational" and that "man differs more from man than man from beast."[21] Man fears another man more than a man-eating tiger; the latter is somewhere in the jungles and it must find you, but man is everywhere. Once a tiger's belly is full it is harmless; but a man's avarice is limitless. The English philosopher Thomas Hobbes wrote that human nature emphasizes our animal nature, leaving each man to live independently of his fellow men, acting only in his own self-interest, without regard for others. This produces what Hobbes called the 'state of war,' a way of life that is certain to prove 'solitary, poor, nasty, brutish, and short.' According to him, human beings are physical objects, "sophisticated machines, all of whose functions and activities can be described and explained in purely mechanistic terms".[22] Hobbes also said that, "Everything we choose to do is strictly determined by this natural inclination to relieve the physical pressures that impinge upon our bodies. Human volition is nothing but the determination of the will by the strongest present desire."[23] It is the satiation of desire of one kind or another that consumes much of life. We live through the body and die as the body. It is not the love of life but the thought '*what else is there?*' that keeps us going. Men are in a state, as the Spanish philosopher Ortega Gasset describes, of 'existential shipwreck', symbolized by a suicide note left behind by a 12-year-old Indian girl who begins with the agonized words: "I hate my life and so I do not want to live."[24] Clearly, there is something horrible at the very core of the human condition. That sense of despair about the tragedy of the human condition has been shared by many creative people. An interesting anecdote is revealed in a recent book about the life of Arthur Koestler by Michael Scammell, *Koestler: The Literary and Political Odyssey of a Twentieth-Century Skeptic* (2009). In the year 1946, Koestler, Jean-Paul Sartre, Simone de Beauvoir, Albert Camus and a few others go for a night-out in Paris. Simone, standing on a bridge over the river Seine says she sees no reason why the two — she and Sartre — should not throw themselves into the river, and Sartre, although drunk, concurs. The absurdity of the human world comes home to many people regardless of the age or gender or eminence or intellect.

Not finding something to hold on to — something to stabilize themselves with, not able to manage pain and pleasure, success and suffering, and buffeted by listlessness and aimlessness — many people, great and ordinary, are clutching at every semblance of support, like a drowning man who makes no distinction between a straw and snake in a stormy sea when all hope is slipping away. Most people are not necessarily 'unhappy' but they lead a life of limited dimension. They have at best a lukewarm relationship with most other people and find no comfort or strength in their company. Increasingly, human connection is offering little joy or comfort, creating an emotional chasm between man and man. Most lives are devoid of what the French call *joie de vivre,* or 'the joy of living'; they do not even live up to what in Latin is called *carpe diem,* live for or seize the day. Many people, these days, have nothing to live for; as someone put it, 'they spend their entire life as if their best friend just died'. The classical cause, for the sake of one's children, is losing its sheen too. Unwilling to take chances, some parents who choose the macabre option of abrupt departure from this world — suicide — are even taking their children with them. It is not always that they are deprived of the good things of life — family, friends, a good job, even good health; but all that still leaves a deep sense of futility. Although this malaise is universal, everyone still feels that they are the 'chosen' ones, that their life is "a diabolical trap set for them by destiny", to paraphrase the words of Václav Havel, the Czech playwright and an ex-President.[25] Most drift because they have nowhere else to go; they live because they are born, they exist because there is nothing else to do. Human institutions and relationships of wife and husband, parent and child, teacher and pupil, and citizen and society are under severe strain, because every one of them requires some 'giving up'. But man is habituated or addicted to grab and greed rather than give and share. This is often illustrated by the story of a die-hard miser who accidentally falls into a ditch. When a passer-by tries to help and says 'give me your hand', the miser hesitates; but when the person says 'take my hand', the miser grabs it! The scripture says that the only thing we take beyond life is what we give, but most people remain moderate versions of the miser and 'take and take', without ever giving anything.

That 'take-give' equation is universal and underpins all human relationships. No relationship is built on equality nor nurtured on that basis. In Nature, there is equity, balance, harmony, but not equality. No two beings are born alike or endowed equally. That is the fundamental law of Nature. The aspiration for equality, lofty as it might appear, is the cause of social breakdown; what is absent in Nature cannot be present in humanity. Man wants to be at once an island and a continent, intimate and independent, autonomous and intertwined, and many 'temporal troubles' come from that tension. Technology, which has helped man not only to survive but also to prevail over all other species on earth, has placed man in a perilous state of 'double jeopardy'; it has induced debilitating dependence on gadgets and appliances; and it has dangerously eroded the need for human interaction in daily life. A gadget is no longer a physical object; it is a 'service' that eliminates a physical activity. A computer and a car are not simply a mix and match of various components; their essence lies in the 'software'; that can be constantly upgraded, which means that more and more of what our brain and body could do are disabled from doing. While the degree and nature of technological addiction and human alienation may vary from society to society, and person to person, there is no doubt that it is a universal phenomenon, cutting across continents and cultures. The combined effect is to denude man of the 'human touch' and to make him more self-absorbed and less tolerant of others, creating the cult of the *individual*. Ironically, at the same time, man is, and more so now than ever before, a competitive species, competing for everything regardless of the need or the means, to such an extent that only with a wee bit of exaggeration did Bertrand Russell say, "If there were people who desired their own happiness more than they desired the unhappiness of others, we would have Paradise in a few years."[26]

Henry Thoreau wrote in the essay titled 'Economy', in his work *Walden* (1854), "The mass of men lead lives of quiet desperation. What is called resignation is confirmed desperation."[27] Things have worsened since the 19th century: desperation is not quiet, but vocal and violent. It has led to depression and destructiveness of the self and of others. Perhaps the saddest thing is that increasingly many people who feel lonely, abandoned, and deprived are not only killing themselves but are also killing those whom they truly love, like their own children, the premise being that the loved ones would be better off dead than being alive in this world without them. The odd thing is that on the face of it and purely in logical terms, the human race has never had it so good. Man is unchallenged on earth; he has acquired awesome powers of creation and destruction. It is even claimed that man can duplicate himself. Yet, man is perhaps the unhappiest creature on earth with the pursuit of happiness as his primary preoccupation, and as his sacred right. Only a few manage to achieve it. It is because most people try to get what they do not have, rather than appreciate what they have. As Mahatma Gandhi said, it is because what we think, what we say, and what we do, are not in harmony. Man constantly seeks unbounded joy and endless happiness but whatever he does is a repudiation of both. It has been said in the scriptures that "immediately after the formation of a man's body, joys and grief's attach themselves to it. Although there is a possibility of either of the two overtaking the person, yet whichever actually overtakes him quickly robs him of his reason like the wind driving away the gathering clouds."[28] The Lebanese-American poet and mystic Khalil Gibran wrote that "your joy is your sorrow unmasked" and that "together they come [joy and sorrow], and when one sits, alone with you at your board, remember that the other is asleep upon your bed."[29] And Helen Keller, whose life was an epitome of suffering, pain, and courage of the rarest kind, wrote: "we could never learn to be brave and patient if there was only joy in the world."[30] But then, joy is joy and is pleasant, and sorrow is sorrow and is unpleasant. Both are states of the mind. Man is unhappy and desperate because he is ruled by his mind, and it is in the intrinsic character of the mind to be restless and avaricious, never satisfied with what it has. The mind of man looks upon another human being at best as a competitor, an arch rival, save a very few 'near and dear'.

Man has always feared anarchism, realizing that if everyone does what he wills to do, the brute might well triumph, and the weak, vulnerable and disadvantaged would suffer. Governance, shorn of all its sophistry, is a process of decision-making and decision implementation, designed to allow diverse people with different abilities and handicaps to live in harmony and security. Because we are complex creatures with competing and colliding priorities, passions, prejudices, needs, and wants, and because we lead complex lives that call for constant 'give and take', and since human tendency is to *take* and not *give*, we need governance at every stage and level of life, governance that is both responsive and responsible, which reflects the tenor of its citizens and yet induces them to rise above themselves. In other words, we need external governance because we do not have internal governance, sometimes called 'spiritual governance', which is necessary for spiritual growth. Because we cannot contain or channel our thoughts, feelings, longings that could create social tensions, we need an agency that regulates our conduct and behavior, and curbs our tendency for avarice and aggression. Some thoughtful people say that such internal spiritual governance, while earlier necessary for individual salvation, is now necessary for species survival. For, as Andrew Harvey puts it, the "massacres of the past, though filled with every form of cruelty... did not menace all existence down to the last dolphin and mouse and fern. There has always been in the human psyche a tendency to rage against wisdom and its demands, but this tendency has escalated through technology and mind control to what can only be called a genocide of wisdom."[31] In the absence of some sort of inner awakening, some sort of spiritual renaissance, all our attempts to make governance capable of addressing global problems, and human conduct more contributory to planetary well-being, will only have marginal effect.

The Quest for 'Good Governance'

We routinely use the word 'governance' to refer to an external power; as something that 'puts us in our place' through inducement, coercion or force. But true governance is equally *internal*. Something or the other, someone or the other, governs or tries to govern in human life. The Athenian politician and general, Themistocles said, "The Athenians govern the Greeks; I govern the Athenians; you, my wife, govern me; your son governs you."[32] But it is the absence of *internal* governance that necessitates external governance. Since we seem incapable of self-governance, we need an extraneous authority to take 'good' decisions and to get them implemented. And since we seem inherently incapable of voluntarily controlling ourselves, we need an external power to perform that function for the common good. But since that 'external power' is also human, subject to the same frailty (not being able to control itself), the problem persists. Indeed, it can become worse unless that 'external control' is of the right kind. The dilemma of man is that some measure of 'governance' is inescapable in life but few, if any, humans have the wisdom necessary to govern others. Human society cannot exist without governance. The problem is that those who are good and worthy shun the process of governance; and the crafty and clever capture the levers of governance. The British-American author Thomas Paine phrased the dilemma well when he said that the best of governance is a necessary evil, and the worst intolerable. Plato wrote that "the punishment which the wise suffer, who refuse to take part in the government, is to live under the government of worse men."[33] The dilemma endures. Every form of governance, from City-State to Nation-State, to the League of Nations to the United Nations, has failed to measure up to its intent and expectations. Mankind remains fragmented and fractured, and has not been able to create any collective institution that can truly project and pursue the human cause. And the human will remain in this state unless he himself changes and transforms from within. We must give serious thought to the question as to why human intellectual and creative capacity, which has been so productive in so many fields, has never been able to actualize Lincoln's elevating concept of 'government *by* the people, of the people and *for* the people', in which everyone can find avenues for full utterance of their inherent potential without exploiting anyone else. The problem is not with the institution; nor with the ingenuity or the lack of its founders; it is the mind of man that does not know how to govern or be governed.

Yet the thirst for 'good governance' is as old as human civilization, as old as the idea of utopia, where everyone lives in a society that enables every individual to rise to his full potential while also contributing to the common good. The air is thick with talk of 'good governance' and 'globalization'; but rarely in conjunction with each other. What the world needs is 'globalized good governance', a paradigm and a process at the global level, which lends itself suitably and sensitively to a truly planetary approach to planetary problems, and which empowers and enables an institution that is charged with that responsibility. The United Nations, as it is now structured and operates, cannot play that part. The truth of the matter is that the earth, as the heart and home of humankind, can no longer be sustained by a post-war fabricated international institutional framework like the United Nations and the World Bank. The main stumbling block is nationalism — which Einstein called 'the measles of mankind', and Erich Fromm, 'our form of incest, …our idolatry, …our insanity' — and our almost compulsive inability to put the world ahead of the nation, and the nation ahead of the individual. Few care to know what their governments do to others ostensibly for their sake. No inhumanity is too much if it is supposed to protect or further 'national interest'. And if a nation is in a 'state of war', declared or undeclared, then all bets are off on what it would not do; blowing up a hospital or bombing a nursery is called 'collateral damage'. The very code that governs 'being human' becomes inoperative, even unpatriotic. The phrase 'good governance' itself has become an oxymoron; governance has to be participatory, consensus oriented, accountable, transparent, responsive, effective, equitable, and inclusive. It is doubtful if we will ever find a paradigm that encompasses all those elements, at least in the present state of mind of humanity. Aldous Huxley summarized the human dilemma and wrote that "one of the many reasons for the bewildering and tragic character of human existence is the fact that social organization is at once necessary and fatal. Men are forever creating such organizations for their own convenience and forever finding themselves the victims of their home-made monsters."[34] We continue to grope, and things are getting no better. There is almost a universal sense of dissatisfaction and disenchantment with the structure of governance, whether it is local or global, municipal or national. Some say we get the governance we deserve; others say it is our leaders who have failed us. The malaise is systemic, not institutional. Whether it is the leaders or the laymen, representatives or the represented, they all come from the same stock, human, and their behavior is a reflection of their position and placement. The bottom-line is the mind, which quickly adjusts to the context and tries to take full advantage to further its own agenda. The prevailing political paradigm, in many ways, perhaps the worst of the lot thus far, is the structure of a sovereign state. Mikhail Bakunin, a Russian political theorist said that "the state then is the most flagrant negation, the most cynical and complete negation of humanity"[35]. The State has almost displaced the world, even the universe, and the family, as the center of human attention and allegiance. The rulers of the modern 'militarized' State exercise more power and control over the citizens than in any other model of governance. Even Plato conceded that the rulers of the State are the only ones to have the privilege of lying. Of course they all do, and more than that, they have the privilege — and legitimacy — to wage war, murder, torture, lie and cheat, all in the name of 'just' governance and to 'protect' the lives and liberty of the people. A citizen is a subject and a supplicant, if not a slave of the State. National interest overrides human rights and morality is the first casualty. Next only to religion, it is the state-sponsored nationalistic fervor that contributes most to human killing.

Although only a few centuries old, the political model of Nation-State serious questions are being raised about its durability and its relevance to the so-called 'flat world' and to solve global problems that require global, not national, solutions. Some argue that it has already become a major source of discontent, division, and disarray in human affairs. Many think that its days are numbered, but no viable alternative is visible on the horizon. Sovereignty has become a straightjacket, shorthand for unquestioned and unaccountable authority, requiring implicit and total acceptance and obedience to its *diktat*. Not only does the modern State trample upon its citizens, but also the very logic of its survival often requires that it should be in a state of hostility with at least one other State, to compete for hegemony, resources, influence, and ideology. The doctrine of absolute State sovereignty has come to mean that the government of the day can do what it chooses to do with its subjects without any outside interference. The world has witnessed rulers like the communist leader Mao Zedong, who preferred to let 30 million of his country's citizens die in the years 1958-1961 due to famine, rather than seek outside help, fearing 'loss of face' and 'erosion' of China's international standing. With rare, if any, exceptions, most of the ruling elites are those who do not believe or practice what was written about the ideal ruler more than three thousand years ago. In the famous Indian classic *Arthasashtra*, Kautilya writes, "In the happiness of his subjects lies his [the King's] happiness; in their welfare his welfare. He shall not consider as good only that which pleases him but treat as beneficial to him whatever pleases his subjects."[36] The State has turned out to be a competitive body which believes that its own survival and strength depend not on its intrinsic worth, but on the demise and weakness of other states. Modern technology has given to the State awesome powers of surveillance, control, and subjugation of its citizens.

The wide disparities in the size, resources, and strength (economic and military) of States, have, among other things, skewed global resource utilization and decision-making. The emergence of the environment as an important global issue has added a new element. In earlier times, human beings largely lived in harmony with Nature, and there was no need for any institutional authority to enforce harmony. The absence of any effective global institutional authority today has pushed global interests to the back burner. What is urgently needed is the cooperation of the States, particularly the strongest ones, in protecting the environment, and thereby ensure the welfare of the unborn generations. The fact is that both individual and global interests are fast becoming causalities at the hands of the modern sovereign State.

The moot question is whether the world would move towards gigantism and centralization, à la the English novelist George Orwell's *Nineteen Eighty-Four* (1949), or shift gears towards a mix of strong grassroots and global governance. Man needs to move at once in two apparently opposing directions: proximate local governance, and institutionalized planetary governance. Many have dreamt of a world government but, given the human condition, it will remain largely a dream unless the mindset of man changes radically. The fact is that not only the States but even the 'citizens of the world' want a world government that is empowered to exercise the kind of powers that national governments currently exercise. Furthermore, one is not even sure if an executive global government would not turn into a kind of Orwellian 'Oceania' (a fictional state), a colossal coercive and possessive apparatus. That risk is always there, but it is debatable which portends a greater risk: the present paralysis and regression caused by the clash of 'national interests', or an imperfect but effective global government. A decade or two ago, one could make a persuasive case from both ends. But no longer now: none of the serious problems the world is now facing, from terrorism to climate change, can be seriously addressed with the status quo. The world needs a strong, truly international, not intergovernmental, organization to take care of the global issues, and to settle the plethora of inter-State and even intra-State problems without giving way to violence and war, and the resultant global catastrophe. As the perennial but abortive 'reform' of the United Nations demonstrates, no true change can occur because those whose consent and cooperation is required are the direct beneficiaries of the present intergovernmental power structure. In the absence of any strong global constituency at the grassroots level, there is no pressure for global governance from any quarter. Even at the national level, interpersonal governance has to be necessarily local. Power has to be proximate to be responsible and responsive. The power to raise revenues and cater to human needs must rest with the representative body closest to the people. The corridors of power have to be within easy reach for policy corrections. The ideal would be to return to the model of City-States and village republics as the principal political centers of governance. And what we now call country or State, would have only those powers and resources that are commensurate with its responsibilities at that level.

That is the only way we can solve the riddle posed by Paul Valéry, the French poet: "If the State is strong, it crushes us, if it is weak, we perish."[37] Sovereignty should be with the people, and the bulk of governance should be at two levels: at the grassroots level, and at the global level. Proximate governance can be strong, representative, and responsible, and global governance can take care of global issues free from the shackles of intergovernmental, 'zero-sum' interplay. Many thoughtful people are of the view that we may be present at a historic time of decay and death of the modern State, but they lament that there is no acceptable successor model. The very technology that has empowered these Nation-States to become so powerful is inexorably weakening their monopoly of power.

No one seems to be clear about how the fate of the 'nation-state' will play itself out, what more calamities and genocides are still in store, how long it will remain as the premier political principle, what will be its death blow. There is however mounting concern that it is fast losing its legitimacy, that it is increasingly becoming an oppressive instrument, even a prime source of immorality, and an impediment to global solutions to globalized problems… We believe and behave as though the State is as 'natural' to the human condition as a spouse: something to live with, whether we like it or not. The origin and purpose that made man embark on this process, namely the need for an external but representative authority to optimize the diversity in the human race for the larger good, has been forgotten. We cannot manage diversity through uniformity; logically that calls for diversity in structures and shades of sovereignty. Further, political, social, economic sovereignties need not be coterminous. While the world is getting economically, electronically, and environmentally intertwined, politically it lies fractured and paralyzed. The State is the stumbling block; or more precisely national governments. There is hardly any thinking about this pivotal subject, be it at the intellectual level or the institutional level. The world today has no road map, no models, no uplifting vision, no new ideas. It is as if the human mind has run out of ideas; or perhaps the status quo seems to suit it. The guiding principles for political reform have to be ascending and proximate power; maximum power at the grassroots and global levels; and power, resources and responsibilities must go hand in hand at each layer of governance: local, national, and international.

Earth and its False Gods

The underlying dictum for any new model of governance has to be the premise that human beings do not own the earth; they are no more than the caretakers and the custodians. The task of conservation, restoration, and rational use of the earth is vitally linked to the question "Who owns the Earth?" The health of the human being and the well-being of the earth are interrelated. It is unlikely that environmental degradation, about which there is heightened awareness now, will cease until the exploitation of the human being is alleviated. The pressures upon those who are themselves exploited, to exploit in turn each other and the environment is too great a temptation. The roots of warfare, causes of environmental exploitation, and the context of human degradation cannot be considered apart from each other; they are woven into the institutionalized fabric of the current state of the world. We cannot insure a safe and secure planet in a world of few masters and many slaves, obscene opulence, and abysmal deprivation. In reality, man has become the guard who robs the bank, the fence that devours the crop, the babysitter who throttles the baby. We are the 'false gods' that rule the earth. According to ancient civilizations and the more recent Gaia theory, the earth is not an inert terrain, replete with rocks and minerals and covered by topsoil, but a vibrant, living organism, as alive as a human being. Nothing in Nature, from an anthill to a snake pit, from the rainforest to a desert, is redundant, and the enforced absence of any of them leaves a void. It is a grand scheme that a million mother computers cannot recreate. A Native American proverb reminds us that "we do not inherit the land from our ancestors; we borrow it from our children."[38] The burden of the parasitical and predatory man on the earth seems to have become just too much even for the resilient and forgiving earth. One of the few issues on which almost all pundits and think tanks, national policy makers and international organizations agree, is that human numbers on the earth are unsustainable. According to them, the most burdensome baggage we — and the earth — carry is our own selves, in terms of sheer human numbers; more precisely, the ones waiting to arrive on earth as humans. If we can shut the doors on them, the planet will be a paradise. There is a paradox here. On the one hand, the growing numbers of the most intelligent, productive, and the 'closest to God' species on a global scale is considered a threat to earthly stability, and on the other hand, the dwindling numbers of the lowly species, from tigers to insects, has become a matter of concern. We have projects and missions to save other species from extinction, but we do everything we can to hasten our extinction. We say that in some parts of the earth, like Japan and Europe, humans are too few, and in other parts, like South Asia, there are too many; the effort is to curtail human births in some parts and to increase in the other parts. So our 'rational' policy is three-fold: to save the tiger, which is a potential man-eater; offer incentives to produce more babies on one side, including through artificial means; and kill babies in the womb, if need be, to drastically reduce the population growth on the other side. And such is the poverty and travesty of our genius that we cannot think, let alone plan, globally and as one species. Our attitude towards the 'others' on earth is laid back, if not downright hostile; it is the *other* man we fear. The existence of species like insects is critical for continuance of life on earth; not that of our fellow humans. It is the *humans* who are expendable, not 'wild life'. The latest assault comes from some environmentalists like James Lovelock who say that the way to solve the problem of climate change is through population control, which is really pointing at the poorer parts of the world. While fewer humans on the earth is good for other reasons, as far as global warming (the chief cause of climate change) is concerned, it is the thinly populated rich countries that contribute many times over to the emission of greenhouse gases. Therefore even if the developing world freezes or rolls back its population, there will be no significant impact on problems such as global warming. Global warming and wealth are linked; even in developing countries it is the rich who are the guilty. In our culture, and even in our sense of moral equivalence, the governing principle of human behavior is 'affordability', not sustainability; the overriding thought seems to be: "if I can earn and pay for it, I can do anything". The very rich can, and the poor cannot, afford what it takes to warm the globe. It is the ultra-affluent who are trashing the planet, not the abysmally poor of say, Africa or Asia. The real baggage or burden is not the numbers; Nature will find a way to handle it in its own way. It is our *behavior*, more specifically our behavior towards Mother Nature.

Man's attitude towards Nature, without whose benevolence he would become extinct, instantly defies all logic and all intelligence. Does it have something to do with our roots? Charles Darwin, at the close of his seminal book *The Descent of Man* (1871), rudely reminds us that whatever man may do and accomplish, he cannot get rid of what he called man's 'lowly origins.' Apart from the questionable qualification of 'lowly', could it be that since man cannot manage to get rid of his animal origin, he has subconsciously harbored a deep-rooted and ambivalent attitude towards animals? Incidentally, this happens to be another snapshot of the Australian biologist Jeremy Griffith's theory that he puts forth in his book, *A Species in Denial* (2003). The touchstone of a species' morality is how its members treat others, within and without the species, particularly the weaker ones. The German philosopher Immanuel Kant wrote: "Two things fill me with constantly increasing admiration and awe, the longer and more earnestly I reflect on them: the starry heavens without and the moral law within."[39] That '*within*', is deeply vulnerable to situations, distractions, rewards, and penalties. Even to the best of us, being moral, like helping someone in obvious distress, is a matter of circumstance, effort and cost; if it is too inconvenient, too pricey, like missing a train or an important appointment, we will pass by pretending we did not really see or, hoping that someone else, less pressed or more compassionate, will stop to help; and if no one does, there is always comfort in the thought 'after all, such is life'. That 'moral flaw' manifests not only in man's dealings with other humans but also in his stance towards other species. Man may have some semblance of a right to mistreat other humans, but not other species. No species, however intelligent, deserves to prevail on earth if it treats other species as cruelly and callously as humans do. It is not killing as such that is heart-rending or abhorrent, but the needless pain and senseless suffering we inflict on animals. One does not have to be an ardent animal activist to shrink in shame at what men do to animals. Mark Twain summed it up well: "All creatures kill…man is the only one…. that kills in malice, the only one that kills for revenge".[40] And for sport and profit as well. It is not that other animals never kill their kith and kin (e.g. polar bears kill baby seals for breakfast) but not very often and when they do, they do it for a good reason, for sheer survival. The human animal, on the other hand, kills all the time, and for reasons as wide as the human emotions from love to hate, from amusement to enrichment, from sport to profiteering, from ransom to revenge to religion. Sometimes, killing is not even the primary purpose; the initial intent could be stealing or rape, but to abort identification, the killing becomes collateral, a calculated act of self-preservation. Science and technology have made killing easier and more methodical, and enable us to enact it on a mass scale with minimum effort. However, in truth and in all fairness, it is not science or technology or the merger of the two that is murderous; it is the *human mind* that is able to conceive and execute such deeds and still be 'in accord' with itself, and find explanations and excuses.

Man's last citadel of pride in 'not being an animal'—that he alone can think, plan, and create, and that animals behave instinctively, while he is clearly calculated and thoughtful in his behavior — is being chipped away. Animals too have minds of their own, they can communicate, show emotion, feel pain, and express grief and empathy. An article in the *National Geographic* magazine noted, "This is the larger lesson of animal cognitive research. It humbles us. We are not alone in our ability to invent and plan..."[41] It does not necessarily mean that we do not have more finely tuned faculties; it simply means that we have no monopoly over any particular capability among the species in Nature. The difference between humans and animals on the one side, and plants and trees on the other side, is also being whittled away by new research. Plants and trees may be permanently stationary, but they too can, as experiments have revealed, register pain and terror when they are about to be ripped apart. It is what some ancient faiths and societies had long believed; they showed reverence even in cutting trees and killing animals. It is amusing how much and how repeatedly man, who aspires to become God, compares himself with animals and chuckles in satisfaction at his conclusion that he fares better. We constantly hear the words 'animals cannot think'. Our mind is made up about the 'obvious': animals may think but they do not *know* that they think; they cannot feel pain; they do not have consciousness, which we do; animals simply live in the present, but we have a sense of the past and future, and so forth. Despite man's belief in his innate or proximate divinity, animals have become man's measure of his worth. If man cannot understand how his own brain functions, through psychology, autopsy or dissection, how can he decode what other species think or know what *they* do not know? For all we know, animals might be thinking that they are superior to humans!

Scientists like Temple Grandin, author of the book, *Animals in Translation: Using the Mysteries of Autism to Decode Animal Behavior* (2005), tells us that humans and animals have the same neurons, but that we use them *differently*. The cells are the same. For example, it is reported that a mouse has 30,000 genes, with 99 percent of them having direct counterparts in humans. The author also argues that autism is a "kind of way station on the road from animals to humans."[42] The sensory powers of animals evolved in a manner suited to that species and necessary for survival in a hostile environment. One or an other animal, as noted before, can see better, hear better, and smell better than man. Dogs, for example, are known to sense the death of their masters thousands of miles away; they have what humans call extrasensory perception (ESP). In fact, it has been said that, initially, humans too had the kind of sensory sharpness and ESP that many animals have, and perhaps we would have continued to have such capabilities, had we not developed the ability to make tools and technology. Animals may live at the level of survival and subsistence, but that also means, unlike man, their mode of existence is *need*-based, not *want*-based. They may not have a sense of past and future; at least, that is what we think, but their mode of living is more farsighted and in harmony with Nature than that of modern man. Maybe they are more spiritual in the true sense of the term.

Among the myriad modes that man adopts to separate himself from the other species is the claim that he is a 'moral animal', which, incidentally, is the title of Robert Wright's book *The Moral Animal* (1994). Everything, from the scriptures to Darwin, asserts that it is *morality* that separates man from animals. Implicit in that belief is that we alone are 'naturally' capable of knowing what is moral and what is not. We like to believe it, but history does not bear it out. Even if we do have that 'capability', the fact that we so often fail to put it into effect makes us more culpable; which is worse than not having such capability at all. No animal, for instance, could have thought of mass extermination as the Final Solution; or massacre as a means of ethnic cleansing; or of 'genocidal rape', which is rape over extended periods to inflict intolerable shame and guilt, to traumatize and to forcibly impregnate the 'enemy' women. And how can we apply human standards of morality or evil to other species whose instincts, needs and rituals of life are different from those of man? When a great white shark brutally forces a female into submission, it *copulates* with her, but it does not *rape* her. For animals, unlike humans, are not moral agents with moral duties to observe. Perhaps man was conceived and designed to be a moral animal, or perhaps morality grew out of survival or reproductive need, but we have by now lost that distinction by virtue of our conduct. Worse still, man has lost the moral discriminatory capacity to distinguish between the moral and the amoral. And if we do know what the moral choice is, we often feel helpless in going *against* it. For, we have come to believe that morality is a fool's choice in the kind of world we have fashioned through our own choices.

Whether morality and, by extension, human behavior have genetic roots has been a subject of evolutionary psychology. Most people agree that being 'moral' is important not only for spiritual reasons but also for social reasons. But opinions, even among scholars, differ as to what 'being moral' means. To some, morality is not a simple choice between good and bad, white and black; one has to make choices between the shades and hues, and between different 'cocktails' of virtue and evil. It is true that there is no simple, single litmus test for morality; it is relative and subjective to time, place, and person. Factors like *where*, *by whom*, and *when* a certain action is performed determine whether that action is moral or not. If a soldier kills in a state of war, it is heroism; if the same person kills at home, even if in self-defense, it becomes a crime. We condone multiple sexual partners, but consider horizontal plurality (i.e., same-gender partners) both a sin and a crime. We cannot codify or shackle what 'being moral' means in the cauldron of *samsara*, the sensory world, in which so many colliding factors have to be balanced in deciding the right thing to do in a given context; in the end, it all boils down to a kind of an intuitive 'gut feeling'. One has to nurture and develop an almost visceral capacity to weigh and choose the right over wrong.

Most of all, humans are bereft of a sense of affinity, bonding, and solidarity. Without some sort of a relationship, we might as well be another species. Hannah Arendt, author of *The Origins of Totalitarianism* (1951) and *The Human Condition* (1958), wrote that "men, not Man, live on the Earth, and inhabit the world."[43] Man becomes 'men' through bonding, and in its absence, humankind remains a conglomeration of disparate individuals, not a cohesive community with shared values and a common destiny. Albert Schweitzer, winner of the Nobel Peace prize (1952) said, "The first step in the evolution of ethics is a sense of solidarity with other human beings."[44] Our bonding increasingly appears to be a bondage; and our solidarity, that of slaves. The Indian mystic Meher Baba said that bondage is not a meaningless episode in the passage of life, and to experience freedom one must experience being caged, just as a fish must come out even momentarily to understand the value of water. The Argentinean writer Jorge Borges summarized a Plutonian hypothesis: "Individuals and things exist in so far as they participate in the species that includes them, which is their permanent reality."[45] At this point, we are only human because we have in its essentials the same body; one has to take a long pause to think of anything else that connects humans selected randomly. The air is thick with talk of globalization, interconnectivity, brotherhood and so on, but in practice we are torn farther apart from each other as ever before. We must realize, as the French writer Antoine de Saint Exupéry put it, "It is another of the miraculous things about mankind that there is no pain nor passion that does not radiate to the ends of the earth. Let a man in a garret but burn with enough intensity and he will set fire to the world."[46] At the same time, the tragedy of the human condition is that the only pain or passion we feel in our consciousness is our own. To act any differently, we need a consciousness change. For human behavior to be any different from what it has come to be, we need a brand new mindset. This is not a new revelation or discovery. Prophets and saints have said the same. Consciousness is both plural and singular. It is the divine force underlying the cosmos, which, in Sanskrit is called *mahat-tattva*, the first of seven cosmic transformations, the primordial Universal Mind or Infinite Intellect. But it is also specific — or appears to be — to every species and every individual. The attempt to merge the individual consciousness into the cosmic consciousness, the *jivatma* into the *paramatma*, as it is described in the Upanishads, is the spiritual journey every individual must embark upon. Consciousness is itself a storehouse of impressions or *vasanas,* carried over from previous lives. And the karmic latencies of those impressions, in turn, influence and condition our behavior. Our consciousness therefore is not only what we happen to have, but what we have earned or acquired, a reward as well as a retribution. The outward extension of consciousness, its practical manifestation is conduct, and the process of this transformation is still a perplexing puzzle. It is clear that for rightful conduct we need the right kind of perception, and for that we need right consciousness. The scriptures emphasize this point. Jainism, for example, places great importance on right perception and says that conduct devoid of right perception and right knowledge is meaningless ritualism, and in the present context, dangerous empiricism. It defines rightful conduct as the absence of skepticism, renunciation of all possessions and avoidance of all sinful and materialistic endeavors. That might be too high a standard for this age and world. The bare minimum ought to be what is called the Golden Rule or principle, which has been variously formulated but which really is something like '*what you would not have done to yourself, do not do to another*' and '*what you dislike, do not do to anyone*'; and putting it more positively, '*whatever you wish that men would do to you, do so to them*'. But even that seems a far cry from the current ebb and flow of modern life whose metaphor is 'I keep what I have and take what you have'.

Ironically, at the same time, as advances in technology have made it possible to undertake a detailed study of human genetic variation, humankind is moving towards intensive amalgamation through travel, trade, and immigration, and increasing inter-cultural and inter-race marriages and sexual unions. But the tragedy is that such coalition has not helped in building bridges across minds; nor has it fostered anything like a global culture. The 'globalized' globe continues to be a fractured world. It may be electronically 'flat', but functionally it is full of potholes. The sorry state of our species is that man has lost the sense of participation in a common mission; his only 'mission' is to expand the frontiers of his personal 'world' regardless of the means; the only aim is never to stop 'getting rich'. We do not see the need or virtue in coming together; indeed no cause worthy of interlinking energies, and no gain in that pain. Philosophers like Plato have argued that 'love directs the bonds of human society.' That still remains lofty and desirable but the state of human emotions belies that. Our expectations are at someone else's expense; our desires are often injurious to fellow humans. Everyone yearns for happiness but actually courts unhappiness by unfavorably comparing oneself with others. Everyone wants happiness and good things in life without doing any good. Everyone wants to dodge the ill effects of evil while doing evil. Man asks 'Why me?' when it comes to change, and 'Why not me?' when it comes to sharing the spoils of the status quo. The phenomenal world is one but the mental worlds are as many as the number of humans on earth. What matters to most people in the real world are their kith and kin, their family and friends; the rest are at best a statistic, at worst, dispensable. Isaiah Berlin was quoted as having said "There are 567 people in the world and I know all of them."[47] Everyone has a similar number. The wide disparity in the way we view the few, and the rest, is one of the triggers for what is wrong in the human world. We shower our attention, affection, and caring for a handful and ignore the rest, as if they are aliens that deserve only suspicion, not support. Human diversity is breathtakingly beautiful; it also hides many deficiencies and discrepancies that defy explanation or any excuse. The stark reality is that with all our blinding insights into the brain, biology, and behavioral psychology, we just do not have a clue about what makes a human, about what a human becomes, and about what divides the best and the rest, the wise man and the fool, the leaders and the followers. We certainly know a lot more about the mechanisms that underlie many cellular processes but very little about the psychic — or *karmic* –– underpinning of human personality. We know that the machine has radically altered the human way of life, but what about the human organism? Does our future lie within our genes or in our technology? Are we the harbingers of the next dominant intelligence on earth, the machine or a mix of machine and man, the former being the preponderant partner? What effect will such an 'evolution' have on human behavior? One widespread view is that in the age of mediocrity and mechanization, what is required to be great or good has become a causality of what Einstein termed as the 'worship of acquisitive success' by contemporary society. Such people argue that our addiction to the 'shortcuts and short terms' of our science-suffused culture aborts the birth of seminal ideas, of truly great works of art, architecture or literature, and that the sheer act of living in our competitive and daunting world denudes greatness. And that our ordinary lives are so exposed to the slew of irresistible sensory pleasures that it requires almost superhuman effort to withstand them and be prepared to pay the price of goodness. Einstein said in the year 1949 that the economic anarchy of the capitalistic society was the real source of evil.

Evil — be Thou my Good

Whether it is economic or environmental, social or religious, evil reigns unchallenged across the length and breadth of the human world. It manifests in multiple ways, like intolerance, discrimination, exploitation of the weak, calculated callousness, wickedness, and cruelty. But they all stem from the same source of supply — mind-controlled human consciousness. The phantom of evil keeps coming back over and over again because that is the centrality of human life. It is wholly human and has nothing to do with our animal antecedents. Evil is usually contrasted with *good*, which describes acts that are subjectively beneficial to the observer. In some religions, evil is an active force, often personified as an entity such as *Satan* (Christianity), *Iblis* (Islam), or *Ahriman* (Zoroastrianism). In Hinduism, it is generally believed that there is no 'problem of evil' as such because it is not deemed to be all that distinct from 'good', and is explained or explained away by doctrines like *dwanda*, *maya*, *karma*, reincarnation, which seek to elevate the believer above both 'good and evil'. The duality of 'good versus evil' is expressed, in some manner or another, by many cultures. But the real 'problem' that has haunted man down the ages and most of all today, is why we find it so difficult to be good and fall such easy prey to evil. It absolves no one; as Rene Descartes said, 'the greatest minds are capable of the greatest vices as well as of the greatest virtues', and we have no idea what truly differentiates one from the other. Often it seems, as Arjuna pleaded with Lord Krishna in the Bhagavad Gita, we are propelled by a mysterious malign force. If that was the fate of Arjuna, the dearest friend of Krishna and an incarnation of Nara of the deity Nara-Narayana in the *Dvapara Yuga*, what about ordinary humans in this sinful *Kali Yuga*? First, we must understand the nature of the beast, and we must acknowledge that evil is not 'existential' or 'irrational' or 'circumstantial'. It is caused, or greatly accentuated, by the very faculty that we are so proud of: that of thought and feeling we experience as human beings. Evil is not 'good' masquerading behind a mask, and it cannot be alchemically altered into 'good' by tolerance or acceptance. Our state of mind parallels that of Milton's *Satan* (*Paradise Lost*; Book IV), whose motto was 'So farewell, Hope; and with Hope farewell, Fear; Farewell, Remorse! all Good to me is lost; Evil, be thou my Good…', Evil is rampant, pervasive but no one admits he is evil. We bemoan that the world is bereft of virtue, but, deep inside, we firmly believe that we are virtuous. And when evil cannot be wished away, we turn a Nelson's eye, and protest our ignorance and innocence. Moral philosophers have told us that indifference to evil is not only an endorsement of evil, but evil itself; there is not much difference between love of evil, and indifference to good or evil.

That indifference is intellectualized, and is really an outcome of our being, as Aristotle said, 'a rational animal'. And that 'rationality' is what allows us to remain indifferent to the other's suffering while leading perfectly 'normal' lives, even 'moral' lives. Instead of being indifferent to the results of our actions, as exhorted by the Bhagavad Gita, we are indifferent to evil, and to the misery of our fellow species. And there is a moral difference between stoic indifference and selfish indifference. The doctrine of *dharma* also says that not performing one's *swadharma*, one's prescribed social obligation, is also evil. The very essence of the Gita is this. While etymologically, 'indifference' means 'no difference', operationally it makes a world of difference in the equation between 'good' and 'evil'. For a species that claims to have high *emotional* intelligence and innate *spiritual* intelligence, the degree and extent of lack of empathy for and bonding with fellow humans is stark and striking. While admittedly all our experiences are bodily experiences and nobody can experience the same experiences as any other, the fact is that we would rather be a slave than share, and rather be in bondage than bond with those outside the narrow but rapidly shrinking circle of 'humans we distinguish as family and friends'. That 'discrimination' leads to a huge chunk of humanity being left uncared for and abandoned. The best of us are indifferent to their plight, and that reduces us to an irrelevant, if not malicious, abstraction. Albert Einstein said that our task must be to widen the circles of compassion to embrace all living creatures and the whole of Nature in its beauty. Helen Keller called the apathy of humans the worst of all evils. Mother Theresa said that the most terrible feeling in life is to feel unwanted and abandoned. Most people convince themselves that they are oppressed (or *downpressed* as Bob Marley would say) by the 'system,' but given a chance, they would have no qualms about sharing its spoils.

'Modern man', intolerant and in the grip of greed, is perhaps the angriest creature on earth. Anger has become the defining signature of man, a reflexive and addictive reaction to frustration and unfulfilled desires, a show of power and control. It is an evil as toxic as hate. It manifests as rudeness, irritation, intemperate words, and hostility, and mars every relationship. Lord Krishna, in answer to the question of Arjuna as to what impels a man to "commit sin, reluctantly indeed… as if by force constrained",[48] answers that it is "desire, it is wrath, begotten by the quality of action (*rajas*); all-consuming, all-polluting, know thou this is our foe on earth."[49] We are so comfortable with and addicted to anger that we use it often as an alibi: '*I said it*' or '*I did it in anger*'. But anger, perhaps more than any other single thing, reflects the extant state of our mind, without the camouflage and the cover of culture. Without anger, there is no avarice, malice loses its sting, and violence becomes toothless. And malice, which is more pernicious than envy and jealousy, has managed to infect the human consciousness; that is why we have not been able to *be* the change we want to see in the world (as Gandhi exhorted us), nor the window through which we must see the world (as Bernard Shaw put it). The 'window' is soiled and hence the world is sullied; every one wallows in misery and self-pity, blaming the society, the system, steeped in self-righteousness. The cumulative effect of the 'toxic' threesome is to fundamentally, perhaps irreversibly, alter the quality of human presence on earth. The British political philosopher John Gray in his much-acclaimed book *Straw Dogs: Thoughts on Humans and Other Animals* (2003), says that humans seem fated to wreck the balance of life on earth, and that they will be trampled on and tossed aside ruthlessly by heaven and earth, much like the straw dogs used as offerings in an ancient Chinese ritual. Nature will not stay forever the silent, stoic, and sullen sufferer.

One of the baffling and enduring paradoxes is how to reconcile the scriptural vision of man and his behavior. The scriptures talk of man's inherent divinity but the reality of human behavior is anything but divine. Man takes pride in his being a 'rational animal', which brings to mind what Bertrand Russell had to say about it: 'All my life I have been searching for evidence which could support that.' Man talks of human dignity and rights but leaves 'no stone unturned' to throw stones at the weak and the vulnerable. The worst part is that man never feels or thinks that he is wrong in his behavior. The world is full of people, to paraphrase Dostoevsky, who claim to love humanity, even die for humanity, but cannot stand the sight of another man for too long without breaking out into a brawl. What holds us back is the fear of social punishment and the prospect of hell after death. But that 'fear' seems to be faltering now, and man has come to believe that he can get away with both crime and sin, outsmart terrestrial law as well as divine justice.

Whether it is man's manifestation of anger, malice, and violence, or his obsessive attachment to sex and money, or the pernicious power of the State, they are all rooted in the human inability to resist the temptations of easy life and evil. Without temptation we are all saints, and all saints struggle with the temptations of the flesh, body, and the devil. Prophets, the noblest of us like Jesus and the Buddha, were tested by temptation by the Devil and by Mara respectively, in the cauldron of worldly life. If temptation means being induced, seduced, and manipulated to do things that seem to give comfort and pleasure but are morally wrong, then much of life is that. The Buddha, on the way to his enlightenment and in his encounter with Mara, identifies temptations as squadrons or 'hosts': the sense organs; boredom; hunger and thirst; craving; sloth and torpor; cowardice; uncertainty, malice coupled with obstinacy, gain, honor, fame; and self-praise and denigration of others. That is a pretty exhaustive but hybrid list of the ways through which we are 'tempted'. It is interesting that things like 'boredom' and 'uncertainty' are in that list. They are states of mind and, in the human world at least, the terminal 'tempter' is the mind itself. It is the mind that strokes the temptations of the body, tempts us to take the primrose path, the path of pleasure, *preyas* as the Upanishads call it, and offers endless explanations and excuses for all our transgressions and trespasses. Some scientists believe that our morality is hardwired into our brains, while others believe that the environment and people close to us help shape our thoughts and actions. But broadly most scientists agree that the struggle between doing good and doing evil resides in the brain. What is not known is if the parameters within which the brain works are a matter of biology or the environment. Some psychologists like Melanie Storry Chan say that our moral compass resides in the ventromedial prefrontal cortex, the area of the brain just behind the forehead which is responsible for highly complex functioning such as empathy and the ability to make moral judgments. It has also been found that individuals who behave dishonestly exhibit increased activity in parts of the prefrontal cortex.

Whether or not man is naturally 'good' or 'unnaturally' bad has been debated since time immemorial. Prophets and saints and mahatmas have sought to distinguish between evil people and evil deeds; and inferentially between good people who do bad things and 'bad people' who do good deeds. In the Sermon on the Mount, Jesus said that no one is entirely good; he even said, "Why do you call me good? No one is good but One, that is, God" (*Matthew, 19.17*). Although interpretations vary on what he meant, the broad message is that only God is perfectly good. Were it not so, where is the place for evil to hide and flourish? But modern man has settled the issue. In the 'matrix of his mind' there is no tangible incentive for 'goodness' at all; the mindset is '*if being bad gets all the 'good things of life', why tread the thankless path of good?*' Yet no one, save perhaps a psychopath, wants to be 'evil'; he just wants some things and if, his mind reasons, that is what it takes to get them and prevail, he cannot be blamed. In other words, being bad is not *his* choice; it is a choice forced upon him by *other* people. Had Hitler got what he wanted — strategic supremacy over Europe — he perhaps would not have gone to war. After all, *he* did not actually; it was Britain that declared war on Germany. And he gained power 'democratically', and an entire nation and tens of millions of people idolized him. They did not think they were bad; they were just being patriotic! Most of all, they were all as 'human' as any of us, as Hannah Arendt reminds us. At the end of the day, we can all 'feel good' about our proclaimed proximity to God, about our 'unique' capacity to differentiate good and evil, and we can endlessly theorize about the duality of good and evil and whether evil is an event or a process. Yet, we cannot shut our eyes to its pervasiveness and predisposition in the human nature. We cannot run away from the unpleasant truth that evil lurks deep inside the human consciousness (where God too has a home), waiting to raise its hideous head at the slightest pretext or provocation.

Modern men are not the only ones baffled and bewitched by evil. The origin and stubborn persistence and pervasiveness of evil in human affairs have long been an enduring subject of theological and scholastic speculation down the ages. It is said in the *Atharvaveda*, one of the oldest of Hindu scriptures, "When the divine architect planned and fashioned the human form, all the evils and virtues entered the mortal frame and made it their home."[50] Over time, virtues seem to have taken a lashing and are in hiding. Some religions tried to 'fix' the problem through a divinely revealed absolute code of conduct like the Ten Commandments of the ancient Hebrews. Some others created a web of *shastras*, or treatises, like the ones enunciated by Manu and Confucius. Some thinkers have tried to reason that human morality plays a role, not as an intrinsic, natural necessity, but as a social need. Those who espouse the utilitarian principle have tried to codify morality simply as 'the greatest good for the greatest numbers' and as 'do unto others as you would have them do unto you.' Implicitly, anything that contravenes this code is deemed evil. In the Hindu epic Mahabharata, the moral tenet 'Do naught unto others which would cause you pain if done to you' (*Mahabharata, 5:1517*) sums up the concept of *dharma*. Vedanta says good and evil, like day and night, are inherent and are really a play of the mind. Charles Darwin, in his book *The Descent of Man* (1871), equated moral sense with conscience, and characterized it as a highly complex sentiment, composed of and evolved from social instinct, reason, self-interest, religious feelings, instruction, and habit. Whether it is natural or acquired, the foremost task is to re-ignite the embers of flickering morality in the human disposition. Evil is something we have to live with; eradicating evil is tantamount to eradicating goodness. But it ought not to be, and need not be, the dominant force in human affairs. We do not have to be so powerless to resist the urge to cause injury to others. There is nothing in our origin or evolution or our culture that explains or justifies the sway and sweep of 'pure' evil in contemporary life. It is not ordained that we should spend much of our limited lifespan trying to nag, nibble, and nullify each other.

Evil has many manifestations, but the one we are concerned with is personal or moral evil. The raw truth of the human condition is that no one is fully free from all evil, whether it is endemic or exogenous. The French playwright and philosopher Octave Mirbeau wrote, "When one tears away the veils and shows them naked, people's souls give off such a pungent smell of decay."[51] There is much that goes on inside our bodies that we do not want to admit to our own conscience. That 'smell' is the byproduct of the way humans have organized their individual and collective lives anchored in individualism, the pregnant price of which goes by the maxims of 'progress' and 'problem solving'. Because we find it hard to share the fruit of our labor, our idea of overcoming any obstacle is elimination, of the situation or the individual. It has now come to such a pass that we are increasingly eliminating ourselves in the name of problem-solving, both as individuals and as a species. To the age-old threats from microbes, biohazards, and pathogens, we can now add the pandemics of suicide and homicide. In the process, our creativity often ends up tampering with the laws of Nature, and we are not wise enough to manage the processes we initiate or invent. The result is that "In a universe of interconnection and interrelationship of all things, each alteration sets into motion unknown and sometimes unknowable consequences."[52]

The evil in man may have had much to do with the way the human species has evolved, but we are now ominously being told that its effect is not confined to humans. And evil could be a tool not for transformation but annihilation. Possible scenarios for a cataclysmic conclusion to the human tenure on earth need not be, as generally assumed, the result of a war or global warming or melting glaciers, or monster earthquakes or crashing Manhattan-sized meteorites. These are still possible or even probable, but it could also be far more insidious and internal, a virus within, the silent but catastrophic deterioration of the human condition. At the turn of this millennium, man is at once narcissistic and nihilistic. It has been said that those whom the gods want to destroy, they make them mad first. Human behavior is bizarre and goes beyond the bounds of self-interest and self-preservation, or even self-belief. The sage Vyasa, the celebrated author of the Mahabharata and many other sacred texts and several *Puranas*, when asked to sum it all up, said, "The act of greatest merit is to help others, and the greatest act of sin is to cause intentional injury to others."[53] Today it requires more effort and will, not to commit that 'greatest sin' but to commit that 'act of greatest merit.' Motive is the real measure of man and in that perspective few are guiltless.

What really bothers most theologians like St. Augustine and many 'god-loving' philosophers like Socrates is not the equation between man and evil, but between God and evil. It has been said that more people have abandoned their faith due to the existence of evil than due to any other reason. If God is good, Almighty and the Creator of everything, how can He create evil, and if He did, He is not all-good. But the confusion lies in extrapolating everything human to God, and in labeling God in terms of human good and human evil. Then again, is evil a 'thing', which, in the words of author Peter Kreeft is something like a "black cloud, or a dangerous storm, or a grimacing face, or dirt"?[54] Or is evil simply the absence of good or a 'lesser good' than that desirable? In his monumental *Summa Theologica*, Saint Thomas Aquinas found only two objections to the existence of God, and one of them was the problem of evil (the other was the apparent ability of natural science to explain everything in our experience without God). Carlos Steel, a researcher and a professor of ancient, medieval and renaissance philosophy, summarizes the Socratic view: "In the discussion on education in the Republic, Socrates lays down the principles which those who speak about the gods must follow if they want to avoid the errors of traditional mythology. The first *typos* of this rational theology is this: 'God is the cause, not of all things, but only of the good.' For 'God, being good, cannot be responsible for everything happening in our life, as is commonly believed, but only for a small part. For we have a far smaller share of good than of evil, and while God must be held to be the sole cause of good, we must look for some other factors than God as cause of the evil.'"[55]

What are those factors? As Steel puts it, God is not responsible for 'most things in human life', since most of them are evil. In this view, God is not the cause of evil, he only guarantees the inevitable decree of fate. In Hindu mythology too, even an avatar of God like Rama and Krishna sometimes say that a certain thing or a happening is the will of *vidhata* (Fate) and one has to accept it, opening the question who or which is the greater power: Fate or God. Or is it that God is Fate but not His spark, even in its most complete manifestation? The more problematic — and practical — question is: if He has nothing to do with evil or is powerless before it, can He have anything to do with fighting or eradicating evil? Implicitly, God becomes marginal in our lives. That directly contradicts the very doctrine of divine avatar, which is precisely to contain, if not eradicate, evil, and to restore *dharma* or righteousness to its rightful place. It means that there cannot be a world free either of evil or goodness; it is a question of balance, which again is sensitive to space and time. Another way of looking at good and evil could be in terms of what really is 'being human'. Two of the attributes of 'being human', according to common belief, are freedom and free will, whether God-given or innate to the human form of life, which together make man, unlike other species, a creature of choice. All his life, almost every minute, man is called upon to make choices. And he makes those choices with the intelligence derived primarily from the brain/mind. The nature of the intelligence determines the character of the choice, the quality of life. The kind of intelligence we have brought to bear on our choice-making, particularly in the last few millenniums, has been such that the choices were based on the criteria that yielded 'evil' in far greater proportion than goodness. The 'evil' choice gives, or rather gives the *appearance* of giving, what man wants. It is not 'evil' that man chooses, but the desires that goodness does not fulfill and evil seems to. The scriptures say that the root of evil is desire. The Hindu sacred texts also say that our unfulfilled desires follow us beyond death. What is emphasized here is not desire, fulfilled or unfulfilled, but man's desire for the fruits of action. It is this that keeps the cycle rolling. The *Maitreya* Upanishad says that, "he who, being overcome by the bright or dark fruits of action, enters a good or an evil womb, so that his course is downward or upward and he wanders around, overcome by the pairs of opposites."[56] Although the state of total desirelessness or desireless action, also called 'choice-less awareness' in Taoism, is extolled as pure bliss, at the practical level, it is really the choice of the *wrong* kind of desires that is at the root of evil. It is not really desire *per se*, but *what* we desire, that creates evil; another cause is the lust for what we call ironically the 'good things of life', necessary for 'good' living, like money and power at the expense of someone else. It is not even perhaps the 'good things' or 'good life' we want, but *how we go about* getting them. Even the scriptures legitimize acquiring money and fulfilling desires, but through righteousness. In the Hindu religion, *artha*, money or wealth, and *kama*, desire for worldly things, constitute two of the four *purusharthas* or goals of human life, but they have to be acquired through *dharma*, which, among other things, is righteous conduct. In short, to ensure that evil does not dominate our lives, we have to change the nature of our desires or rather the way we fulfill them. Evil will then lose its spread and sting. Indeed, none of this is new; it has been said for thousands of years. The point to remember is that the pursuit of desires through wrong means is not imposed by any external force; it is the product of our mind-driven intelligence. It therefore means that, so long as our human intelligence does not change, men will continue to choose the path of desire and evil.

Since nothing is redundant in Nature, or in God's creation, what is the cosmic end served by human evil? Is it the only way to remind us that 'goodness' exists, or does it serve some mysterious purpose? In Jewish mystical writings, evil is viewed as a necessity because without it, there would be no exercise of free will for choosing goodness over evil, and because it allows the infinite love, cascading goodness, and unconditional forgiveness of God to be demonstrated. That, in turn, raises other questions. Does God really need to demonstrate anything, does it mean that for God to get a chance to forgive, we must go on sinning? Evil is 'justified' in another way. In the Hindu doctrine of *dwanda,* everything in Nature comes as a mutually reinforcing pair of opposites: life and death, sunset and sunrise, darkness and light, joy and sorrow; and evil has to be there if we were to know goodness. At the same time, we are endowed with the discriminating capacity to distinguish between the 'opposites' and to make the right choice. On how we use that discriminating capacity hinges the choice we make, of good or evil. The Roman philosopher Cicero said that "the function of wisdom is to discriminate between good and evil." Well, we have a perfect alibi; we have never claimed we have wisdom and in any case it is not that we do not know what is evil. By equating evil with pain, some psychologists like the Danish psychologist Eric Erikson, have postulated that evil is necessary for human development. In modern life, evil is a sort of sidekick to aggressive individualism and our attempt to meddle with and manipulate everything to our advantage. In a universe of interdependence, every alteration triggers a chain reaction, whose end often ends up as evil. The cancerous philosophy of 'having more and bigger is better', more often than not in relation to what someone else has, creates the momentum for a mountain of evil. Our sense of 'feel good' about fame and fortune invariably, though not inevitably, marginalizes morality. Our abhorrence of any kind of 'failure', and veneration of 'success' or appearance of success, implicitly builds the infrastructure for evil. Our consumptive culture of comfort and consumerism, is not only consuming the earth bit by bit, but also breaking down the moral barriers inside us.

The 'problem of evil' as we commonly comprehend, makes us associate evil with noxious actions, bloodcurdling horrors and culpable inaction. But the evil that does the greatest harm, that is commonplace and is barely noticed and gives us the most pain, is the way we treat each other. That evil is rooted in our mind; as a Chinese Buddhist scripture says, "an evil thought is the most dangerous of all thieves."[57] The power of thought, for good or for bad, is enormous. It is the most powerful emitter of energy on earth. Perhaps more than evil actions, it is the sum total of evil thoughts that creates so much negative energy. And we think of evil in the context of others, not our own selves. The Indian saint poet Kabir wrote that he went in search of evil and found it nowhere, but when he looked into his own self, he discovered that no one was more evil than him. It requires a person like Kabir to be able to look inside one's own self. Sometimes, the world outside is compared to a mirror, reflecting our own image, our own character. But a mirror has to be clean to reflect the right image, and the mirror that obscures our vision is the mind. In a famous story in the Mahabharata, prince Yudhisthira (the righteous) and prince Duryodhana (the devious) were asked by their guru to look for an evil and a virtuous man respectively. Both, reflecting their nature returned empty handed. The moral is that we cannot see what is not inside us, evil or good, and the external can only be an extension of the internal. Some say that, like beauty, evil is only in the eye of the beholder. The perspectives of the perpetrator and the victim differ radically. The mind of the perpetrator justifies or greatly reduces the ill effect; and the mind of the victim magnifies or highlights the spin-off effects. One could say the same thing about 'good' too. The question really is not the 'why' of evil but how to handle it without being crushed by it. The simple solution is to get away from its way and do 'good' to as many people as one can and as many times as possible and in as many situations as it is feasible. The only obstacle to be able to do that is within the coils of our consciousness.

The sum and substance of the human way of life, so painstakingly fashioned over thousands of years, is increasingly yielding more evil than good. It is not, as often as it has been said, that man does not know, or even wants to do, what is good, but he often ends up doing what he does not want to do. The '*why*' of this is one of the riddles of the human condition. The answer is what we might call the triple-E syndrome, the three 'E's being *explanation*, *excuse*, and *evasion*. It is these three 'E's that our mind pops up when our conscience pricks, and allows us, literally, to get away with murder or rape as a response to provocation. It has to be said, as Hannah Arendt reminded us, that cruelty, the deliberate infliction of pain (physical, mental or psychological) is not the monopoly of a beast or a barbarian. The human beast, perhaps, beats the rest. Even a visually blind man can sense what man has done and what he is capable of doing, but we are virtually 'blinded' by the three 'E's. It is a trick that the mind plays on us; it makes us believe that we have nothing to do beyond the narrow world of 'kith and kin', our near and dear. The mind even changes the fundamental character of what we do or say, and makes us believe that a cutting word is a sign of confidence, that a massacre is a means to 'feel safe', or that walking over a prostrate body in our path is the only way to go to the other side. Only a human mind can justify the virtual vaporization of tens of thousands of non-combatants in the course of a veritable war to get just one man 'dead or alive'. Only the human mind is consciously capable of justifying to itself the hacking of two people in love as 'killing for family honor', even when one of the two is one's own child. Only a human mind — ironically that of a gifted poet, Marguerite Duras — could make a person say that she was an alcoholic 'because she knew that God did not exist.'[58] The mind can fool us, but not Nature. The American author Eric Hoffer (*Reflections on the Human Condition*, 1973) wrote that "Nature has no compassion. Nature accepts no excuses and the only punishment it knows is death."[59] But what is the *nature* of Nature? More pertinently, what is the nexus between Nature and God? Some say that Nature is the visible visage of God, the major manifestation of divine revelation. And then there are those who worship Nature and see no reason for God, like many ancient cultures and some still extant traditional societies that venerate Nature as the direct divine manifestation. The other view is that it is another creation of God, like man himself, and the sole purpose of this creation is to provide the basis for the human way of life. Modern thought, influenced by science, adopts the latter approach, which is a major factor in the economic and environmental crisis that the world faces today. We want to 'control' and use and misuse Nature, as we would wish to do to another man.

We constantly invent new excuses for the horrors we commit in the name of control and our yearning for hegemony. For, let there be no equivocation, human horror is human horror; there are no parallels in Nature, not in the animal world, nor perhaps in Hell. When we read about the 12 million victims of Nazi and Soviet mass killing policies (during 1933-1944),[60] it is enough to make us sick in the stomach. But what about other, even more disturbing tales, such as that of Kamate, a 'survivor' of the civil war in Congo in the late 1990s: her husband was butchered in front of her eyes, and she was then raped after being forced to lie on top of the pile of her husband's body parts. Kamate passed out, but when she regained consciousness, she heard the screams of her two daughters being raped in the next room.[61] Do such gory accounts shock us enough? Maybe momentarily, a wee bit. Some of us might feel 'horrified', but not enough to make any difference to our comfort level, or to our moral sense of who we are. But those rapists and murderers are also of the same species. Maybe in another context, they too are just like any of the rest of us.

And then, do numbers really matter? Why is 'mass killing' more heinous than any other killing? What is the 'acceptable' number, the threshold to shake us out of our stupor? Had Hitler ordered the killing of only a million or half a million Jews, would he have been less of a monster? Are the killings and rapes carried out by Allied troops and Soviet soldiers in Germany — or elsewhere — any less horrific because they were 'liberating' Europe (and Germany too) from the Nazis? The 'moral difference' is a many-fold extension between a soldier killing in 'war', declared or undeclared, with or without international imprimatur, and a citizen killing in a moment of rage, provoked or unprovoked.

At a more 'practical' level, every day's news seems to be more horrific than the horror of the previous day. Until it happens, even our darkest imagination cannot imagine such a thing; 'sacred cows' are becoming skeletons in the cupboard, tumbling one after another, be it a mother's lofty love, or family ties or bonds of friendship. And money seems to dilute, if not negate every other bonding. For many people, there is not much difference between killing and 'problem-solving' for getting what you think you deserve. All this raises the question: is there any biological and genetic basis to human savagery? If there can be a 'God-gene', why not a 'diabolic' gene? Now scientists say that they have identified what they call a 'hate circuit', which includes structures in the cortex and subcortex. Predictably, scientists disagree on how genes affect human behavior. British evolutionary biologist and author Richard Dawkins (*The Selfish Gene*, 1976; *The God Delusion*, 2006) says we have a 'selfish gene' but denies the existence of a genetic link to human spirituality. According to this hypothesis, the basic unit to be maintained through natural selection is not the individual, who is merely a disposable vehicle, or the group or the species, but the gene. American molecular biologist and author of the book *The God Gene* (2005), Dean Hamer, takes the opposite view and asserts that there is a genetic link to spirituality which is even inheritable. If one eventually proves the existence of a gene for 'selfishness' or for 'spirituality', could it be possible that there is something in the human make-up, a gene for 'savageness' that triggers the malevolence in man that erupts through a certain combination of coincidences and fusion of factors? Richard Dawkins espoused the theory of what he called *memes*, which are 'transmutable units of culture' and which in many ways are similar to genes but with important differences. Memes can mutate overnight, and are largely limited to humans as a possible explanation for the religious affiliations of humans and, maybe, even for the religious and other extensions of extremism.

Thus far, we have been safe in the citadel of our thoughts. What we think is our business, and no one else's; no intruders are allowed, and no one can penetrate our thoughts (at least so far). We think that anybody can think anything, even the most heinous things, and what matters is the deed. This is valid to an extent. One cannot be 'moral in the mind' and callous in his conduct; conversely, one could entertain evil thoughts and do good deeds, at least theoretically. It is true that action, not intent, is the bottom line. But action does not germinate in a vacuum. Khalil Gibran said: "A little knowledge that acts is worth infinitely more than much knowledge that is idle."[62] He also exhorts us to *apply* the words of wisdom of the wise to daily life: 'Wisdom is not in words; wisdom is meaning within words.'

But thoughts that originate in the mind and emotions that come from the heart too have consequences, though unseen and unfelt. Like negative thoughts, negative emotions too can be destructive. It is not a new discovery. For instance, Buddhist tradition has long recognized the transforming power of emotions, and has long advocated the need for such information to be set at the heart of spiritual practice. A moral thought and a selfless feeling can have as great an effect as a moral word or a moral deed. Instead of facing up to the reality of our ambivalent condition and consciousness, we castigate religion, or science or technology, for man's present predicament. In other words, we continue to play the same blame-game we have been playing for long with disastrous consequences. And we still look for alibis and scapegoats. It is the ruse of the mind to evade and escape the responsibility for the misuse of science and technology, and for the systematic subversion of spirituality. Our predicament was foreseen by the sage Vyasa five thousand years ago, in his predictions of what our current age would entail: "The corruption of the spirit, the pursuit of material goals of wealth and power in the guise of spiritual seeking is the greatest evil of all. This will be the root of all misery in the Kali Age, the Age of Untruth."[63]

While evil is classically associated with personal, social, and sexual factors, a relatively recent but increasingly vicious factor is *economic* evil. Almost every traditional evil is laced with, even based on, matters of money. The fact is, nothing loosens us from the moorings of morality as expectations of economic gain; in some parts of the world, there are even reports of sons killing their own fathers to inherit their coveted jobs. Economic 'apartheid', deprivation, injustice, exploitation, asymmetry and disparity have become a major threat to global stability and to human progress. Concurrently, economic inequality rises, as the rich extract an unusually high share of global wealth. When the rich get richer, the powerful get stronger. Perversely, the middle class is moved into the lower class. In this new 'physics of evil', prosperity does not trickle from the rich to the poor, but from the middle class in the wealthier countries to the rich in developing nations, resulting in a few new 'brown or black' billionaires joining the global plutocracy, the 'ruling class' of this century. The global economic 'gap' is not really between the North and the South, but between two types of obscenities — the very, very rich, and the very, very poor across the globe. But rich or poor, man has become a virtual economic 'slave', programmed to perform economic chores almost every waking hour. The mantra of modern man is economic growth, which puts goods ahead of people, and which is fuelled by consumptive consumerism, constant creation and fulfillment of material comforts and their planned obsolescence, and excessive use of natural resources. Our economic 'health' is more important than physical or mental or emotional health; it is the specter of economic 'meltdown' that haunts most people, even more than nuclear Armageddon. The so-called 'revolution of rising expectations' is economic, not spiritual, and the rich, even the 'very rich', are not exempt from it.

Human personality flowers when its different dimensions work in harmony, but when one of them — in this case, the economic dimension — overwhelms everything else, it distorts the total personality. That is exactly what has happened with the dominance of economics in modern human life; in other words, our whole consciousness is geared almost exclusively to the pursuit of earning, saving, spending money, and acquiring and 'enjoying' property. If humanity is to endure as a viable and harmonious entity, we must revisit the role of economics as the religion of modern man. Not only does economics overemphasize the material dimension of human life, it also diminishes the unity of humanity. Economics, even when man was less avaricious than now, has never been a unifying force; on the contrary, it has accentuated the unsavory human instincts. To give practical shape to the oneness of the human race as a viable species, we must put in place a drastic revision in economic thinking. We must get away from our entrenched belief that what we earn we can spend as we wish, subject only to the law of the land. Sometimes what we can economically 'afford', morally we cannot. There is a spiritual aspect too. No one could have captured the essence of the 'economic man' better than Adam Smith, the celebrated author of *The Wealth of Nations* (1776) and often hailed as the Father of Economics, when he wrote that, "this disposition to admire, and almost to worship, the rich and the powerful, and to despise, or, at least, to neglect persons of poor and mean condition, ... is... the great and most universal cause of the corruption of our moral sentiments".[64] Smith also said: "All for ourselves and nothing for other people seems, in every age of the world, to have been the vile maxim of the masters of mankind."[65] Human action has become virtually synonymous with economic activity; the workplace has become more of a 'nest' than home. Instead of being a means, it has become the end. Economic power is more concentrated in fewer countries and people than any other power, save perhaps technological. Economic management has become more difficult than political governance, and economic fortunes have become as volatile as the climate. Indeed, the failure of all experiments in 'good' governance can be attributed to the failure of economic public policy making, and not applying the principles of personal prudence to State policies. Economic deprivation and inequity are debilitating and divisive and widen the gap between man and man, perhaps more than any other single factor. This is not exactly a 'blinding insight'; it is ancient wisdom. The Greek historian and biographer Plutarch (*Parallel Lives*) wrote, "An imbalance between the rich and the poor is the oldest and most fatal ailment of all republics."[66] And the great Plato himself wrote, in his classic

The Republic, that "any city, however small, is in fact divided into two, one the city of the poor, the other of the rich; these are at war with one another...[67] In another of his monumental works, *The Laws*, he said: "The form of law which I should propose... would be as follows: in a state which is desirous of being saved from the greatest of all plagues — not faction, but rather distraction — there should exist among the citizens neither extreme poverty nor, again, excessive wealth, for both are productive of both these evils."[68] That 'evil' of excessive wealth, which has become immeasurably powerful and pungent since then, now threatens not only to rupture human society, but even to retard human evolution.

Economic evil is built into the very process that makes economic life virtually the same as human life. Since human worth is measured in economic terms, few can resist the temptation to amass and enhance their economic wealth regardless of the means and models. The most visible face of economic evil is extreme, 'absolute' poverty on a mass scale. It is 'absolute' because it denies the wherewithal to live as humans on earth. It is 'absolute' because persistent and prolonged deprivation of sufficient and suitable food so emaciates the body and the brain, that their consciousness itself ceases, as it were, to be human. In fact, economic evil is the biggest obstacle to the eradication of food poverty. It creates a 'comfort or acceptance' zone of existence and it becomes a habit from which one does not even *want* to escape. The trappings of that kind of existence simmer discomfort and resentment but also resistance to any real change, either in the surroundings or in the way of life or work. That is why, it is so difficult to 'relocate' or 'rehabilitate' those at the bottom of the ladder in the human society. In relative terms, everyone is 'poor', everyone is 'deprived' and everyone 'hungers' for something or the other. Such poverty, the famous American Harvard economist J.K. Galbraith called *case* poverty. Mass poverty, which is geographically concentrated in parts of Asia and much of Africa, is qualitatively different from the poverty in affluent societies, which is pretty localized and therefore does not change the character of the society as a whole. Further, prolonged starvation or malnutrition insidiously undermines the whole personality of the individual. If the 'very rich' are different *à la* Fitzgerald, the 'very poor' are also very different even from the rest of us, the vast majority who do not fall in either of the 'very' categories. The lives of the extremely poor — usually defined as those who do not earn even a dollar a day to survive on, the bulk of whom are in rural areas — are not only an extension of economic evil but an indictment of the moral smugness of the rest of us. Our consciousness finds no 'problem.' It is part of life and such is the 'world'. Our mind offers the three 'E's — explanation, excuse, evasion — for this too; it 'passes the buck'; pleads both ignorance and innocence; and goes on the offensive and tells us that even the depressing picture drawn is too dismal and negative; and that 'progress' is being made through 'trickle down' economics but it takes time.

Finally, we are told that the rich countries are suffering from 'aid fatigue', and the rest of the world from 'poverty fatigue', We are simply tired of hearing such nomenclature and grim statistics of global poverty. Given the time, every problem gets sorted but how it will be done is another matter. No one can tell the future; so many dates, deadlines and targets have gone into the oblivion of history, but for now, mass poverty is a clear and present threat to global stability, to the environment and to any dreams of a world without war and violence. The tragedy is: it is so needless and calls for so little effort on a global scale. What we need are right public policies and a fraction of the resources expended on armaments.

One of the ironies of the duality of 'good versus evil' is that evil is committed by not just evil people. The callous actions of 'good men' could be more evil than those of 'bad men', that is, if we judge the 'evilness' of those actions by how long the effect lingers. In doing evil deeds, we do harm to other individuals while the dominance of evil in the world does harm to Nature itself. And 'good men' are often passive men and their lives do not add much to the battle with evil. Evil is embedded in what living entails, and has a multiplier effect; it devours everything around and becomes unstoppable. Often we condemn evil but fail to notice it in our own backyard. A 'withering look' or a word that hurts or humiliates another person is evil. Taking advantage of another person is evil; exploitation is evil. The reason we are tempted to put others down, compulsively correct them, and tell them that we are right and they are wrong, is that our ego mistakenly believes that by showing how someone else is wrong, we will feel better. In reality, however, if we pay attention to the way we feel after we put someone down, we will notice that we actually feel worse. Many other evils dot our daily lives: obscene opulence is evil; poverty is evil; discrimination is evil; bigotry is evil; anger on the weak is evil; malice is evil; and not fighting evil is evil. The American essayist Barry Lopez sketches the human dilemma well: "How is one to live a moral and compassionate existence when one is fully aware of the blood, the horror inherent in life, when one finds darkness not only in one's culture but within oneself? If there is a stage at which an individual life becomes truly adult, it must be when one grasps the irony in its unfolding and accepts responsibility for a life lived in the midst of such paradox. One must live in the middle of contradiction, because if all contradictions were eliminated at once, life would collapse. There are simply no answers to some of the great pressing questions. You continue to live them out, making your life a worthy expression of leaning into the light."[69] Evil may seem entrenched in the human psyche but to be moral is not altogether alien to the human species. One part of us wants to be good and moral, but the other part says that that is too exacting and expensive. People are still trapped in the mishmash of moral ambivalence, mundane retribution and senseless jealousy. Great thinkers like Goethe and Dostoevsky said that there was no crime they could not think of, or could not have been committed by them. In essence, crime or sin is a transgression and everyone, sometime or the other transgresses; in that sense, it is natural to the human condition. Transgress we must. The question is, *what* boundaries; knowing which ones is at the core of human transformation. That, in turn, raises issues of 'good' and 'evil' and how to choose, not between one or the other, but between 'two goods' and 'two evils', or more often between a bevy of grays.

We need to ponder over the parallel processes of the rise of materialism and the ascendancy of overarching evil in the past two or three centuries. Assertive materialism fuelled human greed, created the culture of endless 'more', which inevitably made man bid adieu to the moral means that would not earn him the material comforts he yearned for. Acceptance of evil has ceased to be exceptional; it is commonplace now, considered a necessary way of life. The general view is that in today's world, it is simply impossible to be moral in our personal or professional life.

One should be careful not to fall into the mind's soothing trap: explain everything, including evil, and offer scapegoats. Because everything is morally ambivalent and every action has a cause and consequence and nothing occurs in a vacuum, it is always possible to 'explain away' everything by the liberal use of words like 'because' and 'but for'. Materialism itself is a product of science, reason and mind. With all its faults, the mind has advanced knowledge and has improved the living conditions of millions of people. The problem is the longing attribute of the mind, the lust for more; it does not know when and what is enough, and it cannot balance and harmonize alternatives.

Most men have a tendency to distance themselves from other men when the latter fall into 'evil' ways, or 'get into trouble', as we say euphemistically. They adopt a 'holier-than-thou', 'touch-me-not' attitude and look down with disdain on the 'evil doers'. That again is a trick of the mind to obfuscate the reality. For one man who commits a heinous deed, there may be several others who pave the way. It does not matter how many or how few evil men are present in the world; whatever is their number, they are as human as the noblest among us and we cannot disown their thoughts and deeds. One cannot be quite sure that if one is placed in a similar circumstance, one would behave any differently. Even 'evil men' tend to think they are moral, and that they are simply doing a difficult job. Himmler, the Nazi Gestapo chief, for example, reportedly said, while referring to the extermination of Jews, 'Most of *you* must know what it means when a hundred corpses are lying side by side, or five hundred, or a thousand. To have stuck it out and at the same time remained decent fellows, that is what has made us so hard'.[70] In other words, he felt he deserved understanding, sympathy and appreciation for implementing the Final Solution. We cannot lightly dismiss that state of mind. In different degrees and in different words, we all would entertain similar thoughts while committing or condoning evil.

We cannot on the one hand talk of the oneness of humanity, and on the other hand, distance ourselves from the 'evil ones', who can be any of us or all of us. That was the reason why Mahatma Gandhi said condemn the evil *in* man, not the evil man. The reason why Jesus said those who did not sin should cast the first stone. The fact is whatever evil or good any man is capable of, any other man is capable of too. The camouflage of culture can blur to some extent, but once that is removed under some provocation or temptation, the raw nature of our evil shows up. Every man is at once a potential murderer and a mahatma, often a blend of both, and how that blend becomes behavior is hard to grasp. If we want to bask in the reflected glory of good men, we have to equally bear the burden of the acts of bad men. Some scholars like Roel Sterckx even suggest that human morality affects animal behavior, and that the cultivation of virtue in human society was a condition for the spontaneous and orderly working of the animal world, and that changes in human society would spontaneously induce behavioral changes in the animal world.[71] That means that human behavior and animal behavior are connected; perhaps the increased irritability and enhanced aggression in animals, like well-trained temple elephants suddenly turning into killers, could be a reflection of the depravity in the human world. This is an intriguing and potentially perilous line of thought. The odds seem overwhelming. In the current state of the human condition, human fragilities appear to prevail over human strengths. We seem like straws in a storm, reeds in a stream, utterly powerless to control our senses yet powerful enough to play around with the stars. Scriptures, sayings, and teachings are like pebbles thrown into a swirling sea of senses and selfishness. Pettiness and nitpicking, negativity, vanity and spite continue to rule the waves.

Money, Sex, and Power

In any discourse or contemplation of the questions of good and evil, the triad of money, power, and sex invariably arise. They are the ways we affirm our anthropological and ontological affirmations as human beings. That is because man's primary drive is to minimize physical pain and maximize pleasure, and money, power, and sex are the three channels through which he can exercise that drive. While each has a distinct character and is legitimate to human life — even with the scriptures acknowledging it — their combination changes the nature of the compound. Although each of these is dealt with separately in different contexts — for example power in conjunction with passion and love — the thrust and the setting here is the melting pot of the triad. What has happened over the last century is the virtual 'merger' of the three forces, which has become a major complicating factor in our passage to the posthuman future. Even independently, almost nothing historical has happened, nor has any great man or civilization fallen, without any of these three factors playing a pivotal role. They leave a terrible trail of carnage: careers ended, families ripped apart, hearts broken, and human potential wasted.

Money, power, and sex have legitimate — and necessary — places in human life but each of them has been corrupted: money by greed, sex by lust, and power by monopoly. Without some sort of medium like money, it will be impossible to harmonize and optimize collective skills, needs and resources. Without sex there can be no creation. And without power there can be no order. While it is a close call, money — rather our love of money — perhaps is the strongest attachment and affliction. It makes us immeasurably powerful. It is a sentiment well captured by Goethe's character Mephistopheles in the play *Faust*: "If for six stallions, I can pay, Aren't all their powers added to my store? I am a proper man and dash away, as if the legs I had were twenty-four!". Before the advent of 'money', man's 'natural' needs were taken care of *naturally*. After the advent of 'money', particularly paper money, man must have money to have access to things needed even for survival. And given the natures of mind and money, it did not stop there; it went all the way to making man a virtual vassal. Such is money's mastery over the human mind that, should God wish to save us, nothing else will work unless He enables and empowers us to wriggle out of its clasp. Or else, we need a brand new consciousness. Everything is fair not only in love and war — but even more in the matter of making money. But making money can also be virtuous if it helps in the upliftment of others. As a medium of exchange it can be a leveler. In Ayn Rand's novel *Atlas Shrugged* (1957), one of the heroes, Francisco d'Anconia, giving an oration on the meaning of money, says: "The words 'to make money' hold the essence of human morality."

Money and morality are linked because nothing else makes us take so many moral risks for its possession, retention, and aggrandizement. Because, as Karl Marx puts it in his *Economic and Philosophical Manuscripts of 1844*, "Money is the *procurer* between man's need and the object, between his life and his means of life. But *that which* mediates *my* life for me, also *mediates* the existence of other people for me. For me it is the *other* person".[72] Money begets money; in that sense as Marx puts it, it 'became pregnant'. The chief temptation of money lies in the fact that with it we can possess anything, and *that* 'anything' becomes part of us, like another brain or body, hand or leg. Even that '*I am*' could be that which one can acquire with money. Most people, given a choice between money and 'the rest', will choose money; in any case, with money, the 'rest' is easy picking. The problems we face with money, dramatically brought home by the current global financial crisis, are rooted in the nature of money itself, being constitutents of its very design — and they will continue and intensify and implode until money itself and its place in our lives is transformed. That is because money makes money, it bears and seeks interest, and in fact is created in its own absence. Today, one does not have to *have money*, to have the money or the things we need money for. Everything 'human' is monetized, and there is virtually no 'capital' in circulation of any other kind — cultural, natural, social, or spiritual. Millenniums of money creation have left us with nothing else to show or sell. Every innate human skill and natural ability has been taken away from us and mortgaged to money. Every human relationship is now a virtual hostage to money. We depend on money for everything we need to live. Everything, even an individual's worth and value, is a matter of money. It is synonymous with happiness, joy, self-esteem, success — even survival. Money — or the lack of it — is a major trigger for suicides: the list goes all the way from debt-ridden farmers to school girls denied pocket-money. Indeed, life itself has become indistinguishable from money. Although some idealists dream of human society without any manner of money or property, somewhat on the lines of the Marxist maxim 'from each according to his ability, to each according to his need', such a paradigm of human life has never existed and possibly never will; the mix of thoughts and emotions, needs and wants, passions and feelings did not evolve with that end in view. As the Irish social revolutionary William O'Brien once quipped, "when we truly discover love, capitalism will not be possible and Marxism will not be necessary."[73] We have gone a step further — or deeper. We have debased love. We made sure Marxism was stillborn, and we know now that the much-trumpeted triumph of capitalism over socialism has not made the human condition any better. If any, it has widened the chasm between 'good life' and the 'good*ness* of life'. Two of the driving forces in the human mind are avarice and lust for power. Gluttony in what we eat and consume and the desire to dominate others frame our daily life. Much of the time and energy of life is swallowed by the wants of the economic man and the perennial consumer. The stranglehold of 'more' and 'money' on the human mind shows no signs of slackening.

With money as his mascot, man has stopped living in the 'living world', in harmony with other earthly inhabitants and with Nature; he feels he needs them no more. He has created a 'Nature' of his own and made it his link to his fellow humans. The English author Somerset Maugham, in his much acclaimed work *Of Human Bondage* (1915), wrote that "money is like a sixth sense — and you can't make use of the other five without it"[74]. It has become so pervasive and intrusive in human society that there is nothing that even the best of men — be it a saint, or a monk or a *sadhu* (ascetic) — can do without its touch or shadow. More often than not, most of these men have been deeply scarred by its contact. If power is the ultimate aphrodisiac, as the American diplomat Henry Kissinger famously quipped, abundant wealth is the ultimate orgasm, an irresistible titillation. Those who do not have 'enough money' are branded as losers. The really rich automatically climb to the top of the social ladder, the powers-that-be hobnob with them; being seen in their company is a statement of having arrived. As long as two millenniums ago, the Chinese Taoist philosopher Chuang Tzu said: "To have enough is good luck, to have more than enough is harmful. This is true of all things, but especially of money."[75] 'More money' is not just one of the many 'mores' in life; this 'more' causes mayhem, almost alters the very model of thinking, and also plays heavily on how we view people who have money or those who do not have it. With other 'passions' like food, sex, or power, a phase can come when we cannot 'take it' — or even enjoy it — anymore. When something in us says 'enough'. But we can never say that about money. Money was meant as a means, but it is now the end; the substitute has become the actual good. Since everyone cannot make everything, money was expected to help produce and exchange things we need for life — food, shelter, and the trappings of civilization. Today, it produces and exchanges itself and grows independently. Is the power of money but a reflection of the power of evil, or is it simply man's inherent inability to resist anything that gives immediate pleasure? Pleasure, in all its temporal dimensions as remembrance, experienced and anticipated, is a salient part of our mental life; it has a bearing on our spiritual quest. The *Katha* Upanishad says that human beings have to constantly make a choice between things that give permanent joy or immediate pleasure, and the tragedy is that we humans tend to invariably choose the path of immediate pleasure. There are many who think that what gives pleasure is what is 'good', and what gives pain is what is 'bad'. And money is the main means for all pleasures that can be obtained through satiating the senses. For, despite the frowning of the scriptures and the disapproval of saints, its grip over the human mind has never waned; if any, it has only become tighter. The Bible says that one cannot serve God and Mammon at the same time, but that is precisely what man has been trying to do, and has done, one must grudgingly concede, somewhat successfully. What matters is that we need money, we cannot do without it; it is simply a matter of social, even physical, survival. There is a prayer in the Bible that says: "...give me neither poverty nor riches, but give me only my daily bread. Otherwise, I may have too much and disown you and say, 'who is the Lord?' Or I may become poor and steal, and so dishonor the name of my God." (*Proverbs, 30:8-9*)[76]

Someone quipped that to know what God thinks of money, look at those to whom he has given money! Well, it is hard to tell. And it was not always so. Aristotle said: "Money was intended to be used in exchange, but not to increase at interest. And this term 'interest', which means the birth of money from money, is applied to the breeding of money because the offspring resembles the parent. Wherefore of all modes of getting wealth, this is the most unnatural."[77] And Voltaire said: "When it is a question of money, everybody is of the same religion."[78] Few can match the opulence of our God-men, and very few are more ostentatiously religious than the rich. The philosopher Jacob Needleman, author of the book *The New Religions* (1970), believes that our obsession with money and compulsion for material wealth undercut personal authenticity. Money has changed the way one human relates to another, and threatens to turn man into a virtual *Homo economicus*. Man the producer/consumer is gradually losing his 'capacity for communion' with his neighbors. A segregated fellow, insulated from community, corrupted by his concupiscence for material wealth. In a 2006 study, researchers at the

Florida State University wrote: "As countries and cultures developed, money may have allowed people to acquire goods and services that enabled the pursuit of cherished goals, which in turn diminished reliance on friends and family."[79] Money gives power and highlights inequalities. If man is the measure of everything, then money is the measure of man. Deborah Price, author of the book *Money Magic* (2003) says that "making, keeping, and enjoying money isn't just about investments, salaries, inheritances, or dividends… It's also about the games people play around money and their character type in relation to it"[80]. According to Price, "Just about every decision we make, and much of our personality, is formed in some way, shape or form by our beliefs around money."[81] It equals sex as a source of the greatest joy, it equals power as an aphrodisiac, and it equals death as a source of the highest anxiety. The paradox is that, while a century or two ago, man was secretive about sex and more open about money, people today openly proclaim their sexual preferences and peccadilloes, but are silent about their wealth. While sexual satiation has its biological limitations, the desire for money is limitless.

Money's mesmerizing effect on the human mind is mind boggling, and neither reason nor psychoanalysis can adequately explain it. It is irrational and, in fact, ought to be an affront to intelligence; yet we are willing slaves. The human obsession with riches far exceeds the human need for *artha* (wealth) and *kama* (worldly gain). And it often collides with *dharma* or righteousness. In its pursuit, man brushes aside every other norm or need, restraint or constraint. It is an all-consuming passion, respects no relationship, and is capable of unleashing the darkest human instincts. No crime, fratricide, matricide, or patricide is exempt from its tentacles. No amount is too small to steal or kill for. The more one has it, the more he hungers for it. The greed for money overshadows every other greed. The irony is that money defeats the very purpose of having it; it gives neither security nor satisfaction, though the fact makes no dent in man's obsession. A moral man has to be liberated from the vice-like hold of wealth on him; but having money is not immoral. In fact, the Upanishads recognize money, *artha*, as one of the legitimate and righteous aspirations of man. Excessive money leads to obscene opulence, ostentatious lifestyle, reckless attitude and to a sense of being powerful and privileged.

Many hurdles impede man's spiritual progress, and one of the most formidable is the intoxicating incursion of money and materialism into the deepest layers of human consciousness. Can we turn them around and make them stepping stones to human progress? Some think it is possible. Jacob Needleman, for example believes that our long disinclination to grasp the emotional and spiritual effects of money on us lies at the heart of why we have come to know the price of everything, and the value of nothing, and that it could lead us to self-knowledge and turn out to be 'a tool for breaking out' of our mental prison.[82] It is his thesis that in our time the principle of personal gain is embodied in the quest for money and that our obsession with money and compulsion for material wealth undercut personal integrity. Man has been called a 'moral animal,' 'thinking animal,' and 'social animal'. The presumption is that these are the attributes that animals do not have. Above all, man is an 'economic animal' or '*Homo economicus.*' John Stuart Mill defined him as "a being who desires to possess wealth, and who is capable of judging of the comparative efficacy of means for obtaining that end"[83]. What has been called historical materialism or, in the words of Karl Marx, materialist conception of history, proposes that "it is not the consciousness of men that determines their existence, but their social being determines their consciousness."[84] In this view, it is in man's economic incarnation that he becomes a productive person. It is how humans 'make the means to live' that shape their personalities and predispositions. It is the economic processes that delineate the Man—Nature relationship. Making money, saving money and spending money, often all at the same time, become the primary passion and preoccupation. Man's relationship with others is based primarily on their economic use to him, commodities that exist for his economic gain. It is to a large extent, this single-minded pursuit of his economic agenda that has dwarfed his spiritual persona.

Obviously, human society being far more complex than that of the other species and our wants being almost limitless and multiple, some kind of money and some sort of economy are essential to bring order, and for making the human whole more than the sum of its parts. The question is really not *if* we need an economic life, but of *what kind.* The growing importance of the economic aspect of human life, and the attendant economic disparities and inequities within and among societies, raise moral questions. How should a person 'make a living'? How much of it can he use for his needs and wants? What is his obligation to help those less fortunate, who are unable to earn enough to lead a life of bare dignity? And how should he channel his help? Is a person morally entitled to spend as he likes so long as he conforms to the law of the land? How does one become eligible for the aid of other people or of the State? Is a person morally righteous or evil if he earns his wealth legally but does not help others, or does not help them proportionately? How does one morally view a person who illegally and immorally makes millions and spends much of it on charity? Given the so-called triumph of capitalism over socialism in the world and the thirst for spiritualism the world over, these are issues that deserve serious introspection. The American industrialist-philanthropist John D. Rockefeller said "When a man has accumulated a sum of money within the law, that is to say, in the legally correct way, the people no longer have any right to share in the earnings resulting from the accumulation."[85] The 'philosophy' is, what I do with what I earn, accumulate and how I spend, if I am law abiding, is between me and my conscience. This is the refrain, not of the parasites of the society but of the 'honest' and 'honorable'; Rockefeller himself was prince among such people. That doctrine, seemingly flawless, has many loopholes: one, the law regulates only our minimal social obligation, not personal responsibility; two, there is a lot of moral space that is not covered by the State and society; and three, our conscience itself is slumbering and is corrupted by our 'winner-takes-all' culture.

While money is the metaphor for modern man, sex is the signature of our civilization. We associate it with sin and shame, perhaps more than with anything else, and it is also a primary source of sensory pleasure. 'The subject of sex' Edward Carpenter wrote in 1896 at the beginning of his seminal work *Love's Coming of Age*, 'is difficult to deal with'. Several decades later, despite new tools and the emergence of a new scientific field, sexology, the subject has only become more complex and intractable; the fog over it has become more impenetrable. Whatever was the origin and original intent when it sprouted first, its relationship with the human is now double-faced: sex controls man, and it is also controlled by him through technology.

Human sexuality exists today in a sort of moral vacuum, a protean force and a source of pleasure and pain, agony and ecstasy, anxiety and affirmation, a reason for being, and an overpowering cause for killing. There is a battle for the future of sexuality, and how it emerges in the end, and the process leading to it, might have much to do with our own future. In our contemporary culture, people make money off sex, as well as use sex to make money. And use it as a means to acquire power, and use power as a means for sex. At the same time, extreme poverty can induce or seduce a person to trade sex for money. It is the hallmark of the affluent as well as of the extreme poor. The 'in between'— that is, those who do not have to sell sex to buy their basic necessities, but who need money to indulge in cosmetics and high-end consumer goods— do not make a living on sex, but use it sometimes to go higher on the social or professional ladder. The two are intertwined— 'Sex and Money' as they are called. According to one survey that appeared in the business magazine Market Watch some years ago, 'the richer you are... the better sex you have', and that 'the majority of men and women credit their private wealth with achieving a better sex life'. In the survey, 'three-quarters of men cited more frequent sex and a greater variety of partners as the primary benefits of having wealth'.[86] And then we have that special seductive something called 'sex appeal', which is the bedrock of the fashion, entertainment, and movie industries. The cliché goes that, in the advertising and consumer industries, the fail-safe way to attract an audience and to sell is through the projection of sex. While it is socially acceptable to show 'sex appeal' and to use it to make money, it is deemed both a crime and a sin to actually 'sell sex'. We can, legally and even ethically, seduce and sell everything or anybody by the allure or use of sex, save sex itself. The premise is that sex is not a skill, or a product or a commodity. But the irony is, in our society where sex and money are intertwined, a direct trade-off between the two is socially, and in most countries, legally, prohibited.

And then we have two other 'industries' that owe their existence to sex: prostitution and pornography. We may prefer to turn a Nelson's eye to it, but the rude reality is that sex has become so much a part of us — so much our way of life, so much of what we see, hear and read, occupying so much of our psychic space, and its shadow likely to extend so large on the human future — that we have to ask ourselves: are we true to God and His intent? What *was* the intent? God created a 'male' and a 'female' as opposed to two men or two women, to be, in the language of the Bible, fruitful and to multiply by 'becoming one flesh'. And to ensure that nothing man creates could rival that ecstasy, God formed the male and the female *bodies*. Much theological debate has focused on the question: does human sexuality strictly circumscribe to multiplication through procreation, or does it have a pleasurable purpose? Without built-in pleasure, God knew that man might shy away from sex and he made the union ecstatic, but he could not make every act automatic and instantaneous for begetting children. Therefore, sex became a source of both procreation and recreation, and pleasure is the incentive and insurance for multiplication.

Scientists tell us that sexual reproduction appeared over a billion years ago, and it is amazing that it has survived and almost stayed the same for so long. When it came to man, the Greeks thought that a jealous God separated the sexes and dared them to find their other halves before they became infertile. As a sequel, a wag puts it: man spends nine months struggling to find a way out of the womb, and the rest of his life in search of another. Although the dynamics of reproduction have somewhat changed due to technology, the different 'techniques' of mating have not changed (the *Kama Sutra* is still the standard book!), but the urge for sex has grown stronger, fuelled by the power of the visual image, and its grip over the human mind has become even tighter. Basically there are three broad views of sex in human affairs: *Sexual Pragmatism* treats sex as nothing more than just another appetite that is inevitable, an integral part of the pantheon of inherent human desires, no more despicable than our need to eat or breathe. And since you cannot stop it, 'just go with the flow' and allow yourself to go wherever the desire leads you to. In short, all sex is right if it is safe. From the perspective of *Sexual Animalism*, sex is an animal passion that lowers us; a necessary evil since it is the only way to procreate. This view loathes sexuality but tolerates it as a way to leave a legacy to our children. *Sexual Romanticism* sees sex as a creative self-expression, but repressed. It proposes that every human being is born with a healthy sexual desire, but it is twisted by the influence of society and its culture. Of the three, it is the first that has gained the upper hand in recent human history. In the minds of many people, sex is not only a 'basic desire' but, more importantly a desire that can be endlessly satiated with or without money and/or power. To top it, we can still 'make money' and acquire or augment power. With sex we have multiple choices — we can be either a superman or a supermodel, a plain Jane or a Cleopatra, young or old; we can get sex free or pay for it or earn from it; sex can be an instrument of power or of the powerless; it gives us ecstasy and entertainment like nothing else.

And then we have what has come to be called 'spiritual sex'. It has two dimensions: the seamy and the sacred. The seamy or the sordid dimension is its association with pseudo-religious 'gurus' and goons, who exploit the love and devotion of their followers for their personal gratification. While it has always been an occasional aberration, it has become far more frequent in recent times, for two reasons. One, in today's sexually charged culture, it is far more difficult for the people with some religious or spiritual authority to resist the temptation of trespass; it is too difficult to pass up the opportunity. Two, it reflects the sense of disquiet, desperation, and deprivation that mark millions of lives. So many are searching for something to help them overcome a problem, or simply find some solace, that when a charismatic 'spiritual master' comes along and offers some comfort, all taboos break down and offerings are made in flesh to a 'god'.

On the other hand, the sacred dimension of spiritual sex is timeless. It has been a long-held article of faith that sexuality is a potent source of energy, and that if it is controlled, channeled or harvested it could enable man to transcend the bounds of being human. It is believed that sexual energy can be channeled or redirected upward to develop our energy centers, as a way to our spiritual evolution (as, for example, in the Hindu chakra system that comprises seven fields of energy in the human body). Celibacy, enjoined upon priests, nuns and monks, is one way. There are also techniques of spiritual or sacred sex for couples, like *karezza* in the West and *tantra* in India. They are concerned with the conservation and transmutation of sexual energies for spiritual growth. Whichever way one looks at it, we are a sexually lost species. There is so much sexuality and so little satisfaction. Hundreds of books have been written — like the *Kama Sutra* — on how to achieve sexual ecstasy. We have experimented with numerous methods to find sexual peace (monogamy, polygamy, polyandry, casual sex, ceremonial sex, commercial sex, etc.), but lust remains at large, unvanquished, unquenched.

Having examined 'money' and 'sex', let us now look at the third constituent of the triad — *power*. Power closely connects the two, money and sex. Money is power and power is money. Sex is power, too, and power is sex. Power, which is the ability to control the surrounding environment (including individuals) is intrinsic to human nature; it is a means to prevail upon, to control and to subdue another life. Everyone wants to be powerful. No one wants to be weak and vulnerable. Power manifests as coercion, control, and authority. In George Orwell's novel *Nineteen Eighty-Four* (1949), O'Brien, the main antagonist, makes several telling comments about 'power'. While describing the *Party*'s vision of the future, he says (to Winston Smith, the protagonist): 'we are the priests of power' and 'power is in inflicting pain and humiliation'. O'Brien says that there will always be the 'intoxication of power, constantly increasing and constantly growing subtler'. And he tells Winston to visualize the future as a boot trampling on a human face. That description aptly captures the grip of power on the human consciousness. Almost no one — be it a saint or sinner, or a spiritual or sensual or secular person — can deny having harbored, either consciously or unconsciously, a yen for power. As Friedrich Nietzsche chillingly captured the importance of power in human life: being 'good' is that which enhances the feeling of power, the *will* to power, and the power *itself* in man; and 'bad' is that which proceeds from weakness; and 'happiness' is the feeling that the power is increasing — and that resistance has been overcome. And what matters is not contentment, but more power; not peace at any price, but war; not virtue, but competence. And to top it all, the first principle of our humanism is that the weak and the unsuccessful should perish and, indeed, they even ought to be *helped* to perish. Human thirst for power entails, as described by Steven Lukes (*Power: A Radical View*, 1974), an imposition of internal constraints, and those vulnerable to it acquire beliefs that induce them to consent to domination by either coercive or persuasive means. We all know the power of power every minute of our lives. It is a shadow we cannot run away from because that is *our* shadow. How we exercise it — or submit to it — is the test of our character. No high marks on either count. The English historian Lord Acton famously said that 'power corrupts, and absolute power corrupts absolutely'; it is in the nature of power itself to seek unchallenged power. Bernard Loomer, the American theologian said, "The problem of power is as ancient as the age of man. The presence of power is manifest wherever two or more people are gathered together and have any kind of relationship. Its deeper and sometimes darker qualities emerge as soon as the omnipresent factor of inequality makes itself felt."[87] Not only Scott Fitzgerald's 'very rich' but also the 'very powerful' belong to a different genre. The scent of power easily seduces most men. Abraham Lincoln said "Nearly all men can stand the test of adversity, but if you want to test a man's character, give him power."[88] Why the human animal alone is so singularly single-minded and ruthlessly relentless about gaining dominance — physical, psychological or emotional — over another person defies comprehension. What deep-seated urge or sadistic instinct does that fulfill? How does humiliating another person, which dominance is all about, make one feel better or superior? Yet, power is also necessary to protect the weak and the vulnerable, and also for good governance. Man has long tried to find a balance between the two competing factors, but not very successfully, as history shows. Since the possession and retention of power often requires aggressiveness and unscrupulousness, those who wield power rarely happen to be the right kind. It is therefore a state of 'double jeopardy'; good men do not come to power, and power corrupts those who come to power.

End, Means, and Violence

Whether it is pursuit of power, pleasure, or profit, we often face the ethical dilemma: does the end justify the means or do the means justify the end? And to what extent should we tolerate or embrace violence as a means to achieve a just end? What takes precedence in the crucible of life, with so many competing demands, desires, ambitions, temptations, and obligations, is the question. We get mixed messages from the scriptures. Our incapacity — both cognitive and emotional — to mingle, manage and marry them has impeded our search for our real identity and erupts as violence, which tends to spread like a virus. It is, in one sense, the daily dilemma that dogs us every step of the way. It has a bearing on our moral sense of right and wrong and on our modes of values and principles that determine our choices. Leon Trotsky tried to outflank the dichotomy and said that the end may justify the means so long as there is something that justifies the end, signaling the interconnectivity of the two. We often justify our actions as '*there is no other way*', implying several things at the same time: that it is a matter of survival; that the end justifies the means, or that it is a lesser evil in our troubled times. That rationale or defense is proffered by almost everyone, from 'honorable' men to self-serving politicians. If what you want to achieve is 'good', does the manner in which you set out to achieve it matter? The dialectic of Means and Ends is of deep historical, ethical, and philosophical significance. If one cannot, as is often the reality, combine the two, which is more moral and more important — the Means or the End? Then again, the line between the end and the method is not as sharply drawn as we like to think; and often, an end is also a means, and a means is an end, from a different perspective. That is the quandary that crops up ever so often in the drama of life. We often know what we ought to do, but 'end up' doing the opposite for all kinds of reasons, most often because of fear or the lure of the consequences. Most of us agree on what we want in society: peace, justice, love, happiness; but we disagree on how to achieve them. Indeed, in a social fabric based on the supply-and-demand principle, all these are social products like any commodity, the excess of which might reduce their worth and value. Most people also agree that the plethora of problems the world faces have to be resolved or managed, but widely disagree on the ways this can be achieved, since inevitably there is a price to be paid, an inconvenience to be shared. Making someone else bear the entire burden — like making lifestyle changes and paying an economic price for a righteous global end, such as restoring the balance of Nature — is tantamount to adopting wrong means. Sometimes, the end justifies the means; at other times, the means become the measure of righteousness. That message comes loud and clear from the epics like the Mahabharata and the Ramayana. The debate about means and ends once again demonstrates that there are no absolutes in nature, not even in regard to means and ends. The only 'relative absolute' is that the larger good always, whether it is a means or an end, must prevail over the smaller good, be it the means or the end.

The human intellect, or whatever it is that churns inside us, that transforms data into decisions, contemplation into choices, and then comes out as actions and behavior, has not been able to balance and unify the often conflicting pulls and pressures, tensions and temptations, that are innate and incidental to human life, and to ensure that spontaneous individual lives and reflexive actions contribute to, not detract, the common good. What we have 'become' is not what we would *like* to become. The vital interests of the majority of people fall by the wayside on the human march, and the mainstream has often failed to ensure dignity to the dispossessed and to offer hope to the men on the margins. And that is where humankind has almost consistently gone wrong, culminating in the crises that the world faces today. Whatever goes on inside our consciousness that results in choosing a course of action that affects our lives and the lives of others, has more often than not fallen short of the action needed. We live in a world where so many people continue to make the same old decisions and repeatedly suffer the same kind of consequences. Our decisions often reflect our desires, and our desires reflect our 'sense of life' and the state of our consciousness. We rely almost exclusively on our cognitive processes, our 'rational' reasoning capacity, and that by itself has demonstrably been both inadequate and inappropriate. It is easier to go for an individual goal, but when it comes to the world at large, questions arise about equity and proportionality, about whose need is more pressing, and about who shares the costs and how — issues that the human mind is just not adequately equipped to resolve. The matter of 'ends and means' — which incidentally is the title of Aldous Huxley's book (1937) that deals with human behavior — is also a test of man distinguishing himself as a 'moral animal'; after all, for animals, the end is all that matters. Furthermore the consequences of any action form the basis for a moral verdict on the action itself (*consequentialism*). And 'consequences' pertain not only to the desired end but also to the means. Someone said that results are what you expect, and consequences are what you get! The human tendency is to evade and to escape from unwelcome consequences But we cannot avoid the consequences of evading or escaping from consequences. We can dodge responsibilities, but we cannot avoid the consequences of dodging. This applies not only to individuals but also collectively to our species. In the case of individual consequences, they might well linger even after death, and for the species, they can snowball from generation to generation. 'Means' is an action a person engages in, with the intention of bringing about a certain result or an 'end.' The 'end' has initially only an ideal existence, and the resultant End, the actual outcome of the adopted Means, may be quite different from the abstract End for which the Means was adopted in the first place. Both Means and Ends are therefore processes which are in greater or lesser contradiction with one another throughout their development. They are intertwined but not interdependent. Ends do justify the means, and means justify the ends. Means refer to the existing conditions, while the end is the desirable state. That creates conflict and confronts us with a choice. Without 'adequate' tools or means, there can be no end, but the question is what is 'adequate', and perhaps even more importantly, what is 'appropriate' to get that adequacy. Means can also be divided into 'moral' means and 'mandatory' means; the latter refers to what the society or the law prescribes. The doctrine "The end justifies the means," often attributed to the famous or notorious Machiavelli, the author of the classic work *Prince* (1532), captures this school of thought. More accurately, Machiavelli made a sharp distinction between *having* good qualities that are unnecessary and even injurious, and *appearing to have* them, which is useful.

The 'conflict' between means and ends is nowhere more sharply etched in human affairs than on the issues of violence, war and peace. All three are implicit and embedded in Nature, but how they shape up and surface in the morass of life raises important questions. In a world suffused with chaos and hatred, it is 'logical' to ask if the quest for peace itself is morbid and suicidal, the sole preserve of philosophers, evangelists and utopians. Is the idea of peace a mistake, a red herring, to let our worst instincts go unchallenged? Can it ever be practiced as a primary value? If peace is the end, can violence and war be the means? Are we morally secured in being 'benignly' violent to curb or contain 'malignant' violence or to achieve a noble end? Can war of any kind be a means to peace of any ilk? Is any 'peace' better than any 'war'? Can we, for an instance, posit that 'peace' under Nazi occupation was better than the killing of 'innocent' German civilians? It has been said that only three species engage in 'war'— humans, chimpanzees, and ants. Among humans, fighting seems so natural, and warfare so pervasive and historically constant, that we are often tempted to attribute it to some innate predisposition for sadism and slaughter — a gene, perhaps, manifested as a murderous hormone. The earliest archeological evidence of war is from around 12,000 years ago, well before such innovations as capitalism and cities and at the very beginning of settled agricultural life. Sweeping through recorded history, one can find a predilection for warfare among hunter-gatherers, herding and farming people, industrial and even post-industrial societies, democracies, and dictatorships. But then, what is 'war' and what is peace? With changing dynamics of warfare and violence, that question has become more pertinent than ever. And it is nearer home than ever.

Peace has five dimensions: *individual* peace, *family* peace, peace in *society*, peace in the *nation*, and peace on the *planet*. They are like concentric circles with the individual consciousness at the center, which is, in other words, the inner sense of calm and serenity and soulfulness. Further, peace by itself and unto itself is sometimes of little value. What has been called 'positive peace' is part of a triad, the other two being *justice* and *wholeness* (or well-being). The other triad is *peace*-making, *peace*keeping, and *peace* building. In a world that is full of chaos and hatred, violence and venality, some well-meaning 'pragmatists' are tempted to ask if the quest for peace itself is morbid and suicidal, best left to the labors and the levers of philosophers, evangelists and other such hopefuls.

Violent death is snatching more and more people every day, and it seems so random and so pointless. It is happening with increasing rapidity and randomness, and it raises the age-old question why violent, untimely death spares most of us, yet embraces some unlucky few, and what is it that separates the two. It is not death *per se* that is illogical or inexplicable; it is how it gobbles different people differently. It seems to delight in our discomfiture and in our being 'surprised' every time it comes home somewhere. There seems to be no 'rational' reason why someone we know is dead and why we are not. Neither genes, nor health nor habitat or circumstance can explain it. If death — why not, where, when and how — is beyond the play of what we do or do not do in daily life, and if it is not all senseless randomness, then why does it happen the way it happens? The ominous phrase 'wrong time, wrong place' seems scribbled all over our lives. Minutes and inches make a difference in death's fateful lottery. Destiny is a matter of 'detail'. But in every fated action, there is an element of human choice, and in every choice there is an unseen hand of fate. What we do not know are the points of intersection and conjunction. While many 'rationalists' might decry the idea of a deterministic fate, there are few who do not believe in luck, which someone said is 'probability personalized'. For many, good luck is what they have earned, and bad luck is an unfair and unjustified penalty. But they do not mind — and even welcome it — if 'bad luck' visits other people. While we might not end up where we want to be, it is not uncommon that we end up where we need to be. The Jewish Kabbalah teaches that God's drama plays out, right before our very own eyes. Every one of us is among God's cast of players. God's drama requires, like any play, villains, victims and heroes, bystanders, bit players, and active participants. No one plays the same part all the time. Not only what part we play but how we play it has a bearing on what roles we enact in future.

The real theater of war — and peace — is *within* us. While war has been generally viewed as barbarous, the scriptures also recognize that war can be just and even holy, cleansing and even necessary for a moral world, a *dharma yudh*, as it is called in Hinduism, and *jihad* in Islam. From time immemorial, from the Neolithic Age to the Modern Age, man has dreamed of peace, peace within and peace without; peace for the self and peace in the world. "War is peace" was one of the slogans on the façade of the Ministry of Truth (*Minitrue*) in George Orwell's dystopian book *Nineteen Eighty-Four*. A quarter-century after Orwell's imagined future has passed, the phrase sums up the state of the world and the mind of man in a number of ways. One does not really know which is the lesser or the greater evil: the charade of perpetual pseudo-peace, or the formal state of war. Every individual craves for 'peace of mind'. As long as man has been a conscious being, the battle cry for peace has been the constant refrain. Increasingly, that agonizing 'cry', that longing, is leading to suicide. Many *mantras* in the Vedas end with a prayer for universal peace, rendered by the chant *Om shanti, shanti, shanti*. Some scholars say that the very word 'Islam' means peace. The often-used expression '*salaam*' is 'peace be upon you'. Yet, we are living in a world that enjoys little, if any, peace. Everything human is soaked in violence; it has crept into every crevice of our consciousness. It has become virtually impossible to live without violence. Everyone is scarred by it, either as the perpetrator or as the victim, mostly a mix of both. Our heroes, our mythology, our epics, even many of our gods are examples of nonviolence and peace. Hatred, hostility, violence, and wars have become the dominant forces in shaping human history. As Huxley said in his essay *Ends and Means,* every road towards a better state of society is blocked, sooner or later — by war, by threats of war, by preparations for war. Opinions vary on the question whether war-making is purely a human passion, or if it has a solid base in Nature. One can argue from both ends, and it depends on what 'war' is in non-human terms. But one thing is incontrovertible: that man is unique, as Huxley says, in 'organizing the mass murder of his own species', particularly of its young and strong. And as pleasure-seeking creatures, we must admit that there is pleasure in destructiveness. Why do humans, of many affiliations, want or think that they are better off with war? This too has been much debated, and the causes and drives vary from giving a purpose to life, to enjoying the goodies from the lawlessness of war, to being an escape from boredom, the bitter fruit of nationalism, the interests of the military-industrial complex, political ambition of the 'new class', religious righteousness, etc. In Huxley's opinion, the only way to eliminate war is to abolish the arms industry. But these are all symptoms; the root of the trouble is the *mind*, and its offspring, *human culture*.

Not only men but even the gods have used violence to achieve the 'good' end. Down the ages, all *rakshasas* (demons) have been destroyed by the gods through violence, not through inducing repentance or submission or conversion. In the Bhagavad Gita, Krishna proclaims that God will come down to earth from time to time to 'destroy' evil-doers and to protect the righteous. That is because killing in that context is *liberation*. Like death being considered as the end of life, killing as a 'bad' action is also a human cultural attribute. There is a double standard we adopt about killing. We are trained to think that any death other than by disease or debilitation is 'killing', and that any human intervention in the 'process' of death is sinful and unethical. Yet, we do try desperately to ward death off, for example, when someone dear to us is in a critical medical condition, and we plead with the doctors to prolong the patient's life at any cost and by any means; but, since doctors too are human, this is tantamount to human intercession. In this line of thought, the right to bring to a closure the agony and ecstasy of life is not of the 'owner' of that life, but of the disease and the divine will. That 'right' is given by Nature to the bacteria, virus, fungus, or parasite, or to an out-of-control automobile, but not to the one who suffers the consequence. The logic is that, we have no hand in where and how and when we are born, and death should be regarded in similar terms. But we do not adopt the same logic in between; we do not wish to let Nature have much to do with how we live. It is *relative* peace, not perfect bliss, that man craves for, even if he himself is violent within. The real problem is three-fold: As the Buddha said, while peace comes from within, we seek it without. Instead of learning to cope with conflict, we try to eliminate it altogether. We methodically, and even painstakingly, create a culture of violence, and hope and expect that we — in particular, our young — remain untarnished.

As a result, every aspect of human life: personal, social, economic, political and religious, is marked by anger, acrimony, aggression, coercion, callousness and cruelty in thought, word, and deed. It manifests both in interpersonal interactions, and in international affairs — and in our attitude toward Nature. Whether it is climate change or a shattered marriage, the source is the same. The theater of terror is the mind. We cannot solve any problem unless we are able to tame, contain, and channel the rage within. The trouble comes when we try to exorcize it from the face of the earth, as if it is some kind of extraterrestrial force. On the contrary, it might well be only an earthly phenomenon. And like inequality, it would be futile to aim at the opposite, that of absolute nonviolence, perfect peace and a human world devoid of aggression. That would be a wasted effort, and can again do more harm than good. It does not mean that we should condone, encourage or abet the killers and rapists, and follow the adage 'if we cannot stop it, join the party'. Even if it is 'natural' and 'rational', it is not inevitable or universal; we can, as human beings, have the innate ability to go beyond biology and even Nature. What we need to do is to shift our focus from conflict elimination to conflict management or resolution, and transform our instinct for aggression into a force to fight for equity and justice. Nowadays, most adversarial groups seem incapable of negotiating peaceful consensus solutions to problems, especially with those that are perceived as even *more* stubbornly doctrinal than they really are. And we have to look at the scenario from a broader perspective of the species, not of aberrant individuals afflicted with a variety of psychological syndromes, or of even deviant ethnic and religious zealotry. For violence is not, as we instinctively assume, only murder or bodily injury; it can be 'body language; it could be gross insensitivity to the feelings of others.' We condemn violence as if it is some kind of an alien implant. On the other hand, it is innate and built into the very fabric of Nature. Violence also depends on the cause and the purpose behind it. What is the goal? What is the choice? What is the cost of nonviolence? These are some of the questions that need to be addressed. And then, there is what is called 'structural violence', which arises when essential social resources are unfairly distributed, forcing some to lead subhuman lives, in conditions of extreme poverty and disentitlement. Violence has always been the weapon of the oppressor or the conqueror, a means to impose will, and inflict physical or mental injury on another person. It resides in every individual like a volcano, dormant for much of life. Why, when, and how the lava surfaces in some (and not in others) remains unclear. But violence is now the preferred choice of the oppressed and the disadvantaged too; they feel that it is the only way their voice can be heard, the only way to assert their rights and to get their due. Often, we refrain from violence only when we fear the greater violence of the 'other' party.

Although the contemporary human being might appear to be the most violent, the ancestry of human violence goes far back into antiquity. Alongside evolution, man has turned from a prey to a predator, the hunted to a hunter. What he had tried to fight, he has now become. With time, this transformation has only become more pervasive and lethal than ever before, because the tools available to man have become far more deadly. Today, no place or dimension of life is sacrosanct, be it a school or a street, home or workplace, dormitory or a dungeon, sexual or social, urban or rural. Violence is deemed as the short-cut to success, to be 'rich and famous'; no quarrel is too trivial, no cause too lofty. The scriptures are ambivalent about it: while they expressly sanction righteous violence, they leave key questions unanswered — who judges and determines which violence is righteous and which is not? As a result, religion and revenge are merging; one's own life is offered as a wager, as a worthy price for someone else's. The maxim that everything is fair in love and war is truer than ever before. And the common thread is violence, to 'violate' the dignity, integrity and self-respect of an individual or a country. In love, it is merely 'if I can't have you, no one else should'; in war, it is distilled violence. In love, it is the fear of loss of control, and in war, it is absolute control and conquest. While violence is integral to Nature and all species exhibit it in varying ways, human violence is clearly more vicious because it is often laced with loads of malice. And while physical violence is transparent and ugly, the wounding words of verbal violence leave more lasting scars and terribly wrenched souls. While gruesome killings get bigger headlines, it is the subtler and more insidious and incestuous forms of killing that tarnish every life. The *wellspring* of violence has been the subject of long-standing reflection — does violence have its root in biology or ecology? is it genetic or environmental? what combination of factors lead to aggressive behavior? The British historian Arnold Toynbee wrote: "There is a persistent vein of violence and cruelty in human nature. All human beings are responsible for man's inhumanity to man and we all need forgiveness because we know that we are sinning against the light."[89] Some say the villain is the male hormone testosterone, which is present even in women; others say that violence happens simply on the spur of the moment. There are some evolutionary psychologists like Randy Thornhill (*A Natural History of Rape*, 2000), who say that some of the things we abhor most, such as rape, might actually be adaptations from the Stone Age and which are now encoded in our genes. In other words, there could be a 'rape gene' lurking in some dark corner of the consciousness of many men!

Although many scientists disagree on the roots of rape, the fact is that sexual violence now occupies a huge chunk of human violence, and it seems to reveal both an act of violence and an act of lust. Most human relationships have a streak of subtle violence, and this is responsible in no small measure to the coarsening of human life. Our darkest side often erupts in close relationships. It is a clash of egos, each trying to fulfill a desire at the expense of the other, each trying to take more from the other and give, if any, far less. There is probably no such thing as 'non-violence'; it is either 'soft violence' or 'hard violence'. Glaring at another person is soft violence; physically hitting him or her is hard violence. It is doubtful if there has ever been any human being who has led a truly non-violent life. The conundrum is that as a 'social animal', relationships that connect one human to another are integral to human life, but they also erode in different degrees the integrity of human individuality. Every relationship is both potentially synergetic and a restraint. The inability to strike the right balance between the two imperatives of identity and interdependence, intimacy and integrity, leads to intolerance and violence. We think of violence as an act of commission, something we *do*. We have singularly failed to harmonize the need to protect the autonomy of the human subject with the objective of human solidarity. We think it is all right if we directly do not *do* something bad. We are a species steeped in violence and we cannot evade or escape the collective responsibility. Much of our violence stems from the pursuit of money, power, and sex. But it is more than that. Denying dignity is violence; extreme poverty is violence; injustice is violence; intolerance is violence; ill will is violence; evil thought is violence. Non-action in a good cause is violence. Their spin-off is more widespread and long lasting, and they do more damage to humanity than an individual aberration. It has been said that the only thing needed for evil to triumph is for good men to do nothing. That is violence in itself.

Since time immemorial, man has been dreaming about a 'world without war' or peace without war, while at the same time waging war in every conceivable form of collectivity — family, tribe, city-state, kingdom, empire and sovereign state — and destroying every opportunity for enduring peace. But the one 'war' that we must fight (and often do not) is within; in the depths of our own mind and consciousness, between the divine and the demonic, which the Bhagavad Gita says, are innate in every human being. It is a truism that is true that the history of war is the history of humankind. The British historian Eric Hobsbawm calculates that 187 million people have died from wars in the last century. That is more than the total world population a thousand years ago — and about a tenth of the world's population at the beginning of the last 100 years.[90] Experts have long debated if we are 'hardwired' for violence and war, or if it is merely an 'acquired addiction'. Whatever it is, and perhaps a mix of both, modern man has never lived in a world without war, whether his war was for class or caste, ethnic or civil, domestic or gender, religious or race. Technology and warfare have always been intimately connected from the earliest times. Writers like Quincy Wright say that technology has played the same role in modern wars as instinct played in animal warfare. From the 20th century onwards, war has become more menacing, more indiscriminate, more sophisticated, and more like a massacre, and entails more and more cruelty and suffering. What technology has done is to increase the lethal power of a single weapon exponentially, and to dramatically reduce the cumulative cost and make it 'affordable' to many more people and States than ever before. And man now has a weapon of war, the nuclear bomb, which is too terrible to use. How long it will stay that way is anybody's guess.

The apologists of war justify massacres and mass mutilation as a part of Nature, even necessary for its equilibrium, and not exclusive to humans. It bears some reflection and retrospective. One must draw a distinction between violence and war; all wars are violent but not all violence is war. The English poet Alfred Tennyson wrote of 'Nature red in tooth and claw'. But violence and being bloodthirsty is not warlike. Aldous Huxley addressed this issue in another manner: "Conflict is certainly common in the animal kingdom. But, with very rare exceptions, conflict is between isolated individuals. 'War' in the sense of conflict between armies exists among certain species of social insects. But it is significant that these insects do not make war on members of their own species, only on those of other species. Man is probably unique in making war on his own species."[91] Be that as it may, and precisely because it is a singular human invention, war will never end. As Stanley Baldwin, three times prime minister of Britain, put it: "War would end if the dead could return."[92] Should that ever happen, we will not be around to exchange notes, we cannot bet on that. And not many 'rational' men will agree with the Roman philosopher Cicero's words: "I prefer the most unfair peace to the most righteous war."[93] For many, such an attitude would amount to cowardice, and shameful surrender to evil and rank selfishness. Waging war is a struggle for power, for territory; in its essence every war also involves a collision of egos, of rulers, of nations and of societies. According to the 'dualistic view', there exists a completely independent material sphere, given to violence, separate from and opposed to our essential spiritual side. But everything material is however only a symbol and sign, everything external is but a manifestation of the internal, everything coercive is also a free choice. We can make sense of war only with a monistic point of view, i.e., seeing in it the symbolism of what transpires within spiritual activity. We can fantasize that war happens in the heavens, within other planes of being, within the depths of dark spirits. Physical violence or murder is not something substantial in itself, as an independent reality — it is a sign of inward violence, committing evil within the spiritual activity. The nature of war, as a manifestation of material violence, is purely reflective, a sign, symptomatic, not something independent of our essence. War is not the source of evil, but rather a reflection in evil, the sign of the existence of inner evil and sickness in our consciousness. Humans have not found a way to create joy and happiness through service and surrender. The scriptures extol the transformative power of service and that should be the matter of self-training in daily life. If every act we do includes an element of service to someone else, man or God, it could be a potent cleanser of our consciousness. The theosophist Annie Besant said that every individual who happens to be with us at any particular moment is the person given to us by God to serve at that moment. She reminds us that that person could be the one that God wants to help through us. And in serving, we also surrender, and through surrender we can subdue our ego. By subduing our ego we attain a state fit for selfless service.

Without making any headway towards that goal of serving for the sake of service, not for the pleasure of serving, loving not for the sake of love but as an instrument of God, we will never be in harmony. Despite the Biblical exhortation to turn swords into plowshares and spears into pruning hooks, and that no nation shall lift up swords against another nation, wars have been waged, and they have only been gaining in ferocity, brutality, and violence. The arms race among nations is getting more and more ferocious, and exponentially expensive. Man believes that a weapon is power, and power means control and control leads to conquest. For example, since the end of the Second World War in 1945, when peace was supposedly restored in the world, it is estimated that 150 to 160 'wars' were waged around the world till the end of the century, killing an estimated 33 to 40 million people, including civilians.[94] Our resource allocation is the real touchstone for our social priorities. Statistics reveal that the world military expenditure in 2006 is estimated to have reached $1,204 billion in current dollars; this represents a 3.5 per cent increase in real terms since 2005, and a 37 per cent increase over the 10-year period since 1997. One single country, the United States of America, is responsible for about 80 per cent of the increase in 2005, and its military expenditure now accounts for almost half of the world's total. The need for diversion from military expenditure to programs focused on poverty eradication is the constant refrain in every 'economic' international declaration and 'plan of action'. But they remain just that — declarations and plans bereft of political will.

The reality is that man will never exhaust a cause for killing another human being and he will always look for more and more deadly weapons of mass destruction. And war offers the most legitimately lethal way of homicide with the greatest impact. War is pure violence; it is violence on a grand scale, when thousands die and murders are committed in the holy name of national honor; when unspeakable horrors are committed with the silent complicity of millions more, when every canon of 'civilized behavior' is sacrificed with a 'clear conscience' by the perpetrators. War is 'necrophilia,' 'pure sin, with its goals of hatred and destruction.' It bestows on some humans "the godlike power that comes with the license to kill with impunity."[95] It is a time when "murder goes unpunished and is often rewarded."[96] War offers a socially-sanctioned vehicle to unleash man's worst instincts and to fulfill his darkest desires. It is the most corrosive of human activity. The causes for war are as varied as the facets in the human personality. War has done much to dehumanize humanity and to *coarsen* the human condition. And it has provided man with a societal, if not moral, legitimacy for some of his lowest and basest instincts without the need for remorse or retribution or a sense of shame and guilt. If one wants to give free and full play to man's sadistic instincts, one simply needs to join one of the wars that rage around, declared or undeclared: civil wars, ethnic wars, economic wars, religious wars and often a mix of some or all of these. Many times, more people have been murdered or maimed in these conflicts than wars between States. For example, since the civil war broke out in the Democratic Republic of Congo (DRC) in 1998, 3.3 million people were reported to have perished by November 2002, many due to sickness and famine caused by the conflict. The Rwandan genocide of Tutsis and moderate Hutus in the 1990s itself claimed over 800,000 lives. Famine, caused by widespread shortage or non affordability of food, is a symptom of man's inability to share as well as his callousness towards Nature. Despite the undoubted economic gains enjoyed by humanity over the recent past, it is estimated that nearly 70 million people have died due to famine in the 20th century alone. And the recent killings of over 400,000 people in Darfur, Sudan is a reminder that nothing has changed and we, as a species, are addicted to killing each other, whether it is through war or a civil war, or ethnic cleansing or religious reprisal. And if we somehow exhaust all of these options, we will invent new ones. How else can one explain the chilling fact that the world currently spends 11 times more money killing each other than trying to stop the innocent from dying? In another kind of 'war' caused by epidemics like AIDS, millions of people die and many more become orphaned — 40 million people by 2010 in Africa, according to the United Nations. It is a 'civil war' in those lands, but it is a 'moral war' for the rest of us, and we are failing; symptomatic of the state of human consciousness. The real 'famine' rages inside man, caused by chronic shortage of sensitivity, compassion and spirituality. Then again the cause and effect question comes up. Why does Nature/God heap catastrophe after catastrophe over a particular place and over a particular set of people? Does it have something to do with their 'collective *karma*'?

As if all this is not bad enough, there are the mercenaries, private armies, and adventurers who do it for the money or just for the thrill of it. And one has a deadly menu of place and kind to choose from. Every war is a horror, a legalized massacre. It is human invention to murder or maim in a twinkling, a mass of unknown men, women, and children. It is a quick fix to satiate our timeless thirst for blood. From the earliest times, man has had a singular fascination for blood, far before William Harvey's mid-17th century description of the circulation of blood. It came to be recognized as the life principle, long before it was scientifically established; and a feeling of fear, awe and reverence came to be attached to the shedding of blood. Blood rites and blood ceremonies were commonplace among our early ancestors. War offers us the maximum opportunity to spill maximal blood with minimum effort. In Leo Tolstoy's *War and Peace* (1869), Prince Andrei says that the object of warfare is murder. The Prussian military historian Carl von Clausewitz said that war by its basic nature war drives onwards to extremes. And, in the words of American writer Garry Wills, "raping, robbing of civilians and brutalizing and killing of prisoners in war are not anomalies."[97] They are not aberrations, or the zealotry of perverted soldiers, or the dark deeds of desperate minions. Such atrocities are perpetrated not by barbarians or monsters but by ordinary people who are persuaded by war to think that the 'enemy' is a monster, at least not fully human. And maybe, the 'fun' they could not afford on the street, they could in a war. Totally inhuman acts are made acceptable by justifying them in the name of patriotism, national honor and self-defense. The former American President Jimmy Carter said in his Nobel Prize acceptance speech that war may be a necessary evil, but evil it still is and that does not change, and that we will not learn to live in peace by killing each other's children. One could even question the qualification, *necessary*. Like the concept of a 'just war'; a 'necessary war' is not only a questionable concept but also an obnoxious doctrine, like a 'necessary rape', and a 'just mutilation', and a 'right way' of maiming children. In the mind of the perpetrator, every war is 'just'.

The 'justness' and 'justification' come from our history, epics, mythologies, and scriptures. Indeed, war is 'holy' and every atrocity committed is automatically absolved of any human or divine censure. Killing in war is the highest human virtue and getting killed in a war is an assured path to heaven, in spite of whatever sins one might have committed in one's life. Victory sanctifies every moral obscenity. It is always the defeated that are hauled up for 'war crimes', never the victorious, who often go on to commit even more horrendous crimes. War is no different from genocide and mass murder sanctified by the State. War is evil not only because of what waging a war entails, but also because of what it leaves behind, and what follows in the vanquished land — starvation, suffering, social suffocation, and slow death. Before the modern era, wars were still seen as evil, but they were mainly between bands of professional warriors and those affected were the ones whose 'duty was to die and kill'. At least that is the story we would like to believe. But despite all the glory, romanticism and heroism attached to the classical wars, they were still gory and never confined to the combatants, as they left behind orphans, widows, and the wounded.

Although we may extol non-violence as one of the highest human virtues, it is strange that in most cultures and even in religion, mass murder and mutilation are glorified. Dying on the battlefield, the scripture says, is the surest and the shortest route to Heaven, even if the person was evil in life. In the epic Mahabharatha, an anecdote says that prince Yudhisthira was permitted to enter heaven in his own body (a privilege denied to his brothers and wife) because of his unblemished earthly conduct, notwithstanding the lie he uttered to facilitate the killing of his guru Dronacharya. But he is surprised to see his evil cousin Duryodhana in heaven and is told that Duryodhana was there because he 'died on the battlefield'. Death in combat is supposed to absolve a human of all his past villainies! It not only whitewashes 'civilian' sins but elevates the sinner to the pleasures of Paradise! Perhaps it applies not only to those who kill and die in wars but also to those who launch wars! What other incentive is needed for one to wage wars? But what qualifies a conflict to be called a 'war'? In the olden days, the battlefield was the only arena of war, and wars were often waged between sunrise and sunset and were confined to combatants of equal strength or skill. Now it is continuous, multi-fronted and not confined to combat. So, who qualifies to go to heaven? Today, there is intense competition among murderers; many 'suicide bombers' believe that the murder of innocents is a religious duty. Classics like Homer's *Iliad* that glorify wars, paint the terrible as beautiful and evil as honor. In this technological age, wars are fought with weapons that not only decimate the 'enemy', which includes anyone living in a particular place at a particular time, but also decapitate the environment, bring disability across generations, and turn fertile lands into arid forests. We have wars without warriors, battles without battlefields and soldiers who look like space travelers. A 'deserter' is a traitor but an 'escapee' is a hero. And victory or defeat is not decided on the arena of action but by the public perception, which is often manipulated by the media who in turn are manipulated by the ruling class.

With the advent of advanced technologies, both the dynamics and the mechanics of war have changed and along with it the military balances in the world. Alvin and Heidi Toffler in their book *War and Anti-War* (1993) say, "the way we make war reflects the way we make wealth, and the way we make anti-war must reflect the way we make war. In the present technology- intensive wars, a soldier is called a 'system' and the uniform he wears is called Soldier Integrated Protective Suit (SIPS),"[98] designed to kill without combat or being seen. The doctrine of modern war is not to fight but to blow up to bits any of the enemy's habitat, killing all life around, and destroying the infrastructure for a functioning society, and to decapitate, decimate and demoralize the rulers and the people of the 'enemy country' and force them to capitulate body and soul. It is a doctrine designed to maximize suffering, mutilation and murder, deliberately and diabolically. A prisoner of war is an economic commodity, dead or alive, a subject of sadism.

Even assuming that violence and war may be necessary to fight abominable evil or intolerable injustice, and even perhaps to retain or reclaim one's dignity, human beings are morally afloat and emotionally underdeveloped to be able to tread the fine line between necessary and needless violence, egoistic bravado and cowardice from the perspective of human good. Those who plan and prosecute war do not have a divine shield or any moral exaltedness any more than anyone else. Often, they reflect the meaner side of the human spectrum which is needed to acquire power. Often they have the political power to unleash war but not the sagacity and the power to control its conduct and facilitate its conclusion. As a result, many wars go awry, triggering unanticipated damage, laconically, if not sarcastically, called 'collateral damage', which is the kiiling of tens of thousands of non-combatants. That, in turn, generates more enmity and animosity and adds to the cauldron of accumulated hatred in the world. In one sense, the worst part of war comes *after* the war. The dead are gone, mercifully, to a better place. It is the survivors, the victor and the vanquished and the soldier and the civilian alike, who bear the brunt of carrying the ravages for the rest of their lives. A man conditioned by the culture of war will carry the same culture into other walks of life and infect, like a virus, the society at large. The intoxication and thrill of destruction fill their days with wild adrenalin highs, which conjure up grotesque landscapes that are almost hallucinogenic. They become 'killer gods,' accustomed to "killing, carrying out acts of slaughter, with no more forethought than they take to relieve themselves."[99] The species-spin-off is that the essence of human condition gets further coarsened and corroded and the millions who are infected by the war in turn infect millions more every day, triggering a noxious ripple effect in the whole pond of humanity. In today's context, any war, of any type or scale, can escalate into a nuclear or biological Armageddon. The specter of nuclear war is well known, an integral part of almost every doomsday scenario; rather less widely known or discussed is biological warfare. But that seems to be as potentially real as a catastrophic nuclear war. Although some sort of rudimentary germ warfare dates back to at least 400 BCE, when Greek armies hurled arrows dipped in the blood of decomposed bodies, it was child's play compared to the havoc modern-day bacteriological and toxic weapons can cause. We are told that scientists have created mutant viruses and super-bugs (like vaccine-resistant smallpox) for germ warfare. If these pathogens are let loose in error or by design, they may kill billions, but that might not 'yet' lead to species extinction. It is feared that man might soon discover the means to create pathogens completely lethal to everyone, which could result in extinction. Humans, it is said, are almost genetic clones and therefore are much more susceptible than other species to this sort of attack.

Under the ruse of 'necessary evil' and 'national security,' it is the State that has become the greatest perpetrator of violence and evil in the world. The 'State', after all, is another institution and every institution interacts with the outside world through the medium of individual human beings and whatever strengths and fragilities humans can rub off on the institution. Although theoretically, the State is supposed to act on behalf of and be the guarantor of collective will, in truth, the effective link between the State and the citizen is law, which really is fear of force. To be governed by force is no different from being a captive. The classical argument in favor of the State is that its absence is anarchism and the tyranny of the strong and evil. The questionable doctrine of 'necessary evil' is applied. It means that the questionable state ethics are justified for 'greater good', and that although we may not like what State stands for, it must exist to attain a certain objective, which is collective security and justice. As Hannah Arendt wrote in her book *On Violence* (1970), power and violence, though they are distinct phenomena, usually appear together; when one rules absolutely, the other is absent and therefore, she says, to speak of non-violent power is actually redundant. On the contrary, State power is exercised preponderantly through the exclusivity of preventive and punitive power, backed by an elaborate infrastructure comprising of the army, the police, the paramilitary forces, the intelligence agencies and the bureaucracy. With all its lethal resources, the State has not been able to smother social violence. When the wrath of the people is truly roused, even awesome power becomes impotent. The State has become, instead of being a representative institution, a *repressive* institution.

Like almost every human institution, the State too is built on fear, doubt and distrust of human personality. Unless the very character of human aptitudes, inclinations and traits change, nothing can make a decisive difference. By State, we also assume a centralized trickle-down authority, in which our lives are micro-managed by strangers sitting in a far off place, ostensibly to protect us from our dark desires. Being aggressive has become part of being human and human inventiveness alone cannot erase it. The Austrian zoologist Konrad Lorenz in his book *On Aggression* (1963), argues in detail how "both animals and humans are equally endowed with aggressiveness" and that in the case of animals, "aggressive behavior does not lead to the defeat of the other power but becomes a bond of solidarity between the animals." As a result, "aggressive behavior functions to maintain order in the animal world".[100] In contrast, when it comes to us humans, the outcome of aggression is usually the killing of the adversary, and even war, in certain circumstances. In other words, animal aggressiveness is without malice, and human aggressiveness is dripping with it. Steven Pinker argues that human violence cannot be understood without a thorough understanding of the mind. There are both biological and social causes of war and violence. Under certain provocations and promptings, man is capable of both violence and compassion, of waging war and peaceful conflict resolution. Some call human violence a 'testosterone surge', which is "somewhat of a shutdown of the brain which leads to a burst of energy that increases one's 'manliness' factor. The entire body experiences a takeover of pure, unbridled adrenaline. Surely, this is a trait left over from our more primal ancestors, one that was probably helpful when saber-toothed tigers popped out from a bush."[101] Whether it is testosterone or sheer survival, evolution or environment, the footprints of human violence are too indelible to be explained away.

Seeds of Self-destruction

While one can debate about how 'original' human violence is, there is very little doubt about the fact that the way it has unraveled through human history has radically altered the character of human essence. We cannot get away from the stark truth that man is by far the most violent form of life on earth. Whichever way we differentiate one form of violence from another, and call it suicide or homicide, murder or martyrdom, genocide or ecocide, they all point to an uncontrollable urge to intentionally terminate one's life through self-directed injurious acts. Whether it is a byproduct of evolution or Nature's design to contain human delusions of cosmic grandeur, this trait appears deeply implanted in the human psyche. One could also speculate if this has got something to do with our pursuit of bodily indestructibility. If Nature decided to deny eternity to living beings and if human endeavor becomes a threat to that design, then destruction becomes a law of Nature, and the most environmentally economic destruction is self-destruction. Arthur Koestler (Darkness at Noon, 1940) said that mankind is afflicted with a mental disorder that drives us to self-destruction. It is akin to what the Japanese call seppuku or hara-kiri, collective 'stomach-cutting'. But perhaps we are being too hard on ourselves; maybe we are acting as a proxy to Nature and really doing its work by killing ourselves. Maybe this is all part of a grander story. Some thinkers like H.G. Wells have argued that there has been a seismic change in the conditions of the universe and that it signals the 'end of being'. And for that to actualize, man must perish. Perhaps that is why we feel no shame or remorse; on the contrary, we seem to enjoy — even relish — doing things that are palpably harmful for us. But it is not the exclusive preserve of psychologically dysfunctional people; it embraces the ordinary lot, not the stupid and the senseless, but the sober and the sane, not the thoughtless and the vengeful, but the intelligent and the astute. Now, there is no more any predictable or preventable 'pattern' for suicidal behavior; nor any clear psychiatric correlates. Soon, it could be the first impulse and response to any annoyance, difficulty or friction that disturbs and agitates our mind. It almost seems to be a major evolutionary or genetic mutation; the way 'natural selection' has come to operate as 'natural corrective elimination' to contain human rapacity. Evolution, some say, is a continuous process and that, contrary to earlier view, we are not the same as our ancestors, and that the pace of human evolution has actually hastened in modern times. And that we are likely to be very different a millennium or two from now, that is, if we are still around. Evolution itself is the product of two opposing forces, and in the instant case it could well be between self-preservation and self-destruction. Although the 'how' is unclear, the outcome of this could heavily influence the shape of the species. Seething with anger and alienation, afflicted with masochism or intoxicated with martyrdom, we do not seem to care what happens to us, and that includes others, even the near and dear. Paradoxically, that runs parallel with our drive for earthly eternity and obsession with physical appearances and looking 'good'.

Theories are aplenty to explain this paradox, like the Freudian hypothesis that humans have an innate death drive that impels them to pursue their own downfall and death. What we should truly be worried about are not weapons of mass destruction, but about the seeds of self-destruction sprouting inside all of us. The latter is more likely to be the cause of human enfeeblement or extinction than the former. Our whole attitude towards each other and towards Nature is symptomatic. Mass destruction is but self-destruction on a mass scale. The volcano of human violence might be dormant or active, but it is there. And despite recent advances in human psychoanalysis and insights into our motivational drives, we know no means to predict or preempt its eruption. Unable to adjust to what we call technology-driven civilization, our instincts and emotions are showing up the only way they can: self-destructive behavior. And, as our technological power scales new heights and breaks through new frontiers, that pattern of behavior will only deepen and spread. Of all the manifestations of violence, none is more perplexing and tragic as self-destruction, the most prominent forms of which are suicide and homicide. Should there be some kind of observant intelligent beings 'out there' in the cosmos looking down at us, they must wonder 'why these silly puny beings on earth quarrel so much for so little and seem so determined to kill themselves?' But the tongue-in-cheek answer is "you are not 'human' and you do not know what being alive on earth requires." Other than the very meaning of life, perhaps the most enduring mystery is why humans, with so much pain, indignity and decay, not knowing what life is, cling so pathetically and pathologically to life. Much of life is a struggle between survival and suicide, giving life and taking life; and there is no way anyone can tell which of the two will triumph, or when, how and why. Is it the inertia of the known or the fear of the unknown? Is it the embrace of liberty or the rejection of freedom? Is it flight from the 'absurdity' of everyday life or willful exploration of the other world? Is it, as Chesterton said, a refusal to take an interest in existence or in the logical finale to rationality? Who has the inalienable right over his own life? And, finally, is there a divine or a devilish design behind the galloping increase and trivialization of suicide? Looking at the insidious spread and speed, and the all-encompassing nature of suicide, such questions crowd the mind. The French philosopher and Nobel writer Albert Camus said, "There is but one truly serious philosophical problem, and that is suicide. Judging whether life is or is not worth living amounts to answering the fundamental question of philosophy."[102] Equally, one might say that another philosophical and metaphysical question, even greater than why so many choose self-termination, is why so many more choose to continue with life given the meaningless monstrosity, the painful ritual that living entails. Increasingly, the moral difference between those who choose death and those who choose to accept life is crumbling. Our emotions about death are now more mixed up than ever before. Self-destructiveness has always been a part of the human psyche; so is snuffing out someone else's life. Both are different forms of murder. Enforced death has always been an option. Concepts like chastity, family honor have always been viewed as more worthy than life. Some pain, physical and mental, has always been dreaded more than death and dying. Despite the visceral instinct for self-survival, the dark shadow of death appears, for a growing number of people, sunnier than the dark reality of daily life. The motives and triggers have broadened, from the most ridiculous to the most existential. What we now face is a toxic cocktail of suicide, murder, martyrdom, religion, and revenge. Some people are actually eager to blow themselves apart, but in the company of the greatest number of their 'enemies'. We read about people lining up in hundreds to be recruited and trained for this 'job'. We need to ponder deeply over this phenomenon. What is normal and routine for most people, for some mysterious reasons, suddenly becomes a matter of life and death, a banal insult or a setback becomes an intolerable affront for some. Instead of feeling guilty, more and more people feel murder is martyrdom. But martyrdom is not necessarily religious; those who kill and get killed are also called martyrs.

The American writer and satirist Ambrose Bierce wrote that, "There are four kinds of homicide: felonious, excusable, justifiable, and praiseworthy."[103] The character of killing and its morality is a function of the place and person; if it is the murder of an unknown man in war or under orders, it is honorable and patriotic; if it is at home even under threat to life or limb or to save another from murder, it is murder, sometimes deemed grave enough to attract the penalty of death by the law. While 'violent death' has always been a part of human life, suicides and homicides have become so commonplace and frequent in modern society that they are turning out to be as much a threat to human survival as nuclear war or climate change. The irony and tragedy is that just when we *seem* to 'have it all' — health, wealth, longevity, leisure, comfort, entertainment, fun (at least for a large number of people) and we should have every reason to live, many are choosing to 'end it all'. Maybe they do not think they have it all, or what they had was not what they *wanted* or the *way* they wanted it. And it is not the numbers that is striking as much as the range of reasons, practically covering every emotion, occasion, situation and interpersonal interaction inherent in life. Suicide runs parallel with life; often a step ahead for many. The damning verdict on human culture is that in search for a reason for being, for the *raison d'être* of life, many are stumbling upon suicide as an option to what living entails. And unwilling to face up to its share of responsibility, society calls suicide a crime, and those who seek suicide, as weak or ill. Most religions condemn suicide but that has not deterred the millions who have committed suicide over the millennia. The American television talk-show host and satirist Bill Maher said, "Suicide is man's way of telling God 'you can't fire me — I quit'".[104]

Indeed, suicide is both a sin and a crime, an offence against both God and society; society deems it such a grave crime that abetment to it is also treated as an equally heinous kind of crime. The wrath of or the punitive power of the State has made no difference at all to those who prefer suicide. It raises a more fundamental question, articulated, among others by the Harvard Biologist, Edward Wilson in his essay *Is Humanity Suicidal?* (*New York Times Magazine*, 30 May 1993). Wilson calls the human species "an environmental abnormality", and wonders if "it is possible that intelligence in the wrong kind of species was foreordained to be a fatal combination for the biosphere", saying that our species retains hereditary traits that add greatly to our destructive impact. If the past is any guide, nearly a million people 'successfully' commit suicide every year, while anywhere from 10 to 20 million attempt suicide only to survive with indelible scars. According to the World Health Organization, there is a suicide every 40 seconds, one murder every 60 seconds, and one death in armed conflict every 100 seconds.[105] And these figures have only risen over the past decade. Suicide is pretty rampant in many western countries, its number exceeding deaths by motor vehicle accidents, annually. What is truly staggering is not the number but the incredible triviality of the triggers: nothing is too casual, too commonplace or too silly or too sacred. Suicide has become the first and the foremost despondent response to stress and pain, increasingly the preferred solution to problems germane and inherent in the very process of the human way of life. Tragically, an alarming number of children, even before they turn into teenagers are ending their lives provoked by such 'normal' things like a parental reprimand, a peer's teasing, a teacher's scolding, a desire denied. Clearly, something more than the immediate event is at work in their thoughts, something that offsets the instinct for self-preservation, something that makes a person violently — and even painfully — extinguish the flame of his or her own life. It is not mere suffering that leads to suicide; had it been so, most of us would be dead before we turn thirty. It is not that the one who contemplates suicide has lost all taste for earthly life and its attendant allurements. Feelings of crushing hopelessness and helplessness, desperation, and inability to bear the loss have always been apparent factors provoking suicides. But what is now happening is a profound change in the dialectic of thought, especially in man's attitude towards death.

Love of life and desire for death can coexist, but they can seldom be identical. In his subconsciousness, man has a simmering volcano that is capable of persuading him to believe that death is sweet and liberating, a solution to all the tormenting contradictions of life, as a revenge against life, and as a retribution for the inequities of life. Some thinkers like Prof. Stanley Shostak say that like life, death too is evolving, and like life, death too is a facet of the underlying and ceaseless continuity. But what shape that 'evolution' will take is unclear, while it is clearly linked to human behavior. We might well end up as a sterile species with an indeterminate life span. Even about substantially increasing the life span, some experts like Jay Olshansky, a professor of epidemiology and biostatistics, say that the era of large increases in life expectancy may be nearing an end, and that, "there are no lifestyle changes, surgical procedures, vitamins, antioxidants, hormones or techniques of genetic engineering available today with the capacity to repeat the gains in life expectancy that were achieved in the twentieth century". Others disagree; according to them, what they call 'third-stage breakthroughs' will yield hitherto-unknown benefits leading to exponential leaps in wellness and longevity. So much of our moral sense and our values are drawn from our commitment to our progeny and the inevitability of death, should they disappear, man will have to rebuild the entire edifice of human society and redraw the borders of moral worth. Unless man becomes totally different from what he is now, the human form of life would become too heavy and too toxic a baggage for Nature to carry on its back. It will find other ways to cope with the menace, like turning the human mind into a murderous machine. Experts might quibble, but one cannot ignore the fact that man is now prepared to barter with death for many more things than ever before, from the most trivial to the most titanic, from the secular to the sacred. Killing, like evil, is now banal, well within the realm of probability, a temptation that man finds increasingly difficult to resist. And that impulse seems to get stronger with the increase in numbers, and strongest when the fate of the species is involved. For our 'good life', we are willing to embrace anyone else's death, even that of our children and grandchildren. How else can we explain our nonchalance towards climate change? One wonders if this has something to do with a twist somewhere in our age-old quest to transit from death to immortality — what the American '*Immortality Institute*' calls 'conquering the blight of involuntary death'. Nature seems to have responded to this threat to its prerogative by inducing the human mind to impose 'involuntary' death on the non-volunteers. To counter the human thrust towards biological immortality, Nature is broadening the avenues of non-biological mortality. To derail man's dream to be 'God', it is stoking the passions of the beast within him. Evolutionary biologists say that death is not necessary for evolution and its sole function is to spread more quickly by early reproduction than by the longevity of the carrier. It means that if we are able to master the technology for unlimited self-repair of cells and organisms, then Nature would have no problems and there would not be any need for reproduction. On the other hand, some researchers tell us that "the death/birth cycle is part of the very DNA. Rather than overcome death, our challenge becomes to learn how to surrender with grace."[106]

If mortality was imperative for evolution, given the state of *morality* now, what does that foretell about our future? Our blood-soaked history tells us that more than life and self-preservation, man is fascinated by death and self-destruction. He is always searching for new ways to inflict death. Personal suicide is only one manifestation. Through pollution of the water, air and food we depend on, we are actively participating in mass suicide and inter-generational suicide. While there are some people who resort to the extreme step by gulping down a dose of poison, like insecticide or cyanide, most of us commit 'slow suicide' in different ways. While direct suicide catches attention, the insidious one, though deadly, is invisible. The interaction between the consciousness and the subconscious within man is very complex, as noted by psychologists like Sigmund Freud and Carl Jung. The dynamics of that complex interplay seems to be changing in a manner that we cannot comprehend. Nothing is more indicative of the fragility and frustration of modern life than the growing number of suicides; it underscores the inability of the human personality to internalize, to absorb, and to manage the myriad contradictions of what living entails. Suicide and homicide are the visible visages of that inability. Suicide for long has been considered as an unheard cry for help. That remains, but some experts say that there is more to it than that. According to psychologist Paul Joffe, "it's part of a longstanding dance with death, what's known in the psych biz as a 'suicide career'".[107] The people who resort to suicide are not victims but masters of their own fate, people for whom the thought of suicide takes up long-term residence in the brain and for whom the risk of suicide does not fade after a threat or an attempt. Suicidal intent is less a natural response to distress than a virulent ideology. As Paul Joffe puts it: "They feel proud of the power to control their own fate. They feel superior to others in that they have this avenue of power that others don't."[108]

According to this line of logic, although it might appear as an act of powerlessness and helplessness, suicide is another form of exercise of power, or to preempt the exercise of power. It is also a major symptom of the growing influence of violence in the human consciousness, the rumblings that precede the avalanche. This relates not only to collective suicide symbolized by our attitude to the environment, which is an agonizing story by itself, but to individual suicides chosen in the privacy of individual minds. On the one hand, man relentlessly pursues pleasure, and on the other hand, he embraces the 'ultimate pain': self-destruction, triggered by causes ranging from the casual to the sacred. He seeks to gain immortality by hook or by crook, but at the same time, he does not hesitate to volitionally shorten life, his own and of others. He dreads death above all; yet he does not shrink from embracing or inflicting death. As the American psychologist Karl Menninger put it: "It becomes increasingly evident that some of the destruction which curses the earth is self-destruction; the extraordinary propensity of the human being to join hands with external forces in an attack upon his own existence is one of the most remarkable of biological phenomena."[109] While killing is routine in the animal kingdom, opinions differ if animals actually commit suicide. It is reported that altruism leading to death is fairly common and that some animals like dolphins and octopuses do take their own lives. But most experts say that animal suicides are instinctive, not reasoned; though they may go through the processes and do things that might cause death, they cannot conceive of their own death.

The twin killings — suicide and homicide — although distinct, are almost interchangeable. And although they have been a part of human history from the earliest man, they have never been so virulent and widespread as they are today. Traditionally, it has long been thought that these two are antagonistic expressions of human violence, either of which removes the motivating cause and makes the other unnecessary and even impossible. But that is changing, and a particularly alarming 'deathly' development is that of homicide followed by suicide of the perpetrator, which is occurring mainly in partnerships and families. It has now spread to ethnic and religious revenge and zealotry in the form of what are described as 'suicide bombers'. These people are blurring the boundary between suicide as 'auto-homicide', or murder of self, and homicide as murder of another. Both are acts of anger, frustration, alienation, and affirmation of one's identity, dignity, faith. Both are a defiance of the dictum of the sanctity of life, results of the breakdown of natural defenses that let us live and let others live. The equation or equivalence between the two forms of murder has long been debated by sociologists and psychologists, and if any, it has become more tangled and complex. No one is clear what portends, but clearly one's own life or another's life no longer means the same as before. Such an elemental change in the human mindset could not have occurred all on its own; raising the unnerving question if the growing human propensity for self-destruction serves a still mysterious cosmic purpose. Death and destruction play a central role in natural selection and in the equilibrium of Nature. But that is usually not by one's own hand or that of a fellow-species. If a person decides to kill and die at the same time then there is very little to preempt it. That is a new phenomenon in Nature and the killer becomes the most powerful person on earth, and he also becomes the arbiter of what we call 'collateral damage', which means he decides who else gets murdered. The murderer or the martyr (that is, in his mind) becomes the master, whose choice of time and place could mean life or death for others. Unless that mindset changes through consciousness change, this form of violence — homicidal suicide — could well become the apocalyptic pandemic of the future.

In whatever form, death has always been at the epicenter of human creativity and consciousness. Arthur Koestler, who was also the founder of the 'voluntary euthanasia society' *Exit*, wrote before his own suicide: "If the word death were absent from our vocabulary, our great works of literature would have remained unwritten, pyramids and cathedrals would not exist, nor works of religious art, and all art is of religious or magic origin". While death has been a creative inspiration, overcoming death has also been an enduring human passion. And death by violence has been as integral as death by disease and decay. The epidemics of suicide and murder could well be the bitter harvest of our flouting the laws of Nature and of our relentless quest for earthly eternity. Franz Kafka wrote that without the continuous confidence in something indestructible within himself, man cannot live. The scriptures envision spiritual immortality, and science promises physical immortality. Science says now or never, each life is the only chance we have to savor life; the scriptures, on the other hand, assert that now and never are the same. To transcend from 'death to immortality' is part of a prayer at the beginning of the *Brihadaranyaka* Upanishad. And in the *Katha* Upanishad, it is said that those in whose hearts desire is dead and the knots of delusion are untied, become immortal. Nature has provided a sort of biological escape from death through intergenerational or genetic continuity, but what man seeks is individual immortality. We are not content any more with spiritual or symbolic immortality; we want actualized and instant immortality, which makes redundant the 'after-life immortality'. Since the body is made of organic matter which must decay and dissolve, and since life is designed, as Bernard Shaw puts it, 'like a flame that is always burning itself out', human attempt at bodily eternity, through such technologies as cryonics and stem cells, puts man on a collision course with Nature. It is no longer science fiction or fantasies of the rich to perpetuate themselves. People say that it is not only possible but inevitable, that death — the 'ultimate disability or disease' — will be surmounted technologically. Some researchers are talking about the possibility that a person who is identical to you in every way might be brought to life, a sort of technological reincarnation. The enticing, if scary scenario being sketched is eternal youth, indefinite life span and god-like power to create living beings from a single cell. The anomaly is that we might have a situation in which millions of people feel that whatever awaits after death is better than being alive in this world today, and the disturbing prospect of thousands of people paying large sums of money to come 'back from the dead'. Future 'man', if science has its way, might well be like the images of the movie *The Matrix* (1999), in which the human has already become the raw material for the self-perpetuation of nano-tech machinery.

As a species, we think we are the best there is on the earth, but as individuals most people think they are the underdogs, fighting unequal battles on unfair terms. Freud maintained that suicides and homicides are not opposites. Both are killings, the only difference being that homicide is directed against the external world, while suicide is aggression turned inwards. Karl Menninger posits that suicides are sometimes committed to forestall the committing of murder. Similarly, murder is often committed to avert suicide. No species can carry so much 'deadly weight' and toxic load for too long. The human species is ripe for an epochal transition, a revolutionary change, an evolutionary pole-vault; either it will evolve into a better, more moral being, or it will fade away into the black hole of time, one more species that once lived on the earth and had its day under the Sun. Perhaps we are too proximate to notice, but something truly profound, truly awesome, truly horrific, truly benumbing is happening to the human character and personality. Man's threshold of tolerance is fast narrowing; his stoicism in the face of pain and hardship, inconvenience and irritation, annoyance and humiliation, reprimands and insults is lowering day by day dramatically, making man increasingly suicidal and homicidal. It would almost seem as if the human mind is constantly on the lookout, not for reasons to live, but for excuses to cease. And it has increasingly shed its inhibitions about taking another's life. The World Health Organization estimates that every year, more than a million people kill themselves, an increase of 60 percent worldwide in the past 45 years, which means that the cases of suicide far outnumber those of homicides that increased by 50 percent between 1985 and 1994. The truly troubling aspect is not the numbers or the percentage of increases, but that most of the victims quit when they were at their productive best, for reasons mostly trivial. The distinction between suicide and homicide, from a species point of view is immaterial: homicide is a form of suicide and vice versa. Nothing is too trivial or casual, flippant or funny for suicide; murder is holy revenge and suicide-murder is 'preparing to meet God.' Many people today increasingly feel cornered, and the only escape route seems to be to kill. In settling scores, men inflict suffering not only on the 'enemy', but on themselves too. Mohammad Atta, who flew the airplane into the WTC Towers in New York on 11 September 2001, is supposed to have said: "if we do not fight we will suffer. If we do fight we will suffer, but so will they." The old rule of life that 'you don't take what you cannot give' is no longer a barrier to killing. Alarmingly, the individual, society and State increasingly consider killing as a hassle-free and less expensive option to sort out interpersonal and intra-societal discord, disputes and disaffection.

Alarmingly, ever-increasing numbers of people, finding no help among the living, want to join the dead. At their wit's end while facing life's intractable problems, they are telling themselves — and the world — 'enough is enough', there is a limit to every endurance; they just want to end it all, whatever it leads to. Success — which means the desire to get everything we want, when we want and how we want — has become the 'mantra' of self-worth. In human culture, for someone to succeed, another must lose or more importantly, should seem to lose, and when that person happens to be you, you feel you are at a dead end staring into the abyss of death. An eighteen-year-old poor boy in India, not 'faring well' in his studies, hanged himself in the classroom and left a note that said, "I am not a success. God has not helped me."[110] Another relatively new breed of suicides is precipitated by the feeling of insufficiency, a feeling that 'this world is not for me'; for living is an exercise in futility. Despite strict religious strictures, suicide is rapidly spreading and has become the preferred exit route. Way back in August 1975, *Time* magazine carried a cover story that identified suicide as the third major claimant of the lives of young adults in North America, after car wrecks and homicides. In the quarter of a century since, it has become far worse having become as infectious as the common cold. Suicide is said to be steeply rising in Japan, and a recent report noted the dramatic increase in suicide in 'God's own country', the state of Kerala in India, much admired by economists for its high literacy rate and social safety net, and by sociologists because of its communal harmony.

The human mind, whether it is centered in the brain or elsewhere, has enabled and empowered man to become the virtual viceroy of the earth; the viceroy has become the monarch; the representative has dethroned the royalty. But the mind's power is still finite; and it has created a conundrum. Man has become a paradoxical being to whom everything is relative, selective and culture-sensitive, and situation-specific and steeped in self-gratification. Values are now tentative, not absolute and everything is possible and permissible under one or an other circumstance. Thus, we could have an honest thief and a tender murderer, a superstitious atheist, a kind tyrant, and a patriotic traitor. Then there are necessary evils, and just wars; even divine sanction is cited for the slaughter of millions. The human mind is the home of those negative passions which, when they manifest externally, become the primary sources of evil in the world. That evil often takes on the guise of separateness and self-righteousness, both of which come, as Vedanta tells us, from body-identification. Mortal life is tossed between the temptations of evil and the imperatives of morality, a theme that has been explored by many modern writers from Dostoevsky to Graham Greene; the latter wrote about "perfect evil walking the world where perfect good can never walk again."[111] With 'perfect evil walking the world', man has lost his innocence as well as his integrity. In the process, he has crossed perhaps the most fateful of thresholds that allowed the species to survive thus far: love of life and fear of taking another life. The most virulent epidemics in the world are now almost 'senseless' suicides and mass murders, often fused into one. It is becoming increasingly difficult to anticipate how an apparently 'normal' person would react to a 'routine reprimand' or to a 'trivial dispute' or to a 'stressful situation'; it could easily lead to one of the two or even both. Nothing is too trivial for suicide and nothing is too sacred for murder. The epithet 'banal' used by Hannah Arendt to describe human evil applies equally now to killing. It is increasingly becoming a serious option to calm nerves, or to settle scores, be it with a spouse or with society, the preferred choice to cope with frustrations and tragedies of life and the pressures and stresses of competitive life. And 'collateral killing,' a euphemism for killing innocent people, is no longer only a deadly tool of terrorism; it has now gained legitimacy as an essential instrument of State policy, avowedly to protect 'national interest;' the doctrine is that to 'get' one 'wanted man,' it is okay if hundreds of innocents are butchered. Man is on a killing spree, killing of fellow men, of other species, of the environment. Wanton violence, the adoption of coercive tactics to control the will, the intellect, and the limbs of another, has become almost our primary response to weather the storm of life. And it is soaked in malice, which is what distinguishes human violence from other animals. It is invasion of a person's soul. We have come to accept many horrible things as 'necessary evils'. And war, death on the streets brought about by motorized contraptions, subhuman poverty, discrimination, exploitation, injustice and insensitivity as the price of 'progress' and the wages of individualism. And the sophistication of our butchery never stops. Even if we already have enough weaponry to kill every human being on earth ten times over, we will never stop making more weapons with even more murderous power. Because, even if we do not directly handle that power, we still feel vicariously 'powerful', and 'the military industrial complex,' the famous phrase of the American president Dwight Eisenhower, provides the framework for our lives. But all this is an anthropocentric perspective, as if *our* choice controls every event. It is an outlandish thought but maybe, just maybe, we are, by killing each other so effortlessly, compulsively and methodically, in a twisted way, doing Nature's work, namely containing the predatory and parasitic human way of life.

Dialectics of Dharma and Karma

The human impulse for self-righteous self-destruction is both a symptom and a malaise. It comes primarily from our inability to codify our primary duty in a world of contrasts and contradictions, *dwandas* and dualities. Much of what we do is enjoined upon us by religion or society, by custom or culture, but buried deep in the human psyche is an abiding conviction that inexorable fate and evil forces, powerful and complex beyond our comprehension, pervade the human world. These forces now seem to have reached commanding heights of human life and have taken possession of all our faculties. The most horrendous things happen nonchalantly and in the name of 'necessary evil'. And we accept them all as 'just part of life'! Poised on a precipice, we are a flawed species languorously longing for its own early extinction, even secretly, if not sadistically, relishing that thought.

So many things seem so wrong, so many things seem so unfair, so many things seem so inexplicable, and so few real choices in actual life; it all seems so senseless and ruthlessly random. And the much-touted free will and freedom seem illusory. We grope for answers and just when we think there are plausible possibilities we suddenly realize that even more intractable questions are raising their head. Then we ask ourselves: what good is knowledge? Clearly what we actually see and experience in the world and in our lives we cannot accept or even condone, and yet we seem utterly ill-equipped within our own selves to redress any of the incongruities and inequities. If we completely confine the relationship between cause and effect to this world and to this life, it all seems so inept, so amateurish, so pointless and purposeless, so unintelligent and such a waste of energy. And yet we know that nothing in Nature conforms to any such adjectives. How does one reconcile to this dichotomy? Then a flash of lightning hits us. Perhaps the very premise is the real illusion. Why should life be limiting in time and space? What evidence do we have that it is so, that 'death' ends it all? Can something as beautiful and self-generating as life come to a finality of complete closure? Such a line of thought directly leads us to the two of the most sophisticated theological and philosophical doctrines: of *karma* and *dharma.* As words they are ancient, but as ideas their life is even of timeless lineage. If one were to scan history from the mystical or occult point of view, one would trace the curve of cycles according to the rise and fall of the real understanding of *karma* and *dharma.* If we can truly understand their intent and essence and in particular their interplay, many questions that haunt our lives would melt away. If they are rightly interpreted and rightly applied, they can unlock many of life's secrets; a wrong comprehension and misapplication can lead to a person falling from the heaven of Spirit into the hell of matter.

Karma as a major doctrine that offers a rationale of life and death, originated in the Vedic system of thought, later expanded in the early Upanishads and in the Bhagavad Gita. In its elemental sense, *karma* is the physical, mental, and supramental system of neutral rebound, a kind of cosmic causality. Essentially, what it means is that the very being which one experiences on (as a human being in our case) is "governed by an immutable preservation of energy, vibe, and action."[112] It implies that thoughts, words, and deeds in past lives inexorably effect one's current situation. Every individual is thus responsible for the tragedies and triumphs, bad luck and good luck, which are experienced in his current earthly life. It is vital to note that *karma* is not an instrument of the gods, or of a single God; it is rather the physical and spiritual 'physics' of being. Just as gravity "governs the motions of heavenly bodies and objects on the surface of the earth, *karma* governs the motions and happenings of life, both inanimate and animate, unconscious and conscious, in the cosmic realm."[113] What is true of the individual is also true of societies. Though the words and concepts of *karma* and *dharma* are often used separately and each is a full-fledged doctrine, they make better sense if viewed in juxtaposition. Simply put, *dharma* is the subjective dimension of *karma.*

The key to *karma* is *dharma*. *Dharma* is action, and action results in *karma*. By simply performing our various *dharmas* properly we can chip away at *karma*. Any *dharmic* activity cleanses bad *karma* and creates good *karma*. And through *dharmic* behavior one can get everything life has to offer, wealth and prosperity, and attain the final goal of life: not to be born again. Then we come to the ultimate *dharmic* question: why does anyone resort to *adharmic* actions? (that is, actions that are against *dharma*). Is it because *adharma* is man's 'natural' disposition? Or is it because of our lack of discriminating knowledge of *dharma* and *adharma* in the melting pot of life?

It is not that we lack scriptural guidance. *Dharma* is not only the connecting thread of all Hindu and Buddhist religious texts. There are, in addition, specific texts, *dharma-sutras* in Hinduism and *Dhammapada* in Buddhism. Among the texts inspired by the Vedas are the *dharma-sutras*, or the "manuals on *dharma*," which contain codes of conduct and rites as they were practiced in various Vedic schools. Their principal contents address the duties of people at different stages of life, or *ashramas* (student life, household life, retired life, and renounced life); dietary regulations; offenses and expiations; and the rights and duties of kings. They also discuss purification rites, funeral rituals, forms of hospitality, and daily oblations, and they even mention juridical matters. The Buddhist scripture *Dhammapada* consists of 423 verses in Pali uttered by the Buddha on hundreds of occasions for the benefit of a wide range of human beings. Together — *dharma* and *karma* — offer a structure of coherent thought, a practical platform for life, an explanation on why things are what they are and a way to live life fruitfully. What is true of the individual is also true of the species. *Karma* is the causal context of life and after-life; and *dharma* is the cosmic order that underlies and underpins the universe.

The relationship and ratio between work and reward, effort and result is a much-debated question. The two are never simultaneous and that makes it impossible to ensure the outcome. The Bhagavad Gita says that without *karma* or action there is no life, but action and effort have to be for the right cause. Along with *Nishkama karma* (action without attachment to its fruits), one is also forbidden from performing three kinds of actions: *Nishidha karma* (prohibited actions), *Kamya karma* (desire-driven actions), and *Abhichara karma* (black magic). Since life is impossible without actions, human behavior must be circumscribed and circumspect, in accordance with a moral code of conduct, the centerpiece of which is this: do no harm to any living creature by thought, speech or deed, and dedicate all human effort to the divine. It is the sum and substance of spirituality that the Bhagavad Gita (2.47) preaches and touches the heart of human behavior. In the famous verse, "*Karmanyeva adhikaraste ma phalesu kadachana*", which many believe is the best practical scriptural maxim, Lord Krishna tells Arjuna — and through him tells all of humanity — "Seek to perform your duty; but lay not claim to its fruits". For a 'rational' mind it sounds unfair; why should someone else get the credit for what we have done or struggled for, and expended our effort and energy toward? Lord Krishna puts in perspective the question why so often, despite the best effort, the result is not what we desire and someone else benefits. It means that we are only given the chance to act, but not in framing the consequence. Some other time it may work the other way around — then we do not complain or even acknowledge that another person deserved better. Actions that are of a binding nature lose that nature when we do them with equanimity or evenness of mind through the help of pure reason. This principle, indeed, is one of the important tenets of Marxism: namely, from each according to his ability and to each according to the need. In the scriptural sense, the fruits belong to God, and in the economic sense the fruits belong to society, but in fact they are not different. And both — Marxism and the karmic message from God — have proved elusive because to put them into practice runs against the nature of the human mind. And it highlights the connection between *dharma* and *karma. Dharma* is really that *karma* by which one contributes to social good and to Self-realization. *Adharma* is any *karma* that impedes man's social obligations and his path toward spiritual growth. In all human affairs, there are efforts, and there are results, and the *strength* of the effort is the measure of the result. In tune with the human *swabhava* (nature), man generally plans to get the fruits of his work before he even starts any kind of work. The human mind is so endowed that it cannot think of any kind of work without remuneration or reward. In real life, we want reward without effort, and assume that more effort means more 'success' and that any effort is moral if that is our 'duty'. In this logic, a contract killer can say he is doing his 'duty' to his master, that he is being paid to do so and he has no selfish motive. A soldier kills as part of his 'duty' to his country. Buddhism gives particular attention to this aspect. In its eight-fold *Noble Path* are included *Right Livelihood* and *Right Effort*.

In short, *karma* is, in the famous American psychic Edgar Cayce's words, 'memory coming to consciousness', and of interconnectedness, not only of cause and effect but also of individuals and of the universe. It is the casualty of energy which sets up patterns that rule our entire life experience, a universal order to give coherence and management. Every thought, word and deed leaves a *karmic* imprint. Every action involves give and take, and that has a *karmic* effect. *Karmic* effect begins with our birth and with the family that we are born into. One is born into a family where conditions are conducive to give effect to one's *karma* and where one has significant give-and-take accounts with each member of the family, the most with those closest. According to the Spiritual Science Research Foundation, 27 percent of the 'give-and-take' account can be attributed to the spouse, 25 percent to parents 9 percent each to siblings, close friends, colleagues and to people in romantic relationships, and the balance 12 percent to 'others'.[114] Percentages apart, it is obvious that the closer the intimate interactions, the greater will be the *karmic* fallout, both in terms of consuming past *karma* and acquiring new *karma*. A major tenet in the law of *karma* is that every positive deed generates a 'merit' while every negative deed generates a 'demerit' or a sin. Whenever one does a good deed to others, it is bound to give a positive return (in the form of some happiness), apart from a simple thank you from that person! Whenever one inflicts harm, it is bound to give a negative return in the form of sorrow in some form. It cannot be undone by a simple 'Sorry'! The law of *karma* is infallible. As an ancient Hindu text describes: "Your wealth will remain on earth, your cattle will remain in the stables, your wife will come till the entrance door, your relatives and friends will come till the cremation ground, your body will accompany you till the funeral pyre, but on the way beyond this life, only your *karmas* will accompany you". This applies to *dharma* as well. Throughout our lives, we are either settling an old account or creating a new one. If the account cannot be settled in this birth, as is the case most often, it is carried over to the next. We are not consciously aware of the give-and-take accounts generated in our previous births. Even the actions of others towards us are part of our *karma* and consequently, of their *karma*. For one person, it is a 'pay-out'; for the other, it is a 'pay-in', an incremental addition. What is immediately painful can be earned as a credit, and what gives immediate joy can be a debt incurred. And yet, no soul is given more than it can bear to carry — this is the paradoxical blessing hidden in the limitations of time and space. Our perspective on life changes if we perceive it from this perspective. That is why traditional Hindus welcome suffering as a faster way to reduce or redeem their accumulated sins.

One of the often-heard laments is that there is no justice, that the good suffer and the bad have all the luck. Rarely do we think about how unjust we are, making the good suffer and of the times we take pleasure in our own luck at the expense of someone more worthy. It is precisely this perception that the twin doctrines of *karma* and *dharma* address and offer a plausible rationale for. They do that primarily and simply by stretching the span beyond a single life, or a lone form of life, and a particular place in the cosmos. According to this theory, you are repaid by the same amount of pain or pleasure that you caused others with your original action. It also answers another question: what determines character? It says that every thought, word and deed produce what are called *samskaras* or tendencies or potencies, which cling to the astral body after death and are carried over from womb to womb. *Samskaras* also recreate desires in the next birth automatically. For example, a person can experience the desire to steal although he is brought up in a good family and he himself would not understand why he experiences that desire. The *Manu Sastra*, the treatise containing the laws of Manu, says that "a man reaps the appropriate fruit of any act in a body that has the qualities of the frame of mind in which he committed that act."[115] The *karmic* law mandates that every human wish must be fulfilled, and it is this chain that binds man to the wheel of causation. The misfortunes of our lives, according to Indian thinkers, are but the results of our misdeeds; calamities are brought about by our sins. Every tiniest act of caring or dismal deed of shame leaves a trail behind, that stretches over millions of multiple lives. It is said that where and to whom we are born, and even every specific disease we suffer, from colic pain to cancer to leprosy to impotence, are all consequences of specific sins. We reap the rewards of good deeds and pay for bad deeds not only through our behavior, but also how others, particularly the kith and kin, behave towards us, and it works both ways. *Karma* comes into play only in company, not in absolute isolation. Indeed nowhere, being alive, can we be in solitude; other creatures will be around and our actions affect them and their actions affect us. The more intimate the relationship, the more intense is the *karma* we acquire as well as spend. Strong attachments and strong dislikes are carried forward through several lives. It shows that hatred shown towards or by others is also a part of our *karmic* payback, as well as theirs. If someone loves you more than you do or vice versa it is also part of *karmic* reversal. And this applies similarly to groups, communities and clusters of individuals. It is important to note that every action produces a two-fold effect: one, an impression on the mind which one carries when one dies; the second, it creates an impression on the world or on what is called *Akashic* records, a theosophical term which is a kind of universal all-inclusive filing system that records every thought, word, action, emotion and experience that has ever occurred in time and space, the story of every soul since the dawn of creation. It is also referred to as the collective unconscious or the collective subconscious, or Cosmic Mind, or the Book of Life in the Bible. Although every individual life is a product of one's own *karma*, it is still a part of the cosmic scheme, and it has a bearing on and influences the destiny of all life. No action is therefore in isolation either in its cause or in consequence. In its intent it could be a consequence, and in its effect a cause. How a 'consequence' is carried out determines the nature of *karma*, good or bad. Because of the existence of the afflictions (*klesah*), of ignorance (*avidya*), egoism (*asmita*), attachment (*raga*), aversion (*dvesa*) and the clinging to life (*abhinivesah*), we amass and experience *karmas*. We produce *karma* in four ways: through thoughts, through words, through actions, and through the actions of others under our behest or connivance.

In the Hindu trilogy of *karma*, three entities — *sanchita* (the reservoir of all past lives' karmas); *prarabdha* (the portion being experienced in this life) and *agami* (the one we are acquiring in this life by the way we live) — have a more direct bearing on *dharma*. The *karmas* wait for an opening to come to the surface and to express themselves through *klesah*. One strong *karma* may call for a particular birth and body to express itself, and other closely related *karmas* will also be expressed or exhausted through it.

Prarabdha first manifests in the circumstance of our birth — where, when and to whom — and once we expend it we die — not a minute sooner or later. That is the connecting thread through life. Our connections to other humans are ways through which we redeem and replenish our *karma*. This goes on until one attains Self-realization and ceases to create new *karmas*. We need to understand that we are simply living out our karmic destiny. Time is *karma*, the sages say. Everyone has a karmic map. We are often befuddled as to why someone acts a certain way, or lives a certain way; 'how could he?' we mutter. Perhaps that person is sharing the same thought about us. Each of us is programmed with a certain nature, the quintessence of *karma*, the nature required for the fruition of *prarabdha*. In the *Yoga-Sutra*, the ancient Indian sage Patanjali tells us: "Because of virtuous and non-virtuous *karma*, there are [corresponding] pleasurable and painful consequences." The circumstances of our life are the coordinates for *karma*. But we have free will as to how we will deal with these, positively or negatively. If we choose to deal with these negatively, for example, in creating suffering for others, the reactions return to us in more intense or terrible forms. Dealing with circumstances patiently, creating happiness for others, neutralizes the karmic consequences gradually.

The *karma* that is of immediate concern to most people and which they would like to be relieved of by any plausible means is *prarabdha*, which is what one actually experiences in life, and it brings up the questions of both self-effort and God. *Prarabdha karma* is itself of three categories: *ichha* (personally desired), *anichha* (without desire) and *parechha* (due to others' desire). An often-debated, even practical, issue is the clash of *prarabdha* and free will. When a man fails to achieve his desired object, is there a way to find out whether the failure was due to *prarabdha* or due to the deficiency or incompetency of his effort? At what stage should a man stop his effort, when it is supposed to be useless because of his *prarabdha*? Swami Sivananda answered this question and said that though every experience is finally caused by *prarabdha* alone, its connection with one's consciousness constitutes an effort or a fresh deed. Effort is nothing but consciousness of action as related to oneself, whatever be the thing that prompts one to do that action. It is not the action as such but the manner in which it is executed that determines the nature of the result. Experiences which are forced upon oneself or which stem on their own accord without the personal will of the individual are the workings of *prarabdha*. But experiences which result from deliberate and conscious acts that have a pre-meditated background, show that it is a *kriyamana karma* (instant *karma*), though it may be sanctioned by the law of the *prarabdha karma* itself. An experience caused by mere *prarabdha* does not cause another fresh result but is exhausted thereby; but a *kriyamana karma* tends to produce a fresh experience in the future as it is attended by the sense of doership.[116] Yet another view is that man by his own effort, doing *punya* (virtuous deeds) and *prayaschita* (penance), can at least mitigate *prarabdha*. An ancillary view is that only divine mercy can affect the effects of *prarabdha*. The third view is that it is human actions that caused karma and hence human effort is essential and only then would God help. Ramana Maharshi attempts to harmonize all three views: "A man might have performed much *karma* in the past births. A few of these will be chosen for this birth and he will have to enjoy their fruits in this birth. It is something like a slide show where the projectionist picks a few slides to be exhibited at a performance, the remaining slides being reserved for another performance... The different karmas are slides, karmas being the result of past experiences, and the mind is the projector. The projector must be destroyed so that there will be no further reflection and no further slides and no deaths."[117] On the question of the projectionist he said, "Individuals have to suffer their *karmas* but *Iswara* [God] manages to make the best of their *karmas* for his purpose. God manipulates the fruits of *karmas* but he does not add or take away from it. The subconscious of man is a warehouse of good and bad *karma*. *Iswara* chooses from this warehouse what he sees will best suit the spiritual evolution at the time of each man, whether pleasant or painful. Thus, there is nothing arbitrary."[118] Differentiating *karma* and *karta* (God), he said, "...*Karta* means *Iswara*. He is the one who distributes the fruits of actions to each person according to his *karma*. That means that he is the manifest *Brahman*. The real *Brahman* is unmanifest and without motion. It is only the manifest *Brahman* that is named as *Iswara*. He gives the fruit to each person according to his actions (*karma*)". Another modern-day sage Swami Mukhtananda says, "Kabir (the great poet-saint) says in this connection that on the sixth day after the birth of a child, when a special rite is performed, God himself comes down and decides the destiny of the child, and that cannot be altered."[119] It means that God, at that time, transforms part of the *sanchita* into *prarabdha*. But the unanswered question is: on what basis and criteria?

Although it is popularly assumed that 'good deeds' yield good rewards and future 'good births', and that bad deeds yield 'bad births', the question arises as to how to reconcile it with the theory of non-dualism. How can one *perform* 'good' deeds or 'bad' deeds if there is no 'I'? The Advaitic philosopher Ramesh Balsekar explains: Good deeds happen through particular body-mind mechanisms and bad deeds happen through certain body-mind organisms. Both good deeds and bad deeds together form the functioning of Totality at that moment. It is only the human being who says, "good deeds, bad deeds". All are deeds performed, in this life and living by Consciousness, through body-mind organisms according to their natural characteristics.[120] To acquire 'good' *karma* and to expend 'bad' *karma*, one must live in tune with *dharma*. *Dharma* is like a cosmic norm and if one goes against the norm, it can result in bad *karma*. The Hindu *shastras* say that it is *dharma* that holds the universe in balance and maintains the cosmic order. All acts must be judged on their effect, however minute or miniscule, from this paramount principle. There is no neutral act; every one impacts positively or negatively. At the same time, the *dharmic* effect of any act is also circumscribed by the social context of the perpetrator, by the *vruthi*, the duties assigned to the individual as an integral part of the social fabric. It is also said that one should ultimately even be detached from *dharma* and not cling too tightly to it. When the cosmic 'order' and 'balance' are seriously threatened through the ascendancy of evil, God incarnates on earth. *Dharma* is the only friend that accompanies man beyond death. *Dharma* is the stable basis of every aspect of individual and collective life. A man's physical, intellectual, aesthetic, as well as spiritual well-being rests on the observance of *dharma*. Moral conduct sustains man's inner nature. Vedanta firmly emphasizes that the one secret to sound mental health is adherence to moral principles. The great *rishis* of ancient India like Adi Shankara and Vyasa have said that through *dharma* one can attain worldly wealth as well as final beatitude or *moksha*. *Dharma* affects the future according to the *karma* accumulated. Therefore, one's *dharmic* path in the next life is determined by their past *karma*. It is the collision of *karmas* that make a family, a community, what we call a country, and ultimately a particular generation of a particular species. In that sense, the package or baggage an individual carries contains not only a bit of his own *sanchita* but also a bit of the collective *sanchita*, of a group of souls somehow linked together over past lives. That is the 'missing link' in mass deaths, in war, or a flood, or an earthquake or an accident. The doctrine of *dharma* too applies to all these categories. In short, we have all created the causes that compel us to experience horrific results in some of our finite lives, 'putting' ourselves in a collective situation to experience the cumulative results and share the bitter fruits. There are many reasons beyond our knowing that could cause a particular group of people to come together at the 'right' time to experience horrendous events. We must find a way to cleanse our collective *karma* to be able to ascend to a higher plateau of consciousness. Cleansing and ascension require inner focus, not external searching. Practice of virtue and righteous conduct are also cleansers. In Buddhism, there are three types of virtue: first there is the virtue that is not embraced by either means or discernment, and this is called merely meritorious virtue. Then there is the virtue that is embraced by the discernment, that is realization of selflessness, and this is called virtue that is merely conducive to liberation. Finally, there is virtue that is embraced by both means and discernment, and this is called the virtue of the Mahayana.[121] The third is considered the highest. 'Means' refers to compassion for all sentient beings, and 'discernment' to focus on full awakening. In the Indian epic Mahabharata, it is said that righteousness and its reverse arise from one's acts producing happiness or misery to others, and they both affect one's future life with respect to the happiness and misery enjoyed or endured therein.

The doctrine of *dharma* is also very subtle and complex, and there are so many *dharmas*, some situational and person-specific, and some universal and eternal, which makes it difficult to harmonize them. The axiom that *dharma* protects those that protect it is variously interpreted. And it is often used to justify *adharmic* actions. And that it is okay, for example, to slay an evil person through evil ways. And the two examples often cited in the Hindu epics are the killing of Vali while he was fighting his brother Sugriva, and the killing of the unarmed Karna on the battlefield of Kurukshetra by Arjuna, at the urging of his charioteer Lord Krishna himself who incarnated on earth to restore *dharma*. It means that both *dharma* and *adharma*, right and wrong, are contextual and contingent upon the greater good or lesser evil. The message is that one cannot protect *adharma* or evil through *dharma* or personal piety, and if anyone, however noble they might be and are actually practicing their own *swadharma*, they must be punished or sacrificed at the altar of the greater *dharma* or collective good. In a way, it means that the end justifies the means but it does not mean the converse. How to balance and blend the two is a daily conundrum. Almost all choices we make raise such questions. And we do not have the kind of 'intelligence' that is needed. It is not only a question of the nature of karmic action, or of ends and means, but also of the perpetrator. For example, it is *dharmic* for the State to kill even if it violates the law; an individual cannot. What a soldier or policeman can do in the call of duty, the same person cannot in a different setting. Some actions are *dharmic* or mandatory in marriage and are prohibited outside or even deemed a sin. Whether an act is *dharmic* or *adharmic* is also a matter of culture and context. Ravana even justified his abduction of Sita as *dharmic* according to the *dharma* of the *rakshasas*, the demons. Rama triumphed because his *swadharma* was more *dharmic* than Ravana's *swadharma*, which was based on coercion, force, and cruelty. As an aside, it is worth remembering that the wives of both Rama and Ravana are two of the five greatest *Pativratas* in the Hindu pantheon of chaste wives, and both were adherents of *pativrata dharma*, which demands total devotion to the husband and to regard him as God-incarnate. It is so powerful that even gods are powerless before this *dharma*. It is a clash of wills of two persons observant of the same *dharma*: Mandodari, the wife of Ravana, could not save her husband, while Sita — not really Rama — triumphed, not because she was superior but because the *pativrata* power of Mandodari was powerless in the face of Ravana's *adharma*. The only rule of thumb so to speak, in every *dharmic* dilemma is to look at it from the other person's perspective.

The Buddha taught that one should live in a *dharmic* way that would produce no more *karma* while enduring whatever karmic reactions destiny brings. This, he said, would free one from further rebirth. The Buddha also said that understanding *dharma* is as difficult as catching a snake; if you do not do it properly it can kill you. Our intellect can be blurred and clouded by the power exerted upon it by the senses. Our senses are very potent, and their power is such that what they desire can produce an impact on the mind and the intellect to such an extent that the mind can think and the intellect can understand things only in terms of the senses. The Upanishads warn us against this fall, and offer the path of *dharma* to prevent the fall. There are many *dharmas*, specific to a person or time or a circumstance, but the one that is given particular importance is *swadharma*, which means the mode of life and duty that is natural to us and consistent with our social status. In the Bhagavad Gita, Lord Krishna tells Arjuna, in his exhortation to bear arms and fight even his own revered grandfather and guru, that it is better to do one's *swadharma* imperfectly rather than emulating *paradharma*, another person's *dharma*, and that doing the latter is against the very personal nature of our being. One of the major contributory causes to social unrest is that everyone neglects their own duty and tries to perform someone else's. The practical problem in this age and time is: what is *swadharma* and how does one decode *swadharma*? Modern life is a complex web and entails several, often conflicting duties and responsibilities (between personal and professional, religious and social, for instance), and it is very difficult to grasp where the 'balance of *dharma*' lies in a given context. To acquire that capacity, we must free ourselves from the toxic hold of *ragas* (attachments) and *dweshas* (hostility, avarice). If we can do that and align our *karma* or conduct to *swadharma*, life will become both meaningful and joyous.

The present age, the *Kali Yuga* in the Hindu cycle of eternal time, foretold as the most *adharmic* or immoral of all, has a silver lining. Because evil will be so pervasive and entrenched, the standards of 'being moral' also come down considerably, so that with minimum effort in the right direction, one can attain the same results as those that required Herculean effort in the earlier *yugas*. That which was achieved through contemplation in the *Satya Yuga*, through sacrifices in the *Treta Yuga*, and through worship of God in the *Dvapara Yuga*, may be attained through *kirtana* or loud chanting of God's name in this *Kali Yuga* or the Iron Age. In our sinful age, even a sincere desire to do good is good enough; just *not* doing harm can be deemed as virtuous. All of our desires and deeds are conditioned by the external world, which is not an ideal world. However romantic and idyllic it might be, we cannot exchange *yugas* or our lives with those of our ancestors. The nature and entitlements of every life are specific, and even the same person, if he were to relive in another *yuga*, cannot act the same. There is a story in the Mahabharata: When Bhima, one of the five 'righteous' Pandavas, the son of god Vayu (wind), meets Hanuman (also a son of Vayu, and who is the great so-called 'monkey-god' of another epic, Ramayana), Bhima asks his 'elder brother' to show him the gigantic form that he [Hanuman] had assumed in the Ramayana, while crossing the ocean in search of Sita, the abducted wife of Rama. Hanuman chuckles and says, 'that was in another *yuga*, and even *I* cannot recreate it…'

4

The Sacred, the Secular, and the Profane

The Three Strands

To make some sense of his present malaise, and to find a way out of the labyrinths of life, to retain some sense of sanity in an increasingly inscrutable world, man searches for symbols and signposts, crutches and coordinates, searchlights and lodestars. However much we might demur and deny, none of us are truly comfortable with who we think we are or have become, and we are desperate to define ourselves in a better light. At the same time, and much as we may quibble and cavil at the world around us, we also know deep within that the world is but our own visible shadow, the external projection of the world within. This angst, this seeking, invariably draws us into the domain of the three strands — the sacred, the secular, and the profane — that drive the human thought. We tend to think that if we can manage to put a tag on an event or happening as one of those three then it would make our lives easier. We want to venerate the sacred, embrace the secular, and shun the profane. But such clarity eludes the human mind. The human mind has always instinctively viewed the sacred and profane or the holy and the desecrated as belonging to two distinct classes, as two worlds between which there can be nothing in common. Although, everything is God's creation or His representation, or so we like to say, the mental divide between the sacred and the sacrilegious, or the holy and the unholy, permeates every walk and circumstance in life. And that mental divide has led man to 'assign' sacredness to things around him: sacred space, sacred time, sacred name, sacred Nature, sacred texts, sacred ideals, sacred words, sacred music, sacred art, and sacred place. As a theological concept, Rudolf Otto (The Idea of the Holy, 1917) defined 'holy' as something that is 'non-rational, non-sensory experience or feeling whose primary and immediate object is outside the self'. The 'sacred' is strewn all over, in every walk of life. The place of worship is a sacred space, and in many cultures, certain times are deemed holy or auspicious (for example, the concept of muhurta in Hinduism). Religious festivals are ritualized sacred events of mythical origins, and participating in them means stepping out of the ordinary time into a sacred time. There is even a holy hour of death in many religions. Truly religious or spiritual teachers and exponents are called holy, and their very proximity is deemed a blessing. The utterance or chanting of some words, like the mantras in Hinduism, or even the sounds of these words, it is believed, carry the power of a miracle. At a practical level, almost everyone has certain things 'sacred' or 'sacrosanct', which are not necessarily holy; which are so fundamental that they are non-negotiable; the expression 'sacred cow' [for the Hindus] symbolizes that spirit. Being 'secular' is a badge of being 'modern'. Broadly, it means not being overly or ostentatiously religious, but being tolerant to other faiths, and being prepared to share equal public space with all religions. Being 'secular' is sometimes used as a symbol of not being superstitious, and having a scientific temper. It is often applied to the institution of the State, in the sense that the instruments of the State do not support or promote any particular religion and of governance not being theocratic. And although we do not speak much about the word 'profane' except as an expression of vulgar language — as in 'profanity' — its place in human consciousness is no less native.

Something that is *profane*, then, would literally mean 'against the temple' or even 'far from the temple', where 'temple' refers to the *method* of worship, not to a structure or a building. In fact, the very origin of the word 'profane' is from its Latin '*in front of the temple*' or '*outside the temple*', referring to entities and structures not belonging to the Church. Though we view the sacred, the secular, and the profane as antithetical forces flowing from the way we practice religion or apply science and technology, the truth is that all three are independently intrinsic to human nature. Then we have something we pejoratively call 'superstition', thrown on the way. For some, sacred itself is superstition, and for some others, superstition is that which *they* do not like and *others* believe in. Just as a mirror reflects only what is in front of it, and just as we cannot throw up what is not already inside us, so it is with our actions and our thoughts, the feelings and emotions within. We cannot assume that the sacred is something *endogenous* and that the profane is *exogenous*; or that being secular is innate in our culture. Or dismiss as 'superstition' something that we cannot 'prove' or we cannot find 'evidence' for. All three— the sacred, the secular, and the profane — constantly crisscross and crosswalk in our consciousness, and we, being unable to harmonize them, create artificial walls at the most superficial level, which manifest in a variety of ways in our behavior. The 'balance of the blend of these three strands' shapes our psychic personality, defines our reflexive responses to life's vicissitudes. It is an important input to human transformation.

Somewhat simplistically, we think that what is not sacred must be secular, and what is not vulgar or profane must be holy, and what science cannot corroborate must be superstition. We view secular as something that is sacred sans superstition and practical without profanity. Just as there is profanity in the symbol of the sacred — religious behavior — there could be the sacred in the synonym for the vulgar — sex. That which incites hatred cannot be sacred and that which creates life, of the saint and the sinner alike, cannot be profane by itself. Indeed, in the contemporary world, more profanity oozes out of religious zealotry than perhaps from any other single source, but, the faithful zealots themselves think they are doing their 'sacred' duty in committing those horrors. Few people in India would see anything profane in the dumping of human waste or religious refuse (or even toxic industrial effluent) into the 'sacred' River Ganges, which they literally worship as a goddess. It does seem that in the womb of the sacred lies the 'savage', and that with the halo of the holy around us there is no depth below which the human will not sink. The shield of the mind fired by the sacred is impervious to any sense of guilt. The 'sacred' as a concept is associated with mystical awe or rapture, the veneration of something larger than what the mind can live with. The secular is what the mind can confine and confide in confidence. Even space and time are divided into the sacred and the secular. A place of worship is sacred, and a place of gambling or prostitution is profane. Situations arise where the Sacred *and* the Profane go hand in hand, one more apparent duality that frames — and festers — our life, constantly challenging us to choose or to harmonize. For many Hindus, certain times of the day like the hours before the dawn (*Brahma muhurta*) are considered sacred, and certain other time periods in a day (*Rahukala*) are considered inauspicious. The same act performed at different times of the day is believed to yield different results, underscoring the idea that nothing in creation, space, and time is equal. In the Old Testament, God tells Moses not to come any closer and to remove his sandals as he is standing on the holy ground. For the best part of man's earthly existence, it was the sacred, the holy, the spiritual, the sublime, and the supernatural that were dominant in his life. Even though we tend to scoff, they played an important emotional part in seeing us through torrid times — and they still do for the believer as well as the rationalist.

At the most basic level, everything that a human does today is heavily influenced by three strands of knowledge that are embodied by and embedded in what we call religion, science and technology. At the practical level, the questions that confront us are: who is a truly religious person? who is a genuinely spiritual person? and, what is a scientific state of mind? The human consciousness harbors a bewildering array of thoughts, passions, prejudices, feelings, and emotions, and how they collide or combine and emerge through behavior has been an enduring enigma. These thoughts or rather the *way* they are applied, give shape to our behavior and cast their shadow on how we act and react in everyday life. Since all three — religion, science and technology — are governed by different inherent dynamics, they leave gaps and apparent inconsistencies in the totality of the circumstance of life. The relationships between science and religion on the one side, and science and technology on the other side, have been particular fields of inquiry ever since modern science became the preponderant force in human affairs. Such has been its transformative impact that predicting the shape of science fifty years from now is as hazardous as predicting the geopolitical landscape of the world. In one word, modern man will go wherever science will lead him. It has now become a crunch factor in any human endeavor to ensure that human destiny does not totally slip away from human hands. Every endeavor has — or proclaims to have — the same central objective, which is to better the human condition. But the players are governed by different dynamics, and are inherently multifaceted. Therefore, forging a lasting and mutually reinforcing relationship calls for a plurality of points of contact and cohabitation. But things have not been static also. The relationship between science and technology has been the most advanced. Technology has been a part of human endeavor long before science, and perhaps even before religion came aboard. Technology *per se* did not prevent humans to live in equilibrium with other species and Nature, but the focus on science substantially changed that. With the injection of science into technology, leading to their virtual fusion, man has become the unchallenged monarch on Earth. It has also fundamentally altered the tenor and quality of human life. The 'double-helix' of science and technology courts and feeds on man's inherent languor, his distaste for work and effort, and on his love for comfort and convenience, thus propelling him often to choose the wrong over the right. The velocity of science-based technological change has run ahead of the ability of the human intellect to grasp, absorb, and adjust. Technology is letting us do things that once seemed like science fiction; from thoughtless navigation to limitless recollection, machines have made nearly every facet of our lives facile. But in doing so, they have also taken away skills that were once second-nature to the human. A growing concern is that technologies like the internet (and the general abundance of technology in our daily lives) may, in fact, be making us stupid — and that our dependency on technology will become so intense that, in the near future, our brain might lose even the meager cognitive power it now enjoys. Technological impact has another dimension. What used to take decades, if not centuries, from invention to application, has shrunk to a few years, leaving little or no time for assessing its implications and impact, often leading to a hasty and flawed decision making. Among the plethora of issues that confront mankind, one of them is the quality of 'scientific decision making', which is increasingly being shaped by the personal qualities of scientists. The irresistible appeal of 'techno-science' lies in the human mind's irresistible attraction to the three 'C's — comfort, convenience, and control.

When we even think of the sacred, religion instantly crops up. The shape, form, and direction of religious activity in the world has become another issue with overarching implications. Religion has been a huge factor in human life, but the way it impacts modern life raises the question if it is a relic from the wild wilderness of our prehistoric past, when nobody had the faintest idea what was going on, or if it is an adolescent attempt to meet our irrepressible need to know, or even perhaps, if it is a pure something that is perverted in practice by the human mind. With the human mind now crossing hitherto uncrossed thresholds of life and death, religious fervor or fundamentalism has become a 'sacred terror', as reflected by the title of a book by Daniel Benjamin and Steven Simon (*The Age of Sacred Terror*, 2002). It is this very sacred terror that seems to be offering an outlet for some of the darkest shadows lurking deep inside the human consciousness. Since religious zealotry is clothed in a divine garb — like in the battle cry *Deus Vult* ('God wills it') of the First Crusade, or *Jihad* in recent times — the hallucinating human mind, harboring malice and bolstered by real or illusionary religious victimization, has transformed the psychological profile of man and made him a ticking time bomb. Since no individual is a mental carbon copy of another, we do not know where the fuse is hidden, and when it is set to go off and with what effect. Religion can be and has been a powerful moral force, but also, when a 'believer' convinces himself that his religion is in peril or when any of its sanctified or sacred symbols — a pig or a cow, a statue or a forbidden picture — are parodied or defiled, the reach and the depth of the resultant 'holy slaughter' is awesome and awful. Whether or not religious terror is a perversion of the 'spirit' of every religion is beside the point, even pointless: the mind loves it, and who can stop the mind? It is said that there is never enough religion in the world to make people love one another, but just enough or plenty to make them hate one another. And that 'hate' can translate into horrendous behavior. And those who incite, encourage, revel, and rejoice in such 'sacred' terror are not freaks or sadists but ordinary folks. They are normal people who consider themselves to be 'god-fearing' and 'good' people, and religious leaders. They do not feel 'bad' or remorseful because they believe that they are doing 'God's work'. James Haught's book *Holy Horrors* (1990), gives a gory historical account of holy human depravity. The historical evidence shows that to 'appease', to 'please', to 'satiate', to 'beseech' God, man has not stopped at anything: nothing is sacrosanct, no sacrifice or sacrilege is unthinkable, nothing is too degrading or demeaning. Underscoring the point that the history of religion is a history of horror, Haught quotes the words of a Christian cleric who boasted, after one of the Crusades, that 'in the temple of Solomon, one rode in blood up to the knees and even to the bridles of horses'. And all that, in this view, was not barbaric; it was bolstered by the just and marvelous judgment of God! We cannot easily dismiss the current crop of zealots as another abominable aberration like the maniacs of the Middle Ages, or as expressions of localized lunacy of deranged or brainwashed bigots. They too are 'human', and that cause is religion; and every religion, every kind of faith, every culture has been privy to such horrors, which are not only bloodcurdling but even beyond our imagination. How can that which is deemed 'sacred' propel man to do such things to another human? Such is the sway and power of religion and science over the human mind that, tempting as it is, we cannot just leave them to their present motivation and momentum, and simply hope — like the character Wilkins Micawber in Charles Dickens's novel *David Copperfield* (1850), — that man will somehow muddle through the crises that he faces, and that religion will, in a flash of divine insight or revelation, loosen its venomous fangs, or that science, triggered by a moral angst of scientists, will become a healing balm. The catharsis must come from within.

Religion, Spirituality, and Science — the Struggle for Supremacy

Instinctively, we associate 'sacred' with religion, spirituality and the divine, and 'secular' with 'morally neutral' things relating to the physical, worldly and material matter and science. After all that has happened in the name of religion, and after all that science has done to the human condition, it might be legitimate to ponder if anything that transpires under the signature of religion is any longer 'sacred', and if science (rather, what some scientists do for profit or power) is 'safe'. We need fundamental rethinking on both fronts to harness their potential and power for the good of mankind. What constitutes 'religion' has long been a matter of both sacred and secular thought. While there is no unanimity, what perhaps one can broadly agree is that it is a body of thought and knowledge that makes us do or follow — or not do or not follow — certain procedures, symbols, rituals, worship, etc., that are drawn from the scriptures, traditions, and beliefs, often with supernatural or transcendental underpinnings; and that religion influences, among other things, the way we relate to a Supreme, Higher power, or to a God, or to afterlife. It is sometimes used synonymously with 'faith' or a 'belief system'. Although most people identify religious impulses with God, the French sociologist Emile Durkheim wrote that one of the distinctive traits of religious thought is the division of the world into two domains, one containing all that is sacred, and the other containing all that is profane. Durkheim emphasized the social nature of religious thought and even argued that the sacred/profane dichotomy was not equivalent to good/evil: the sacred could be good or evil, and the profane could be either as well. In common usage, the shorthand for sacred is scripture. While every religious person swears by the 'scriptures', what he usually implies are the sacred books of his holy religion, as opposed to the false, if not profane, writings on which all 'other' faiths are based. It is this 'double vision' about scriptures that causes most problems. Some interject another category into this context — the sinful, those things that the scriptures expressly prohibit. Leaving aside the sinful side, 'sacred' is associated with religion and God; 'secular' with rationality, temporality and science; and 'profane' with the vulgar and the obscene. And then we have this rather elusive domain called 'spirituality' or spiritualism, which in one sense distinguishes itself as being none of the above; not science, not technology, not religion. Spirituality or spiritualism concerns itself with the 'matters of the spirit'; it is the search to know our true selves, which is also to 'know God'. In some countries like the United States, spiritualism has been the fastest-growing 'religious group' in the last ten years, and this movement denies any particular religious denomination or practicing affiliation. That is in one way encouraging (followers can become better human beings), and in another way dangerous (they can fall prey to pseudo-spiritualists and nihilist cults).

Science works in the world of knowledge, which is human; spirituality operates in the field of the inner world, which is divine. Spirituality is said to be about faith; and science, about fact. But both seek answers to the same questions, such as 'what is life?' Neither science nor spirituality has clear answers yet, but they both claim that it does not negate the validity of their observations and results. The Austrian physicist Erwin Schrödinger in his celebrated work *What is Life?* (1944), addressed the question "how can the events in space and time which take place within the spatial boundary of a living organism be accounted for by physics and chemistry?" and his 'preliminary answer' was that the "obvious inability of present-day physics and chemistry to account for such events is no reason at all for doubting that they can be accounted for by those scientists". The same sense is shared by spiritualists. In the spiritual perspective, as described in all the great wisdom traditions, there are three levels of existence: physical, mental, and spiritual. Science has until recently (and barring some notable exceptions) denied the spiritual dimension. Even in regard to mental processes, science argued that they are simply biochemical processes germane to the brain itself. Hence, the only mode of knowing the real, it posited, was by observing the objective, physical world through sensory empiricism. But in the end, these are all metaphors intended to convey a sense of something or some idea that cannot be clearly defined. While the 'modern mind' looks at everything as an opposite of another, many indigenous cultures have had a more holistic view. They thought, felt and lived in unity with Nature — even in killing they were respectful. They had empiricism, and they had an intimate, profound, and sensitive relationship with Nature, in their beliefs, actions, and consequences. They emphasized kinship, interdependence, and reciprocity with Nature, as well as care, respect, and reverence for Nature.

Operationally, it is the practice of religion and the products of science that dominate our lives. But they are no longer independent of each other; the 'fruits' of technology are used in religious practices, and scientific inquiry draws upon the scriptures. And, despite predictions for over three centuries by social scientists about an impending dissolution of religion, that humans will outgrow their belief in the supernatural with the onslaught of modernism, religion is very much alive and kicking, even if one cannot vouchsafe for its robust health. It is now widely accepted that the 'theory of secularization' — which states that the unstoppable sweep of 'secular' modernization will hasten the 'death of religion' — is now passé, and that the world now, to borrow a phrase from Peter L. Berger, one of the foremost advocates of the secularization theory, is as 'furiously religious' as at any time in history. It is even being said that the time has come 'to carry the secularization doctrine to the graveyard of failed theories, and there to whisper *requiescat in pace* [rest in peace]'[1]. There are those who argue that religious growth has occurred not because of any development in human capacities or divine grace, but because of a predisposition toward religious experience that was always innate but only gradually awakened. Coupled with a brooding sense of uneasiness and wrenching angst, religiosity has come to be seen as the 'Aladdin's Lamp', the rubbing of which helps us overcome all our travails. 'Secularization' might be in retreat, but not modernization powered by science and technology. The other tenet of secularization, separation of private belief and public behavior also has not worked. Religion is now more in the public domain than ever before. So much of our 'living space' is public that it is unrealistic to think that it can be isolated at home. The real problem is not religion's impact socially, but that we do not apply or practice what religions prescribe as desirable values in human behavior on the street or at the workplace. Religion is on the ascendancy, but religious values have been relegated to the background. We must remember that every religion reflects the place and time of its origin. In that sense, religious morality seems skewed for the present context. For example, it places too much emphasis on sexual behavior and not on social conduct. That has affected both social values and personal piety. Sex, more than any single thing, straddles the domain between the sacred and the profane. The mindset is that if we are sexually straight it is okay to be socially deviant. Sexual transgressions are more severely dealt with than social crimes. This imbalance has to be set right both for the sake of religion and society. For instance, adultery is both a crime and a sin, but adulteration, in most societies, is almost accepted or condoned as a part of economic life. This is, in fact, part of a larger problem which was incisively probed by the American theologian Reinhold Niebuhr in his book *Moral Man and Immoral Society: A Study of Ethics and Politics* (1932). Niebuhr dealt with the growing gap between our private and public personas, and argued that while we know a lot about how to apply morality to our individual existence, we know very little about how to apply it to our *aggregate* existence, whether as nations, organizations, or communities. Modern, science-based technology (*techno-science*, as some like to call it), arguably the defining intellectual venture of our age, has itself become what we may call 'secular' religion, and it promises to give us what 'sacred' religions promised but could not deliver — eternal life on earth. Techno-science has escalated the size and scope of human inventiveness to such a degree that everything is mass-scale, almost absolute and universal: production, consumption, culture, creativity — and extermination. And paradoxically, contrary to the incompatibility and tension that is supposed to exist between the sacred and the secular — religion and science — what we have instead is cohabitation between the two. Moreover, there is hostility and rage between religions and even within the same religion, between different denominations or sects. No *jihadi* or a religious fanatic targets any scientist, however much what the latter says and does violates the basic tenets of his religion. The fanatic targets only those who profess and practice another faith.

The human mind is neither equipped nor trained to handle the avalanche of raw information on the one hand, and the disappearing distance between discovery and adaptation, creativity and adjustment, on the other. While it has without doubt enhanced the physical quality of life of the vast majority of humans (marginally for most and qualitatively for some others), science has also given birth to what M.D. Aeschliman calls 'murderous science', by which he refers to the role of modern science in atrocities like Nazi human experimentation, genocide, sterilization. Enhancement, that is the key concept that drives human ambition. We want to *enhance* everything — from body to brain — and move from 'noble stoicism' to distilled joy. And science dangles that primrose prospect. The fact is that science is not as clear-eyed or candid as we like to think. Time and again, one 'established' theory has been overtaken by another until that meets a similar fate, or it sometimes goes back to the beginning. Climate change and global warming are telling examples of our pathological — and pathetic — inability to grasp the import of the risks we face. It is mind-boggling but symptomatic of our state of mind that with possibly the very future of humanity and even life on earth at such clear and present danger, we still dither and debate. Our intellect cannot make up its mind if it is simply another natural vagary of the weather or if it presages an impending catastrophe. But such is the inebriating influence of science, that, in the words of a pioneering thinker in the field of science and religion, Denis Alexander, "the new atheists, as they have been dubbed by the media, those such as Dawkins, Atkins and Dennett, have declared their opposition to religion in the name of science, suggesting that science has all the answers that we need to know."[2] Skepticism or downright hostility toward religion did not begin with these 'new atheists'. While technology and belief in a supernatural power were able to coexist, science from its very inception looked upon itself as the antithesis of faith, but that might be somewhat of an oversimplification, as many scientists have said. Despite the popular impression that scientists are hostile to faith, many celebrated scientists are believers in something that is beyond the control of human intelligence. Contrary to popular perception, 'scientists' are not a homogenous lot, nor is one quite sure who qualifies to be called a 'scientist'. And the 'facts' and 'findings' of science, change constantly, and no particular scientific theory is cast in concrete or considered unassailable. Even 'scientific skepticism' is also science. Many branches of science like geology found no incompatibility with religious principles. Some even speculate that it might be possible that our studies in earth science may so improve our understanding as to permit geology to re-enforce religion, and might even help in codifying ethical rules of conduct. Many great scientists were 'believers' in its broadest sense. Isaac Newton, whose discovery of the laws of gravity reshaped our understanding of the universe, said: "This most beautiful system could only proceed from the dominion of an intelligent and powerful being."[3]

The British anthropologist Alfred Russel Wallace, co-discoverer of the theory of natural selection along with Darwin, was an ardent advocate of spiritualism and wrote: "I am thankful I can see much to admire in all religions. To the mass of mankind religion of some kind is a necessity. But whether there be a God and whatever be His nature; whether we have an immortal soul or not, or whatever may be our state after death, I can have no fear of having to suffer for the study of nature and the search for truth…"[4] And in the book *What We Believe but Cannot Prove* (2006), many scientists and 'rational thinkers' enumerate the kinds of things they believed, which we often ridicule as supernatural or superstitious. The title of the book reflects the opinions of scientists like Richard Dawkins, Freeman Dyson — "there are true mathematical statements that cannot be proved".[5] The book quotes Dawkins as saying that "science proceeds by having hunches, by making guesses, by having hypotheses, sometimes inspired by poetic thoughts, by aesthetic thoughts even, and then science goes about trying to demonstrate it experimentally or observationally."[6] That description hardly sounds 'scientific', and it raises the question, who is a 'scientist'? Is he some kind of a 'saint' in white robes laboring in a laboratory mindless of any material gain, or is he just another human being pursuing a profession, and morally — or materially — no different from others in that pursuit? Whoever he is or he is not, and whether or not he is to be held accountable for higher ethical norms, given the repercussions of his work, the fact that many 'scientists' *feel* that way is encouraging for the future, for forging a partnership between science and spirituality. If science accepts that there are forces beyond 'proof', and if spiritualists concede that empirical knowledge of the laws of Nature and of the universe could be an input to man's spiritual quest, that by itself is a huge step forward toward reconciliation between science and the spirit of religion. The American physician-geneticist Francis Collins, described the Human Genome Project (HGP) as the first glimpse of our own instruction book, previously known only to God. In his book *The Language of God: A Scientist Presents Evidence for Belief* (2006), Collins says that scientific discoveries are an 'opportunity to worship', and that he was an atheist in his early years, but later walking through the Cascade Mountains in Washington State, USA, he had an epiphany, a kind of divine inspiration, and came to the view that man could not be a moral animal without the aid of a God-endowed moral law. Collins also said, "One of the great tragedies of our time is this impression that has been created that science and religion have to be at war."[7] The British astrophysicist Arthur Eddington wrote, "We have learnt that the exploration of the external world by the methods of the physical sciences leads not to a concrete reality but to a shadow world of symbols."[8] And the Nobel physicist Max Planck, who is regarded as the father of modern quantum theory said that "science cannot solve the ultimate mystery of Nature. And that is because, in the last analysis, we ourselves are part of Nature, and, therefore, part of the mystery that we are trying to solve."[9]

Setting aside, for the moment, both the semantics and the skeptics, nuances and niceties, the fact is that religion and scientific technology, two of the most transformational forces in the universe, have thus far been unable to work complementarily, science relying primarily on empiricism, and religion on revelation. For at least three or four centuries, modern man has been trying to broker what the American author Ken Wilber calls the '*marriage of science and soul*', the integration of science and religion. It has to be a marriage, not of convenience but, in Wilber's words, an 'agreement acceptable in their own terms'. Historically, the relationship between religion and science has followed four paths: irreconcilable *antagonism*; *interdependence* (no overlap); *complementarity* through dialogue; and *integration* or enforced takeover of one of the two.

The stark reality is that science and religion have never made easy bedfellows, because science, in exploring the universe, time, and space, or how humans have come about on earth, has not found either the evidence or the need for God, thus cutting away at the very root of religion. Moreover, more avowedly religious and spiritual persons are willing to acknowledge the fact that scientific inquiry has a legitimate role in the search for the Truth, than there are scientists prepared to extend the same courtesy and accommodation to religion. The *raison d'être* of religious faith is its allure of healing the wounds of human existence and of elevating man to the higher realms of ethereal existence. Yet, the history of religions is soaked in blood, sacrifice, and vengeance. The brutal facts of the history of religions pose stark questions about the intertwining of religion and violence. Some historians like Rene Girard even claim that in that intertwining lies the origin of human culture. For centuries, religion and science have been circling each other, gingerly and suspiciously courting with intermittent episodes of amity and hostility, love and hate. The British mathematician and philosopher Alfred Whitehead wrote that more than anything else, the 'future of civilization depends on the way the two most powerful forces of history, science and religion, settle into a relationship with each other'.[10] But what kind of 'marriage' should it be — one of convenience, sort of cohabitation, each retaining its identity and individuality, sharing common space and coming together to mutual advantage? Or should it be like science and technology, a kind of merger, complete surrender to each other, becoming altogether a different personality? Some even argue that forcing an artificial rapprochement and cohabitation could do more harm than good; each, being distinct, should be left in its own natural territory. The scope and the undercurrents of this question are huge and have been the subject of hundreds of books and articles. Be that as it may, no one can argue that humanity will gain anything by the total isolation or breakdown of communication. Furthermore, although some diehard scientists still deny everything that religion is supposed to stand for, fields like quantum physics are validating some ancient beliefs. While the union of science and technology has been a mixed blessing, the prospect of bridges, not necessarily betrothal, between these two can be nothing but a blessing. Some sort of belief system (we call it religion, organized or unorganized, informal or implicit) has always been a part of human presence on earth. And whether in killing or in cohabitation, in making love or in waging a war, humans have almost always used scientific tools and machines.

Man has been called a tool of tools and a complex machine. The machine has made man both a master and a vassal; both creator and the terminator. Technology and transformation have almost become interchangeable. Pundits debate if change is inherent in technology or in people. Some say that technology changes; that people do not; and that the human animal is the same. Some believe that the change comes not from the nature of technology *per se*, but by what technology allows people to do differently. Others argue that technology is simply another knife in your hand; what you do with it depends on your state of mind at that moment. For some, more specifically the so-called *Generation Y*, technology is integral to their everyday lives, entertainment and socializing; something that allows them to lead, as they say, a 'full life'. But that 'fullness' conceals gnawing emptiness. It opens the door not to the world within, but to the brewing apocalypse within, an implosion triggered by enfeeblement in the garb of enhancement. Thus far, man has managed a reasonable balance between adapting to the external environment and cultural change. Now, he is trying to become a 'new and improved' product through biological, especially genetic interventions. Again, some see this is as a way to ethically ameliorate human nature and transform man into a better being; others see this as the final affront and assault on Nature — and God.

Since the first use of stone tools by Paleolithic man around two million years ago, man has been inseparable from some kind or other of an artificial prop. In one sense, man survived because he became a 'handyman', able to make and use a range of tools, not only to survive but to also prevail. The story of human evolution is the story of tools. The man-machine relationship has changed but mostly in one direction: towards the dominance of the machine, and the subjugation of man. We are at a stage when robots might take over the tasks of men, when humans might have 'brain implants' that would allow them to think at the speeds of today's microprocessors. And information technology is hurtling towards a point where machines will become smarter than their makers. We read about scientists creating a 'Frankenrobot', a robot controlled exclusively by living brain tissue, stitched together from cultured rat neurons.[11] Clearly all scientific 'advances' have far-reaching implications for human future, but much of it takes place away from the public gaze, and the lay public also behave as if it is a 'scientific' issue and of no particular consequence to their lives. Although scientific advances more directly impact our lives than religion, we are more cognizant of religion than science. While we try to regulate the minutest things of daily life, we are totally complacent about matters that could fundamentally alter the context and content of human life on earth. It is not as though science is all bad; even if it is all good, those who are the intended beneficiaries, the public at large and the civil society, must be made participants in setting its agenda and direction.

Many philosophers have commented upon the technological character of the modern world and on the dominance of the technological way of thinking, what the German philosopher Martin Heidegger called 'machination', which is 'the challenging-forth of nature and the making of nature as a by product'. 'Machination' leads to the 'loss of enchantment with the world', what Einstein called the ability to 'stand rapt in awe'. On the one hand, science is trying to qualitatively enhance brainpower, and on the other hand, technology is marshalling that power to increase machine power. The basic assumption is that the human brain is a marvelous 'neutral' machine, much like a computer hard drive, that it simply gathers, stockpiles, and processes data to be tapped as and when we need it. But this theory, we are told, does not hold water because every time "we recall it, our brain writes it down again and during this re-storage, it is also reprocessed. In time, the fact is gradually transferred to the cerebral cortex and is separated from the context in which it was originally learned."[12] So, if 'the brain lies to you' and our decision making is inherently flawed, what do we do? But then of course, who is the actual decision maker? In the race between the powerful but 'lying' brain, and a robot that can 'think' and become a 'partner', what could be the outcome? No one has a clue how all this will impact on the consciousness, culture, and creativity of future generations. Man could either be another 'endangered species' or become a machine with a mind, akin to Mary Shelley's *Frankenstein* (1818), where the 'victor' runs the risk of losing his own life, if not his very soul. Mary Shelley's Victor (the scientist in the novel) carries an uncanny resemblance to what modern man is attempting. Victor's quest is for God-like power and glory. He tries to create a new species that can defy disease and death; he thinks natural laws are not immutable. What he gets is loneliness, desolation and complete failure, and in the end he is terrified of his own creation. Our dependence on machines is such that if the machine succeeds, we are supermen, and if it fails, we are sub-animals in the sense that we cannot do what even animals can. Man is like a domesticated pet unable to survive in its own natural habitat. What we have for company, as we 'brood on the brink', is a machine which perhaps knows its 'mind' more than we know our own. For, contrary to what we think, the 'things' around us, while being transient and ephemeral, have a 'life' of their own; once created, they acquire a self-sustaining momentum and they may, in certain cases, outlast their creator.

Transhumanism and Technology

Goethe's Faust sells his soul to the devil in return for power over the physical world. This is often interpreted as a metaphor for the tyranny of industrial technology. Few issues divide some of our best minds as does the question how science-based technology is likely to transform the human condition. For example, Nick Bostrom, philosopher and advocate of transhumanism, says that human nature is "a work-in-progress, a half-baked beginning that we can learn to remold in desirable ways."[13] Transhumanists believe that progress, understood as betterment over time, is inherent in Nature and innate in culture; and that the human species in its current form does not represent the end of our development but rather a comparatively early phase. Evolution is tantamount to progress in biology. Technological advances amount to progress in culture. The direction of 'progress' is set, and the task of the transhumanist technology is to press on the pedal of progress. The other term sometimes used synonymously is posthumanism, a state or a condition in which basic capacities so radically exceed those of present-day humans as to be no longer unambiguously human by our current norms. It begins when man begins to overcome his own limitations, but is still identifiable as a human person. It could be a symbiosis of human and artificial intelligence, or uploaded consciousnesses, or the result of making many smaller but cumulatively profound technological augmentations to a biological human. Others argue that we will never have sufficient wisdom to make ourselves fundamentally different from what we are. The Japanese-American philosopher Francis Fukuyama describes transhumanism as one of 'the world's most dangerous ideas'. But whatever be the ultimate outcome, we are on the threshold of changing human nature by direct biochemical intervention. The synergies and confluence of nanotechnology, biotechnology, information technology, and cognitive science (NBIC) can either enhance man beyond recognition, or extinguish human life as we know it. Serious concern is being expressed by scientists like Raymond Kurzweil that the capacity for 'self-replication' (that is, to be able to make carbon copies of oneself), applied to biotechnology could go terribly wrong or could fall into the wrong hands. The exclusiveness of the actors involved — science, technology, business, and government — and the resultant exclusion of the public who could be the unintended victims is also a source of great concern.

It is also being predicted that there could be 'horizontal transfer of genes', that is from one species to another, as it was said to be the case in the earliest stages of life on earth when, in the words of Freeman Dyson, 'life was a community of cells of various kinds, sharing their genetic information'... evolution then was a 'communal affair'.[14] If this were to recur in the future world, that would be even more technologically deterministic. As for nanotechnology, which is based on the ability to manipulate matter at the atomic and molecular levels, some pundits speculate that, in the hands of a malicious megalomaniac, it could well cause the extinction of intelligent life on earth by releasing 'biosphere-eating' *nanobots* into the environment. The technology that produces such destructive *nanobots* is much easier to develop than a technology that provides a shield against such man-made creations. It is an issue of profound import and implications for our future, and it is surprising that so little work has been done on this subject. Leaving it to scientists and the political class could well be as catastrophic as the danger itself. Man is now capable of creating microscopic robots that can perform repair at the cellular level and, it is claimed, revive the dead through cryonic technology. Clearly, the moral gap between what we can do and what we *ought* to do is dramatically narrowing, thus opening either a 'Pandora's box' or a 'can of worms', we are not sure.

What anthropologists call culture, which broadly means patterns of human activity in a social setting, has always heavily influenced the human condition, and, in the modern age, culture is shaped by science and technology. Although recent evidence indicates that some other species like chimpanzees used tools like leaf sponges, man alone has been called a tool-making animal, and it was his ability to convert natural materials into tools that tilted the scales in his favor in the struggle for survival. As some historians of technology have noted, "Societies tend to mold themselves around their tools. Tools change the user, in ways that are unanticipated."[15] Technology at once empowers and enfeebles the human condition and carries certain grave evolutionary implications for the future. We have become slaves to gadgets, and a recent study indicates that our addiction to machines is not only for convenience but also for comfort, as a recipe for loneliness and as a substitute for 'emotional company'. When the telephone was first introduced, Oscar Wilde was told how it worked: "...a bell rings and you go down the hall to see who is calling", and Wilde quipped with his usual wit, "just like a servant."[16] The irony is that, over time, the servant became the master, and turned the master into a subject. When human beings become troublesome, and human relationships such a hassle, and when a machine seems to serve the same purpose with greater diligence, why bother about opinionated humans? The British philosopher C.E.M. Joad described modern man's view of sexual desire as "a buzzing bluebottle that needed to be swatted promptly before it distracted a man of intellect from higher things".[17] So, for 'higher things', if we cannot find a human mate, a machine might well do! That would seductively save man from having to deal with another human's moods, passions, and demands. We are now being told that "by the year 2050, your lover may be a…robot" and that "robots as sex toys should already be in the market within five years."[18] There could soon be a time when one 'human' sexual partner might say to the other, "If you have sex with a robot, I am leaving you", or purely as a matter of precaution, when one goes on a business trip, "please take your robot because I happen to worry about the red light district."[19]

Technology is also becoming a primrose path on the quest for bodily betterment. Hitherto, the human had essentially accepted the body he was born with, and within that limitation worked towards making it healthier and stronger. It is being predicted that one day, parents will be able to choose genes for their children, genes that increase athletic ability or musical talents, and so on. What science is trying to do now is to go beyond that 'limitation', as in the case of, for example, the eye. It is being predicted that soon human beings might be able to experience *3-D virtual reality* through glasses and contact lenses that beam images directly to their retinas. With such devices, we are told, we will be able to block the 'real world' entirely and 'live' in a virtual world. Another 'limitation' has been that the genes get 'mixed up' at birth; the offspring inherits them from at least two sources, the mother and father. One way to ensure genetic 'purity', or even 'excellence', it is claimed, is cloning, which really is to artificially produce identical twins. Although it is said that cloning success in animals does not necessarily extend to humans, and "no one knows why some species are tougher to clone than others,"[20] already the world's first human clone, a girl dubbed 'Eve', is claimed to have been created, and several thousands are said to be waiting to be cloned. We will be creating what we may call adult identical twins, the idea being there is nothing wrong in parents being enabled, if they can afford it, to give their children something that some other children already have. This brings us to the possibility that if human intervention is likely to alter the 'basic features of birth', it nullifies the theory of Karma, at the least. If a certain group of human beings continue cloning themselves from one generation to another, the likelihood is that the genetic pool of the human race would remain frozen and identical. On the other hand, as the British molecular geneticist Johnjoe McFadden argues, whether we like it or not, if humanity is not to become an endangered species, we must face up to the challenges of genetic engineering. It is posited that while natural selection took care of the defective genes by weeding them out, in the earlier times, modern medicine lets us survive them and, in the process, while we live longer, the undesirable genes become weaker. Thus, we have two diametrically different visions, and like much else in life, it depends on individual perception.

Whether a cloned man will resemble a being from Huxley's *Brave New World* or Mary Shelley's *Frankenstein* or the idyllic world of *Utopia*, whether such a man would be on par with the Buddha or a Stalin or a Hitler, it is anybody's guess. Science is supposed to be a search for truth and meaning, and technology is supposed to help man overcome the limitations of natural laws. It is modern man's ability to fuse the two that has endowed him with such power that he himself is fearful of it. After the first atomic explosion, Albert Einstein remarked that everything in the world has changed except man. He said, "Only two things are infinite, the universe and human stupidity, and I am not sure about the former."[21]

Like much else in the human world, science and technology are double-edged weapons, both a boon and a bane, a mixed blessing. They have ameliorated the living conditions of millions but left behind billions in abject poverty. For mass poverty is caused not only by economic and social exclusion, but also by technological exclusion. The fact is that the largesse of science-based technology has largely bypassed the majority of mankind. Our greater comprehension of the neurological and biochemical basis of the human brain, and of the biological basis of human nature, can give us new insights and instruments for social engineering and spiritual awareness. But instead of throwing up a superman or spiritual men, it could also lead to the creation of a physically powerful man with a weak and vile mind. Hence, instead of being a 'noble savage', man is all set to become a 'toxic technological animal', totally dependent on machines for everything other than eating, sleeping, and sex. Through contraceptives, science and technology have decoupled sexual pleasure and reproduction, and abortion has detached the fates of the mother and the fetus. Children are no longer the price or purpose of pregnancy; artificial insemination and in vitro fertilization have removed sexual activity as a necessary condition for human multiplication. And if science bestows the boon of 'eternal life', then children may be wholly dispensed with, and then sex will become, as some biologists dub it, an "evolutionary accident…during the evolutionary bootstrap phase of our history."[22] We have sleeping aids, and maybe in the not-too-distant future, the stomach may become superfluous and predigested food can get straight into the bloodstream.

Science and technology are now trying to dig into the deepest layer of the human condition: the faculties of thinking and feeling. No 'sacred cows' hold them back; no 'final frontiers' are final. While a full-fledged 'thinking' computer is a scientific possibility, a 'feeling' computer is another matter altogether. The odds about a merger between man and machine are long and formidable. In the first place, we do not know the biological origins of feelings and emotions. A 'thinking' or 'organic' computer may be ruthlessly rational and its decision-making process may be superior to ours. Devoid of emotions, feelings and tenderness, such a computer may be more substantially efficient, but not even nervously human. For example, if his mental calculus reaches the conclusion that the world is better off without humans, he will destroy mankind, say, by pressing the nuclear button. But in the process he will also destroy himself and the very world he is trying to save! That is what clinical reasoning leads to.

Since the emergence of science-based technology as a transforming force three or four centuries ago, many observant people have expressed concern about its adverse impact. The 'Luddite' revolt in 19th century England was one such voice. Ralph Waldo Emerson said, "Things are in the saddle, and ride mankind."[23] With the exponential increase in the power of science and technology in the 20th century, many writers and historians like Aldous Huxley, Arnold Toynbee, Bertrand Russell and Mahatma Gandhi tried to awaken humanity to the potential risks and dangers. The French historian and philosopher Jacques Ellul wrote, "Technology is not content with *being*, or in our world, with being the *principal or determining factor*. Technology has become a system."[24] It is a system that is driven by its own dynamics and is propelled by its own momentum. Not all, however, are alarmists, some are downright euphoric. The economist Paul Zane Pilzer (*God Wants You to be Rich*, 1997) wrote that technology is the chosen instrument which will make everyone rich and transform the world into a land of plenty and prosperity. Similarly, Michael G. Zey wrote in his book *Seizing the Future*, that "humankind will extend its control over many of the forces of Nature that have stood outside its dominion since the beginning of time".[25] According to him, the human species in the present century is about to burst through the boundaries of Nature and unleash the power of its technology and ingenuity, hurtling itself to the next stage of evolution, and human life will be disease-free and its span will be doubled, deserts will bloom and man will colonize Mars. It is now believed that if a person's cells can be extracted and saved before his death, that person could later be 'recreated' through cloning.

All these rosy predictions miss one central point: man and his mind. Together they make human responses wholly unfathomable, and that is why 'the lessons of history' have been of little value in predicting future events or shaping political, social, economic and ecological changes. We have a tendency to look back at the past as better than it was, look at the present as worse than it is, and the future with more apprehension than it warrants. And so often, we seem to know what needs to be done but find ourselves unable to do it. That is the endemic gap between 'knowing' and 'doing' that bedevils human life. Technically, pundits like Zey predict all that might be possible, but man is more interested in prevailing over another man and ravaging Planet Earth than in his own well-being. All that science can do is to somehow keep man alive when he is better off being dead; to somehow lengthen life with scant regard for the quality of life.

Limits of Science, and the Science of Limits

Despite its virtuosity and immense creativity, we have to bear in mind that there are two frontiers that science cannot cross given the limits inherent in the human species. John Barrow points out in his book *Impossibility* (1999), that there are limits to scientific inquiry imposed by the deficiencies of the human mind, and that our brain evolved in such a way as to meet the demands of our immediate environment. He argues that much of what lies outside this small circle may also lie outside our understanding, that there are limits to human discovery, and that there are things that are ultimately unknowable, undoable, or unreachable.[26] According to Eddington, instead of knowledge of substance, science gives us knowledge purely of structure, and instead of revealing a strict determinism in Nature, science has to be content with probabilities. It cannot 'cure the disease of death' and it cannot create 'artificial consciousness', or so it was assumed till the late 20th century. Scientists now say that they are on the 'cusp of immortality', or at least on the verge of extending the human life span to an extent that mortality loses its sting. Computer scientists like Raymond Kurzweil, forecast a growing convergence of humans and intelligent machines, leading to immortality and to humans existing as 'software' that can operate in various bodies. He predicts that by the year 2029, a $1,000 personal computer will be 1,000 times more powerful than the human brain, and that soon we will be able to reprogramme our body's stone-age software to halt, then reverse aging; and then the power of nanotechnology will enable us to live forever. In short, death will also be brought under control, within the ambit of choice. If death does strike and if one wants to come back to life, the scenario would be like this: "…clcse-up of his right wrist, a red medical-alert bracelet instructs the finders of his dead body to act quickly, administer calcium blockers and blood thinners, pack his corpse in ice water, balance his pH and call the 800 number of a firm that will helicopter paramedics to begin cryonic suspension'[27]. The person would then be woken up from death when a cure is found for the disease that caused his death. Eventually, it is predicted, an all-powerful 'God Computer' will emerge, which will be the savior of mankind. This computer will have the ability to reach into the past and resurrect dead human beings, and create a paradise on earth. Champions of the God Computer theory include American mathematician Vernor Vinge (who predicted in 1993 that superhuman intelligence will arrive within the next thirty years and that the human era will end), and inventor Raymond Kurzweil. One more major proponent of the idea that a super God Computer will save mankind is physicist Frank Tipler, who spells out his theory in painstaking detail — including mathematical proofs — in his book, *The Physics of Immortality* (1994). When opinions come from such distinguished scholars, it becomes difficult to choose between being elated or alarmed, or amused — or marvel at how delusionary the human mind can be, or wonder if it is also a part of the Vedantic *maya*, the cosmic illusion. But the more intriguing, if not scary, question is: even if a fraction of such scenarios actualize, what kind of a human society will emerge from it? It is hard for us to visualize because there are so many imponderable and unknowable variables that would come into play.

That pregnant probability is for the future, but now we have to grapple with the ethical and social implications of human cloning, and of supermodels "selling cells from their bodies to make hundreds of 'perfect' human clones for tomorrow's parents."[28] It has been reported that humans have acquired the capacity to create headless mice through removal of genes in the embryo that control the development of the head. But the body would have the capacity to keep the organs functional for use as transplants.[29] Would that 'body' have a life as we understand it to be? A 'headless body' is said to be a step towards 'curing death' and ensuring immortality! At least Mary Shelley's *Frankenstein* had a head and a 'feeling heart'! In another 'exciting' direction, maybe science will implant an 'organic computer' in the place of the missing head! Slowly but surely, what once used to be 'science fiction', seems to be fast becoming dead serious stuff.

Yet mankind cannot turn its back on science and technology and turn the world into a Luddite Land or an Amish Enclave, just as we cannot stop wearing clothes. We cannot stop making tools, but we can stop making horrendous weapons that often fail to kill the targeted enemy, but instead, kill thousands of innocents. We cannot put biotechnology back into the bottle, but we can certainly stop messing with the basics of life and genes. While in earlier times, there was a long intervening time lag between scientific discovery and technological and commercial or practical application, which allowed time to assess the impact on the human personality, that chain of events is now telescoped. What used to take several decades or centuries, barely takes a decade or even less today. And the greed for quick profits overwhelms the need for proper technological and ethical assessments, which should be as important as the traditional techno-economic assessment.

While the threat of a nuclear Armageddon has somewhat lessened but has not entirely vanished (as long as it is within human reach, so long that threat will remain), biotechnology now threatens to change the fundamentals of life and Nature. We read about the extremely rapid degeneration of the genetic patrimony of humankind, with a potential for hereditary illnesses, which already is increasing in tandem with the cure of certain diseases; and also about 'direct gene control', *imminently possible* production of 'mechanizing and de-mechanizing' bacteria for the 'biologically induced' modification of human behavior and intervention in the processes of the human psyche; and of many other unsettling and unintelligible research agenda. The problem is that science can often start a journey but it has no control over where it ends; there is no knowing which dynamic gets initiated and how it unfolds and impinges on earthly life. Time and again, we have seen that ultimately discoveries have little to do with the initial intent; they are often unintended byproducts or products of chance and coincidence. We may be thus far lucky but not for too long. That is why one gets uneasy when we read predictions that are not too far removed: for example, in futurist Michio Kaku's words, man might be able to, from now onwards, 'alter and synthesize new forms of life... and to attain control over matter itself.'[30] It also assumes that there is no force in the Universe other than human will and no law besides human law.

The nub of the problem is three-fold. *One*, the human mind has not evolved, and may never do so in a way that it can wisely exercise the power that science and technology have placed in human hands. In that sense, the very invention of science might have been a deviant, an aberration in human evolution. In another sense, human cognitive creativity, meant to enhance the human condition, has outstripped human emotional capacity. The mind is monopolistic, defensive, distrustful and divisive, and these are not the qualities one should have while wielding such power. And the human institutions man has fashioned to handle that power are ill-equipped to provide him with the needed restraint, farsightedness, and wisdom. *Two*, society is substantively shut out from exercising any influence on the direction of and the priorities for research and development (R&D). *Three*, it is the startling differences that persist within the scientific community, on 'scientific facts', that confuse the common man and stretch the credibility of science. The differences are not nuances but contradictory conclusions on the same 'basic facts.' Take climate change, for example, a matter of gravest importance. Some like the American environmentalist William McKibben warn of possible catastrophic consequences from phenomena like global warming caused beyond any reasonable doubt, by human behavior. For instance, greenhouse gas emissions have dramatically grown since pre-industrial times, with an increase of about 70 percent between 1970 and 2004, triggered by human activity and chiefly through the release of carbon dioxide. Since the end of the 19th century, the earth's average surface temperature has increased by 0.3-0.6°C. Over the last 40 years, the rise has been 0.2-0.3°C. Recent years have been the warmest since 1860, the year when regular instrumental records became available. According to the report by the UN's Intergovernmental Panel on Climate Change (IPCC), 30 percent of animal and plant species will be vulnerable to extinction if global temperatures rose by 1.5 to 2.5°C. It says that the world's economically underdeveloped societies would be the worst hit by climate change, and warns that the increasing levels of greenhouse gases would change rainfall patterns, intensify tropical storms, hasten the melting of Arctic ice and mountain glaciers, and accelerate the risk of drought, famine, and flooding. The carbon dioxide levels are now at the level of the Permian extinction, which occurred some 230 million years ago and led to the extinction of 70 percent of all life on earth. That was caused by natural global warming; the current global warming is man-made. While all this sounds scary, there are those who say that climate science has been 'steadily corrupted' and has "blossomed to assume the undeserved status of dogma."[31] They argue that climate is a part of Nature and the present climate change is not qualitatively any different from the previous ones. They maintain that humanity will survive this one as it did the others, and will come out stronger and more vibrant. Dozens of books are being published supporting both viewpoints. This controversy mirrors the dilemma that a layman faces in coping with science.

We read every day about 'scientific findings' that directly contradict 'scientifically proven facts' of just a few years vintage. One day, chocolate is bad for the heart, and another day it is declared good. While granting that it is to some extent inherent in empirical and deductive intelligence, such volatility and dramatic divergences are unsettling to an already insecure, nervous and troubled mind that apprehends the worst and does not know what to do. If nothing else, it undermines the confidence in science itself, and even more in human intellect and integrity. Bernard Shaw, perhaps somewhat sweepingly, said "Science is always wrong. It never solves a problem without creating ten more."[32] Compounding the problem is the growing influence of profit-seeking R&D corporations in critical areas like biomedical research, encouraged by governments to reduce the budgetary burden and by scientists as options for additional income generation. Universities have become companies and scientists have become entrepreneurs. As a result, scientific priorities are skewed, reflecting the concerns of the industry rather than those of the public, particularly those of the meek and the marginalized. Man must evolve into a better being with a more balanced consciousness than he has now, to be able to ensure that these technologies are used for the good of man and the benefit of the world.

The creators of mechanical devices are often granted the status of gods. In the case of religion, we have the scriptures to turn to for authenticity, however ambivalent they might appear to be; but science has none. Science has made man knowledgeable, not a knowing person; it is equally intolerant of dissent and difference; and it is more elitist than religion. And its sights are set on the horizons far removed from the mundane lives of the ordinary. Just as religion has turned away from understanding the meaning of man and from being a calming influence for corrosive impulses, science has turned to catering to the conveniences and comforts of the articulate and the affluent, and to perfecting the means of human destruction. It is coming close to the admonition of Thomas Huxley who said, "Science commits suicide when it adopts a creed."[33] Man has changed course from 'finding' God to 'playing' God. Scientists claim that they have found what they call the 'God particle,' "a mysterious subatomic fragment that permeates the entire universe", which is said to explain how "everything is the way it is."[34] It is necessary to ask, in the words of the Persian mathematician Omar Khayyam, "Where have we come from? Where are we going? What is the meaning of our lives?"[35]

Instead of seeing God in the 'poorest of the poor,' as Mother Teresa did, and trying to better their subhuman condition with the aid of science and technology, scientists embark upon attention-grabbing projects like the Human Genome Project, that often begin with a bang and end in a whimper. The fact is, we cannot whitewash or wish away either man's thirst for spirituality or the reality of scientific power. Any agenda for human betterment or transformation must include how to bring about a rapprochement between the two. Since the discovery of DNA's fundamental structure by James Watson and Francis Crick less than 50 years ago, man's capacity to look at his own genome and his ability to artificially create identical twins has exponentially increased. It is also generally acknowledged that many fundamental questions like 'what is life?', 'what is human?', why is man so unpredictable?' remain unanswered. Science and scientists rarely exercise self-restraint; they get carried away by the 'logic of their success', and there is often big money involved. Human cloning, we are told, is already a technical possibility and what is technically within our reach, man has always clasped. Frontier technologies, particularly biotechnology, might alter the very way we perceive ourselves and turn upside down our ideas of life, death, sex, heredity, and intelligence. New evidence and new theories are emerging, which question some of the 'sacred cows' of science. For example, there is serious scientific speculation that consciousness does not reside solely in the brain, and that it could be in every cell of the body; and also that all our cells (not just brain cells but millions of cells in the muscles, skeleton, gut, skin, and blood) 'talk' to one another in a kind of network that keeps our experience of consciousness going seamlessly even as billions of cells die and billions of others are produced.[36] Scientists are even whispering the dreaded word 'soul.' It may be premature even to speculate where all this will lead to. But surely man will not be the same, nor will be the world.

Opinions vary on whether new technologies would usher in the *Brave New World* of Aldous Huxley, make man a 'dehumanized happy slave' or a technicized Utopian. Already the world is governed by a technocracy, and if the mold of man itself is mechanized, the human condition will no longer be human. Technology has already created a 'virtual world'; maybe, it will create a 'virtual man'. Technology can be a boon for the betterment of the human condition too. We already have distance learning and healing, annihilating the gap between the giver and the recipient. The education and health gaps can be bridged online. It might be possible for robotic machines to diagnose ailments and even treat patients. Can all these advances coalesce and provide the momentum for a posthuman future in which man, retaining his present form of life, moves on to the higher stage of evolution with a new consciousness, a mishmash of mind-machine-heart? Maybe with a brain that is directed by 'implanted micro machines' and a heart whose latent energy is unleashed by other similar machines. Science fiction has come true; but that 'being' will not be human. The being may be more 'efficient,' live longer and challenge the gods, but it will not be human. The term 'Brave New World' (the title of the 1932 book by Aldous Huxley) has become "almost a reflex for commentators worried we are rushing headlong toward a sterilized posthuman society, engineered to joyless joy."[37] Huxley's book has an arresting passage in which the protagonist 'Mr. Savage' says, "I don't want comfort. I want God, I want poetry, I want real danger, I want freedom, I want goodness, I want sin." The 'interrogator' Mustapha Mond replies, "In fact, you are claiming the right to be unhappy." The Savage then says defiantly, "All right then, I'm claiming the right to be unhappy."[38] More than seventy-five years later, man is more robotic and unhappier, and if push comes to shove, he is even prepared to be a robot if only that would make him any less unhappy.

The fact is that, technology, not tradition, is on the cutting edge of change, arguably the most transformative agent in human history. And it has become a self-sustainable system, as the French technological determinist Jacques Ellul noted. Technology is driven by its own dynamic, independent of human control. The most transformative technology, besides biotechnology, is what is called 'virtual culture' or 'cyber culture', powered by the Internet and the World Wide Web (WWW), a 'new nervous system', which you cannot see but touch. Some fear that the web is assuming the role of the collective mind of mankind, and that soon it will be the sole point of reference for all our 'knowing'. Written text is replaced by the versatile 'hypertext', computer-displayed information that is referenced to other text residing elsewhere, which can be rapidly accessed. Information processing technologies are described as extensions of the human mind, which some call 'psychotechnologies'. Combined with biotechnologies like genetic engineering and cloning, man might be able to manipulate both his body and life more architectonically than ever before. At the same time, the human world bristles with glaring and unconscionable oddities. For instance, it is estimated that every five seconds one human in the world goes blind, that thirty-seven million people in the world are blind, that 124 million are visually impaired, and that the world population of the blind might rise to 75 million by the year 2020 (if current trends continue). But then, there will be electronic eyes everywhere to watch us, and to 'see' for us.[39] Direct brain-to-computer interfacing, the stuff of science fiction, we are now being told, could be a reality. We could have robotic dogs, servants, soldiers, and machines that "tune into the full spectrum of emotional broadcasting."[40] Scientists are predicting that soon the development of computers that match and vastly exceed the capabilities of the human brain will be no less important than the evolution of human intelligence itself, some hundreds of generations ago, and that by the close of this century non-biological intelligence will be ubiquitous. There will be few humans without some form of artificial intelligence, which is growing at a doubly exponential rate; whereas biological intelligence is basically at a standstill.

So much is being said about where science is going to take us, it is hard to retain any semblance of balance, to come to any reasoned view on what is good and what is bad from the species point of view. Even if a fraction of these predictions come true, how would they affect the human personality and behavior? After all, if we go by the logic of Richard Dawkins (*The Selfish Gene*, 1976), "We are survival machines, robot vehicles blindly programmed to preserve the selfish molecules known as genes."[41] Further, as noted by Stephen Talbott, "a technologically motivated globalization shows every sign of simply obliterating the local and thereby sacrificing the truly global as well", and that technology "consists of the machinery embodying our one-sidedly abstract habits of mind."[42] That habit of mind, in effect, erodes the very autonomy of human existence, and makes man, what one might call, a 'terminally tentative' personality, disabled and incapable of doing anything by himself. The mind itself is a reflexive habit. Richard Soutar, the American pioneer in neurofeedback explains: "Our neurophysiological organization is such that we routinize our responses to all situations and once the routines are established to act reflexively or automatically to the fast majority of future situations unless they are novel. As a consequence we tend to become prisoners of our own habitual patterns."[43] Science may debate about the existence or absence of the 'selfish gene' or a 'spiritual gene' (the two need not necessarily be antagonistic), but nothing is worse than a 'scientific almighty' or 'selfish science.' What is truly terrifying about science-based technology is its transformational character, its ability to transform the mindset and mode of living of people almost effortlessly, to accentuate divisions and differences, and to empower 'small numbers of people to kill ever larger numbers of people'.[44] But the same power could be used for the good of the world.

Innovation and Integrity

A long-standing debate concerns scientific innovation and integrity. The question is: does a scientist carry a heavier ethical responsibility than others because what he does as part of his work affects the lives of all of us? While what all of us do to eke out a livelihood affects others, the question is should some be held up to higher standards of integrity simply because what they do and how they do it as part of their work might carry greater implications for our well-being and even for the future of humankind? Opinions vary. Some argue that a scientist is not a free agent and he does what he is called upon to do, and that he cannot be held responsible for its fallout. The ethical and moral accounting has to be done by his masters, be it the state or university or any other institution. Others counter and say that creativity is god-like and there cannot be moral equivalence between the innovators and the rest. Clearly, there is merit in both propositions. And there are examples on both sides. Sometimes, one must draw a moral line in the legitimate pursuit of a noble ideal; crossing that line then transforms what is right into wrong. Clearly, there is awesome power in the hands of scientists, but they too are human; some of them perhaps are *too* human, caught in the same web of worldly life, of envy, ill-will, avarice and ambition, and of survival and success. After all, a scientist is not a saint; one should not expect higher standards of selflessness than from the best among the rest. Most scientists seem to think they are not morally responsible if the fruits of their work are misused or lead to questionable ends. Sometimes, the stream of history has been shifted by a single discovery. For instance, what would have happened if Einstein had not written that famous letter (which he regretted later) to Franklin Roosevelt about the awesome power and the feasibility of splitting an atom and of the work being done in this area by the Nazis? As it turned out, the Nazis were nowhere near making the atomic bomb at that time. Was it the hand of destiny that wrote that letter, and Einstein was simply the human medium? Was it the birth of the force that God chose for eventual human destruction? Was it, and is it, sinful for scientists to participate in research to make weapons of war and destruction, even though they play no part in their actual use? Are they like the executioners or hired killers, who have no 'personal ill will' and just 'do a job'? Scientific research, once started, acquires its own momentum, often drifting towards undesirable directions, carried away by the ambitions of the scientists. Science has become, in the words of Ravi Ravindra, another "intellectual orthodoxy,"[45] more dogmatic and intolerant than even religion. It prides itself on its objectivity, which, as Ravindra points out, is really "inter-subjectivity." While science is propelled by its own momentum, its fruits fall into the laps of our rulers who use them to pursue their own interests and instincts. For instance, even if it could be argued that the atomic bomb was necessary to preempt Hitler and to bring the War to an end, there was no ethical justification for developing the far more destructive hydrogen bomb by Edward Teller and his ilk, which itself was partly an offshoot of the strained relations between Robert Oppenheimer and Edward Teller.

When it comes to society, scientists are, as it were, a breed apart; there are important differences among them, ranging from atheism to different perceptions of divinity. If they can be inspired collectively to strive for the common good, their contribution could have a profound positive effect on the human condition. But if they are holed up in an Ivory Tower, cut off from the concerns of the common man, and use their enormous creativity for competitive gain and esoteric or irrelevant purposes, it would have disastrous consequences. Whether good or bad, what they do and what they do not do has a ripple effect. The entry of the corporate sector into scientific research has further compromised the integrity and credibility of science. With more and more resources diverted for scientific research, the bulk of global research projects is focused on military-related purposes. Comparatively, little is directed exclusively towards human betterment, and science now has little time and fewer resources to serve as a tool of transformation. If man cannot control technology, can technology control itself? Is there a natural limit to technological advancement, as mass has at the speed of light? For the foreseeable future, one has to work on the assumption that science and technology would not self-correct themselves internally, given the sort of winnowing they need, nor would scientists and technologists or their masters make any serious effort to change their course. Also, science would not be a tool to lift the marginalized or to ameliorate the human condition. Such a possibility could have a chance only if the lay public or the common man, not the social elite or the rich and powerful, are actively involved in setting the scientific agenda. There is also a need for global surveillance of scientific research for which an appropriate institutional framework might be required. If the impact of research is not limited to a country or a region, then its dynamic and direction should not also be limited.

Religion and its Future

Perhaps the biggest and weightiest question the world faces today is about how religion will impact on our lives and on the future viability of the human race. While it is too late to imagine how the world would have been without religion, it is opportune now to consider what needs to be done to make religion and its attendant attributes soothing, benign, and unifying. Could we ever have a single religion and a single codified scripture? All religions profess to be based on direct divine revelation or sanction, and although there may be many gods in some religions, there is, all scriptures acknowledge, only one Supreme Being, only one God. The attributes of that God in all religions are the same — omniscience, omnipotence, omnipresence, and omnibenevolence. Even in the so-called polytheistic religion, Hinduism, the core conception of God is no different from that of the monotheistic religions like Judaism, Christianity, Zoroastrianism, and Islam. *Brahman*, the Supreme God of the Upanishads is described as the One that is beyond description, indestructible, imperishable, an all-embracing, all-pervasive force, and other than which there is nothing else in the cosmos. The *Kena* Upanishad[46] amplifies:

- "That which cannot be expressed in words but by which the tongue speaks — know that to be *Brahman*. *Brahman* is not the Being who is worshiped of men.
- That which is not comprehended by the mind but by which the mind comprehends — know that to be *Brahman*. *Brahman* is not the Being who is worshiped of men.
- That which is not seen by the eye but by which the eye sees — know that to be *Brahman*. *Brahman* is not the being who is worshiped of men.

- That which is not heard by the ear but by which the ear hears — know that to be *Brahman*. *Brahman* is not the Being who is worshiped of men.
- That which is not drawn by the breath, but by which the breath is drawn—know that to be *Brahman*. *Brahman* is not the Being who is worshiped of men."

Many of these attributes figure in Islam too, about Allah. For example, it is said that Allah is One, without any partners. He has no sharers in His essence, attributes, actions, or rulings. He is the sole Creator of all that exists, has existed, and will ever exist. Everything other than Him is His creation... He alone controls all events, causes, and effects, and no power exists independently of His power. Nothing happens outside of His will... He is not qualified by the laws of His creation.[47] The description of God in the New Testament is the same; He is described in such terms as the One pure in spirit, perfectly free, creator of the world, holy and good, all-powerful, and worthy of mankind's love and worship. In fact, there are more differences between the attributes of God in the Old Testament and the New Testament, than between those given in the Qu'ran and the New Testament. All religions preach the same in terms of how we should conduct ourselves on earth; to show love, kindness, compassion, charity, altruism; not do to others that which we do not want done to us; and that what we do on earth has a bearing on what happens after our death. No doubt there are important differences: for example, Hindus worship God as an idol, and Islam prohibits it. But there exist vital differences *within* the same religion — between Catholics and Protestants, in Christianity, and between Shias and Sunnis, in Islam — and sometimes more animosity towards other sects of the same religion than towards outsiders. What is truly incomprehensible is why, with so much in common, religion evokes such intensity, animosity, and vitriol, sufficient to murder a neighbor or a friend or a child. The one casuality of religious virulence is the very morality that all religions prescribe and preach as the human essence. And although the fangs of acerbic religion are sharper and its fallout deadlier, this is not a new phenomenon. It is as old as the birth of religion, which means it has distorted the human personality and consciousness for several millenniums. And why is the 'Almighty, All-merciful, All-good God' keeping silent and letting such horrors happen for 'His sake'? Does it matter to Him that so many of His 'believers' of one religion are committing so many sins to 'save' Him from the 'believers' of another religion? Does it bother Him that, when He is the source of all religions, each claims monopoly and exclusivity and commits unspeakable atrocities? Does any of this, and murder under the cover of martyrdom serve any cosmic or divine purpose? If so, what could that purpose possibly be? We will not have answers to any such questions because either the kind of intelligence we have is not good enough or knowing the answers might do more harm than good to us. But what we can and must do is to take a serious and holistic look at the very role, function and purpose of religion as it has come to mean in human affairs.

Religion, Swami Vivekananda said, is "the manifestation of the divinity already in man" and "the idea which is raising the brute unto man, and man unto God."[48] We seem far from that ideal. Despite utopian dreams, we will almost certainly never have a unified global religion, or a single scripture or a 'unified God'. Then, where is religion, as the foundational force in the human consciousness, headed? Looking at what goes on in the name of religion, one feels both dazed and disgusted. On the one hand, one sees the reason why religion was conceived or revealed. Since man by nature could not be trusted to be ethical and egalitarian, religion was meant to instill a sense of fear and moral responsibility to do the right thing in life. It was a way for people to have hope that, when things go horribly wrong sometimes, as they are bound to, religion was to give balance and comfort in the thought that there is a supreme being watching over us who will take care of us. But on the other hand, we see people viscerally hating each other purely based on religion and nothing else, and passing judgments on someone, based on the nature of his faith, even before they get to know that individual. And we view and read about ordinary 'god-fearing' people committing unspeakable horrors on those who profess an 'enemy' religion. As the world simmers, as knowledge explodes, and as the existential context of life changes, people change as well, simply to stay alive. For religion to remain relevant and effective as a source of spiritual guidance and emotional support, to bear suffering stoically, it too must change. But religion draws its inspiration and inspires precisely because it is supposed to be timeless, eternal as the direct word of God. So, if it strays merely to survive, it loses its legitimacy and its appeal. But if it remains frozen, it loses its relevance and invites ridicule.

Caught on the horns of a paradoxical quandary, the world's great religions find themselves at a critical juncture. Desperately clinging to values and beliefs that are often thousands of years old, they find it increasingly difficult to provide the spiritual guidance and moral strength necessary to face the challenges of modern life. So the question is: can the great religious traditions of the world winnow and reinvent themselves in order to show the world how to address the needs and hopes of a complex, materialistic, twenty-first-century world that is increasingly becoming skeptical, if not antagonistic, to religious impulse and trying to embrace something about which everyone has a particular understanding and vision: spirituality. We must remember that when we refer to a 'religion' or 'religions of the world', what we are in fact alluding to are the interpretations of their religious texts and the interaction with the religious institutions. And we must also remember that we live in a world where we often crave more for the very thing we despise; religion is no exception. We want to embark on a search for the sacred; yet we want to live in a secular society. People throng to places of religious symbols but there is nothing 'religious' about the ambience of their life. We want to annihilate the 'social' symbols of profanity — pornography, prostitution, sexual permissiveness; yet we harbor profanity in our mind which manifests as ill will, envy and malice. The world is shrinking geographically, and people of different faiths are forced to live together; yet it does not seem to be rounding off the rough edges of religious practice or fostering greater desire to learn from each other. Many people talk of all religions being different paths to the same God, but a lot more people perhaps than ever before are prepared to kill and be killed to protect their 'God'. It is hard to synthesize and harmonize all these strands and arrive at a common platform, and extrapolate the likely future of religion as it is currently organized. What is clear is that we cannot isolate and segregate religion, or rather what it entails inside us, from the state of our consciousness and the pulls and pressures it will be subjected to.

What has actually happened is that man, unable to integrate and assimilate the different demands of religiosity, has turned into a marauder, masquerading as a monk, making the brute less brutish than man. In a sizeable number of people, faith or the manner of its misrepresentation, has become a deadly tool, a holy license to exercise leverage through violence. Some say that a 'religious impulse' is a basic built-in feature in the human machine, and that was put in by God. While every religion, save Buddhism, expressly affirms God, most people believe God to be, as William James described in his classic *The Varieties of Religious Experience* (1902), a 'larger power', a power that is independent of us and as something larger than our conscious selves; and in our union with that power we will find our greatest peace. Instead of helping us to attain that peace, organized religions have been so compromised that many people are driven to the conclusion, in the words of Sigmund Freud, that "when a man is freed of religion, he has a better chance to live a normal and wholesome life."[49] Charles Colton, an English clergyman, aptly wrote, "Men will wrangle for religion; write for it; fight for it; die for it; anything but live for it."[50] And Ambrose Bierce, an American satirist dubbed 'Bitter Bierce', wrote, "Religion, a daughter of Hope and Fear, explaining to Ignorance the nature of the Unknowable."[51] So, who is the villain and who is the victim — religion or man? We must understand that even if religion or a scripture was divinely inspired or revealed, its perception, comprehension and practice pass through the filter of human consciousness dominated by the mind. The filter seems to alter the character. Furthermore, few really 'know' their own religion, nor have they studied their own scriptures. Perhaps, had they been fully informed and had they understood its true essence, the scope for religious extremism and absolutism might have been greatly minimized. Scholars are debating if religious vengeance and violence are only motivated and triggered by the perceived threat to one's religion, or if there is more to it than meets the eye. What makes people blow themselves into bits just to make sure others meet the same dreadful fate? And, for the record, such religious extremism is not confined to Islam. Of course, every religious 'revolutionary' protests that he is only defending his religion, which is his sacred duty. Clearly, religion has in it something which when mixed with the latent tendencies of the human mind becomes a volatile and violent passion that explodes. At the same time, we cannot infer that religious impulse is inappropriate to the human form of life; on the other hand, even many scientists are talking about the existence of a 'God gene' or a 'God particle' inside all of us.

The roots of religious violence have of late received much scholarly attention. Basically there are two typologies: one external, the other internal. The first typology looks for causes outside religion and puts it solely on human frailties, culture, and civilization. The other argues that the very doctrine of faith or dogmatic belief and what it entails, inexorably leads to violence. It could be a combination of both. A distorted, faulty or inadequate comprehension of the 'spirit' of religion adds fuel to the fire inherent in the human mind. Once we envision God as a vertical authority above us, not innate in another human, and that our primary loyalty is to Him, not to another man, and when we become convinced that others who do not share this vision are doing injury to Him, then the gates are thrown open wide for hatred and violence. 'God' then comes before 'goodness', divinity before tolerance. When religion and its symbols — places of worship, ways of salvation, divine revelation — become scarce by its denial to others, the sacred gets sullied, and intolerance and violence follow as night follows day. The only way to halt the march of religious 'fundamentalism' or 'fanaticism', both loaded words with pejorative meanings, is to rob or rid every religion of its monopoly. It is man's instinctive need for 'monopoly' — of faith, power, access, property, wealth, pleasure — that causes much social strain and which seems to be a particular human trait. It is in fact a logical extension of the desire to control without competition, which is the more basic human instinct. In matters of faith, this monopolistic tendency is more extreme and becomes evangelical and aggressive. Without monopoly, there would be no need for conversion, no need to 'defend' any particular faith or a specific religion. It should be made socially 'hip' to be seen as practicing more than one religion. Believing should not require belonging, and practice ought not to be a 'take it' or 'leave it' package, and any place of worship must be a place of sanctuary and sanctity open to all.

Spiritualism and Self-fulfillment

One of the questions that many thoughtful people wrestle with is, if we are so exalted, why do we behave so abominably? If we have any semblance of divinity about us how can any of us, be it a 'terrorist' or a psychopath or religious extremist do what they actually do? And, as R.D. Ranade framed it, 'if the *Atman* (soul) is capable of being realized even while the body lasts, why is it that *all* people do not realize him in their lifetime, or yet again, if he can be realized by some, what can we regard to be their qualifications for that realization?'[52] The search for an answer to this question goes to the heart of the search for truth. Down the ages, the yearning for spiritual awakening of the human soul has been typified by the travails of those who believed that they were more than a body randomly born, leading a rudderless ritual of a life, and doomed to die by sheer wear and tear, decay and disease. Traditionally, spiritualism sans religious roots was perceived as a threat to organized authority, and the spiritualist, as a kind of upstart, someone who is trying to cut corners. Spiritualism today has acquired an altogether different context and content. Partly as a reaction to what religion has come to stand for, and partly as a way to cope with the stress and tension of our combative life style, many people, across cultures and ages, are embracing that moving target we call spiritualism. Celebrities, movie stars, writers, business tycoons, and social bigwigs are jumping onto this bandwagon. And when it comes to their much-advertised passion for spiritualism, none of them find it incongruous with their life priorities, or with what they do in their daily lives. What was deemed superstition and paranormal not too long ago, to be shunned by any 'rational' person, is now fashionable. The explosion and popularity of things and practitioners like divination, fortune tellers, tarot cards, palm reading, crystal balls, clairvoyance, telepathy, black magic, ghosts, etc., is at once a broadening of the frontiers of knowledge, and a desperate search for help to cope with the 'unbearable emptiness' of modern life. There are some who say that even this 'pseudo-spiritualism' is not all bad, that a spiritual journey that begins with an 'impure' motive can practically serve a greater purpose and can be transformed into a collective spiritual quest. The spiritual life is no longer a specialist concern, restricted to those who belong to religious traditions. The spirituality movement has now become a motley revolution, embracing diverse sections of the society and induced by different interests. In them lies probably the hope that, despite the god-men and gurus, a spiritual renaissance of mankind will emerge out of this 'selfish spiritualism' and opportunism. One of the fundamental aspects of the spiritual renaissance ought to be the realization that much, if not most, of the sorrow in the world is generated by our present states of consciousness, in which each one of us acts as if he is the center of the universe. That we act in this manner is not surprising, given that each one of us exists within a separate physical body, with private thoughts and private sensations that nobody else can hear or feel. This state of consciousness is at the root of our rampant indifference to the needs and feelings of others. The others are "not me" — so, "what do I care if they feel pain when I hurt them, if I try to get ahead of them, or if I steal from them or even kill them for a cause?" All this is rationalized in our mind.

We cannot precisely define it, but a broad definition of spiritualism could be found in the words of Ursula King, author of the book *Spirituality and Society in the New Millennium* (2001): "...spirituality is now understood anthropologically as an exploration into what is involved in becoming fully human."[53] Someone said spirituality is a journey from the external world of names and forms to the subtle world of energy, to the innermost core of our being. In practical terms, it has come to be the metaphor for man's discontent with the state of his being, a statement of modern man's search for a meaning other than in material comforts and worldly gains. Very often, the cacophony of spirituality is so boisterous that the spirit of spirituality is obscured, giving it a bad name and scaring off the real seekers. Its ambit is very wide, and it encompasses a wide spectrum of people and quests — from atheism to total identification with God, psychic healing to ghost-busting, from transcendental meditation to corporate excellence, fashion designers to fortune tellers, from mediums that 'talk to the dead' to merchants of death, ramp-walkers to the recluse, and those who, in the words of Aldous Huxley, want to 'be a bit kinder'. But search without the essence has led many people to the sanctuary of suicide, to the ashram of a guru, to the conclave of a cult — and to mindless, or maybe 'mind-full' murder. If a person deeply believes he is not only doing his religious duty but in so doing has become a 'spiritual being', then we must conclude the malaise is far deeper than an individual hallucination or misdirected zealotry. Many thoughtful scientists are also coming round to the view that man is more than a material being. The Australian neurophysiologist John Eccles, for instance, said, "I maintain that the human mystery is incredibly demeaned by scientific reductionism, with its claim in promissory materialism to account eventually for all of the spiritual world in terms of patterns of neuronal activity. This belief must be classed as a superstition. . . . we have to recognize that we are spiritual beings with souls existing in a spiritual world as well as material beings with bodies and brains existing in a material world."[54]

The hunger for spiritualism, although a new found 'love', is as hoary as man himself. Noble as it is and deemed a shorter route to God than any other way, spiritualism is also not an end by itself. It is a way to fully fulfill our inherent potential and to, as it were, externalize the divinity dwelling inside, and in so doing obliterate the distance between any two humans, indeed any two beings. The essential question is, are we spiritual beings having a human experience or human beings having a spiritual experience? If we are human beings experiencing a spiritual experience, then it means that our personality and thoughts are primary, and being spiritual becomes a desirable goal towards which we labor in everything we do. If we are the other kind, then, it means that, first and foremost, we are qualitatively different from who or what we assume we are, and the 'I' of the self is but a reflection in this 'personal pond' of the all-pervading Almighty. The essence and substance of this thought is best captured in the four famous Upanishadic *mahavakyas* (great sayings): *Prajanam Brahman* (Consciousness is *Brahman*); *Ayam Atma Brahman* (The *Atman*, or self, is *Brahman*); *Aham Brahmasmi* (I am the God) and *Tatvam Asi* (Thou art That). So essential are they to spiritual life that they are the *mantras* that are taught when a person is initiated as a *sanyasi* (someone who renounces everything worldly).

Striving towards that kind of vision is the heart of spiritualism, which is also sometimes dismissed as mysticism. In fact, many scientists are themselves turning to mysticism, and it is said that the favorite study of a good many of them is *The Secret Doctrine* (1888), written by the mystic and the master of occultism and theosophy Helena Blavatsky.[55] The essential difference between the scientific and the scriptural view of the human being is that, while science posits that man is wholly a physical being, the scripture says he is essentially a spiritual being. The awakening of the slumbering spiritual side of man is important not only to redefine the man-to-man relationship, but also the man-Nature relationship. In many ways, man's schizophrenic nexus with Nature is a snapshot of the overall human condition. Unless we set it right, nothing else will make the needed difference. We are a part of Nature; we are reliant on Nature; but we methodically destroy Nature. We must move towards a new pattern of partnership with Nature, which has been called *deep* or *spiritual ecology*.

Deep ecology is based on the premise that all living beings are separate but are equal parts of the web of life, that animals and plants, and also human species, possess awareness and intuition, and perception; probably some are capable of experiencing fear, jealousy, friendship, pain and shame as well. As one ecologist said, "Each time we harm Nature, we cut a little piece of our own flesh."[56] It echoes the message of the Upanishads that voice the living credo of the ancients. One of the central messages of the Upanishads is that one should strive to see all creatures in himself, and himself in all creatures and everything that exists in the cosmos; living or non-living is the manifestation of the divine. The Upanishads say that there are two selves — the many individual selves and the one Universal Self, whose locus is the 'cave of the heart'. The *Mundaka* Upanishad likens these two selves to 'two birds of the same appearance who sit in the same tree'.[57] A Shinto saying captures the essence: 'Even in a single leaf of a tree, or a tender blade of grass, the awe-inspiring Deity manifests Itself'.[58] But, to actualize that realization and to rise up to that level, reason and intelligence are not good enough or even inappropriate, which is another pivotal message of the Vedas and the Upanishads. Our inability to connect with the non-human animals and with Nature, stems from the same source that divides one man from another, which is our inability to go beyond the boundary of the physical body.

For a fuller understanding of spiritualism, it is useful to take a peek into another branch of ancient human knowledge often dubbed as mysticism and magic, and also sometimes called the oldest known religion: occult or occult science. The word 'occult' itself comes from the Latin word *Occults* (clandestine, hidden, secret), referring to the 'knowledge of the hidden'. Somewhat similar to the spiritual way, the occult approach requires us to literally become the very thing we wish to investigate — or at least to participate in it. It is like the Vedantic view that we must become God to truly relate to God. Again, like spirituality, the occult system always operates from within to without, and prefers to investigate Nature by participating within its processes, rather than interpreting its outward manifestation. The widespread violence and evil in the world today, where power, perfidy, and physical force hold sway, has reflexively propelled many persons to embrace spirituality as an escape route, not as a means for betterment. It has become the refuge of the discontented and the disenchanted. And then there is the question of the nexus between spirituality and religion. The question is whether one could be spiritual without being religious. Or, can one be religious and yet not be spiritual? Being spiritual is often identified with religious extremism, so there are some who feel repelled by what goes on in the name of religion and who tend to lead a spiritual life while demonstrably being anti-religious. The big question then is: if inheritable spiritual genes are present in human beings — as some scientists like Dean Hamer posit (*The God Gene*, 2004) — then why are the roles of the spiritual genes in human behavior so passive and subdued in most men, while the monster or evil genes seem so active and alive in the human gene pool? One possible explanation could be that the evil genes are the stronger ones, rooted as they are in the mind, and the mind being the dominant part of consciousness, these genes shape and control human predisposition more than the spiritual ones. Evangelists reject the idea that faith can be reduced to chemical reactions in the brain, and humanists refuse to accept that religion is inherent in people's make-up. In any event, we cannot adduce it as an alibi for our ruinous behavior. After all, predisposition is not predetermination. As Dean Hamer says "our genes predispose us to believe. But they don't tell us what to believe in" and again that, "what we do with our spiritual genes, however, is very much up to us."[59] That is what being human is all about: to choose from among what we have, inside or outside, within or without. Hamer himself says at the end of his book that it "is important to distinguish between believing and the *act* of believing, which is one of the greatest gifts of being human."[60] And to that, one might add, believing or even the act of believing, and acting on that belief are altogether different. Much of our malaise comes, not from ignorance of what is right, but from our almost pathological inability to put what we *know* is right to practical effect. But what is the role of spirituality in a man who lives in the sensory world, where he has to perform multiple chores just to stay afloat? Should he renounce and retreat from one or the other? Can he be spiritual by simply 'being good'?

But, even at a conceptual level, are we quite sure what 'doing good' really is? We may not be sure enough to say, but deep inside we know what the right thing is, in a given situation. Our not 'doing' good is due to a combination of several factors: that we do not know what the correct course of action is; that it is not 'profitable', not even 'practical'. The fact is, performing good acts is not that easy without a moral foundation. No Christian turns the other cheek anymore. No Hindu sees divinity in every human being. Under pressure and in response to the other's actions, it is so easy to 'pay back in the same coin,' an eye for an eye. Just as a garland requires a thread to string the flowers, a moral life requires the thread of spirituality. Theoretically, one can be spiritual without being religious; secular and spiritual are not antagonistic. A genuinely spiritual life makes religion an asset, not a hindrance, in overcoming the stress and temptations of modern life. Spirituality has to be adapted to the demands of daily life.

Spirituality has to be integrated into the processes of our thought and has to be built into the fabric of everyday life; it is neither escapism nor an unearthly and utopian dream. Spirituality does not entail a saintly life; a *sanyasi* (the one who renounces all worldly attachments) need not be a greater spiritualist than a householder. Indeed, in the Hindu religious thought, the *dharma* of a truthful householder is higher than that of a *sanyasi*. And the Gita says that a true *sanyasi* is not one who renounces earthly activities or one who renounces all desires. He is the one who is detached from the fruits of his actions. In that sense, a *sanyasi* is no different from a *karma yogi*, the one who acts according to his *swadharma*, without attachment to the consequences and results. The essence of spirituality is, as the Upanishadic thought says, to identify, indeed fuse, oneself with everyone as inseparable parts of the cosmic whole, that is the *Brahman*. Once that state is attained, one becomes incapable of injuring any one, in thought, word or deed. That might be too lofty a state for present-day men. But that is clearly not possible with the kind of consciousness that man has nurtured. Making man less hostile to his fellow men and more instinctively capable of relating to the other's suffering is what is expected of spirituality. That is the key to compassion. The Tibetan scholar Thupten Rinpoche says, "To develop true compassion, first we must know that suffering is real and that sufferings hurt."[61] Compassion 'is the very essence of a spiritual life, and the main practice of those who have devoted their lives to attaining enlightenment'. Compassion is a 'mind that is motivated by cherishing other living beings and wishes to release them from their suffering.'[62] The world may be unreal, but suffering is real. Even those who do not commit any sin cannot escape suffering. Nothing is nobler than alleviating the other's sufferings. The French philosopher Simone Weil wrote that the capacity to give one's attention to a sufferer is very rare and almost a miracle. That is because our mind looks at life as a zero-sum game; if we give something we lose it; whereas the truth is that what we finally take, is what we give, not what we take. In the act of helping a sufferer, the one that gains most is the giver, much more than the recipient. The Buddha said that if only we knew what he knew of the benefits of giving, we will not eat a single meal without sharing it with the hungry. In Jainism, what is called *Satavedaniya karma* is accumulated by showing mercy to all living beings, by sharing the unhappiness of unhappy people and reducing their misery. It is also worth noting that in Jainism, a soul's *karma* changes even with the thoughts and not just the actions. Thus, those who think evil of someone will endure '*karm-bandh*' or an increment in bad *karma*. Human consciousness, at the present level and condition, is incapable of that kind of sharing, much less the absolute surrender of ego, of everything we do, as envisioned in the scriptures. Sharing has a bigger meaning than sharing of good fortune between two individuals. What we also lack is the sense that we all share the same space on the same planet and a common fate. We are so consumed with our individual fates that we seem utterly oblivious to what happens to the rest.

Laboring only for personal salvation and praying without social concern is not true spirituality. Because prayer then becomes a petition, and a place of worship becomes a place for barter. Indeed, prayer without piety and worship without compassion, like virginity without chastity, is a ruse to lure God. And God, if He is anything we imagine Him to be, is not likely to fall for it. In the Bhagavad Gita, responding to Arjuna's question why man commits *adharma*, Lord Krishna says it is because man turns his back on society. He tells Arjuna that he (Arjuna) lives in society; society does not live in him. As Swami Vivekananda so eloquently proclaimed, the search for God and service to man, indeed service to all creatures, are one and the same; anything less, anything else is an affront to God. One cannot be spiritual if one causes injury to others; although spiritualism is essential, that by itself is not sufficient. Doing good and being truly happy with others' happiness should be turned into a habit, and such an instinctive act requires a trained heart and that training comes from God-centered spirituality. One who marginalizes or manipulates God cannot be truly spiritual.

In pondering over the innate but hopelessly hidden spirituality in man, we cannot blink at the religious savagery of the previous and present centuries. Although savagery and brutality are not endemic to any particular part of the human personality, few things in the human world are more appalling and more 'rationally inexplicable' than slaughter and savagery in the cause of religion. Religion has been used to justify everything we denounce in human affairs, through the use of labels like 'just war' and 'religious duty'. Even holy men like St. Augustine and St. Thomas Aquinas justified 'just wars.' In 1095, Pope Urban II made a qualitative and religious leap when, at the time of the First Crusade of the middle ages, he used the Latin term '*bellum sacrum*' (holy war) instead of '*bellum justum*' (just war). He reportedly said "If you go and kill the infidel, you will be forgiven *immediately* — Paradise."[63] It is said that in 1,300 years of Islamic history, people have fought for 1,100 years.[64] In fact, religious wars have always been fought in one form or another. We cannot run away from the historical fact that religion transforms human personality and somehow brings out the very best and the worst in us; the best can make man a god, and the worst can make him a fiend. We cannot typecast or stereotype the kinds of people concerned. Anyone can be of either kind, divine or destructive; what tilts the scales we do not know. Some anthropologists assert that it is savagery that distinguishes the animal from human, implying that animals indulge in savagery whereas humans do not. But history has a different tale to tell. It has explained away every act of savagery as an aberration, but so much has accumulated and has become so commonplace that we cannot shut our eyes to the ugly fact that it is inherent in human nature. And it is becoming increasingly difficult for a man to accept that another man's allegiance to a different belief-system is no threat to the integrity of his own allegiance. Two things seem certain; one, even if misdirected, the grip of religion on the human consciousness has never flagged; and two, religion, in some form or the other, will continue to be a dominant dimension of human life. It is therefore important that we come to grips with religious violence. While its destructiveness cannot be denied, the power of religion could also be turned into a potent tool for human transformation. Organized or unorganized, formal or informal, personal or impersonal, monotheistic or pantheistic, religion in some form or the other has to remain an important part of human life. The diverse religions of the world will continue nibbling and gnawing at each other unless either God intervenes or human consciousness itself changes. There is no moral or spiritual reason why one cannot be a Hindu and a Muslim, a Christian and a Jew, at the same time. But such a choice is clearly not possible with the mind-controlled consciousness. But this consciousness, with its multi-faceted capabilities, can transform religion itself into a tool. A spiritual person, since he cares for his fellow mortals, can do much in purging religion of extremism and intolerance. He can exercise his influence in inducing religion to rid itself of its rigid exclusivity and monopolistic and intolerant edges. If that happens, the gap between religion and spirituality will become progressively narrow, and the combined force of religion and spirituality could be a formidable positive force.

Knowledge and Desire

Man may be, as the Greek philosopher Sophocles characterized, 'the greatest marvel' on earth, but that does not necessarily translate into him being the desirable being. Without spirituality, man cannot afford to stand still for too long, either as an unfinished product (as de Chardin said) or as a transitional being (as Sri Aurobindo put it). Man either becomes an agent of moral change or rides the crest of negative forces to his doom. The philosophy and axioms of the Upanishads, the Sermon on the Mount or the Sermon at Sarnath (of the Buddha), the teachings of Zoroaster, Mahaveer or Muhammad, and the sayings of saints and sages have been part of the human consciousness for thousands of years — without leading to any directional difference in human behavior. We hear or read the teachings of the Buddha or Jesus, of Rumi or Ramakrishna or Ramana, and having done that, we merrily relapse into our lives of negativity and nitpicking, of pleasure and 'progress'. The fact is that their teachings could not pierce the impregnable shield of our mind-centered consciousness. That is because we try to 'become' a Buddhist or a Christian, not Buddha-like or Christ-like. We treat the scriptures and sayings of the prophets and sages as another source of empiricism and knowledge. But Truth, as the Upanishads proclaim, has to be realized, not merely known. One has always wondered why man has paid such a terrible price for eating the fruit from the *Tree of Knowledge*. Does it have something to do with the nature of knowledge itself? Osho explains that the Biblical parable has immense insight. Why has man fallen from grace through knowledge? Because knowledge creates distance, because knowledge creates the 'I' and 'Thou', because knowledge creates subject and object, the knower and the known, the observer and the observed. Knowledge is basically schizophrenic; it creates a split. And then there is no way to bridge it. That is why the more man becomes knowledgeable, the less he is religious. The more educated a man, the less is the possibility for him to approach God.[65] Osho also says that "Knowledge is the curse, the calamity, the cancer. It is through knowledge that man becomes divided from the whole. Knowledge creates distance."[66] And that knowledge has to be negated. All that we have gathered is just rubbish. The ultimate remains beyond our grasp. As Osho further puts it, "What we have gathered are only facts, truth remains untouched by our efforts".[67] Here is a conundrum: if we know nothing, how can we blame knowledge for creating the distance and dividing man from the whole? Knowledge, like truth has several depths. Every species has knowledge necessary for that form of life. Our knowledge is at the depth of shallow subsistence, and there are many deeper depths that are even beyond our imagination. So, at once we know nothing and know something. Our knowledge, derived from reason and intelligence, is sufficient to create the distance but not enough to know the whole, the Truth. Even if man develops the capability to 'download' the contents of the brain into a supercomputer and replicate consciousness very soon, as is being claimed, and evade 'death', some depths of knowledge will ever remain beyond our reach. Vedanta says that true knowledge is self-knowledge, higher than the knowledge of the Vedas itself, and by embarking on that journey man may attain both *moksha* (liberation) and *jnana* (knowledge). The Indian scripture *Ashtavakra Samhita* says that "the world appears from the ignorance of the Self and disappears with the knowledge of the Self, even as the snake appears from the non-recognition of the rope and disappears with its recognition."[68] But then, when man attains that state he will have transcended the bounds of being human.

American New Age author Gary Zukav, whose well-known works include *The Seat of the Soul* and *The Dancing Wu Li Masters*, says, "The logics and understandings of the five-sensory personality are in the mind. They are the products of the intellect. The higher order of logics and understandings that is capable of meaningfully reflecting the soul comes from the heart."[69] We must harvest, to borrow the phrase of American author Elaine Matthews, *the heartbeat of intelligence* (which is incidentally the title of her book). Man's pillaging and poisoning of the earth, and the persistence of the pestilence of benumbing mass poverty on earth, spring from the same source: denial of living space and legitimacy of the 'other' of all sorts: other species, other sex, or other man. Disregard of the 'total order' has become our bane now.

Behind the denial of 'others' are our unending desires. Man is essentially a creature of desire of all hues. There is not a minute that he does not desire something. For him, desire is life and life is desire. The more we know the more we desire. Perhaps the oldest scripture of all, the *Rig Veda* simply says that 'desire links non-being to being'. Throbbing, pulsating desire is the starting point of any achievement and the stepping stone to civilization. Often, we long for forbidden things, and desire denied is the springhead of frustration, unhappiness, and aggression. In fact, desire, deeply felt, has a life of its own. The American author Napoleon Hill (*Think and Grow Rich*, 1937) wrote that, "when your desires are strong enough, you will appear to possess superhuman powers to achieve."[70] Every wish, Vedanta tells us, will be realized even if it takes a million births. The state of *desirelessness*, being devoid of *tanha* (desire or craving), is the state that Buddhism prescribes to rid oneself of *dukkha* (suffering or sorrow), and to attain *nirvana*, the final liberation. The forces of desire and hatred trap us in cyclic existence and consequential suffering. The paradox, however, is that the desire to be without desire is another kind of desire. But like right action and wrong action, there are right desires and wrong desires, the distinction being the nature of the effect of their fulfillment. To have the right desires is not easy, as it requires a totally new mindset. The composite of human thoughts and desires, perhaps more than human actions, is what shapes the human world, and because of their toxic and noxious nature, human future inevitably gets sullied. Our thoughts, as Thomas Hobbes noted, run over everything, holy, profane, chaste, ugly, obscene, without shame or blame — but they leave imprints on the cosmos. And we have no mode or mechanism or even the will to cleanse them. Religion, whose purpose was to accomplish this task, has itself gone awry. Of all the areas in which the human cognitive potential has failed human destiny, it is its inability to navigate the religious stream in the human consciousness. We seem to be adrift somewhere between the boundaries of religion, social ethics, morality and spirituality, which until rather recently were more or less in harmony, at least not openly antagonistic. For a human life to be wholesome, all the four have to be in tandem, if not integrated; alarmingly, as time passes, the gaps are widening and the distortions are lengthening. We need radical winnowing, shifting of gears and direction, and the tools to achieve that objective. Science must cease to be the handmaiden of technology, and has to become a tool in human transformation. Even to come close to that goal, the mind must be dethroned and de-fanged. In the Bhagavad Gita, Lord Krishna tells Arjuna: "The mind *(manas)* which follows the rambling senses, makes the Soul (*buddhi*) as helpless as the boat which the wind leads astray upon the waters."[71] Man has to become essentially a spiritual being, not a mental being; much less an immortal predatory physical being, which is precisely what science is trying to do through technologies like cryonics and genetic engineering, offering, as they say, a choice between a cold storage and a coffin (or a cemetery) to every man. Our idea of strength is physical, agility is mental and life's goal is to make it perpetual. Nietzsche's superman exercises power not over others, but over himself. That, at its core, is spirituality.

According to Sri Aurobindo, for man to change from an "ignorant mental being misusing, or not effectively using, his knowledge, moved by ego and governed by vital desires and passions and the needs of the body, unspiritual and superficial in his outlook, ignorant of his own self and the forces that drive and use him,"[72] to a spiritual being at peace with himself and with the world around, calls for nothing less than a consciousness change, which is to ascend to higher layers of consciousness. According to Tibetan Buddhism, there are eight different kinds of consciousnesses. Of them, the first four are called inconstant consciousnesses, the fifth is sensory, the sixth is mental. The seventh and eighth consciousnesses are 'constant'; the seventh is called afflicted consciousness, in the sense that it refers to the most basic level of mental affliction or the root of *kleshas*; it is the basis for the 'I' and 'mine' fixations; the eighth consciousness is called the 'ground consciousness', the ground for the rise of all other consciousnesses. Every act of an individual has an imprint, which is stored in the eighth consciousness, and these latencies manifest later by entering the sixth consciousness, or the mental, which is the most important. The challenge is to create an environment that is conducive to elevate individual consciousness on a scale sufficient for a species-wide spiritual change.

Sri Aurobindo says, "Only a spiritual change, an evolution of his being from the superficial mental towards the deeper spiritual consciousness, can make a real and effective difference." According to him, "A change of consciousness is the major fact of the next evolutionary transformation, and the consciousness itself, by its own mutation, will impose and effect any necessary mutation of the body."[73] Much would depend on what we truly wish for our own selves as, "you are never given a wish without also being given the power to make it true. You may have to work for it, however."[74] But to truly and wholly wish well of others we need wisdom and compassion. We may use the word consciousness a million times and think we know what we are talking about, but in the end, in the words of the American psychologist William James, consciousness remains 'the most mysterious thing in the world'. But we do know or *think* we know that consciousness is the key, the root of all experience, the difference — or the continuum — between life and death. All evolution is to move from consciousness to consciousness. The very purpose of all life, some say, especially human life, is to evolve into a higher consciousness at each stage. Some like Jeremy Griffith postulate that it is this 'glitch' in human consciousness that blocks our final evolution to, what Griffith calls, 'God-Man.' Whether it is a 'God-Man' or, like in the advertisements of our consumer products, a 'new and improved' man, what man needs is a qualitative consciousness change. Only through that can we change the nature of the power of our knowing, or rather the power within us that determines what we know. We must continue to believe that man still has a fair chance to 'rise above himself'. We are free to choose our future, and we do exactly that every minute of our lives. Maybe a better word would be 'to make,' not 'to choose'. Future is not some magical thing on a dusky distant horizon, it is the morrow of every day. The next minute is as much the future as the next millennium. If, as Plato said, time is a moving image of eternity, and the future, as Jorge Luis Borges put it, is 'a mere construction of our hopes,' then our collective hope has to be that humanity could yet find its utterance and liberation. It is this that offers scope for man to change himself, and hope to change his future. It is this that gives immediacy and importance to human effort. And it is never too late for change or hope. And then the teasing question: is human effort really and solely 'human effort'? Or is that also an illusion, an invention of the human mind to lull us into complacency?

Conceptualizing and comprehending consciousness is as difficult as identifying what constitutes human content and human essence. The word is used differently by different people. Some say that "consciousness could be the final frontier in man's quest to know what life is really all about. At the broadest level, being conscious is to be awake and aware, having a sense of self, and a feeling of embodiment, of knowing the difference between you and the world around."[75] Our brain, we are told, will never understand its 'own consciousness' because it is not equipped to understand itself. In terms of consciousness, humans claim that what distinguishes them from animals is an awareness that can communicate complex information with a sense of self-referral, and that information culled from the outside world passes through our senses through the brain's electromagnetic field to neurons in the brain and then back again to the field, creating a self-referring loop that could be the key to consciousness. Essentially it means that consciousness is a product of over 100 billion electrically active neurons of the brain. It has also been said that the basic problem is that our subjective experience of consciousness does not correspond to the neurophysiology of our brain and that we really do not know how all the physically distinct information in our brain is somehow bound together to the subjective image: the so-called 'binding problem'. There is also a view that consciousness continues after a person's brain has stopped functioning, and he has been declared clinically dead. The conclusion is, consciousness ultimately cannot be defined, only realized, like the Self in the Upanishads. Mark Hamilton, in his book *God-Man: Our Final Evolution* (1998), said that man did not have a consciousness till about as late as 3,000 years ago, reflecting the thesis expounded in Julian Jaynes's much acclaimed book, *The Origin of Consciousness in the Breakdown of the Bicameral Mind* (1976). He argued that until as recently as two or one thousand years, human beings were not *conscious* and their behavior was directed by what he called 'auditory hallucinations', which they thought came from the voice of their chief, king or gods. According to Jaynes, the change came when man along with other primates functioned by mimicked or learned reactions, what Hamilton calls 'automatic guidance system.' Bicameral means a combination of the left and the right halves of the brain, and the development of consciousness is a result of the neglect of the right-brain and the dominance of the left-brain. Bicameral can also be a combination of the inquisitive capacity of the heart and the reasoning capacity of the brain — the mind. Man was forced to develop consciousness in order to survive as his hallucinating voices no longer provided guidance for survival. In other words, what is called consciousness is synonymous with mind-centered intelligence and reasoning faculties. They became the guidance system, which since then has been the dominant force in human consciousness, and conduct, in the world. Researchers like Mark Hamilton have been of the view that mankind might be in the middle of taking an evolutionary leap into a far more competitive species. Hamilton describes what he calls a *Neo-Tech* World, in which the God-Man will "enjoy Six Ultimate Gifts such as spectacular love and sex, and a slim, sexy body; superior intelligence; millionaire wealth; exceptional health and longevity; an exciting profit-building and profound security and safety". The God-Man "also attracts two other gifts, including beautiful women, powerful men, and rich and famous friends." He "will become the Sun at the center of your personal universe."[76] In Hamilton's *Neo-Tech* World, man will say adieu to his 'bicameral mentality' as mind 'becomes its own authority.' This is truly breathtaking and scary stuff, a blend of euphoria and Utopia or pure nightmare. In other words, the world will have more of the 'mind thing' that brought man to the brink of the abyss, even the feeble stirrings of feeling and emotions will forever be snuffed out, and the mind will, aided by technology, make the man of reason a demi-god with a sexy body and super intelligence. This has to be the scariest doomsday scenario, the ultimate triumph of the material man over the spiritual man. To call this carnal man 'God-Man' must rank as the strangest of ironies. Let us first cross the threshold of 'good-man.' Other scientists and thinkers sketch a different scenario, more plausible and more desirable, in which man will learn to strengthen heart-generated intuition and intelligence, and restore the balance in the consciousness, which Hamilton calls bicameral mentality and which he implies has been a drag on human evolution.

The Masters and their Message

Yet another paradox stands out in human history: despite the fact that the genetic difference between any two individuals is at little as 0.2 percent, there is a yawning gap between one human and another in terms of their personalities and behavior. A few among us become great, noble, and exemplary, while the rest lead mundane, materialistic lives, trapped in the coils of *samsara*. In a world seething with disillusionment, desperation and despair, with God choosing to, or so it seems, stay away, more and more people are looking for gurus, guides, guardians and guardian angels, magic wands and mystical mantras. But too often, wise words seem to fall on deaf ears. But it is not as if we are impervious to external inspiration; quite a few rational, sane and 'sensible' people fall prey to the teachings of pseudo-spiritualists and charlatans. Why do so many people ignore Jesus, the Buddha, Zoroaster, Mother Teresa, Mahatma Gandhi and Martin Luther, and follow the likes of Jim Jones, David Koresh, Sun Myung Moon, Luc Jouret and Mother Ann Lee. While prophets and 'cult' leaders are of a different genre, it is not an accident that they all administered their message dipped in religion. The word 'religion' has that power. It is but rare that a true atheist becomes a mass leader with a fanatical following. But the question is, what, for example, could have induced more than 900 ordinary human beings to stand patiently in line for hours to drink poison, 'inspired' by another man (Jim Jones), while they failed to draw any hope from the lives and legacy of prophets and saints? And let us not forget Adolf Hitler, who 'inspired' a whole nation. In everyday life too, everyone is constantly, albeit fleetingly, 'inspired' by a motley mix of individuals and influences, from movies to lyrics to rabble-rousing leaders. The human mind is at once impervious and porous, but which characteristic prevails when and under what circumstances, is something that continues to be baffling. We are not sure if it is the individual that matters or the nature of the input or influence. Despite steady decadence down the ages, few among us, while still leading human lives, have managed to transcend the bounds of being human. In that rare category come those whom we simply call 'masters', or as the theosophist Annie Besant called 'masters of compassion'. The term embraces everyone, from a teacher in a classroom all the way to sublime spiritual personalities, those who have mastered their minds and have realized within their own selves their oneness with the Supreme, devoting their earthly life to inspire the mass of mankind to embark upon the same spiritual journey. Spiritual Masters have taught the timeless spiritual truths in a variety of ways, and in different idioms, essentially reflecting the environment and period of their time. And they have all said that they too were human and what they could achieve anyone else can. They invariably added that we should not act upon their message simply because they have said so, but only after applying the full range of faculties and our reflective and deliberative capacity. That most people, except a select few, have not measured up to the message of these

Masters, is cause for deep reflection. Is it the hostile hold of the mind over the human consciousness that prevents the kind of transformation they were able to achieve? And is it the ingenuity of our mind to let us 'learn' something but not let us act upon it? The exhortation of the Masters that we must apply our own minds before practicing their teachings also seems to beg the question, so to speak. If we have that 'capacity' we would not need a master, but it is also said that a master or a 'guru' should be implicitly obeyed. Then again, the scriptures say that the mind is feeble and fickle, and that there are limits to where the intellect can take us. Who qualifies to be a 'master' and a 'guru'? And, to what extent and how should we 'adapt' their teachings to suit our age and time? There are no off-the-shelf answers, but one must recognize the fact that whether it is scriptural sayings or a master's teachings, the medium is the mind, and the mind puts its own stamp on them and doctors them according to its own predilections. Either such teachings cannot pierce the armor of the mind, or, if they do, they get corrupted by the mind. The 'message' is conditioned by the medium and for any knowledge to be consummated the credentials of the individual are important.

Man may fall easy prey to evil, but that does not prevent him from aspiring to be both good and great. But in the melting pot of the human condition, the concepts of good and great do not easily mix. Most good men have been faceless, and most great men have been unscrupulous. It is easier to be good than great. From a species perspective, who is more crucial for its evolution? What triggers greatness or what camouflages goodness, is a riddle. How does a Michelangelo or a Leonardo da Vinci, or an Einstein or a Picasso or a Napoleon differ from the rest? And how do sinners turn into saints? Edmund Burke once said that all that is required for evil to prevail is for good men to do nothing. What about great men? Do they carry lesser responsibilities or are they exempted because often they are not good men? There have been a few in history who were both great and good, like Krishna, Christ, Zoroaster, the Buddha, Muhammad, Mahaveer and Guru Nanak. What made them so transcendental and so lofty, and such a huge cut above the rest? One explanation, the easiest, is that they were the 'chosen' ones or, in Hindu parlance, '*avatars*'. But, barring Krishna, they all disclaimed any divinity. The Buddha, who, according to Osho, was the greatest breakthrough that humanity has known up to now, for instance, said that he was not an exceptional person, that he did not have any special powers, and that what he did anyone could, if he applied himself. In our time, it was Gandhi who said the same thing: 'my life is my message'. And if we can brace ourselves to 'believe' the so-called mediums, Gandhi sent a 'message' even while being dead. A voice, purportedly of Mahatma Gandhi, manifested in the séance room of British medium Leslie Flint on 21 June 1961. The voice said "…Fear dominates the hearts and minds of man. And we know that, unless something is done about this before it is too late, the disastrous consequences are so tremendous that one hardly dares to think about it. Today your world stands on the bridge as it were of destruction. Anytime that bridge, which is in itself so unreliable that it is doubtful if it will sustain the weight that is placed upon it, because man himself, unconsciously, and in some ways consciously, has brought into being such a condition of confusion, such a condition of hatred and intolerance."[77] This reveals yet another 'gap' in human knowledge that defies bridging. But what we do know is that these men's greatness came not from their intellect and not even from what they preached. And they lived from the deepest recesses and depths of their heart, not of their mind. Their footprints on the sands of time have imprints far deeper than those of reason and science. Einstein, a great scientist but also a great spiritualist, wrote that although our time is distinguished by great achievements in the fields of science and technology, human beings have every reason to place the proclaimers of high moral standards and values above the devotees of objective truth. What humanity owes to the Buddha, Moses and Jesus ranks far higher than all the achievements of the inquiring and constructive minds. People like the Buddha and Gandhi were born as humans, but transcended the limits and constraints inherent in 'being human' not by marshalling their mind-driven intellect but by attaining a higher level of consciousness.

Any radical change in the dynamics that govern the environment of human life is well nigh impossible with the present mode of cognition and perception. And that can be changed only through transformation of the human consciousness, which is filled with anger, fear, malice, and greed. There are levels of our consciousness which are too deep for us to understand, but that is where our problems are rooted and the solutions lie. For a real and lasting spiritual upliftment, the human consciousness must cease to be mind-centered. Sri Aurobindo and the Mother, his spiritual companion, called for an *Operation of Consciousness* or *Supramental Consciousness*, which they said, "gives form to matter. It fashions matter by sending out the corresponding vibration, as today we fashion thoughts with the word."[78] The path that they proposed was to penetrate the four layers of the mind: intellectual, emotional, sensory, and physical. How can we, mundane mental men, accomplish such a stupendous task? When the mind is like an ocean tossed about by a typhoon, how can we question it? When the mind is brimming with venom and vermin, how can we cleanse it? When the mind is taken over by separateness, divisiveness, and intolerance, how can we transform it into an instrument of Oneness heralding Universal Consciousness? Can man evolve out of this suffocating civilization, the crippling infirmities of his mind and body, and become a kinder and a gentler being? Is there a spring, a switch, a lever, or a trigger hidden somewhere in the human organism, that can alter the very dynamic of our consciousness? Can man's 'earthly God,' *science*, help? Can religion, shorn of its bigotry and absolutism, help mobilize the latent energies in the human body? New technologies, we are told, might enable man to download his mind into computers and reinvent himself. Such is our state of mind that we are confused what it portends and if we should be excited or alarmed.

The war is within; the crucible is the consciousness. It is consciousness that determines the human condition and shapes human behavior. It is what differentiates modern man from men of yore. It is consciousness that lets us separate the past from the present, and the present from the future, the important from the immediate. The ancient or the primitive man lived in the natural state; we exist in a synthetic state. The gap between the primitive men and their creator or Nature was much narrower. Their nobility, truthfulness, selflessness, and righteousness were not the outcomes of daily battles within between good and evil or right and wrong, but they were outcomes of their first impulses, spontaneous and effortless. Madame Blavatsky believed that the primal or the original man lived by intuition, not reason, by the heart, not by the mind. And the French mathematician and philosopher Blaise Pascal said, "Our intellect holds the same position in the world of thought as our body occupies in the expanse of Nature",[79] and our reason is always deceived by false shadows. Elaine Matthews wrote that "the brain is not our only source of intelligence, that we have a second kind of intelligence which Nature intended to act in biological Dynamic with our brain intelligence: intelligence of the heart."[80] The Indian sage Meher Baba characterized the transition from sensation to reason as one such step (in human evolution); the transition from reason to intuition will be another.

To make any progress towards that goal, one has to journey inside, embark on an odyssey within. And it must be in tune with the direction of terrestrial evolution, which is the evolution of consciousness. Man must realize that the cosmos is loftier than creation, that he is merely a part and not the whole, and that his sensory world is constricted. For example, "our eyes can visualize only 3-dimensional configurations, while remaining oblivious to the panoply of subliminal energies from other dimensionalities interwoven into a flowing pattern."[81] Our eyes can see only certain things; our ears can hear only certain sounds. Indeed, many animals can see, hear, and smell much better than humans; but those faculties are indispensable for their kind of life. Only our brain is bigger, but it is often a mixed blessing. It has brought us this far, but to take us much farther we need a new captain at the controls. Our intellect is too handicapped to cross all hurdles. Stanford professor William Tiller says: "The break with the past will come, in part, by accepting that, like light and sound, our present band of cognition gives us a window on only a very small portion of Nature's total modes of expression."[82] Tiller discusses the 'supersensible domains of Nature', and says that space and time are "not necessarily the only variables or the best variables for cognition of the broader domains of Nature."[83] Sometimes, we 'just feel' something intuitively before our cognition comes to the same conclusion. Einstein, for example, is said to have, "felt within his body the truth of the relationship $E=mc^2$, and then had to work backwards to formulate his intuition into mathematical terminology."[84] All spiritual leaders and all truly creative people transcended the limits of their sensory systems and their brain-generated empirical intelligence. Man can become a 'whole man' only by reaching down to the deepest levels of his being. The English poet P.B. Shelley said, "Man who man would be, Must rule the empire of himself."[85] In so doing, man must pay heed to the wise words of the American Indian Chief Oren Lyons: "Keep in mind the Seventh Generation to come."[86] Today man behaves as if there will be no generation to come; indeed with his narcissistic and nihilistic bent of mind, he might be instrumental in ending all generations with this generation. Man needs a kind of consciousness with which he does not, in the words of Sri Aurobindo, "follow good for a reward now on earth or in another existence, but for the sake of good, and no longer shuns evil for fear of punishment on earth later on in this life or else in another life or in hell, but because to follow evil is a degradation and affliction of its being and a fall from its innate and imperative endeavour."[87] A heart-centered consciousness would open the way to a new vision of mystical transformation and spiritual creativity.

Whether it is due to man straying from the *dharmic* (righteous) path as many devout Hindus believe, or due to the ripening of his true being, or due to a still mysterious process, man is, perhaps, as never before, a slave of his senses, a captive of an enfeebling civilization. Man remains steeped in self-righteousness, while doing 'good' or 'bad', and in a stupor of selfishness, necessary or unnecessary. Although his ego is destroying him he still clings to it. To halt the drift into the abyss, brooding on the brink will not do. Sooner than later, he will tumble over. Man must shift the center of gravity of his consciousness from his ego-mind to the inner heart. That, in turn requires nothing less than overhauling the entire architecture of our culture and civilization, of our terminal dependency on technology, and of the infrastructure of human value systems and institutions. For too long, man has been lamenting his fate, bemoaning the world around, blaming the 'system' and at the same time eager to 'share its spoils.' It is now time for some spine, some nerve, some resolve, and some action. Our mind's fascination with explanations is fascinating but troublesome. Why must everything be explainable and according to what criteria? Time and again, we see the 'unexplainable' being 'explained', and what were thought to have been 'explained' suddenly appearing as though they are 'yet to be fully explained.' We do not need 'explanations' for what we do or do not. Most choices and consequences are simple and straightforward. What is important is not what we know through an explanation; it is what we do with what happens to us. Often, an explanation is an escape and an evasion. It is at once an aphrodisiac and opium: it excites our senses, makes us feel good about ourselves and induces stupor. For too long, have we believed in the dictum of Descartes: 'I think, therefore I am'. It is time to tell ourselves and believe in 'I feel, therefore I am.'

Feeling is deeper and more 'un-spoilt' than thinking. And it is fear that stalks many lives: fear of our dark desires, fear of disease, fear of an accident, fear of failure, fear of losing a job or a loved one, fear of old age, fear of death, fear of hell… Although consciousness is universal and integrated, the 'reality' is that it is splintered into myriad parts. To restore and realign those myriad parts, we need divine powers. But we too can do something. The psychiatrist Ernest Pecci says: "Moreover, even a small group of properly entrained individuals can have an exponential effect upon the general level of consciousness on the population of the planet."[88] What is needed is a coalition of the concerned scientists, spiritualists, and anyone for that matter who cares for something beside himself and the shrinking circle of his near and dear. The fact is, Elaine Matthews writes, "Our DNA as it is now cannot help us survive the world we have created," and that "it is our emotions which will determine whether or not we survive."[89] She says that human survival or extinction will not be a matter of a God sitting in heaven passing judgments against the *evil* ones and in favor of the *good* ones, but "will be a natural selection, a process built into our genes from the beginning of the human race."[90] But 'natural selection' and 'Nature' are not antithetical to each other, why must they be so to God? They could be His instruments like anything else in life. According to one hypothesis in Christianity, "evolution from primitive, cellular forms up to the level of hominid creatures may well have occurred by exclusively physical laws and processes; but these would have been incapable of producing the superior genetic make-up of a being physically apt for, and hence requiring, a rational soul. Hence, it is said, a last-minute *supernatural* intervention at the moment of Adam's conception would have been necessary in order to give his embryonic body the genetic constitution and physical features of a true human being."[91] In effect, it means we alone are the direct creatures of God.

The scriptures say that God manifests himself in myriad ways in all living beings, more so in the human form of life, and that means we must act towards another person as if he is God. But the scriptures also say that in every human being, there are three forces at work: human, divine, and demonic, and our outward personality and our actions and reactions are the shifting strands of their struggle for supremacy. In the Bhagavad Gita, Lord Krishna says that "The divine properties are designed for liberation; the demonical for bondage."[92] While the struggle is eternal, it does seem like the demon inside is prevailing over the divine within. We can talk of unity in diversity and universal brotherhood and common destiny for another thousand years if we last that long, but they will remain just that, full of words and piety, signifying nothing. The bitter truth is that another man in our reckoning is a necessary nuisance, an opportunistic option, something you have to live with. We spend much of life trying to get along with, get away from, get over from and get back at other humans. The yawning gap between the desirable and the practical, knowing and doing, haunts human life. Unless man finds a way to bridge, or at least significantly narrow, the gap, and learn to look at life outside our bodies as no different from the one inside, there is not much that man can do to reverse the downhill slide. The problem, once again, is consciousness itself; or more precisely the mind-centric consciousness that man of this age or *yuga* has acquired or is fated to have. It is only through consciousness that man can attain transcendence. And nothing will change unless this changes. But then, if it is fated not to change, can it change? We will never know the answer unless we try. And if we have belief and faith and act selflessly in the larger interests and do God's own work, we can change and/or God will help us change. It is the myriad small things of daily life that really matter, that make a difference to mankind. The tragedy of the contemporary human society is that more people appear to 'die for God' than to 'live for God,' which is more difficult and involves multiple choices and needs a new mindset.

Cleansing Consciousness and Cultivating Love

For any spiritual progress, the imperative is to cleanse and elevate our consciousness. Through millenniums of struggle for survival and cultivating culture and creating a civilization, our consciousness is loaded with impurities, aggression, and avarice. They have distorted human personality and have become impediments to human progress. Everyone needs a 'spiritual cleansing bath' to rid ourselves of the toxins inherent in human life. Other traits like spontaneous compassion, kindness and love, while not altogether vanquished, have become mute and meek. The defining difference is that while to men and women of yore and yonder, making a moral choice came more naturally or without too much struggle, for us it requires a herculean, often debilitating, effort. If it was the ordinary then, being righteous, it is an exception now. They, the humans of the earlier *yugas*, did not have to wage an internal war every time they had to do the right thing or to suppress an evil thought; but that is not the case now. If human beings who lived say forty or fifty thousand years ago had to go through what we have to in our daily lives, the constant and corrosive struggle not to knowingly do wrong to someone else, they could not have lived the lives they led. In this tumultuous time and turbulent period, ill will has almost become irresistible. Few are satisfied with their own gratification of good; many want others to bite the dust. The result is to warp and corrupt the myriad often moral choices that our transient lives entail. It manifests in multiple forms ranging from broken homes to religious intolerance, from ethnic cleansing to virulent nationalism. Man's tool-making capacity, which helped him survive and prevail over other species and Nature, has turned out to be his nemesis; he is making weapons too terrible to be used, but too irresistible to be piled up. A weapon has a 'life' and momentum of its own. Our addiction to gadgets has made us so dependent and debilitated that we are now easy prey to every passing vulture and virus.

There is no virtue more valued, and no state of mind more wished for than love. We all want love in our lives, to love and be loved — there is little doubt about that — but love has come to mean or convey so many things that it may actually mean nothing at all, or nothing to do with 'love'. Although we cannot neatly package love in a few crisp words, the fact is that no other emotion has inspired, enthralled, excited and exasperated more people, and has played a larger role in human relationships and in the destiny of the species. Alfred Tennyson wrote that it is better to have loved and lost, than to have never loved at all. Emily Dickinson wrote, 'Love in its essence is spiritual, and for a seeker the love of all life is to love God'. On one thing all spiritual teachings agree. Love, in its transformative effect, is alchemy. It can, as nothing else, enable us to be radically different from what we are born to be, or have turned out to be; to rise above ourselves; to overcome much of the malaise that afflicts us. It can turn the barren soil of our soul into a garden of flowers; it is the inexhaustible elixir. It is the poet's life breath and a philosopher's stone. Through love we can forgive ourselves and forgive others. An act or even thought of true love can erase bad *karma* and open the gates of good *karma*. The simplest way to cultivate love is through sharing and generous giving, regardless of reward and reciprocity. Although universal love, and love of the divine, are extolled as true love, personal love, love of another person can be transformed to service universal or divine love. Any form of life, any sentient being is but a symbol, a spark, a microcosm — of the macrocosm, of the universe, and of the Supreme. Any love we send out returns in a regenerating spiral and radiates all around. The bedrock of all love is Self-love, which is the love of the Supreme whose earthly expression is all life on earth. One does not 'fall' in love; one rises in love of any kind, personal, interpersonal, intimate, or inconsequential. It is the cleanser of the consciousness. It is the best medicine for the malaise of man, the best antidote for fear and insecurity; and a single heart can swamp and suffuse the entire world. It is a kind of condition that is blind to the loved one's flaws and sees only the virtues, not weaknesses but strengths, not what is wrong but what is right. Love may or may not cover a multitude of sins, as the Bible says, but it does cleanse our own soul. It is through unconditional love that one can exhibit cascading compassion. Love is to be free; one does not hold another with love; or 'belong' through love. Only in the state of love is it possible to experience what is best in 'being human'.

The question then is: if, as the Beatles' lyric goes, 'all you need is love', why is it so elusive, so slippery? A more troubling thought is: has our tumultuous passage through evolution, coupled with the corruption of our culture, transformed love to the extent that its place in our life is just that of another means, yet another gimmick, to get what we want of and from life, and from other humans? Could it be that we are really 'in love' with hate, and that on some layer of our consciousness we have come to believe that hate gets us more out of life than that fluffy, wooly love? Love seems to slip too easily into hatred, which is the intense, visceral dislike of another person, a dislike so consuming that it will stop at nothing to destroy that person. We do not only hate someone else for wrongs, real or perceived, done to us. There are many more people in the world who hate themselves, and so intensely that they destroy themselves. The wall between love and hate, sometimes called the two sides of the same coin, has become porous, and the acts done in the name of love, for the sake of an individual or a religion or a country or God, have come to be barely distinguishable from those done in hate. People feel good about themselves because such acts are done for 'love', no matter if the very object of 'love' gets destroyed. The American poet Henry Longfellow wrote that the sweetest thing in the world is love, and the next sweetest is hate. Freud said that humans, unlike dogs, are incapable of pure love and always have to mix love and hate. Now, scientists say that indeed the two — love and hate — are connected, and that "brain scans of people, shown images of individuals they hated, revealed a pattern of brain activity that partly occurs in areas also activated by romantic love."[93] It was also reported that the same sections of the brain that trigger intense love are also the 'areas of addiction', say, to cigarettes, drugs or alcohol, which means that we can not only hate but even feel good about hating, as we do when we are addicted to something or someone, and might even experience withdrawal symptoms if deprived of the 'ecstasy of hate'. That might be why we see so little remorse or regret in hurting or humiliating someone whom we are supposed to love; when the boundary is blurred, it makes little difference how we react. Maybe hate is not only addictive but contagious too; that is why we see so many copycat 'hate crimes', and why they often snowball into mob frenzy. Much as we would like to ostracize hate from the human world, we must bear in mind that the law of Nature is that something can come from nothing; that if we exhibit any emotion, whether it is love or hate, it can only come from within; if it is not already there, whatever is the occasion or provocation, it cannot be directed towards another person. In other words, we cannot hate anyone without having already provided a haven for hate inside us. We germinate hate; we incubate hate; therefore we show hatred. The enemy, if one were to look for a villain, is not an external malevolent force bent on destroying humankind; the enemy is ensconced within.

It is a truism, but it is not good enough to say that the way to conquer hate is love; far too many people think that hate gets them more out of life than love. Loving must become non-obligatory, non-reciprocal, a reflexive 'habit', no longer at the mercy of the mind. The first step towards making 'love a habit' is 'acceptance'; of ourselves and of other people. As the 'success guru' Chris Widener, puts it, "we become aware of love whenever we choose to accept people without judging them, commence the gentle effort of giving without any thought of getting something in return. And we should 'practice' acceptance, not tolerance, which is not being negative. True love is a completely pure and unencumbered form of giving. It is not bestowed on a perfect person but in seeing perfectly the imperfections. The word 'love', as we generally use it, means something quite different from true love. It is conditional love — giving in order to get; it is a bargain, a trade agreement." Widener adds "in order to love we must recognize what is the same within us and in all living beings. The love in us can unite with the love in others but two bodies can never become one."[94] According to psychologist James Hillman, "when love moves the heart, something else is perceived in the idolized object, which poetic language tries to capture. The meeting between lover and beloved is heart to heart, like that between sculptor and model, between hand and stone." Hillman adds, "a heart's image lies within each person. It is what we truly reveal when we fall helplessly in love, for then we are opened to display who we most truly are, giving a glimpse of our soul's genius." It was heart's image, Hillman says, which "Michelangelo called, *immagni cuor*, that he tried to capture when he sculpted the portraits of the figures of religion or myth."[95] Jack Kornfield, one of the leading Buddhist teachers of America, says that, "what type of universe we create, what we choose to plant, what we bring forth in the garden of our heart will create our future. It is through our intentions that we can shape or direct the patterns of our heart and mind."[96] While the natural state of Nature is a harmony of opposites, human intelligence has not found a way to reconcile the pairs of opposites that Vedanta calls *dwanda*, (duality): identity and interdependence, intimacy and isolation, competition and cooperation, pain and pleasure, personal gain and common good. Bereft of the knowledge of his true nature and the reason for his being, much of man's life is spent battling the three 'B's: burden of the body, brittleness of life, and, in the famous phrase of Hannah Arendt, the banality of evil. Swami Vivekananda with his usual unforgiving candor wrote, "We have seen how the greater portion of our life must of necessity be filled with evils, however we may resist, and that this mass of evil is practically almost infinite for us. We have been struggling to remedy this since the beginning of time, yet everything remains very much the same. The more we discover remedies, the more we find ourselves beset by subtler evils."[97] Our falling easy prey to evil is a direct consequence of our inability to roll back the tide of rampant materialism, to rise to our full 'sacred' potential, which some thoughtful people say has directly brought us to the "greatest dilemma in human history: the possibility of our own extinction as well as the possible destruction of our planet."[98]

5

From Mind to Heart — the Odyssey Within

Harmonizing the Head and Heart

The one attribute that distinguishes man from other living creatures on earth, it is commonly believed, is his *intelligence*; the ability to gather data and information, assemble and analyze it, and arrive at a conclusion fundamentally different from any of the original facts and incipient inputs. In other words, 'transform' a particular 'fact' into an altogether dissimilar and distinct entity. At this turbulent time in human history, we must face up to the central 'fact' without which no problem we face, personal or collective, can be solved. It is that what makes our lives so noxious is nothing but our 'intelligence', the force that drives everything external but germinates internally. Unless we set this right, nothing will work as we wish; our problems will mount, and their sheer weight will lead to an implosion. And the only way to set it right is to change the nature of the 'intelligence' that we bring to bear in our everyday lives. And the only way to change its 'nature' is to change that which is the source of supply, which has been for a long while the mind. Although we have come to accept the preeminence of the mind as a given reality, there has long been also a search for an alternative source and fountain of intelligence that lets us be a variant from a vassal of the mind. But we have not made much headway, because that very search is controlled and directed by the very force we want to change — *the mind.* We have been living in this state of logjam, impasse, and paralysis for almost all recorded history. That search has now acquired added importance and urgency as we gather speed in our slide towards catastrophe. Many thoughtful people are coming to realize that somehow we must wriggle out of the suffocating grip of the mind if we were to survive as an 'intelligent' species on earth beyond a 'century or two'. And that 'search' takes us to the heart of human transformation — the human heart.

The scriptures have tirelessly told us that besides being an individual with a personal, social, and political legitimacy, man has a higher calling, a loftier mission, and a deeper dimension. But we are not very clear how we can reach that 'higher', 'loftier' and 'deeper' level, not only as individuals, but also as a 'chosen' species. But we *do* know that *that* dimension can *only* be spiritual. We also know that that dimension is within; it is in the 'inner space' from which we operate as individuals and as a species. And we also know that only that can take us to a paradigm shift in our awareness, comprehension, and prioritization, which is what is needed at this pivot in history of human endeavor. It is this dimension that promises us to lead an integrated life, combining work and worship, the sacred and the secular, and help us to disconnect 'doing' and the sense of doership. It is this dimension that allows us to go deep inside and cleanse ourselves of the toxins, vermin, and venom from our consciousness. There is an emerging school of thought which posits that during our long and tortuous evolution, the nature of the intelligence that governs our lives underwent a profound change, a development that led to our straying from the path intended by Nature. And that straying was to marginalize, if not eliminate, the intelligence of the heart and to rely exclusively on the brain as our source of intelligence. Man today — good, bad, ugly — is preeminently the handiwork of the mind, more precisely the 'ego-mind', which really is the villain, as explained in Vedanta, the one that causes all our travails and troubles, the stumbling block to our salvation. In the ancient *Sanatana dharma* that is Hinduism, it is believed that the soul reincarnates over and over again because of the unfulfilled desires of the ego-mind, until the ultimate desire to merge with God is fulfilled. Then all individuality, including the separate self, gets dissolved into the cosmic consciousness. Our mind, it would seem, messes up not only this life, but also our liberation from the wheel of incarnation and reincarnation, cycle of birth and birth, death and death. It is the one that stands not just between man and man but also between man and God. And we seem haplessly and hopelessly trapped in the web of our mind, with no help seemingly in sight. The Upanishads say that the cause of bondage and the source of liberation are in the mind. The *Advaita* philosophy holds that mistaking the transitory things for real constitutes bondage. It also says that it is the mind that makes us make that mistake. This is the dilemma: how can we transform the cause of bondage into a springboard for liberation, to turn shackles into silken threads that bind us together. It is this conundrum that has tied us into knots, that has frustrated and paralyzed all human endeavor to set man free, and that has denied the dream of man to become a nobler living being. The scriptural and traditional methods of 'mind control' practiced by saints and *rishis* — scriptural *sadhanas* like *japa* (repetition of *mantras*), and *tapas* (yogic meditation) — are too difficult for an ordinary person. As a result, it seemed, until very recently, that we are doomed to drift towards destruction. Now science is discovering that human behavior need not be at the total mercy of our mind, and that the way forward is the 'way of the heart'. Harnessing the full potential of the heart has emerged as one of the few areas where science and spirituality meet.

Today, we know that the physical heart not only keeps us alive but is also the locus of many important human qualities that allow the human organism to function holistically. Our perceptions, mental and emotional attitudes, immune system, reaction times, and decision-making capabilities are all directly related to the realm of our heart. All education, all growing up is mind-centered. Children are taught to use their head in school, to direct it toward analytical thought, but not to calm it down or balance it with heart intelligence. The idiom and idea of 'heart intelligence' is at once ancient and post-modern. Poets, philosophers, bards, sages, shamans, rishis and mystics have spoken plainly about the intelligence of the heart throughout the reaches of time. The teachings of the world's religions and prophets all hint that the heart is at the epicenter of Eternal Knowledge or the place of *real* knowing. A new branch of empirical and experimental knowledge, the 'science of the heart', is now solving some old mysteries and opening new doors to our understanding to what goes on inside us.

Heart intelligence, it is believed, arises from an actual, biological process that is just as real, and as important as the process involving the brain intelligence. Further, it is "only by evolving full heart intelligence will we become fully brain intelligent."[1] In fact, it is the disconnection between the heart and the brain intelligence and the resultant disharmony, that is said to be responsible for much of what is wrong with the human world. It has prevented us, the argument goes, from becoming whole, complete, and to function as spiritual beings living in harmony with Nature. By harmonizing the heart and head through love we can take our consciousness and intelligence to a higher plateau of existence. For several centuries, human character and conduct were deprived of any input other than the machinations of the mind. Mind reigned supreme over man. However, it was not a one-way street. Human environment and habits also affected the mind. Mind and man have been so intertwined that we forget that the mind did not always play the dominant role that it plays in modern life. The heart seems more 'original' than the brain. A fetus, we are told, develops the heart much sooner than the brain. The human brain took several thousands of years to grow to the present size and weight; the heart has been the same organically. For long, the heart guided and guarded man while the brain was still a 'baby' and growing. In the life of the prehistoric or primitive man, the heart held its place alongside the brain. After all, the heart was the only organ he could actually sense and hear. It manifested in myriad ways: intuition, instinct, sixth sense, extra sensory perception, etc., to help him anticipate danger and look for safety. He could only survive by raw instinct without the aid of fire and tools. As the brain grew bigger and tightened its hold on man, the heart went into enforced recess.

The subtler and spiritual heart has long been, perhaps for hundreds, if not thousands of years sidelined, smothered, and silenced. In the *Voice of Silence* (1889), Helena Blavatsky teaches us to separate the real from the false, the ever-fleeting from the everlasting and, above all, the head-learning from soul-wisdom, the 'Eye' from the 'Heart' doctrine. It will take extraordinary effort for the heart to once again come to the mainstream from the margins. The accent has always been on boosting brainpower, not harnessing heart energy. Even if we can wipe the slate clean and rewrite the syntax of our living and reverse or change the mind and the mental modules, it could still be insufficient to put heart back on track. We have to cultivate mindfulness, a state of consciousness that Zen Buddhism advocates, without being mind-full or being filled with mind. The American poet Robert Frost wrote that half of our mistakes in life arise from *thinking* when we ought to feel, and *feeling* when we ought to think. The paradox is that man without a mind is a zombie, but with mind as his master, he could become a veritable monster. In any serious attempt to get to grips with our cognitive faculties of information processing, knowledge application, choice making, and perceptive powers, we must bear in mind five central factors: (1) Intentionally or accidentally, the mind has turned out to be the unchallenged monarch of man and of the universe; (2) As a result of this unmerited elevation of the mind, human personality has become a hostage to all its attributes and limitations; (3) Our quality of life reflects the quality of our decision making and problem solving, which, at present, are governed by distorted dynamics germinated in the mind; (4) To go out of the confining and corrupting clutches of the mind, we need to find another countervailing power; and (5) That spiritual power — the human heart — is also within us, but for a variety of reasons has been somnambulant and dormant and therefore needs to be reawakened and renewed.

Man — A 'Mental Case'

Much of our misery and sorrow, pain and suffering in life spring from an imbalance among the forces, impulses, instincts, and emotions that control and condition our behavior; in short, the imbalance between mind and heart. The links between man and the mind, on the one side, and the mind and consciousness, on the other, have been issues of deep reflection and study from time immemorial. A nascent field of inquiry, for long only spiritual but of late scientific too, is the nexus between mind and heart, in other words, the role of the heart in human consciousness. Above everything else, man is, not necessarily in a pejorative sense but increasingly accurately, a 'mental case', mentally manipulated in varying degrees and ways. Not only that, we are also held in a 'mental cage', and it increasingly seems that the kind of future we will have, will depend on how we stand in relation to that cage. Man has always been driven around by the mind, but now, either the mind itself has lost its moorings or it seems to have acquired a sinister agenda. One of the most challenging and incredibly complex and difficult areas of research is the attempt to quantify a mental state that causes a particular behavior. It is far more difficult to study internal stimuli than external ones. Although the research is currently focused on 'negatives' like drug use, alcoholics, and chronic sex offenders, hope lingers that any breakthrough there can have wider and elevating applications. The mind has become the dominating, if not deterministic, force in the human world to the extent that the two are indistinguishable. Albert Einstein once said, "The intuitive mind is a sacred gift and the rational mind is a faithful servant. We have created a society that honors the servant and has forgotten the gift."[2] What Einstein called 'intuitive mind' others call *heart intelligence*. It is the same rational mind that induces some of us to believe that it is acceptable if two-thirds of humanity perishes in an all-out nuclear war. It is the same intelligence that impelled man to commit countless atrocities and horrendous acts in the name of religion and national honor. And it is this rational mind that justifies biocide and genocide for a 'pleasant' life on earth. Dumping everything from human and toxic wastes to radioactive 'spent fuel' on earth is the preferred 'solution' to the problems created by human civilization. The earth has "become 'harlot earth,' in the words of Francis Bacon, whose secrets were to be wrung from it and its substance made totally available for human use on any scale one wanted to operate."[3] We have ceased to take care of creation in a 'shepherdly manner;' as a trustee or as a custodian, much less as God's regent on earth. Much of human endeavor has been directed not at how man should fit into the natural world, but at how the wealth of the world should be made to quench the human thirst for material prosperity. The question is: did something go terribly awry in human evolution that changed the human personality and brought about the present pass? Was the dominance of the mind an evolutionary need or a byproduct? And what is 'mind'? Is mind purely physical or is it paranormal? Is it another name for the brain or a different entity? Is it an alien implant or innate and integral to the human? Do the other non-human animals, particularly primates like our closest cousin, the chimpanzee, have a mind? What is its place and role in the human consciousness? Is it a boon or a bane or a blend of both?

The answers to such questions cover a broad spectrum of human inquiry, and there are no clear answers. The very word 'mind' is used in a variety of meanings in English as well as in other languages. But the striking fact is that with all its power and hold over the human condition, no one really has a good word to say about the mind except perhaps tyrants, paranoid cult leaders and 'Secret Services' of various countries, to whom coercive 'mind control' is a favorite tool to bend the human will. The mind has been called a smokescreen, a monkey, one that is mischievous, malicious, feeble, fickle, dualistic, divisive, devious etc. Also the mind is congenitally constrained in its capacity. It cannot cope with the formless, the *no*-thing; it cannot know what is going on at a level deeper than that of thought. True knowledge is deeper than thought. What we actually detect at a mental level is just a small amount of what is actually happening — the tip of the iceberg. We only get to see the objectified part, not the holistic whole. The mind operates in pairs of opposites and therefore it cannot 'grasp' the non-dual. The Buddhist *Dhammapada* compares the mind to a fluttering fish drawn from its watery abode and thrown on land. It has also been compared to a lake. Just as one can see one's reflection on the water, or the stone at the bottom, when the lake is calm and clear, not muddy and ruffled, similarly, if we can keep the mind pure and still, we can have a vision of our true self. In practical terms, the mind lets us get away with selective, inconsistent, and insensitive behavior, and endlessly offers explanations and excuses. By its inherent attribute of self-justification, the mind robs man of the ability for self-inquiry and it blurs our moral vision. The *Jyotirbindu* Upanishad says that there is a world so long as there is a mind, and that the world ceases to exist as a separate entity when the mind is annihilated. In the Mahabharata (*Santi parva*, *section XXXVIII*), it is said that there are two causes for all mental sorrow: delusion of the mind and the accession of distress. Distress comes from unfulfilled desires and desire incubates in the mind.

A Sikh scripture says, "The conscious mind is engrossed in sexual desire, anger, and *Maya*. The conscious mind is awake only to falsehood, corruption, and attachment. It gathers in the assets of sin and greed."[4] Milton, reflecting the same spirit, wrote, "The mind is its own place, and in itself, can make heaven of Hell, and a hell of Heaven."[5] And Rene Descartes said, "The greatest minds are capable of the greatest vices as well as of the greatest virtues."[6] For The Buddha, "All wrong-doing arises because of mind. If mind is transformed can wrong-doing remain?"[7] The great Adi Shankara, the celebrated exponent of the *Advaita* school of philosophy in Hinduism, compared the mind to a tiger prowling in the forest of the senses. Arjuna, in the Bhagavad Gita, drew the analogy of the wind to allude to the waywardness of the mind. But one wonders if it is the mind that is really the monkey, or if it has made a monkey of man and is enjoying a laugh. The Gita says, "*manojaya eva mahajayah*", the conquest of the mind is the greatest victory. The paradox here is that in one breath we talk of man and mind as indistinguishable, and and the next moment, we talk of the control, conquest of the mind by man. In ancient Vedic thought, the mind is described as one of the *ashta-prakritis*:

earth, air, water, fire, ether, mind, reason, and egoism. The Gita further says that the mind or *manas* controls the sense organs or *indriyas*. The mind is compared to the horses of a chariot, whose leash is held by *buddhi*, the discriminatory intellect and the charioteer. The chariot will move in the right direction only if the horses are controlled and directed by the charioteer through the leash. The mind cannot be allowed to be the decision maker; it has to be only the implementer. The sacred Sikh scripture *Adi Granth* says, "The restless mind is not fixed on one spot". Both scriptures and psychologists closely identify the mind with the many things that afflict mankind. Foremost among them is malice, which the French renaissance philosopher Michel de Montaigne called the 'tart-sweet titillation of malicious pleasure.'

The very foundation of contemporary culture and modern civilization has been the rational, thinking mind. What do the head and the heart have in common? According to Kathy Hurley and Theodorre Donson, pioneers in the development of the *Enneagram* model of personality types, "*Nothing*, if we are satisfied within our lives the way they are. *Everything*, if we are searching for personal truth and the meaning of our lives."[8] They blame contemporary culture for having "caused the human heart to be placed on the endangered species list", and remark that "at this point in time the overdevelopment of the mind and the underdevelopment of the heart are at such extremes as to endanger the existence of humanity itself."[9] Many great souls like the theosophist George Gurdjieff believe that harmonizing the head and the heart, along with the hands, the three centers of our intellectual, emotional, and locomotive life, is necessary to become a genuine person.[10] To bring about a better balance in the human decision making and behavior, we must go beyond the conceptual boundaries of the traditional — and sterile — body-brain-mind prototype, which has been a staple for much of the philosophical, scholarly and scientific discourse for several centuries. The Austrian philosopher Ludwig Wittgenstein said, "What is troubling is the tendency to believe that the mind is like a little man within".[11] The broad scriptural view is that the mind is useful and even indispensible; for the ultimate spiritual pursuit like God-realization one must transcend the medium of the mind. Some saints even say that man minus mind is God. Although there are some who hold the view that the brain-mind relationship is not fully decodable by finite procedures, the broad scientific assumption being our mental states are clearly connected to the physical states of the brain, and that physical laws apply equally to the brain. It is expected that progress in neurobiology will soon be able to explain the brain-mind relationship fully. Recent insights into brain research involving consciousness are inducing many scientists to believe that they will soon crack the 'mystery of the mind'. Maybe, but can that alter the makeup of the mind and make it a benevolent force? The bigger, larger-than-life question that humanity faces is the paradigm of 'heart to heart' communication, *seena ba seena*, as it is called in Sufism. Is it possible in today's world that is at once militarized and mechanized?

Whether it is a born blank slate or a soiled white sheet, or a ghost-in-the-machine or a god-gone-awry, the mind is much of what we are and will be, if we stay the course, and will determine what becomes of the human species. We have a far better neurological and biochemical understanding of the way the brain works, than of the origin, locus, and the functioning of the mind; and even less of how the mind influences our consciousness. We now know fairly clearly the basic structure of the human brain. It consists of three parts — neocortex, limbic system, and brain stem — which is why it is sometimes called the *triune* brain. We also know that there are two sides in the neocortex, left and right, that control the two 'modes' of thinking. The left is logical, rational, and objective; and the right is intuitive, holistic, and subjective. It is also generally believed that inadequate coordination and mutually complementary interfacing in the triune brain and the two hemispheres might be responsible for the erratic, often, bizarre, behavior of humans, and for their highly individualistic personalities. Our knowledge of the origin, locus, and function of the mind is far hazier. Science simply equates it with the brain. But we do know that the human mind has been indispensible to human survival.

Prince Arjuna, the great archer-hero of the epic Mahabharata, compared the mind to the wind and asked Lord Krishna how he could bring it under control. In answer, Lord Krishna prescribed *abhyasa* (constant practice) and *vairagya* (renunciation). The *Mandukya* Upanishad, in fact, recognizes this and says that the mind can be brought under control only by an unrelenting effort like that which would be required to empty an ocean, drop by drop, with the help of a blade of grass. One can read it either as a measure of the effort involved, or as an impossibility. Swami Vivekananda called the mind a 'mad monkey.' Ramana Maharshi said, "The thought 'I' is the first thought of the mind; and that is egoity. It is from that whence egoity originates that breath also originates. Therefore, when the mind becomes quiescent, the breath is controlled, and when the breath is controlled the mind becomes quiescent."[12] And again, the mind cannot know the self, for how can it know that which is beyond mind? So it is impossible even for a *Jnani* to explain his state in words, "which is only of the mind". To know it is to *be* it. There is no other way.[13] Meher Baba, another Indian mystic, said that a fast mind is sick, a slow mind is sound, and a still mind is divine.[14] All these are words of wisdom, but to pursue these paths it requires spiritual qualities lacking in most humans. And the mind is not going to play dead when its dominance is threatened. Rabindranath Tagore, the great humanist, said that man lives in a cage built by himself and is confined within his limitations. That cage is a mental cage, and the limitations are his blind faith in the intellect incubated in the mind. Sri Aurobindo's disciple Satprem said, "This physical mind is precisely what suffocates us insidiously, multifariously, and quite implacably. It is our cage. The very wall of our human bowl." He then adds: "And perhaps our species is indeed reaching the time of suffocation."[15] No one seems to have a good word to say about the mind, and yet that is what we are and have. So, how do we go forward?

Above all, the mind is a metaphor for power, control, and conquest. Since the beginning of recorded history, humans have lusted after power and control over their fellow humans, and until about a century ago, the means were brute force, religion, or propaganda. Mind control is the principal tool to prevail and it could be so subtle that the perpetrator is not even conscious of it. The mind itself is a tool, the process of control is mental, and the controller is also a mind. It is the battle of minds. While according to the scriptures, the control of the mind is a spiritual tool, in today's world it has become a tool of conquest. In the Hindu scripture *Padma Purana,* it is said that if you are able to control your mind, then you need not go visiting holy places; wherever you are, that place would be holy. The premise is that, through mind control we can control our senses, and that removes all obstacles to spiritual growth. Although it is now an essential weapon in the armor of every State, the urge to induce others to do what we wish, not what they want, is in-built in the human personality and implicit in human relationships. In different degrees and ways we all try to do that in our daily lives. All life is mind control, and no one is immune or invulnerable. On the contrary, everything we think, say, and do, is an amalgam of influences and impressions. George Eliot aptly captured the human vulnerability in her book *Middlemarch*: "for there is no creature whose inward being is so strong that it is not greatly determined by what lies outside it". It does not mean that our behavior is entirely externally conditioned; it means that our internal defences are not impregnable. Beginning with the 20th century, invasive techniques and technologies have been developed that tinker with our heads and command and control us. In the hands of the State, these techniques and technologies become immeasurably more powerful and menacing, especially if they are directed to produce 'programmed humans', or 'human robots' for particular missions. There has also been another strand in human affairs. It is to use the versatility and power of the mind as the solution for much of what afflicts mankind and as the sublime path to individual salvation. Both are grounded on the same basic premise, namely that an individual's very way of thinking, behavior and dynamics of decision making can be fundamentally altered through control and proper channeling of mind power. The premise is unquestionable and many great men have achieved great results. But it has to be seen as a spiritual tool; not social, political, or of the State. Ramana Maharshi used to talk about having a thorn in your palm — so you break off another thorn and dig out the first one, then throw both of them away. The use of the mind is like that. Without a spiritual basis, mind control becomes 'coercive persuasion', 'brainwashing', 'mind-manipulation', not for the individual's benefit, but to induce the person to obey someone else's will without overt use of physical force. The acronym *BITE* is sometimes used to describe destructive mind control: behavior control; information control; thought control; and emotional control. The often-cited description of such control is contained in the classic work of George Orwell, *Nineteen Eighty-Four*. It is now a favorite weapon in the hands of every State. The aim is to enforce compliance and conformity, and to silence dissent and opposition. Mind control, also called the ultimate weapon of terror, the favorite tool of totalitarian regimes, has now gained legitimacy and is often assumed as necessary for 'orderly governance.' Shorn of scientific jargon, what is being attempted is the alteration of the historic human condition, and perhaps nature's design, through control of the human mind by penetrating the barrier of the brain. Roger Penrose, whose pioneering work has helped us understand the working of the mind, wrote in his *Shadows of the Mind* (1994), that "though we believe ourselves to represent the pinnacle of intelligence in the animal kingdom, this intelligence seems sadly inadequate to handle many of the problems that our society continues to confront us with."[16]

Feelings like love and compassion, sympathy and sacrifice, adoration and altruism are not individual-specific, but that is not the case with thoughts. You may *feel* like another person, but you can never *think* like him. The mind exists as memory and expresses itself as desire. Buddhism says that desire leads to suffering, and Vedanta holds that the desireless state is the ultimate spirituality. It is desire that rules our lives. Many people's secret desires fostered by the mind have little to do with themselves or what they need, even want; they are 'negative emotions' about other people. Too often, people measure their happiness on the scale of other's misery. Somewhere deep inside our consciousness lurk desires that we would not like to acknowledge even to our own selves. One whole chapter in the Bhagavad Gita (XVI) deals with the war that rages within every human — indeed in every living being — between the *asura* (demonic) and the *daiva* (divine) tendencies. The demonic trait manifests in daily life in multiple ways from a wounding word and a deliberate slight, to calculated callousness and sadistic cruelty. The headwater of the 'victim syndrome', which has besmirched human behavior more than anything else, is the mind. It is through this prism that we look at every event, individual and life itself. The feeling that we are wronged, that we got a raw deal, that everyone is 'out to get you', that fate has been cruel, that God has forsaken you (even Jesus felt that way on the Cross), prevents us from leading fruitful lives and to contribute to the common good. Such is the dexterity of the mind that it makes even an oppressor think he is oppressed; it can make a sadist think he is sinless, a monster think that he is a martyr; and make a despot think that that is his manifest destiny. But maybe, not wholly without reason! Such is the genius of the mind that it obfuscates the difference, and by constantly shifting and shuffling, it does not let us know who we are. Every man becomes at once a victim and an oppressor, sometimes at the same time and sometimes at different times; sometimes towards the same person and sometimes towards different persons. The one who does not oppress is the one who does not have the capacity to oppress; those who do not exploit are those who do not have the ability to exploit; the one who does not seek to control is the one who is powerless to control. When we do sometimes manage to recognize or realize that we have indeed wronged or hurt another person, the mind immediately proffers an explanation and an excuse, it mitigates, to condone, if not justify the act — 'it is not *your* fault'; '*you* could not help it'; 'what else can *you* do', etc. By aborting every attempt to see ourselves as we really are, it deadens our discriminating capacity and leads us to choose the path of pleasure and gratification. It is the mind that transformed money from a means to a monarch, from a facility for easier exchange of services to an intoxicating, all-powerful and all-encompassing factor in human life. The mind values everything from its value or benefit to someone else. Someone quipped that we would not mind losing a fortune if only we are assured that no one will pick it up. Peter Ouspensky (*The Psychology of Man's Possible Evolution*, 1950) makes the rather disconcerting claim that "the strangest and most fantastic fact about negative emotions is that people actually worship them."[17] People would prefer the suffering engendered by the unholy emotions to the enjoyment promised by the pleasures of positive thoughts. Most people hug negative emotions tight, since, if they are taken away, "they would simply collapse and go up in smoke", for, they have nothing else inside them![18]

But in most of us, the mind — feeble and frail, or mischievous and malicious it may be — proves to be stronger than the heart. Most actions and words germinate as thoughts. We have more control over our actions than on our words, and more control over our words than on our thoughts. It is said that thought is as much a thing like a 'yonder piece of stone'. It has weight, color, size, shape, and form. It is a force like gravitation, cohesion, or repulsion. Thought can travel, move, and even heal. A pure thought, the Upanishad says, is sharper than the edge of a razor. Everyone is surrounded by and floating in an ocean of thought. Thinking is divided into four kinds: symbolic (through words); instinctive (fear of death); impulsive (lust, greed, fear); and habitual (of body, food, bathing). Thought affects the thinker as well as the outside world through what are called 'radiating vibrations'. The human mind is a beehive of negativity which judges others, not itself. We see the flaws in others, but not in ourselves. Even more insidious, it does not allow us to be even conscious of that. Often, the fault we see in others is the one we refuse to acknowledge in ourselves. Indeed, if we do not have it, we cannot even notice it in others. By judging another person, you define yourself. There is nothing negative about using every opportunity to our advantage; what is reprehensible is to work overtime to deny just opportunities to others. At its core, negativity is a state of being, a state of mind, which sees life as a zero-sum game; it cannot conceive of a state where everyone can win; it is a state in which if someone wins, another has to lose; if you prosper, another must be prostrate. It is the arrogant exercise of power over the weak and the vulnerable, the defenseless and the deprived. Negativity is the lurking monster in all of us. Noxious thoughts damage not only one's own body and being, but spread outwards seeping into other bodies and beings.

The toxic seeds of indifference, intolerance, and injustice germinate in the fertile soil of the mind. They are the fountainhead of most of our problems, from failed marriages to social strife and religious bigotry. Many of us think that we just have to live with these abominable traits in us. But in reality, we have much more power over negative emotions than we think, particularly when we already know how dangerous they are, and how urgent the struggle is. But to rid oneself of negative thoughts calls for uncommon will, effort and training, that only a few can summon. Negativity clogs up our consciousness, just as cholesterol does our arteries. We need powerful cleansers, what are called *antarkarana suddhi* and *samskara suddhi* in Sanskrit, cleaning of the consciousness, and cleansing of the accumulated *karmic* imprints, the leftovers of past lives. Mind and heart, reason and intuition, intellect and emotion have to be in concert in a wholesome human being. But to put this into practice, "the culture of the mind," as Gandhi said, "must be subservient to the culture of the heart."[19] One compassionate heart can induce a far greater ripple effect than the combined intellect of a hundred minds. Intuition has been described as the 'inner voice' or the 'murmur within'; the 'whisperings of the cosmic spirit' or the 'channel to our better self'. It is in the heart — called *anahata* in Sanskrit — that love manifests and gives us a sense of responsibility and pure behavior towards others. It can take us to a place of deep reflection, love, universal compassion, and detachment and can contribute more to connectivity and oneness than the intellectualization of the human condition. What man needs is the temperance and tenderness of his heart as well as the cold and calculating calculus of his mind. The mind is needed to outsmart other species. The heart, on the other hand, is required to build bridges with other humans, to bring out the best in oneself and in others. It is the access point for experiencing God, the route to the divine dimension of man. We are all wise to our physical heart, but we are yet to realize fully that we have also an emotional heart, a psychological heart, and a spiritual heart. The theosophist Gottfried de Purucker described the heart as: "…the organ of the god within us, of the divine-spiritual: here in the physical heart considered now as a spiritual organ — and not merely as a vital pump, which it is also — is the god within; not in person, but its ray touches the heart and fills it as it were with its auric presence — a holy of holies. Out of the heart come all the great issues of life. Here is where conscience abides, and love and peace and perfect self-confidence, and hope, and divine wisdom. Their seat is in the mystic heart of which the physical organ is the physical vital instrument"[20] The love that emanates from the heart alone can transform and elevate the human condition. As Mother Teresa said, "in this life we cannot do great things; we can do only small things with great love."[21] Mahatma Gandhi used to say that true love is to put another person's welfare ahead of yours; anything else is business, just give-and-take. It is the love-laced heart that can be spontaneous, instinctive, and intuitive. It is only through love of others, and love of God that man can fulfill his promise and potential.

Harboring Holistic Heart

Any study of human behavior, any attempt to ameliorate the human condition that ignores the heart is fated to fail, as feelings and emotions are as integral as reason, thought, and intelligence, if not more. Feeling is more spontaneous than thought. Nietzsche said that thoughts are the shadows of feelings — always darker, emptier, and simpler. And Thoreau said that to see things correctly one must have felt them. Thoughts come from the mind, and feelings from the heart. Our inability to synergize the heart and mind has prevented us from realizing our full potential. While other organs have more or less operationally complemented one another, the disharmony between these two has remained a road-block on our evolutionary path. Much of the turbulence and turmoil in the human condition comes from a reversal of roles: mind becoming the controller of consciousness, and man turning into its vassal. To attain the state of final evolution, man needs to reach out and dive deep into his heart. Man must be able to distinguish between what Joseph Pearce calls the intelligence of the heart and the intellect of the head. The heart itself has been in a state of hypnotic hibernation for at least around three milleniums; the spirit of life is trapped in the camouflaged caves of the heart. Our persistent inability to tread what we know to be the right path, the stranglehold of malice on our consciousness, and our paralysis in making any headway towards the goal of universal brotherhood, are reflective of the apparent triumph of our head over our heart in the yin and yang confrontation within our consciousness. "It is very hard to get your heart and head to think alike; in my case, they're not even friendly!"[22] quipped Woody Allen in his movie *Crimes and Misdemeanors.* The evangelist Billy Graham contended that hot heads and cold hearts never solved anything. Author Somerset Maugham chipped in, "I'll give you my opinion of the human race in a nutshell…their heart is in the right place, but their head is a thoroughly inefficient organ"[23] Albert Einstein maintained that the present-day problems cannot be solved with the mindset we were in when we created them. The New Age writer Elaine Matthews says, "Passion and joy, goodness and beauty, love and compassion are the birthright of every human being, built into our genes and intended by Nature to speak in every beat of our heart", and asks, "why then do so few of us experience these wondrous qualities in ourselves and in our lives?"[24] In her opinion, "In order for a sentient being to achieve a high level of intelligence and to continue growing and expanding in that intelligence, Nature has to move that being out of the realm of instinct into the realm of choice."[25] But to avoid the risks involved in such a movement, Nature has provided the evolving human being with "a second level of intelligence which would temper and balance the choices made by the brain. That level is heart intelligence 'designed' by Nature to give the intelligence of our brain a holistic view of its world as well as a humane, compassionate ground on which to base its world-views and decision making; its choices."[26] In his book, *Biology of Transcendence: a Blueprint of the Human Spirit* (2002), Joseph C. Pearce makes the same point by contending that the evolutionary structure of the brain and its interfacing with the heart were designed by Nature to reach beyond our innate evolutionary capacities.

The Upanishads proclaim that the lotus of the heart is the locus of the divine and of love, kindness, and goodness. According to the *Mundaka* Upanishad, *Hridayam sannidhya* — 'the One Source resides in the heart'. The *Kaivalya* Upanishad describes the heart-lotus as perfectly pure, free from all *rajasic* and *tamasic* dirt, free from all passions and delusions, containing within it the orbs of the sun, the moon, and fire. The *Chandogya* Upanishad says that as far as the universe extends, thus far extends the space within the heart. And the *Mundaka* Upanishad makes the awesome assertion that when the knot of the heart is finally opened, the mind will stop ranting, all doubts will be cleared, that you will stop running around knowing that you have finally arrived, as you behold the portal of the gateway to immortality. The import of all these maxims is that we need go no farther than our own heart to know the 'knower', to experience the divine. Yet, at some hazy but fateful time in evolution, human consciousness became mind-centric and the 'knot of the heart', the *Hridaya Granthi* in Sanskrit, got tightened, marking perhaps the beginning of the decadence of the god-like species. Man before *that* time, was like any other animal, free from guilt and deception. Rudolf Steiner wrote that "God, having vanished from the world, is reborn in the depths of the human heart". But, ensconced in the heart, He seems to have gone into deep slumber or, appalled at what He could observe, decided not to intervene. Whatever it is, it was the rise of the asymmetry between the heart and mind — which some experts like the American psychologist Julian Jaynes (*The Origin of Consciousness in the Breakdown of the Bicameral Mind*, 1976) have dated as recent as the second millennium BCE — that has resulted in the transformation of consciousness into the kind we presently have. With the dawn of dominance of the mind over the human consciousness in human evolution, the emotional and spiritual prowess of man has weakened, and the holistic human heart became a mere physical entity. In the words of James Hillman, "the [spiritual heart] had first to become a machine and the machine become a spare part, interchangeable from any chest to any other".[27]

It is inconceivable, but there was indeed a time, which is most of the history of habitation on earth, when the heart was the primary source of intuitive intelligence, the center of consciousness, the source of love, and the seat of the soul in the world of humans. Although the heart has its own nervous system and is, in effect, a 'specialized brain, at some point in evolution, for reasons still not clear, the heart got relegated to the margins, and the brain-dominated mind came to the center-stage of consciousness. It is this lopsidedness, this disharmony, that leads to faulty decision making, flawed prioritization, and a warped way of being and thinking. Its corrective measure involves a different paradigm which entails treating the human heart not as a magnificent muscular pump — which pumps more than seven liters of blood per minute through some 96,000 kilometers of blood vessels in the human body, a distance approximately 2.5 times the circumference of the earth — but as a generator of complex and multiple physiological patterns that have a vital bearing on human consciousness. Recent research has discovered that the heart, which has an inherent wisdom, independent of any other system or organ of the body, has an electrical field many times more powerful than that of the brain. James Lynch (*Language of the Heart*, 1986), goes to the extent of linking the vascular changes registered in the fluctuations of our blood pressure with what he calls 'the language of the heart', which is integral to the health of the emotional life of all of us. Researchers have demonstrated that the heart routinely engages in a rational dialogue with the brain and the body via the nervous system and other pathways, and that the messages the heart sends to the brain not only affect physiological health but also profoundly influence perception, emotions and, most significantly, behavior. It is actually the central player in setting the frequency signatures of all bodily systems, ranging from the brain to the blood cells. The heart has neural cells, amounting to about 60 to 65 percent of the total cells in the heart, similar to those found in the brain and, being autogenic, it does not require a signal from the brain to beat and pulsate to maintain balance.

Although the human has been around for hundreds of millenniums on earth, the consciousness he has now, in relative terms, is 'brand new'. And man, until very recently, has been relying primarily on intuition and instinct, the 'gut' feeling, with intelligence and logical thought playing merely a secondary role. Mark Hamilton (*God-Man: Our Final Evolution*, 1998) contends that mankind is still going to undergo one more evolutionary leap into a far more competitive being called God-Man. In the 1960s and 1970s, psychologists John and Beatrice Lacey found that the heart did not mechanically respond to signals from the brain, but was selective in its response, and that the heart actually sent messages back to the brain and the brain listened. And in 1983, the heart was reclassified as an endocrine gland, the source of a new hormone that affects the blood vessels, kidneys, adrenal glands, and regulatory regions in the brain. In 1991, the concept of a functional 'heart brain' was introduced, which decides when to trigger an emotion without the direct involvement of the 'other brain'. New discoveries now offer a comprehensive overview of the heart's intrinsic nervous system which enables it to process information, learn, remember and produce feelings, and then transmit that information from one cell to another. All these and related studies demonstrate that the human heart is a highly complex, self-organized sensory organ with its own functional intrinsic brain.[28] Recent research has also shown that the human body and organs are highly complex, 'non-linear' organisms; which means that the whole is more than the sum of its parts. The human heart, for instance, is now seen as a non-linear, self-balancing system that functions not only as a powerful endocrine gland, but also as a powerful electromagnetic generator and receiver, whose energy field is said to be 5,000 times stronger than that of the brain.

Although the efforts and resources directed in this direction are meager, it is already becoming evident that our heart is an extraordinarily versatile and sensitive organ whose domain of feelings is a parallel (though connected) source of energy, electromagnetic field, and intelligence. This new perspective on the heart's functioning explains how the seemingly complex, disparate information of the body's behaviors, molecular biology, and genes is organized into a single coherent picture. That perspective is now being called 'Heart Wave' — the body's master key, which reflects, organizes, synchronizes, and synergizes the various 'behavioral waves' of the body. Although mainstream science has thus far been largely responsible for the relative neglect of the heart by ignoring emotions, and making reason, logic, and intelligence the primary determinants of human conduct and culture, it is now on the frontline of the effort to restore heart to its rightful place. Researchers suggest a strong link between heart energy and intuition as a systemic process involving both heart and brain working together to decode intuitive information. We have to awaken the somnambulant angels of the heart and destroy the rampaging demons of the mind. In our effort to alter the human condition, the heart has to be at once the locus and the focus, the catalyst and the conductor of the orchestra.

The Chinese philosopher Mencius maintained that, "No man is without a merciful and tender heart; no man is without a heart for shame and indignation; no man is without a heart to give away and yield; no man is without a heart for right and wrong. A merciful and tender heart is the seed of love; a heart of shame and indignation is the seed of right; a heart to give away and yield is the seed of courtesy; a heart for right and wrong is the seed of wisdom."[29] A holistic heart allows these seeds to sprout and flourish. According to the Buddhist *Heart doctrine*, a divine or a spiritual spark is the essential source of individual consciousness. It is the quantum Self, or the real "I," within a human being. Although every heart is specific, hearts seem to have more in common than human minds. We often say 'heart-to-heart', not 'brain-to-brain' or 'mind-to-mind'.

Path-breaking research on heart intelligence, by the American Institute of HeartMath (IHM), has shown that the heart's "intelligence" affects emotions and physical health — especially when it comes to handling stress — and specifically what you can do to balance heart rhythms, reduce stress hormones, and boost your immune system. The "intelligence" refers both to the heart's "brain," or the 40,000 neurons found in the heart (the same number in the brain itself), and the intuitive signals the heart sends, including feelings of love, happiness, care, and appreciation. When such positive emotions are felt, it is said that they not only change patterns of activity in the nervous system but also reduce the production of the stress hormone called cortisol. When there is less cortisol, there is more DHEA (dehydroepiandrosterone), the so-called fountain-of-youth hormone known to have anti-aging effects on many of the body's systems. What is called the *HeartMath Solution* outlines ten steps for harnessing the power of the heart's intelligence, including ways to manage one's emotions and keep energy levels high. One of the most important is the 'Freeze-Frame' technique for calming the nervous system, improving clarity of thought and perception, and boosting productivity. The heart is said to communicate with the brain and body through four pathways: neurological (nervous system), biophysical (pulse waves), biochemical (hormones), and energetic (electromagnetic fields). At the dawn of civilization, heart intelligence manifested itself in ways that are now called intuition, instinct, the sixth sense, and extrasensory perception, to help man sense danger and look for safety. The prehistoric man, in truth the primal man, was genuinely more human than the 'civilized' man; he was less divided, more in harmony with Nature, and more synergistic in his behavior, perhaps violent by necessity but less malicious and more creative without the aid of technology. Man did not have a fully developed brain then, but had a fully functioning heart to provide the needed energy and momentum. In all probability, it was man's heart that triggered the formation of his genius. It is the excessive intellectualization of the human condition that coarsened it and has brought man to the present pernicious pass. The way forward is perhaps a step backward. Henri Bergson, the French philosopher and Nobel Laureate argued that intuition was deeper than the intellect, and declared that the next human quality to develop is intuition. No fundamental change in the human psyche and condition is possible with the consciousness man has evolved. Heart transplantation, the life-saving medical procedure, is throwing new light on the heart as a source of cellular memory, stretching beyond the finality of death. New areas of research in cellular biology like energy cardiology, and cardio energetics suggest that the heart's biophysical energy and information travel throughout the body and reach the surface of the skin, and the sounds generated by the beating heart too store energy and information, and traverse through the fluids and make their way to the outside of the skin and eventually go out into space. It is being said that someday science might well be able to develop some sort of a 'heart print', a kind of a road map to lay bare the world of emotions within, to destroy our negative emotions and empower us to experience the nobler emotions more spontaneously. And the prospect is dangled when "machines will be able to partially fulfill the work of an introspective mind", and "handheld gadgets will be able to take a complete heart print of an individual and point out the dark secrets of her heart".[30]

While on the one hand, man is trying to realign the human condition with the heart as the fulcrum, on the other hand, mainstream research is focusing on 'boosting brain power' as the silver bullet to solve all human problems. Much hangs on which will win the race; it would be even better if we could harmonize both. Research is also indicating that there are several 'silent areas' or apparently inactive zones in the brain whose precise role is unclear, and it is being speculated that they may be the gateways to supra-sensory cognition that is not based on reality as we currently understand, nor on subject-object dichotomy. If science succeeds, minds may, we are being reassured, directly communicate with each other, babies can be custom-made, man will have X-ray vision with a terminator mind, and life can stretch so long that death becomes a mere theoretical possibility. But man could also become more of a mental being and his brain-guided behavior could be even more nihilistic. He would then become even more suicidal, murderous, fratricidal, and fractious. Life itself is now reduced to a mental construct, bereft of aliveness, awareness, a deadened abstraction or travesty of who we are. There are already more 'mentally' ill people, some declared and many undeclared, than the physically ill, and more people suffer from mental impairment than physical disorder. According to the World Health Organization, some 400 million people globally suffer from some kind of mental disorder, accounting for about 12 percent of all disease and half of all measurable handicaps (2001 figures).[31] If the mind is the most powerful and dominant force, what is it about it that makes us so prone to be so sick as to be able to kill other humans so casually (or kill ourselves so banally) and not be even conscious that we are so afflicted? Is the kind of mind that we happen to have had, an evolutionary tool no longer appropriate to the human form of life? And frontier brain research is also trying to break into the citadel of the unconscious. Sigmund Freud theorized the unconscious to be a deep cavern of dark desires. Psychologist Abraham Maslow disputed it. The unconscious, he said, is not merely an undesirable evil; it "carries in it also the roots of creativeness, of joy, of happiness, of goodness, of its own human ethics and values."[32] To place this in mind-heart terms, the 'bad unconscious' is largely centered in the mind, and the 'good unconscious' is rooted in the heart. However, we must recognize that emotions and reasoning complement each other and help man to make reasonably sound decisions. But man must dislodge the mind from its pre-eminence in human culture. To borrow a political phrase, we need power-sharing, a compact of cohabitation between the mind and the heart. If a mix of experience and emotion, intelligence and intuition could be made to govern human behavior, it could profoundly change the phenomenal world, and make man a better being, and the species a more moral organism. The French philosopher and Nobel Laureate Henri Bergson had argued that intuition was deeper than the intellect and declared that the next human quality to develop is intuition. The intellect, he said, looks at the outward world. The intuition is a faculty belonging to the inner life, related more to instinct that emphasizes in the organism life-preserving energies.[33] Theosophist Annie Besant said that the intellect has to be "subordinated to the higher spiritual quality, which realizes the unity in diversity and therefore comes to realize the divine Self in man. That is the next step forward, looking at consciousness."[34] Mind and heart have to march in step as there is growing evidence that both play a critical role in controlling bodily functions and conditioning emotional responses.

Fortunately, even some among those who worship the god of mind and have delved deep into its magic and mystery have begun to acknowledge its limitations arising from its inherent character. They do not disown the mind but want to transcend it. Sri Aurobindo asserted that "It is only through a decisive transformation of the mind and an emergence into a higher stage of consciousness that man can come face to face with the realization of all that has remained his dream and his aspiration through the ages. Vedanta characterizes the mind as a storehouse of enormous energy, and yet utterly inadequate to probe into subjects such as the meaning of man and the foundation of the universe. The essence of all such ancient wisdom and increasingly nascent insights is that, although inadequate, the mind is everything; the mind can unravel many mysteries, but not really what we want to, and ought to, know. William Tiller (*Science and Human Transformation*, 1997) believes that as we ride the 'River of Life', the great consciousness adventure, we perceive events around us, but, more often than not, we do not perceive the truth and the reality behind those events. Some wise men say that truth itself is reality, which is never fully comprehensible through our finite intellect. Pearl Buck said that what she learnt in her life is that there is a kaleidoscope of truths, not the absolute truth. Theosophist G. de Purucker, for example, says that "Truth may be defined as that which is Reality; and present human intelligence can make but approximate advances or approaches to this Cosmic Real which is measureless in its profundity and in its infinite reaches, and therefore never fully comprehensible by any finite intellect"[35] What we take as reality is actually a convolution between what is real on the one hand and our mindset or the belief structure on the other hand. It is said that "we can only comprehend truth to the extent to which it resonates with some portion of already perceived reality."[36] In the theosophical text *Agni Yoga*, from the teachings of one of the founders of theosophy, Master Morya, who was also the guru of Madame Blavatsy, it is written that, "To behold with the eyes of the heart; to listen with the ears of the heart of the roar of the world; to peer into the future with the comprehension of the heart; to remember the cumulations of the past through the heart; thus must one impetuously advance upon the path of ascent. Creativeness encompasses the fiery potentiality, and is impregnated with the sacred fire of the heart."[37] Blavatsky herself asserted that "even ignorance is better than head-learning with no soul-wisdom to illuminate and guide it."[38] She compared the mind to a mirror and said, "it gathers dust while it reflects. It needs the gentle breezes of the soul-wisdom to brush away the dust of our illusions."[39] According to late Arnold Keyserling, the great 20th century European philosopher and author, our head-centered and ego-dominated consciousness operates at the lowest level, equivalent to the ground state of the atoms, where all electrons are in the lowest energy position.

The universality and unity of 'consciousness' is also illustrated through a famous episode in the life of Adi Shankara. On his way to the temple of Viswanatha in Varanasi, Shri Adi Shankaracharya encounters a sweeper (a low-caste *chandala*) and asks him to step aside and give way. The sweeper (none other than Lord Siva, the main deity of the temple that Shankaracharya was going to pray to) asks *who* should move away from *whom* — whether one body made of food from another made of food, or one consciousness from another consciousness. The sweeper then says 'Is there any difference between the reflection of the sun in the waters of the Ganga and its reflection in the water in a ditch in the quarters of the outcastes? Or between the very space in a gold pot and in a mud pot?' Shankaracharya realizes the profound truth in the question, and prostrates himself in front of the sweeper (who, in reality, is Shiva Himself). It is consciousness that unifies as well as differentiates one man from another man; indeed one living being from another. It provides the common thread as well as the individual identity.

Restoring Equilibrium in Human Consciousness

Our current consciousness, in one sense, is the 'abnormal' or 'unnatural,' not the 'normal' or natural consciousness. The American philosopher and scientist Norman Livergood says, "The conspiracy to reduce consciousness to intellectual awareness of the physical world has been in evidence for at least five thousand years." He says that "over the centuries the mental and psychic powers that only mystics and seers now possess have been filtered out of most people"[40] and our current intellect-based awareness is highly abnormal and unnatural. It is this conspiracy that has brought humanity to the brink of the abyss. Our 'normal' but really 'abnormal' consciousness lost some of its 'normal' powers like intuition, inspiration, and a range of perceptions we call extrasensory since, as theorized by occultists like Colin Wilson, we no longer 'need' them. Or, to put it more accurately, that is because these powers have been rendered redundant by our materialistic civilization. One could even argue that it was the loss of those 'powers' that brought about the imbalance in the human condition and led to the total dominance of the human consciousness by the brain-mind. But those 'powers' are essential attributes of the human condition and are still needed for human betterment, and perhaps for survival. And that will be possible only if the human heart comes out of the shadows and margins. Elaine Matthews puts it across aptly: "We can only move into a higher dimension of awareness when we have full heart intelligence, which implies that our triune (three-in-one) brain will have become one brain, functioning perfectly as a seamless whole. When this happens we will live our lives as unique individuals with full intelligence, aware at all times that we are also a part of the whole, The One."[41] It would then be possible to awaken the 'Buddha' within each human being, who, Osho said, has been put to deep sleep. But it is a delusion to think that simply wishing, writing, and reading or even praying will bring about the 'Buddha'. It will stay as a 'pious' wish and a desirable state. The biggest bottleneck to human betterment since the time of the 'first humans' to the 'modern man' is the disconnect between the 'devotedly desired' and the 'practical actuality;' the gap, as noted earlier, between knowing and doing, belief and behavior, precept and practice. We must put together a 'tool box' for that purpose, drawn from both scriptures and science. William Tiller says that the heart *chakra* should open first in the human transformation to a significantly higher level of both consciousness and energy flow.[42] How to activate heart chakra energy has to be on the frontline of both science and spirituality. But first we must learn or relearn to 'live— and learn —in our hearts' what it is to be humanely human as a way to restore balance between intellectual intelligence and intuitive intelligence. As Elaine Matthews puts it, "Only by evolving full heart intelligence will we become fully brain intelligent."[43] She asserts that if we could mobilize what she calls the 'heartbeat of intelligence,' begin turning things around in a generation or less, and with wisdom, we could take over our own biological evolution and become, at least in spirit 'spiritual beings,' and restore our bond with the rest of the cosmos.

The mind brooks no rival or even a parallel. It is the perennial source of ego. We have come to identify ego with the whole of our being. Sogyal Rinpoche, the Tibetan Dzogchen Lama and scholar (*The Tibetan Book of Living and Dying*, 1992) says, "In Tibetan, ego is called *dak dzin*, which means 'grasping to a self.' Ego is then defined as incessant movements of grasping at a delusory notion of 'I' and 'mine', self and other, and all the concepts, ideas, desires, and activity that will sustain that false construction. The thought that we might ever become egoless terrifies us. To be egoless, ego whispers to us, is to lose all the rich romance of being human, to be reduced to a colorless robot or a brain-dead vegetable." Sogyal Rinpoche goes on to say, "to end the bizarre tyranny of ego is why we take the spiritual path, but the resourcefulness of ego is almost infinite, and it can at every stage sabotage and prevent our desire to be free of it."[44] The *Kathopanishad* clearly rules out the mind's capability to lead us to the summit of consciousness. But the mind, like the ego, cannot be gotten rid of easily. The Bhagavad Gita says that a man's own self could be a friend or a foe. If he stays a captive of his mind, the mind could be the foe; if he awakens his heart and lets it lead him, it would be a friend. Meher Baba emphasizes the paramount need for the emancipation of consciousness from the limitations of the mind and says that "to throw off the limiting mind is no easy thing. The chief difficulty lies in the fact that the mind has to be annihilated through the mind itself."[45] History has shown that it is not possible to overcome or surmount the mind through mind control. We have to outflank and work around it and strengthen an alternative source.

It means restoring the lost balance of our consciousness. What is needed is a counterforce, a force that induces equilibrium in the human consciousness. For this, there has to be a seminal shift in the human effort from controlling the mind to complementing it. The focus of human evolution has to be on the restoration of the balance and harmony within the processes that turn human thought into human behavior. Ancient cultures intuitively recognized the existence of an independent source of intelligence, wisdom, and subtle energy to balance or reinforce the mind, but the mind-dominated modern civilization has hardly paid any attention to it. To counterweigh mind-power we have to empower the heart. The heart is the repository of iove, tenderness, compassion, mercy, and sacrifice. Cynthia Kneen, a Buddhist scholar and the author of the book *Awake Mind, Open Heart* (2002), says that 'having a heart' is the willingness to be exposed, to be touched nakedly by the world, not being weak or sentimental. It is the seat of the soul and the abode of God in man. A Persian Sufi mystic Mansur Al-Hallaj who had attained communion with God by diving deep into the innermost recesses of his being, said "you can break a temple; you can break a mosque; but you must never break the human heart, because the heart is the very dwelling place of the Lord."[46] It is through this heart that one can overcome the limitations and fragilities of sense perceptions. While the physical heart needs constant blood supply, the spiritual heart can be nurtured through nutrients like solitude, meditation, and prayer. If the mind is a gift of God, the heart is God's abode. If the mind is the wall between God and man, the heart is the bridge. We need to break walls and build bridges, and foremost among them is the wall of the mind and the bridge of the heart. Psychologists like Mihaly Csikszentmihalyi and Alan Watts argue that the human brain has a natural, evolution-based negativity. That negativity might have been necessary for sheer survival, but it has remained entrenched and has come to occupy the entire inner space of man and has become the 'natural' disposition of the human organism. If kept under check and tempered with morality, that 'negativity' could become a cautionary restraint. A dose of negativity is necessary for self-preservation, but often it hijacks the whole consciousness. When that happens, it makes man a menace. If the brain is innately 'negative', the heart is naturally 'positive'. If the first impulse of the brain is to see the shades and the shadows, the instinct of the heart is to see the light and the sunshine.

Even if we are not fully cognizant of the larger-than-pump role of the heart, we all know that emotions play a profound role in life and that the heart has some vague connection to them. One of the most popular words and the cause of many 'modern' maladies goes by the ubiquitous word 'stress', which really is the destructive dichotomy between the head and the heart. The fact is that the mind will not quit or quietly disappear into the sunset, with man waving an affectionate adieu from the shore. But it is not necessary or even desirable for the mind to vanish. Without mind, man is dead meat; he cannot survive without it, and if he does, other species, so long under its yoke, will seize the chance to settle their deadly scores. Man needs the energy and crafty intelligence of the mind, but he needs the energy and compassionate intelligence of the heart even more. The great French writer and aviator Antoine de Saint-Exupéry had some insight into this phenomenon when he wrote in *The Little Prince* (1943), "...And now here is my secret, a very simple secret: it is only with the heart that one can see rightly; what is essential is invisible to the eye."[47] Theosophist de Purucker said, "The Buddha within you is watching you. Your own inner Buddha has his eye, mystically speaking, on you. His hand is reached compassionately downward toward you, so to speak, but you must reach up and clasp that hand by your own unaided will and aspiration."[48] It is our feelings, not thoughts, that let us clasp that hand. As Swami Vivekananda said, the 'power of the prophets' lay, not in intellect, but in their feelings. In his words, "Feel like a Christ, and you will be a Christ; feel like a Buddha, and you will be a Buddha."[49] That is what separates a sage or a seer from the multitude of human beings. It is the feeling that is the life, the strength, and the vitality, without which any amount of intellectual activity cannot reach God. Intellect is like the limbs without the power of locomotion.[50] Swami Vivekananda also said that "if you do (feel) you are growing in oneness. If you do not feel for others, you may be the most intellectual giant ever lived, but you will be nothing, you are but dry intellect and you will remain so."[51]

The insights that modern science with powerful penetrating tools is gathering, is what the *rishis* of ancient India were able to discern through their intuitive insight into the depths of the human soul by summoning the spiritual energy of their hearts. The heart, unlike the mind, is inherently pure. The *Maha Narayana* Upanishad speaks of a "small, sinless and pure lotus of the heart which is the residence of the Supreme."[52] The *Isha* Upanishad says that in the heart of all things, of whatever there is in the universe, dwells the Lord. And the *Katha* Upanishad says that the Supreme Person, of the size of a thumb dwells forever in the heart of all beings. The Bible says, "Blessed are the pure in heart: for they shall see God" (*Matthew, 5:8*). Not only does the brain dominate our body, it has now devised extensions of itself in the form of electromagnetic energy embodied in devices like cell phones and computers. The human intellect has had things its way for the last several hundreds of years, and the result is the hapless but hazardous human being that man is today and the warped mental world he sees around. The mind is essentially a factory that manufactures thoughts, a factory in a perpetual production mode.

The French philosopher René Descartes famously said, 'I think, therefore I am.' What is forgotten is 'You can be what you feel' too. Just as every thought, positive or negative, is a force in nature and affects everyone else, so is every feeling and emotion. If a thought outlives a life, an emotion can transform a life. Just as thought can be sharpened and trained, so can feeling be nourished and nurtured. It is the interplay and tension between thinking and feeling, thought and emotion, that straddle the human consciousness and create what one might call pendulum personalities, often oscillating between apparent opposites. No one can deny the power of thought but one should not decry the power of feeling or emotion. Blaise Pascal wrote, "There is internal war in man between reason and the passions…. because he has both, he must be at war; since he cannot have peace with one without being at war with the other. Thus he is always divided and in opposition to himself."[53] That would be tantamount to a 'house divided against itself', which has been the malaise of mankind for several centuries, if not millenniums. Tibetan Lama Sogyal Rinpoche said, "We are so addicted to looking outside ourselves that we have lost access to our inner being almost completely. We are terrified to look inward, because our culture has given us no idea of what we will find. We may even think that if we do, we will be in danger of madness. This is one of the last and most resourceful ploys of ego to prevent us from discovering our real nature."[54] Intelligence and intuition have to act in unison. If intelligence is our reasoning faculty, intuition is 'taught from within,' a spontaneous perception, an impulsive knowledge that is outside the realm of reasoning. Intelligence we cultivate and acquire; intuition, already germinated, has to be incubated.

'Be a master *of* mind rather than mastered *by* mind' says a Zen maxim. The fact, however, is that the mind's hold over the body is total and lethal. What we call 'human civilization,' 'scientific temper' and 'progress' are all built on the foundation of intellectual excellence, a product of the mind. How does an ordinary human being, battling with his body, mind and the senses, drowning in the sea of *samsara*, the phenomenal world, cleanse and control the mind, the force that controls him? Persistent practice, non-attachment, meditation and prayer, are the remedies suggested by the scriptures, though they are clearly not sufficient in the way that they are put into effect. Prayer, it is said, is how we speak to God and meditation is when God speaks to us. Prayer and its power have not changed; it is the one who prays who has changed; it is what we want from God that has changed. We have put prayer outside the realm of our overall behavior; even from our sense of morality, right and wrong. Prayer has become a petition, instead of a conversation with or contemplation of the divine; meditation is identified with mental concentration instead of, in the Buddha's words, a means for witnessing or watching one's own mind; and non-attachment to the fruits of our efforts. We pride ourselves on our capacity for logic, reason, and rationality. We worship intellect, intelligence, and intellectuals, and view intellectualization as strength, and scoff and snigger at feelings, emotions, and tenderness, and consider them weaknesses. Intelligence has become the sole measure of human worth, and intelligence quotient (IQ), the primary passport to social esteem. It is intelligence that is common to experts, scientists, specialists, scholars, and pundits of all hues and persuasions. Without 'intelligence' we cannot live. We need to move away from the monopoly of brain/mind germinated intelligence and towards a blend of intellectual, emotional, and spiritual intelligence.

Mastering the Mind and Harnessing the Heart

A radical change in the context and content of the human condition could be attempted through two routes. One way could be to stay the course, try to cleanse, control and calm the mind, and try to go on to a higher but still mental consciousness. The other path could be to continue to cleanse and control the mind, but develop another source of internal energy as a means to neutralize the negativity of the mind and to change the energy balance in human consciousness. In either case, the question that arises is whether an individual man alone or a group of like-minded men could reach those levels, or must it or does it have to be be a species-spread process? Adopting the first route, some men could become extraordinary beings with exceptional mental and spiritual abilities, while the rest will be what they are pretty much now. Even if it were not to be a species-scale consortium that embraces the spectrum of humanity, which clearly is impossible, we would certainly need a 'critical mass' of kindred souls for a species-wide lift-off. A single man does make a difference — no selfless effort is in vain — but for a whole species to reach a higher plateau of evolution, a broader base is required. We need a global community of men and women who see themselves as citizens of the world, who care about what happens to people beyond their immediate families, and who weigh their actions keeping in mind the quality of life of generations to come and above all, who are in a state of harmony within their selves.

Many great souls have tirelessly told us that it is the absence of harmony and equilibrium in our lives as well as inside us that makes us so brittle and ambivalent. The Roman emperor and stoic philosopher Marcus Aurelius said that he who lives in harmony with himself lives in harmony with the universe. What prevents inner harmony is the ego, which really is the 'sense of separateness' that often tends to become a 'sense of superiority'. Everyone has an ego as part of the instinct of self-preservation, the *aham*, but it should not lead to *ahamkara* (arrogance) and *agraha* (anger). The three 'A's combined — *aham*, *ahamkara*, and *agraha*, or oversized ego, arrogance, and uncontrolled anger — become a toxic triad, a menacing mélange, and make the mindset intolerant, vain, prone to praise and flattery and self-righteousness. The ego blinds us to our faults and magnifies the faults of others; it makes the person incapable of even a passing thought that he or she could be wrong on any matter. In western psychotherapy, the ego is part of a triumvirate, the mediator between the other two parts, 'id', the primitive power of the senses and the 'super-ego', the moral conscience. In Vedantic philosophy, ego is compared to a stick that seems to divide the water into two, which makes you feel that you are one and I am another. And that when the ego disappears, one realizes *Brahman* as one's own inner consciousness. All scriptures are unanimous that the human ego is the chief impediment to human enlightenment and they prescribe ways to overcome it. Scriptures like the Upanishads and the Bhagavad Gita identify the ego as the chief obstacle to Self-realization. And the ego not only enslaves us to the mind but also cuts us off from the heart. The poet Khalil Gibran says, "The world that moves with you is your heart, which is the world itself."[55] The formidable power of science and psychology are directed towards enhancing the efficiency of the mind. As if we are not quarrelsome enough, learned professors even teach us how to hone our argumentative skills! The byline is 'Never mind the truth, be smart! Be competitive, be aggressive! Winning is all that matters, be a killjoy! If you are not happy or prosperous, see to it that others too are not.' The Buddhist *Dhammapada* exhorts man to make haste in doing good and to check our mind from evil. The paradox is that to check the mind we need the mind, and mind cannot at once be the problem and the solution, and mind control, even if it is the remedy, is not within the reach of ordinary folks. The path of the mind is the one that man followed in recorded history. And we know the outcome; we see the outcome; we *are* the outcome. The world is mind's handiwork; the jarring voices of suffering are its music; the evil that is strident and triumphant is its legacy.

Some spiritual thinkers like Swami Vivekananda were of the view that just like an animal, man with the help of instinct matured into a rational man. And by the process of conscious effort, rational man also can mature into an intuitive, super-rational man. There is tremendous spiritual energy in every person but it is latent, often stifled. It is the outpouring and unleashing of this energy that gave mankind a Buddha, a Christ, a Muhammad and a Ramakrishna. As Napoleon, of all persons, remarked on his death bed in St. Helena, the power of the spirit is mightier than the power of the sword. It is once again the same spiritual energy that can show the way to a fuller realization of man's true potential. But, to achieve that, man needs to journey inwards, turn his sights from the stars to his soul. The irony is that man makes his destiny but cannot make his day: no one can be sure if he will see the next sunrise or sunset but he can contribute to the very process of evolution by his thoughts and deeds. He cannot predict or change the nature of the next minute, but he can change the very climate that sustains life. He cannot prevent his own decay but he can destroy the planet.

It has often been said that the universe within, mirrors the universe outside, that which one does not have, one cannot project, be it hate or love; and there is no problem that man faces that is beyond his innate capacity to tackle it. That truism has practical implications. It means that we cannot just stay as we are and hope that the world will be okay. Man is a microcosm of the cosmos, and the universe is a man magnified billions of times. It is the inability of man to reach out and tap the spring inside, that is the problem. He has methodically sidelined probably the most important source of energy inside the heart, and focuses entirely on his mental capacities. It is the distancing of the self from the heart that has cut off the spiritual guidance and nourishment that the heart alone can provide. Throughout the ages, the heart has been referred to as a source of not only virtue and love, but also of compassion and a flowing spring of intelligence. "Many ancient cultures, including the Mesopotamian, Egyptian, Babylonian, and Greek, assert that the heart is the primary organ responsible for influencing and directing our emotions and our decision-making ability. Similar perspectives of the heart as a source of intelligence are found in Hebrew, Christian, Chinese, Hindu, and Islamic traditions. For example, the Old Testament saying "For as a man thinketh in his heart, so is he" (*Proverbs, 23:7*), is further developed in the New Testament (*Luke, 5:22*), "What reason ye in your hearts?"[56] According to the ancient Hindu texts, for a long time in human evolution, the center of the human personality was not the brain; it was the heart. Before that, it was not even the heart; it was still lower, near the navel. It appears that what we metaphorically say 'gut-feeling' is literally feelings drawn from the gut.

On the subject of the intellect, which is often used interchangeably with 'intelligence', although some draw distinction, Swami Vivekananda said, "First, it is absolutely necessary to clear the intellectual portion, although we know that intellectuality is almost nothing; for it is the heart that is of most importance. It is through the heart that the Lord is seen, and not through the intellect. The intellect is only the street-cleaner, cleansing the path for us, a secondary worker, the policeman; but the policeman is not a positive necessity for the workings of society."[57] The Sufi saint Hazrat Ibn Arabi in his famous book 'Fusus-ul-Hukm' said: "Those who have come to know Allah, through His own self-disclosure to them, they did not come to know Him via their minds, have known him with the light which Allah imparted to their hearts and minds."[58] The heart is caring and compassionate and less self-serving than the mind. It is less susceptible to the negative external environment. Extremism, fanaticism, intolerance, obduracy, one-dimensional visions, these are all attributes of the mind. Tenderness, kindness, sensitivity, love are the very grain of the heart. The mind is exclusive and intrusive; the heart is inclusive and subtle. The mind seeks hegemony; the heart, harmony. The voice of the heart is soft and light, but is often drowned in the cacophony coming from the mind. Its attributes are intuition, insight, sixth sense, gut-feeling, knowledge without thought, and so on. While we put all our talents to assiduously cultivate the mind, the heart is left to its own rhythm and relentless beat.

That 'beat' of the heart starts very early, barely 21 days after conception, and by then it is already pumping (through a closed circulatory system) blood whose type is different from that of the mother. With the help of new tools and techniques, science is showing that "the heart begins to beat in the unborn fetus even before the brain is formed so it appears that the heart truly holds primary status as the initiator of human life."[59] It has also been said that there is "a spot in the heart which is the first to live in the fetus and the last to die."[60] Thus far, our perception of identity, who we are and what we want to be, is identified with the brain-mind. Thus far, this entire 'heart thing' has been relegated to the realm of the philosophical, spiritual speculation, and New Age mysticism. Since the waning years of the last bloody century, new light is being thrown by researchers on a new source of energy called L-energy, centered in the human heart, which has a memory and intelligence of its own, which is independent and beyond the control of the brain. It is part of a new discipline, cellular memory, which postulates that cells contain clues to our personalities, tastes, and histories independent of other genetic codes or brain cells. Some remarkable stories of heart transplant recipients throw fresh light, and indicate that hearts may have memories beyond bodies. It is reported that some people who underwent heart-transplant surgeries suddenly acquired the tastes of the heart donors. In a moving 'story', Paul Pearsall (*The Heart's Code*, 1999; p.7), under the heading *The heart that found its body's killer*, recounts a case in which a little girl, who received a transplanted heart from a murdered girl, managed to identify the donor's killer; based on her 'evidence', the murderer was even convicted. The scientific explanation offered is that the heart is loaded with molecules that contain memory, which go along with the heart into another body. These molecules can then form memories of rhythmic patterns like the nerve cells in the brain that store patterns of events to form memories.

Scientists have found that the heart has its own independent nervous system, not only memory, a complex system referred to as 'the brain in the heart', sometimes called the 'third brain', the other two being the one in the head and the other in the stomach. Medical science is exploring the physiological mechanisms by which the heart communicates with the brain, thereby influencing information processing, perceptions, emotions, and health. Researchers have found that the heart can record a whole event and that it is possible to induce the heart into states of love. It is said that "there are at least forty thousand neurons (nerve cells) in the heart — as many as are found in various subcortical centers of the brain."[61] It means that hearts too can think and feel, learn and carry one's personal code and that a heart's biophysical energy and information travels throughout the body and reaches the surface of the skin. Evidence is mounting that the heart, "instead of simply pumping blood, may actually direct and align many systems in the body so that they can function in harmony with one another" and that although it is "in constant communication with the brain, scientists are discovering that our hearts may actually be the 'intelligent force' behind the intuitive thoughts and feelings we all experience."[62]

Some researchers also think that the heart is a *balance* organ whose function is to balance and regulate the physical, mental, and emotional natures. The phrase *Heart Intelligence* is now widely used as a metaphor for the independent wisdom inherent in the heart. The heart is the source of natural love and the task is to nurture and expand it until it fills the entire being. Maybe the heart does not solve problems, but it dissolves them. In short, it tells us that the heart is not only a source of independent but integrated source of energy in the body, but also that hearts can communicate with other hearts. Rollin McCraty, the lead researcher at the Institute of HeartMath, says that "the planet is really moving through a paradigm shift. A shift from the head to the heart. The heart is the base frequency that we're hard-wired to live in."[63] These findings reinforce the long held view in 'esoteric circles' that the heart sends us intuitive signals to govern our lives, if only we listen and pay heed.

The scriptures, prophets and poets have long recognized the spiritual role of the human heart, and as the favored abode of God. God is everywhere and in everything, but the 'cave of the heart' or the 'lotus of the heart' is his abode, his nest. The Upanishads give great prominence to the heart in their conception of the universe and divinity. The *Shvetashvatara* Upanishad says that in the heart of creatures the self is hidden. The *Katha* Upanishad warns man that the ascent to the summit of consciousness is not from the mind and the path is 'sharp like a razor's edge.' The *Manduka* Upanishad speaks of the Self dwelling hidden in the heart as the source of love, to be known through love but not through thought. In the Bhagavad Gita, Lord Krishna tells Arjuna that God dwells in the hearts of all human beings. The ancient Greeks were divided over the respective roles of the heart and the brain. Socrates habitually listened to and obeyed an 'inner voice' which he called the *daimonion*, a sort of 'voice of God'. Mahatma Gandhi said the only tyrant he accepted in the world is the still, small voice within. That voice comes from the heart. Some, like Aristotle and Homer, speculated that the heart was the seat in which intelligence rested. The heart in the human system is the 'access point for experiencing God'; the route to the divine dimension of man. Some strongly contend that the path to paradise and the gate to heaven are through the heart. In the 17th century, Descartes felt that the flow of blood from the heart to the brain served the purpose of producing 'animal spirits' which animated the body. Spiritualists viewed the heart in terms of divinity. God is omniscient, formless, and featureless; he is also manifest within the human heart as its innermost self. Sri Ramakrishna, the great Indian sage, said, "You should remember that the heart of the devotee is the abode of God. He dwells, no doubt, in all beings, but He especially manifests Himself in the heart of the devotee. The heart of the devotee is the drawing room of God."[64] The notion that God dwells within is not exclusive to the Vedantic thought. The Russian Orthodox Church exhorts, "find a place in your heart, and speak there with the Lord. It is the Lord's reception room."[65]

The philosopher Blaise Pascal wrote, "It is the heart which perceives God and not the reason."[66] Khalil Gibran wrote "the world that walks with you is your heart, and the heart is all that you think the world." Jalal ad-Din Rumi, the thirteenth century Sufi saint said that "the light that shines in the eye is really the light of the heart, and the light that fills the heart is the light of God, which is pure and separate from the light of intellect and senses."[67] Gandhi said that morality is rooted in the purity of one's heart, and that moral goodness comes from the primacy of the heart in human consciousness. Prophet Muhammad was often referred to as an 'unlettered prophet' which, Rumi clarified, was not because he was unable to write or learn, but because his knowledge and wisdom were innate, not acquired. That innateness was the intuition of the heart, not intelligence of the mind. No truly great problem was ever solved solely through the rational approach. Nor any great work got done purely through diligent deductive application. The intellectual commodity might be the most overrated article in the efforts of man to find his true utterance. Most great men, at great moments when they had to take momentous decisions, turned to their intuition rather than to intellect to guide them towards the right thing. Wolfgang Mozart, whose musical genius was unquestioned, said: "Neither a lofty degree of intelligence nor imagination, nor both together, go to the making of a genius. Love, love, that is the soul of genius."[68] That love comes from the heart. Helen Keller, although blind was still able to say that "the best and most beautiful things in the world cannot be seen or even touched. They must be felt with the heart." And Kahlil Gibran wrote that beauty is not in the face; it is a 'light in the heart'. Shakespeare summed it up "Go to your bosom; knock there, and ask your heart what it doth know".

The genius of Mozart or Rembrandt, or the spiritual virtuosity of St. Francis or Ramakrishna was not intellectual; it was inspiration, intuition, and divine grace. It is not the intellectual strength that propels a prophet or unites a *bhakta* (a devotee) with God or, for that matter, brings solace to so many troubled souls. The Buddha's reaction to seeing an emaciated old man or a corpse was not mental; if it was, he would have at once turned back the chariot to the palace and to the soft bosom of his lovely wife. Jesus' anguished prayer on the cross 'Father, forgive them; for they know not what they do,' was not a cry of reason or of desperation; had it been so he would have asked God to exterminate his tormentors. It was not knowledge or learning that enabled great men to alter the course of human history for the better. It was their spiritual energy arising from their hearts. The 'inner voice' of Gandhi and the 'voice within' of Tolstoy, the 'voices' that Joan of Arc heard, all came from deep within their hearts. When asked who he was, the Buddha replied, 'I am the *Awakened One*'. That awakened state and the Buddha's infinite compassion were of the heart, not born of his reasoning capacity. If the Buddha turned to his mind for answers to what he saw — old age, debility, disease, and death — he would have been deluged with explanations and he would have remained happily married to Yasodhara and become a 'king of kings'. And humanity would have lost by far one of its greatest creations. Of course, it is another matter that men made the Buddha a 'God', and after paying ritual obeisance violated every one of his teachings. For that matter, that is true also of Jesus, Muhammad, and every other religious or spiritual source. In the human mind, belief and behavior are disconnected. What man needs is a blend of the robust reasoning and calculation of the mind, and the love and emotions of the heart; he needs a mind in a state of 'awareness' and a heart that is in the throes of 'tenderness.' Osho said that "heart has no logic, but sensitivity, and perceptivity". He also said that the "truth is not known by the mind; truth is felt by the heart; by your totality, by you, not by your mind; by you as an organic entity."[69] Man must rein in the mind and rekindle the inner heart as a source of energy, memory, and spirituality. The mind must be trained to listen to the heart, and the heart has to be tempered by the discriminative ability of the mind.

The human species must learn how to listen to the spiritual, but still, voice of the heart. To save the human race from the fury of Nature or the folly of man, or the wrath of God, we must quicken and energize the heart and temper the mind. It is only then, as the American Indian Chief Seattle reminds us, that man can hear "the rustle of an insect's wings" and "the soft sound of the wind darting over the face of the pond."[70] It is by the restoration of a reverential relationship with Nature that we can halt the coarsening of the human spirit. We feel right, but think and do wrong, on so many issues. Feeling is of the heart, thinking is of the mind, and action is of the body. Too often do we comfort ourselves by saying, 'but I couldn't help it.' It is because the voice of feeling is drowned in the noise of the thought. By energizing the heart we can enhance the influence of emotions and feelings in molding the human personality. Morality and ethics, piety and prayer, that do not translate into character and behavior, into the nuts and bolts of daily life, are shallow self-deceptions. Whether or not prayer is a direct dialogue with God, it cannot be a free pass to ride roughshod over other human beings. What ought to be a matter of concern for the future of mankind is that more and more people are able to separate what we might call their 'sacred' side from their 'operational' side.

That 'separation' is wider when we are part of a 'mob', with the anonymity that group participation affords. Something happens to the human psyche when it finds itself unknown and unrecognized by fellow humans, and the darkest of desires, unknown even to one's own 'conscious consciousness', erupt like lava from a suddenly active volcano. And it then manifests in man's rawest persona. In Orwell's *Nineteen Eighty-Four*, the antagonist and interrogator O'Brien chillingly tells the protagonist and the victim-cum-hero Winston Smith that, "by the year 2050, at the very latest, not a single human being will be alive who could understand such a conversation as we are having now... The whole climate of thought will be different. In fact, there will be no thought, as we understand it now. Orthodoxy means not thinking — not needing to think. Orthodoxy is unconsciousness." The instrument for that end is mind control. External mind control is bad but easy; internal control is good but difficult. But in human society, implicit obedience to another human being can be destructive because no one is worthy of that kind of surrender. And yet, that is what the human mind wants and is naturally inclined towards power, control, obedience; but once it clashes with a stringer or a more powerful mind, and when it knows that resistance entails a higher cost, it meekly capitulates. The mind then makes the bully a coward, who is asked to bend and crawl. So few, if any, know how to wield power wisely and be able, as God does, to put the interest of the surrendered above his own interest. Aldous Huxley visualized such a society and wrote: "And it seems to me perfectly in the cards that there will be within the next generation or so a pharmacological method of making people love their servitude, and producing... a kind of painless concentration camp for entire societies, so that people will in fact have their liberties taken away from them but will rather enjoy it, because they will be distracted from any desire to rebel by propaganda, brainwashing, or brainwashing enhanced by pharmacological methods."[71] Another 'vision' is that of O'Brien, in Orwell's *Nineteen Eighty-Four*, who tells Winston, while torturing him, that his crime was not to "make the act of submission which is the price of sanity."[72] Once one makes the absolute surrender, it hardly matters what one gets called, sane or insane. Is there anything in us that is proximate to that possibility?

And is there anything in our construct that can help us to go on the path of the heart? In his book *The God Gene: How Faith is Hardwired into Our Genes* (2004), American geneticist Dean Hamer says that human spirituality has an innate genetic component to it, and claims to have discovered precisely such a gene (VMAT2) which is capable of what he calls self-transcendence. Recent research on how to harness heart energy and intelligence might be able to help alter the dynamics and balance of human consciousness. If there could be a gene for selfishness, why should not there be a 'spiritual gene'? After all, everything in Nature is dual or *dwanda* as it is called in Sanskrit! Can genes play a significant role in faith and spirituality? Pioneering research is also being undertaken in fields like linking "the weirdness of the quantum world to mysteries of the macro world (such as consciousness) and on quantum consciousness."[73]

While science tries to probe into the mysteries of the mind to further the human cause, spirituality harks back to harnessing the primordial power of the heart to better the human condition. Phrases such as 'another heart', 'heart of heart', 'heart in heart', 'inner heart', 'right heart', 'spiritual heart', and 'holistic heart' are used to describe this phenomenon. All these seek to convey the same message: that there is far, far more to the heart than its ceaseless beat and exquisite rhythm and awesome pumping power, and that for the good of man we must learn to tap the boundless spirituality and love inherent but dormant in the human heart. It is through this heart, the 'inner sanctum' as the sage Ramakrishna used to call it, that man can reach a higher state of consciousness and make himself a more harmonious being. The Indian mystic Meher Baba said that "the heart, which in its own way feels the unity of life, finds fulfillment in love, sacrifice and service."[74] The route to human transformation is through the heart. But it does not mean abandoning the mind or exorcising the brain and turning our back on logic, reason or research. Meher Baba further says that "The mind ought to work in tandem with the heart, subordinating factual knowledge to intuitive perceptions. The mind has a place in practical life but its role begins after the heart has its say. Spiritual understanding is born of harmony between mind and heart."[75]

The human species must evolve into a species that is in harmony, not in hate, and walk with compassion as its companion; only then will the illusion of separateness yield to Brotherhood and Oneness. The *Book of Golden Precepts* says, "Behold, there is the goal of beatitude and there the long road of suffering. Thou must choose the one or the other across the cycles to come."[76] The Buddhist *Dhammapada* says, "You shall wander in the darkness and see not till you have found the eternal light."[77] Struggle we might with all our feeble strength, we will remain wandering in the dim forest of darkness unless we restore the right balance between head and heart in the human consciousness. We ceaselessly talk of one world and one humanity, but in reality everyone lives in a mental world of one's own. Humanity may be six plus billion, but for most people, for all practical purposes, it is at best a hundred, the people one 'knows'; the rest is a demographic statistic, the less the better. Human growth in numbers is considered a serious threat to the earth's carrying capacity. In less than a hundred years, the number of humans on earth is expected to touch ten billion. But the irony that escapes many is this — the 'large' number of humans that constitutes that threat on earth is still far less than that of any other species. When the numbers of any other species, be it a tiger or a python or an insect, go down dramatically, we call them 'endangered species', a cause for concern. Many of the world's problems are ascribed to overpopulation. In other words, on a global scale, we want to increase the tiger population and decrease the human population. We prefer a man-eater to man — maybe not without good reason — and for the good of the world! Normally, we try to increase the numbers of those who are the strongest and the smartest. What we are trying to do with our own kind is just the opposite. Perhaps the greatest indictment of human ingenuity is that we have not found a way to make human presence on earth positive and enriching, or a way to harness human energy and power for human good and for planetary enrichment. No one has ever told us the basis for the 'optimum human population', the 'desirable' human numbers for the continuance of life on earth, or the unit for such determination. Low productivity and human rapacity for resources should be of equal, if not greater, concern. It is human behavior that is the bigger problem; not human population growth. It is the human 'way of life' that causes havoc; not how many humans 'live' on earth at any given time. Even if the human population is frozen or gets reduced, none of the problems man is facing are likely to disappear; we will become more brazen, greedier, and even more consumptive. It is human 'civilization' that is the problem. Behind civilization is the mind. Nature has a built-in, self-correcting mechanism, including a way of controlling how many of which species should inhabit the earth at any point. Predator and prey coexist without either becoming extinct, or when a new species arises. Nothing is an accident in Nature; not 'natural disasters', and not even the 'human population explosion.' Nature has its own number for the numbers of all forms of life, and it will, in its own way, take care of the balance and the earth's carrying capacity. Perhaps, we are doing Nature's work by killing each other for so many reasons that we will soon run out of reasons that will not lead to such killing.

Whether it is a 'population problem' or climate change, or galloping moral decadence or even growing indifference, intolerance and insensitivity, they all stem from the same source — the world within; the vortex in which our thoughts arise, incubate, mature, mutate, and burst out as behavior. Judging by the nature and character of our behavior, something is seriously and terribly amiss inside. The process or processes that entail information gathering, discriminatory analysis, decision making and prioritization must be transformed. It is at that level and depth of dimension that we must induce and channel change, a change that has never been attempted before since the advent of man on earth. For there has developed a serious imbalance within the rubrics of intelligence and energy that come to play when thoughts, feelings, passions, and emotions fight for mastery of our 'conscious' and 'subconscious' consciousness. The war is within; the battleground is consciousness. The antagonists are mind and heart. It is a war that must be waged, but it is a war that must have neither a victor nor a vanquished. What we need is both a détente and a entente, a structure of sharing that allows each of us to play cooperative and complementary roles in shaping our thoughts, and in what we say and do.

6

Contours of Consciousness Change

Consciousness — All there is

All our lives we think and talk of 'my' life, 'my' body, 'my' thoughts, 'my' feelings, 'my' pain , 'my' sorrow, 'my' destiny, and so on. So, what is this mysterious *me* or *mine* that makes us what we are, distinct from any other, or feel in a manner that is particular only to ourselves? And what makes us different from an ant, or for that matter, a plant or a tree? We come face to face with these questions after exhausting ourselves with a multitude of metaphors and an avalanche of analyses. Perhaps the questions become easier to answer if phrased differently: What is it that separates humans of one *yuga* or age from those of another time, or an infant from an adolescent and the young from an adult? What is it that we need to change, without changing which nothing else is worth changing, to behave differently? What is it that we need to connect to, to attain the goal of universal brotherhood or the kingdom of God on earth? The answer, unquestionably, is *Consciousness* — the mystery of mysteries, the enigma of all riddles, the final frontier of all human struggle and seeking. Its ambit embraces a variety of fields of human knowledge, such as religion, mysticism, theosophy, occultism, science, psychology, etc. Anything that we are aware of at a given moment forms part of our consciousness, but we are not 'conscious' of it, which makes conscious experience at once the most familiar and most mysterious aspect of our lives. Long the focus of esoteric thought and of intellectual inquiry, the study of consciousness has, over the past century, acquired added relevance and respectability as man struggles to build a 'bridge' to the future. Millions of people across cultures and continents, perhaps for the first time in their lives, are beginning to realize how much they have been let down and deceived by the various institutions and ideas they have long cherished as sacred, and that for any decisive change in the world, there should be no safe havens or 'sacred cows'. Parallel to that disquiet there is also simmering optimism, a deeply felt gut- feeling in many thoughtful people that, although we are wholly unaware, there are forces at work in our seemingly rotten world that are pushing us towards a new dawn. In New Age circles, there is considerable talk of a new — and final — level of consciousness that is said to be pervading the planet, as a prelude to a radically altered state of the human condition. In the words of David Wilcock, researcher of ancient civilizations and consciousness science "humanity is on the verge of a near-spontaneous metamorphosis into a more highly evolved state of consciousness"[1]. This 'shift in human consciousness', it is believed, leads up to the year 2012 which would trigger a "discontinuous mega-event where 'time and space collapse"[2]. Whether or not this prophecy too is fated to be yet another failed one, hyperbole or an imminent happening, there is little doubt that something at the very core of human condition, at a depth deeper than we can discern, is changing. And the effect is both positive and negative. The negative is all too vivid and visible — bloodcurdling cruelty, mindless massacres, unspeakable crimes for lust, wealth and power. It seems as though we wait daily, if not eagerly at least compliantly, to read or hear far more macabre 'news' to 'entertain' ourselves. Less visible but potentially positive is the appearance of stunningly gifted children in unprecedented numbers across the world, the emergence of innovative and integrated holistic modalities, people becoming less "religious" and more "spiritual," and the dawning of new communities and social structures based on partnership principles. Whichever scenario seems more plausible, it must have some bearing on our consciousness. While the spotlight is on a plethora of crises — economic, ecological, ethnic, political, moral, religious — the real crisis is the one of consciousness. We often read and hear abour corruption in public life, corporate corruption, and so on, but but the real 'corruption' is the insidious corruption of the consciousness. Unless we address *this* issue, no problem that human society is now grappling with can be seriously addressed. The fact is that human consciousness must change, for man to go anywhere other than over the 'edge of the brink'. Albert Einstein, with his uncommon ability to go to the heart of any issue, said that "No problem can be solved from the same level of consciousness that created it"[3]

For all change is a change in the level or states of consciousness. Whatever any man has ever accomplished has entailed raising the consciousness to a different level. Whatever atrocity anyone has committed was possible only because something in his consciousness went awry. In both cases, 'consciousness' includes the conscious, subconscious, and the superconscious. Not only is there no unanimity, among psychologists or even the scriptures, about what constitutes consciousness, but there is no unanimity either about how many levels of consciousness there are. However, what psychologists call an 'altered level of consciousness', is *dhyana* or *samadhi*, for the Hindus; *nirvana*, for the Buddhists; *fana*, for the Sufis; *pneuma*, for the Christians; and *kensho* or *satori*, for the Zen Buddhists. Consciousness is not only individual and universal; it is the one that at once connects and separates life and death and afterlife, all three of which are, in essence, altered states of consciousness. Although life after death still defies human imagination, there is also growing acceptance in scientific and parapsychology circles that 'death' is not wholesale wiping out or total annihilation of all that a sentient, self-conscious, thinking human being is, that some sort of human essence or an element of human personality survives, and that death is no different from a passage to another state of consciousness. What are called NDEs — near death experiences — and what are dubbed as 'cross-correspondences', over a span of thirty years, from the 'dead' psychic researcher F.W.H. Myers, induce even skeptics to give some credibility to the idea of life, death, and afterlife being altered states of consciousness. But whether or not any consciousness at any level survives death, there is little doubt that the future of the human race will hinge on the nature and level of consciousness that the succeeding generations of humans will possess. And what they will 'possess' will have much to do with how *we lead* our lives. That process is already underway; there is little doubt that everything human, including human consciousness, is in the throes of a profound transformation. The challenge is to take charge of this process, to bring to bear other subtle forces on it, other than the ones we currently rely upon like science and technology, forces such as spirituality and heart energy, and steer this process in the desirable direction.

The word *consciousness* itself is derived from the Latin *conscientia*, which primarily means 'moral conscience'. In the literal sense, *conscientia* (or con scientia) means 'knowledge-with', that is, shared knowledge. One of the abiding mysteries of life is not only what life is, but what constitutes the fullness of a person, an individual independent of another individual. Have we always been like this, a bunch of individuals whose world ends at the boundary of their bodies and the rest theoretical, at best a necessary nuisance? Not so, say many epics, cultures, and calendars. For example, from the Mayan perspective, it all began barely 26,000 years ago, a time that marked, according to psychologists Barry and Janae Weinhold, 'the beginning of humanity's psychological individuation', which means moving from being unconsciously united with the Creator or Ground of Being, to choosing to become divided from the Creator and developing separate individual consciousness.[4] In the current paradigm of existence, space, time, and matter constitute the primary 'things' of reality. They are the *a priori* assumptions, the premise for the paradigm. But within this framework, consciousness appears inexplicable. A paradigm shift will occur when we learn to experience consciousness as something fundamental and everything else as derivative. And it will materialize when we move towards the goal of collective global consciousness, through the stages of individual global consciousness and group global consciousness. At a generic level, consciousness is inherent in everything from an atom to a human; and all evolution and growth is to attain higher and higher levels of consciousness. The theosophist and great visionary Annie Besant said, "To begin with a definition of terms: consciousness and life are identical, two names for one thing as regarded from within and from without. There is no life without consciousness; there is no consciousness without life"[5]. According to theosophy, the difference between life or 'web of life' as Annie Besant calls it, in different 'kingdoms' — the mineral, vegetable, animal, and human — is the level or plane of consciousness. British psychologist Stuart Sutherland once wrote: "Consciousness is a fascinating but elusive phenomenon; it is impossible to specify what it is, what it does, or why it evolved. Nothing worth reading has been written on it."[6] Hopefully things are a bit clearer today. Consciousness is the 'awareness of awareness'; it is also sometimes compared to air, which can be compressed to varying degrees of density in containers of different shapes and sizes. Some New Age thinkers believe that it is by the bridge of consciousness that the age-old conflict between science and religion could be solved, possibly opening the way to the realization that "Consciousness" is God, and that we are the creators of our own universe. If we can actualize that realization, we can then become players in the ongoing evolution of consciousness and of our own transformation.

Complex and incomprehensible as consciousness might seem, it is still useful to lay bare a few comprehensible parameters. At the deepest level in every human there is an irreducible, irreplaceable, 'content of consciousness', unique to the individual and yet all encompassing. We give the appearance of being 'stand-alone'; we are born separately, we live separately, and die separately. But multiplicity, the Upanishads have proclaimed, is only apparent — it is an appearance, if not illusion, the *leela* of *maya*. According to the American author Ken Wilber, consciousness is never experienced in the plural, only in the singular. Indeed, in the words of the Indian Advaita philosopher Ramesh Balsekar, there is only consciousness; there is neither creation nor destruction, neither birth nor death, neither destiny nor free will, neither any path nor any achievement. David Shiang (*God Does Not Play Dice*, 2008) calls God a 'gold mine of consciousness'. It is consciousness, not our sense organs, that either earns *punya*, the credit in the karmic ledger, arising from good deeds, words, and thoughts, or incurs *papa*, the debit entry in the same ledger due to our bad deeds. The fountainhead of desire is consciousness, and it is desire, as Krishna told Arjuna in the Bhagavad Gita, that makes us transgress against our own will. According to ancient Vedic insight, all matter is energy, and energy is nothing but consciousness. According to the Indian system of yoga, the key to attain a higher consciousness is the awakening or activation of the *kundalini* energy, located at the lower end of the spinal cord, which according to Ramana Maharshi, is 'nothing but the natural energy of the Self, where Self is the universal consciousness (*Paramatma*) present in every being', and that the 'individual mind of thoughts cloaks this natural energy from unadulterated expression'. That subtle energy is the divine guiding force behind our continuing evolution towards higher dimensions of consciousness. At the individual level, consciousness manifests as our thoughts, feelings, articulations, and actions. Every action, every thought, every idle word creates waves and sets up reactions. According to the Universal Law, when one thinks a thought or feels an emotion, that thought or that emotion makes an impression on the Universal Consciousness. Nothing is lost or is in vain. Everything that happens is within the Universal Consciousness. Our reactions to past thoughts and actions become our fate, destiny, and karma. An individual's fate is simply the rebounding effects of previous choices remembered by his soul. At the species level, fate is the fallout or hangover of our predecessors' actions over millions of years of evolution. And yet the primary actions that keep us alive, such as breathing, seeing, hearing, touching, and even tasting, take place without our conscious participation or without us stopping to think about them. Even our automatic, purposeful behavior, such as solving most of our routine problems happens without the aid of our full consciousness. Consciousness, like thin air, cannot be grasped or held on to. Consciousness is ageless, formless, colorless, and genderless. Just as air permeates the entire atmosphere, consciousness permeates the entire human body. While it can never be located, it is very real, as real as life itself. Consciousness is that which at once separates and connects — one human to another human, one generation to another generation, one *yuga* to another *yuga*, or age. Researchers are now saying that what separates our early childhood from our adulthood is the state of consciousness, and that a child is not simply a miniature adult; nor is an adult simply a blown-up baby. In short, in terms of consciousness, children and adults are, as described by Alison Gopnik (*The Philosophical Baby*, 2009), 'different forms of *Homo sapiens*'. And yet, they are all reflections of the same universal consciousness, much like the reflections of the same sun in different forms of water on earth, be it the water of the Ganga or of the gutter. According to Advaita philosophy, the universe and everything in it are not God's creation; they — and countless others we have no idea of — are all divine *disclosures*, forms through which He lets us see, touch, and relate with Him as a mark of His mercy.

To understand both the 'why' and the 'why not' of human behavior, and the slide down the moral hill, we must come to grips with the question of consciousness. It has many dimensions and depths. In one sense, consciousness is not different from what we think is the objective reality of the world. The world outside is *us*; it is our consciousness. The subject and the object are one. The words of the British astrophysicist Arthur Eddington (*Space, Time and Gravitation*, 1920) offer a useful analogy: 'We have found a strange footprint on the shores of the unknown. We have devised profound theories, one after another, to account for its origins. At last, we have succeeded in reconstructing the creature that made the footprint. And lo! It is our own.' In another sense, consciousness is always *of something* and lasts no more than a millisecond. Because these seconds succeed each other continuously it gives the impression that consciousness is permanent. At another level, consciousness is what both unites and separates one living being from another. It was what made the humans of the earlier ages so different from us. In the epics, we read about the heroic deeds of great men and wonder 'how could they do it?' and 'how could they be so utterly selfless?' The answer is that the consciousness with which they functioned as a species was of a different genre, qualitatively different from the ones we have; as different as human from another animal. Judging by the basics of our behavior, it does appear that the men of the past had a different and a more moral and *dharmic* consciousness than the men of this age. That is what the Hindu cyclical time and passage of *yugas* is all about. To do the right thing was not an epic struggle at that time. To be compassionate in one's personal life did not require supreme sacrifice. Such a hypothesis is also shared by anthrophilosopher Owen Barfield. He argued that the perception of primitive man, what he called 'original' participation, was a kind of thinking, and in those primordial days, perceiving and thinking had not yet split apart, as they have for us. According to Owen, at first, humanity perceived itself as One with all things, which he called 'pantheism' (*Saving the Appearances: a Study in Idolatry*, 1988). What he calls participation and others call intuition, is something that we share with animals. Over several millenniums, and as the brain grew bigger and bigger, our intuitive capacity got marginalized and our 'intellectual' capacity became the dominant force in human affairs. That was the need of the hour, the wages of survival. But it also changed the balance and content of human consciousness, which, in turn, changed human personality and character, which again, in their turn, impacted on human behavior and conduct. Consciousness is the key, not merely conduct, to 'being a better being'. Our sense of separateness stems from our sense that we alone have a 'conscious' consciousness and that we are therefore entitled to ride roughshod over everyone else. There is no such thing as 'unconsciousness'; it is a question of different layers and kinds of consciousness. The Spanish novelist Miguel de Unamuno wrote that, "The only way to give finality to the world is to give it consciousness."[7] If we can do that, the world will cease to be a mere word that signifies very little for us, and the earth will become 'Mother Earth', and we will probably treat other species with a little more humaneness. In the Bhagavad Gita, Lord Krishna says there are two kinds of attributes in the living world, the divine and the demonic; while the proportions might vary, most human beings manifest both attributes in their behavior. Lord Krishna explains the attributes that lead to a demonic life — lust for worldly wealth, wrath which comes when lust is obstructed, and greed for gratification. As a bare minimum, no one, save the psychopath and the sadist, ought to be able to derive pleasure in the pain of another human, indeed any other living being. Being kind and considerate should not require an epic struggle; and as the Buddha metaphorically puts it, we should not be able to eat a single meal without sharing. That kind of change could come only with a change in the consciousness.

The challenge is that consciousness is not static, either for an individual or a species, and yet we have to be able to orchestrate the change. The impulse and impetus for that change must come from both the universe within and the world without. Continuance of the *status quo* on either front is inimical to human growth. And lack of growth is death, and growth unbridled is chaos. The direction of growth is also important; suffering, it is said, is due to wrong direction. The Russian philosopher and mystic Peter Ouspensky uses the term 'consciousness' for the "designation of a complex of all psychic functions in general, or for their separate manifestations." He says that "it is necessary to regard consciousness as distinct from the commonly understood psychic functions: thought, feeling and sensation. Over and above all this, consciousness has several exactly definable forms or phases, in each one of which thoughts, feelings and sensations can function, giving in each different results. Thus consciousness (be it this or something other) is a background upon which thoughts, feelings and sensations reveal themselves."[8] The nexus between mind and consciousness has long been a subject of intense speculation and considerable research. It cuts across many fields like religion, philosophy, psychology, epistemology, neuroscience, cybernetics. There are differences even among scientists. One school of thought is that once we fully comprehend the chemical and electrical processes in the brain, both mysteries — of the mind and of consciousness — will be resolved. Oth-ers say it arises else-where: in some even sub-tler, yet-un-dis-cov-ered brain pro-cesses, or per-haps what is condescendingly, if not contemptuously, referred to as mind-stuff quite dis-tinct from the brain. Spiritualists say that consciousness is singular and cosmic, not separate and personal, and not realizing this is at the root of the problem, and that our destiny lies in transiting from the corporeal to the cosmic consciousness, which the *Mandukya* Upanishad describes as the fourth state of consciousness, extending beyond the wakeful and the two dream states. The universe of consciousness is the most mysterious, and on how deep we can delve might depend our spiritual progress.

Paramahamsa Yogananda, the Indian spiritual master (*The Autobiography of a Yogi*, 1946) said, "The so-called miraculous powers of a great master are a natural accompaniment to his exact understanding of subtle laws that operate in the inner cosmos of consciousness."[9] Experts like the American psychologist Julian Jaynes (*The Origin of Consciousness in the Breakdown of the Bicameral Mind*, 1976) say consciousness is not perception or cognition. It is a bundle that includes thoughts, emotions, feelings, sensations, sentiments, memory and self-awareness. Everything, in the cauldron of life, churns and changes — body, mind, personality, sexuality — but something stays. We do not look, say, think, and feel the same throughout our lives, but in the totality of life on earth and in the tapestry of creation, there are no carbon copies. The residue, the one we cannot define but still constitutes the continuity, is consciousness, and it separates the living from the dead. The essential question is, if consciousness is not constant and the one we now have is different from that of our predecessors, and if human consciousness is qualitatively different from that of other species, how much and what is the nature of consciousness that must remain in us, for us to be called 'human'? This is an important question in the context of consciousness change and in the agenda for human transformation. How much of consciousness, if any and in what form, has survived the tens of thousands of generations that have passed is debatable, but what one can infer is that human consciousness at the operational level has been profoundly transformed over the long struggle for human survival. In his book Julian Jaynes proposes that ancient consciousness was radically different from modern consciousness. He suggests that ancient human beings had no sense of an interior, directing self. Rather, they accepted commands from what appeared to them to be an externalized agency, which they obeyed blindly, without question. He wrote 'that ancient peoples did not access consciousness (did not possess an introspective mind-space), but instead had their behavior directed by auditory hallucinations, which they interpreted as the voice of their chief, king, or the gods'. Jaynes was of the view 'that the change from this mode of thinking (which he called the bicameral mind) to consciousness (construed as self-identification of interior mental states) occurred over a period of centuries about three thousand years ago and was based on the development of metaphorical language and the emergence of writing.'[10] Jaynes proposes that a series of unprecedented environmental stresses in the second millennium BCE forced the two halves of the brain to merge into what he terms *unicamerality*. A cultural, rather than a biological, transformation. The stresses might have included natural disasters like floods, population growth, forced migrations, warfare, trade, and the development of writing.

Irrespective of whether the heart was in the driver's seat or the mind, or for that matter the navel, through human evolution, the two instruments or agents for human transformation have always been the mind and the heart. The Dalai Lama said, "The key to transforming our hearts and minds is to have an understanding of the way our thoughts and emotions work."[11] And the way to that is by identifying the opposing sides in our inner conflicts, positive and negative thoughts and emotions; by examining how thoughts and emotions arise; and through sustained efforts to cultivate the positive aspects within us and through what he calls 'constant familiarity'. The Buddhist scripture *Sutta Nipata* says that if a man's thoughts are unsteady, if he does not know the true law, if his peace of mind is troubled, his knowledge will never be perfect. According to the Dalai Lama, "The nature of human thoughts and emotions is such that the more you engage in them, and the more you develop them, the more powerful they become. Therefore we have to develop love and compassion consciously in order to enhance their strength."[12] Modern man takes great pride in his civilization and views it as the crowning glory of his consciousness. Implied in that pride is that the 'pre-civilized' man was 'barbaric', perhaps not even worthy to be called fully human. Based on the new archeological and anthropological findings, several scholars now believe that there was a Golden Age, a spiritual one, spanning thousands of years, before the advent of the mind-driven civilization, which for unknown reasons perished without a trace. There were civilizations more 'civilized' in the true spirit than the current one, even in the Stone Age, and the 'tribal man' was a better human being than the 'technology man.' Some occultists like Madame Blavatsky believed that the earliest humans were giants, both physically and spiritually, and may even have had a third eye! Feeling, to them, was what thought is to modern man. Modern civilization has been built almost exclusively on mind power and material progress, measured by how much we spend and plunder the bounty of the earth and its exquisite ecosystem. Man is so 'civilized' and so 'clever' that he does not realize that to harm Nature is to 'cut a piece of his own flesh,' and that the extinction of any other species is a step towards his own extinction.

Some things need constant remembrance and one of them is this: every species is specially endowed and equipped strictly and solely for that form of life, and every condition is inherently tightly conditioned, including the human one. No form of life, ant or human, is capable of knowing the essence of any other form of life. Every species is naturally gifted with certain advantages or abilities that are innate to that species and essential for its survival, but extraordinary, if not unnecessary for, or non-existent in, others. Flying is natural to birds, but impossible for wingless creatures. Many species can see, smell, and hear better than humans. The speed of a cheetah is hard to rival, but its speed is limited to short distances. Many mammals can swim, but not as naturally and adroitly as fish. Some birds use star patterns to navigate; some use the position of the sun; some can hear low-frequency sound waves; some may use the earth's gravitational and magnetic fields. That birds fly but man cannot, that dogs can sense emotions and man cannot, does not make them superior to man. So is the case with man; that certain things he can do better than a fish or a cat or a dog does not make him a greater being. In fact, many of the scientific 'accomplishments' of man were rooted in adapting to the natural functions of other species, even insects.

Hallmark of Human Intelligence

Everything in the world is *appearance* derived from our senses. That is the message both from the scriptures and, of late, from science. Vedanta says that the world is nothing but a manifestation of the *Brahman*, but that we mistake it as the phenomenal world because of *maya*, which also is divine manifestation. This means that what human intelligence actually sees and perceives is the appearance, not the actuality. The noted Australian 'Nobel' neurologist John Eccles pointed out a truth that materialists, including scientists and ordinary people, do not readily grasp. He argued that there is no sight or sound 'out there' in the world, no touch or taste, no beauty or ugliness, no sensation of light or objects. All these are created in subjectivity; they exist only in consciousness. Such 'scientific inference' is nothing but Vedantic revelation, embedded in the concepts of *avidya* and *maya*. The operative term for consciousness is 'intelligence'. The source of our conduct is 'intelligence', and therefore if our conduct is to change, 'intelligence' must change. As individuals, we differ from one another, more than in our physical frame, in our ability to understand complex issues, to adapt effectively to the envelop of the environment, to deal with cognitive complexity, to learn from observation and experience, to engage in various forms of reasoning, to overcome obstacles, and even in terms of how we relate to one another. In one word, as commonly understood, we differ in our 'intelligence'. One of the central issues that philosophers have been debating over for centuries is the nature of human intelligence. One of the questions often debated is if we acquired our uncommon capacity for rational thought (and all that goes with it) as a result of some special act of creation, or if it just happened as a result of evolution through natural selection. Theologians like William Paley (*Natural Theology*, 1802) argued that complex biological structures, such as the human eye, offer evidence of a creator. Rationalists like Richard Dawkins have refuted that argument by citing the enormous time spans involved, the selective advantages conferred by even small incremental improvements in such a sensory organ, and the fact that the eye has evolved separately in various forms of life. But the question is, while the human species has been around for millions of years, when, why, and how did 'intelligence' suddenly appear about 100,000 to 150,000 years ago? Some even say it is much more recent, about 30,000 years or even 3,000 years ago. And what prevented 'intelligence' from evolving even earlier than that? Some occultists and theosophists question the basic premise that our hoary ancestors did not have 'intelligence'. They say that in fact the 'original humans' were far more enlightened, if not intelligent. Madame Blavatsky in fact calls our ancient ancestors "animal *plus a living god* within his physical shell."[13] If it were so, did 'intelligence' actually transform us from 'god in animal form' to 'animal in human form'?

Without a proper understanding of concepts like mind and consciousness, and heart as an organ of cognition, we cannot comprehend or come to terms with 'intelligence'. But this much, drawing from the balance sheet of what intelligence has done to our species thus far, we can 'rationally' infer: we cannot retain the same type of intelligence and expect any kind of real transformation. For, the intelligence that created the problem in the first instance cannot be the problem solver. And, there can be no change in the type of intelligence, unless a change is brought about in the very source of that intelligence — consciousness. 'Intelligence' is a generic term often used to describe some or all of our mental capacities, such as to reason, to plan, to analyze and solve problems, to think abstractly, to comprehend complex ideas, to use language, and to learn quickly, and to adopt effectively to environment. In other words, 'intelligence' is most often used simply to denote nothing more than *information processing*. Intelligence, in our times, is equated with being brilliant, bright, smart, and socially savvy. It has monetarized and militarized human society; the only two kinds of 'intelligence'-derived powers that we respect are money and the 'barrel of the gun'. Our society values intelligence and clear thinking much more than integrity and *clean* thinking; not the quality of decisions, but their speed. Not even physical beauty and strength are so valued. Even actresses, supermodels, and beautiful women want 'highly intelligent' men to 'father' their babies. Marilyn Monroe presumably married Joe DiMaggio, the baseball legend, for his physical prowess, not for his cerebral brilliance, and later, Arthur Miller, the playwright, for his creative intelligence, not for his looks; her rumored 'affair' with John Kennedy was presumably for a brush with his presidential power. Intelligence is often contrasted with intuition. Intelligence, it is usually posited, you can inherit, sharpen, and enhance through application and training. On the other hand, intuition, sometimes called 'gut feeling', it is said, you cannot do much to enhance externally. Brain- or mind-generated intelligence dominates human life today. Should there be any extraterrestrial 'intelligence' (in forms that we cannot even recognize) 'staring us in our face', as astronomer Martin Rees surmises, they must be perplexed as to how any 'intelligent' beings could behave the way we do, and be so quarrelsome, reckless, and destructive. The fact of the matter is that our intelligence has not given us the tools to enable us, at a minimum, not to oppress when we can oppress, not to exploit when we can exploit, to be kind when we can get away with cruelty, to be just when we get nothing out of it — that is practical morality and true spirituality. In reality, it lets us get away with cruelty and callousness, injury and insensitivity, pollution and profligacy, wanton waste and vandalism. Our intelligence adopts double, indeed manifold standards when it comes to morality. We need intelligence that expands the ambit of morality from personal purity to social relevance, and includes acts that are collectively compatible. For example, adulteration should be as reprehensible as, if not more than, adultery, and morality should be as important at the workplace as, if not more than, at home. We must remember that even the smallest act that we do (or do not) is a moral choice. In turn, this brings up related questions. Why is man so prone to evil, and why does goodness take such a struggle to surface? We may all condemn evil, which we often think is what people we do not like do to us, and not what *we* do to them. The French writer and social philosopher Simone Weil aptly said, "Evil, when we are in its power, is not felt as evil, but as a necessity, even a duty." She added, "I would suggest that barbarism be considered as a permanent and universal human characteristic which becomes more or less pronounced according to the play of circumstances."[14]

People who commit atrocities, wage wars, and kill thousands, often do not think that they are doing anything out of the way, but just that they are doing their duty or that they are compelled by circumstances to do so. Such is the genius of our intelligence. If morality and spirituality are "hardwired into our genes,"[15] as Dean Hamer says, then why are they so subdued in the human condition? Is there any genetic basis to saintliness? Why do some humans reach the 'high end of human continuum' while the vast majority remain at the lower end? Although several probable theories have been advanced, the science of genes has so far been silent on this. Dean Hamer argues that indeed "spirituality is one of our basic inheritances; it is, in fact, an instinct." He says that spirituality "has a biological mechanism akin to birdsong although a far more complex and nuanced one" and that we "have a genetic predisposition to spiritual belief."[16] While Hamer's theory awaits the test of scientific replicability — even Hamer says that it is not '*the*' gene but '*a*' gene — it at least offers a glimmer of hope that the very genetic manipulation that is dangerously violating the laws of Nature and encroaching on God's preserve, would also clear a path to human betterment. Along with the discovery of the heart as a source of intelligence and energy independent of the brain, this could, if it does not meet the same fate as other short-lived theories, be the Holy Grail of the human search for the origins of spirituality. And it could be the master key to the meaning of the universe referred to by Jalal ad-Din Rumi, the great Afghan-Persian mystic, when he said that if men knew the splendors of the spiritual universe, they would hardly look elsewhere.

Well, we will have to see. Men of Rumi's time were differently 'intelligent'. Firstly, we will debate to death what 'spiritual universe' really is. Secondly, how does one see the spiritual universe when our minds are full of the physical universe that is soaked in sensual pleasures? Last, even if we could 'see' the spiritual universe, how long will that gaze remain focused? We also read about the ongoing research on 'applying quantum mechanics to consciousness, spirituality and human potential.' What is still unclear is if all the exciting insights and ideas like heart coherence and heart code and God-gene, etc., are sufficient to design the transcendental 'operational' tools for human transformation. Piero Scaruffi, the Italian poet, philosopher and scientist who has done pioneering work on the issue of quantum consciousness, says that a new "consciousness is unlikely to arise from classical properties of matter" but that quantum theory "allows for a new concept of matter altogether, which may well leave cracks for consciousness, for something that is not purely material or extra-material."[17] Scaruffi says that in the quantum model of consciousness, a virtual nervous system could be produced which can direct the behavior of the real nervous system, and that consciousness is (can be) driven by quantum laws, even if the brain's behavior can be described by classical laws.[18] It is impossible for the lay mind to comprehend their implications for human transformation. There may be some promise and potential, but that has to be properly harnessed for the common good, and should not be allowed to end up in some military laboratory, manufacturing some sort of 'supermen soldiers' or 'terminators' who can see but cannot be seen, who may have a consciousness but no conscience, and who can kill but cannot be killed. It is really hard to discern what all these portend for the future, and whether they could catalyze into a new human consciousness presaging a New Man. But there is little doubt that for any kind of human progress we must ascend to higher levels of consciousness. What is not so clear is where we are on the ladder of consciousness. Is the present a beginning of the beginning, or the end of the beginning, or beginning of the end in the evolution of consciousness? Is it the twilight of the dawn or dusk? We really do not have the consensual answers within the realm of human capacity. But what we do know is that our consciousness is the wellspring and springboard of much of what man has accomplished, as well as of what afflicts modern man. The Buddha said that "certain fundamental afflictions of the mind are the source of the distress we experience". Given the dominance of the mind, those 'afflictions' are *ipso facto* the afflictions of our consciousness. Our consciousness created a culture and a context of life that became increasingly distanced from its moral moorings as well as from the milieu of Nature. And those afflictions transformed man into a narcissistic and nihilistic creature, steeped in self-righteousness, self-love, and self-hate. Mind-controlled consciousness has become a divisive and destructive force and has pushed man on a collision course with Nature. And our 'conscience', the one expected to check our vanity and venality and serve as a moral watch dog, is simply overwhelmed by the increasingly assertive evil in our consciousness. We are tuned to think that if we have a working 'conscience' our innate 'goodness' is impregnable. That is another ruse the mind plants on us to leave consciousness to its wiles, and to get us bogged down in the morass of conscience. If our consciousness is sullied and scheming, there is little conscience can do. On the other hand, if we have a genuinely compassionate consciousness, perhaps we do not need a conscience. The truth of the matter is that in 'good conscience' we can do bad things, but not with a good *consciousness*. With consciousness of the right kind, we will not be able to hurt, insult, or humiliate another person, because he or she will be seen as an extension or projection of our own selves. With conscience, a man might not murder, but he can still kill with words or do deliberate things that bring intense suffering to others if his very *Being* is violent; and he deludes himself that he is 'good' and 'decent'. What has been variously called the 'inner voice', or 'voice within' or the 'still voice' or 'voice of silence', has to be anchored in our consciousness, not conscience. If morality is rooted in the subsoil of consciousness, not the topsoil of conscience, then we will be naturally and spontaneously malice-free and non-violent in thought, word, and deed; we cannot be any otherwise. What is based on conscience is a matter of fear, punishment, and greed. To make man a better being, conscience is a poor proxy for consciousness. In the sense that conscience is supposed to make us feel guilty when we do bad things, does not let us do things we want to do or not to do things 'when someone is looking', it is a limiting virtue that is wholly inadequate to solve any of the problems that beset us. It is the uprooting of our moral instinct that led to the erosion of the universal values and principles around which we could wrap our lives. And that has unleashed all the dark forces, internal and external. We need consciousness-change, not conscience-pricking. Indeed, that will be a throw-back to the previous ages like the *Tretha* and the *Krita Yugas* — and perhaps to the living world of Nature. We have forgotten that we came from Nature and will go back to Nature when our time is done.

In human consciousness, despite our pride in our reasoning capacity, belief plays a big part; indeed life hinges on it; without some sort of belief in someone or something, it is almost impossible to go through the grind and grime of life; but our beliefs — and disbeliefs — are selective; and our 'behavior' scarcely conforms to our beliefs. Certain things we cannot directly sense but we still believe; others, we just disbelieve; both are projections of the mind. Oftentimes — and it is happening more and more these days — it is belief, not disbelief, that is making us commit atrocities, without the slightest tremor or trepidation. And our much-valued conscience poses no problem. Still, in matters of faith, one should not seek 'proof'. 'Proof' itself is not infallible. Because, if it is infallible, then he who offers and he who accepts proof would likewise and equally be infallible, which we know is not true. Faith, as Tolstoy said, is the force of life; and as Tagore wrote, "Faith is the Bird that feels the Light when the dawn is still dark."[19] And Soren Kierkegaard called faith the highest passion in a human being.[20] The New Testament says, "We walk by faith, not by sight."[21] Faith is abject acceptance of things unknown since they transcend the 'powers of human conception', and on which, as a theosophist principle puts it, 'all speculation is impossible.' We must accept that certain knowledge we might never have, because we do not need to know it for just 'being human.' Nature is built on the principle of 'need-to-know'. Just as some animals can see, hear, and smell better than humans, maybe there are some among humans who could see and sense things that other humans cannot. Those are the prophets, saints, and *rishis*. We must recognize, therefore, that some knowledge and some answers might remain hidden from the prying perception of humans, and that some other knowledge might be known only to a few among us, obscured as it remains from the vision of the rest of us.

If human transformation does not materialize with the power of human 'intelligence', a 'burst of evolution' could do it for us; and maybe send us back to being a simian again, to start all over again, this time, and hopefully, under a more watchful eye of Nature, evolve into a less self-destructive form of life. Evolution is propelled by the weakness of one species, which opens the door to the advent of the next one. Our intellect's chronic inability to distinguish between what a thing actually is and what it seems through the filter of our senses, has attained criticality, and is warping everything we think and do. For that to change, we need nothing less than a new consciousness. We should not forget that historic man, the present man, the one revealed to us by archaeology and anthropology, is of recent vintage, and that prehistoric man was on earth for a much longer time and might well have been a better human. His life, in the words of John Gray, was of noble idleness and his world a partial paradise. Gray adds that almost certainly the Paleolithic humanity was better off. True or not, it is a sobering thought and a devastating verdict on human civilization. Going back to the forgotten past may not be such a bad idea, but in the design of Nature and life, it is not possible. We also know in our hearts, if not in the mind, that things cannot continue much longer the way they are now, and, unless somehow something fundamental changes, the human race might not last beyond this century.

Our mind-dominated 'intelligence' is obsessed with pleasure and pain; everything we do, pursue and value is to maximize the former and to eliminate the latter, to the exclusion of almost everything else. Indeed that is the measure of our life, the essence of 'happiness' and the touchstone of 'success'. The problem from which stems much of our misery is that we do not know how to harness the duo; instead we are governed by them; they are our masters. The scriptures tell us to treat both pleasure and pain with equal fortitude and equanimity, but our 'intelligence' refuses to relent; yet, we really do not know what is true 'pleasure' and real 'pain'. When Samuel Johnson was asked what pleasure men take in making beasts of themselves, he answered that "he who makes a beast of himself gets rid of the pain of being a man."[22] The ingrained idea is that being human itself is a story of anguish, anxiety, and pain. For thousands of years, through religion, psychoanalysis, and science, men have been laboring to overcome this condition. Men far less corrupt and coarse than us have tried and failed. It might be because man wants pleasure and no pain, whereas the two are one of the many pairs of apparent, not real, opposites that are innate in nature. Vedanta says that pleasure and pain, like bondage and liberation, are the manifestations of the ego-mind. Philosophers such as Jeremy Bentham, Baruch Spinoza, and Descartes have hypothesized "that the sensations of pain and pleasure are part of a continuum. There is strong evidence for biological connections between the neurochemical pathways used for the perception of pain and those involved in the perception of pleasure and other psychological rewards."[23]

Through the turbulent passage of life, pain and pleasure hold us in thrall and cause the ebbs and flows, the highs and lows of life. The English jurist and philosopher Jeremy Bentham wrote, "Nature has placed mankind under the governance of two sovereign masters, pain and pleasure. It is for them alone to point out what we ought to do, as well as to determine what we shall do. On the one hand the standard of right and wrong, on the other the chain of causes and effects, are fastened to their throne. They govern us in all we do, in all we say, in all we think…"[24] Neither pain nor pleasure can exist without the other; alone, neither has legs to stand upon. We must learn to turn them into tools and means for a greater cause, not as ends in themselves. But it is the nature of the human mind which seeks to separate them, to shun pain and to embrace pleasure. It is the mind that drags the consciousness towards the 'painful' pursuit of pleasure, which is synonymous with happiness, the holy grail of the human condition.

Our 'intelligence' might not be able to rid us of the constancy of pain of some sort or the other, or give us eternal pleasure, but that does not deter it from dangling the vision of eternal life before us. That has been an age-old quest: to become an angel on earth beyond the reach of decay, disease, and death. While that prospect has remained a dream, science reassures us that there is now, or soon will be, a real 'prospect for immortality', for those who are about to die or are just dead, or for those who want to 'take a not-so-brief-a-break' and are willing to be deep frozen and stored away, to be brought back to life fifty or hundred or five hundred years hence. We are also told by 'experts' like Robert Ettinger (*The Prospect for Immortality,* 1962), "Indeed, in theory, it is possible even now."[25] So, our 'cemeteries' will turn into dormitories. In other words, if civilization endures, humans eventually will achieve biological immortality; whether this happens soon or later is of no consequence in the saga of the species and its successors. We are further enlightened that it is not that unnatural or uncommon as we presume, and "that some animals of the lower orders (Rotifera, Tardigrada, Anguilla), some vegetable seeds and some microbes can have all internal activity interrupted for a long time by being reduced in temperature to close to absolute zero — and then, upon being thawed, resume all normal functions again."[26] What science is trying to do is to extend to superior organisms what is natural to lower organisms. For science, everything is one and once, one body, one life, and one death; and life and death are the exact opposites, and the only way to cure the problems of life is to prolong it indefinitely; or at least make it so stretched that death, if it were to occur, becomes pointless or profitless. Science may offer us extended longevity, even eternity, but it has no recipe for happiness or a solution to any of the social problems. Already, for more and more people, the volitional embrace of death seems less forbidding than life, and more alluring than what living in this world is demanding of them, and if one must live for hundreds of years, life will become more hellish than hell. Then men might prefer to escape to the scriptural hell. As the theologian Carol Zaleski noted, speaking of a mortality that aims only at keeping the body alive, "To be given everlasting longevity without being remade for eternal life is to live under a curse."[27] 'Being remade' involves a spiritual not a scientific process.

The spiritual view is perhaps best espoused in the Indian spiritual school of thought popularly known as Vedanta. Swami Krishnananda in his commentary on the *Katha* Upanishad expounds this school and says, "The *Nasadiya sukta* in the Veda says that both death and immortality are the shadows of the Eternal. Even immortality is a reflection cast by it. Life and death are relativistic counterparts of each other and they become a mystery, an enigma before us when we try to understand them with our intellect working through our sensory perception."[28] Vedanta says that everything in life, indeed life itself, and death are the creations of *maya* and *avidya*, they are mere illusions. That creates a problem because although they are illusions, the suffering they cause is real, not an illusion. That is why the ancient Indian *Sankhya* philosophy, considered as one of the oldest philosophical systems in India, treats suffering as the central problem in human life. So did the Buddha. Setting aside for a moment scriptural characterizations, even according to the utopian scientific scenario, the operative part is, *if civilization endures*, suggesting that it may not, if the present mindset and resultant mayhem were to continue. There are many thoughtful people who fear that human civilization might well collapse by its own profligacy and toxic overweight. And if somehow it does not, and human conduct on earth remains unchanged, and if humans try to attain bodily permanence without consciousness change, it will be the gravest challenge man has ever thrown to Nature. It could, so to speak, turn the tables and simply speed up and widen the self-destructive tendencies in man, a process that appears to be already under way.

Moral Decadence and Consciousness Change

One of our major assumptions about the human condition, as opposed to our fellow animals, is that we are 'moral beings', that is, we assume that we alone are capable of knowing what is right and what is wrong, and with that knowledge, that we alone are capable of putting the common good ahead of our personal advantage. That increasingly shaky assumption is the foundation of our sense of self-importance and superiority. In reality, our conduct both as individuals and as a species never actually measured up to it. On the other hand, it has become our license for our unspeakable cruelty towards animals, and also towards other humans who we think are 'less human' — people of other races, ethnicity, even religion. Although we want to be good, moral, and godly, the true signature of our species has regressed into moral depravity. It is not merely our conduct but our very consciousness that is depraved. Whether it is man's assault on Nature or the intolerance of another man, it stems from selfishness whose character changes when it goes beyond the needs of survival. In common parlance and in social etiquette, there are few words that one dreads more than being called 'selfish'. Indeed, we may prefer being called cruel or callous but not 'selfish', obviously oblivious to the fact that the 'shoe fits' us as well, if not better. As Jane Austen said, most of us are selfish in practice, though not in principle. But the real problem of man is not selfishness; it is not self-preservation; nor is it concern for one's own well-being or devotion to one's own advantage; it is not even not being altruistic. It is 'otherness'. It is not, as Oscar Wilde wryly noted, to live as one wishes to, but to demand of others to live as *we* wish them to; not to live like us, but like what we determine. In one sense, everything we do is selfish; otherwise we would not do it. It is inherent in every choice; if we choose what we value most or what is most beneficial to us, that becomes a 'selfish' act that best serves our purpose in comparison to any other alternative. The question is what impact it has on 'others', particularly those more vulnerable than we are.

Another name for 'otherness' is self-righteousness; which is a kind of erroneous appeasement as well as self-deception, that smug sense of almost awesome moral superiority derived from the visceral conviction that our beliefs, values, actions or affiliations are the righteous ones. We appear almost pathologically or neurologically addicted to being incapable of feeling empathy for our opponents, of accepting any dissent or condoning any criticism. And that 'addiction' can be more pernicious socially than any hallucinogenic drug. That comes in the way of finding practical solutions to any problem. In the long run, that could be the trigger for self-destruction. From self-righteousness comes vanity; from vanity, pride; from pride comes intolerance, and from intolerance stems animosity, and from animosity springs violence and war. It is as removed from righteousness as light from darkness; as *dharma* from *adharma*. The Upanishads exhort man to follow *dharma* (the righteous path) in obtaining *artha* (wealth or material prosperity) and *kama* (sensory pleasures) and even *moksha* (liberation). Righteousness is to act in accord with the divine or moral law, to put the other person ahead of oneself. Self-righteousness is to be convinced of one's own absolute righteousness; to view everything from the prism or prison of self-benefit.

The self-righteous think, feel, and believe so strongly that they are right and righteous, their sense of certainty is so impregnable, that they try to control others' lives; indeed mold the world to their image, turning a blind eye, so to speak, to the cracks in their own face. They are chronic 'fault-finders' and compulsive 'correctors'; judgmental without the slightest self-awareness that they are so; indeed, they will be aghast with disbelief — and deeply hurt — that anyone should think so. Sarada Devi, affectionately called *Mother* by her devotees, and the spiritual partner of the sage Ramakrishna, said, "I tell you one thing my child — if you want peace, do not find fault with others. Rather, see your own faults."[29] Ramakrishna's foremost disciple Vivekananda elaborated on this and said, "Condemn none: if you can stretch out a helping hand, do so. If you cannot, fold your hands, bless your brothers, and let them go their own way."[30] Emerson said " that which we call sin in others, is experiment for us". The more dangerous part is that self-righteous people not only convince themselves that they are the sole repositories of 'revealed truth'; it is that they see themselves as 'victims' of injustice and exploitation. There is a growing number of that breed now, which could easily set the stage for greater domestic, social, religious, and ethnic tension and turbulence. In some form or to some degree, everyone is self-righteous. And to believe that we are *not* self-righteous is also, perhaps, an even greater level of self-righteousness — because, that makes us judge others from our belief that we are not self-righteous, which is really the signal signature of self-righteousness. Many confuse self-righteousness with self-belief or self-esteem, or even spirituality. That is why few, not even saints, are able to escape the spell cast by self-righteousness. These saints are like the elder brother in the Biblical parable of the '*Prodigal Son*' who is also — as Timothy Keller notes in his book *The Prodigal God* (2008) — 'lost' through his self-righteousness. Whatever label we may use, selfishness, self-centeredness, self-righteousness, they are all defenses of the 'ego-mind' in dealing with the external world in satiating its insatiable wants and demands. Biologists and evolutionary psychologists have long pondered over whether this almost reflexive trait in our behavior is inherent or acquired, and whether it has become entrenched in our psyche beyond evolutionary imperative. Philosophers like Georg Hegel argued that the 'other' is an integral constituent in self-consciousness. He wrote that "Each consciousness pursues the death of the other."[31] That pursuit takes different ways, from physical killing to control, and getting others to do what we want regardless of their will. There is considerable ambiguity about the import of terms such as selfishness and self-centeredness, self-esteem, self-belief, and self-love; indeed about the term *self* itself. The *Self* in the scriptures is God, and in daily use, it is the individual person.

It is also said that what one does not have, one cannot give, and that includes love or hate. Therefore, to be able to love another person, one must love oneself. Spiritually, self-love is no different from love of God. But self-love is not self-absorption, to look at everything solely from the prism of self-benefit. It means that by themselves, self-love or self-centeredness or self-righteousness are neither good nor bad; it is where and towards whom it is directed that makes the difference. Whatever be the nuances of these terms the basic question is, why do humans find it so difficult, more than any other species, to combine, cooperate, and collectivize their efforts? Evolutionary psychology argues that humans do have cooperative instincts but that they are reciprocal; that is, we become altruistic when there is something to be gained. In other words, cooperation too is a 'subtle form of selfishness.' Some call this a cynical travesty of human nature, and evolutionary psychology is accused of being "a blatant attempt to discredit our altruistically orientated instinctive self or soul as nothing more than a subtle form of selfishness in our makeup."[32] They say that articulating such theories could, on the one hand, make some people fatalistic (*I can't help my selfishness*) or, on the other hand, despondent (*what a horrible being I am*). In sociobiology, DNA is immortal and the only purpose of genes is self-preservation. But the problem is that human behavior is inexplicable even in terms of selfishness and self-centeredness. Whether selfishness is an inherent or an acquired trait or a dated evolutionary necessity, the human condition seems to have crossed that frontier. Mankind's selfishness is beyond any discernible self-benefit, and its recklessness borders on self-destruction. The 'mind and me' centered civilization, in turn, has shaped the human condition and behavior.

Man, in the words of John Gray, is a product of blind evolutionary drift; perhaps the very dynamic of survival in prehistoric times ingrained in man the imperative of greed and grabbing. Yet man is the most explorative creature on earth, explorative of his fellow-men, of other species, of Nature, and even of God, but not explorative enough of his own soul. And hence he is the most exploitative. The self-righteous mind is so ingenious that it makes the exploiter believe he is the exploited; it makes the oppressor believe he is the oppressed, and it makes the villain believe he is the victim. It makes man think that he is at once the most virtuous and the most victimized, a Mahatma and a martyr. In the rush of civilization, most men are torn apart from their moral moorings, doomed to lead a mechanized life, without a clue as to what they are supposed to do or what is happening to them or where they are drifting, other than towards death. Every minute we are dying, but it does not change a whit how we live. Yet everyone complains, feels helpless, blames and badmouths the world, the system, and drowns in sensual pleasure and material trappings. While the individual is a virtual cog in a mighty soulless machine, those who control the levers of power, science, technology, wealth, and weapons, not knowing how to use them wisely, are busy acquiring 'more' of everything, plundering Nature, ravaging the earth, and pushing mankind — and the planet — towards the precipice.

To be fair, it is not that we are evil; at least not all the time; indeed we may even be good 'at heart'; we mean well, at least, so we tell ourselves. In our view, it is the *other* fellow who is evil. To paraphrase Jesus on the cross, often 'we know not what we do'; nor *how* we do what we do. One direct result of man's moral decadence, and indifference to the means adopted, has been the steady escalation of physical and moral violence. What is mystifying is that such violence is totally unnecessary either for his survival or even for his supremacy on earth. Man's behavioral pattern is very difficult to reconcile with much of what the scriptures and saints say of him — how 'near perfect' he is, so close to God, the only form of life that can arrest the cycle of birth and death, and so on. He is able to live with such behavior because of his state of self-righteous denial. Violence might be oozing out of every crevice of his consciousness, but from time immemorial man has dreamed of peace, peace within and peace without, peace for self and peace in the world, of a world without hostility and animosity in interpersonal and interstate relations. The scriptures like the Vedas abound in 'mantras' meant for universal peace; they all end with the invocation of '*shanti*' or peace and tranquility. Similarly the very word 'Islam' means peace; the Islamic greeting is 'peace be upon you'. Yet, violence, killings, and wars have been the constant companions of humankind. The word 'peace' is often used to mean the absence of war, but most of those who wage war claim that they are fighting for peace. What makes the humans thirst for war? Is it simply a byproduct of the thing we call life? Aldous Huxley delved into this theme and writes, "War is a purely human phenomenon... man is unique in organizing the mass murder of his own species" And again, "War is not a law of nature, nor even a law of human nature. It exists because men wish it to exist... It is enormously difficult for us to change our wishes in this matter; but the enormously difficult is not the impossible."[33]

One can argue that violent responses are natural responses, and that man is no exception; but man should be able to stop their escalation and virulence. Which combination of factors and forces result in what effect is hard to anticipate. The same individual or consciousness is capable of reacting in different ways to different situations or at different times. But we cannot wholly wish away, or slyly sidestep, human violence that is often laced with malice. Horrific events have happened so consistently in human history that it is not possible to 'rationalize' them as aberrations or the malevolence of a few individuals. The greatest myth is that the human being is a peaceful being. Pitirim Sorokin, in his book, *Social and Cultural Dynamics* (1957), noted that in the past 800 years, most of the world's countries spent about half that time in warfare. Fighting, according to him, is seemingly so natural to the human temperament that no amount of education can cure this universal malady. And that goes for culture too. We have to accept the reality of the deep roots of destructiveness in the human psyche. What man has been trying to achieve is external peace without internal peace, and establish order in the world in the absence of harmony in the consciousness. Time and again it is noted that what we do not have inside we cannot project outside, and what we feel inside cannot but find external expression. That applies to war and peace. And the simple absence of war or even violence does not amount to peace. *Ahimsa* or nonviolence is not *shanti* or peace. It is the negation of any kind of force or coercion in human behavior. Peace is a rare sublime state that humanity has seldom, if at all, experienced. The 'paradox of peace' is that the more we chant the 'mantra' of being at peace with ourselves, or with others or with Nature or God, the more it gets distant. Everyone is avowedly, if not ostentatiously, for peace; no one wants violence or war, save perhaps a psychopath. But for the most part, peace is just a means. Everyone wants something — control, conquest, land, resources, — and peace provides them the opportunity to exercise or fulfill that want. Even those who wage war claim that they are fighting for peace. The massacre of thousands of non-combatants is publicly touted as the necessary price of peace. We are getting pretty close to George Orwell's fictional superstate *Oceania*, teeming with Thought Police, Thought Crimes, Ministry of Truth, and Big Brother, where "War is Peace. Freedom is Slavery" and "Ignorance is Strength."[34] The constitution of UNESCO famously declared that since wars begin in the minds of men, it is in the minds of men that the defenses of peace have to be constructed. What was meant by 'mind' was consciousness. The mind *per se* is the problem, not the solution. In the cauldron of our consciousness, our way of wanting peace is not letting others be at peace; deep inside, what we desire is not peace but victory; we demand surrender, not shared sacrifice.

Many things man wants to be (and, even more, does not want to be), but, after millions of years of evolution, millenniums of progress and centuries of science, man remains finite and fragile, vulnerable and wayward, troubled and tentative, ignorant and arrogant. It would do a world of good if we could demystify and demythify our ingrained and unshakeable beliefs about ourselves. We cannot speak for the other *yugas* or the Biblical times, but we, the mammalian mortals of this millennium, are a blessed species with many blemishes, exquisitely endowed but severely flawed. And the flaws and blemishes are showing up more and more prominently, like festering pimples on our face. Then again, like all other planetary beings, we too have to function within certain physical, psychic, and mental limits. Emmanuel Kant is said to have observed that "we, as humans, do not possess the capacity to fully comprehend reality."[35] And Einstein talked of the insufficiency of the mind to understand more deeply the harmony of the Universe which we try to formulate as 'laws of nature' — and then go on to show condescension or contempt towards them. Whatever it is, fate or free will, man is so enfeebled and conditioned by the external environment that unless it changes, man will not change. The external environment can change only if man changes his internal environment, his very consciousness. The French novelist Marcel Proust wrote, "The real voyage of discovery consists not in seeking new landscapes but in having new eyes."[36] We know 'the landscape' of the human malaise; the 'new eyes' we need are new cognitive thinking and perceptive powers, independent of the mind.

Although most people are too immersed in the minutiae of mundane life, there is an emerging broad consensus that the human species is passing through a period of epochal transition. There is deep unsettling uncertainty about everything. The epicenter of that 'uncertainty' is in the brain, which manifests in the way we absorb what goes on around us and in the way we act and react. Our brain does not have sufficient information or capacity to know what is out there or what is in store. None of us can be any different from what we are with the consciousness we have. As Stanislav Grof, founder of the field of *transpersonal psychology* says, a radical inner transformation and a rise to a new level of consciousness might be the only real hope to solve any of the problems the world faces, and the only hope for human survival. The 20th century American 'mythologist' and author Joseph Campbell brought the issue down to the practical level and said that when we quit thinking primarily about ourselves and our own self-preservation, we undergo a truly heroic transformation of consciousness. And personal transformation can have global reach, for 'we are the world'. American self-help guru and author Wayne Dyer says that transformation is going beyond our form. But we must first cross that barrier to such 'thinking'. Despite random flashes of shame or guilt or remorse, none of us can behave any better with the consciousness we have. And none of us can truly quench the fires of anger, avarice, rage, revenge, envy, and malice that scald our souls given the kind of fuel we pour into our vitals. We are changing the world at an unprecedented velocity, but the kind of change that our consciousness is undergoing is accentuating the very traits that threaten our existence. There is a tendency to talk of change and transformation as something exceptional and unique to the humans. On the contrary, ceaseless change is the 'natural' state of Nature, and it is embedded in every form of life. The world consists of patterns of relentless transformation of energy and matter. Life from birth to death is itself a process of transformation, the unfolding of a plurality of inter-weavings of cycles and discontinuous transitions. And as we are an amalgam of multiple identities, every identity should be anchored in transformation, which means we should grow, not diminish, in every identity. In one sense, transformation is to harmonize and come to terms with our multicentered personality. Vedanta says that all living beings are subject to a six-fold change (*sad-vikara*): birth, growth, transformation, decay, disease, and death. In addition to this inherent transformation, there has always existed in human life another kind of 'induced' or 'enforced' transformation. Often the line between innate and induced, virtual and actual, natural and induced gets blurred. Ancient traditions and systems like yoga, alchemy, and Shamanism are replete with examples of psychic transformations. While in the ancient schools of human transformation, symbols, metaphors, analogies, parables, and myths played central roles, some say that our conceptual system, how we think, how we talk, and how we react, is fundamentally metaphorical in nature. Goethe said that "All phenomena are merely metaphorical."[37] The mind has also been called metaphorical or as a pattern that connects. But the mind has made itself the monarch of consciousness and a monkey of man; that must change, and that is the change that is the need of the hour.

Clearly, consciousness change at the deepest level, and more foundational than perhaps ever attempted by man, is the key to a better world and for human renaissance. Change of consciousness is a change of state. It is the only way to cool and heal the planet. It is the only path to do things differently, to change our personal habits and predispositions, our lifestyles. We do not know how many decades or years we have, before we reach a tipping point beyond which nothing we do could possibly rescue us from irreversible damage. There is a serious likelihood that current paradigms of human habitation, or even thought or even culture, will not be able to halt our march towards the extinction of humanity and probably of most other living organisms on this planet. What we need to do is 'involution' (as in esoteric philosophy), through consciousness change. We view evolution as 'progress', which has made us what we are, masters of everything we see and touch. But there is a side effect. The very core of our being and our consciousness has been shaped by our 'fight or flight' reactions to life-threatening situations, which include, in the words of Dawson Church (*The Genie in Your Genes*, 2007), "shunting of blood away from the gut to the large muscles of the extremities to provide greater strength in combat or speed of locomotion away from a site of potential peril, increased blood flow to the brain to improve decision making, dilatation of the pupils to provide better vision, quicker clotting of the blood to reduce loss from lacerations or internal hemorrhage, and a host of other reactions that occur automatically and instantaneously."[38] The downside of our rise from what Darwin called 'lowly origin' to the present eminence is that the embedded habits, instincts, impulses, and responses now pose a threat to the further evolution of man himself. All evolution is, in effect, consciousness change, and that is inexorable. Each level of evolution stands upon the shoulders of the previous level (mind on top of life, which is on top of matter), but each successive phase increases the rate of acceleration. The consciousness we have is not the one our ancestors had not too long ago. If we are to believe pundits like Julian Jaynes, our consciousness dates back to barely 3,000 years, a fraction of a second in the human tenure on earth. Much of the damage, therefore, happened during this fraction, when man moved from a bicameral 'animal' mentality to 'human consciousness'. But the combination of that 'baggage' and what we have fashioned as our modern or post-modern way of life, might either make us a human monster, not a 'God-Man', or lead us to an early extinction, not to our 'final evolution'. It is not only the personality of man that has become decadent; even his consciousness is deviant.

Our mind-dominated consciousness is conditioned, and in that condition its content is corrupted. And content determines conduct. There is nothing that we see, think, and do which is unaffected by our consciousness; indeed, they are its external manifestations. Anything within the realms of thought, feeling, and emotion cannot escape its influence. As philosophers like have Kant pointed out, what we relate to is not the 'world as it is' but the world filtered through our consciousness. If consciousness is corrupted, so is our perception of the reality of the world. We must find the means to a cathartic purging of the insides of our inner being. Cleansing is normal to every organism but what we need now is an 'accelerated purgation'. We are running against time; so much toxic filth has accumulated within. And individual consciousness catharsis, if it is inclusive of a cross-section of people, can make a species-scale difference. For there is growing evidence to suggest that a 'collective consciousness' does exist at some level, connecting the consciousness of every individual person into a coherent combined entity of awareness. Although science has long been convinced of the existence of gravitational, electric, and magnetic fields, significant research in the frontier science of parapsychology, or the study of psychic ('psi') phenomena, indicates the possible existence of other types of fields — including *thought* fields. This collective consciousness offers us ways to address humanity's toxic triangle of indifference, intolerance, and injustice, and to try and stem the callous abuse of our planet, symbolized by wars, wanton destruction, and waste. It suggests that a field of awareness and intelligence exists between human beings, that we influence each other in many subtle and potent ways, and that our collective wisdom and creativity can be harnessed for the common good much more than we do presently. While collective consciousness can be used as a platform for shared knowledge, beliefs, and ideas, and as a basis for a 'division of labor in society', which is the title of a book by the French philosopher Emile Durkheim, some other thinkers like Douglas Hofstadter and Peter Russell refer to what they term Collective or Symbiotic Intelligence, which is shared or group intelligence that emerges from the collaboration and competition of many disparate individuals, which is more than the sum of individual intelligences, and more likely to be more positive. There is strong evidence that we can develop and work with our collective consciousness to produce and enhance empathy, understanding, and respect for each other. In our increasingly diverse and divisive world, where we are challenged by extremely complex and daunting problems, cultivating these capacities could not only promote the common good but also ensure our survival. While for science the existence of collective consciousness might be an exciting discovery, the scriptures are replete with references to it. While science talks of connectivity, the scriptures refer to it unity, as the all-embracing Oneness; the multiple manifestations of the divine enjoying or engaged in different experiences. Terms such as Cosmic Consciousness, Christ Consciousness and Krishna Consciousness are used to describe this phenomenon. In the Sikh religion, a scripture becomes a scripture only when it is filtered through the collective consciousness and experience of a people. As each of us works to clear the dross and debris of our personal foibles, the cholesterol of our spiritual arteries — individual hurts, ill will, explosive angers, and dark urges

— we will be contributing in a small way to the clearing of our negative contribution in the collective consciousness.

History is replete with accounts of those who have evolved inwardly to higher states of consciousness, who went beyond the realm of empiricism, reason, and experiment, beyond what we call the 'scientific method'. Such people are examples of what each and every one of us is innately capable of; they are the beacons that show us what we must strive towards. There is nothing 'unnatural' or out of the ordinary about them — whom we call saints, seers, rishis, and mahatmas — in terms of their biology and anatomy, brain and heart. Their daily oblations are the same as ours; they have the same sense organs as we do — and are subject to the same temptations as any of us; sometimes, they too succumb to them... In short, they too are human beings, just like anyone else that walked this earth, and will walk in the future. The only difference is that they attained a state of consciousness that empowered them to liberate themselves from a limited, artificially derived sense of identity, and to fathom a deeper peace and security within. The difference between prince Siddhartha and Gautama Buddha, and in our own times, Mohandas and Mahatma is simply a 'level' of consciousness. One could even say that the Buddha and Christ were not individuals; they were states or levels of consciousness. The individual we call by that name today is only a symbol and an instrument. It is not easy for the human form of life to 'make the cut', and it was not easy even in the past when life was far simpler and the temptations and transgressions far fewer. In the past, the number of such people was very small. A full-blown Buddha or Christ or maybe even a Mahatma or Maharshi is not possible in our times. Yet, our times are more perilous than their times and we need them as never before. As the Global Millennium[39] project report puts it. "Never before has humanity been on the verge of devastating the Earth's biosphere and crippling its ecological foundations for countless generations to come. Never before has the entire human family been required to work together to build a sustainable and meaningful future. Never before have so many people been called to make such sweeping changes in so little time". Which means more than ever before we need a 'battalion of mini-Buddhas' and mini-Christs, men and women who are prepared to undertake the inward journey to cleanse their consciousness. For the many crises that the world faces — moral decadence, climate change, gaping holes in the ozone cover, eroding rainforests, divisive politics, polluted rivers, acid rain, devastating droughts, mass poverty, over-exploitation of natural resources, religious savagery, pandemics of homicide and suicide, and a host of other crises — all arise in one way or another from a corrupted human consciousness.

We have to tackle our malaise and malice at the level of perception, not experience; at the level of cognition, not comprehension. We have to confront them beyond the 'intellectual' processes of the brain, and before they crystallize as reality and infect every thought, word and deed, feeling, emotion, and passion. By the time we comprehend, by the time we actualize, by the time we experience, it is already too late to change the outcome. We can truly change our conduct and character — and destiny — through consciousness-change; it is the only paradigm of change that does not throw up greater problems than the ones it is supposed to resolve. Given the state of the world, that kind of change seems like a rainbow on the horizon or a mirage in the desert — alluring but beyond grasp. But maybe not: perhaps, as some speculate, the so-called 'doomsday date' of the Mayan prophecy of 21 December 2012 might actually be the beginning of a human consciousness revolution, what Owen Waters calls *The Shift*. We must induce the 'shift' because we can no longer overlook the many design flaws inherent in our modern lifestyles that perilously neglect to account for our interdependence with Nature. We must find a way to transform our self-centered materialism into respect for life, and move from a state of callous ignorance to sensitive awareness. The crisis the world faces, we must realize is the crisis of consciousness.

7

Transformation and God

Three Paths to Human Transformation

The daunting human dilemma is this: carrying the baggage of culture, evolution and civilization, with a consciousness that is filled with mind-muddled malice, how should we make sense of what we truly want to be and what we wish to seek from Nature and God? With all our intelligence, ingenuity and creativity that we believe rivals the divine, we have no clue where we are headed or indeed where we want to head. Should we try to create a 'paradise on earth' or work to go to paradise? What are we expected to do in the interval between birth and death on earth? Whether we are divine artifacts or 'fortuitous accidents of cosmic architecture', what is our mission — and mandate on earth? What is our real 'story'? Is it because of our long fall from the sublime grace of a natural, instinctual innocence to a toxic state of anarchist ignorance, from being the pride of the Creator to one who faults Him for his poor craftsmanship? Or is it our inverse 'transformation' from an innately divine being into a species steeped in narcissism and nihilism, from an essentially spiritual personality to a purely sensual predator? Whichever way it is, whether we are in a state of denial or decadence, we are groping in the twilight zone between a dying 'way of life' on life-support, and an emerging way trying to find its feet. Old identities and values are being deconstructed without any alternatives on the horizon. We are a species at odds with itself; no other species fears its own kind as we do. Everyone feels despairing purposelessness; but no one can name the 'problem'. Economic, physical, and political insecurity, — and fear, almost visceral fear — of death, of change, of failure, of decline, of debility, above all of 'others', of the unknown — stalk our lives, eroding trust, interdependence and the potential of collective effort for the common good. What we aspire for and what we want to be are a blend of many tenuous things; and the three dimensions that make us who we are — physical, mental and spiritual — are out of sync. We long to shake off our shackles, lighten the load on our back, soar into the sky, dive into our soul and become a kind of 'human angel'. We can only speculate on or surmise, to use the words of the biologist Robert Wright, the 'logic of human destiny'; but what we do know is that the human lot seems pretty dismal. Whether or not, as the biologist Stephen Jay Gould puts it, we are here by the 'luck of the draw', or because God put us here as His pristine proxy, the fact is that we are alive in the 'here and now', and that ought to be the governing ground reality. Another such 'reality' is that we are the dominant form of life on this planet in terms of our plundering power, not in our enriching ability. We are also not the most numerous species; others far outnumber us and their relationship with the planet is more balanced; they give and take, although unconsciously, in equal measure. That is why their populations, which do fluctuate like the human, do not pose a threat to Nature. The irony is that we are unchallenged on earth, but we behave as if we are under attack and fear for our lives. Most of us might be 'alive' in the physical sense, but we are neither 'awake' nor 'aware' in the real and full sense. We take great pride in *being human* and yet we strive relentlessly to overcome the confines of human flesh and fate.

The trouble is, we are not quite sure what we should 'become'; whether we should choose the 'ignorant innocence' of an animal, or learn to live with the limits and limitations of our 'knowledge'. We are not happy with what we are but we feel trapped in this body and in this life. We want to be many things, do many things, soar in the sky, save our soul, enjoy eternal bliss, but we do not know what to do with our body. Without it we do not exist. And if we do not exist, we go nowhere, temporally or spiritually, and with it we become a prey to desire, disease, decay, and death. We cannot 'undo' our birth or embrace the life-after. Such is our dilemma and we seem fated to search, struggle, and suffer and die.

It is this deep disaffection with what Nature has assigned to the human lot that drives the destiny we want to make for ourselves. That is the bedrock and benchmark — of our age-old yearning for what we variously call alchemy, cathartic change, paradigm shift, transcendence, metamorphosis, and transformation. Our perspective on transformation, like much else, is riddled with paradoxes. We are transformed all the time; yet we struggle for transformation. The only constant, as the cliché goes, is change: but when it comes down to our own lives, we prefer the comfort of the *status quo*. The only change we want is 'exchange' on our own terms; that is, to keep what we like about ourselves, and exchange what we do not like with what we like in others. When we do want to alter our conditional existence, we do not want to leave that to the gods of fate or to the laws of Nature, or to chance or randomness. We want to control the process, prepackage the product. The most puzzling aspect of us as a species is our immense capacity for transformational change, individually and collectively. Equally puzzling is our inability to induce the right kind of change, to transcend the boundary of direct personal gain, to strive for anything that is not immediately useful. We confuse change of conditions, which is what we aspire for to better our lives, with the 'change of condition', which is transformation. What we need is change within; while we try to do to change the external circumstance. We need inner illumination; not searchlights into the sky.

In the final analysis, the current global crises are but a direct reflection of the level of consciousness evolution of the human spirit. All those tremors have the same epicenter: the consciousness. None of them can be resolved without a radical inner transformation and an elevation to a nobler plateau of consciousness. To put it differently, we must find a way out of the mental labyrinth of assumptions, beliefs, and paradigms that have governed human life so far. We have to imbibe path-breaking human values, spontaneous sensitivity to the suffering of others, acceptance and adoption of a simpler and less ostentatious lifestyle, and a heightened awareness of the ecological impact of our every action or inaction. Many thoughtful people have come to realize that a radical inner transformation, or transformational evolution and rise to a nobler plateau of consciousness, are the only hope for the resolution of any of the grave problems the world faces. It means that we must be able to 'experience' experience differently; to transform our understanding of ourselves and of the world around us. And it means that *a priori* we have to rethink our concepts and ideas about things such as chance, luck, serendipity, or accident that underpin our sense of reality, and the difference between 'fact' and fantasy'. We have to rethink our conceptual comprehension of and relationship with Nature and God. We implicitly assume that what we cannot experience, cannot exist, that what we cannot know or predict even, Nature cannot do; and our idea of God is a reflection of our ultimate fantasy, an image of the best of what we want to become. And we presume that what we view as a 'fact' is the unassailable truth. We cannot reorder the world outside and make it peaceful, harmonious, and trouble-free if we harbor indifference, intolerance, malice, hatred, jealousy, and violence in our minds and hearts. If we cannot desist from deriving joy from the misery of others, how can the world be at peace with itself? The truth of the matter is that we simply do not have the wherewithal, the tools and the goods, inside us for what it takes to 'fix' things outside, or to know what is right and to do it effortlessly or even to be able to listen to our own 'inner voice', which Shakespeare's Cardinal Wolsey calls 'still and quiet conscience' (Henry VIII). Wolsey's rueful lament that had he served his God with half the zeal he served his king, he would not at his age have left himself naked to his enemies, fits us like a shoe. Metaphorically speaking, the 'king' we are servile to is the troika of pleasure, power, and profit, and the 'enemies' we are *naked* to are anger, greed, indifference, malice, and violence.

This means that the simple but seminal choice before mankind is either to completely and consciously modify and mutate himself (transformation, for short) practically leaving no trace behind — or to face a future that is so nightmarish that people might actually prefer death to life. We have to modify and transform while knowing that we are transforming ourselves. But the idea of 'transformation' itself gives us the jitters. That is because we somewhat facilely assume that to be 'transformed' is to undergo some exceptional, transcendental experience, or to go through something similar to the Buddha's *Night of Enlightenment*, or to display exceptional heroism or altruism or to be personally touched by God. We do not have to be saints or supermen or possess supernatural powers to transform ourselves. But we must be clear about what we want to become, where we end up, and what we end up as. If we embark on a voyage without knowing the destination, we cannot choose the vessel appropriate for the journey, and as a result show up somewhere else or simply sink on the way.

At a very practical, almost automatic level, 'transformation' is what we want all the time. Every desire — for wealth, fame fortune, for good health, good looks, good job, and so on — is transformational. But these are at the outermost, superficial level. The 'transformation' we must strive towards to save ourselves and our soul is at the deepest level that we are capable of envisioning. Only then can we bring it to the level of choices we make for living. A Buddhist adage says "all know the way; but few actually walk it". It is that 'walking' that we should do as the essence of transformation we seek. Our sense of self, our idea of identity of who we are in relation to other humans, other species, Nature and God, has to change. It is to train oneself to put the other person's good ahead of our own good in every circumstance. To rephrase the thought, it is to look at every person as someone in need of God's help through you. That might still fall far short of the famed Upanishadic axiom '*Tatvamasi*' (thou art that), but it will be a big step forward. In other words, the focus has to be not so much or only on the content but on the context, and we must rid ourselves of the negatives like anger, pride, greed, vanity, and malice. It is like draining out vile water and discovering a spring of freshwater welling within. It means transformation of our character and personality, that is, to go beyond the hypnotic pursuit of money, sex, and power into a harmonious state of living at peace with life, Nature, and God. It means bringing about a new understanding of the things that dominate our thought processes. It is to realize that, as the American author Norman Brown puts it, the essence of money is in its absolute worthlessness; that sex is an expression, not a substitute, of erotic love; and power that is of no benefit to others is tyranny. Transformation is not about hereafter, not about what happens when we are dead and gone; it is about here and now, while we are still alive and existent. Any change that does not affect our 'self-righteously self-destructive' behavior, the signature of our 'civilized' life, for the better, is cosmetic, and the illusion of change is more destructive than the *status quo*. What we sow is what sprouts from the ground below; if the subsoil or the seed are of the wrong kind, the plant or the tree cannot be any different. Transformation that could positively impact human behavior, although spiritual in its essence, need not entail any particular religious ritual or spiritual affiliation. But tireless practice and non-attachment to the fruits of practice (*abhyyasa* and *vairagya* in Sanskrit) are required for any spiritual or behavioral progress. These are the two composite core principles on which the entire Yoga system rests, and the ones that Lord Krishna told Arjuna (*Bhagavad Gita, 6.35*) are essential to control the wayward mind. We need to nurture an attitude of incessant effort to attain and maintain a state of stable equanimity; and we must learn to let go of the many attachments, aversions, fears, and false identities — even entitlements — that are clouding our vision of the world and thwarting our evolutionary destiny. At a superficial level, persistent practice and unattached effort seem incompatible with and antagonistic to each other: we are required, at the same time, to 'never give up' and to 'let go', to 'never cling' and to 'shed'. Practice requires the exercise of the will, while non-attachment seems more a matter of surrender. At a deeper level, practice and non-attachment work together and complement each other; they are like the two wings of a bird. The two are complementary parts of yoga, each requiring the other for its full expression. *Abhyasa* is sometimes described as a process of canalization and re-conditioning, and *vairagya* as a process of de-conditioning. Persistent practice and ceaseless effort lead us towards the right direction; and not being attached to any particular outcome of any action allows us to continue our inner journey without being diverted by the *dwandas* or the pairs of opposites of life.

Transform or turn terminal — that is the defining human choice of this century. But in one sense, it is not a 'choice' at all; because, that which is constant and continuous is not something we can choose. The question really is about its direction. Trans-formation or 'transcendence', as some like to call it, has been at once the clarion call of the mystics and the mavericks, the 'New Age' buzzword, the meeting point of the sacred and the secular, a heady mix of myth and the mundane, the boundary between the absolute and the absurd. Many have spoken about human transformation in myriad ways: as a conversion, as a discovery of the sacred, as rebirth, regeneration, and so on. One of the innumerable claims we make of our uniqueness is that the humans alone are capable of self-transcendence and conscious evolution. We cannot be transformed into something we are not innately, or something that we do not have within. In essence, it is to actualize a latent potentiality through an internal process emerging from the deepest depths of the psyche. In fact, even alchemy, which was practiced by scientists like Newton, was not, as noted by Carl Jung, merely a conversion of base metals into gold, but was far deeper; it was the mixing of chemicals using a symbolic form of reasoning to discern the ultimate truth. But transformation, above all of consciousness, externally or internally induced, is not an end by itself, only a means to better the human condition and conduct. That means, it has to be progressive, not regressive. Progressive transformation implies that which leads from darkness to light, from fragmentation to wholeness, from separateness to oneness, and above all from a mind-driven to a heart-centered consciousness. It is also to change our perspective of our presence in the cosmos. It is to realize that we live, in the words of astronaut Edgar Mitchell, in a "little civilization on this planet, in this little solar system, in this rather average galaxy, which is only one of billions of galaxies"[1]. What we want is transformation on our own terms, to selectively take everything without giving up anything that needs to be relinquished. Yet the paradox is that transformation, or generically ceaseless change, takes place all the time in life and in Nature. Every subatomic particle interaction comprises of the annihilation of the original particle and the creation of new subatomic particles, a continual dance of transformation, of mass changing into energy and energy into mass. Indeed, creation *is* transformation, evolution is transformation, a fetus becoming a baby is transformation, the process of dying is transformation, art is transformation, music is transformation, and an idea is transformation. In today's 'visual' and 'virtual' world, the effect of television is transformation, the Internet is transformation, the transition from ape to man was transformation, and now, man into 'something' else will be transformation. What that 'something' is, will be the question and challenge for us to explore.

Although we call it change, not transformation, we all want to change many things in our lives: job, partner, fortune, house, gadget, etc. We want continuity in some and change in others with a view to bettering our lives. Furthermore, powered by science, the human condition is dramatically transforming more than ever before in human history, making man almost a new species. As if this is not unsettling enough, recent reports proclaim that scientists have created artificial life in the laboratory, avowedly opening the door to making and manipulating 'life', a development that could possibly prove, according to *The Economist* magazine "mankind's mastery over nature in a way more profound than even the detonation of the first atomic bomb"[2], calling into question much of the very basis of creation. That is, in a very real sense, transformation of the highest, if not the deepest, order. What is more transformative than creating life? By any rationale we should be relieved, elated, and excited. But whether it is *that* or making man 'immortal', which science says will soon become a real possibility, we are far from happy; so few are in a celebratory mood. So, why are we so apprehensive of our future when we have it so good? Why are we so fearful of our own power, so concerned about our creativity? Everyone is for transformation so long as someone else pays the price and goes through the grind. No one wants to be transformed except on one's own terms. And we want reality to be more *real* than the world we live in, we want to be insulated from the fruits of our own failings, to be a lotus in a toxic pool poisoned by our own mind. In a world where so much consciousness is concentrated on physical phenomena, almost any effort to abstract from the phenomenal world and divert it to the spiritual world is a herculean task. How does one reconcile to this confusion and move forward? The answer is, we need to 'transform' transformation from the temporal to the transcendental, from the pursuit of personal growth to species-upliftment. The American writer Joseph Campbell said that when we quit thinking primarily about ourselves and our own self-preservation, we undergo a truly heroic transformation of consciousness, which is what mankind needs. While there is a broad consensus that mankind is poised for a major 'transformation', the actual 'jump' will imply far more than a cosmetic change, some 'fixing' and 'plumbing' or even course correction of the existing order of things. The irreducible imperative is a new perspective on reality through cathartic change, to overturn assumptions of our imagination, to purge the bowels of our basic being of bitterness and bile accumulated over millenniums of evolution and centuries of 'civilized' life. In short, it translates into evolution from the physical to the spiritual dimension.

If the meaningful survival of the human species hinges on that kind of transformation, how do we incubate, induce, and guide that complex process? Will it all be a wholly human affair, so to speak, all in the 'family' and none of the business of anyone else? As autonomous individuals with bodies and brains that cannot be shared, will it all be a matter between 'me', 'my God', and nothing in between, and the rest, in a manner of speaking, can well 'go to hell'? If destiny, as someone wryly wrote, is a tyrant's mandate for crime and a fool's excuse for failure, where does human effort begin and end? Is every man, in the words of Helena Blavatsky "weaving thread by thread around himself, as a spider does his cobweb; and this destiny is guided either by the heavenly voice of the invisible *prototype* outside of us, or by our more intimate *astral*, or inner man, who is but too often the evil genius of the embodied entity called man"[3]. What we need to 'overcome', to transcend, for therapeutic human transformation, is the stranglehold of the mind over our consciousness. Although visions vary and desires differ, men have always dreamt of a kind of transcendence that goes beyond the processes of life and death. As Sri Aurobindo puts it, man should strive to become more than himself. In becoming more than himself, man becomes true to himself. In becoming true to himself, he fulfils God's premise in his creation. Everyone, at some point or the other, feels that he is not living up to his full potential, that much of his life is spent wandering in the wasteland, that all of life's labor is directed towards simply staying alive and keeping death at bay. But simply 'staying alive' consumes so much energy that man has little left to know 'what it feels to be alive'. The kind of transformation that excites modern man is that of an *immortal superman*, with the capacity, so to speak, to reorder the stars to fit his good fortune, to live long, if not eternally, with the vigor of youth, to eat once again the 'fruit of the tree of knowledge', this time not of the good and evil mentioned in the Bible, but of pleasure and power. It is grounded on the perception that life is both dualistic and linear. Our identity and destiny, so we convinced ourselves, lay in being separately successful — from Nature, God and above all, from each other; to prevail not only at work but in every relationship, and that creates a lot of negative energy. The dreaded 'L' word is 'loser', who really is anyone who refuses to walk over another prostrate man. All this is part of our 'culture', the theater of life, the scene of action. True transformation of the human condition must come from within, but it will be stillborn or distorted without the transformation of the human context of life. If everything is left as it is and our yardsticks of success and social esteem, values and worth, risk and reward, remain untransformed, then the human species will have to be content with the current paradigms of transformation. Any genuine human transformation has to be holistic, aimed at our inner being that takes us to a higher level of existence. The Bible offers one such vision: "Do not be conformed to this world, but be transformed by the renewal of your mind, that by testing you may discern what is the will of God, what is good and acceptable and perfect" (*Romans 12:2*). What remains hazy is the probable end product: whether we should strive toward *Man plus* or *Man minus*, or a brand new being or something even more than that. Put differently, do we aspire to become an altogether new form of life on earth, or an improved and substantially reinforced life but with our basic capacities radically altered?

While science is trying to make man a whole by himself, a creature of pure physicality, the spiritual path exhorts him to become a critical part of something larger or something altogether different from his phenomenal existence. And while science is trying to make the body impregnable and the individual the pivot of the universe, the scriptural path, although there are significant variations within, is body-dissolution and ego-annihilation, and making God central to life, seeking 'eternal life', which is, as the *Chandogya* Upanishad puts it, to be 'lifted to the region of the deity'[4] or in the words of the great Sri Adi Shankara, 'absorption in divinity'[5].

Through the scriptures, God promises to remake man if we keep faith in him. The Hebrew Scriptures refer to prophets who look forward to the future because God promises new things. "I am about to do a new thing" says God in Isaiah 43:19. The Bible closes in Revelation 21:5 with God saying, "See, I am making all things new". The Bhagavad Gita is nothing but a treatise of transformation, a catalyst that transforms the 'battle of life' into a 'battle of truth', a blueprint for the birth of a better man. It offers a menu of choices to help us remake our raw existence, and more importantly, it offers tools for transformation — from action to knowledge to devotion, in its eighteen chapters.

The scientific path, which is sometimes referred to as *Transhumanistic transformation*, is to be liberated from the vagaries of biological shackles, to cling to the body, make it more seductive, make the organs unimpaired, make human tenure eternal on earth and soak the cosmos with human intelligence. The underlying premise or promise is that once we are freed from the boundaries of our limiting bodies, human intelligence will leapfrog from the human organism to machines, making high-tech machines more human, though not biological. Man will then become a new species, *Homo cyberneticus*. With the aid of technological connectivity, science is hopeful that humanity will soon become a coherent species. Other than the invisible 'hand of God', it is our almost compulsive inclination to insert ourselves into technological contraptions as a short cut to solve every problem we face, that will have a deep and decisive bearing on human destiny. It is now very clear that our growing fascination for the apparent invincibility of sophisticated machinery, and an attendant desire to trade human sweat for metal in order to attain superhuman powers, will have a profound bearing on the direction of human transformation. Indeed, *transformation* is itself a code word for acquiring superhuman powers, which is really what we want. The avatar man wants to become has little, if any, to do with the divine avatars. It is hard even for pundits to foresee what would happen if the current rate of technological innovation continues uninterrupted for another millennium. Would we develop a working knowledge of all natural law and the know-how to keep the cells of our bodies endlessly renewing themselves, thus pre-empting death? Would 'beam transport', à la *Star Trek*, become possible, enabling man to de-materialize and re-materialize matter? Would computers be thought-activated and designed on an atomic scale? Above all, how would man behave, with those powers, towards another human? Do we then need a God as we now perceive and project?

For, in the scriptural frame of reference, God, as, for example, described in the Bahá'í Faith, is the single, personal, inaccessible, omniscient, omnipresent, imperishable, and almighty God, the architect of creating, reshaping and making things anew, constantly turning things, cleansing the gathering dirt and making the world fit for the righteous. In the scientific scenario, man is the cause and consequence of everything, the virtual end of biology, and the universe is but an arena for his triumph, his mission to transform the universe in his own visage. Excluding the likes of 'accidental' posthumanity, induced through mutation or post-apocalyptic scenarios or becoming floating angels or gods in disguise, these are the two paths, the two choices, and the two challenges that are often offered.

There is a third one too, the path of 'conscious' consciousness-change: transformation of that which precedes action and becomes behavior, and quells, if not conquers, one's own innate or acquired weaknesses and limitations. But we cannot remove the filth and foulness, the dirt and slime that lies *inside*;

whatever we do will only be a 'Band-Aid' approach. A central message from the history of human transformation is that only with a fundamental change in the inside can we bring about a change in the outside, and that transformation has to be two-pronged. Just as a bird cannot fly with one wing, any *modus operandi* for a radical alteration of the human condition has to be a train on two tracks, not a monorail. And there cannot be any 'sacred cows'. Transgression is a part of transformation, we go nowhere without crossing a frontier; but it must have the right limits and lines. Instead of overcoming or combating our real enemies that nestle within and nibble away at our essence, we transgress the laws of Nature. Our consciousness is full to the brim with toxins, crowded with no standing room, and we cannot put anything in unless we take something out. But for cleansing we need a cleanser, and we are befuddled about what it could be and where to find it. Both scriptural salvation and scientific immortality overly, though not singularly, emphasize individual liberation and body betterment or spiritual enhancement at the implicit expense of terrestrial responsibility and species-scale spin-off. Any improvement within the reach of the mass of mankind, it is assumed, has to be a 'trickle-down' byproduct of personal 'growth'. In that sense, the desire for self-salvation is the ultimate temptation, and physical immortality is an impediment to spiritual evolution. So many factors crowd in when we seriously think about transformation that it becomes almost impossible for us, the garden-variety human beings, to see clarity and unity. A contemporary spiritual guru, Sri Chinmoy, summed it up well: 'the animal in us needs immediate transformation. The human in us needs conscious liberation. The divine in us needs perfect revelation. The Supreme in us needs complete manifestation. To see God, we need transformation. To be invited by God we need liberation. To be loved by God we need revelation. To be immortalized by God we need manifestation.' By revelation, Sri Chinmoy meant sharing the fruits of realization and by manifestation he meant perceiving all life on earth as divine.[6]

We have to bring about a symbiosis between science and spirit, what Jeremy Rifkin called transition 'to biosphere consciousness' (*The Empathic Civilization*, 2009). The premise is that new communication technologies, enhanced awareness of the potential of renewable energies, discoveries in evolutionary biology, neuro-cognitive science, are pushing us to recognize that human beings are biologically empathic and our true nature is not rational, acquisitive, and aggressive, and that we are, in the words of Rifkin, 'deeply connected with each other in the ecosystems that make up the biosphere'. The assumption is that each of us, at the core of our biology, is not an autonomous, self-centered, and materialistic being. Whether we can translate that 'empathic connectivity' into the consciousnesses of the multitude and realize that one's daily consumption of energy and other resources ultimately affects the lives of every other human being and every other creature that inhabits the earth, is the question. And we need to put in place the mechanism or modality that allows innate empathic sensitivity to nurture and mature, leading to consciousness-change.

Although human culture and modern civilization have radically altered the dynamic of every experience from birth to death, our abysmal ignorance, about the fundamentals of birth, life, and death, has become a forbidding barrier to further evolution. We must remember that the contingencies of happenings that led to human arrival are simply a sequel to the blind, amoral, and aggressive march of evolution. Even in evolutionary terms we face an anomaly. Natural selection, the engine behind evolution, is supposed to make organisms more suitable and fit for their environment. But that is not happening in the human world. It is possibly because the environment itself is getting worse, caused by the dominant organism and, in turn, weakening the organism itself. It is hard to foresee how this incestuous 'story' will reach its climax. Then again we quibble and quarrel over the 'story'. Some scoff and say it is the usual 'doom and gloom' stuff of half-baked heretics, that human organism is not getting weaker but stronger; that we are living longer and healthier than ever before; that the human body is breaking many barriers either in speed of motion or in scaling heights or in endurance. And, as for the 'problem of the environment', solving that problem too is well within the realm of human ingenuity. Debates and dialogues go on but we just cannot seem to get anything right about anything that truly matters; often, we seem shackled by our own intellectuality, paralyzed by analysis. At times, it does seem that someone out there — or up there — is out to cut us to size, and is enjoying our discomfiture. Although outer space is no longer so dark, deep, and forbidding, the inner space remains impregnable. We still ruminate if we are the products of ascent from animals, or descent from angels, of evolution or involution, or a product of a still unknown process, or that somewhere, somehow, something went terribly awry in the metamorphosis of or transition from Spirit into matter. We still squabble if man is simply another manifestation of matter, a coincidental cauldron of atoms and molecules, with no particular purpose, as science suggests, or if he is a sublime spark of the Supreme Spirit intended to eventually dissolve into the Infinite, as the scriptures propound.

Despite occasional bursts of grandeur and glory, the human form of earthly life has not yet risen up to its full measure and seems paralyzed by its inherent instincts and impulses, emotions and passions. The world of matter outside and the world of spirit inside have been out of tune. That inefficiency, most of all, is manifested outwardly in man's 'natural' inability to put other humans on the same footing as his own, by the reflex to view another person at best as a competitor, usually as an adversary, all to savor what life has to offer. Neither angelic descent nor animal ascent can account for this predisposition. Blavatsky wrote, "With right knowledge, or at any rate with a confident conviction that our neighbors will no more work to hurt us than we would think of harming them, the two-thirds of the World's evil would vanish into thin air."[7] We have not found the 'right' knowledge and the dance of evil on earth is deafening. According to Blavatsky, the only decree of the absolute of Nature is that we should live in harmony in the world of matter as it is in the world of spirit. We have not found harmony in either kind. Although one might argue that 'blind' reverence led to the virtual extinction of some animals and reason has virtually transformed us into craftier beings, there are signs that we are headed the same way as the animals. Man's attitude toward Nature has always been, from the first days to the morrow of this millennium, ambivalent, ranging from standing, in Einstein's words, rapt in awe, to condescension and contempt, and we still have not found the right fix. The ambivalence comes from the fact that we have forgotten, as Thomas Berry reminds us, that the human story is part of the earth story, not the other way, and that we see ourselves as a transcendent mode of being, independent of the earth community. Berry also says that there is a radical discontinuity in the governing principles of the universe, as we tend to assume that the natural world is somehow lacking the spiritual mode of living and that man did not emerge out of the normal evolutionary processes. It is this basic assumption and its reckless translation into our economic life that has given rise to the planetary physical alterations which some scientists like Alexey Dmitriev say are a part of a larger paradigm of global change in the vital processes of living organisms, or of life itself, which may lead to a total revision of the range of species and life on earth. Perhaps our penchant for self-destruction is a part of or a prelude to that paradigm shift. Apocalyptic or prescient, all signs point to the strong probability that the current cusp of change is not cyclical but seismic, not transient but tectonic. And it is also self evident that man, as he has now evolved into, with the consciousness that he has, cannot cope with what will be required to ensure that such a shift does not become cataclysmic. Our vision is not good enough to see if the faint light at the end of the tunnel is the edge of the way out or the headlights of an oncoming train. Our loves, hates, triumphs and tragedies, passions and foibles are played out within the inexorable march of insentient time. Both our ignorance and arrogance are incorrigible.

All this agoraphobia, all this thoughtful torment, all this wiggle and wriggle, is grounded in the rickety base that man is the master, that he matters most, and that his premature disappearance from this particular planet will make God a virtual orphan, a cosmic calamity so disastrous that earth itself may be left without a *raison d'être*. Although that is the general working hypothesis of modern life, the fact of the matter is that there is very little evidence to support this, save our exaggerated sense of our manifest destiny. While experts might differ on how long, given *good* behavior, human species might last on earth, the numbers range from a few hundreds to more than a million years. Although there is broad agreement that our behavior is not exactly exemplary and therefore we might not last the full stretch, surely we deserve to last longer than a century or two, or even another millennium. But it depends, as never before, on us. While the genetic, biological, social, and psychological basis of behavior is a subject of scholarly discourse, the stark fact is that both individually and collectively we have no control over our conduct. That is more glaring when it comes to our conduct in company, in human interfacings that call for a tradeoff between giving and taking, sacrifice and sharing. In both ancient Greek and Hindu thought, rebirth is conditioned by behavior. And it is not only what we do to each other, it is also what we think of each other that forms the determinant. A pre-Socratic philosopher Empedocles asked, 'Do you not see that you are devouring each other in the thought processes of your mind?' And in the Hindu *Manusmriti* it is said, "he whose flesh I eat in this life, will devour mine in the next".[8] Our bad behavior also has planetary implications. Fueled by human avarice and ambition, greed and gluttony, the economic growth machine has pushed our planet well beyond its ecological stamina. The inference is increasingly becoming irresistible that with the kind of consciousness we presently have, the driving force behind behavior, our generation just does not have the will, wit, and wisdom to arrest and reverse the course on the scale that is needed. And the date of reckoning, the time for the 'end of the world' kind of change, according to the Mayan calendar, for example, is not far; it could be as soon as 21 December 2012. It is said to be the start of the World of the Fifth Sun, "a new era resulting from and signified by the solar meridian crossing the galactic equator, and the earth aligning itself with the center of the galaxy."[9] According to the Mayans, this date indicates the beginning of what they termed, "The Prophecy of the Sun," and denotes the dramatic transition from one major phase of our world into another era. It begins a new 26,000-year cycle through the next era, or the Age of Peace. The technological singularity concept (the dawn of superhuman intelligence and the end of the human era predicted by Vernor Vinge) parallels this, only at a date roughly three decades from 2000, in the year 2030. According to Carlos Barrios (*The Book of Destiny*, 2009), a famed Mayan ceremonial priest and spiritual guide, we are at the cusp of the era when peace begins, when people live in harmony with Mother Earth; we are no longer in the World of the Fourth Sun, but we are not yet in the World of the Fifth Sun. This is the time of transition, a period of passage, the threshold to a new era.

One does not have to be an all-seeing seer, a crystal gazer or a futurologist or a Nostradamus to say that while everything in life and in Nature constantly change the present turmoil is clearly extraordinary, beyond the natural flux of Nature, beyond the flow of space and rhythm of Time, bound inextricably with human will and actions. Along with a sense of fateful foreboding, the troubling thought also curls up: could all this sense of gloom and doom and hype and hyperbole turn out to be yet another false alarm? Will it soon be shattered by that magical thing — hope — that keeps most men alive, defying all reason and logic? Described as pearly and white-winged, capable of healing all sorrows and bring peace, hope is the only thing, according to Greek mythology, that remained in the forbidden box that Pandora opened and later, to our eternal relief, let out. In the dynamic of 'life', imagination is more fruitful than knowledge, dreams more alluring than facts, and hope more 'life-giving' than experience. It is such fearless hope that inspired some mystics and philosophers to envision, despite modern man's crass materialism, that man, within the circumstance of his own space and time, is capable of transforming himself into a nobler being, a god. The theosophist Annie Besant foresaw, far away in 1914, a wave of mysticism sweeping over the world and philosopher Hans Jonas saw a historical sequence of development that moves from 'objectification' to 'interiorization', from religious knowledge to its subjective application. A more recent report prepared for the *Millennium Project* (1992), under the auspices of the United Nations, addressed fundamental questions such as, "Is there a countervailing set of indicators that shows that we humans may be waking up to our predicament? Is there a set of trends that shows that we are beginning to consciously organize ourselves to respond to the ecological, social, and spiritual challenges we face? Is a new kind of experiential or first-hand spirituality emerging?"

The report concludes on a note of soaring optimism, "From this inquiry, we have concluded that a new global culture and consciousness have taken root and are beginning to grow in the world". This assessment represents a huge hope for paradigm shift in consciousness, "as distinct and momentous as that which occurred in the transition from the agricultural era to the industrial era roughly three hundred years ago."[10] Further it makes an exciting but astonishing statement that, "the most distinctive feature of this emerging era is not technological change, but a change in human consciousness." The report calls this consciousness, the 'reflective/living-systems' paradigm or perspective, which has two distinctive features: 1) an enhanced capacity to step aside and non-judgmentally look at ourselves and the world; and 2) to see the earth and the cosmos as interconnected, living systems.[11] We have to take these findings with the import they deserve, but the world we outwardly see barely offers any hint. Even assuming that there is a wave of consciousness-change in the world, the question is: is there a 'critical mass' and is it strong enough to coalesce into an unstoppable movement for species-scale transformation? What such minimal 'critical' mass should be is hard to calculate, but we do know the true test of such a 'wave of change'. It is the spontaneous, unlabored and almost 'ordinary' or 'default' ability to derive genuine happiness from the happiness of others or, at the very, very least, not being able to derive even a semblance of satisfaction at the misery of others. If any shift in human consciousness does not lead, at the least, to this development, then that change or transformation is labor lost, effort gone in vain.

Be that as it may, we have so far prepared ourselves for every threat and contingency by focusing on the external environment, by inventing new technologies to 'fix' problems, to fill 'gaps' between what we want and what we cannot get. The German theologian Dietrich Bonhoeffer talked of getting rid of the 'God of gaps'. One 'gap' we need to fill is between being and becoming, between what we are and what we should become; what we are is a gift of God and what we become is our way of showing gratitude to God. But we must overcome our hubris about what man, even more, ought to do, both as an individual and as a species. It is true that, whether it is divine design or human dexterity, humankind has managed to surmount seemingly hopeless odds. In our own lives we see that things can unrecognizably change any minute. Be that as it may, the problem is not with the human hand; it is with our *mind.* When our limited, conditioned mind finally opens up to the infinity of the mystery which has been repressed until then, a person often finds himself drowning in the ocean of limitless implausibility. For, when the mind is finally divorced from all its previous premises and understandings, it suddenly stands upon the brink of the limitless abyss. It is at this point where some sink, some swim, some fall off the cliff, and a few learn to fly. This is the 'vertiginous uncertainty' of life, of blinding incomprehension, of immense possibilities, few probabilities, and thus far two certainties.

Unlike ever before, the earth itself is the issue, at stake; Nature itself has a stupendous stake. And never before has the entire humanity been called upon to make a shared sacrifice. Never before were so many human beings of one generation required to make such changes in their 'life style'. That is the difference between then and now. We tend to think that every 'mind' is specific and autonomous to each individual but, some great 'minds' like the Swiss psychiatrist Carl Jung have said, the subconscious of our minds are all somehow connected or are part of a universal source, which the Upanishads called the Universal Mind. The intriguing question is: can we re-establish and strengthen the connectivity that seems to surface from time to time through a mysterious process? That could be a big boost to the task ahead, which is that we must change everything between conception to action, the way we think, the way we take decisions, the way we analyze and assimilate knowledge, the way we prioritize and the way we relate to the universe. And for that we must go down, or 'up', to the deepest depths — or to the starry heights — of our consciousness. Tolstoy wrote: "All human history, from the earliest times to our own day, may be considered as a movement of the consciousness, both of individuals and of homogeneous groups, from lower ideas to higher ones."[12] The 'higher idea' now has to be, 'conscious consciousness change' as a means to make man a genuinely and naturally compassionate being. Gillian Ross (*The Search for the Pearl*, 1993) said that mysticism and compassion are inseparable and that "we are entering the most challenging decade of our history. To meet this challenge, the onus is upon each one of us to help shift human consciousness beyond the limitations of personal ego."[13]

We must remember that consciousness itself is two-fold. The universal or cosmic is what pervades all physical bodies, inclusive of all animate and inanimate beings, and the specific is the same consciousness animating a particular body in the wakeful state, called *jagritasthana* in Vedanta, the *Atman* or the soul in the individual body. Liberation, salvation, *moksha* or *nirvana* or true transformation, whichever way one wants to describe it, is the extinguishment of the divisive consciousness in the all-enveloping oneness of the divine. In the Hindu conception of the divine, the 'human soul in the human body' is the abode of the divine. To align our behavior with this realization, we need a new 'conscious' consciousness in which intellect is driven by intuition and intuition is directed by intellect. In the language of science fiction it has been called the 'Captain Kirk principle', named after the captain of the famous American television serial *Star Trek*, who harmonized the super rationality of Mr. Spock and the hyperemotional sensitivity of Dr. McCoy.[14] We can take heart from the fact that science fiction has so often turned into scientific fact and that this too would fall into that category. But fictional fantasy can also become a real-life nightmare. While what is needed is a consciousness born of a blend of intuition and intellect, what modern man is attempting to do is to take control of his fate solely through the intellect and denying God His due. In so doing, he is destroying everything that joins one to another and lends dignity to life.

The Phenomenon Humans Call God

If 'transformation' is complex, confusing, and riddled with contradictions, even more forbidding but fascinating is another phenomenon that we humans call God. G.K. Chesterton wrote, "Whether you say that God made the dog or the dog made God does not seem to matter; that is only one of the sterile disputations of the too subtle theologians"[15]. Whatever it is, that single syllable conveys more meaning and hope, and consecrates more awe, despair, and devotion than any other in human imagination. It is the one word, or the very thought of it, that is capable of the greatest ecstasy, akin to the thrill of passionate romantic love, strong enough to brave any odds and transcend any barriers. Equally, it could elicit derisive ridicule and scorn we rarely exhibit to another human. While pronouncing God's 'death', as some philosophers, atheists and scientists have done, we do not even show the courtesy, decorum and mourning we bestow on a human acquaintance. While burying, we do not even leave a decent epitaph on his tomb — we are in too much of a hurry to go along to the next funeral of a human. We say He is almighty, all-knowing, all-seeing, but behave as if He cannot see through our brazen behavior or that he does not really mean what he says. All through our tempestuous tenure on earth, we have struggled with the God-factor, the extra factor in every equation that defies even the laws of Nature and blurs the boundary between the possible and the impossible, between the infinite and finite. While it is true that some are more passionate seekers than others, and some can brave the burden of life better than others, there is hardly anyone who has grown into adulthood without wondering and ruminating about God. In the Bhagavad Gita, Lord Krishna says that four kinds of people worship Him — or 'seek the face of God' — (1) those who are in distress or world-weary; (2) those who desire worldly things or earthly happiness; (3) those who seek *jnana*, knowledge; and (4) those who want to merge themselves into Him. He says that the last category are dearest to Him, for "he alone loves me because I am myself: the last and only goal of his devoted heart." An enchanting description of divine love is expressed in the Hindu text called *Mahimandala Gita* by saint Arakkhita Das, "Therefore, O mind, listen to the grace of devotion; one who has an empty mind knows *that*, knows nothing apart from *that*, knows the world to be *that*, wanders alone and shuns company, has *that* for company, feels only *that*, has no fears and knows nothing apart from *that*, so that one knows only *that* and doing so meditates in *that*, sleeps in *that*, sings in *that*;"[16] That ***that*** is God. But *that* one word has also been the greatest source of denial, derision, friction, fratricide, and bloodshed. Where God is a cause, blood never stops flowing in the human world. We now have an incendiary mix: religious bloodthirst and global interdependence. In God's mind that could be the greatest human betrayal — people killing each other to 'protect' Him, the one who is the cause and consequence, the sustainer and the destroyer, the source and salvation. The irony is that every religion prohibits killing save for a just cause. Buddhism, perhaps the one religion that elevates it to the deepest and highest level, says that "He should not kill a living being, nor cause it to be killed, nor should he incite another to kill. Do not injure any being, either strong or weak in the world."

Still we use killing to settle scores with a fellow man and to 'protect' God. Since we do not know how to relate to Him, and because we do not know the nature of His true Being or Non-Being, our mind does the simplest of all: turn Him into a human, a close friend or a loving parent. The Upanishads proclaim that God is 'that' through which all things are born, and having been born, 'that' by which they live, and 'that' into which they enter while leaving. And they further say that, he who meditates on God (*Brahman*), as Non-Being, he himself will cease to exist and as a Being shall always exist; the attributes we identify God with, as a support, savior, almighty, we will become that.[17] It means that which we deeply meditate upon as the embodiment of God and that which we seek from Him with a pure heart, we will be transformed into that. His dispositions, his apparent intentions, the aims of his kingship, we interpret in human terms. God is both immaculate but invisible, light and sublime and abysmal darkness: light because He alone can show the way; darkness because of the perception of his inscrutability and impenetrability to the human condition. As we have not been able to relate to that God, we have failed to absorb and assimilate the divine into our daily life. Though, the scriptures say that He is within each of us and embedded in every being, He is, in terms of actual experience, as remote as the stars and as inscrutable as the cosmos. Vedanta says that it is the mysterious *Maya* or grand illusion that obscures our vision and befuddles our mind, but *Maya* is also His creation. Does it mean that it is He who is keeping us away from Him? Some indeed speculate that God first arose as an illusion, and that the subsequent history of the idea of God is, in some sense, the evolution of an illusion. Some others say that God became a primordial need once humans discovered that they were mortal. So many, so often have pronounced His demise, but those newscasters themselves are all dead or soon will be, but He remains the dominant force in human consciousness. There is no human emotion that someone or the other has not felt towards God, from love to hate, indifference to intense ecstasy, reverence to ridicule. For some, He is all there is. For some, He is a necessary nuisance, and for others, an opportunistic option. The scriptures are the principal source of our vision of God. The purpose of human life itself has been described as the seeking of the 'companionship' of God, or as Sri Adi Shankara had put it, 'absorption in divinity'. Saints put God at the core of their consciousness; they love and live for Him, and some, like the Hindu mystical singer Mirabai were actually 'in love' with God (Krishna) and considered themselves 'married' to Him. Only prophets and mystics can really visualize Him, if not actually see and converse with Him; they are the people 'from whom God hid nothing'. They are the ones who, attaining a higher state of consciousness, engage in a series of transcendent encounters with God, and through their contemplation, find a way to God.

The remarkable fact is, as the physicist Erwin Schrodinger put it, "the mystics of many centuries, independently, yet in perfect harmony with each other (somewhat like the particles in an ideal gas) have described, each of them, the unique experience of his or her life in terms that can be condensed in the phrase: *Deus Factus Sum* (I have become God)."[18] Some of the majesty of God is captured in the song *Everyday God*: "Creator God we encounter you in the beauty of creation; Companion God we encounter you in the warmth of friendship; Loving God we encounter you in the embrace of a loved one; Merciful God we encounter you in the search for justice. Mysterious God in our restlessness we search for you, we desire you and we are confident in your assured presence, now and forever." Another mystic, the sage Ramakrishna, was said to have been in routine communion with Kali, the Hindu Goddess. Quite simply, what separates a Ramakrishna from the rest is *consciousness*, what has been described as a kind of inner transformative consciousness of God. Meister Eckhart, a German mystic wrote in his sermon *The Nearness of the Kingdom*, "Our salvation depends upon our knowing and recognizing the Chief Good which is God Himself. I have a capacity in my soul for taking in God entirely. I am as sure as I live that nothing is so near to me as God. God is nearer to me than I am to myself; my existence depends on the nearness and presence of God. He is also near things of wood and stone, but they know it not. If a piece of wood became as aware of the nearness of God as an archangel is, the piece of wood would be as happy as an archangel. For this reason man is happier than the inanimate wood, because he knows and understands how God is near him."[19] To realize God, one must walk the razor's edge that both separates and straddles mysticism and madness.

Not only mystics and saints — the boundary between the two is really blurred — it was even said that our very early ancestors were able to directly mix, mingle, and match with the divine on earth; a devotee was reverential but not subservient or servile. Perhaps because we cultivated false values and turned to God, not to savor His Company but to seek competitive favors, and lived our lives in direct contradiction to His dictums, the Almighty might have chosen to become a symbol or a stone in a place of worship. Our consciousness and conscience got sullied with self-righteous selfishness, no longer fit for divine habitation. Although much of our life is a desperate cry for divine help, in the face of His stubborn silence, we really do not know what we should do. And as a result, we are left wondering, in the words of Nietzsche, if man is one of God's blunders, or if God is one of man's blunders. Whether one 'believes' in God or not is perhaps the most frequently asked question; a question that almost everyone has had to address at some point or the other. The answer to that question is supposed to determine if the person is religious or not, and rational or not. Kierkegaard captured the dichotomy of the divine dilemma and wrote, "If I am capable of grasping God objectively, I do not believe, but precisely because I cannot do this, I must believe."[20]

Man can defy, denounce, or deny, but not ignore the intangible, unknowable entity of God, or rather '*The God-idea*', as Annie Besant preferred to call it. We view God in a variety of ways: as an explanation (of the universe), as an excuse (for our foibles), as a helper (when in trouble), as a judge (in after-life), as a scapegoat (for our sins), as a parachute (when everything else fails). And even our denial is an assertion of our innocence. Expressions like 'Oh, my God', 'God knows', 'God help us', 'God forbid', 'Thank God', all these dot the daily lives of the theist, the agnostic, and the atheist. The real problem for many 'rationalists' is really not God, but God *as we picture Him to be*. Some say that the fault is not God's but ours, our interpretation of how He is projected in the scriptures. In other words, we have adopted towards God the same double standards we show in the world — ignoring those divine traits that do not suit us, and highlighting those that appeal to our greed. This is the theme that Gerald Schroeder develops in his recent book *God According to God* (2009). He says that the God revealed in the Bible is 100 percent compatible with the world as we know it today. It is our misconception of God that causes the disparity and heartburn. Eric Hoffer (*Reflections on the Human Condition*, 1973) said that man invents God in the image of his longings, in the image of what he wants to be, then proceeds to imitate that image, view with it, and then strive to overcome it. While we keep speculating about how He looks, and interpret or misinterpret and bemoan his alleged indifference to the torrid time we have on earth, the question God must be agonizing over is: How could He have gone so wrong? What ought He to do with this paradoxical and perplexing species, so blessed in its creation and so flawed in its behavior?

Whether God is a pervasive, personal or impersonal presence, a particle or a primordial force, a magician or a mathematician, pure energy or a stream of light (Zoroastrian *Ahura Mazda*), a 'Supreme Fascist' (Paul Erdos) or a Sublime Spirit, the Father in heaven or embedded in every object, omnipotent as the scriptures say, or powerless as today's 'neo-realists' say, the enigma of God is the ultimate mix of magic and mystery. Whether God is for real or simply an illusion or a delusion of a desperate or devious mind, is not likely to be resolved as long as we remain confined to human faculties and endowments. Generations from now, men will continue to be born, and will live and die wondering 'if He is, or He is not' and what He has to do with their lives. That ignorance, that unawareness is all the more galling for the human intelligence as, for example, the Upanishads say that God is the subtle essence of all phenomenal existence and gross manifestation; that He is the one who makes the fire burn, the sun to shine, the wind to blow, that the underlying all-resplendence and all-power, even of the gods and elements, is His power. In the *Kaivalya* Upanishad, the *Brahman* describes Himself in the following words: 'without arms and legs am I, of unthinkable power; I see without eyes, and I hear without ears. I know all, and am different from all. None can know me. I am always the Intelligence'; and 'For me there is neither merit nor demerit, I suffer no destruction, I have no birth, nor any self-identity with the body and the organs'. Even the Buddha who saw everything, and transcended the bounds of the human condition perhaps more than any other man, could not or did not give a definitive answer to the 'question' of God, either because that knowledge is too hazardous to our intelligence or irrelevant to his focus, which was to ease our suffering. But that begs the question: how can God, if He is anything like the one we imagine, be irrelevant to 'suffering'? Who or what else can alleviate our misery? By ignoring the 'God question' has the Buddha done any better? But the Buddha single-handedly changed the focus of spiritual search. Before the Buddha, the search was fundamentally a concern with God. After the Buddha, we have an option. The Buddha offered another way of cleansing the human consciousness and making compassion the vocation and destination of man. But can we do that without factoring in the divine? That is the question. The answer increasingly is a nay.

The Buddha's enigmatic silence has not deterred the rest. Unable to pin Him down or capture His essence, we have showered Him with a variety of names and adjectives: a magician, a mathematician, a circle whose center is everywhere and circumference nowhere; almighty, creator, observer, pervasive, vengeful, merciful, transcendent, immanent, Father up there, omnipotent, omniscient, spirit, light, compassion, love, grace, and a myriad more. As an acronym, God has been described as AWESOME: **A**lmighty, **W**onderful, **E**verlasting, **S**ustaining, **O**mnipotent, **M**erciful, and **E**ternal. The Upanishads call Him *Brahman*; in Islam, he is *Allah*; he is *Ahura Mazda* for the Zoroastrians; *Jehovah* for the Jews; and the Father in Heaven for the Christians. Some of the scriptural names have a common connotation. For example, *Christos* is the Greek version of the word *Krishna*, the Hindu God. In fact, God has numerous names in every religion. It has also been said that although God's names are countless, His name is not known to anyone, not even to the gods. But it has also been said that God 'signed' His name on everything in creation. He is both immanent and transcendent; He takes every form in the universe, yet His form is inconceivable. A great exponent of *Bhakti Yoga* (the path of divine devotion), Chaitanya Mahaprabhu said that God has millions and millions of names, and because there is no difference between God's name and Himself, each one of these names has the same potency as God. Philosophers of all antiquity and cultures and civilizations have exhausted themselves in their description of their concept of God. For Seneca, God is the soul of the universe; for Spinoza, God and Nature are one; for Aristotle, God is not where we believe Him to be, He is in ourselves; for Hermes, all is full of God; for Eckhart, God is all and all is God; for Tolstoy, God cannot be recognized except in one's self; and for the Sufi saint Muhyiddin Ibn Arabi, all things subsist in Allah, much like the Upanishadic *Brahman*. The two forms of the Upanishadic *Brahman* are the formed and the unformed, the mortal and the immortal, the stationary and the moving, the actual and the yon.

While such were the hoary thoughts of our ancestors, H.G. Wells (*God: The Invisible King*, 1917) aptly summed up the modern man's perception of God and wrote that "God comes we know not whence, into the conflict of life. He works in men and through men. He is a spirit, a single spirit and a single person; he has begun and he will never end. He is the immortal part and leader of mankind. He has motives, he has characteristics, he has an aim. He is by our poor scales of measurement, boundless love, boundless courage, boundless generosity. He is thought and a steadfast will. He is our friend and brother and the light of the world."[21] Perhaps the practical human need for God was best captured by the French philosopher Voltaire who, especially in his sunset years, came to believe that a 'rewarding and avenging' God was essential to keep man on the moral path. A society of atheists can only subsist, he felt, if they are all philosophers and since that is not going to happen, he said famously, "If God did not exist, it would be necessary to invent him."[22] Some have tried to see God in Nature, in fact, as Nature itself. Some of our greatest thinkers like Spinoza and scientists of earlier centuries — Michael Faraday, for instance — believed that all natural laws are the principles upon which God designs and controls His universe. Thoreau said his profession was to 'always find God in Nature'. The debate about where we are posited relative to God covers a wide spectrum of human knowledge — axiological, theological, ontological, cosmological, historical, and practical. Much of religion, and increasingly of science too, boils down to our, one might say, stormy, relationship with God. It varies from the sublime to the absurd, from silly to sacrilegious. Some have likened it to the relationship between a dead father and his surviving off-spring. Others have argued that God once 'lived' but 'died' several millenniums ago, and that it is his spirit that continues to control the affairs of the planetary system, just as some believe that the souls of one's departed ancestors continue to play a leading role in their lives. Setting aside such inanity, the truth is that 'knowing God' has been man's mandate for ages. It is at once deemed the most difficult and the easiest. It is the most difficult with a consciousness that is corrupted. It is the easiest with a cleansed consciousness. Meister Eckhart said that no man desires anything so eagerly as God desires to bring men to the knowledge of Himself. In its true depth, it defines us, more than Him. Human thought, from the primal days to this millennium, has always been ambivalent and paradoxical about the 'phenomenon of God'. And it also starkly highlights, perhaps more than anything else, how limited, restricted and suffocating, so utterly banal, our imagination and vision are. We envision Him to be what the best of us wants to be: superman, mighty, unfailingly kind, unquestioningly responsive to what anyone asks. We want God to at once manifest Himself to us whenever we call upon Him; that His sole business is to help us out. We want Him to be worthy of our faith and give His glimpses; solid, concrete, and tangible, not vague visions. We want Him to measure up to higher standards than what we ourselves practice; all because He is God and we are human. Man's basic nature is to seek that which transcends his own existence; he worships that which is supremely superhuman, that which has a sense of the miraculous — and God fits that bill. God's grace, that is, if He exists, we think, is our natural right, and to give it to us is His reason for being God, forgetting that what is grace is not given freely or under compulsion; it is discretionary. We want to prove or disprove God by His epistemic need and necessity. That is, if we think we can 'explain' everything — the origin and design of the universe, the origin of living beings, the advent of man, etc. — He does not have to exist and therefore He does not exist, and if He did at some point, now that we know better, He should do what we do in such circumstances: wither away and vanish! We can only visualize God as utterly incomprehensible or wholly utilitarian, all-powerful or ineffective, an unsolvable mystery or the outpourings of what Henry Fielding and Edward Gibbon called 'amiable weaknesses of human nature'. The real mystery is not God; it is the mind and its relationship to God: is God the creation of our mind, or is God the creator of the mind? And then the troubling thought: this ambiguity about God, does this have a divine purpose and if somehow, sometime, it finally ends, then what? How would that affect human behavior and mindset?

God does exist — even denial is a kind of effervescent existence. The real problem is that in either case — affirmation or absence — it does not seem to make any moral difference to our earthly behavior. In today's world, a 'believer' can be as ruthless as a non-believer; and an intellectual denial of a Scriptural God of 'rewards and punishments' need not necessarily mean callousness. Our mind disconnects religious ritual and ethical conduct, devotion and behavior. It makes us 'feel good' about our faith in God but does not let us 'be good' in our relations with other humans. The problem is that the scriptures enjoin us to both love and fear God but that is a difficult mix. We are supposed to love Him for what He is, and fear Him for what we are. In the Quran, Allah repeatedly instructs and warns "fear only Allah", or "those who fear Allah are the fortunate ones." The Sikh scripture *Guru Granth Sahib* says that, without the fear of God everything, all that is fashioned is false. The Bible (*Proverbs 1:7*) says that the fear of the Lord is the beginning of knowledge: Fear is generally considered a negative emotion and, if that is so, why does God tell us to fear Him? The answer to that has less to do with God and more to do with men. First, we love God for what He is and fear Him for what we are. Second, fear is not always negative; indeed fear keeps us alive; we should not fear to fear. Third, what we fear most is not the action but its consequences; we fear God because He knows everything, even our darkest thoughts, and thoughts too have a consequence. Lastly, by fearing God, we are rid of the fear of everyone else and everything else. That is why fear of God has been called a transformative power. At the back of it all is the tacit assumption that God is a key player in human destiny, but the perception of how exactly God becomes involved in human history and what direction the ultimate course of humanity will take under His watchful eye, varies considerably from one religion to another. But even God must come through the gate of the human mind, and by the time he comes through, God Himself is transformed; the mind attaches to Him what it *wants* to see in Him. Like everything else in the human realm, the mind wants to 'own' God, and in so doing, it disconnects devotion to God from behavior that God expressly forbids. We forget that what we make ourselves, what we become is what God cares and wants. If we are reverential to Him and scornful to fellow-men it pleases him not. The real mystery of God is not so much about his true identity or whether he is inherently comprehensible or incomprehensible, or even if he is with form (*saguna*) or without form (*nirguna*), but about His *leelas*, a Sanskrit term which means the play or ways of God. We might be desirous of knowing, in the words of Stephen Hawking the 'mind of God' or as Einstein described 'His thoughts'; great saints and *rishis* have wrestled with this question. When they are face to face with Him, they do not ask questions or try to probe his mind; they surrender.

The scriptural vision of the inherent interplay between God and man has been a subject of many disquisitions and expositions. In summary, it could be broadly divided into three belief systems: (1) we are not God, but He is closer than the closest; (2) we are part of God, like the sparks flying from a hot iron rod, or the reflections of the same light on water in myriad pots; and (3) we are 'God', not '*a* god'; nothing added, nothing taken and nothing else.

In Vedantic terms, the first system is called *Dualism*, the second qualifies as *Monism*, and the third is *Advaita*. And then we have the two of the four *Mahavakyas*, great axioms, of the Upanishads: *Aham brahmasmi* (I am God); *Tatvamasi* (Thou art that), where 'that' refers to the *Brahman*, the Supreme all-encompassing Consciousness, the subtle Entity which forms the essence of all universe. This maxim comes from an Upanishadic story, in which the rishi Uddalaka asks his son Svetaketu to cut open a fruit plucked from a tree. When asked what he can see inside, Svetaketu replies, 'I see small seeds'. Uddalaka then tells his son to break open one seed, and asks, 'What do you see inside?' Svetaketu obviously replies, 'I see nothing'. Uddalaka then gives the explanation: 'In that Nothing which you cannot see is the power of the whole of that tree, the whole of life comes from that nothing; the gross, which is visible, is the effect, the cause of which is the subtlest essence; at the heart of that hidden mystery is *thou art that.'* When one is referring to oneself, one uses the first axiom and when referring to another person, the second. The essence, however, of '*I*', '*you*', '*they*', '*the world*' is the same. The great Sri Adi Shankara, the principal exponent of the Advaitic school of thought of Hinduism wrote, '*Brahma satyam jagat mithya, jivo brahmaiva naparah*' — Brahman is the only truth, the world is an illusion, and there is ultimately no difference between Brahman and the individual self. According to the Upanishads, the very purpose of human birth is God-realization, which is also called Self-realization and is tantamount to liberation from the cycle of birth and death. That possibility or privilege is allotted only to a human being, not to any other creature as per this scripture.

Ramana Maharshi, perhaps the greatest 20th century exponent of the *Advaita* philosophy, said, "I say the Self is not reached. You are the Self; you are already That."[23] In other words, Ramana erased the qualification 'ultimately' and conceptually merged the self with the *Brahman*. The claim that 'I am nothing but God' might appear as the ultimate arrogance but, on deeper reflection, it is the mark of ultimate humility. In any other self-identification such as 'I am the servant of God' or 'I am a reflection of God', two identities are assumed — the '*I*' and the *God*, in that order. In the affirmation "I am God', there is only one God; everything else, most of all, the ego, vanishes. With that disappearance, the only barrier between man and God crumbles. While God is always man, man becomes God once that barrier crumbles. It has also been said that everyone has the intrinsic knowledge of his divinity; it is overshadowed by the mind and by the act of its incessant thinking, through which we have to identify ourselves. But to be able to 'feel' that way, to transcend the mind, one must ascend to a higher level of consciousness and a deeper plateau of awareness. 'God' is not a matter of discovery, something to be found hidden somewhere in a cave in the cosmos. It is not also a question of His existence or absence; that issue cannot be conclusively settled because we cannot, within the parameters of human intelligence, either demonstrate God as either a logical contradiction or a reasonable probability. It is one of awareness within. And it is how we apply that awareness to everyday existence. One of the commonly attributed characteristics of God is omniscience, also called *sarvantaryami* in Sanskrit. The *Atharva Veda* describes the all-seeing Lord Varuna, the god of the 'celestial ocean', on these lines: 'the great guardian among these (gods) sees as if from anear. He that thinketh he is moving stealthily — all this the gods know. If a man stands, walks, or sneaks about, if he goes slinking away, if he goes into his hiding-place; if two persons sit together and scheme, king Varuna is there as a third, and knows it.'[24] The *Kathopanishad* says that God regulates all souls during all states, of being awake, in a dream and in deep sleep, and even after death and liberation. The Vedas have described God, as quoted by Swami Vivekananda in his famous address to the *World Parliament of Religions* (1893), as the One "by whose command the wind blows, the fire burns, the clouds rain and death stalks upon the earth."[25] Tolstoy said that, "Man in order to be really a man must conceive the idea of God in himself."[26] In mystical terms, it is referred to as 'to reduce oneself to Oneness'. It has often been said that not even a blade of grass moves without divine will. Emily Bronte wrote in her poem *No Coward Soul is Mine*, "O God within my breast. Almighty, ever-present Deity!"[27] Sri Aurobindo wrote, "Thou who pervadest all the worlds below, Yet sitst above, Master of all who work and rule and know, Servant of Love! Thou who disdainest not the worm to be, Nor even the clod, Therefore we know by that humility, That thou art God."[28]

With the level of consciousness few have to truly relate to maxims like 'Thou art that', the great majority of humans believe in something, some entity, some force, some higher and superior or supernatural or extraterrestrial phenomenon. The world has always had a spectrum of skeptics, agnostics and atheists, some of them of high intellect. Those who profess religious agnosticism argue that, 'we know neither a Creator nor have knowledge about one. If there is a God, we know it not.'[29] They say that the very idea of God contradicts the theories of Big Bang and evolution. Some have pronounced the death of God for a whole lot of reasons, from ineffectiveness to redundancy. They fault Him for sin and suffering on Earth, for the 'triumph' of evil and the vulnerability of virtue. The imminence of the death of God has also been predicted by the likes of Nietzsche — 'God is dead. God remains dead. And we have killed him' — to Thomas Altizer, a professor of religion, who wrote, "We must recognize that the death of God is a historical event: God has died in our time, in our history, in our existence."[30] In the same context in which Nietzsche's Madman announced the divine death, he also wrote of 'the noise of gravediggers burying God' and of 'divine decomposition'. Paul Tillich, the German-American protestant theologian and an avowed anti-supernaturalist, said that the only non-symbolic statement that could be made about God was that He was being Himself, since He is beyond essence and existence; therefore, to argue that God exists is to deny Him. To say that God has died is to say that He has ceased to exist as a transcendent, supernatural being and has become fully immanent in the world, heralding an essential identity between the human and the divine. Such a 'denial' is, in effect, an affirmation close to *Advaitic* philosophy. Just as we deny God because He did not, for instance, stop the Holocaust, God too can abandon us for disobeying every command of His. He is alive but we have erased Him from our canvas by the way we live; and the chief instrument of that 'killing' is by the way we have incorporated into our lives that body of knowledge that claims to be His direct word — religion. But God is too big for any one religion — or religion itself; or any book or word, even His own. And between His 'Word' and ours, something has terribly gone wrong. Or is it part of divine dispensation or displeasure? In the Bible, it is said "Therefore, as I live, saith the Lord God, I will prepare thee unto blood, and blood shall pursue thee: sith thou hast not hated blood, even blood shall pursue thee" (*Ezekiel, 35:6*). Religions continue to inspire the noblest of our passions and aspirations; yet they can turn demonic and betray our inhumanness when our capacity for self-transcendence yields to malice and violence. Religious myth and ritual could then be marshaled to energize and rationalize the destructive choices and actions. And we seem to carry, within us, a far lesser sense of shame and guilt about 'divine' murders and massacres, than those due to other causes. Faith-empowered mayhem and martyrdom has come to mean holy bloodletting. Any pangs of crisis of faith seem, at best, fleeting. After all, we are doing all that for 'His sake', how can *He* object and find fault with us? One could well argue that our perception of the divine is also not immune to inherent human debauchery, or that, had it not been for the 'fear of God', man might have been a man-eater on the prowl.

Meanwhile, God seems quite happy to let us quibble and quarrel, unwilling or unable to set the record straight. Once again, we are left guessing the 'mind of God'. In his book *And Man Created God* (2000), George Mynchenberg argues: 'if there is a God, we know it not', and that the creation of God became necessary to explain things man could not explain any other way. The Scottish critic William Archer said, "I suggest that the anthropomorphic god-idea is not a harmless infirmity of human thought, but a very noxious fallacy, which is largely responsible for the calamities the world is at present enduring".[31] The famous science-fiction author Arthur Clarke wrote, "It may be that our role on this planet is not to worship God, but to create him."[32] Nietzsche asked, "Which is it, is man one of God's blunders or is God one of man's?"[33] American philosopher George Santayana (*The Life of Reason*, 1905) wrote, "That fear first created the gods is perhaps as true as anything so brief could be on so great a subject."[34] Stephen Hawking identified belief in God with a deficiency in mathematics. Does that solve the mystery why so many believe in God, deficient as most people are in mathematics! But it is, after all, mathematics that appears to resolve the puzzle about Providence. Physicist Stephen Unwin, in his book *The Probability of God* (2003), claimed that by applying a mathematical equation developed over 200 years ago by philosopher Thomas Bayes, and the basic rules of the Probability Theory, he had 'subjectively' calculated that there is 67 percent mathematical probability that God exists. That subjectivity and the 33 percent deficit were more than sufficient for skeptics like Michael Shermer and Richard Dawkins to twist the 'probability proof' and argue that God, of the kind we usually allude to, does not exist. And then we have Mark Hamilton who said that man will soon become *God-Man*, a mind-driven super-intelligent being, a magic blend of God and Man; one could even say the best of both. In our desperation to 'find God' we are leaving no stone unturned, no means unexplored, sacred or sexual. New Age gurus like Ken Wilber and David Deida have written books on 'finding God through Sex' and claimed that one can deepen the relationship between man and God and achieve oneness with God 'through waves of deep sex', of 'lovemaking as transcendent of human condition' and of 'awakening the One of spirit through two of the flesh'. It is easy to be judgmental and denounce them as drivel, but then that kind of 'sex' could be fundamentally different from the one we crave for.

By and large, we cannot any longer refrain from the 'rational' inference that man has preferred, when the chips are down, the world of desire and decadence to the world of temperance and divinity. The disconnection between belief and behavior which defines the human condition extends to the question of God; we 'believe' in God but behave abominably. Both belief and disbelief have become delusions, to be selectively used or misused. The two questions asked by the Greek Sophist Antiphon (5th century BCE) are still relevant: Which actions are right or wrong? Why should one perform right actions, and avoid the wrong ones? Neither the fear of society, instilled by the State, nor the fear of God, which someone like the American author Neale Walsch ascribed to religion, have proved equal to the task of keeping man tied to his moral moorings. Someone have quipped that maybe it is time to give up on religion and go back to God — or God in another man! Another reality we must face up to is that, religion cannot any longer ensure morality, which for long has been closely intertwined. Whether or not religion is needed for morality, today's reality is that religion seems to evoke brazen behavior in the minds of some of its zealots. We must find new bearings, a new road map, so to speak, in our consciousness to keep man on the moral track independent of fear or favor of society or God, to be thoughtful and sensitive to a fellow man, to go to the aid of someone in distress and, above all, to avoid insulting and injuring, in word or in deed, any living being, particularly those who are in no position to return the 'favor'. In the best of times, in the previous *yugas* or ages when being moral required very little effort, this was easy and 'natural'. We are living at a time and in a world in which every unspeakable horror is overtaken the very next day by something more horrific. American author Pearl Buck (*The Good Earth*, 1931) wrote that 'when men destroy their old gods, they will find new ones to take their place.[35] Our new gods are money, power, intellect, and technology.

The irony is that most people say God is Almighty, omnipotent and the cosmic creator, sustainer and destroyer, but they still think that *their* God needs their 'help' to defend Himself against the followers of 'another God.' They say God is everywhere and in all forms of life, and yet they massacre fellow humans to build a temple or a mosque at a specific spot. And they aver that those who do not believe in 'their God' are 'virtual atheists'. Moreover, the followers are not only convinced that such 'atheists' will go to hell, but assume that it is their religious duty to hasten that 'going'! An avowed 'rationalist' would ask, omnipotent and omniscient that God is, He should have known what He was going to get by creating a creature like man. Einstein once asked, "How much choice did God have in constructing the universe?"[36] We could also add: 'and in making man?' Does He now regret it, looking at the mess men have made and the menace they have become? An enchanting theological question is: does God have needs that man alone, with his vanity and vulnerabilities, pride and ego, can meet? Is God lonely and even incomplete without the evil that man alone is capable of? All these questions and concepts of old God, new God, and tomorrow's God, and why God is tolerant to evil are rooted in the premise that God is meant for man and any human failure is a divine deficiency. Echoing the ancient Greek philosopher Epicurus, man wants to put God in the dock by saying that if He can prevent evil but is not able to, then He is not omnipotent; if He is able to but not willing, then He is not benevolent; if He is both able and willing, then why does evil have its way on Earth? And if He is neither able nor willing, then He is not God. The verdict, in this line of thought is that God is a human creation to neutralize the imperfections inherent in the human condition. That 'logic', that 'verdict' illustrates our innate disposition to make God one of 'us', subject to our 'cause and effect' condition, bound by human morality. In other words we 'know' God just as we know any other external object. At a more practical level, our gods, as George Santayana said, are fashioned as reflections of our image and to be servants of our interests. If we adopt the Upanishadic concept of *Brahman*, the all-embracing, all-encompassing, all-inclusive God, without which nothing else is, this agony and anguish would vanish. The Upanishads also proclaim *Aham Brahmasmi*: I am *Brahman*, the all-encompassing Almighty. To attain that level of consciousness, one must see everything and everybody, not simply as manifestations of God, but as God. If one thinks of oneself as God and everyone else as man, or worse still as 'necessary nuisance', one would be making a mockery of that sacred maxim. The sage Ramakrishna, perhaps one of the most evolved modern-day spiritual souls, clarified modern man's predicament with his usual candor and simplicity. He compared modern man to the rishis who attained that state of consciousness, by saying, "But in *Kali Yuga*, the life of a man depends entirely on food. How can he have the consciousness that *Brahman* alone is real and the world illusory? In the Kali Yuga, it is difficult to have the feeling 'I am not the body, I am not the mind. I am not the twenty-four cosmic principles. I am beyond pleasure and pain. I am above disease and grief, old age and death. However you may reason and argue, the feeling that the body is identical with the soul will somehow crop from an unexpected quarter. I never feel like saying 'I am Brahman.' I say 'Thou art my Lord and I am Thy servant'."[37] If a truly great spiritual soul like Ramakrishna felt that way, who are we to imagine we are divine essence? As for being human, according to *Gurbani*, the Sikh scripture, one is not qualified to be called a human being just because he is born in a human form, and deprived of the divine understanding, people become beasts and demons.[38]

We cannot get a fix on the 'phenomenon' or the paradox and so we try all kinds of permutations and combinations to pin it down within the confines of our thought. As David Shiang puts it, "the question of God is ultimately one of knowledge vs. ignorance; not faith vs. reason" (*God Does Not Play Dice*, 2008). The problem is that we want to be 'logical' about something that is conceptually beyond our thinking; we want to apply 'facts' which are no more than conjectures and unsupported assumptions to 'prove' divine non-existence or incompetence. That confusion is best exemplified by our intellectual assumption that Darwinian natural selection conceptually and logically negates God, that it offers stellar proof of atheism. In the words of Richard Dawkins, that it enabled man to be 'an intellectually fulfilled atheist'. The year 2009 happened to be both the 200th birth anniversary of Darwin as well as the 150th year of publication of his work *The Origin of the Species*, which has been hailed by the *National Geographic* magazine (February, 2009) as the 'the most incendiary book in the history of science'. It is interesting to learn from a recent book by Adrian Desmond and James Moore (*Darwin's Sacred Cause*, 2009) that the 'sacred cause' that imbued Darwin to discover evolution was emancipation and abolishing of slavery, which he considered a 'sin'. The words 'sacred' and 'sin' inevitably drag us toward divinity. Evolution and natural selection are simply processes; but who is the 'Engineer' who is controlling the process, the conductor controlling the orchestra? Darwin's theory assumes the existence of something we call replicators; but who is the replicator and the regulator? We think that God must create everything the way we produce, but if we can use instruments and techniques in the laboratory, why cannot God do so in the divine laboratory? As Francis Collins, who led the Human Genome project puts it, "If God, who is all powerful and who is not limited by space and time, chose to use the mechanism of evolution to create you and me, who are we to say that wasn't an absolutely elegant plan? And if God has now given us the intelligence and the opportunity to discover his methods that is something to celebrate."[39] In a similar vein, Michael Behe, professor of biochemistry asks: 'If he wanted to make it [life] by the playing out of natural law, then who were we to object?' It is a measure of the human mind that thinks that it is not possible to believe both in God and evolution, and that the mechanism of creation excludes random mutation and natural selection. Some thinkers have tried to use everyday analogies to explain creation. The British philosopher William Paley (*Natural Theology*, 1803), for example, likened the universe to a watch, arguing that if we were to discover a watch in the natural environment then, due to its order, complexity, and purpose, we would rightly infer that it was the work of an intelligent designer; these features are the marks of a design. The universe, Paley argued, exhibits the same order, complexity, and purpose, and so it too can be seen to have been produced by a Creator. In the book *Signature in the Cell* (2009), Stephen Meyer exposes the increasingly evident brittleness of materialist explanations of life's origins and argues that the digital code embedded in the DNA points inexorably to a designing intelligence and addresses the question that Darwin's theory of natural selection did not: how did the very first life begin? Meyer does not necessarily pitch for a God as the catalytic agent, but contends that such an agent is the most likely cause of the specified information in the double helix and in the information processing systems of the cell. Although some question the premise that complexity by itself cannot demonstrate intent, and rhetorically ask 'who designed the designer?', new discoveries are tilting the scientific scales in favor of transcendental Intelligent Design (ID) as the only rational — and probable and most likely — explanation.

Despite the history of animosity between religions and the scientific skeptics, the good thing now is that, coupled with growing intellectual interest in myth, mythology, and occultism, the spiritual traditions of the world are engaged in a serious conversation with one another, without claiming to be the only path to the Truth, in a way they never were before, and that is bound to create a climate of clarity and consensus. Albeit the fact that it is still fragile, there is a worldwide ecumenism now, a momentum towards understanding other traditions because they are no longer 'out there,' far away; they are us. That gives us hope. But we still have to face the problems of a world with all-but-dissolved-divinity, and religions that continue to be deeply distrustful of each other.

Free will, Fate, and Surrender

In such a climate of consciousness, we are both polarized and paralyzed and do not know how to strike the right balance between human will and divine omnipotence. What we face everyday are lives out of control, events out of control, joy and happiness always a stretch away, our loved ones in despair.

It all seems so 'unfair'. And we wonder, is there such a thing as destiny oblivious to human will and effort? Is it merely the name we assign to that legion of strong forces that we ourselves have set in motion, a net consisting of our accumulated motives, desires, and actions from out of the past, immediate or distant? And 'why me?' Faith and free will: which one is the determinant and a compulsive catalyst in human life? Is man's fate man's choice or God's choice? Is fate a matter of fatalism and free will of free choice? Does our free will make redundant the concept of predestination? Is *Prarabdha karma* fate or free will? Is free will God's gift to man or is it also an illusion? Does what we believe really have the power to change the forces affecting our life? Is faith the bridge between free will and fate? Is surrender, to God (through free will) and to man (by force), the only way out? The function of fate or the element of chance in the universe is a theme that runs from ancient to modern times, through all religions and all cultures. Whether man is the architect of his own fate, or fate is the arbiter of his destiny, has long been argued about. The range of beliefs vary all the way from anointing fate as the supreme force on earth, to what the ancient Indian text *Yoga Vasistha* describes as 'fashioned by fools'. Much of scientific supposition often tends towards a rigid, mechanical interpretation of the laws of nature based on very narrow mathematical principles; and we attempt to apply the same rigid scheme to human life. Some have sought to represent nature as a system of linked causes and effects which, once started (who knows how?), goes on automatically like a machine without the interposition of any influences from outside the system. In spiritual terms, we choose the reasons and lessons for a particular incarnation before we are born. While on earth our spiritual memory is clouded from all but the most enlightened, to prevent it from distracting us from the fulfillment of our purpose in life. We have the free will necessary for us to gain the experience we came for. We are presented with the circumstances that give us opportunities to learn our chosen lessons. Our free will may avoid these lessons, in which case we will continue to be presented with conditions suitable for the fulfillment of our chosen purpose. Thus, we have free will throughout our time here. The Islamic saint Hazrat Ali Murtaza, a companion of Prophet Muhammad, when asked to differentiate free will and fate, replied that he could lift his one foot from earth to keep standing out of his free will, but if he lifted the second foot, he would fall down. It means that man has some powers to exercise his free will, though Nature does not allow him to do everything out of his free will. While we have the power of choice on certain matters, we do not have control over issues such as the selection of life, death, children, parents, fame, etc.

Fate is a fact of life; indeed, life itself is fated. The ancient Indian poet Bharthari wrote (*Satakatraya*) that no hand can ever efface fate's sentence written on the brow; and 'whom fate has chosen to persecute; finds every refuge in vain' (*The Praise of Destiny*). Shakespeare compared fate to the wind and tide that cannot be resisted. Sherlock Holmes once told Watson, when we hear the steps on the stair walking into our life, and we know not whether for good or ill, they are of fate. Not a day passes in life without our coming face to face with one central fact of earthly existence: we bring to bear no decisive control over the myriad things we do in life; everything seems so random, so senseless, and so absurd. The short name for that is fate. We all know that things happen with or without our consent; we know that things have consequences, some to our liking and some to our dismay; yet we desire to deceive fate and maneuver the consequences to our advantage. When things go right we credit them to our effort; when they do not, we blame it on fate. We beseech God to rescue us when we are in trouble wrought by our own fate, putting Him in a quandary, being asked to violate his own law that for everything there is a sequel. Even the gods, it is said, are not immune to the will of fate, *vidhi*, as it is called in Sanskrit. Divine avatars too could not escape that law; indeed they did not make an attempt to escape by drawing upon the powers of divinity. This unpredictability, this brittleness, the uncertainty of the next moment, the disconnection between the sequences of events, seems to be increasing, not diminishing, despite our vastly expanded knowledge of the universe and our supposed 'conquest' of Nature.

Science too has traveled a good distance in trying to understand the determinants of human life. It has moved from Newton's mechanistic 'clockwork' universe, through Einstein's discovery that neither time nor space are as we perceive them to be, to quantum physics, that far from following the principles of cause and effect, reality at its most foundational level is indeterministic. The physicist Freeman Dyson recently wrote, "the more I examine the universe and the details of its architecture, the more evidence I find that the universe in some sense knew we were coming". And Paul Davies, who in the past had denied divine existence, wrote, "there is something going on behind it all". If we are 'superbly placed in the right sort of solar system, in the right place, in the right sort of galaxy, at the right time to be able to study the rest of the universe, then who ensured it? But all through and since the inception of human thought, whether it is free will or fate or faith or destiny or knowledge of God or the ways of Nature, the aim has always been to 'control'. The irony is that we have 'control' in some measure, but not over the intended consequences. Indeed, our very effort to acquire control over Nature and life seems to be having the opposite effect. Even fate itself seems fated; it too has no control over its delivery and disposition. The reality of life is that, nothing else is as dissimilar, as divergent and as disparate as fate; all other differences, physiological, biological, racial are no match for fate. The same set of circumstances or the same configurations appear to yield different results for different individuals. We cannot even tell how much of what we imagine as human will or effort is not fate in disguise. There is a difference between the 'irremediable event' and how we react to it. They are part of the same, the two sides of the same coin. Charles Swindoll wrote that life is 10 percent of what actually happens to us, and 90 percent of how we react to it. One can quibble with the percentages, but there is little doubt that our attitude or the mindset we bring to bear has much to do with how an event affects us. But some will argue that that our reaction itself is part of our predetermined fate.

While we can debate how deterministic fate is in life, we all agree that our final fate is death, at least as of now. It is said that when the gods created man, they assigned death to man and kept life to themselves. What we humans call life is but the process of dying and a prelude to death, and how we prepare for the process is the call of manhood; and the gods must be laughing at our desperate attempts to wiggle out of it. Like Shakespeare's Romeo we are all 'Fortune's fools'. An English proverb says that 'he who is fated to be hanged shall never be drowned'. As the French proverb goes, you often meet your fate on the road you take to avoid it. No matter how deep we dig into the bowels of Nature, and advance in narrowing the possibilities and probabilities of life, we always run up against indeterminate contingencies outside the context under inquiry and laws of casualty. That raises the troubling question: is human effort really a waste of effort? Some say that what we call 'effort' is itself the divine will at play, and that we are simply the medium of a certain action that has to be done at a certain time and at a certain place on earth. According to the *karma* theory, the present effort is a past consequence; we reap the fruits, good or bad, of our past actions, which means that while we can influence our future life through our present effort, the present fate cannot be changed. Others say, as it is said in the *Yoga Vasistha*, that "without doubt a former fault is extinguished by the current good qualities."[40] The fact is there will never be a definitive conclusion, and we cannot discern whether fate has a life of its own or it is subjective insufficiency of human knowledge, or if it is a divine instrument to maintain order. Indeterminism or fate or fortune or chance seems ingrained in the complexity of human life. And every culture has tried to grapple with it in multiple ways. The Romans, for example, worshipped it as a deity. Fortune is also compared to a wheel. In actuality, much of human effort is to get out of fate's cruel grasp and make life profitable, productive, and pleasant. Even accepting grudgingly that many things in life could go wrong and that often, as Murphy's law postulates, when things can go wrong they will go wrong, we still want to mitigate the adverse effect by the search for some kind of a 'middle path', in which fate may determine what will be in one's life but, how that actualizes becomes a matter of man's own choice.

We all may say, at a moment of helpless exasperation, 'such is life' or 'life is unfair', but as the French author La Rochefoucauld puts it wittily, but truly, "All of us have sufficient fortitude to bear the misfortunes of others."[41] While most people will concur that fate or destiny does have a role to play in life, what is open to debate is whether it is frozen or flexible, and how much of it is amenable to human effort? In fact, all life is, to use a popular phrase, to bend fate 'like Beckham' to our will, and make destiny dance to our tunes. Phrases like 'it is my fate', 'fate of earth', 'human destiny' and 'designs of destiny' have become clichés. Cutting across cultures and continents and up and down the ages, there have always been two kinds of people: those who believe in 'letting things happen' and those who believe in 'making things happen'. The subtle difference between the two, notwithstanding, the underlying idea is some sort of predetermination, absence of choice, and the presence of a power that determines the outcome of an event before it occurs. The difference implies some sort of negation or dilution of another frequently used term 'free will', which, in its absolute sense, means that we are the masters of our fate with total control over our actions and their consequences. Although the existence of free will is the foundation of science and it implies that through our actions we can control the future, many great scientists like Einstein ('*I am a determinist; I do not believe in free will*') have supported the notion that we cannot affect the future any more than we can change the past. David Shiang, in his book *God Does Not Play Dice*, says that the solution to the free will problem can be summed up in five simple words: you cannot affect the future; he goes on, "our future may be 'before us' and not yet traveled but the road is already designed". According to the *Advaita* philosophy, the 'problem' arises because we, under the spell of '*maya*', fail to differentiate between reality and appearance. We will never be in a position to say what *really* is or what *really* happens, but we can only say what will be observed in any specific individual case. Any *reality* is nothing more than that. "For there to be fate, there would have to be someone to whom separate things could happen or who could observe other things happening in some predetermined manner. For there to be free will, there would have to be someone who could choose between separate things. All these ways of thinking belong to the illusory world of duality."[42] In the present context, in which appearance is the only reality that we know, the important issue is how fate and free will impinge on human behavior and their impact on the future of the species. The way man is behaving, so irrational, suicidal, and destructive, makes us believe that we are simply playing out our fate according to the directions of our destiny. Between the two 'absolutes' of fate and free will, some settle for the middle ground: that is, the conviction that there are external forces that influence, if not determine, our individual and collective lives; but it leaves a lot of room and scope for our will and wisdom to make our choices and pave our passage into the posthuman future. We do feel overwhelmed by forces that apparently defy our decisions and flout our control and yet we constantly exercise choices that lead to consequences which again are not always what we intended to yield. The apparent contrasts of chaos and cosmos, chance and cause, accident and purpose, order and disorder mark much of human life. Man has long bemoaned the vagaries of *vidhi* (destiny) or the fickleness of fate for apparently harassing good men and favoring evil ones. Some like

Saint Augustine opined that fate *is* God's will, and Greek tragedy viewed it as a deterministic power that ruled humans and even the gods.

Both logic and prudence argue in favor of the 'middle' course; that is, let fate play its games but do your utmost to spice it to your taste. Translated into theological terms, it is tantamount to believing in divine omnipotence and omnipresence, but behaving as if human effort can make a decisive difference. And since every effort has a consequence we should ensure that that consequence is positive and beneficial to others. We have no other rational alternative except absolute inaction or absolute anarchy. Then, we come to the practical question. If we can make a difference with our behavior, what should we do to improve the odds in our favor and to better the destiny of the species? One view is that by assessing the way we manage our past and present, we can make reasonable assumptions about our future. It has also been said that fate is the outcome of the past, and free will, that of the present.[43] H.P. Blavatsky stated that the "destiny of every man and the birth of every child, whose life is already traced in the Astral Light — not fatalistically, but only because the future, like the past, is ever alive in the present".[44] Setting aside for a moment the question of divine will, we are left with two 'moral aims' related to how we behave towards others. The greatest good to the greatest numbers might not always be the answer but it is still the closest. A close second could be non-injury to fellow humans, if not to life, in thought, word, and deed. We must not forget, not even for a moment, that all three are postscripts of the past and postcards of the future. And their fall out impacts other people, particularly the defenseless. While thought has a subtle effect, word creates a cascading context, but human deeds directly determine human destiny. The Upanishads underlined the virtue in one's own actions, "As a man acts, so does he become. A man of good deeds becomes good; a man of evil deeds becomes evil. A man becomes pure through pure deeds; impure through impure deeds."[45] If these two principles, greatest good and non-injury, motivate human effort, then we might stand a fair chance of deserving divine grace. Jainism gives more importance to self-effort or *purushartha* than even fate or *karma*. The scriptures also highlight the importance of divine grace and mercy as indispensable to help us navigate in the turbulent waters of human life. Many saints have welcomed what is fated as divine grace, but most mortals pray for grace to spare them from the vagaries of fate.

We forget the fact that the fate we bemoan is the fate we have made for ourselves through the continuum of our thoughts, words, and actions; we create fate every day, nay every minute, we live by our behavior. Our fate is our fortune. The principle we apply to human interaction, that there is no action without consequence, that we must take responsibility for our actions, we do not apply to life as a whole. Down the ages, we have put fate outside the vortex of our actions. The belief that the 'force of destiny' always seems to outwit human ingenuity is ingrained in human consciousness, and that theme has been the stuff of mythology and great works like Sophocles's *Oedipus Rex*, Spanish poet Duque de Rivas' play *Don Álvaro* that the great Italian composer Francesco Verdi transformed into *La Forza del Destino* ('The Force of Destiny'), Thornton Wilder's *The Bridge of San Luis Rey*, and Shakespeare's *Macbeth*. The same theme occurs in the Indian epic Mahabharata, in which Yudhisthira, the personification of *dharma* or righteousness, succumbs to the temptation of playing the game of dice twice and, losing his kingdom, gets banished to the forest. In all these works, foreknowledge or forewarnings could not prevent the inevitable fate. In one sense, it is a tussle for control between the past and present, and the present and future. Emerson said that "Fate is nothing but the deeds committed in a prior state of existence."[46]

God certainly can do what he wishes, but if he injects Himself into our lives whenever *we* want Him to, then will He be undermining His own greatest gift to man — freedom and free will — that make, or rather are supposed to make man a free moral agent? That kind of thinking is typical of human thought. As Arthur Schopenhauer noted, 'every man takes the limits of his own field of vision for the limits of the world' — and of God. On the contrary, one can also suggest that that mode of thinking does not diminish or negate the divine sovereignty or omnipotence. In fact it enhances; it shows God to be, in human terms, a true 'democrat'; not an autocrat or a tyrant of the Old Testament. God allows His subjects to have a lot of elbow room to lead responsible and responsive, autonomous lives without interference; and yet He retains the power to alleviate the woes of the righteous and to ensure that the balance between good over evil is not overly tilted towards evil. But the tricky question is the question Abraham asked Yahweh, the Jewish God, when he was told that God was planning to destroy the cities of Sodom and Gomorrah: Would God let good men be destroyed while slaying the evil ones and what are the minimum human numbers required for the species to escape divine wrath? The promised number was ten then; the actual, the righteous were three; what could it be now, for over 6 billion humans? What is the *tipping point* for divine destruction in this millennium? How much sin can we accumulate and how many sinners can we 'accommodate' amidst us without inviting divine intercession? Clearly, with freedom comes responsibility, and with choice comes consequences. Had it not been so, God could well have created robots programmed to be His unflinching devotees. With such 'humans', He could also have created a world of perfect peace and harmony, without wars and or violence. That is His dilemma and that is why He is so choosy and scarce in His dealings with us. And His behavior towards us is dependent on our behavior toward our fellow-humans and towards other animals. We cannot expect God to be pleased with us if we shower praises on him and pray fervently while we abuse and ill treat His other creations. We, personally and socially, do not know why we behave the way we do. The problem is that our behavior affects other people more than ourselves, and that affects their behavior and so on, eventually affecting the whole species. Our actions are so obviously irrational and opposed to self-interest that it seems that we are driven by forces we cannot comprehend. But we are rational enough to know that nothing is without consequence. The least of good deeds or the best of bad deeds can yield results proportionate to the deed. The Buddha advised his disciples, "Do not to overlook tiny good actions, thinking they are of no benefit; even tiny drops of water in the end will fill a huge vessel." At the same time, he cautioned his disciples: "Do not overlook negative actions merely because they are small; however small a spark may be, it can burn down a haystack as big as a mountain."[47] In Buddhism, perhaps more than in any other religion, intention decides whether *karma* is good or bad. We tend to forget that the most transformative force in the universe is God and that the very essence, meaning, and purpose of divinity is transcendent transformation. One can say that transformation is God and through the path of surrender we can, or rather God will, transform into His likeness. God is thus the means as well as the end, the way and the destination of scriptural transformation.

Absolute, unconditional, total self-surrender to God or *saranagati*, the scripture says, elicits the quickest response from the divine and absolves us from all sin. That is because in surrender, the ego dissolves the quickest, like salt in water or butter in sunlight. And once the ego goes, nothing stands and God comes home. Two examples are often offered from the Hindu epics to illustrate this insight. The one from Bhagavatham is the *Gajendra moksham*, literally the 'liberation of the king of elephants'. It is the story of a giant elephant caught by a crocodile in a pond and after exhausting all its strength, the elephant totally surrenders itself to the all-encompassing God, and the Almighty comes to its rescue and slays the crocodile. There are two conclusions one can draw from this story. One, the elephant fought the crocodile for a thousand years and exhausted all its strength before it sought divine help and God came down to its rescue. Two, none of its numerous companions, with whom the elephant was playing at that time came to help when their king was fighting for its life. The other example from the Mahabharata is the *Draupadi Vastra Haran*, the disrobing of Princess Draupadi, the wife of the five Pandava princes. When Yudhisthira loses his kingdom (and his brothers and finally his wife Draupadi) in a game of dice, and is banished to the forest, Draupadi is dishonored in the open court of King Dhritarashtra. Although some scholars say that she was dragged by her robe, and that no attempt was made to physically disrobe her (as a later addition to the narrative), it is commonly believed that such an attempt was indeed made, and that Lord Krishna came to her succor. Here too, Krishna comes to Draupadi's rescue not only after she exhausts all her strength, but also after giving up all external resistance, joining both her hands and totally surrendering to Him. And here too, no one, not even the great Bhishma and the guru Drona, who are present at the scene, come to her aid. The only person who speaks up is the *mantri* or the minister Vidura, a man of great wisdom and a *Nirahankaari* (man without arrogance), a *Nishchalamanaska* (man with a still mind), a man in whose name stands a whole moral treatise called *Vidura Neeti*. From these two anecdotes, five messages spring out for the common man: (1) evil begets evil; (2) no one can escape his or her destiny; (3) total surrender requires total effort; (4) when we truly need help, no one will respond and God alone will aid us in His own way; and 5) when seeking His help, we must give up the baggage and burden of our being, most of all, the ego.

According to the scriptures, absolute surrender to God is both the simplest and the most difficult state to attain. It is simple because its path is straight and smooth. All religions advocate this path of 'letting go'. The very root of the word *Islam* means peace and surrender. In Christianity, the holy cross is a symbol of spiritual surrender; the faithful are exhorted to make Jesus not only their savior but also their Lord. Buddhists are told to throw themselves into the abode of the Buddha. The concept of surrender, *saranagati* or *prapathi*, is also an integral part of *Bhakti Yoga* and an important aspect in Hinduism, particularly in *Vaishnavism*, in which it is extolled as a direct means of attaining *moksha* or liberation from the cycle of birth and rebirth. The Vedas, Upanishads, Puranas, and the epics also exhort devotees to take the path of *saranagati*. Saints such as Sri Adi Shankaracharya and Sri Madhvacharya gave immense importance to *saranagati*. This act of total self-surrender at the feet of the Supreme Being is hailed as the pinnacle of *bhakti yoga*. It does not require any pre-requisite rituals and can be followed by all, irrespective of caste, creed or sex.

The six ingredients of *saranagati* are rendered as: "*Anukulyasya sankalpa pratikulyasya varjanam*; *raksisyati iti visvaso goptrtve varanam tatha*; *atma-niksepa karpanye sas-vidha saranagati*." They translate as: (1) acceptance of that which is favorable to bhagavad-bhajana, or 'singing the praise of the Lord'; (2) remembrance of God; (3) rejection of that which is unfavorable; (4) firm faith in the Lord as one's protector; (5) deliberate acceptance of the Lord as one's guardian and nourisher; and (6) submission of the self, and humility. Saranagati is possible through both self-sacrifice (*Sadhana bhakti*) and self-forgetfulness (*Raga bhakti*). The former path is calculated, and the latter is automatic and continuous. In the Bhagavad Gita, Lord Krishna explicitly and repeatedly tells Arjuna and through him to all of us, "*Sarva-dharman parityajya mam ekam saranam vraja*; *aham tvam sarva-papebhyo moksayisyami ma sucah*" — 'let go all duties and take refuge or shelter in God, surrender everything; that God will project and absolve you from all sins'. The concept of 'surrender to God' is also there in the Bible.

Spiritual surrender is considered as the highest form of devotion or *bhakti*. If one can attain such a state, God, it is said, would respond in the form and way of our wish. Which means, in a sense, the roles would be reversed, between the devotee and the deity. In a culture where winning is lauded and surrender is equated with losing, or is considered a negative attribute, it is to finally 'give up' any hope of victory. We even say that 'surrender to evil' is itself evil. But in the divine context it becomes a supreme virtue, a sacred duty. And it is not even surrender *per se*; it has to be so absolute and unconditional that there is nothing left with you or in you or about you. In such a state, the difference and distance between the devotee and the divine crumbles. *Saranagati* is simply the annihilation of ego, and without the ego, the scriptures tell us, man is God, or rather what is inherent becomes manifest; it is like when a stone first becomes a statue in the hands of a sculptor, and then a god in the mind of a *bhakta* or devotee. The idea is that God is your creator, He is in you: indeed He is you, and life before divine surrender is life away from home; it is like a river finally finding peace in the ocean. When you surrender willfully, you take refuge in the protection of the Supreme, and when you take such a refuge you do not have to care for yourself. Even in everyday life, we so often feel relieved in surrender; then you do not have to fight anymore; you have no responsibility and the one you surrender to takes all responsibility. Then there is no conflict between our will and someone else's wish, between our ego and another person's or Force's power. After a time the mind realizes that surrendering causes less pain than resisting. In the case of God, in surrender you triumph; even achieve liberation.

But our mind is used to either control or subordination, it can only be a master or a slave; and it can effortlessly oscillate between the two. We surrender all the time to someone or something, for survival, or as an easy way out, and sometimes to stoop to conquer; there is an element of expediency, coercion, and force in all these actions. When it comes to God, we want to be the boss, we want him to be at our beck and call, respond without whimper to our every call for help. We would rather accept enforced surrender to another human, than willingly give up something we do not own to someone who is its rightful owner. It is based on the premise that everything — our life, property, our time on earth, our rights, our values — belongs to God, that we are only the trustees, and surrender is returning to the rightful owner when we feel we can no longer shoulder that responsibility. Spiritual surrender is only an ascent and evolution is no descent or defeat; it is finding God by removing the veil that separates. But it is difficult because it calls upon us to do the hardest thing in life: to shed our ego, the '*I*-identity'. But if man could do that or at least wholeheartedly make an attempt, then God might come calling and even become his *sarathi* or charioteer, as He did for Arjuna in the great battle at *Kurukshetra*, in the Mahabharata, or come to our doorstep and wait for our call, as He did for Pundarikaksha, a great devotee in Hindu mythology. But God will not bear arms and fight our battles. Just as Lord Krishna vowed that He would not even fight for Arjuna in Kurukshetra, and did not violate His vow even under extreme provocation when the great Bhishma seemed invincible on the battlefield. In our case too, we must fight our battles with our own arms, but when we finally surrender, our battle then becomes His battle. Which means that we should make human effort wholly human, and the result and outcome wholly divine.

God's existence, omnipotence or omnipresence is not irrelevant, but that does not diminish the potency of human effort. It is man's malevolence that is the issue. Just as gravity is a reality whether one believes in it or not, so is God. If God, as a Force that creates and controls the Cosmos, is altogether missing, He cannot obviously do anything to anyone. But if He is anything like the Biblical or Quranic or Upanishadic God, and if man is resolute to hasten his own extinction, He might not stop him. But if man wants to get back from the abyss of moral decadence and sincerely tries to go on to a higher level of consciousness, God might give a hand; nay, even carry him on His shoulders. And none will be happier than Gaia, Mother Earth over this. If man wholeheartedly asks for help, deep from the 'lotus of his heart,' help will come from a Consciousness far superior to the human intellect, in ways that are unimaginable. Gerard Hopkins in his poem *God's Grandeur* said, "The world is charged with the grandeur of God."[48] The British philosopher and mystic Paul Brunton once asked Ramana Maharshi the question uppermost in most minds: "Will the world soon enter a new era of friendliness and mutual help, or will it go down into chaos and war?"; Ramana Maharshi replied, "There is One Who governs the world, and it is His lookout to look after the world. He Who has given life to the world knows how to sustain it also. It is He Who bears the burden of the world, not you."[49] Sure He does, but in His myriad manifestations, what is our responsibility? Sri Aurobindo wrote, "Our life is a paradox with God for key."[50] And that "the force of man can be driven by God's force. Then is he a miracle doing miracles?"[51] But we want to capture the key and discard God. American preacher Barbara Brown Taylor said, "As a general rule, I would say that human beings never behave more badly towards one another than when they believe they are protecting God."[52] We want God as a symbol of human hostility, a source of ultimate pleasure and unending happiness, and a permanent troubleshooter, sometimes all at the same time or at different times. Long ago, St. Paul the Apostle said that men and women have turned their backs on God and, consequently, have become perverse in their behavior.

Faith, Divinity, and Doubt

Odern man's posture towards God is so complex with so many contradictions, that it is almost impossible to draw any across-the-board conclusions. Perhaps a good starting point might be to desist from any such inferences, because the same man is capable of devotion and doubt, implicit faith and bizarre behavior. It is all a matter of 'balance of advantage', which gives us instantaneous gratification. Although we value certainty and faith, some consider the transition from certainty to doubt and devotion to rebellion as a sign of spiritual progress. Despite our armor of arrogance, the 'dynamic of doubt' rules our lives. We are uncertain and distrustful of everything, and everyone; including or above all, ourselves. We just do not know how we will behave in a certain circumstance, in a state of certainty or doubt. Both certainty and doubt are double-edged. The Buddha called doubt a 'dreadful habit'. Our doubt is so deep that we do not know what things we cannot — and must not — change and have to accept, and things that we can — and must — change. The common phrase is 'these days you cannot trust anybody'. Such is our state of mind that we cannot even trust ourselves, let alone others. We are not even sure at times if God is a friend or a foe; is he having fun at our misery? Or is he as helpless as any of us? We are a bundle of contradictions when it comes to the interplay of belief and behavior. Sometimes we think it is okay to think honorably and act dishonorably, to mean well and behave abominably. Sometimes we do not behave the way we believe, and at other times we behave better than we believe. Some devout people believe that it does not offend their religion if they are prayerful but treat others shabbily; that malice in the mind is okay as long as the lips are prayerful. Even the scriptures advise us not to 'believe' or follow any exhortation without applying our discerning, discriminatory faculties. The Buddha said, believe only what you yourself test and judge to be true. At the same time, the sanctity of faith is also extolled. The Bhagavad Gita says that 'man is made of faith, and as his faith is, so he is'; the Buddhist scripture *Sutta Nipata* says that 'by faith you shall be free and go beyond the world of death'; and the Quran says that 'God has endeared faith on to you and has made it beautiful in your hearts'. In a world of unrest and uncertainty, turmoil and torment, with a feeble and fickle force at the controls, how can we sift the wheat from the chaff, and choose not between black and white but among a galaxy of grays. So often, either we are paralyzed or confused and end up making wrong choices. Doubt too is thought, of the mind, and faith is an emotion, of the heart. But both are tools; we should not end up as *their* tools. But who is that 'we'? Once again it is the mind.

One of the great problems with religions is that they seem to let us off easily for bad social behavior, or at least we tend to think that 'being religious' is to be absolved from the need to be humane. Our motto seems to be: it is God that matters, not men. While it is true that most people do not know, much less understand, their own religions, let alone of others, that seems to have little bearing on their conditioning and content of actions. Jesus, for example, said in his *Sermon on the Mount*, 'whosoever shall smite you on your right cheek, turn to him the other also' and 'love your enemies', but no one does that — or never did — and yet deem themselves good Christians. Buddhism perhaps more than other religions, lays great stress on good intentions, but the social conduct of many Buddhists is no different from that of others. In Islam, faith is incomplete without virtuous action, but that does not prevent a jihadist from blowing up innocent people and children. The Upanishads proclaimed *Aham brahmasmi* and *Tatvam asi*, implying that divinity is inherent in all living beings, but no Hindu even remotely comes close to following that in his behavior. Our mind plants the seed of ambiguity, misgiving, and doubt, *samsaya* or *sandeha* in Sanskrit, and offers many explanations and excuses for our non-behavior as well as misbehavior. Whether to engage our intellect as faith or doubt is the question. Voltaire said that doubt is uncomfortable and certainty is ridiculous. We seek certainty in absurdity. At the practical level, doubt is what consumes all of us and few, if any, humans have been spared from it. Even Christ on the Cross and many saints could not retain total faith in times of unbearable torment or suffering. Doubt torments much of our mundane life because nothing seems to happen as we wish and when we wish. Not everything happens as we wish, because we do not control all the forces that influence the outcomes, and our wishes often are unrealistic. But without some sort of faith in something or someone, life is impossible. When no one can assure a certain result to anything, we tend to think that life itself is a progression of approximation. No matter that we cannot be certain of anything, but when it comes to divinity, we want foolproof, ironclad certitude. There are no guarantees in life, and in our futile search we seek God as a guarantor; and when He does not appear to oblige and we cannot read His mind, we call him inscrutable. We turn to God as a matter of 'best belief' or a 'safe bet', or out of dire need to help us out of our doubt-laden predicament. And, from God, we expect nothing less than immediate, unquestioned and total affirmative response or implicit obedience, failing which we say He is no God. Yet, what we expect from God we do not show towards other humans, much less other creatures on earth. We want 'proof' for everything, and more so for God; while in the case of human affairs it is the prosecution that must establish guilt beyond 'reasonable doubt', in the matter of God, it is He who has to convince us beyond a 'shadow of doubt'. To quote the Greek philosopher Aeschylus (*Agamemnon*), we want God to help 'quit us of our toils', to carry our burden on His back.

Throughout human history, faith and free will, the two principal modes of belief, the two wings of the human spirit, have been a part of human consciousness in varying degrees of conflict or compatibility. Our inability to bring about amity or division of labor, so to speak, between these two strands of human thought is responsible in no small measure, among other things, to the acrimony between religion and science. In fact, science is used as a cover by those who want to decry divinity. They ask for scientific 'proof' for the existence of God. While they accept many things on hearsay and on 'best belief' basis, when it comes to God they settle for nothing less than absolute evidence. They do not accept deductive dialectic; they want direct proof like mathematical formulae or the properties of physics. They dismiss arguments like 'nothing else explains the existence of the universe' as a leap of blind faith, but they invoke as high a leap of faith to deny God. Richard Dawkins wrote the bestseller *The God Delusion* (2006), and included in that a chapter tellingly titled '*Why there almost certainly is no God*'. Dawkins seems almost not sure. *Almost* is the operative word. The gap between the almost and the actual is the widest in the world. With that kind of caveat, one can, without the fear of contradiction, rewrite that title as 'Why there *almost certainly is* a God'.

Whether the rewards of reason or the benign fall out of faith is more enduring has been a subject of much philosophical inquiry from the Greeks down to the moderns. Each has had its own ardent, if not 'fanatical', defenders and detractors, often with very little 'faith' or 'rationality'. The fact is that neither of them is an absolute, wholly autonomous of the other. Indeed, the human mind is incapable of functioning wholly either on unquestioned faith or on pure reason. Most of the time, perhaps all the time, we wander in the twilight between knowledge and ignorance, faith and doubt, and no one knows where and when they meet or clash. It is part of the eternal play of *dwandas* or duality, between pairs of opposites. We think we are free only until the next minute; we are bonded-slaves of the senses and confuse shadows for the substance, and, as Vedanta tells us, as long as that doubt remains we will never be free or know what is real and unreal. Most of us are not what we want to be, and our mind proffers many explanations and excuses. And despite all the negatives associated with it, doubt is essential for any introspection or inquiry or creativity; it can be the beginning, not the end, of wisdom. Only the ignorant and a fool are soaked in certainty. But for doubt, we would all be dead by now. Whether it is divine design or Nature's way of retaining its mystery, human knowledge and intellect do not lend themselves to infallibility or even definitiveness. And faith provides, despite all the absurdities and incongruities of life, hope that the dawn can be better than the night. Reason itself is based on faith in ourselves, if in nothing else; and if rationality is something like conforming one's beliefs to the highest norms of thought, then faith is the highest kind of rationality. Whether one calls it faith or rationality or the lack of it, the fact is that both are branches of what man is capable of understanding, and that understanding leaves gaping holes; there is much that cannot be explained away by either of them. We need to combine faith and rationality, and in so doing, transcend both to make some sense of our lives; but the human mind seems congenitally incapable of weaving them together into a fabric. We pursue parallel tracks that got twisted with time, faith increasingly a hostage to ribald religiosity, and rationality becoming a tool of self-glorification. Our unflinching, some would say 'irrational', faith in deductive reasoning and logical thought that is itself beyond reason, has given us many false gods and goddesses. Luck has so far held faith with us but that seems to have run its course and now, we are on our own. As chance comes in at each stage in the progress of our knowledge, we are likely to be unaware that we are on the brink of a deeper level of reality of uncertainty which will make us more prone to error. If we continue on the same path with the same mindset, chances are we will make catastrophic choices that could drastically shorten the life span of the human species on earth. St. Teresa said that when one experiences the highest states of ecstasy, "intellect and senses both swoon away."[53] For ordinary living, they need not 'swoon away' but they ought not to shun higher varieties of awareness. Whether or not man had an 'untainted mind, heaven's first gift' (Aeschylus) which got tainted through culture, or if mind itself is a latter-day alien intrusion, the source of mischief and malaise is the mind, a 'sort of Trojan Horse or Pandora's Chest,' which is adept at offering explanations and excuses for inaction and wrong actions and does not let us stay on the straight path. It creates in us, a paranoia of persecution, of being a victim, that everyone is 'out to get us.' It enables us to do horrible things to another human and still 'sleep like a baby.'

Faith, Jesus said, can move mountains (*Matthew 17:21*). And, belief it has also been said, makes faith a fact. For Tolstoy, faith is the force of life; and for Tagore, faith is the bird that sings when the dawn is still dark.[54] The bird knows it by instinct; we do not, because we rely on reason, and reason wants to see 'bright light' before it lets us wake up. The power of faith, like the power of thought, is immense; but it is a power that is barely harnessed by mankind. And just as the power of thought, if misguided, can be our worst enemy, similarly the power of faith if misdirected, like the modern-day religious fanaticism, can destroy our very soul and make us a monster... Faith, in short, is one that you trust but cannot prove, but that must be well harnessed. Usually, the word 'faith' is used in the context of God, religion, and theology, but not exclusively; we have 'faith' in people too. Some view faith as the logical, natural progression of good reasoning, while many others call it superstition, a 'soft option' to life's challenges. But faith has to be tempered by questioning; and questioning should be able to throw light, not enable evasive action. In the Gita, Krishna tells Arjuna not to blindly accept what even He tells him, but to reflect upon the advice given, use his discretion and make his choice. The Buddha told his disciples not to accept anything because "some great man said it or because it is found in a book or because the majority of people believe it."[55] The truth is that, there is no magic formula or method to mix faith and doubt, because faith is, in the words of William Wordsworth, a passionate intuition, while doubt is the driving force of reasoned certainty. They do not easily blend; indeed, they are two shades of the same light. Paul Tillich said doubt is not the opposite of faith; it is one element of faith.

Within the contours of consciousness, doubt is a product of the mind, and faith that of the heart. Only when they both occupy equal but connected parts in the consciousness, will it be possible to have faith-based intelligence. So far, they have remained disparate and hostile to each other and have forced man to choose between the two. One of the mysterious things in Nature is that belief in anything, be it magic or logic or God itself, is transformational, a prerequisite for the success of the instrument as well as the intended effort. If you do not believe in God, for example, He *cannot* help you even if He wants to. And if you believe with a pure heart, He will have to 'do something' even if you do not worship Him. Belief leads to passion, and passionate effort enhances the chances of success manifold. Indeed, compassion is nothing more than passionate concern for someone else. It is based on the moral premise that if we have in our power to abort something bad from occurring, without giving up something nearly as important, it is wrong not to do so. It is to try giving more than we take in every situation, when that giving does not affect our vital needs. It is to feel morally and collectively responsible for the persistence of scourges like mass poverty and pain and suffering due to material want. How do? we earn our living and how much are we entitled to keep, for the pursuit of comfort and pleasure and avoidance of pain, when what we save and give in the process helps other people lead better lives? How do we balance our own happiness (and that of others we love and value), with the happiness of strangers? We must make sharing a default mode in everyday life. At the most fundamental level, we must review what is meant by ethical life, being a 'good human being', and about things that make us 'feel' good — or bad — about ourselves. But in our lives today, instead of a heart of compassion we manifest 'hard-heartedness', which both the Old Testament and the New Testament often speak about. We must believe that if we sincerely seek His help, it will surely come by. It is a message that resonates through all the scriptures and epics. In the Ramayana, the demon Ravana drives his brother Vibhishana away from Lanka because the latter had dared to suggest reconciliation with Rama. Vibhishana then crosses over to take refuge in Rama's camp, but is stopped at the gates by Rama's aides. Rama, deemed as a *dharmic* incarnation, signals them to let Vibhishana in, and proclaims in crystal-clear words that he [Rama] will not abandon even the murderer of millions of Brahmins (considered to be the highest sin), if he seeks refuge in Him and says, "the moment a creature turns his face towards Me, the sins incurred by it through millions of lives are washed away."[56] The message is repeated by Lord Krishna in the Bhagavad Gita.

The Bible says: "if we sin deliberately after receiving the knowledge of the truth, there no longer remains a sacrifice for sins, but a fearful prospect of judgment, and a fury of fire."[57] What must happen might happen, but what has not yet need not, at least until it actually happens. Ignorance can be bliss, handicap, or even hope. According to the Biblical *Book of Revelation*, at the end of human tenure on earth, the epic battle between good and evil will take place, and beasts would appear in the heavens and wage war on God and His angels. *Revelation* puts God on the winning side — the human experiment would draw to its finality. The scripture tells us that the way to avert or abort the Apocalypse is to 'turn,' repent, and return to God, the Jesus way. Some theologians say that it is man's separation or alienation from God that has precipitated all the human misery. It is sometimes said, particularly in Islamic theology, that sincere prayers can change the way events unfold, and that true worship and sincere submission to God can raise the believer above the normal ways of Nature. It is also viewed as the deepest fulfillment of the human spirit. It is the same promise that Lord Krishna makes to Arjuna in the Bhagavad Gita: "Merge thy mind in Me; be My devotee; sacrifice to Me; prostrate thyself before Me; thou shall come even to Me; I pledge thee My troth; thou art dear to Me."[58] God's word is simple, clear, and straightforward. But we find it very hard to 'take God on His word' and to 'seek refuge in Him.' We are full of doubt and disbelief and find it almost impossible to take anything or anyone, other than our own selves, seriously. The mind says, 'Where is the proof?' But where is the proof for 'proof'? We associate rationality with reason, knowledge with intelligence, and proof with truth. This temporal trinity of reason, intelligence, and proof have blinded and brought mankind to the 'brink of the precipice.' But we want 'proof' for that too. You see an abyss ahead but you want proof for that! As the American professor of philosophy and author Peter Kreeft says, "You cannot scientifically prove that the only acceptable proofs are scientific proofs. You cannot prove logically or empirically that only logical or empirical proofs are acceptable as proofs. You cannot prove it logically because its contradiction does not entail a contradiction, and you cannot prove it empirically because neither a proof nor the criterion of acceptability are empirical entities. Thus scientism (the premise that only scientific proofs count as proofs) is not scientific; it is a dogma of faith, a religion."[59] Self-absorbed, dissatisfied, and disillusioned with both science and religion, many are turning to a motley mix of mystics and mavericks, guns and gurus, scriptures and science fiction, to anyone or anything that seems to promise hope, however slender or sleight of mind it might be. The hope is that humanity might still get rid of its ennui, reclaim its élan and keep its tryst with its destiny. A nobler calling for man is ahead of him. Ideas and idealism are still valid. Caring and compassion still count. The still surviving human goodness must converge and coalesce and become a positive force for the good of the global community. The immediate task is to create the 'minimum mass' of men who not only combine, at least in partial measure, the intellect of Aristotle, the humanism of Einstein, and the sagacity of Gandhi, but are also capable of welding their individual energies into a systemic whole. Each person becomes both a participatory actor as well as an agent who will replicate the same context in two or more persons, culminating in the uplift of the mass of humanity.

It is not only philosophers and scholars who have pondered over the question of 'what to do with God'. Almost every 'who is who' in every walk of life, from saints to scientists, celebrities to the common folk have said something or the other, some thought-provoking, some hair-splitting, some profound, and some utterly pedestrian things. To recognize that God exists, that God is "there," is to believe in God. To recognize that God is "an ever present help in trouble" — that God is *here* — means having faith in God. At the end of it all, the magic and the mystery, the lure and the allure of God still endures. That is not going to change any time soon — despite God-gene and God-particle — and we will all probably die drowning in that divine black hole. Even to stay afloat in that black hole, which is what the state of the world now is, we need *That* right now, whatever we might think it is, an idea, an ideal or an idol, a Father or a Force, a comedian or a mathematician. We have to fall back upon what Voltaire said: if God does not exist, we have to invent Him. And if He is in eclipse, we must remove the cover. And if 'we are in exile' from God as the Flemish mystic John of Ruysbroeck said, then we must redeem ourselves through our conduct on earth. Whether or not science proves the existence of a 'God-particle' or a 'God-gene', God will remain as a matter of 'best belief' and last resort. We have simply run out of all other options to change course and save ourselves. And that brings up the 'mother of all questions': Can a species-saving tectonic transformation occur without divine acquiescence, if not intervention? If we cannot control the way we live, how can we manage the alchemy of our transformation? Does it all depend on what we mean by 'transformation'? Is it to ease the birth pangs of the advent of the posthumans, our 'successor species', that is, to play the role we are playing on earth but with vastly technology-enhanced intelligence? Or will it really be an 'improved version of the human species'? Ray Kurzweil opted for the latter and said that he would define the next human species as that species that inherently extends our own horizons. We did not stay on the ground, we did not stay on the planet, and we are not staying within the limitations of our biology. Kurzweil hit the nail on the head when he positioned technological manipulation of the human organism on the same footing as our ability to fly a plane or sending a man to the moon. But he was also the one who warned of the unintended consequences of 'self-replicating' nanobiotechnology. The danger is not only in the know-how getting into the hands of 'terrorists' but, even more, the product itself being or becoming a potential Frankenstein.

Transcendence, immanence, and indifference of God

Our multidimensional relationship with 'God' brings up an important issue: the apparent dichotomy in divinity and how it affects our lives. One of the principal attributes most religions associate with divinity is immanence, which means the omnipresence of the divine essence. Or that the omnipotent divine force, the all-encompassing divine being, pervades through — and beyond and behind — all things that exist, and is able to influence them. The axiological question then is: if God is in everything, is everywhere and knows everything, and can do anything, why is the human world — let us, for a change, leave other creatures aside — so full of exploitation, misery, unhappiness, and evil? And why do evil-doers seem to have all the fun and luck? And why does not God step in every time we are in trouble? It is our 'suffering', not divine potency or prevarication that is the issue. In other words, is our suffering the evidence against, the reason to doubt His immanence? This age-old question has cropped up every time a horrific thing happened in human history. And it crops up whenever a personal tragedy strikes. When an earthquake swallows up children, or a child dies in an automobile accident, or a friend succumbs to a deadly disease (almost everyday occurrences in practically everyone's life today), we ask 'why' and point the finger at God. At a time when 'casual' suicide and 'reflexive' murder have become both prosaic and pandemic, it is impossible for the human mind to insulate the divine from the dastardly, the god from the gory. What we are saying is that God must face the consequences for our wrong choices because He gave us the freedom to choose. The image of an apathetic and indifferent, if not callous, God and the corresponding ideal of a solitary, autonomous self comes to the mind, both of which are socially and spiritually destitute. In a sense, the answer depends on how one deals with the six implicit assumptions: (1) that God is caring and cares for what happens to us; (2) that God is beholden and accountable to us because we are, after all, *human*; (3) that we, the 'virtuous', are 'innocent' not only in relation to other humans but also in relation to other species; (4) that we are worthy of divine help; (5) that 'suffering' is pain unnatural to the human condition; and (6) that the time-frame is this, our present life. For none of the above assumptions do we have, in the human language, any 'evidence', much less any 'proof'. There is no such being as an 'innocent victim' or a 'virtuous sufferer.' Life is unthinkable — maybe untenable — without pain, as it is without pleasure. And both are highly individualistic. None of us (not even a serial killer) really thinks he is evil — on the contrary, he thinks he is a *victim*— and our sole test of divine intervention is our personal present life. And we forget that by relieving any particular person from suffering, God might have to let someone else suffer, someone who may be less deserving of suffering and more in need of His help. Even if we ignore for the moment the karma theory and the transmigration of souls and rebirth with a bearing on past lives, we should not forget that God is, as described in the scriptures, not only kind and forgiving but also just and fair. In the Bible, He is called 'a just God and a Savior'. And being 'just' might sometimes require some to suffer: 'and God proclaimed that He will slay the wicked and shelter the virtuous'. The Bible contains many examples of divine punishment for transgressors. For example, it says: "For we know Him who said, 'Vengeance is Mine, I will repay' (*Hebrews 10:30*). And when the people of Egypt set themselves up against God, He threatened that "the land of Egypt shall be desolate and waste; and they shall know that I am the Lord" (*Ezekiel 29:9*). And He alone knows where to draw the line between punishment and forgiveness, and how to 'punish' or 'forgive'. In the Hindu epics it is said that the greatest act of divine mercy is to slay an erring *bhakta* or devotee; such a person directly merges into Him.

And then we have a category of events which, in law, are called 'acts of God', not related to what God does but what, in our mind, he should have done and did not, causing us suffering and bereavement. When Nature does not behave as we want it to, we call it an 'act of God'. Even if we directly cause an event that we do not like, we call that outcome (for instance, a flood) an act of God. Going by this 'logic', we can 'explain' away global warming as an act of God. Despite the indictment of God as a Father who does not care about the suffering of his children, there are also some avowed atheists who have lately discovered the conventional God. Such as, for example, Antony Flew, dubbed the world's most famous philosopher of atheism, who initially proposed that one must presuppose atheism until evidence of God surfaces, and later came to advocate deism of the Aristotelian kind.[60] Flew came to the conclusion, like many others, that the existence of a super-intelligence is the only good explanation for the origin of life and the complexity of Nature. While statistics vary, and belief or skepticism in God is too subjective, personal, and emotional to lend itself to simple *yes* or *no* answers, there is also a wide gap between 'belief' and 'behavior'. The fact is that there are a good number of people who have serious reservations about God as portrayed by the scriptures. According to one estimate (2005 figures), about 2.3 percent of the world's population describes itself as atheist, while a further 11.9 percent is described as non-theist.[61] In a nutshell, one could say that after millions of words written and spoken about God, the human perception of divinity remains as hazy and as confused as ever. We just cannot make up our minds and in the end, we have to go by our 'gut feeling' and bring it down to the basics. In the words of the theosophist Annie Besant, our goal ought to be to manifest "sympathy with all that feels, that swift response to every human need"[62] to become 'Masters of compassion'. She suggested a simple maxim: "nor let us forget that the person who happens to be with us at any given moment is the person given to us by the Master to serve at that moment."[63] That is a beautiful way of expressing divinity. To be able to serve not for the sake of the pleasure of serving but for the sake of serving, is the true test of spirituality. To attain that state, we must be able to not merely see God in every one, but also see everyone as God. For that, we need a brand new consciousness; and for that, we need divine grace. And for that, again, we need *vairagya*, non-attachment or renunciation of the fruits of one's labor and *abhyasa*, spiritual discipline and practice. What the scriptures call Self-realization is transformation. The famous maxim of the Upanishads, *Tatvamasi* (Thou art that), is the ultimate transformation, the consciousness that you are nothing else and nothing but God. To become "the subtle essence in which all that exists has its self," which the *Chandogya* Upanishad talks about, is the goal of spiritual transformation.

It is unlikely, as saints like Sri Aurobindo implied, that the sheer force of evolution, unless directed by God, could induce the movement of spirit into matter and raise humanity to a higher level, to a 'consciousness of super-manhood'. In Sri Aurobindo's soaring vision, the final 'evolution' is the *divinization* of matter itself, the ushering in of a completely new 'divine' way of existence on earth, what he called 'life divine', that will lead to greater unity, mutuality, and harmony within humanity. Transformation to this kind of 'Gnostic' being requires both psychic and spiritual transformation. Whether or not evolution is goal-oriented or simply an adaptation to a circumstance, and whether or not we are but a bunch of genes or memes fighting for living space, the fate of our species would depend on the creation of a context of life conducive to purposeful transformation. And we must change completely our perspective on the environment. We must recapture the spirit of religions like Hinduism where there is no such thing as the 'environment'; it is simply divinity. We are far too dysfunctional, divided, and dissipated as a collective and coherent entity on earth to make the kind of mutations needed at the very core of our being. Mankind must find a way to increase, if only incrementally, the inflows of the 'divine essence' into daily life, and recapture both 'the primal fear and pristine love of God'. Human evolution itself has demonstrated that the mind-dominated consciousness will not change solely through human effort, because we are mental beings, and that true consciousness change entails loosening the grip of the mind, which our own mind will resist with all its available strength. The route to human transformation is consciousness change, and that is what God will induce if He wants to help us. If humankind ever becomes enabled to establish a kingdom of righteousness on earth, it would happen only through consciousness change. And for God to bestow His grace, we need to manifest devotion with compassion. Annie Besant said that "the word 'devotion' is the key to all true progress in the spiritual life."[64] Devotion is an intense attachment and love of anyone, but in spiritual life it relates to God. In true devotion, both towards another individual or to God, the ego evaporates and the boundary between the two blurs or disappears. Devotion is the tissue that connects man with God. The lives of saints demonstrate the transformative power of devotion combined with cascading compassion for fellow creatures. Much of classical religious fervor is devotion so strong that the distinction between a devotee and the divine disappears. The foremost example in Hindu thought is the devotion-cum-absolute surrender of the *Gopikas* towards Lord Krishna, and the interplay between the two symbolized in what has come to be called the *Raas Lila*, the cosmic dance of love performed by Lord Krishna, a child all of seven years in the midst of His devotees. It symbolizes the interplay between the aspiring and the yearning human soul and the divine and transcendental love; it is about how the One relates to His many. Such is its sacredness and spiritual significance that in the Bhagavata Purana, it was affirmed that whoever hears or describes the *Raas Lila* attains Krishna's pure loving devotion (*Sudha bhakti*). Ridiculously, it is sometimes portrayed — a projection of the limitations and frailties of our mind — as an erotic extravaganza. Swami Vivekananda said that it is the external expression of divine play that takes place in every human heart between the individual and the universal soul.

Clearly, neither is that ideal within the reach of most men, nor will such harmony be able to manifest in the minds of modern men, the 'pure love' of God — "love that is stain-less, motionless, and that one feels only for the sake of love" that Sri Ramakrishna said was beyond even *dharma* and *adharma*.[65] And also, neither will we ever have "the comfort of certainty about the ways of God",[66] nor will we ever know what His plans are for our future. All the knowledge we have assiduously accumulated is of no avail; in fact, it is this mind-centered knowledge that is the burden breaking our back. It is the human capacity to acquire, access, assess, and use knowledge far beyond the needs of simple survival that has allowed humanity to prevail and eventually to dominate; but it is, in Einstein's words, slowly strangulating the 'holy curiosity' of spiritual inquiry. 'Knowledge' figures prominently in the scriptures. Knowledge, in Christianity, is one of the gifts of the Holy Spirit; and in Islam, Prophet Muhammad declared himself to be the 'city of knowledge'. In Hinduism, it is divided into two kinds, *paroksha-jnana* (indirect knowledge) and *aparoksha-jnana* (direct knowledge). What we commonly call knowledge is really raw data; knowledge is what you imbibe; data is what is accessible; wisdom is the use of knowledge for the good of the world. It is being claimed that, "all of the information which all of mankind has ever recorded in books can be carried around in a pamphlet in your hand..."[67] Information, it has been said, no longer has the proverbial nexus with power because technology makes it accessible to everyone. It is more important to connect, judge, and choose. And unused and unusable information, like cholesterol, clogs the arteries of advancement. We have to unlearn what we have learned so far. The scriptures and saints have consistently told us that the ultimate end and aim of life is the union with God. As Tagore said, "This is the ultimate end of man, to find the One which is in him; which is his truth, which is his soul; the key with which he opens the gate of the spiritual life, the heavenly kingdom."[68] There are some who say that in endowing us what we have, God gave up part of his own power and therefore we are doubly accountable to God: for our own actions and as His proxy.

Rabbi Norman Lamm (*Faith and Doubt*, 1971) wrote: "The drama of human existence is predicated upon the divine grant of Freedom to Man. But such Freedom for Man implies that God has willingly surrendered part of his control; that he has paradoxically, willed that things may go against his Will."[69] The question that crosses the doubting mind is: will God regret his 'giving up' and deem us betrayers of His trust? If, as the Quran says, 'there is always a third person listening when two people whisper', and if God is closer to you than your nose, God then knows our every fleeting thought, every word spoken, and every act done or not done. If we are 'naked' and cannot hide anything before God, what are we supposed to do to save ourselves? We cannot hide and we will not change. A fair way to proceed is to put ourselves in God's shoes and imagine what we would do to Him if he behaves the way we do. Any human jury would pronounce that He has betrayed our trust and mandate, and would probably put Him away for good. Although we may be wary of phrasing the issue in this way, what man is really trying to do by becoming immortal and by freeing himself from the consequences of his actions, is to make God passé, or redundant, or at least bring Him into disrepute. Alexander Pope wrote, "Tis this, Though Man's a fool, yet God is wise."[70] But can that save man? For, as philosopher Soren Kierkegaard said, "Man is capable of nothing; it is God who gives everything, who gives man faith."[71] God is merciful, but He is also just, and being just means being fair, fair to all His creations. Will Nature, which is but a practical extension of God, continue to be indulgent? If we are rational beings, as we claim to be, we should know the answer is 'not likely'. If human consciousness stays static and the mind rules the roost, our relationship with God, with Nature and with our own inner selves cannot change in any sweeping way, and we need to do a lot more while God needs to do nothing. He will simply relapse into His '*yoganidra*', His cosmic sleep, and Man will have to do all that needs to be done to ease the earth of the human burden. With the mind and weapons he has, that will not be an uphill task. Already, we see the tell-tale signs. In the Hindu doctrine of *avatars* (incarnations), God descends to earth to eradicate evil and restore righteousness from time to time. But it has also another import. Truly, God did not have to become human to do what he wanted to do; it was to show that man can become God. It was predicted, as mentioned earlier, that the last *avatar* would be *Kalki*, at the end of this *Yuga,* to re-establish righteousness on earth. Significantly, it was said that the minds of men who live at the end of the Kali Age shall be reawakened, and shall be, in the words of the Hindu scripture *Vishnu Purana*, 'as pellucid as crystal'. According to Vedic philosophy, the human body is composed of seven basic sheaths: matter, life, mind, super mind or gnosis, bliss, becoming, and being. Human evolution, it is said, has passed through the first four sheaths, constituting what the human today 'is'. To make further progress through the last three sheaths — bliss, becoming, and being (*Sat, Chit*, and *Ananda*) — the human needs the grace of the divine force. This is because these sheaths lie beyond the realm of the physical world and are in the spiritual world. The tenth avatar will help mankind cross the last three layers of consciousness and merge with the divine. It means that God will induce consciousness-change as a prelude to final transformation. Without that even God cannot change us or save us.

'Critical Mass' and the 'Hundredth Monkey'

God may love us a little more than other creatures — so we would like to flatter ourselves — but by our malevolent conduct and by our stubborn refusal to mend our ways, we must be leaving Him with little choice but to wring His hands in despair. God is kind, compassionate, and merciful, but also just, which means that He has no favorites and holds all His creation equally accountable for its choices and actions. And He too has, like all of us, his own *swadharma*; his righteous duty and obligation that is cosmic, overarching, and the one that sustains the universe or 'multiverse' as some cosmologists like to call it (to signify that there are millions, if not billions of worlds). His *swadharma*, in so far as earth is concerned, is to restore the moral order on earth, with or without man. Let us not forget that, even on earth, we are simply the 'human portion' of His being, not the entirety of His manifestation. Somehow our 'intelligence' has never been able to grasp this primal truth and to come to terms with it. The root cause of man's narcissistic and nihilistic bent of mind is the way he thinks and looks at himself, at the universe, and at God. Every man thinks he is at once the epicenter of the universe as well as a victim of circumstance, of fate, or of an 'unfair' God. The perception of 'being a victim' leads to indifference and intolerance and to violence, which then becomes a statement, a protest, a way to redeem one's self-esteem and to feel 'good' about oneself. Increasingly, in a ruthlessly competitive world, in the minds of the weak and vulnerable, and the marginalized, violence is the weapon of choice, the only way they feel their voice will be heard. The only alternatives to them appear to be surrender or suicide. Since even the oppressor feels he is a victim, violence then becomes the preferred means to 'settle scores' not only with the 'oppressor' but with the world. Thus violence breeds violence, and soon it becomes the behavioral norm, for settling disputes of every hue and character. Although violence is more extreme and endemic now, it has been integral to human nature and history. Indeed it is inseperable from or indistinguishable from everything we call human. Prehistory was so violent that some anthropologists estimate that almost 40 percent of deaths were due to fighting. Since power comes with the possession of weapons, the race is for more and more destructive weapons than what the potential adversary has or is likely to have. The only way to get out of this syndrome is to attain a different content of consciousness. It may be a higher consciousness, or a prehistoric one or a 'bicameral' one. What really matters is that humans need a consciousness change to advance any further or at least not to stumble over the brink. Vaclav Havel, the playwright, said that without a global revolution in the sphere of human consciousness nothing will change for the better and the impending catastrophe will be unavoidable. This very imperative was reflected in St. Paul's letter to the Romans: "Do not conform any longer to the pattern of this world, but be transformed by the renewing of your mind. Then you will be able to test and approve what God's will is — his good, pleasing and perfect will" (*Romans 12:2*).[72] 'Renewing of your mind' is nothing but consciousness change. The principal thrust of the Bhagavad Gita is consciousness change. The tenet to treat pain and pleasure, joy and sorrow on the same footing and to do all work without attachment to its rewards or returns is tantamount to consciousness change. It is only through consciousness change that spiritual transformation becomes possible. It is only through consciousness change that the hold of the 'empirical ego' is destroyed and the suffocating sense of separateness disappears.

While such is the drift of the scriptures, the direction of scientific effort should be to 'fix' the brain circuits, to transform self-centeredness into altruism, animosity into compassion, indifference into benevolence, and hatred into love. We can never say 'never' with science, but to think that by manipulating or boosting the brain we can master the mind, much less the consciousness, seems a huge stretch of credulity. Brain surgery can hardly be a substitute for spiritual transformation. At this moment in man's tenure on earth, we must, with all the wisdom we are capable of mustering, face up to one fact. Maybe it was possible in the distant past, but it does seem highly improbable that with our present-day body and mind-consciousness we can incrementally ease into a spiritual something, capable of expressing and experiencing higher life. We must become innovative enough to destroy everything man has come to stand for, without destroying what man is meant to be. In the end, it is God's choice, and the dynamics of divine intervention in human affairs can hardly be comprehended by us with the present consciousness.

No one grudges what man has achieved; the problem is with what man has *become*. Man may pretend to be the master of the universe but hardly has any mastery over his own life, and that will not change. But we must do our bit. We must find a way to tap not only the dormant or unused areas of the mind but also the latent and the for-long-discarded part of consciousness — heart intelligence and energy. The heart has been described as the interface of body, mind, and spirit, and it can take us on the most important journey: that of self-discovery. From there to knowledge of God, which the scriptures say is the true purpose of human life, is only a step away. The Indian mystic and philosopher Jiddu Krishnamurti said, "The mind moves from the known to the known, and it cannot reach out into the unknown."[73] The real answers to real questions like who, what, and why we are, and what becomes of us after death, are in the realm of the spirit, not of matter, they are in the realm of the heart, not of the mind. To ensure that man lives in harmony and amity with other men and with Nature, we need a completely new perception of reality and of our relationship with the universe and God. That 'relationship' has been the focus of the scriptures, and has been the subject of intense study, conjecture, and speculation. It is pretty straightforward in the scriptures: God is the origin, the creator, the sustainer; indeed God and His creation are one. Human birth entitles and empowers a soul to find a way to God.

In our obsession with 'knowing' God, we forget that despite his stupendous accomplishments, man has serious sense limitations. Many other species have sharper and more evolved capacities — they can hear and see better, move quicker and live longer. Just as that does not make them better beings, so is it with man. Man knows, through scientific experimentation, of the existence of much more than the eye can see, of much more than the hand can touch, and of much more than the ear can hear. We must go beyond the sensory power to spiritual power. Ken Wilber says, "It is often said that in today's modern and postmodern world, the forces of darkness are upon us. But I think not; in the Dark and the Deep there are truths that can always heal. It is not the forces of darkness but of shallowness that everywhere threaten the true, and the good, and the beautiful, and that ironically announce themselves as deep and profound. It is an exuberant and fearless shallowness that everywhere is the modern danger, the modern threat, and that everywhere nonetheless calls to us as savior."[74] It is that 'fearless shallowness' that we must fear, that 'exuberant' complacency.

There are some analysts who see differently. They are more optimistic and see shadowy signs of human renaissance, feel the birth pangs of a more humane human. Much of the 'feel good' about the future stems from technology. But there are also others who see signs of more fundamental and deeper reasons not to despair. They feel deep within their own hearts a shift towards the intuitive heart and as a result, they feel that humankind's ability to move beyond limitations and experience fulfillment has exponentially grown. Many people are trying to change their priorities and values. The increasing interest in spirituality and religious practices of all kinds, albeit sporadic and sparse, illustrates that people are looking for something more than a life of unrelenting avarice and blinding ambition. They are searching, going within themselves, for meaning and purpose in their lives. So many are people's wants and such is the sense of desperation that even for purely material things, like a job or a loan or a visa, or to destroy a rival or someone they envy, many are turning to 'spiritual service providers' who promise to service everything except the soul. Spirituality is the fashion of the day and salvation is now big business. We need to change the balance of forces that control consciousness, which means that the grip of the mind should be loosened. P.D. Ouspensky said, "We must start with the idea that without efforts evolution is impossible; without help, it is also impossible. After this we must understand that in the way of development, man must become a *different being*, and we must learn and understand in what sense and in which direction man must become a different being; that is, what a different being means."[75] For Ouspensky, evolution into a different being does not happen en masse for humanity; it is selective, since everyone does not want it strongly enough and long enough. To become a new being, man must acquire new faculties that he does not possess, but also those that he does not have but thinks he has, what Ouspesnsky calls the 'missing link'.

Man's fate might well rest on his ability to control what Jalal ad-Din Rumi characterized as the "duck of gluttony, the cock of concupiscence, the peacock of ambition and ostentation and the crow of bad desires."[76] And on our ability to turn our gaze and senses inwards to see that the wish-fulfilling philosopher's stone is inside us. The Upanishads emphasize, as the Indian philosopher R.D. Ranade put it, the need for a dual process of 'introversion' and 'catharsis'. Sri Sai Baba said, "Our senses have been created by God with a tendency to move outward, and so, man always looks outside himself and not inside."[77] Rarely, a wise man, desirous of immortal life, looks at his inner self with his eye turned inward. The 'catharsis' consists in returning to the righteous path, and the Upanishads clearly state that through intellect alone, man can never realize the Self or God. In fact, they say knowledge is more dangerous than ignorance: 'Into blinding darkness enter those who worship ignorance, and into deeper darkness those who worship knowledge alone'. Most people are almost hypnotically heading towards that 'deeper darkness'. But such is human thought that all this sounds so academic or esoteric; what we fear is the reality of the darkness of this life, not of the dark shadows of afterlife. But then again, maybe, just let us hope, it is still not too late to save ourselves from meeting a dismal fate; maybe there is still a window open to retreat from the brink of the abyss. Although drowned in the shrill sounds of civilization and materialism, there is, even if sparse and splintered, a subtle spiritual awakening in the nethermost depths of several troubled souls. But that awakening must be able to gather sufficient momentum and be self-sustaining in order to fuel further growth. The critical context for a species-scale evolutionary transformation that is revolutionary in its impact is *critical mass*, which, once assembled, becomes such a gale or force that it sweeps aside everything on the way. In thermodynamics, at a 'critical point' or a 'tipping point' (temperature and pressure) a 'phase boundary' ceases to exist, as for instance, when water turns to vapor. The critical mass is to kick off or jump-start to reach the critical point of no return. Once we attain such a criticality, it could then trigger a cascade of consciousness-change. The idea of raising consciousness through reaching critical mass is being promoted by a number of New Age spiritualists!

How an idea becomes an avalanche, a small change becomes a global phenomenon, has long intrigued human imagination. It is an important field of inquiry because, diverse, disparate and inherently divisive as the human race is, it is almost impossible for all human beings to embrace the same idea or ideal, particularly when it calls for sacrifice or acceptance of any hardship. That has been a stumbling block to human progress. Researchers have now discovered a behavioral phenomenon that they call the *Hundredth Monkey effect*: when a limited number of people know something in a new way, it remains the conscious property of only those people. However, there is a point at which if just one more person tunes-in to the new awareness, that new awareness is picked up by everyone else. It answers the lament 'what can *I* do?' The profound meaning and message is that individuals — even a single one — matter. And that although the exact number varies, when only a limited number of people know a new way, it may remain in the consciousness of those people only, but if just one more person tunes-in, it might be possible that the new knowledge and awareness may spread unstoppably across consciousnesses, and lead to species-scale transformation. Much of the previous effort might have failed because we were always missing that 'one person' and the 'consciousness to consciousness' contagion. We must believe and behave as if everyone and anyone could be the 'hundredth monkey', capable of making the decisive difference to induce a leap in our consciousness. It can, in turn, create the context and conditions to solve hitherto intractable problems like nuclear proliferation, energy crises, climate change and global warming.

Since the evolution of *Homo sapiens*, every major evolutionary change coincided with, indeed was preceded by, shifts in human consciousness, some temperate and some tectonic. Something happens which breaks the previous equilibrium, and suddenly it becomes advantageous for new things to develop. For something to happen, something needs to be present in the first place which is capable of evolving. A trigger event or a circumstance might inspire or influence consciousness to suddenly evolve into a radically different form. Just as the advent of human consciousness ruptured the 'world of apes', the rising of new consciousness will doubtless disrupt the world of humans. It would induce rapid positive changes in the collective consciousness of humankind, the kind of changes that might make us suddenly realize that we can actually live in peace and work together and share common space on this space, on this tiny outpost in the Milky Way, and still have a rollicking time at it. It is a kind of change that alters our perception and perspective on the priorities of life. Some philosophers compare the self of man to a seed, a member of the old plant when humanity was closer to Nature. But now, the capsule is wide open. Henceforth, one of the two things, they extrapolate, may happen to it: either it may abide alone, isolated from the rest of the earth, growing dryer and dryer, until it withers up and crumbles; or, by uniting with the earth it could blossom into a fresh life of its own.

Whether we are the 'associates of apes or angels', 'divinity messed up by *maya*', or naked men dressed up in culture, at the end of the day, whether we blossom or fritter away depends on us and on how we relate to the totality of life. It is not inconceivable that those things in the world that are so trying and make us tremble, could be the fertile womb in which human potential could incubate into its promise. Unfortunately, we have developed a mindset that disconnects many things that need to be connected; for example, prayer and personality, conscience and conduct, belief and behavior, power and responsibility. What are at stake in our actions are not only our personal lives but also the direction and destination of human evolution. The German philosopher Schrodinger wrote, "In fact every individual life, indeed every day in the life of an individual, *has* to represent a part, however small, of evolution [of our species], a chisel-stroke, however insignificant, on the eternally unfinished statue of our species."[78] Indeed, the most charitable view of the human species is that we are still a 'work in progress', and every thought, word and act of every individual is an input. We are a part, not only of a colossal cosmic context, but also of an unimaginably bigger process of creation. After millions of years of evolution, millenniums of culture and centuries of civilization, do we have within us what it takes to behave as parts of a larger whole? Can we begin to germinate the thought that all sentient beings on earth have an equal moral standing? We think of sin as a grave moral transgression or murder, rape, etc. But sin can be as trivial as the denial of something that is someone else's due, or deliberately hurting others, particularly the defenseless. For example, the Hindu scripture *Padma Purana* says that things like back biting, seeing faults in others and demeaning their efforts, acquiring others' land by unfair means, killing innocent animals, telling lies, showing disrespect to the guests, etc., are all considered to be sinful deeds. It also says that anyone who obstructs a hungry man from having his food, or a thirsty person from quenching his thirst, commits a sin similar to that of killing a *brahmin*. And sin can be economic and ecological too. If we apply all these yardsticks, few of us would be considered sinless. We are precariously perched, in the words of Graham Greene, "on the dangerous edge of things", and on "what it always has been — the narrow boundary between loyalty and disloyalty, between fidelity and infidelity, the mind's contradictions, the paradox one carries within oneself."[79] Call it the brink of the abyss or the edge, or the '*edge of the brink of abyss*'; the truth is, we cannot tarry too long without tumbling over. We must simply and swiftly get onto the high road of transformation or call it quits, and use whatever little time we have to taste all the forbidden fruits on the planet of pleasure.

The crux of transformation is cleansing, change, and growth. All three are part of the self-adjustment inherent in Nature and in the Natural world, there is no need for any external intervention. Human beings, also a part of Nature, are not exempt, but the human has harnessed an external force — technology — to trigger fundamental changes in his context and content of living. Technology, as Schumacher (*Small is Beautiful*, 1973) noted, unlike the laws of Nature, is not self-limiting and self-correcting, but it is now the primary force behind man's attempt to remake himself. He is going outside the laws of Nature and that takes him into unchartered waters.

Cleansing is an important requirement for spiritual progress, it is sometimes described as a way of 'soul cleansing'. In Sanskrit, it is called *samskara suddhi*, which means cleansing of the past impressions recorded in the mind. Both change and growth are inherent in Nature and every form of life goes through the two. Natural growth occurs without effort, whereas transformation requires the elements of choice and action. The best things in life are hidden within, but we cannot find them since we know not the way. All our stimulation and satiation are external. As the young narrator of Steven Spielberg's new television science fiction mini-series *Taken* so aptly remarked, "It's like trying to find your way back from what you've become to who you know you could have been."[80] That is the gap to fill, the transformation that we need to make happen. Filling that gap also involves achieving greater understanding of why intolerance not acceptance, competition not cooperation, aggression not accommodation, has come to occupy so much of our psychic space. We must fathom why man as he is, scripturally so close to divinity and so well endowed, behaves so recklessly. It is high time that we reclaimed the lost essence and realized our full potential, which great masters have told is manifest in everything we do, the divinity nesting in the 'cave of the heart'. It is a kind of transformation that allows the species to ultimately transcend into the posthuman 'human' phase of evolution. It is not what science is trying to do with biotechnology and nanotechnology; it is, as it were, to transform a small core group of humans into 'immortal supermen.' It has to be a transformation that allows us to harness our spiritual potential. But we need spiritual infrastructure for spiritual transformation. Our behavior, individually and collectively, is inextricably entwined with our culture and civilization, and for them to change we need a new context of life. Given the state of knowledge and our ability (or the lack of it), it would be an uphill task. We are like the "fishes that are taken in an evil net and as the birds that are caught in the snare" (*Ecclesiastes 9:12*)[81] and however much we whine and wriggle, we cannot come out without help from a source beyond our own species.

Equally, we cannot, in the words of the sage Aurobindo, simply wait for "some tremendous dawn of God."[82] We must make ourselves worthy, but how? The conundrum is that the human condition cannot change unless human behavior changes, and human behavior will not change unless human consciousness changes, and that cannot happen unless the hold of the mind on consciousness slackens, and that cannot come to be because we are essentially mental beings. And then, as many human inventions have shown, what we deem impossible or improbable could become possible. This is the idea captured in the *The Black Swan Theory*. One single sighting of a black swan in Australia in the 17th century changed the connotation of the 'Black Swan' metaphor, from 'perceived impossible' to 'improbably' to 'possible'. It highlights a fateful limitation to our learning from observations or experience and the brittleness of our knowledge. After all, the historical fact is that almost all consequential events in history, which seemed beyond the realm of possibility, came unexpected, which we convince ourselves as rational or predictable in hindsight.

Still, to try to make the impossible possible, to remove the sting from the unexpected, to dream till dawn, and to ask not only 'why' when we see misery, but also 'why not' when we want to reach out to a better life, that is much of the stuff of the best of human effort. But the bulk of it is to preserve the *status quo*. We need to discover self-interest in change. As Delbert Thiessen points out, "It is not from the benevolence of the butcher, the brewer, or the baker, that we expect our dinner, but from their regard to their own interest."[83] But the point of departure has to be that although we might appear to be the masters of the universe, we are not masters of our lives, not even of the next minute. There is a superior force or process that stretches before birth and beyond death that has a big say on how human life, indeed all life, unfolds, and how and when it ends up in the womb of Eternity. In the Bible, it is said, "And we, who with unveiled faces all reflect the Lord's glory, are being transformed into his likeness with ever-increasing glory, which comes from the Lord, who is the Spirit." (*2 Corinthians 3:18*).[84] But that 'unveiled face' is now defiled and we want to push Him aside and play His part in human transformation. Not only that, we are 'transforming' God himself, judging Him, instead of fearing His judgment. Too often, our quest for 'meaning' is a means to acquire more wealth, not wisdom, more temporal power not spiritual power.

Many people feel many things that muddle up their minds and unsettle them, but it is given to a few to find the words that capture that sense of the blend of hope and fear. One such person is that little girl, Anne Frank, and the words in her famous diary: "I see the world gradually being turned into a wilderness. I hear the ever-approaching thunder, which will destroy us too. I can feel the sufferings of millions and yet, if I look up into the heavens, I think, it will all come right, that this cruelty too will end, and that peace and tranquility will return again."[85] But the 'flicker' is too feeble to turn into a light robust enough to lead us 'from darkness to light' — *Tamaso Ma Jyotir Gamaya*, as the Upanishads proclaim. The prayer is to be led from the world we experience, which is a world of darkness, towards the Supreme Light, the divine. We need the guidance of the divine hand. The way to gain that 'guidance' is to do our *dharma*, individually and collectively. By doing our *swadharma*, our individual '*dharma*', which is an input into the species-*dharma*, we can mold our destiny and change or even dissolve our 'karma', which is the sum of every thought, every word, every emotion, and every act of commission and omission experienced by every human being born on earth. The Italian Catholic priest Thomas Aquinas wrote, "Three things are necessary for the salvation of man: to know what he ought to believe; to know what he ought to desire; and to know what he ought to do."[86] At this juncture in our tortuous tenure on earth, we seem to have failed all the three '*knows*'; we just do not know what to believe and our belief has no bearing on our behavior; we have no control over our desires; and above all, we have no clue as to what we should do to make a difference.

Sri Aurobindo wrote in *Savitri*: "Man must overcome or miss his higher fate. This is the inner war without escape."[87] In most cases, that war is too subtle to be noticed and it continues from life to life. Sri Aurobindo also said that the human, as he is now poised, is not the final rung on the evolutionary ladder, and that the transformation of man into a spiritual being must happen within Nature because, according to him, the divine Reality must itself manifest in Nature. He said that, "an evolution of consciousness is the central motive of terrestrial existence."[88] Elaine Matthews echoes the same view: "the transformational impulse may well be the most powerful impetus behind human evolution."[89] Nothing in life is accidental or redundant. Nothing stands in solitude. Everything is part of a process. And nothing is a copy of anything else. Every individual and species is a particular and unique package, a piece of cosmic matrix, specially designed for that particular form of life to exist, survive, and multiply on earth at that particular time. What that species knows and could know, or is allowed to know, is also constrained and contained. Every creature, from a mosquito to a predator, instinctively performs a cosmogonical function that flows out of its form, the abrupt absence of which over time could cripple the delicate balance inherent in Nature. That is why there is no sin in a tiger killing a deer, but if a deer, with a gun, kills a tiger, that becomes a sin. Humans alone, it is said, can sin and also blush; sin because we know we are sinning, and blush because we cannot hide the secret pleasure we get out of it. Transform we will be, smiling or scowling, with or without our cooperation. It is a question of direction. The direction man has now apparently chosen is to be a 'Matrix-like' man, to attain immortality like the gods, which really is to become 'beings outside time' and make the future meaningless; an experiment no man has ever ventured before. Even within the confines of intelligence we have, one could sense that unless there is an evolution of consciousness, that will be an apocalyptic catastrophe. Mortal man is bad enough on earth; Nature does not need beings on earth with the ambition — and ability — to 'play God'. If, as Goethe said, the greatest act of faith occurs when man finally decides he is not God, perhaps the greatest mortal risk arises when the human mind fancies itself the architect and arbiter of life on earth. The human brain, which will continue to be the manager and manipulator of human life, was not designed for an immortal man. Scientists talk of replicating or 'downloading' the brain, but it is not clear what it means and implies. Can the brain work indefinitely, and if it does, will it be the same? Can we arrest its 'aging'? And even if we could, the question is about the mind and consciousness. What are the genetic implications that would lead to stagnation of the genetic pool and eventually lead to early extinction, earlier than of a mortal man? Purely physical immortality, which is focused really not on life but on death, could be the last straw on Nature's/God's back. Rather, we must seek to be worthy of God's help. And God will judge us, not by what we do to Him — it hardly matters to him — but by what we do to each other. We want divine grace but we cannot bring ourselves to treat each other with civility and dignity. We want a divine hand to bail us out of our troubles, but we would rather smother than hug someone in distress. The German philosopher Martin Heidegger, one of the past century's most perceptive thinkers, summing up the state of humanity famously said, 'only a god can save us.'

Transformation, Nature, and Science

Whatever be the state of divine disposition or displeasure or weariness with mankind, the transformation we must strive towards is one of consciousness that enables us to change not simply the way we relate, but the very way we relate 'to the way we relate'; to change not only the way we analyze and understand, but the very way we understand 'the way we understand'; and to change the way we perceive and react to virtually every experience from birth to death. As Heidegger said, echoing the Vedantic wisdom, we should shift the focus from looking at everything from the perspective of a being, to an inquiry into the content of *being* itself. That requires summoning of the deepest inner reserves to somehow change the content of our consciousness and context of human life. Consciousness change, lofty as it is, is still a means. The goal ought to be to virtually become a 'compassionate species', whose first impulse would be cooperation, not competition. A way towards that goal, according to some researchers like Alison Gopnik, is to retain or recapture the consciousness of a baby, which they say is more naturally compassionate — and more evolved with more neural pathways — than the consciousness of adults. With the kind of consciousness we have, we have fashioned a world that reminds us of the words of General Omar Bradley (a hero of World War II): "The world has achieved brilliance without wisdom, and power without conscience. Ours is a world of nuclear giants and ethical infants."[90] For enabling a conscience to serve as a moral compass and as a 'light of God in the darkness of His absence', we need, quite simply, a new 'adult' consciousness. The fact is that simply having a conscience, whatever it might actually be, has not helped much in managing human passions and attributes like anger, hatred, intolerance, and malice. Baring his soul, Gandhi wrote, in his autobiography, that although God governed every breath of his life, he felt very far from God, and that "the evil passions within that keep me so far from Him, and yet I cannot get away from them."[91] It is the same lament as that of St. Paul and many others, who fought relentless, often losing wars within to subdue and conquer their sensual passions and cravings. A passion or a craving by itself is neither good nor bad; if they contribute to good action they are good; and they are evil when they lead to bad actions. Although many do not admit frontally, the assumption is that self-interest and altruism are inherent opposites. And yet we do know that conscious pursuit of self-interest is not necessarily incompatible with its attainment, and that the thrill of a selfless act far outweighs the short-term gains from a selfish act. Our moral responses are varied and circumscribed because they are anchored in our conscience, not in our consciousness.

Our moral sense, so to speak, should be delinked from the state of our conscience and be directly rooted in our consciousness. Then we do not have to bank on the so-called 'prick' of conscience; then things such as not hurting anyone by word or deed, spontaneously helping someone in need of help, become a part of 'just being alive'. Then God might do the same to us as what we do to our fellow humans. He might then be too glad to forgive and give a reprieve, offer us another chance to endure on earth for the full length of our tour of duty, and go on to meet our destiny with the sense that we have not failed our maker. Saint Ramakrishna, with his uncanny directness and simplicity, asked, "How may we conquer the old Adam in us?" He went on to say, "When the fruit grows out of the flower, the petals of the flower drop off of themselves. So, when the divinity in thee increases, the weaknesses of thy human nature will all vanish of their own accord."[92] The Indian spiritual guru, Eknath Easwaran suggests the example of a hummingbird to show how one can live in harmony with Nature: "A hummingbird threads its long, delicate bill into the center of the flower, not even touching the petals, and sips its breakfast. A moment later it is gone, having drunk only what was necessary and leaving the flower pollinated. Precise, efficient, agile, respectful: I think humanity can find no better teacher in the art of living."[93] The world will be a far better place and life immeasurably more fulfilling if only we can learn, as Dante said, to find tranquility through that true love that makes us desire no more than what we have, nor covet what others have, for our selfish benefit.

That sounds simple but it goes against the grain of what man has come to stand for, what evolution has made us to be: greedy with an insatiable appetite for 'more' of everything. That can truly change not at the level of conduct but only at the depth of consciousness. Albert Einstein said, "No problem can be solved from the same level of consciousness that created it."[94] The French philosopher and Jesuit priest Pierre Teilhard de Chardin said that we are not physical beings with spiritual experience, but spiritual beings with physical experience. In other words, being spiritual is the true purpose of 'being wholly human'. That again is a truism, but how can we make that practical? We have been talking of spiritualism for thousands of years, from saints like Saint Teresa to Mother Teresa, from scientists like Einstein and Oppenheimer to Narlikar; and now even business tycoons and movie stars have joined the bandwagon. But we are nowhere near becoming a spiritual being; if any, we are more sensual — and sexual — than ever before.

We are more confused than ever; not sure about what spirituality entails, much less how to attain it. It has been variously called 'going beyond the world of proof and reason', 'journey within', 'realm of faith, mystery and belief', 'way to our well-being', 'and selfless service', 'communion with God', and so on. And its relationship with religion remains fuzzy; it is not possible to be truly religious without being spiritual. But what is less clear is whether we can be truly spiritual without being religious in its truest sense. We may not be able to turn spiritualism into a formula, but we know what it is not, by elimination, if not by affirmation. In transformative terms, religious transformation tends to make a person more shrill and strident, while spiritual transformation makes a person softer and subtler. In the former, the mind plays the dominant role while in the latter it has to be the heart. The way to spirituality and to true transformation ought to be to transform our understanding of the heart not as the one which simply keeps us alive, but as one that gives meaning to life; as an organ of intelligence, cognition, and comprehension, much like the brain. With the heart in its rightful place in our consciousness, we must orchestrate the process of conscientious change, beginning with our own selves. Gandhi said that we must *be* the change we want to see in the world. And we cannot be the 'change' unless we are able to reverse what we have injected into our ego-centered consciousness for hundreds, if not thousands of years.

We must reverse the corrosive corruption of consciousness, due to which 'a man fails to express a given emotion, makes him at the same time unable to know whether he has expressed it or not'.[95] In other words, he is not conscious of his own duplicity. Equally important is to get out of our addiction of short-cuts and quick-fixes of technology, and get 'addicted' to love, kindness, and compassion. Researchers are saying that the way the brain is structured, it might be possible to 'self-dope' ourselves to socially beneficial behavior. That is an intriguing possibility, but right now developments in bio-, cyber-, nuclear, and nanotechnologies open up new dangers of error or terror, and in our interconnected world, they could pose risks, even a remote probability of which becomes unthinkable. Unless 'we, the people', not only the scientific or the political community, get a hold on the dialectics and direction of science-based technology, no positive or spiritual transformation can be induced in the human condition. Technology is continuously transforming us and will continue to do so *ad infinitum*, and experts predict that the transition from modern man to nanotechnology-improved man might well be more dramatic and drastic than from the Ice Age to this millennium. It is hard to visualize how the human persona will change if human beings resort to internal and external technological enhancements, not only to overcome any 'natural' impairment but to qualitatively improve their physical and mental powers. Maybe, after a century or two, which incidentally is the time some environmentalists give to human tenure on earth, babies might be born incubated in the laboratory with myopic eyes, and have an organic Blackberry instead of a brain!

If we were to preempt that possibility, however slim and far fetched it might be, we must stimulate another, a humanely human kind of transformation, triggered by 'self-reinforcement' of desirable qualities, instead of gadgetry or mechanized add-ons and plug-ins. Sages, rishis, and spiritualists have long dreamed of transforming self-consciousness into cosmic consciousness, in which one lives in perfect harmony with the universe without the sense of separation. And through that sense of oneness, we will be able to cease to identify ourselves with the present part we are playing in the divine drama, but instead identify with the play as a whole and its Director. Paramahamsa Yogananda, the acclaimed author of *The Autobiography of a Yogi* (1946) said, "The so-called miraculous powers of a great master are a natural accompaniment to his exact understanding of subtle laws that operate in the inner cosmos of consciousness."[96] That ability within the limits set by Nature for the human form of life is another matter. To acquire that capacity might need transformation not only of the 'conscious consciousness' but also of the 'unconscious consciousness'. A guru of positive thinking wrote, "There is consciousness of the ego and the world around you, and there is consciousness of the Real Self, the Real You."[97] Vedanta calls the cosmic or pure consciousness, *cit*, which in fact is singular. Whichever kind of consciousness it might be, it must make it possible to ignite our latent faculties of *viveka* (discriminative capacity) and *vairagya* (renunciation of the fruits of one's effort), bring the intelligences of the mind and heart into a state of harmony and equilibrium, and through that, fundamentally alter the nature of our thinking and feelings, thoughts and emotions. We must go beyond brain-based, sensory cognition and comprehension, and discover new dimensions of consciousness. And we must shed, like a snake that sheds its skin, the fallacy that what we cannot experience does not exist, what we cannot comprehend is fanciful, and that our current paradigm of intelligence is unmatched in the universe. In short, what is needed is a shift in our sense of identity and awareness of ourselves and the world around. Only then we would be able to seek answers to fundamental questions such as 'who am I?', 'what is life?' and 'what am I supposed to do?' and 'where do I go from here?' That could also, in turn, empower us to cleanse our psychic space of our obsessive fear of death and pursuit of sensual pleasure, prurient thrills, power for control and wanton wealth, and help us not to be such a pathological prisoner of anger, greed, and violence. Only then we might be capable of desisting from nagging, nibbling, and negating each other till death does us apart, and begin to view, relate and behave towards another person as if we are him. And then, how do we deal with death? It is doubtful if we will ever be able to look at death as being as normal as the rite of passage from youth to old age. Or as the humanist Rabindranath Tagore put it, "Death is not extinguishing the light; it is putting out the lamp because the dawn has come"[98]. At the least, we should not live as if there is no death, or die as if we never lived. Even if we cannot do any of them, we must, above all or at the least, exorcize malice, the one attribute that can scorch everything by its very proximity, from our consciousness.

The chief obstacle to transformation is the disequilibrium and dysfunction within, our inability to find in the depth of our soul, values worth living for and worth dying for. If we cannot induce synergy within our own consciousness, how can we hope to bring about bliss and peace on earth? For mankind to make any serious dent on the plethora of problems that threaten to hasten its own extinction, we must recognize that the root of the malaise is the closing down of inspirational love, and that the remedy can only come through a return to heart intelligence. For that, we need a new paradigm of human cognition, a joint venture between the intelligences of the head and the heart, each supplementing as well as moderating the natural traits of the other, leading to the evolution of a new consciousness. The odyssey towards heart intelligence has been described as "one of the most exciting, thrilling explorations you will ever take, a journey that will bring more fulfillment and wonder than you have ever imagined, and open doors that you never even knew existed — a journey into your own inner heart. As you venture into your heart and discover your other intelligence that resides there, your heart intelligence — you will connect with its potent energy and begin to trust its power to create the life you are truly meant to live. You will know that your most reliant guide, your most loyal ally, and your truest source of wisdom and pov er reside, not in your mind alone, but deep within you — right in the very center of your being — in your heart."[99] The first step in that journey of discovery is to alter our understanding of the role of heart in life, not merely as an indefatigable muscular mechanism that pumps blood throughout the body, but as a kind of organic machine, an independent source of memory, energy, and intelligence, what Joseph Chilton Pearce calls the 'fourth brain'. For long, the existence inside us of another heart — the spiritual heart — has been spoken about by the scriptures and by saints. Sri Adi Shankara described it as, "That being, of the size of a thumb, dwells deep within the heart. He is the lord of time, past and future. Having attained him, one fears no more. He, verily, is the immortal Self."[100] Sometimes it is referred to as 'the lotus of the heart'. Sri Chinmoy said that inside the ordinary human heart is the divine heart, and inside the divine heart is the soul. In his recent book *The Death of Religion and the Rebirth of Spirit* (2007), Pearce pleads that humanity must rise above its lower, instinctual 'brain' to allow 'our newest brain' — the 'fourth brain' — to blossom, which, he says, will bring about a higher stage in evolution that prizes love and altruism. Our culture and civilization have been the creations of the 'third brain', and in turn they have heavily conditioned our consciousness. They have fashioned a living context in which our image is more important than our ideas, our decisions are governed by desires, and our desires have no bearing on our stated, conscious goals of life. According to Pearce, the biggest impediments to this new order are religion and science, which together promote violence and arrogance. However troubling that thought might be, the fact is that what man is now is the product of organized religion and orthodox science, and unless their grip is loosened, humanity will continue to drift towards the abyss. Every religion must undergo a process of 'winnowing' and 'weeding out' and renounce its delusions of monopoly on divinity and Truth. We must, as Advaita and the doctrine of *Perennial Philosophy* exhort, recognize that the world of matter and individualistic consciousness are rooted in what Huxley called 'Divine Ground', and that to realize it we need 'unitive knowledge' and for that, again, we need to be pure in heart and pure in spirit. While God is Absolute, truth is not; and if truth indeed is Absolute, the fabric of our intelligence is not tailored to fit it. Pearl Buck wrote that truth is as people find it, and kaleidoscopic in its variety. But it is the power of the mind to make us think — and believe — that what we think is the truth, that it is the only truth. And the mind leads us to believe, inferentially, that the other side of the question is false; and that leads to intolerance. Science, in the words of Owen Barfield, needs 'redemption' and redirection. What we lack is not knowledge, spiritual or scientific; it is proper and integral application that is missing. Such a paradigm must enable us to harness our innate capacity for direct knowledge, for immediate insight, without observation or deductive reason, and without abandoning our unique ability to assemble, analyze, and decide; in short, make man worthy of the famous *Hamlet* dictum of Shakespeare: "in action how like an angel! in apprehension how like a god! the beauty of the world, the paragon of animals!"[101] Can science help? Researchers are saying that there could be a 'God-center' in the brain, by stimulating which, with repeated practice, one could attain a state of serenity, bliss, and ecstasy. What spiritualists call 'realization' could then be a neurochemical phenomenon and be 'imaged and anatomically localized'. Happiness, the 'scientific speculation' continues, would then be independent of a cause, and could be triggered at will. So could be perhaps, the sense of the Advaitic oneness, the loosening of the grip of the '*I*-consciousnesses'. Spirituality could then be codified and monitored and managed.

When our mind is attuned to our emotions, it is enriched and made more constructive; and when our emotions are illuminated by our mind, they become more practicable. With the heart and the mind working in harmony, we will cease to be a species feared both by man and beast. God willing, many conflicts that bedevil our lives will become more manageable — from suffocating self-righteousness, to our hopeless inability even to ever imagine that we could be wrong on any issue, to narrow nationalism, which Einstein called the measles of mankind, and rampant consumerism, which is the root cause of environmental degradation, to virulent religiosity whose twin brother is neo-secularism. Only then will the power of man cease to be the peril of the planet, and human presence be a positive proximity. We will then be able to resume our march on the evolutionary path and move on to what Elaine Matthews called the 'higher dimension of awareness.'[102] We might then even be able to understand, if not realize the Upanishadic exhortation to see ourselves as eternal beings presently dreaming the dream of evolution, a dream whose culmination is a different level of 'awareness' or 'awakefulness', towards which all of our attention and energy should be focused.

8

Models and Metaphors for Human Transformation

Lessons from the Living World

The terms 'awareness' and 'wakefulness' often occur in spiritual and religious writings. In such contexts, the ideas they embrace are far more profound, inclusive, and elevating than we normally associate them with: awareness implies *watchfulness*, and wakefulness brings to mind a *state of alertness*. We are 'alive' in different dimensions and 'asleep' in different degrees. One could be 'aware' without being 'awake' and 'awake' without being 'aware'. In spiritual parlance, these notions refer to our state of 'separateness', that is, the way we view ourselves in relation to other humans, non-humans, and to Nature and God. While in our mundane world we are more 'aware' and 'awake' if we are more absorbed with our body and personal lives, it is the opposite in the spiritual sense: the more *detached* we are, the more 'aware' and 'awake' we become. It is a way to destroy the distance between two living beings, which, in turn, will destroy the distance between man and God. In different languages the meaning and import of the word 'aware' varies. For example, in Japanese the phrase '*mono no aware*' is a comprehensive concept that embraces within its ambit attributes we cherish in life: beauty, harmony, sensitivity, empathy, and simplicity. When the Buddha was asked who he was, he replied that he was neither a god nor an angel, and then enigmatically added 'I am awake'. Different scholars and pundits might interpret these three words differently, but they all agree that in 'becoming' a Buddha, Prince Gautama attained a higher, perhaps the ultimate, plateau of consciousness any living being can.

The transition from Prince Siddhartha to Gautama Buddha, what H.P. Blavatsky (*The Secret Doctrine*) called 'the mystery of Buddha', was transformation at the highest and deepest levels through consciousness-change. In Buddhism, 'transformation' itself means awakening a deep awareness of our oneness with all others, even with the world of Nature. Such an awareness will allow caring, compassion, and love to replace indifference, intolerance and hatred as our primary reflexes. The path it prescribes is the path of consciousness change. That ought to be the aim, the goal and direction of transformation we should strive and seek.

Dissatisfied as we are with what we are, and subject as we are to a multitude of constraints, enticements, and temptations, we want to be, all at once and in one leap, a 'saintly superman', to enjoy all good things of life and still be 'good', to experiment with every conceivable or, if we could, even inconceivable experience and still be sinless, to be invulnerable to disease and death but be vulnerable enough to emotions like love. And then, if we must die, we want nothing else but to go to Heaven with our body intact. In Blavatsky's words, used in a different context, it is like 'trying to bottle up the primordial Chaos, to put a printed label on Eternity'. At a more mundane level, we have tried everything, scripturally and scientifically, intellectually and intuitively, and even summoned gods and gurus, to be simply 'healthy and happy', but to no avail. If anything, we are falling behind; things are worse than ever before, at least in the minds of millions. That is largely because that 'health' and 'happiness', like much of everything else in life, is comparative and competitive. But the quest continues. Some see hope in science, some in the innate nature of man; some expect an avatar to save us; some think that the best service we can do to the world of Nature is to quietly dissolve into the sunset. We always feel the need for something tangible; something we can relate to. Where do we look for light and lucidity, metaphors and models? The answer lies in the living world of Nature. An avatar does not have to be a man — or a god. In fact, most of the *avatars* in Hinduism were neither. Maybe, having completed a full circle, from a fish to a perfect man to a *poorna avatar* (complete incarnation), the cycle is going to begin again. Not necessarily as God manifesting as a creepy creature or a winged bird, but with man being given the knowledge and wisdom to *know* what he needs to know to transform himself. But we must realize one basic fact in Nature: we cannot become what we already are not; transformation is to bring out what is implicit, hidden, and camouflaged. A species cannot become another species; and every species is at the same time empowered and conditioned depending on its assigned place on earth. And yet everything is always in a condition of continuous transformation.

Even a stone, for that matter. The nineteenth century *Natural Theology* tradition of seeking sermons in stones symbolizes the essence of man's tendency to find the meaning of existence, his place in the universe, and his responsibility as an individual. Nature bristles with change, transformation, and metamorphosis. Growth, inherent in Nature, is a mysterious process independent of human will. The growth of a seed into a tree is transformation. Jesus used the parable of a mustard seed transforming into a tree with 'great branches' to explain the growth of the Kingdom of God on Earth. And through our lives, we are using what environmental historian Paul Josephson (*Industrialized Nature*, 2002) called brute-force technologies, which transform or rather traumatize the biosphere, the living world, and the earth, and which turn forests into 'cellulose factories', oceans into giant fish ponds, and prairies into bio-industrial landscape. When it comes to such exploitative transformation, all nations, all 'isms', all ideologies are united; the quarrel is over the question of how to share the spoils. Human creativity has transformed the biosphere through several ways such as the invention of fire, language, agriculture, culture, civilization, and science and technology. While transforming the very basis of life engaged in active metabolism, man has also transformed himself, the two processes becoming interactive and increasingly indistinguishable and destructive of both. We must realize and recognize that our relentless pillage, and corruption of Nature with concoctions of dangerous chemicals, is irreparably damaging the biosphere, and insidiously altering the very biology of the human organism, a danger that pioneering environmentalists like Rachel Carson (*Silent Spring*, 1962) have so vividly portrayed.

Our skewed 'transformational' abilities are not directed only against Nature. Natural selection, experts tell us, does not operate in the human sphere exactly as it does in the rest of the living world. Unlike other species, what we know and learn is passed onto our descendents through education, through institutions that nurture transformative practices, through our cultural and religious traditions, and so forth. The hope is that, as we begin to get a deeper understanding of our potential, its enormous range, and how we are both the beneficiaries and the victims of the cultures we live in, we will be able to harness and direct our pregnant potential in the right direction. Transform we must, but we must also remember that, in a crooked way, transformation was what most tyrants and gurus of fanatical cults have tried to engineer in the human psyche, from Genghis Khan to Pol Pot to Jim Jones, at such a horrendous cost. They found what they saw in man — a hindrance to their ambition — and tried to change man as a way to erase an obstacle. But the very idea of transformation involving our personal lives makes us uneasy because it means being something we are not throughout our lives, and that we instinctively resist as a reaction to our fear of the unknown. But, for any change in the mass the individual has to be the basic unit; a society is but a conglomeration of individuals; and in our interconnectedness, the consciousness of each must reflect itself in the consciousness of all. To put the matter simply, because we are the world, the vision that transforms us transforms the world. Some things require repetition, and one such thing is that transformation is not an exotic phenomenon. It is *in situ*, ingrained in Nature and in life. We are 'transformed' all the time, from birth to death and beyond death. The rites of passage — from infancy to adolescence, from youth to old age and indeed death itself — are nothing but transformation. Even in this very life, there is nothing in us that connects to our past, not even memory; we might not even remember many things that happened. Both body and mind change continuously. So, who or what is this '*I*', beyond which we cannot even envision, and we strive so much to keep it alive and appease its every whim and fancy?

The paradox is that we are transformed ceaselessly, but still remain essentially the same. But what that 'same' is, we cannot fathom. The process of transformation is never sudden, never like a low-pressure area strengthening into a cyclonic thunderstorm overnight. It is rather a process of subtle, almost imperceptible change, much like a gentle breeze that gathers incrementally greater momentum to form a strong wind, and eventually becomes another kind of thunderstorm. The 'temporal trajectory' of human transformation is akin to this latter kind of thunderstorm. But first, we have to embrace and energize a *conscious* transformation, so to speak, in which we play our part. The best 'modern' example is Mahatma Gandhi. By his own effort — and God's choice — 'Mohandas' became a 'Mahatma'. What he called *My Experiments With Truth* (the title of his autobiography) is a tale of transformation — from a sensual man into a spiritual man, from a violent man into an apostle of non-violence, from a shy young man into a charismatic leader, from a self-confessed coward, into a man who took on, and toppled, a mighty empire: in short, the transformation from a mere man into a Mahatma. Gandhi transformed, not his life, but himself, by relentlessly chipping away at his imperfections; he did not become a 'perfect man', but a *transformed* man. He was the one man, extraordinarily ordinary, as susceptible to senses as any of us — 'a hapless unprepossessing youth whose only distinction is a marked fear of the dark'[1] — who, as it were, reincarnated without dying, into an altogether different man, an embryonic posthuman, if you will. Perhaps more than any other contemporary human, Gandhi was the symbol of transformation delineated in scriptures like the Sermon on the Mount and the Bhagavad Gita. He remained physically the same, but controlled his mind and transformed his consciousness by turning to his heart — the inner voice — for guidance and inspiration. He proved that man can be spiritually transformed while still living in the material world, and that bodily immortality is not necessary, that it is even counterproductive. In so doing, he told us that all of us can, too. How did this Mahatma do it? What was that 'critical point'? Gandhi was appalled at what he saw of himself and simply decided, deep within himself, to do something about his own condition, not the conditions around. On that dark night at the obscure railway station of Maritzburg, in South Africa, which he himself later described as the most defining moment of his life, he was thrown out of a First Class compartment of a train because he was not a 'white man'. It was at that point that he decided to do something rare in human struggle: never to *yield* to force and never to *use* force. In other words, he chose to transform himself, to fight the real enemy, within, not the world around. We must first ignite deep within a desire to cleanse and change ourselves, and then find our own *Maritzburg*, a spark of our own that will shake us out of our complacency, inertia, and 'quiet desperation', and jump start the process of inner transformation.

To simply stay put, to hang in, to linger and languish and die when the hour strikes, might be comforting. But any choice of *status quo* is the choice of death as a species. Assuming that we summon our will to opt for radical transformation of the right kind, where do we go for guidance and a roadmap? What did our ancestors do? They turned to religion and scriptures. But the record is clear. Only a few saints, *rishis*, and sages have been able to draw upon them for inspiration and for practical help. The very tools and techniques they advocated like total surrender to God, mind control, and detachment from the fruits of one's effort were beyond the capacity of most mortal men. What the other potent transformational force, science-based technology, has been doing is to focus on the body, make it impregnable and immortal. As we have noted before, without a fundamental change in the mindset of man, such a focus could make man a virtual monster and could well hasten human extinction. What are we left with?

Before we proceed any further, we must face up to one basic problem. Human transformation cannot happen at the level of behavior; we need to dive far deeper into our own selves and change the forces that influence our decision making. Unless the way we choose and decide is changed, we cannot be any different from what we are. Our responses and reactions, indeed our perception of our 'problems' and our mindset about possible solutions must therefore change. Only then would sharing become intrinsic to the human way of life; and sharing then cures the malaise of separatism, not only of suffering. The burden of the body is what we carry on our backs. It is the body that we cannot get away from. The question is, Satprem, the disciple of Sri Aurobindo, speculated, will the body of the successor species have 'five fins, wings or a third eye?' Satprem said that "our deficiency is not only a lack of imagination about the future but above all an incapacity to conceive of anything but an improvement or an extension of the present."[2] Would the future man be able to loosen himself from his moorings and levitate as St. Teresa of Avila reportedly did, and as Maharishi Mahesh Yogi's Transcendental Meditation claims we can do, with proper yogic practice? That raises a more basic question. What is our duty in relation to the species that would inherit our mantle as the dominant form of life on earth? If, as the illustrious evolutionary biologist Julian Huxley wrote, "Man is not merely the latest dominant type produced by evolution, but its sole active agent on earth. His destiny is to be responsible for the whole future of the evolutionary process on this planet..."[3] Then how do we approach it?

A related question is: where is science headed in the field of human transformation? On that single question could depend how the future of the human species unfolds. Science by far is the most unpredictably transforming power in the world, and opinions even among scientists vary so widely that it is hard to even make an informed projection of its probable direction and impact. In 2001, a study examined three major forces that will shape the 21st century: Erosion, Technological transformation, and Corporate concentration — 'ETC'[4]. *Erosion* refers to the forces eroding our ecosystems, human cultures, and equitable societies. *Corporate concentration* is going to be, according to this study, a major threat with corporations converging and merging and intruding into the entire human living space and, as author Pat Mooney says, "No one gains more from knowing and controlling genomics than your insurance company", and "What happens to genetic privacy when your doctor is also your insurance agent?"[5] The kind of 'transformation' in the human condition that science is trying to kick start is technological. With regard to the third force, *Technological transformation*, the study says, "As the critical elements for human survival (our biological environment and our cultural diversity) collapse, powerful new technologies are being brought forward to manipulate our world."[6] Not only the world, but our own bodies have become the laboratories of manipulation. The thrust of the scientific effort is to cling to the 'gross' body, the outermost extension of our indwelling divinity. Science aims to make our body stronger; keep it ticking forever; rid it of decay and disease and even death; its dream is to make man a nanotech 'terminator' who can 'romance the robot', conquer space, and at some point, abandon this planet after sucking out every ounce of its juice and emigrate to 'other earths'. In one sense, science is planning to use technology as a short cut to salvation, leaving the body structurally in the 'as is where is' state, and subsume the next phase of evolution. The closest theological parallel is the Hindu ideal of *jivanmukta*; a state of blissful consciousness that can be reached, or more accurately realized, only through supreme spiritual practice in this very body. According to Advaitic philosophy, one who has actually realized God or the *Brahman* is a *jivanmukta*; he is liberated while still living. Such a being continues to live in a material body, because of the momentum of the *prarabdha karma* that has already started taking fruit. But he accumulates no further karma, because all *agamin karma* and *sancita karma* are 'burnt' in the knowledge of '*brahmajnana*'. The body eventually dies, and the *jivanmukta* is said to have attained *videhamukti*. Science-based technology is trying to catapult man into that kind of being by manipulating the body through technology. The aim is to keep the anatomy intact, but alter the various phases of life; stretch out the youth and middle age, and compress the last years of aging and dying, and make the life span so long that death simply becomes theoretical and optional. While the ostensible goal is to make man an 'immortal superman', the same force, technology, is drastically emaciating the body by enticing man to turn to a machine to perform the many functions that Nature intended the body to perform. Soren Kierkegaard wrote that with the power of human invention, "the human race became afraid of itself, fosters the fantastic, and then trembles before it."[7] The fantasy is to prolong the present life indefinitely in the present body and to colonize the cosmos with the same consciousness. We should tremble before it because we have no idea where we will end up. There is mounting evidence to justify a re-examination of basic assumptions that may perhaps lead to a re-definition of what constitutes the essence of scientific endeavor and how it should be conducted. The historical focus of science by a process of physical trial and error is the primary reason why scientific discoveries often generate unpredictable and dangerous effects that could not be foreseen and cannot easily be controlled. That has to yield place to a new mode of approach that minimizes that risk. It is not abdication of science or a throwback to the days of the Paleolithic man, but a broadening of its scope of inquiry and ensuring more inclusive social and spiritual inputs into its prioritization and goal-setting.

What science-based technology is doing, with increasing virtuosity, is empowering man with awesome destructive power. With the ascendancy of the mind, man already became a malicious being, and science has immensely darkened his darker side. Unlike any previous time in the history of human horror, even a small group of men today, even a single individual for that matter, can kill or main thousands. Earlier that kind of power was the monopoly of the State; it is no longer so. In fact, the State itself is fighting a losing battle, relegating itself to a state of disrepute in the public mind. While the destructive potential of nuclear weapons is well known, what is less realized is the potentially deadly power of biotechnology. One comparison of the destructive capability of different weapons of genocide reveals the following disturbing statistics: one tonne of the nerve gas Sarin (used in a Tokyo subway attack in 1995) could kill up to 8,000 people; a one-megaton hydrogen bomb could kill up to 1.9 million people; and, finally, just 100 kg of the deadly Anthrax dropped over a city under favorable weather conditions is capable of wiping out up to three million people. Biowarfare, including agro-terrorism and 'ethnically targeted' attacks are so inexpensive, anonymous, and effective, that there is nothing to stop their use or deployment[8]. The world is already unable to cope with that kind of murderous power in the hands of the State. If that power gets into the hands of a 'driven' individual or a devious 'charismatic' cult leader, the consequences could be catastrophic. While for global consciousness change we need a 'critical' mass, a handful of individuals now can exploit science in order to create new instruments of mass destruction. Nick Bostrom, Director of Oxford's Future of Humanity Institute, sketches several apocalyptic scenarios, besides nuclear holocaust, that threaten humankind, such as the deliberate misuse of nanotechnology, badly programmed super intelligence, and out-of-control global warming. One could add to that list of calamities things like unstoppable pandemics, asteroids from outer space, human cloning, etc. 'Rolling back the specter of a warming planet', might well be the greatest challenge faced by modern man. That could be the gravest challenge man faces now. Scientists are saying that the prehistoric human race came close to extinction because of drastic climate change, and we cannot be so lucky every time. Yet these are all what the human intellect can imagine and project, but there could be scenarios that we cannot even speculate. A pointer can be the past. Time and again, humankind has shown that our destructive creativity and our malevolence have run far ahead of our 'creative constructivism' and benevolence. We have not been able to balance passion, an attribute of the mind, and compassion of the heart; we have not been able to make passion compassionate, and compassion, passionate. Passion without compassion ultimately leads to hubris and self-exaltation. Compassion without passion might be momentary and fleeting. Compassion makes passion others-centered. Passion makes compassion operative and effective. At a more foundational level, the human species has failed, from its inception to the present times, to govern itself. Indeed the word 'governance' is ill-suited to the human species. We have not managed to find a way to share what the planet offers us without killing ourselves and endangering the earth. We cannot 'govern' our passions, drives, and desires as individuals. Successive models of political governance from city-State to the Sovereign States to the United Nations have proven unequal to their tasks and mandates. The world faces far greater problems and dangers than ever before, and what it calls for is global governance and a World Government.

That is a tall order, and calls for extraordinary effort and a serious quest for new avenues and models of change. But all such avenues and ideas will be still born given man's present make-up, and the consciousness that drives his actions. If scripture and science cannot provide us the 'models' for our metamorphosis, the only resort we have is to turn to what man has always turned to when he is in 'deep trouble' or at an impasse: the universe of Nature. Nature is nothing if not transformation. The change of seasons from spring to fall to winter is transformation. A single seed becoming a mighty tree is transformation. An egg becoming a bird is transformation. And thoughtful humans have long looked to the natural world for guidance and illumination, seeking analogy, metaphor, and messages in all quarters of the animate and inanimate worlds. Nature invariably holds up a mirror so we can more clearly see the ongoing processes of growth, renewal, and transformation in the living world. If that were so, then where can we find similes for our present plight and future pointers? The answer ironically seems to revolve around three creatures that we instinctively detest and spurn: *insects* (like ants, bees and termites), the *caterpillar*, and the *rat*.

Of Man and Mice

Taking the last creature first, the particular type that is relevant to the present human predicament is the lemming, a small rodent that is found in vast numbers in the Arctic. Rodents have been around for about 57 million years, and form about forty percent of all mammal species on earth. Much as we detest them, we seem more and more drawn to them. Increasingly, science is turning to this lowly creature, the rodent, for therapeutic testing. We read a headline that says, "Infertile men can bank on mice for kids",[9] and the story goes on to say that mice have been used to make human sperm, and what it means is that "an infertile man could have a baby by giving up one of his teeth and agreeing to involve a mouse in the process of reproduction."[10] In other words, in a twist of exquisite irony, we have more in common with mice than what the Scottish poet Robert Burns gave us to believe: "*The best laid schemes o' Mice an' Men, gang aft agley*" (the best-laid plans of mice and men often go awry). So, if all else fails, man can turn to the lowly and much-despised mouse to see that he does not become extinct! We are now told that in the case of both mice and men, it is the structure of the odorant molecule, not solely experience or culture, that determines the smells they love or loathe. In simple terms, both humans and mice are attracted by the same odors. Scientists even say that the mouse genome might be even more important than the human genome to medicine and human welfare, because as much as 99 percent of mouse genes have analogues in humans and, more important, the genes appear in the same order in the two genomes.[11] The scientists are even dangling before us the possibility of eternal youth and life spans of up to 125 years based on a genetic breakthrough, of all things, on rodents. The analogy does not end there. The human race seems to increasingly resemble another rodent, the lemming. One of the most fascinating aspects of this small rodent is its ability to survive in a predominantly harsh environment like the Arctic, despite being a staple prey for bigger animals and birds. Lemmings remain active throughout the Arctic winter without freezing to death. Lemmings are good swimmers and can cross a body of water in search of a new habitat. Although accounts of lemmings committing mass suicide by jumping off a cliff remains a myth, large migrations across water triggered by a search for new habitat inevitably results in exhaustion, drowning, and accidental mass death. Lemmings are also often pushed into the sea as more and more lemmings arrive at the shore. For still unknown reasons, lemming numbers wildly fluctuate, reaching a peak every three or four years. Lemming suicide is a frequently used metaphor in reference to people who go along unquestioningly with popular opinion, with potentially dangerous or fatal consequences.[12]

Although experts tell us that it is not true, the myth of the 'Lemming Suicide Plunge', is now a part of anecdotal folklore. It stems from an old belief that lemmings, apparently overcome by deep-rooted impulses, deliberately hurtle themselves over a cliff in millions, only to be dashed to their death on the rocks below, or to drown in the turbulent sea. It is part myth and part real: actually, the pressure for food, space or mates becomes too intense and then they sometimes kill each other. Even setting aside allegations that the Walt Disney documentary *White Wilderness* propagated the myth of lemming mass suicides, the parallels one can draw between humans and these rodents are uncanny and unsettling. The fact is that suicide is fast approaching pandemic proportions in humans, not yet in numbers, but in triviality of cause and impulsiveness. No one can now predict which word or action will provoke a suicide or a homicide. Lemmings are notorious for wild and inexplicable population explosions, alternating between rocketing numbers and near extinction. While, unlike humans, they might not deliberately kill themselves, they, like humans, kill each other when the competition for food, space, and mates becomes too intense. There are clear parallels with us. Human population numbers and rates of fertility also fluctuate, not in terms of time but of space. It is said that there are over sixty countries in which fertility is lower than the replacement level, while in some other parts of the world, the situation resembles that of lemmings on the cliff. The number of humans on earth is expected to gallop, according to the United Nations, from 6.7 billion to 9.2 billion by 2050. Ironically, while we quibble and quarrel about everything, on one thing most people in the world agree: we are far too many for our own good, and if only we can somehow stabilize or even bring down our numbers, earth will become a heaven!

Population density, combined with mass poverty is so explosive in some parts of the world that millions are migrating, like lemmings, to distant lands where they often find themselves rootless and adrift. And the pressure for food, jobs, living space and pursuit of pleasure, power, and profit is becoming so intense that the twin pandemics of suicide and homicide are increasingly finding favor in the mainstream humankind as an 'honorable' option to manage any problem. Turning the tables, perhaps Nature is adopting a human technique — population control — to cope with a universal problem: predatory human behavior. Like lemmings, we too migrate in large numbers when population density becomes too great and we too, after nearly two million years of evolution, have arrived at the edge of a cliff, with an abyss in front and with howling winds behind; we too are increasingly dying together in large numbers due to Nature's fury or man-made massacres. And lemming-like, more men and women are meeting only to mate and then go their separate ways, and they too have a capacity for reproduction year round. And humans too are essentially solitary by nature and, like these creatures, the stronger ones drive away the weaker ones. Lemmings are also known to be cannibalistic during times of food stress; increasingly so are we, at least metaphorically, if not yet literally. And we too are more murderous in clusters and as members of mobs. In fact, we do 'better' than the lemmings; we kill by complacency, for example, by just ignoring the living conditions of millions; conditions that are so subhuman that it amounts to both 'slow suicide' and 'mass murder'. We cannot read the mind of a lemming, but the human mind seems to have become an exterminator driven by murderous rage to annihilate everything around.

The Butterfly

The other analogy that Nature offers, perhaps the most enchanting and tantalizing, is that of the ugly *caterpillar* and its transformation into one of the most beautiful creatures on earth, the butterfly. It is fascinating because it involves the metamorphosis of a creature we loathe — the caterpillar — into one that we admire and want to emulate — the butterfly. And Nature — or the hand of God — is at its most transformative in this case. The breathtaking transformation of a caterpillar into a butterfly through the virtual death of pupation has led to much speculation about analogies to human fate and transformation. The great Russian short-story writer Anton Chekhov perhaps best captured 'the anomaly of the anomaly' when he wrote, "In nature, a repulsive caterpillar turns into a lovely butterfly. But with humans, it is the other way around: a lovely butterfly turns into a repulsive caterpillar". The challenge is to turn 'the other way around' around, shed what is ugly and abominable in us and become a kinder, gentler being, and be 'awake', because, as Thoreau put it, 'to be awake is to be alive'. The transformation of the creepy caterpillar has yielded some of the most beautiful poems and verses in literature. Chinese philosopher Chuang Tzu wrote, "I do not know whether I was then a man dreaming I was a butterfly, or whether I am now a butterfly dreaming I am a man"[13] Why did not God create a butterfly directly like the millions of other insects he created? The reason perhaps is that God wanted us to see the transformation that even an earthly being is capable of. Our earthly life can be compared to the caterpillar stage; our physical body to the larva; the emergence of the soul from our dying or dead body to that of a butterfly from the pupa. It is a mysterious process, particularly pupation, without which there can be no transformation, no butterfly. The butterfly, also called a 'flying flower', is the symbol of beauty, freedom, and victory. During its first life, an egg hatches and the larva is born, growing into a pubescent caterpillar. As an earthbound creature, the caterpillar crawls on the ground. After the completion of its life as a caterpillar, a great change occurs. It begins to weave a thread around itself and an entire new life begins. The caterpillar encases itself in a chrysalis that becomes a chamber for its final metamorphosis into a butterfly. Although the butterfly appears far different from the caterpillar, the butterfly is the eventual manifestation of structures that are latent in the caterpillar. The amazing thing is that distinct stages of development into a butterfly— egg, caterpillar, cocoon, butterfly— all are very different from each other, and each phase has a specific purpose, orchestrated by God, not the butterfly, although the caterpillar has to cooperate and be involved in some aspects of these changes. Researchers have noted that some of the rudimentary structures of the pupa are already present in the mature caterpillar, even during the embryonic development in the egg. In its passage from one form to another, the butterfly draws upon these structures which were earlier underdeveloped or camouflaged by other more dominant features. In short, the butterfly is not a different being or a newer form of life than the caterpillar; through a magical process it so transforms itself that it bears no physical resemblance to its own form, and an earthbound crawling creature suddenly becomes bird-like.

What lessons can we draw from this 'Miracle in Nature'? Why Nature endowed only the caterpillar with this capability, and what cosmic cause it serves, we do not know, and if it will let man emulate the lowly caterpillar we can only wonder. Clearly that kind of power is not of the caterpillar but of the divine. There is much to learn from this fragile but exquisite creature, the butterfly, but in our behavior, at this point of time, we are more like the voracious caterpillar. Like the caterpillar, we do not know what 'enough' for us is. The caterpillar spends as much as 90 percent of its time eating; we are close to that in our appetite for resources. We must note that in this kind of transformation, what actually happens is that at a certain stage, some innate but hidden features come to the fore and assume commanding positions while others, till then dominant disappear.[14] Who orchestrates and fine tunes this complicated process. What 'intelligence' does the caterpillar have? Can our 'intelligence' match that of the creepy creature? For our own transformation, we must find a way to subdue or eliminate the obnoxious features that have come to dominate our lives, and draw upon the dormant but latent nobler features. The butterfly chooses to be born twice in one lifetime and lives two complete lives. In this way, butterflies tell us that we live forever, that life is continuum, that transformation even in 'one life' is possible. It visibly illustrates what the Bhagavad Gita says, that what we deem as death is but another phase of life, not the finale. The physical aspects and forms of the butterfly during the four stages of its life teach us the meaning of metamorphosis and the limits of transformation. Metamorphosis is more than physical change that happens between the stages of caterpillar and butterfly. Just as the body of a 'creepy' caterpillar dies and becomes a winged being, we must induce the death of the ego-self to become a new and 'improved' product. To come out of the cocoon, the pupa agonizingly struggles and in the process, it becomes stronger: which is a lesson for us that struggle and suffering are necessary for real change. Just as each time a butterfly flaps its colorful wings, it leaves behind a glow of iridescent light behind, our lives also could leave a trail of compassion. We can learn humility from the butterfly: to accept where we are in our stage of growth. We can learn from the butterfly that vulnerability is part of the process of living, and being soft can be a strength, and that death is a step towards life. Like a caterpillar, which eats its way out of its egg, and then starts eating the leaves of its host plant until it grows too big for its old skin, we too seem ravenous in our assault on Nature. In the case of the caterpillar, it must first become a curious creature, alive but not fully, and then build for itself the chrysalis or pupa, a quiet house, a safe place for it to grow into its true form. Without becoming a pupa, a caterpillar cannot become a butterfly.

The crucial issue is, what could the human equivalent of a pupa be? An indeterminate intermediate being? Or more probably, a state of consciousness that is half human and half successor sub-species? How much of what we have must we shed, and how much of what is inherent but hidden must be activated? And how do we acquire that kind of capacity and intelligence? This is the contingency that Sri Aurobindo visualized. According to him, 'between this supramental being and humanity, there would be transitional beings, who would be human in birth and form, but whose consciousness would approach that of the supramental being. These transitional beings would appear prior to that of the full supramental being, and would constitute an intermediate stage in the Earth's evolution, through which the soul would pass in its growth towards its divine manifestation as the supramental being on earth.'[15]

Perhaps the telling clue in the transformation of the caterpillar is that to trigger the process, it creates a safe environment around itself, a sort of buffer from the world, a place where it can simply be without the enabling environment; the caterpillar will only be a caterpillar, not a soaring butterfly. To change the condition, we must change the context, which is as much internal as external. We must do the same as that creepy creature: go within and create a conducive and compatible environment, as close to the divine as possible, around and within us. The butterfly is an excellent example of the inevitability of our march towards consciousness. Each human being is absolutely unique — one of the many species of 'butterfly' — but the process of transformation will inexorably lead each of us to the same outcome. In the words of Genece Hamby, "Our world and organizations have been run by caterpillars who, with an insatiable appetite to have more, have destroyed their environment. People, in the caterpillar stage of transformation, step over others in their path in order to reach their ego-centered goals. They want to have the most money and the best that money can buy and have little conscience as to how the needs of others are met."[16]

Our own chrysalis, our cocoon, which is the sum of our culture and our civilization we have created and nurtured, will not let the 'human butterfly' to happen. We are too much of a 'caterpillar', perhaps more creepy and avaricious than the real one itself. Like the caterpillar that first eats the leaf it hatches on and goes after other sources, we too are 'eating' on the earth and searching for other planets to replicate the ravage. It is significant that the chrysalis or pupa is already formed beneath the skin of the caterpillar, and emerges in its final form as the caterpillar sheds its skin for the last time. In Nature, what is not innate or implicit cannot be even 'transformed'. We need a fundamental change inside ourselves to bring about a transformative environment outside and to break free from our own cocoon. The 'transformation' we have induced is not internal but external, and that too not conducive to our spiritual growth but to pollute and poison the very environment that sustains life on earth. And the word 'others' which has come to signify and symbolize separateness and self-centeredness has to become a unifier. The test of transformation is how our life impacts on the lives of 'others'. Helping 'others' should not be a humanitarian response; it must be a *human* response, not a matter of barter but for the sake of our own soul. And for any of that 'wish list' to become 'natural' to man, not a labored 'civilized' response, we must 'unlearn' many things that have seeped into our consciousness as part of our culture, and we must radically change the way we perceive ourselves and the world outside. We must unlearn to look at everything in an either/or way. We must unlearn that in every situation, one must prevail and another must yield, that alternatives are necessarily opposites. We have to nurture a mindset that looks at another person as really oneself in another body. And for that, we must change the forces that influence our perception, which, in turn, means fundamentally changing the content and character of the things that make us what we are: education, parenting, dialectics of economics, thirst for power and control, entertainment, religion, science, technology, and so on. And we must learn to look within. In her book, *A Message for Humanity: The Call of God's Angels at a Time of Global Crisis* (2001), Karyn Martin-Kuri, wrote that, with our preoccupation with waging battles on multiple fronts, economic, environmental and religious, we are missing the greatest battle, the most deadly one, that of the inner nature of the human being. And also that, "every time we think a negative thought or commit an act of jealousy, greed, or hatred, we hold the angels at bay. The angels want to help us, but they are powerless, except in extreme cases, unless we create an atmosphere of love and kindness within which they can intercede for us. When God gave us free will, he gave us the opportunity to determine our fate. In hearing and acting on the messages from the angels, we come closer to God."[17] To create that 'atmosphere of love and kindness' and to cleanse ourselves of greed, jealousy, malice, and hatred, which has been a timeless longing of the human race, nothing short of transformational catharsis will do.

All tangible human effort towards transformation is now almost exclusively scientific. It is essentially three-pronged. *One*, through technologies like cryonics, science is trying to eliminate the irrevocable nature of death, to make it *optional*. *Two*, through nanotechnology, and using what are being called 'enhancement technologies', it is fundamentally changing the biological 'boundaries' of the human body; we can or, so we are told, soon will be able to, enhance the operational capacity of almost every single organ beyond the natural limits of the human species. Once that happens, everything will be transformed — the human way of life, human values, cultures, priorities, and perceptions. *Three*, it is hoping that through technologies like the Internet, the world will be integrated and mankind will achieve the age-old dream of universal brotherhood, and turn the conglomerate of a disparate human society into a coherent and connected community. The human species, science expects, will then be transformed into a '*superorganism*', a term loaded with irony when we realize it does not refer to the likes of angels or gods, but to insects.

Analogy of Insects

Such a contingency brings us to the third possible 'model' of human transformation — the world of insects. The physical transformation of an insect from one stage of its life cycle to another is called metamorphosis. Insects may undergo gradual metamorphosis, where transformation is subtle, or complete metamorphosis, where each stage of the life cycle appears quite different from the others. With more than a million species on earth, the ubiquitous insect can be found in the soil beneath our feet, in the air above our head, on and in the bodies of the plants and animals around us. They are integral and essential to life on earth. But we tend to think that we are better off without them. In our search to reorder and reorganize the human world, as a way to enhance our interdependence, scientists are turning their attention to a class of insects they call 'social insects', like the ants, which, it is said, make up an incredible 20 percent of the animal biomass on the planet. No mere masses of bugs, the habitats of these insects seem to be highly integrated functional units whose members communicate, cooperate, and coordinate their efforts at such activities as defending their group, searching for food, building homes, and caring for their young, much as we humans try to do. The expectation is that a future digital human society might well resemble an ant heap, a beehive, or a termite colony. Many thoughtful people have for long been captivated by the similarities — some real, some euphoric — between anthills and human societies. In the view of the biologist E.O. Wilson, ants are metaphors for men, and men for ants. Margaret Atwood, in her review of Wilson's book *Anthill* (2010), says, "Though there are no symphony orchestras, secret police or schools of philosophy, both ants and men conduct wars, divide into specialized castes of workers, build cities, maintain infant nurseries and cemeteries, take slaves, practice agriculture, and indulge in occasional cannibalism, though ant societies are more energetic, altruistic, and efficient than human ones"[18] But the analogy of the ant is ancient and scriptural. *The Book of Proverbs* says, "Go to the ant; thou sluggard. Consider her ways and be wise". The advice is to emulate the organization and industry of the ant. Thoreau, referring to ants, wrote (*Walden*), 'the more you think of it; the less the difference' between man and ant. Aristotle and Karl Marx, among others, argued that humans are social animals, and Marx wrote that, 'each individual has no more torn himself from the navel-string of his tribe or community, than each bee has freed itself from connexion with the hive'

(*Capital*). According to thinkers like Peter Kropotkin (*Mutual Aid: A Factor of Evolution*, 1902), the pinnacle of 'social perfection' is occupied by ants and bees.

But the 'perfect' order of anthill also evokes robotic regimentation and fascist tyranny. Ants are essential to human life, but as Atwood puts it "too few ants would be a disaster; but so would too many". While the organizational order and almost perfect division of labor in ant colonies has long been envied, modern science is trying to bring it closer home. The thesis is that the drift of human development over the past ten thousand years has been towards bigger and bigger collaborative units, consequent economic specialization, social order, and progressive interconnectedness, all of which could culminate in the emergence of a cohesive, global 'superorganism'. In other words, through connectivity, man kindles consciousness change, which will then pave the way to a just society and transformation. By clasping the global interconnectedness that technology enables and empowers, humankind will be able to get rid of its divisive and destructive tendencies, achieve a better division of labor and synergize its energy. Critics counter and say that, unlike in ants, it is competition that distinguishes us, not only between nations and societies but also between communities, religions, and individuals. They say that we are more like plants: a seed becomes a tree and fills out available space, crowding out all competitors. Although science now embraces the ant, it is ancient wisdom that we have much to learn from the lowly and loathsome insect. As Hobbes noted, human society is driven by strive and conflict. The reason why the human world never really had a 'communist' society and why real socialism never had a chance is because we are governed by 'reason'. An ant or a bee, as Dostoevsky noted, knows the formula of an anthill or a beehive respectively; only humankind does not know the formula suited to its genius. What we call the 'human way of life' is for every individual to incessantly seek the 'perfect security of pleasure' and 'problem-free happiness', and leave the fortunes of the community to its benevolent or malevolent fallout. For bees and ants, the common good is indistinguishable from the individual good, and they are apparently able to live their lives in accordance with the dictum that the scriptures exhort humans to cultivate as the habit of coexistence — one for all and all for one. For man, joy consists in comparing himself and competing. Social insects lack reason and so are unaware of the fruits of their own labor and faults of their leaders. And it is hard to envision technology being able to change all that and make man behave like a bee or an ant with the kind of consciousness we have.

The Rainbow

The breathtaking beauty of the "transformation" of a raindrop into a rainbow is another ray of hope. It tells us that if we can put in place the right context, nothing is beyond the horizon of human reach, that man can be transformed to his deepest depth. The magical mystery of the rainbow has long inspired and transfixed the human imagination, and is the stuff of legend and myth in ancient cultures and religions. If nothing in Nature is an accident or redundant, what purpose does the rainbow serve and what message does it convey? Man himself has been compared to a rainbow, a mosaic of all seven colors, symbolizing his multi-faceted, multi-dimensional complexity. In Hindu mythology, the rainbow is referred to as *Indradhanush* or the bow of Indra, the king of gods. And in Greek mythology, it is considered as a path made by the messenger Iris between Earth and Heaven. Some ancient indigenous cultures like the Cree American Indians believed that when the world becomes completely corrupted, the earth is ravaged, the waters are blackened, when birds fall from the skies, forests are destroyed, and the air is so thick it can be touched, mankind would turn to what they called the 'Warriors of the Rainbow', the keepers of the legends, stories, cultures, and values of the 'earth people'. These 'warriors' would go to the far corners of the world and spread love, harmony, and brotherhood, and cleanse the world of poisons and restore the purity and sanctity of the earth.[19] The prophecy of another Native American Indian tribe, the Hopi, says, "When the earth is dying, there shall arise a new tribe of all colors and all creeds. This tribe shall be called *The Warriors of the Rainbow*, and it will put its faith in actions not words."[20] After all, a legend is a happening waiting in the wings, and the way a rainbow actually materializes offers hope that anything is possible if a certain conjunction of factors and forces can be induced. Just as many different colors combine to make the rapturous rainbow, we too need a magical process to harmonize the myriad divisions of humanity into a coherent community. Just as a rainbow constitutes a symbol of unity in diversity, which displays a colorful image of different colors, not mixed or fused, but alongside one another, so should humanity not seek uniformity or homogeneity, but learn the art of cooperative coexistence. In another sense, what the rainbow in the sky illustrates is what the Upanishads tirelessly teach, that the Reality is One; diversity and multiplicity are only appearances.

Human Effort and Divine Dispensation

Whichever way we go on the path of our labyrinthine evolution, the way of the ant or bee or the rodent or the butterfly, depends on two kinds of choices—ours and God's. Our choice, among other things, stems from the state and nature of our knowledge. In the scheme of the Scriptures, ***knowledge*** of one's self and of the universe (called *anfus* and *aafaaq* in Islam; *atmanjnana* and *shristijnana* in Hinduism), along with ***divine grace*** (or ***will***) constitute the two agents of change and the two triggers of transformation. It is the will to 'know' that made man, according to the Bible and the Quran, even superior to the angels. The Upanishads say that all come in will, consist of will, abide in will, and exhorts man to meditate on Will, and such a person indeed is *Brahman.*

The problem is that our will to acquire knowledge is often stronger than our insight into the limits — and temptations — of knowledge. While God hoped that the combination of reason and Revelation would enable man to be a wise viceroy on earth, man has found a way through the mind to subvert both. Our will takes the shape of 'want', and 'want' becomes thought, word and action and in the process gets sullied. In one Hindu ritual, the person chants, 'I will absolve myself from the sins of my behaving as I wish, talking as I wish and indulging in drinking and eating as I wish.' In the Christian theological doctrine of 'total depravity', the Fallen man is utterly incapable of truly choosing God or bettering himself, and he needs God's Grace to escape God's wrath. It is man's apostasy from God that is responsible for the wretched state of the world. The Hindu scripture *Yagnavalkya smruti* says that effort is what you do in this life, and destiny is the expression of efforts made in previous lives; the self-effort of the present life determines the future destiny of our soul. In other words, the fruits in the form of debits (unrighteous acts) and credits (righteous acts) created by the self-effort of this birth will be reaped in future lives. Upon the death of this body, the only thing that goes with the soul is our *karmic* actions. But 'will' is not action, and we know very little about how 'will' translates — or does not — into behavior. Then again, we are bewildered how, as the Bhagavad Gita exhorts, one can be detached from the fruits of action in the midst of ceaseless action, and how one can annihilate avarice while living in a world suffused with sensory pleasure.

Whether human effort can be corrected solely through human will has been a subject of intense theological debate for long. It perhaps depends on the timeframe and our understanding — or interpretation — of the words and concepts: will, effort and grace, and of how they interface. Swiss philosopher Frithjof Schuon (*Roots of the Human Condition*, 1991) says that man's whole nature, vocation, and duty is to know totally, to will freely, and to love nobly. All three seem to be woefully wobbly. Knowing has not helped us much in doing the right thing; our will has not made us any wiser. And love today has no soft feathers, only sharp teeth. The Buddha said 'only when you reject all help you are freed'. And one might add, 'only when you do not want to cling to something can you truly enjoy having it'. Life is inextricably tied to action and, as a Sikh scripture says, 'without self-effort or exertion one cannot even jump over the footprint of an animal'. Hannah Arendt wrote that pain and effort are so ingrained in the human condition that we cannot remove them without changing life itself, and that an effortless life would be a lifeless life. Sustained effort, *nishkamakarma*, can make the 'moment of the miracle' not so miraculous; it can make the supernatural natural, the extraordinary ordinary. But making it possible is not the same as making it happen. Since every effort is a question of 'choice', what impels us to choose a particular path? Is that entirely an exercise of free will and our analytical capacity? Is it all self-induced and self-devised or self-inflicted? Is it something that gets done *by* us or *through* us? We might say all good things about will, action, and effort, but it is an illusion to think that we 'rationally' and volitionally choose anything. There are no absolutes in life, and many a time, we are unable to do things we are capable of doing or do things we do not want to do. It is not as if we think through, identify the options, choose the most cost-effective and correct alternative, and implement it. It is usually a convoluted, unconscious process that becomes action. We all agree that we make choices and every choice leads to consequences, and that we are responsible for our actions — and silences. But behind that truism lie several subtleties. The question is why and how we 'choose' something over another alternative? The fact is that we really do not know what happens inside us before a thought, a feeling, or an emotion germinates and then becomes behavior. Is it confined to our own personality, parentage, and predilections, or to other factors and forces — divine will, fate or *karma* — that become deterministic? The key is the mind. Whether the effect is positive or negative, it is caused by our own mind; the mind is the conduit for *karma* as well as its consequence. And the outcome can be many times more expansive than the original karmic action. According to the Buddhist scholar Nagarjuna, if we cheat one person, we will be cheated by other persons in one thousand lifetimes. Kahlil Gibran wrote that we choose our joys and sorrows long before we experience them. There is a Sanskrit proverb that says '*Buddhi karmanusaray*', meaning the mind works according to karma. It means that effort, even if it is intentional, is not wholly of the human will, and the choices we make are a function of the outcome we are destined to cause or trigger. Put differently, it means that the nature of the effort we make is programmed to fit the predetermined result. That 'program' is nothing but the actions and efforts of countless lives. Nothing happens to us that we did not cause ourselves. A Buddhist teaching says that through endless time we have all done everything any human — and non human — can do. We have all been murderers, molesters, mothers, fathers, brothers, doctors, and every possible thing. All these actions have sown seeds that come to fruition through future lives. They come to fruition not only through what we do, but also through what others do to us. The pain caused by someone else's actions might be the 'harvest' of a seed sown long ago by us.

But what about that mighty force, the human will or will power, in the shaping of our destiny? The debate between, in the words of Rumi, 'necessitations and the partisans of free will' is timeless, and is at the root of morality and religion. Whether the two are really independent of each other or really complementary, and where one ends and the other begins, and how the two could be harmonized, are age-old questions. If our actions are devoid of will then we are blameless, and if we are wholly empowered by our actions, then the divine becomes ornamental. Such is the degree of ambivalence and ambiguity that even within the same religion, if not the same scripture, different passages appear to give different messages. If God is the sole source of knowledge and power in the universe, and is everything, everywhere, inside and outside, as the Upanishads proclaim, then how could the human will be any different? On the other hand, another Hindu scripture *Yoga Vasishta*, seems to offer another message; it extols human will as the paramount force. Learned commentators try to reconcile and bring out the nuances, but for the uninitiated and the ordinary, it all aggravates their state of confusion about the true nature of their identity, essence, and empowerment. In the end, it all comes down to that one word: 'choice'. For what we call 'will' is really the faculty of choice, the immediate cause of action. And choice means the refusal of one alternative and the assent to another. Every choice has a consequence and every consequence calls for another choice. And choice can be volitional or involuntary, and it also brings up the question of levels of consciousness. Who controls the consciousness, controls choice.

What we have to ponder over is this. Of the millions or billions of choices we make in a lifetime, how many, if any, are truly free, unfettered, and volitional? We think we have the 'freedom of choice', but in actuality we are managed and manipulated to make the choices someone else wishes us to make. We actually have less freedom and little choice. We may have been free in exercising our will, but not in choosing what we willed. The daily reality is that there is hardly anything that we can truly and wholly do but not out of necessity, and we should perhaps thank God for that; for, had it not been so, the consequences would have been catastrophic. Will becomes wish and wish turns into a want, and then the mind goes berserk. For the sake of what man believes to be 'freedom' — political, economic — he seems prepared to surrender his free will. To fulfill his wants, his sensual desires, man is prepared to sell his soul and sup with the devil. That is no longer a fictional scenario or a theoretical possibility. Scientists are predicting that soon behavioral engineers and neuroscientists will be able to so condition our brains that every choice we think we are making is really what the State or someone else wants us to think we are making, the concretization of the scenarios of Aldous Huxley's *Brave New World* (1931) and B.F. Skinner's *Walden Two* (1948). In one sense, free will in the human context is an oxymoron; it is really an attribute of God; and so is unfettered sovereignty. As the Creator of the world, God is sovereign in the true sense of the term. He has chosen to bring into existence a world of substantially free agents. God's relationship with His creation is dynamic, not deterministic. He has foreknowledge of everything that will ever occur as a direct result of the future free will choices, without Himself being the free agent that causes them. Still, we must acknowledge the fact that the human intellect is either unsuitable or insufficient to definitively settle the equation between human effort and divine devotion in shaping human destiny. On the one hand, the scriptures maintain that no amount of self-effort can be enough to intuitively perceive divinity, and on the other, they proclaim that Divine help cannot come without utmost effort and spiritual discipline. The Bhagavad

Gita simultaneously advocates the two apparently adversarial practices of *abhyasa*, ceaseless effort, and *vairagya*, renunciation of the fruits of that very effort; to strive as if effort is everything and to surrender to God as if anything else is useless. The Indian scripture almost dismisses the divine role in human affairs and extols human will and effort. Perhaps the debate in one way exemplifies the limits of human intelligence. After all, what we choose to call human will is but a divine manifest.

One could say that *karma* is God's law of perfect justice, through which He makes sure that a good or a bad thought, word or deed is rewarded or punished, partially or wholly, on this earth. Logically, it means that He can change anything He wants. The story of Markandeya in the Hindu scriptures, in which Lord Shiva intervenes and saves a boy from predetermined death, a part of his karma, illustrates this point. In another story, coincidentally narrated by the same sage Markandeya to King Yudhisthira in the Mahabharata (*Vana parva*), Yama, the king of death restores Satyavan to life as a boon to his virtuous wife Savitri. One of the names of Lord Vishnu in Hinduism, *Dharmadhyaksha*, according to Sri Adi Shankara's interpretation, means the One who directly sees the merits (*dharma*) and demerits (*adharma*) of beings by bestowing their due rewards on them. What we do not know is what should we do and what we ought not to do to make Him bestow his grace or mercy. But even if God wants to do something, the actual 'doer' is man himself. As German theologian and writer Dorothea Soelle puts it, "God has no other hands than ours. If the sick are to be healed, it is our hands that will heal them. If the lonely and the frightened are to be comforted, it is our embrace, not God's, that will comfort them."[21] All creation and all creatures are 'God's own hands' and He deploys them as he deems necessary and suitable. The architecture of life itself is divine. Life on earth is based on such superhuman fine-tuning and extraordinary combination of forces and factors, that all of it cannot simply be dismissed as cosmic randomness or fortuitous coincidence. Some scientists say that but for a certain 'tweaking' of some 'cosmological constraints', the universe would have been filled only with huge black holes or would have been totally devoid of stars. Hugh Ross in his paper *Limits for the Universe* lists 47 items in the universe like gravitation, oxygen and ozone levels in the atmosphere, magnetic field and nuclear force and their precise presence as evidence for design in the universe.[22] Others like Stephen Gould and James Wilson turn the 'evidence' around and say if the world were designed by God, things would be more perfect — inferentially, our lives would be better.

We might know the precise 'mix and match', but clearly both human will and divine disposition will have much to do with human future. Whether we go off the cliff like the lemmings, unable to bear the burden of 'civilized' life, or develop a 'human pupa' to become a 'human butterfly', or emulate the ant or the bee and reorder human society with a perfect 'division of labor', or just implode from the pandemics of suicide and homicide, would depend, in the final reckoning, on the content and balance in our consciousness between the two intelligences of mind and heart. For, without a catharsis of consciousness there cannot be, as all human history shows, any comprehensive change in human behavior. It is only then that man can achieve, in Sri Aurobindo's words, "the change from a mental being to a spiritual being."[23] For us, to make any advance towards a consciousness that we are not isolated bodies adrift in a sea of matter but are connected souls in an ocean of spirit, we need a consciousness change. We must induce congruence between three parallel processes: evolutionary imperatives, technological change, and spiritual transcendence, similar to what French Jesuit philosopher Pierre Teilhard de Chardin called '*Omega point*', the maximum level of complexity and consciousness towards which the universe appears to be evolving. The journey of our healing, reclaiming, re-unifying all that is separate in us and our spiritual evolution are one and the same — evolution in consciousness. There is nothing else going on — regardless of what anything that appears to be, or looks like, or is believed to be. There is nothing but the ongoing process of liberation, the evolution of consciousness. To change the internal image of reality, we need a consciousness change. For us to overcome the twin drags of attachment and separateness and cultivate what is called 'holy indifference' or non-attachment to the fruits of one's labor and the Oneness of all Life, we need consciousness change. In the Chinese Consciousness-Only school of Buddhism, Buddhahood is not a goal to be attained through the acquisition of new knowledge or new conceptual understanding, but it is the end product of a fundamental internal transformation, which is the transformation of consciousness. And which means that, we need to go 'behind behavior' and the façade of 'social civility', and change what transpires inside us before it comes out and impacts the world: consciousness. Man could then be still a man, but cease to be a threat to life on earth, and acquire a compassionate consciousness. For real consciousness change we need to bring the heart to the epicenter of human consciousness. Acquiring the skills and techniques to tap the boundless positive energy of the heart ought to be on top of the human agenda — scientific as well as spiritual. The foreword to Paul Pearsall's book *The Heart's Code*, suggests that if the 20th century had been the Century of the Brain, the 21st should be made the 'Century of the Heart.'[24] Some others say that the challenge of the 21st century is to trigger what they call the '*Silent Revolution of the Heart*', an inner revolution that would help us move from hatred and fear to compassion and love, from darkness to light, and from separatism to wholeness. That would mean concretizing the maxim of the *Brihadaranyaka* Upanishad: *Tamaso ma jyotir gamaya*; lead us from darkness of the mind to the light of the heart. That would mean shifting the focus of intellectual and scientific spotlight towards finding ways to design the tools required to unleash the intuitive intelligence and energy of the heart. The heart can then be a powerful force for spiritual transformation of the human species.

Can we do it?

Can we do all this on our own, with our own will, wit and wisdom, body, mind and heart? We should not be afraid to admit that we need help; that is wisdom. In life, we seek help so many times from so many people but when it comes to something so seminal, something that man never attempted before — human transformation through induced consciousness-change — we want to do it all alone. It is for this generation of men to create the context and conditions that are both necessary and sufficient for Nature/God to lend a helping hand. And in that 'context and conditions' we must figure out what 'being human' ought to be in relation to non-humans. Although we are hardly 'humane' to other humans, as a species we have no moral right to treat other species the way we do the 'human' way. Every insult, every act of indifference, intolerance and injustice and malevolence, cruelty and violence exacts a cost, and the costs continually add up until the time comes when we, as a species, are called upon to recompense the cosmos. How soon or how far we cannot tell, but surely we will. In Nature, stagnation is the sure road to extinction. How to trigger and direct a metamorphosis that would negate the effects of stagnation and *status quo* is a huge challenge. And if it is not ordained and orchestrated soon, there is a reasoned and reasonable probability that the human species might not endure on earth for more than a century or two. Whether that would be a catastrophe for man or a welcome opportunity for other species is another matter. But since we are human, our interest lies in our continuity. Death for an individual and extinction for a species may be, when everything else fails, the Final Solution, but only after exhausting everything else. Shakespeare said, "All the world is a stage; and all the men and women merely players. And one man in his time plays many parts."[25] Once you are a player, you will not quit until your part is finished, or you drop dead, or the director brings down the curtains; the players change, the parts change, but the play goes on. In the cosmic play, in the divine drama, we constantly change and exchange parts. But every part, *memsahib* or a maid, saint or a sinner, mahatma or a monster, is what we have ordered for ourselves. Why and how someone happens to fall into any of these typologies has little to do with his merit or demerit in this life. And depending on how well — or badly — we play those parts, the roles can be turned around. According to some Eastern religions, even the form of life can change — an animal into a man and vice versa, as an episode in the Hindu epic Mahabharata illustrates. In that episode, a kindly saint, Jadabharatha, who took care of an orphaned deer and got obsessively attached to it, becomes a deer in his next life, and later becomes a man again.

Humans have been around for quite a while, over a million years (no more than a blink of the cosmic eye), and the question that arises is: are we at the end of the beginning, or at the beginning of the end, on the cosmic scale? According to the Hindu concept of cyclical Time, we are at the beginning of the beginning of the last of the four major *yugas*, or ages, the sinful age of *Kali Yuga*. Brian Swimme tells us that, "the human species is the youngest, freshest, most immature, newest species of all the advanced life forms in the planet. We have only just arrived. If we can remain resilient, if we can continue our questioning, our developing, our hoping, if we can live in awe and in the depths of wonder, we will continue moving into the only process that now matters — our authentic maturation as a species. It is in this way and only this way that we will enable the Earth to bloom once again."[26] The fact is that for the 'Earth to bloom' again, two things are crucial: at the most fundamental and deepest level, our perceptions and priorities must change; and we must remove the cobwebs that camouflage our relationship with God and 'get it right with God'. After all our labyrinthine labors, we will be 'back to God'. The great German poet Goethe (*Faust*, 1808) wrote, "As man is, so is his God. And thus is God oft strangely odd."[27] Joseph Campbell said, God is a metaphor that transcends all levels of intellectual thought; indeed even in terms of a conceptual framework. In fact, our understanding – rather the lack of it — of underlying forces and of God is linked. David Anderson said, "The God or Gods we worship are more a part of us than we realize… Only by understanding how in our own minds we have defined their nature can we begin to understand the underlying forces that make us behave the way we do."[28] The famous physicist Richard Feynman said that God was invented to explain mystery, to understand things we do not understand, and as our understanding grows, the need of God diminishes. And despite the resurgence of 'believers' in the human world, we are more adrift than ever before. Not only are we drifting in the sea of *samsara*, the phenomenal world of sin and suffering, but also, we find ourselves clutching to God to save us. But what would it take for God to grasp our outstretched hand?

One analogy is that of a grazing cow. Those who swear by free will say that the cow is unfettered and grazes wherever it wants. Those who say that 'divine will' guides everything, believe that the cow is tightly tethered; it simply cannot go beyond a few paces by itself. The third stand is that although the cow is tethered, the rope is long and the cow can go very far but within preset parameters; God or fate or karma, whatever one prefers to call it, decides how tight and how long the rope should be. The sage Ramakrishna often used the third scenario to describe the nexus between God and man. We crave for divine help, but we shun those who crave for *our* help. We must remember that the distance between man and man is the gap between man and God. The fail-safe way to improve our standing with God is to improve our equation with other humans. Gandhi said, "I know that I shall never know God if I do not wrestle with and against evil even at the cost of life itself."[29] God will not offer His holy hand unless we help one another. Once, a man asked Jesus

Christ, "Lord, are only a few people going to be saved?" Christ replied, "Make every effort to enter through the narrow door, because many, I tell you, will try to enter and will not be able to."[30] The door is narrow but open, and the price for entry is struggle and surrender, just as the caterpillar struggles to come out of the pupa before becoming a butterfly. The sage Ramakrishna said: If we take one step towards God, He will take ten steps towards us. It is also said that what you earn by your compassionate effort, even God cannot take it away from you; on the other hand, He would multiply it manifold. It is a sterile exercise debating if our relationship with God should be 'Creator-created', 'Father-child', 'Director-actor', and so on. The Spanish philosopher Miguel de Unamuno (*Tragic Sense of Life*, 2005) draws a distinction between 'God idea' and 'God Himself', and says, "Those who believe that they believe in God, but without passion in their hearts, without anguish in mind, without uncertainty, without doubt, without an element of despair even in their consolation, believe only in the God idea, not God Himself."[31] Unamuno says that God and man, in effect, mutually create one another, and that "We need God, not in order to understand the *why*, but in order to feel and sustain the ultimate *wherefore*, to give a meaning to the universe."[32] Einstein said, "I want to know how God created this world. I am not interested in this or that phenomenon, in the spectrum of this or that element. I want to know His thoughts; the rest are details."[33] But then, as they say, the devil is in the detail!

The one connecting thread in all human thought is that man has a stirring part in the Cosmic Play, and that God has nothing much to do but save us when we stumble, or punish us when we sin, and that when such an intervention is not possible by His staying away from earth, He must come down and be one of us, to rescue the faithful and the righteous, and slay the wicked. As Richard Feynman puts it, "The theory that it is all arranged as a stage for God to watch man's struggle for good and evil seems inadequate."[34] It is deeply ingrained in the human consciousness that human birth is the pinnacle of creation and evolution. According to an estimate, it takes more than 8 million previous incarnations of lower forms of life to be born as a human! If that were so, what a mess we have made of it! Be that all as it may, the real tragedy is that we want to 'know' God, but we make no effort to know ourselves. We want to read His thoughts, reach close to Him, but behave directly in defiance of what we know He wants us to do. The New Testament says, "For the foolishness of God is wiser than man's wisdom, and the weakness of God is stronger than man's strength" (*1 Corinthians 1:25*).

Indeed any juxtaposition of a divine attribute with human intelligence is incongruous. We are 'human'; our consciousness is human; our wisdom or the lack of it is human. That is our boundary and circumstance of life on earth. So much has been said and written about God and man that it is easy to miss the wood for the trees. We must come to some kind of a *modus vivendi* and a *modus operandi*, a new understanding and a new way of putting that understanding into practice. It should be based on four essential principles: (1) We must revisit the man–God relationship and seek 'God within man' rather than seek 'man within God', in other words, not seek God as an external benevolent force; (2) We must change our awareness of God in our consciousness and see, as the Bhagavad Gita exhorts, His *amsa* or spark in everything and everywhere and in every act as an oblation. For purposes of practicality, we must, since we cannot see the 'invisible' divine within, train ourselves (as Swami Vivekananda said) to see the 'visible' God in every other person. Gandhi said "If you cannot find God in the next person you meet, it is a waste of time looking for him any further"[35]; (3) Religion might help, but our relationship with God must be autonomous; we do not need an intermediary between God and us, it has to be personal and embedded in everything we do; (4) As Paulo Coelho puts it, we must turn daily chores into divine tasks. For every thought we entertain, every word we speak, and every action we perform has a cause and a sequel spread over multiple lives, and the only way that divine grace could be attracted is to render everything as an act of total surrender to Him. The sage Aurobindo wrote that the first word of the *Integral Yoga* (complete union into and with the divine) is surrender; its last word is also surrender. The Hindu scriptures say that the only *dharma* (required and prescribed) of the *Kali Yuga* is chanting — seeing God through sound, as it were — and reflecting upon the holy name of God, through which every sin gets cleansed away, just as the rays of the summer sun melt hard ice. In the ancient Hindu scripture *Skanda Purana*, Lord Sadashiva (one of the Gods of the Holy Trinity — Brahma, Shiva and Vishnu) tells the celestial sage Narada that in the sinful *Kali Yuga*, the way to attain liberation (*moksha*) is by chanting two sacred mantras: '*Gopijana-vallabha-charanau sharanam prapadye*' (I take shelter at the feet of He who is the beloved of the gopis); and '*Namo gopijana-vallabhabhyam*' (Obeisance to the divine couple, who are dear to the gopis). Sadashiva clarifies that these mantras can be recited even by the greatest sinners, at any time or place, without any ritual or purification; but the mantras *cannot* be recited by those who are not devoted to Krishna or Hari, even if such persons are the noblest and the best of men.

It has also been said that God's names like 'Rama' are more powerful than the God incarnate Himself who bears that name. In the Hindu epic Ramayana, Hanuman even tells Rama that he valued Rama's name more than Rama himself, because He (Rama), even though a divine avatar, was still a mortal whereas *Rama nama* was eternal. In fact, by chanting that name, Hanuman gains the strength to fly across the ocean to Lanka, and even to move a whole mountain. For human transformation, of the color and character that modern man needs at this juncture on the evolutionary path, what we need is an ascent in the form of human effort, and the descent of divine grace towards man. Mother Teresa said, "God does not require us to succeed; he only requires that we try."[36] But to try we need faith, and faith falters, as Mother Teresa herself admitted. But if we keep trying, we shall overcome. Cleansing and purification must be a continuum of life, for life without smut and sin is impossible. That is why most religious rituals are processes of purification. They enjoin us not only to purify ourselves but also to keep the elements of Nature pure. Zoroastrianism preaches that the four elements of Nature — fire, water, air, and earth — should be kept pure and all its customs, including the way they dispose of the dead, have that objective. We must recapture reverence and rapture for Nature. We must try to move from a passive and, more often, helpless acquiescence of life and make it, in its own right, through our thought, word, and deed, a positive force in the cause of the cosmos. The human function is to fight, evil, injustice, and suffering. We must begin to see another person as a subject in his own life, not as an object in ours. And consider the distance between him and ourself as the distance between two of our own organs.

Man without God

The unsettling thought is that if our behavior is so unbecoming even with the vast majority of us being 'believers', how would it be if humankind truly banishes God even as a phenomenon of fear, if not of faith? It would be a kind of biblical 'backlash' towards God. If He banishes us from His Garden of Eden for eating the forbidden fruit, we return the 'compliment' to Him — and expel Him from our *Empire on Earth* by letting evil reign supreme in our lives. With no one or nowhere to turn to, and '*Tomorrow's God*' as elusive as '*Yesterday's God*', would we become more responsible and compassionate? Or with no one to judge us and with no reward or punishment, would we become more demonic and destructive? On the one hand, we say that God has become irrelevant and redundant; and on the other hand, complain and ask, if God cannot help us in distress, what is the difference between God and ourself or another human being? Although the overwhelming majority of people affirm belief in a spiritual after-life, and also that our conduct here has a bearing on what happens to us after death, that hardly bothers us in our daily dealings with other people. Human beings who believe in unfettered free will fare no better. And our innate sense of right and wrong has found a way to do horrible deeds without guilt or shame. For that to change, and for our behavior to change, *that which drives* our behavior must change — consciousness. In that process, we can use every help we can get from anywhere, even outer space. Perhaps our attempt to pierce the skies and go, like the crew of the fictional spaceship *Enterprise*, where no man has gone before into outer space, could be turned into a journey into *inner* space, and enable us to feel and touch God within our own being. If we can somehow cut loose from the forces that tie us down, like gravity, could that allow us to reach a new level or depth of consciousness? Eugene Cernan, who spent three earth days on the moon as part of the Apollo 17 mission echoed such hope and wrote that although he was not an overly spiritual person, that vision from outer space made him realize the spirituality of existence, and the existence of a Supreme Being. In the empirical arena, scientists are conducting experiments on the effect of intention and emotion on DNA; on the measurable molecular changes in the DNA molecule emanating from human desires, intentions, and emotions. Clearly, a new paradigm of energetic communication occurring within the body at the atomic and quantum levels seems to be emerging. It is said that the study of human nature at the molecular level is of such import that it could potentially alter the application of biological knowledge for good or evil and help us to influence the evolution of our species. New research is indicating that "the human brain hardware system has a remarkable functional resemblance to the Internet hardware system which now spans our globe. They believe that this resemblance is such that it can be logically defended that an independent software system, a global mind, will equally miraculously emerge from it in a way which may be comparable with the miraculous emergence of the individual human mind from the individual human brain."[37] Scientists who are researching how the mind really works are raising the tantalizing possibility of discovering "how strong and deeply rooted is the bond that ties us to others, or in other words how bizarre it would be to conceive of an '*I*' without an *us*."[38] In another emerging area of research that gives hope to those who emphasize the importance of 'heart intelligence', it is claimed that several of the brain's electrical rhythms, such as the alpha and beta rhythms, are naturally synchronized to the rhythm of the heart, and that this heart–brain synchronization significantly increases when an individual is in a physiologically coherent mode. As Paul Pearsall (*The Heart's Code*, 1999) aptly puts it: "An irrational world brings us only misery, but a millennium in which the gifted brain is moderated and instructed by a gentle heart could bring us a shared paradise on earth."[39] This synchronization is likely to be mediated at least in part by electromagnetic field interactions. This is important, as synchronization between the heart and the brain is involved in the processes that give rise to intuition, creativity, and optimal performance. Many great saints as well as thinkers have repeatedly underlined the fact that we can only relate and realize not by what Huxley called 'discursive reasoning' or deductive inference, but by 'direct intuition', and the source of that intuition is not the mind but the heart. Some gentle souls see growing harmony, congruence and convergence between science and spirituality, and recall the observation of the 20th century German 'Nobel' physicist and a pioneer in quantum mechanics, Werner Heisenberg, that "in the history of human thinking, the most fruitful developments frequently take place at those points where two different lines of thought meet."[40] Heart intelligence is one such area. Along with the solitary domain of spiritualism, science is embarking on the same search. The awakening of a consciousness of the heart could unite the scientific and the mystic ways to form a spiritual-scientific view of our multidimensional humanity. It could completely alter the basics of human behavior and man's very perception of his place and role in the universe. Some people think that humankind is poised at such a juncture when the deep insights of mysticism could become scientifically applicable in practical life, which could open the clogged path to a state of heightened awareness and a new consciousness. Scientists have identified what they describe as a "hate circuit" in the brain, specific areas of the brain whose activity is triggered when, for example, the subject sees a person he hates. Such findings raise hope of the tantalizing possibility of special 'brain clinics' where we could have our brain's hate circuits 'fixed' in order to become better human beings. On another front, recent scientific discoveries in fields like quantum physics are coming close to the idea of a single unified force behind the universe, which is very similar to the Upanishad concept of an all-embracing *Brahman* and man as a participant in a seamless existence. If every cell in any part of the body contains a chromosomal DNA that carries the complete code for the entire host, then, some scientists speculate, it is possible that an unseen governing system might very well run on a somewhat similar process, and that everything in the universe, bacteria to a blade of grass, might have a soul, which is in effect a coded reflection of God. That is, quite simply back to *Brahman*.

Promise of Science

Despite the rather troubled track record of science and its popular association with mechanized materialism and nibbling negation of God, it is still the closest on earth to divine power. Till very recently, that power was to prevent or abort reproduction or to terminate life; now we can 'make life in a laboratory'. But it would be churlish to decry or deny the potential benefits from the scientific quest in our efforts to better ourselves and to 'soft land' into the posthuman future. But without a spiritual underpinning, it is more likely to lead us down the primrose path of dalliance and decadence. On the hopeful side, a spiritual ferment is finding utterance and outlet in multiple ways among a growing number of people, albeit nebulous. Disenchanted with organized religion, repelled by crass materialism, many are groping for an anchor in their lives. Rudolf Steiner, the Austrian philosopher who claimed that his knowledge of prehistory and the evolution and nature of mankind were given to him as divine revelation from God, warned that materialism has thrown man down into such depths that a mighty concentration of forces is necessary to raise him again, and that man is now subject to illnesses of the nervous system which are veritable epidemics of the life of the soul. Perhaps the two principal reasons why all previous labors had failed were that the human consciousness remained mind-dominated and the initiatives did not coalesce into a species-scale mutation. Species-scale transformation or uplift, particularly for a creature so diversified and highly evolved as the human, is a daunting task, a task that embraces many intertwined dimensions. Some efforts are needed at the level of an individual being; some, at the layer of a group, community, or nation; some, in those who are at the helm of human affairs in every walk of life. Above all, we need a consciousness-change and a 'critical mass' to reach the 'critical point'. Conceptually, critical mass refers to a group of awakened, self-reflexive people whose collective influence and energy is sufficient and strong enough for a paradigm shift in human consciousness, the bedrock of which is the effortless ability of an individual to identify with humanity as a whole and live and act accordingly. How big or small, the number of such people which can coalesce into a global collective consciousness is hard to guess. The founder of Transcendental Meditation, Maharishi Mahesh Yogi put that figure as one tenth of one percent of mankind, which at the present level of population (seven billion plus) amounts to roughly seven million. Another Indian guru and mystic Osho said that five percent of the 'human seed base' is needed for genuine species-scale awakening.

Whatever is the 'cut-off number' of the 'critical mass' for human transformation, we must recognize that it all comes down to one word: consciousness. All there is, is nothing but consciousness; really, we do not know the *world*; we know only the response of our consciousness to impressions made upon it from what we presume to be the world. The response of consciousness itself is a function of the level of consciousness, and how these impressions are processed determines how we behave; and how we behave in the final analysis will influence how we will evolve. Whether that will lead to the advent of a higher form of life, whose very life is love and creed-compassion, whether it will give a chance for the 'baby Buddha' to be born within each of us, or whether it will exorcize malice from every crevice of our consciousness and cleanse it of all toxicity and negativity and make us better men, we cannot tell. In any case, we must ensure that the mind is not the sole constituent force in the decision making. Compassion, which has been called the Law of all Laws, is now hiding in some corner of our consciousness, afraid to show up and fearing ridicule. In her classic book *The Voice of the Silence* (1889), Helena Blavatsky makes compassion speak to us: "Now bend thy head and listen well, O Bodhisattva — Compassion speaks and saith: Can there be bliss when all that lives must suffer? Shalt thou be saved and hear the whole world cry?"[41] We must somehow retrieve compassion from the fringe margin and bring it to the center stage in our lives, make it the touchstone of morality. Shedding a tear, which Byron said is the dew of compassion, does more than give comfort to the needy and the suffering; it cleanses the conscience. For that, we need a new paradigm of intelligence that underscores our consciousness and in which both mind and heart play complementary roles. For any of that to happen, we need a powerful spark, a spur, a stimulus, an *agent provocateur* that brushes aside all inertia and opposition. That could come from the rumblings of restlessness, yearning, longing, and churning that sweep the globe without finding an utterance or an outlet. And, in turn, for any of these to happen, we desperately need in abundance both mercy and grace of God — mercy for our trespasses, and grace for our transformation. For, God too has a stake in our future; indeed, even more than we do. What we have invested is much less compared to what He has put into the 'human experiment', whether it is making us in His own image, or as the only blessed form of life on earth with the potential to directly dissolve into Him, as the Upanishads proclaim. In Hindu scriptures like the *Vishnu Purana*, it is written that the final *avatar* of God, *Kalki*, will not only restore *dharma* on earth but will also awaken the minds of all those who live at the end of our age. This means that the advent of the next avatar might also entail and result in consciousness change. Hopefully, God has not yet wholly given up on man. Human transformation, at this moment of truth in human evolution, will open the pathway to becoming a 'better being' and take the human race to its tryst with destiny. We have to undertake this task, as Lord Krishna tells Aruba in the Bhagavad Gita, as a service and surrender to God. To paraphrase the words of the Soto Zen priest Shunryu Suzuki, in so doing, 'we should burn ourselves completely, like a good bonfire, leaving no trace of ourselves.'

By leaving nothing we become everything, and by finishing ourselves we complete God's work — which is the reason for our being, our mission on earth. Sages like Sri Aurobindo have dreamed of man overcoming his limiting nature and emerging as a new species, a Gnostic 'divinized' being. And saints like Augustine emphasized that only through God's will can human beings progress into higher beings, for we have no inherent power to overcome our innate limitations. We know we are 'limited' in many ways; what we are not sure of are the 'limitations of the limits'. The scriptures say that God has given man the power of choice, of reasoning, and of discrimination between right and wrong, and consequently made him accountable to his actions. And it is made clear that, as the Quran puts it, none charged with his burden shall bear another's burden, and that whosoever goes the right way does so for his own good, and whosoever strays from the right path does so for his own hurt. The only way we can truly do the good we want to do, and not stray from the *dharmic* path, is through purification of the consciousness, what is called *chita suddhi* in Sanskrit, and *melanoma* in Greek. Our mind-driven consciousness, the product of billions of years of evolution, is so full of ill will and intolerance that we will, more often than not, choose the path of the pleasant or sensory pleasure, *preyas*, over the one of goodness, *sreyas*. All that is 'pleasant' need not necessarily be bad, but to choose the one that gives pleasure but that is not bad, to perform one's own *swadharma* without encroaching on an other's, requires a kind of surgical subtlety and spiritual sensitivity that most of us are incapable of. The clarion call of our time is cathartic consciousness change.

An Epitaph for Mankind

The message for our future is crystal clear. We must remember that the deadliest weapon of mass destruction is the human mind. Hitherto it was preying on other species; now it has turned a 'man-eater'. Rather, it has turned man into a virtual cannibal, making him kill other humans for as many reasons as the mind can come up with. And it has virtually 'occupied' the human consciousness. Nothing positive is possible unless the mind is dislodged from its position of preeminence. And that is not possible unless we find a countervailing force to checkmate and balance the monopoly of the mind. Given the configuration of the inner forces that drive our behavior, that can only be the awakening our dormant heart intelligence. Nothing else will work; everything else is Band-Aid on a gangrenous wound. While we would like to leave behind the human baggage, become a monarch butterfly and soar into the sky with wondrous wings, it is more likely that our present mind-dominated consciousness will make us meet the fate of the lemming jumping off the cliff en masse, or get pushed over by the pressures of our way of life. It is idle (and futile) to speculate if God is or is not, or who or which is the primary mover and shaker in human life — human effort or divine energy. In truth, they are the same. But purely pragmatically, for man's sake we should hope that He or It *is there*, alive and not averse to helping us. Without His special grace, humanity is no more than its own unchanging dust heap.[42] It is clear that neither individual action nor abnegation, personal resolve nor renunciation, will help man achieve consciousness transformation: we need the 'descent of the divine Spirit' into our consciousness.

Our effort should be two-fold: to create the conducive context for divine descent; and to move from 'vertical' transformation, that is, individual growth, to 'horizontal' transformation, that is, create the 'critical mass'. That takes us back to the nagging question: when and how does divine help materialize in human life and what are the prerequisites? The most reasonable assumption might be that it materializes, as the Holocaust survivor, Corrie ten Boom (*The Hiding Place*, 1971) wrote, only when the best of human effort is done with the faith that 'God's power alone be free to work'. And that Power is exercised through 'His image on earth'. God's grace makes human effort tangible but does not take its place. What we do not know is the mix and meeting point between human will and divine disposition in the vortex of daily life. We must also remember that when things became too bad on earth, God chose to become an *avatar* in myriad forms, including the human form. He chose to use human hands and the human body — not the human mind — to do His work. Human behavior, which in its barest essence is how we treat other beings, can influence divine disposition. For whatever reasons He made us as we are — limited, frail, and subject to pain and sorrow — in taking human form, God did not spare himself to show that in the cause of creation no one is exempt from the natural laws of life on earth. Indeed, the *avatars* of God suffered more than ordinary men. In the Christian belief, God chose to enter human history in the person of Christ, and in so doing sent his 'only son' to bear unbearable pain and to die for the sins of the faithful. That was not of necessity, but of His choice; out of love, not out of need. In spiritual terms, total, unattached effort— *Nishkamakarma* in Sanskrit — is another way to God. But first, we must abstain from *Nishiddhakarma*, forbidden acts in daily life, which is even more difficult than *Nishkamakarma*. We instinctively tend to do that which we are not supposed to do. Things that are bad for us seduce us easily. But things that are actually good for us fail to appeal to us; we shun them compulsively, finding powerful explanations and excuses to justify our procrastination or state of denial. The mind cannot resist both temptation and trespassing.

Without getting bogged down with the nuances of conflicting *dharmas* and the relativity of righteousness, we must remember that we often tend to mistake what is pernicious and dangerous for what is useful and desirable, and what appears as good to us with what is truly good. We must remember that we cannot do a wrong thing even for a good cause; not even for a divine cause, and even if we are seemingly selfless. We must cultivate a culture that induces fraternal affection for humanity and a compassionate sensitivity to all life — and a pious love and adoration of the divine. We must draw an indelible line between spiritual surrender and capitulation to force, tradition, terror, or tyranny as a matter of expediency. This surrender is elective, liberating, and ennobling. Capitulation is enforced, diminishing, and denudes us of our dignity, which is the most precious human trait. In evolutionary terms, going up to the next level is giving up the baggage of the present level, which is to surrender the comfort and inertia of the *status quo*, our predispositions, preferences, prejudices, and our mind-driven thought processes. How to fine tune and fuse self-effort and spiritual surrender, self-belief and self-abnegating faith — two apparently antithetical forces — and how to actualize it, is the defining dilemma that mankind confronts.

As individuals, we will have to make choices that will impact on us all. If we persist on this noxious path of hate, with the attitude of an eye for an eye, with the desecration of Nature, trembling with fear and riddled with egoism, we will disappear as the dominant race of this planet. If we become conscious of the oneness of life, and realize that we all form part of a great organism, and that we should respect one another and be grateful to Mother? Earth for its forbearance, then we will move directly into the path of positive growth. And if we do not and stay the course of the *status quo*, then, whatever might happen or not, we will have forfeited our moral legitimacy to linger a minute longer. Our Planet Earth, the Sun, the Moon, the stars, the galaxy, and the cosmos — and God — are awaiting our decision. The choice is here. The time is now. It is the crunch time, the daunting hour. The bell tolls for us all. And if we — this generation and perhaps the two that follow — fail or falter, the epitaph on the human grave might well read thus: "Here rest the remains of the species *Homo sapiens*, a creation so majestically sculpted, so munificently blessed, by Nature and by the Master; it had its own golden moment, under the high heaven and on indulgent earth, to make man a god on earth; yet, it so senselessly, so needlessly, squandered itself; confused, not knowing what to do in the brief interlude of a single lifetime, it turned on itself, leading to its premature passage — and even the All-mighty Allah, the All-pervasive *Brahman*, the All-merciful Father in Heaven — could not do anything."

References and Notes

Chapter - 1
Man in Context

1. Adam Ferguson. An Essay on the History of Civil Society. 1767. Accessed at: http://socserv2.socsci.mcmaster.ca/~econ/ugcm/3ll3/ferguson/civil1
2. Swami Vivekananda's Address at the World's Parliament of Religions (1893, Chicago, USA). Accessed at: http://www. belurmath. org/s wamivive kananda _works.htm
3. H.P. Blavatsky. The Secret Doctrine. Volume 3. p.13. Accessed at:http:// www.translife.co.za/Theosophy/Secret Doctrine, The_HPBlavatsky.pdf
4. Cited in: Helen Vendler. A Powerful, Strong Torrent. The New York Review of Books, USA. 12 June 2008. p.64.
5. Cited in: Helen Vendler. A Powerful, Strong Torrent. The New York Review of Books, USA. 12 June 2008. p.64.
6. Cited in: Susan Bridle. Comprehensive Compassion. An Interview with Brian Swimme. 2001. Accessed at: http://www.wie.org/j19/swimme.asp
7. Winston Churchill. Never Despair. 1955. Speech to the House of Commons, UK. 1 March 1955.
8. Immortal Words: an Anthology. 1963. Bharatiya Vidya Bhavan. Bombay, India. Moral Law. p.142.
9. The Apostle Paul. Romans 7:15. Accessed at: http://faculty. cua.edu/ pennington/Canon%20Law/Romans7.htm
10. Mass Suicide. A Holology Special Report written by Freydis. Accessed at: http://www.holology.com/suicide.html
11. Owen Barfield. Introducing Rudolf Steiner. Accessed at: http:// www.rsarchive.org/RelAuthors/BarfieldOwen/introducing _rudolf_steiner.php
12. Cited in: The Conscious Creation of a New Paradigm. Interview with Dr. William A. Tiller. The Spirit of Ma'at. Vol.2, No.8. Accessed at: http:// spiritofmaat.com/archive/mar2/tiller1.htm

13. Edwin Arnold. The Light of Asia. 1974. The Theosophical Publishing House, Adyar, Chennai, India. Book III, p.33.
14. Swami Nirmalananda Giri. Commentary on the Katha Upanishad. From the Unreal to the Real: Eternal Values. Spiritual Writings, Atma Jyoti Ashram. Accessed at: http://www.atmajyoti.org/up_katha_upanishad_7.asp
15. Carl Sagan. Who Speaks for Earth? Transcript from the final program in the *Cosmos* television series first shown in 1980 on the Public Broadcasting System, USA. Accessed at: http://www.cooperativeindividualism.org/sagan_cosmos_ who_ speaks_for_earth.html
16. Adam Ferguson. An Essay on the History of Civil Society. 1767. Part First. Of the General Characteristics of Human Nature. Section I. Accessed at: http://socserv2.socsci.mcmaster.ca/~econ/ugcm/3ll3/ferguson/civil1
17. Swami Nityaswarupananda (tr.) Ashtavakra Gita. 2001. Sri Ramanasramam. Tiruvannamalai, India. Chapter 1. p.5.
18. John Milton. Paradise Lost. Book I, The Argument, p.182. The Poetical Works of John Milton. Edited by H.C. Beeching. 1944. Oxford University Press, London. UK.
19. Richard Lewontin. The Wars Over Evolution. The New York Review of Books, USA. 20 October 2005. p.52.
20. William Irwin Thompson. BrainyQuote.com. Popular Quotations. Accessed at: http://www.brainyquote.com/quotes/quotes/w/williamit306481.html
21. Swami Sivananda. Sarva Gita Sara. 1999. The Divine Life Society Publications. P.O. Shivanandanagar, Himalayas, Uttar Pradesh, India. pp.173–174.
22. N.S. Rajaram. Nostradamus and Beyond: Visions of Yuga-Sandhi. 2002. Rupa & Co. New Delhi, India. p.73.
23. Pierre Baldi. The Shattered Self: The End of Natural Evolution. 2002. The MIT Press. USA. p.42.
24. Daniel Goleman. Emotional Intelligence. Accessed at: http://www.susanohanian.org/show_commentary.php?id=307
25. Motherhood is Possible at 100. The Deccan Chronicle. Hyderabad, India. 18 July 2008. p.20.
26. V.S. Ramachandran. Mirror Neurons and Imitation Learning as the Driving Force Behind "the Great Leap Forward" in Human Evolution. Edge: The Third Culture. Accessed at : http://www.edge.org/3rd_culture/ramachandran/ramachandran _p1.html
27. Now Chimpanzees Might Get the Rights Reserved for Humans. The Deccan Chronicle. Hyderabad, India. 15 July 2008. p.15.
28. Voltaire. The Quote Garden.com. Quotations about Prejudice. Accessed at: http://www.quotegarden.com/prejudice.html
29. Karl Popper. All the Best Quotes. Intolerance Quotes. Accessed at: http://allthebestquotes.com/theme/intolerance.htm
30. The Mahabharata. Book 12: Santi Parva: Rajadharmanusasana Parva: Section XXI. Accessed at: http://www.sacred-texts.com/hin/m12/m12a021.htm

31. Bardor Tulku Rinpoche. Why We should Give up Anger. 2005. Densal, Issue 1703. June 2005. Karma Triyana Dharmachakra. Accessed at: http://www.kagyu.org/ktd/densal/archives/1703/anger.php
32. Anger and Islam. Is Anger Lawful Or Not? Accessed at: http://www.islamawareness.net/Anger/anger.html
33. The Buddha. ThinkExist.com. Accessed at: http://thinkexist. com/quotes/with/keyword/anger
34. Sri Aurobindo. The Human Cycle. 3rd edition. 1999. Sri Aurobindo Ashram Publications. Pondicherry, India. p.176.
35. Mind Power. The Deccan Chronicle. Hyderabad, India. 7 January 2008. p.6
36. Cited in: Laura Moncur. Edgar Allen Poe's Birthday, 19 January 1809. Accessed at: http://www.quotationspage.com/special.php3?file=w980118
37. Cited in: Wikipedia. Man's Search for Meaning. Viktor Frankl. 1946. Accessed at: http://en.wikipedia.org/wiki/Man's_ Search_for_Meaning.
38. Helen Keller. WisdomQuotes.com. Accessed at: http://www.wisdomquotes.com/topics/suffering/
39. Cited in: Maurice S. Friedman. Martin Buber: The Life of Dialogue. Accessed at: http://www.religion-online.org/showchapter.asp?title=459&C=386
40. Kali Yuga. The Mahabharata. Vana Parva, Section CLXXXIX. Translated by Sri Kisari Mohan Ganguli. Accessed at: http://www.hinduism.co.za/kaliyuga.htm
41. Cited in: Joyce Carol Oates. The Treasure of Comanche County. The New York Review of Books, USA. 20 October 2005.
42. Neale D. Walsch. Tomorrow's God: Our Greatest Spiritual Challenge. 2004. Hodder Mobius. London, UK. pp.3-4.
43. Arthur Koestler. Accessed at: http://en.wikiquote.org/wiki/Talk:Arthur_Koestler
44. Cited in: Editorial Reviews. Publishers Weekly. John E. Mack. Passport to the Cosmos: Human Transformation and Alien Encounters. 1999. Accessed at: http://www.amazon.com/Passport-Cosmos-Human-Transformation-Encounters/dp/0517705680
45. Cited in: Brian T. Prosser and Andrew Ward. University of Aberdeen. 2007. Kierkegaard's "Mystery Of Unrighteousness" In The Information Age. Accessed at: http://www.abdn.ac.uk/philosophy/endsandmeans/vol5no2/prosser_ward.shtml
46. Swami Sivananda. Sarva Gita Sara. 1999. The Divine Life Society Publications. P.O. Shivanandanagar, Himalayas, Uttar Pradesh, India. p.108.
47. Cited in: Soil and Health Library, Social Criticism Library. Alexis Carrel. Man, The Unknown. 1935. Chapter I: The Need of a Better Knowledge of Man. p.1 Accessed at: http://www.soilandhealth.org/03sov/0303critic/030310carrel/Carrel-ch1.htm
48. Elaine Matthews. The Heartbeat of Intelligence. 2002. Writer's Showcase. New York, USA. p.109.

49. Lao Tzu. ThinkExist.com. Heart Quotes. Accessed at: http://thinkexist.com/quotations/heart/
50. Edward O. Wilson. Consilience: The Unity of Knowledge. 1998. Alfred & Knopf. New York, USA. pp. 261-262.
51. Mind Power. The Deccan Chronicle. Hyderabad, India. p.6.
52. Osho. Mind is the Creation of Society; Heart Has No Logic. The Deccan Chronicle. Hyderabad, India. Sunday, 22 June 2008. II.
53. Osho. Shaking the Inner Snake Awake. The Psychology of the Esoteric. Accessed at: http://www.activemeditation.com/OtherModalities/Yoga/Yoga1.html#top
54. Osho. Why "Osho Active Meditations"? The Psychology of the Esoteric, #4. Accessed at: http://www.oshoatlanta.com/whyactive.html
55. Osho. Shaking the Inner Snake Awake. The Psychology of the Esoteric. Accessed at: http://www.activemeditation.com/OtherModalities/Yoga/Yoga1.html#top
56. Excerpted from: Osho. Shaking the Inner Snake Awake. The Psychology of the Esoteric. Reproduced in The Times of India. 24 April 2006. p.2.
57. Cited in: Annie B. Bond. Hindu Heart Consciousness: Integrating Thought and Feeling. Adapted from Christina Becker. The Heart of the Matter. 2004. (Chiron Publications). Accessed at: http://www.care2.com/greenliving/hindu-heart-consciousness.html
58. Swami Gambhirananda (tr.). Isa Upanisad with the Commentary of Sankaracarya. Advaita Ashrama. 5 Delhi Entally Road, Calcutta, India. p.3.

Chapter - 2
The Human Condition

1. G. Xenopoulos. The Secret of Countess Valerena. 1904. Accessed at: http://www.allthelyrics.com/ forum/greek-lyrics-translation /23789-first-sentences-an-isoun-allos.html
2. Swami Sivananda. Sarva Gita Sara. 1999. The Divine Life Society Publications. P.O. Shivanandanagar, Himalayas, Uttar Pradesh, India. p.155.
3. R.D. Ranade. A Constructive Survey of Upanishadic Philosophy. 1968. Bharatiya Vidya Bhavan, Chowpatty, Bombay, India. pp.241-242.
4. The Vedic Foundation. Bhartiya Scriptures. Accessed at: http://www.thevedicfoundation.org/authentic_hinduism/bhartiya_scriptures.htm
5. Practical Vedanta. Ramakrishna - Vivekananda Center of New York, USA. Accessed at: http://www.ramakrishna.org/activities/message/weekly_message7.htm
6. Ramana Maharshi. Readings in the Theory of Karma: Evolution from Lower Forms. Accessed at: http://baharna.com/karma/1_Readings.htm
7. El Morya On Karma and Reincarnation. El Morya from Agni Yoga Society. The Inner Life - Book 2 (1938) – 304. Accessed at: http://www. reversespins.com/agnikarma.html

8. The Times of India, Hyderabad, India. 5 July 2008, p.14. To undergo the litmus test. Experience life after death. Soma Chakraverthy.
9. Nicholas Wade. Changing Regions of Genome Suggest Evolution is Still Occurring in Humans. 2006. The New York Times. Volume 126, Issue 9: Tuesday, 7 March 2006. Accessed at: http://tech.mit.edu/V126/N9/9long5.html
10. Sri Aurobindo. Philosophy and Spiritualism of Sri Aurobindo. Supramental Existence. Accessed at: http://en.wikipedia.org/wiki/Sri_Aurobindo
11. Jerry Boone. Graduating from Life. 2008. The Times of India, Hyderabad, India. 27 July 2008. p.17.
12. William James. Habit. 2003. Kessinger Publishing, USA. p.3.
13. The Buddha's Words on Kindness (Metta Sutta). Accessed at: http://dharma.ncf.ca/introduction/sutras/metta-sutra.html
14. P.D. Sharma. Immortal Quotations and Proverbs. 2003.Navneet Publications. Mumbai, India. p.23.
15. Rodney Collin. The Mirror of Light. 1959. Vincent Stuart, London, UK. p.18.
16. Thomas Berry. Ethics and Ecology. (Harvard Lecture, 9 April 1996). Accessed at: www.earth-community.org/images/Ethics Ecology 1996.pdf
17. Cited in: Mark Titchner. Black Magic Mind War. 2003. Frieze Magazine, Issue 74, April 2003. Accessed at: http://www.frieze.com/issue/article/black_magic_mind_war.
18. Max L. Stackhouse. Torture, Terrorism and Theology: The Need for a Universal Ethic. The Christian Century, 8 October 1986. pp.861-863. Accessed at: http://www.religion-online.org/showarticle. asp?title=117
19. David Livingstone Smith, Why We Lie: The Evolutionary Roots of Deception and the Unconscious Mind. 2004. St. Martin's Press, New York, USA. Accessed at : http://www.amazon.com/Why-Lie-Evolutionary-Deception-Unconscious/dp/0312310390/ref=cm_cr_ pr_product_ top#reader_0312310390
20. Vedanta Network. Ramakrishna Vedanta Society of Boston, USA. Vivekananda's Quotes. Accessed at: http://www.vivekananda.org/quotes.aspx
21. Annie Besant. Bhagavad-Gita. 10.20. 2003. The Theosophical Publishing House, India. p.145.
22. Cited in: Carl R. Trueman. Redeeming Hate. 2008. Issue Number 19, March 2008. Accessed at: http://byfaithonline.com/page/ordinary-life/redeeming-hate
23. Cited in: Osho. Love Completely to Wave Final God Bye. The Deccan Chronicle, Hyderabad, India. 7 July 2008. p.II.
24. Brian Urquhart. The UN and the Race Against Death. 2008. The New York Review of Books. USA. 26 June 2008.
25. Working Minds. Quotations from Albert Einstein. Accessed at: http://www.working-minds.com/AEquotes.htm
26. Mayan Prophecy 2012: Entering Our Galactic Day. Accessed at: http://www.december212012.com/articles/mayan/7.shtml

27. Mayan Prophecy 2012: Entering Our Galactic Day. Accessed at: http://www.december212012.com/articles/mayan/7.shtml
28. Mayan Prophecy 2012: Entering Our Galactic Day. Accessed at: http://www.december212012.com/articles/mayan/7.shtml
29. Cited in: Care2 Share. Jonathan Huie Share book. Accessed at: http://www.care2.com/c2c/share/detail/1451674
30. Cited in: Laura Moncur. Edgar Allen Poe's Birthday, January 19, 1809. Accessed at: http://www.quotationspage.com/special.php3? file=w980118
31. Ascension Gateway, Famous Spiritual Quotes, Don Miguel Ruiz Quotes, Accessed at: http://www.ascensiongateway.com/quotes/don-miguel-ruiz/index.htm
32. T.S. Eliot Quotes. Famous Poets and Poems. Accessed at : http://famouspoetsandpoems.com/poets/t__s__eliot/quotes
33. Macrohistory and World Report. Changing Hinduism, Jains and Buddhists, to 500 CE. The Upanishads. Accessed at: http://www.fsmitha.com/h1/ch05b-ind.htm
34. Cited in: Pico Iyer. Holy Restlessness. [Review of the book "The Religious Case Against Belief" by James P.Carse]. The New York Review of Books. USA. 26 June 2008. p. 37.
35. Robert Darnton. The Library in the New Age. 2008. The New York Review of Books, USA. 12 June 2008. p.72.
36. Robert Darnton. The Library in the New Age. 2008. The New York Review of Books. USA. 12 June 2008. p.1.
37. Peter Drucker. Knowledge Management, The Next Information Revolution. Accessed at: http://www.greatmanagement.org/articles/535/1/The-Next-Information-Revolution/Page1.html
38. Cited in: Global Oneness, Science and Spirituality: Marrying Science And Spirituality. Accessed at: http://www.experiencefestival.com/a/Science_and_spirituality/id/221066
39. M.K. Gandhi. Satyagraha in South-Africa. Accessed at: http://www.forget-me.net/en/Gandhi/satyagraha.pdf
40. J. Bottum. First Things. What T.S. Eliot Almost Believed. 1995. Accessed at: http://www.leaderu.com/ftissues/ft9508/articles/bottum.html
41. P.D. Sharma. Immortal Quotations and Proverbs. 2003. Navneet Publications. Mumbai, India. p. 67.
42. P.D. Sharma. Immortal Quotations and Proverbs. 2003. Navneet Publications. Mumbai, India. p. 35.
43. Cited in: Suma Varughese. Enlightenment - The End of Suffering. The Guru's Role. Life Positive. Eknath Easwaran. The Upanishads. Accessed at: http://www.lifepositive.com/Spirit/Enlightenment/The_End_of_Suffering72005.asp
44. Cited in: Shirley Galloway. The Razor's Edge. 1994. Accessed at: http://www.cyberpat.com/shirlsite/essays/razor.html

45. Alexis Carrel. Man the Unknown. 1938. Halcyon House, New York, USA. p.4.
46. Shunryu Suzuki. Zen Mind, Beginner's Mind. 2004. Shambhala Publications, Inc. Boston, USA. Part Three, Right Understanding. p.136.
47. Cited in: William McNeill and Karen S. Feldman (eds.). Continental Philosophy: An Anthology (Blackwell Philosophy Anthologies). 1998. Blackwell Publishers, USA. p.81.
48. Swami Nirmalananda Giri. Commentary on the Katha Upanishad. The Immortal Self. Spiritual Writings, Atma Jyoti Ashram. Accessed at: http://www.atmajyoti.org/up_katha_upanishad_10.asp
49. Cited in: Wikisource, The Complete Works of Swami Vivekananda, by Swami Vivekananda, Volume 7, Accessed at: http://en.wikisource. org/wiki/The_Complete_Works_of_ Swami_Vivekananda/Volume_7/Epistles_-_Third_Series/XXXVI_Miss_Noble
50. Cited in: Pico Iyer. Holy Restlessness. [Review of the book "The Religious Case Against Belief" by James P. Carse]. The New York Review of Books. USA. 26 June 2008. p.38.
51. Cited in: Swami Ranganathananda. Vedanta, Science and Religion. The Approach to Truth in Vedanta. 2010. IndiaTimes Spirituality. Accessed at http://spirituality.indiatimes.com/articleshow/msid-1089740,prtpage-1.cms
52. Cited in: Lauren de Boer. Science as Wisdom: The New Story as a Way Forward. Interview with Brian Swimme. 1997. Earth Light Magazine. Sample Articles and Reviews. Issue 26, Summer 1997. p.10-11, 15, 22. Accessed at: http://www.earthlight.org/interview26.html
53. Cited in: Understanding Hinduism. The Mahabharata, Vana Parva, Section CLXXXIX. Kisari Mohan Ganguli. Future History of the World. Kali Yuga. Accessed at: http://www.hinduism.co.za/kaliyuga.htm
54. Cited in: Understanding Hinduism. From Srimad Bhagavat Mahapurana. The Evils of Kaliyuga. Book 12, Discourse 2. Rendered into English by C.L. Goswami, M.A. Shastri. Accessed at: http://www.hinduism.co.za/kaliyuga.htm
55. Cited in: Understanding Hinduism. From Srimad Bhagavat Mahapurana. The Evils of Kaliyuga. Book 12, Discourse 2. Rendered into English by C.L. Goswami, M.A. Shastri. Accessed at: http://www.hinduism.co.za/kaliyuga.htm
56. Wikipedia. Eschatology. Accessed at: http://en.wikipedia.org/wiki/Eschatology
57. Cited in: Rabbi Raymond Beyda. The Best Policy. Parshas Noach. Table Talk. Accessed at: http://www.torah.org/learning/tabletalk/5765/noach.html
58. Peter Singer. Children at War. 2005. University of California Press, USA. Accessed at: http://www.amazon.com/Children-at-War-P-W-Singer/dp/0375423494
59. Cited in: Caroline Moorehead. The Warrior Children. 2005. [Review of the book "Children at War" by P.W. Singer]. The New York Review Books, USA. 1 December 2005. p.46.

60. Cited in: Caroline Moorehead. The Warrior Children. 2005. [Review of the book "Children at War" by P.W. Singer]. The New York Review Books, USA. 1 December 2005. p.46.
61. Shana Pate. CliffsTestPrep Praxis II: Social Studies Content Knowledge Test (0081). Behavioral Science, Human Culture. Wiley Publishing, Inc. p.85.
62. Jay Earley. Social Evolution and the Planetary Crisis. Accessed at: http://www.earley.org/Transformation/social_evolution_.htm
63. Cited in: What is Culture? Human Culture: an Introduction to the Characteristics of Culture and the Methods used by Anthropologists to Study It. Behavioral Sciences Department, Palomar College, San Marcos, California, USA. 2009. Accessed at: http://anthro.palomar.edu/culture/culture_1.htm
64. Cited in: Miroslav Pecujlic, Gregory Blue and Anouar Abdel-Malek (eds.). Science and Technology in the Transformation of the World – Volume 1. Section III Biology, medicine and the future of mankind. The United Nations University. Accessed at: http://www.unu.edu/unupress/unupbooks/uu39se/uu39se09.htm
65. Cited in: Miroslav Pecujlic, Gregory Blue and Anouar Abdel-Malek (eds.). Science and Technology in the Transformation of the World – Volume 1. Section III Biology, medicine and the future of mankind. The United Nations University. Accessed at: http://www.unu.edu/unupress/unupbooks/uu39se/uu39se09.htm
66. Cited in: Miroslav Pecujlic, Gregory Blue and Anouar Abdel-Malek (eds.). Science and Technology in the Transformation of the World – Volume 1. Section III Biology, medicine and the future of mankind. The United Nations University. Accessed at: http://www.unu.edu/unupress/unupbooks/uu39se/uu39se09.htm
67. Cited in: Frank Kermode. Heroic Milton: Happy Birthday. 2009. [Review of the book "John Milton: Life, Work, and Thought" by Gordon Campbell and Thomas N. Corns. Oxford University Press. 488 pp.] New York Review of Books, USA. 26 February 2009. p.28.
68. Rewriting Human Prehistory. The Economist. UK. 30 October 2004. p.81.
69. Kate Wong. Digging Deeper: Q&A with Peter Brown. Scientific American, USA. 27 October 2004. p.16. Accessed at: http://www.scientificamerican.com/article.cfm?id=digging-deeper-qa-with-pe
70. Cited in: Quotations Paul Johnson. [Modern Times: A History of the World from the 1920s to the Year 2000]. ConservativeForum.org. Accessed at: http:/ /www.conservativeforum.org/authquot.asp? ID=855
71. Sidney J. Harris. BrainyQuote. Accessed at: http://www. brainyquote.com/quotes/quotes/s/sydneyjha152323.html
72. Ralph Waldo Emerson. BrainyQuote. Accessed at: http://www. brainyquote.com/quotes/quotes/r/ralphwaldo397348.html
73. Aleister Crowley. BrainyQuote. Accessed at: http://www. brainyquote.com/quotes/quotes/a/aleistercr156791.html

74. Cited in: Allen Watson. Why Do We Judge People? Circle of Atonement. Accessed at: http://www.circleofa.org/articles/WhyDoWeJudge.php

75. Giacomo Leopardi. ThinkExist. Accessed at: http://thinkexist.com/quotation/no_human_trait_deserves_less_tolerance_in/184205.html

76. Andy Coghlan. Pollution Triggers Bizarre Behaviour in Animals. New Scientist. 3 September 2004. Accessed at: http://www.newscientist.com/article/dn6343-pollution-triggers-bizarre-behaviour-in-animals.html

77. Andy Coghlan. Pollution Triggers Bizarre Behaviour in Animals. New Scientist. 3 September 2004. Accessed at: http://www.newscientist.com/article/dn6343-pollution-triggers-bizarre-behaviour-in-animals.html

78. Cited in: Mike Adams. Interview with Randall Fitzgerald, author of *The Hundred-Year Lie*, on the Prevalence of Toxic Chemicals. NaturalNews. 21 June 2006. Accessed at: http://www. naturalnews.com/019434.html

79. Cited in: Peter Schwartz. Man vs. Nature. Environmentalism. 1999. Ayn Rand Center for Individual Rights, Washington DC, USA. Sacramento Bee, 23 April 1999. Accessed at: http://www.aynrand.org /site/News2?page= NewsArticle&id=5200&news_iv_ctrl=1084

80. Mark Townsend and Jason Burke. Earth 'Will Expire by 2050'. The Observer. The Guardian, 7 July 2002. Accessed at: http://www.guardian.co.uk/uk/2002/jul/07/research.waste

81. P.D. Sharma. Immortal Quotations and Proverbs. 2003. Navneet Publications. Mumbai, India. p.21.

82. P.D. Sharma. Immortal Quotations and Proverbs. 2003. Navneet Publications. Mumbai, India. p.21

83. Publilius Syrus. The Quote Garden. Accessed at: http://www.quotegarden.com/civilization.html

84. C.P. Snow. The Quote Garden. Accessed at: http://www.quotegarden.com/civilization.html

85. Geoffrey O'Brien. When Hollywood Dared. New York Review of Books, USA. 2-15 July 2009. p.6.

86. Anthony Robbins. ThinkExist. Accessed at: http://thinkexist.com/quotes/with/keyword/entertainment/

87. Hannah Arendt. BrainyQuote. Accessed at: http://www.brainyquote.com/quotes/quotes/h/hannaharen402663.html

88. Cited in: Agence France Presse. Water, the Looming Source of World Conflict. Global Policy Forum. 20 March 2001. Accessed at: http://www.globalpolicy.org/component/content/article/198/40338.html

89. Cited in: Eddy Dow. The Rich Are Different. The New York Times Books. 13 November 1988. Accessed at: http://www.nytimes.com/1988/11/13/books/l-the-rich-are-different-907188.html?page wanted=1

90. Cited in: Matthew J. Bruccoli. Some Sort of Epic Grandeur. The Life of F. Scott Fitzgerald. 2002. The Drunkard's Holiday, 1925-1931. University of South Carolina Press, Columbia, South Carolina, USA. p.228.

91. Cited in: PoemHunter. Quotations from Ernest Hemingway. Accessed at: http:/ /www.poemhunter.com/quotations/famous.asp?people= Ernest% 20Hemingway&p=5
92. Cited in: Learn Peace, a Peace Pledge Union Project. Aldous Huxley. Ends and Means. Some Causes of War. Accessed at: http://www.ppu.org.uk/learn/ infodocs/people/pp-huxley1.html
93. Christopher Lasch. The True and Only Heaven: Progress and its Critics. 1991. W.W. Norton & Company Inc., New York, USA.
94. Christopher Lasch. The True and Only Heaven: Progress and its Critics. W.W. Norton & Company Inc., New York, USA.
95. Deborah Butterfield. Toccata and Fugue: The Hegemony of the Eye/I and the Wisdom of the Ear. 1993. Trumpeter. Vol.10, No.3. Accessed at: http:// trumpeter.athabascau.ca/index.php/trumpet/article/view/383/609
96. Oscar Wilde. ThinkExist. Accessed at: http://thinkexist.com/quotation/ there_are_many_things_that_we_would_throw_away_if/326088.html
97. Christine Kenneally. Of Ants and Men: Compare the Two Civilizations, and Who Wins? 2008. [Review of the book 'The Superorganism: the Beauty, Elegance, and Strangeness of Insect Societies' by Bert Holldobler and E.O. Wilson.] Accessed at: http://www.slate.com/id/2205472.
98. Tim Flannery. The Superior Civilization. 2009. [Review of the book 'The Superorganism: the Beauty, Elegance, and Strangeness of Insect Societies' by Bert Holldobler and E.O. Wilson.] New York Review of Books, USA. 26 February 2009. p.23.
99. Cited in: Elizabeth A. Pector. Lumina Dei:Lights of Accessed at: http:// www.synspectrum.com/ld.html
100. Roger Segelken. What's in the 1% Difference Between Chimps and Humans (DNA). Medical News Today. 20 December 2003. Accessed at: http:// www.medicalnewstoday.com/articles/4945.php
101. Anthropology.net. Gene Regulation, the Driving Force in Human Evolution. 13 August 2007. Accessed at: http://anthropology.net/2007/08/13/gene-regulation-the-driving-force-in-human-evolution/
102. Cited in: Therese Littleton. What's So Special About Being Human? Interview with Ian Tattersall, author of the book "Becoming Human: Evolution and Human Uniqueness." Accessed at: http://www.human-nature.com/interviews/ tattersall.html
103. Cited in: Editorial Reviews From Publishers Weekly. [Review of the book "God's Messengers: What Animals Teach Us About the Divine" by Linda Anderson and Allen Anderson]. Accessed at : http://www.amazon.com/Gods-Messengers-Animals-Teach-Divine/dp/1577312465
104. Cited in: Kate Douglas. Are We Still Evolving? New Scientist Magazine. Issue 2542. UK. 11 March 2006.
105. Georgia Purdom. Human Evolution — Faster Than a Speeding Bullet. Answers in Genesis. 30 January 2008. Accessed at: http://www.answersingenesis.org/ articles/aid/v3/n1/faster-than-speeding-bullet

106. James B. Delong. The Arrow of Cultural Evolution. [Review of the book "Nonzero: the Logic of Human Destiny" by Robert Wright]. Amazon.Com Customer Reviews, 19 June 2000. Accessed at: http://www.amazon.com/review/product/0679758941?showViewpoints=1

107. Cited in: William H. McNeill. Bigger and Better? 2004. [Review of the book "The Escape from Hunger and Premature Death, 1700-2100: Europe, America, and the Third World" by Robert William Fogel]. The New York Review of Books, USA. 21 October 2004. p.61.

108. The Times of India, Hyderabad, India, 27 October 2008, p.16.

Chapter - 3
Of Human Baggage and Bondage

1. Cited in : Live Science, Health Identical Twins Not So Identical by Robert Roy Britt, LiveScience Senior Writer, 8 July 2005, Accessed at: http://www.livescience.com/health/050708_identical_twins.html

2. Susan Greenfield. The Private Life of the Brain: Emotions, Consciousness, and the Secret of the Self. 2000. John Wiley Publishers. New York, USA. p. 9.

3. Susan Greenfield. The Private Life of the Brain: Emotions, Consciousness, and the Secret of the Self. 2000. John Wiley Publishers. New York, USA. pp.181-182.

4. Niles Eldredge. Why We Do It: Rethinking Sex and the Selfish Gene. 2004. W.W. Norton. New York, USA. p.15.

5. Cited in: Morrison Institute for population and resource studies, Human Genome Diversity Project, Summary Document, II Introduction to the Human Genome Diversity (HGD) Project, Accessed at: http://www.stanford.edu/group/morrinst/hgdp/summary93.html

6. Havelock Ellis. The Dance of Life. 1923. Cambridge, Massachusetts,USA. p. 352.

7. Cited in: Mayan End Age 12-21-2012. Predictions about the Spiritual Mother. Accessed at: http://www.adishakti.org/mayan_end_times_prophecy_12-21-2012.htm

8. Cited in: Odell Shepard (ed.). The Heart of Thoreau's Journals. 1961. Dover Publications. New York, USA. p.149.

9. Edward O. Wilson, In Search of Nature. Nature's Abundance: Is Humanity Suicidal? 1996. Island Press. USA. p.190.

10. Cited in: Wikipedia. Anti-environmentalism. Accessed at: http://en.wikipedia.org/wiki/Anti-environmentalism.

11. David Holcberg. The Environmental Evil. Capitalism Magazine. USA. 18 July 2000.

12. Alan Curuba. State of Fear by Michael Crichton: Exposing the Global Warming Sham. Capitalism Magazine. USA. 15 February 2005.

13. Jeremy Griffith. Beyond the Human Condition. 1991. Introduction. The World Transformation Movement, Sydney, Australia.
14. Cited in: The Eternal Wisdom: Central Sayings of Great Sages of All Times. 1993. Sri Aurobindo Ashram Publications. Pondicherry, India. p.80.
15. Jayant V. Narlikar. Man, Nature and the Universe. Prakrti: the Integral Vision, Vol. 5 (Man in Nature, edited by Baidyanath Saraswati). 1995. Indira Gandhi National Centre for the Arts, New Delhi, India. Accessed at: http://ignca.nic.in/ps_05003.htm
16. M.K. Gandhi. My Religion. (Bharatan Kumarappa, ed.). Navajivan Trust. Ahmedabad, India.
17. Cited in: Divine Wisdoms: Over the Horizon's Limit. Human Knowledge. 20 August 2007. Accessed at: http://divinewisdoms. wordpress.com/2007/08/20/human-knowledge/
18. Richard Lewontin. The Wars Over Evolution. The New York Review of Books, USA. 20 October 2005. p. 52.
19. Steven Pinker. The Blank Slate: the Modern Denial of Human Nature. 2002. Penguin Books. New York, USA. p. 329.
20. The Eternal Wisdom: Central Sayings of Great Sages of All Times. 1993. Sri Aurobindo Ashram Publications.Pondicherry,India. p. 483.
21. John Wilmot. PoemHunter.com. A Satyre Against Mankind. Accessed at: http://www.poemhunter.com/poem/a-satyre-against-mankind/
22. Cited in: Hobbes's Leviathan. Philosophy Pages: Britannica, Internet Guide Selection. Accessed at: http://www.philoso phypages.com/hy/3x.htm
23. Cited in: Hobbes's Leviathan. Philosophy Pages: Britannica, Internet Guide Selection. Accessed at: http://www.philosophypages .com/hy/3x.htm
24. The Times of India. Hyderabad, India. 25 November 2007. p.10.
25. Václav Havel (President of the Czech Republic). Speech delivered at the Gala Evening 'Václav Havel: The Playwright as President' at the City University of New York, Graduate Center, New York, USA. 20 September 2002. Accessed at: http://old.hrad.cz/president/Havel/speeches/2002/2009_uk.html
26. The Deccan Chronicle. Hyderabad, India. 30 October 2004. p.1.
27. Cited in: Trivia-Library.com. Origins of Sayings - The Mass of Men Lead Lives of Quiet Desperation. Accessed at: http://www.trivia-library.com/b/origins-of-sayings-the-mass-of-men-lead-lives-of-quiet-desperation.htm
28. Kisari Mohan Ganguli. The Mahabharata of Krishna-Dwaipayana Vyasa. 2008. Book 12. Part I, Section XXVIII. BiblioBazaar. p.72.
29. Khalil Gibran. The Prophet. 2006. Jaico Publishing House. India. pp. 36-37.
30. The Hindu. Hyderabad, India. 2 November 2004. p. 2.
31. Andrew Harvey. The Return of the Mother. 2001. Tarcher/Putnam. New York, USA. p.12.
32. Cited in: Robert Andrews. The Concise Columbia Dictionary of Quotations. 1989. Columbia University Press, USA. p.113.
33. Plato. WorldofQuotes.com: Historic Quotes and Proverbs Archive. Accessed at: http://www.worldofquotes.com/topic/Government/2/index.html

34. Aldous Huxley. Finest Quotes.com. Accessed at: http://www.finestquotes.com/select_quote-category-Organization-page-0.htm

35. Mikhail Bakunin. Ethics: Morality of the State. Accessed at: http://flag.blackened.net/revolt/anarchists/bakunin/writings/ethics_ state.html

36. S.K. Agarwal. Towards Improving Governance. Kautilya on Governance, Self-Discipline, and Riches. 2008. Academic Foundation. New Delhi, India. p. 22.

37. Cited in: Robert Andrews. The Concise Columbia Dictionary of Quotations. 1989. Columbia University Press. USA. p. 253.

38. Cited in: The Times of India. Hyderabad, India. 25 October 2004. p. 2.

39. Immanuel Kant. Philosophy Paradise. Famous Philosophy Quotes. Accessed at: http://www.philosophyparadise.com/quotes/kant.html

40. Mark Twain. TwainQuotes.com. Directory of Mark Twain's maxims, quotations, and various opinions. Accessed at: http://www. twainquotes.com/Malice.html

41. Virginia Morell. Animal Minds: Minds of their Own. National Geographic Magazine. USA. March 2008. p. 33.

42. Temple Grandin and Catherine Johnson. Animals In Translation: Using the Mysteries of Autism to Decode Animal Behavior. 2005. Scribner. New York, USA. p. 6.

43. Cited in: New World Encyclopedia. Hannah Arendt: Thought and Works. The Human Condition. Accessed at: http://www. newworldencyclopedia.org/entry/Hannah_Arendt# The_Human_ Condition

44. Albert Schweitzer. ThinkExist.com. Accessed at: http://thinkexist.com/quotation/the_first_step_in_the_evolution_ of_ethics_is_a/146835.html

45. Eliot Weinberger (ed.). Jorge Luis Borges: Selected Non-Fictions. 1999. Penguin Books. New York, USA. p. 127.

46. Cited in: Antoine de Saint-Exupéry. Wikiquote. Wind, Sand and Stars (1939). Accessed at: http://en.wikiquote.org/wiki/Antoine_ de_Saint_Exupéry

47. Isaiah Berlin. A Letter on Human Nature. The New York Review of Books, USA. 23 September 2004. p. 20.

48. Annie Besant. The Bhagavad Gita. The Theosophical Publishing House. Adyar, Chennai, India. 3:36, 37. p. 58.

49. Annie Besant. The Bhagavad Gita. The Theosophical Publishing House. Adyar, Chennai, India. 3:36. p. 58.

50. Sacred Space. The Times of India. Hyderabad, India. 14 August 2004.

51. Octave Mirbeau. The Quote Garden. Accessed at: http://www.quotegarden.com/soul.html

52. Cited in: Examining the Raw Truths of Life. The Trouble with Oneness: Individualism has its Own Kind of Blow-back, or Collateral Damage. 17 June 2008. Accessed at: http://theforbiddenblog. wordpress.com/category/humankind/

53. The Times of India. Hyderabad, India. 26 August 2004. p. 2.

54. Peter Kreeft. The Problem of Evil. Accessed at: http://www. peterkreeft.com/topics/evil.htm#top
55. Carlos Steel. Does Evil Have a Cause? Augustine's Perplexity and Thomas's Answer. 1994. The Review of Metaphysics. Vol. 48. pp..251-273.
56. Robert Ernest Hume (tr.). The Thirteen Principal Upanishads: Translated from the Sanskrit, with an Outline of the Philosophy of the Upanishads, and an Annotated Bibliography. 1921. Oxford University Press, London, UK. pp.417-418. Accessed at: http://www.archive.org/stream/thirteenprincipa028442mbp#page/n7/mode/2up/search/maitri+upanishad
57. Cited in: The Eternal Wisdom: Central Sayings of Great Sages of All Times. 1993. Sri Aurobindo Ashram Publications. Pondicherry, India. p. 370.
58. Edmund White. In Love with Duras. The New York Review of Books, USA. 26 June 2008. p. 30.
59. Cited in: Eric Hoffer. Wikiquote. Reflections on the Human Condition (1973). Accessed at: http://en.wikiquote.org/wiki/Eric_Hoffer
60. Timothy Snyder. Holocaust: the Ignored Reality. The New York Review of Books, USA. 16 July 2009. p. 15.
61. Adam Hochschild. Rape of the Congo. The New York Review of Books, USA. 13 August 2009. p. 18.
62. Khalil Gibran. BrainyQuote.com. Accessed at: http://www.brainyquote.com/quotes/authors/k/kahlil_gibran.html
63. N.S. Rajaram. Nostradamus and Beyond: Visions of Yuga-Sandhi. 2002. Rupa & Co. New Delhi, India. p. 76.
64. Adam Smith. The Theory of Moral Sentiments; Or, An Essay Towards an Analysis of the Principles by Which Men Naturally Judge Concerning the Conduct and Character, First of Their Neighbours, and Afterwards of Themselves. 1853. Part I: Of Propriety. Chapter III. Henry G. Bohn. London, UK. p. 84.
65. Cited in: Adam Smith. Wikiquote. The Wealth of Nations (1776). Book III, Chapter IV. Accessed at: http://en.wikiquote.org/wiki/Adam_Smith
66. Plutarch. BrainyQuote.com. Accessed at: http://www.brainyquote. com/quotes/quotes/p/plutarch109440.html
67. Plato. [Benjamin Jowett, tr.]. The Republic. Book IV. 2008. BiblioBazaar. p. 153.
68. Plato. [Benjamin Jowett, Tr.]. The Laws. Book V. 2008. Forgotten Books. p. 127.
69. Cited in: A Journey of Hope. A Fresh Start. Exploring news Vistas. Accessed at: http://legendoftheearth.wordpress.com/2009/08/16/exploring-new-vistas/
70. Cited in: Jonathan Wallace. An Auschwitz Alphabet. What I Learned from Auschwitz. Accessed at: http://www.spectacle.org/695/essay.html
71. Roel Sterckx. The Animal and the Daemon in Early China. 2002. State University of New York Press. Albany, USA. p. 162.

72. Karl Marx. Economic and Philosophic Manuscripts of 1844 : The Power of Money. Accessed at: http://www.marxists.org/archive/marx/works/1844/manuscripts/power.htm
73. Cited in : Gaiam Life: Stream of Consciousness. Accessed at: http://blog.gaiam.com/quotes/authors/will-obrien/59940
74. Somerset Maugham. ThinkExist.com. Money Quotes. Accessed at: http://thinkexist.com/quotations/money
75. P.D. Sharma. Immortal Quotations and Proverbs. 2003. Navneet Publications. Mumbai, India. p. 88.
76. Cited in: Nigel Goh. Money, Sex and Power. Eagles VantagePoint. Accessed at: http://www.vantagepoint.com.sg/Money_ Goh_2008.html
77. Cited in: Philosophy Resource Center, George J. Irbe's Favorite Quotes from Aristotle on Selected Topics. Education and Living. The Radical Academy. Accessed at: http://www.radicalacademy.com/philosophicalquotations33.htm
78. Voltaire. ThinkExist.com. Voltaire Quotes. Accessed at: http://thinkexist.com/quotation/when_its_a_question_of_money-everybody_is_of_the/8412.html
79. Cited in: Jill Elish. The Florida State University News. Two Sides of the Same Coin: Money Spurs Changes for Better and Worse. Accessed at: http://www.fsu.edu/news/2006/11/20/two.sides/
80. Cited in: Money Magic. New World Library. Accessed at: http://www.newworldlibrary.com/BooksProducts/ProductDetails/tabid/64/SKU/12449/Default.aspx
81. Cited in: Frances Lefkowitz. Money Changes Everything: Exploring Your Attitudes Toward Money Can be the First Step in Making Personal and Global Transformations. CBS MoneyWatch.com. September 2004. Accessed at: http://findarticles.com/p/articles/mi_m0NAH/is_8_34/ai_n6191102/
82. Cited in: Editorial Reviews. Publishers Weekly. Jacob Needleman. Money and the Meaning of Life. 1994. Accessed at: http://www.amazon.com/Money-MeaFning-Life-Jacob-Needleman/dp/0385262426
83. Cited in: Mill on Political Economy: Collected Works Vol.II. Introduction by V.W. Balden. The Forum at the Online Library of Liberty, A Project of Liberty Fund. Accessed at: http://oll.libertyfund.org/index.php?option=com_content&task= view&id=524&Itemid=278
84. Cited in: Karl Marx. A Contribution to the Critique of Political Economy. 1859. Preface. Accessed at: http://www.marxists.org/archive/marx/works/1859/critique-pol-economy/preface.htm
85. Cited in: Inequality.Org. CEOs and Business Leaders. Accessed at: http://www.demos.org/inequality/quotes.cfm
86. Cited in: Thomas Kostigen. More Money, Better Sex. MSN Money. MarketWatch. 10 February 2007. Accessed at: http://articles. money central.msn.com/CollegeAndFamily/LoveAndMoney/More Money BetterSex.aspx
87. Bernard Loomer. Two Conceptions of Power. 1976. [Process Studies, vol.6, no.1, Spring, pp.5-32]. Accessed at: http://www.religion-online.org/showarticle.asp?title=2359

88. Cited in: Ray Blunt. Leadership in the Crucible: the Paradox of Character and Power. GovLeaders.org. Accessed at: http://govleaders.org/crucible.htm
89. Arnold Tonybee. Human Savagery Cracks Thin Veneer. Los Angeles Times. USA. Sunday, 6 September 1970.
90. Cited in: Paul D'Amato. No More Blood for Oil: The Socialist Alternative to a System of Violence and Poverty. A World Without War. SocialistWorker.org. 17 January 2003. p.11. Accessed at: http://socialistworker.org/2003-1/436/436_11_WorldWithoutWar.shtml
91. Cited in: Peace Pledge Union: Working for Peace. The Case for Constructive Peace. Accessed at: http://www.ppu.org.uk/e_publications/huxleycase1.html
92. Cited in: Be a Hero for a Better World. Anti-War Quotes. Accessed at: http://www.betterworld.net/quotes/nowar-quotes.htm
93. Cited in: Be a Hero for a Better World. Anti-War Quotes. Accessed at:http://www.betterworld.net/quotes/nowar-quotes.htm
94. Alvin and Heidi Toffler. War and Anti-War: Survival at the Dawn of the 21st Century. 1993. Little, Brown and Company. Boston, USA. p. 13.
95. Chris Hedges. On War. The New York Review of Books, USA. 16 December 2004. Accessed at: http://www.nybooks.com/articles/archives/2004/dec/16/on-war/
96. Chris Hedges. On War. The New York Review of Books, USA. 16 December 2004. Accessed at: http://www.nybooks.com/articles/archives/2004/dec/16/on-war/
97. Garry Wills. What is a Just War? The New York Review of Books, USA. 18 November 2004. p. 32.
98. Alvin and Heidi Toffler. War and Anti-War: Survival at the Dawn of the 21st Century. 1993. Little, Brown and Company. Boston, USA. p. 119.
99. Chris Hedges. On War. The New York Review of Books, USA. 16 December 2004. p. 12.
100. Cited in: Miroslav Pecujlic, Gregory Blue and Anouar Abdel-Malek (eds.). Science and Techncl0gy in the Transformation of the World – Volume 1. Section III Biology, medicine and the future of mankind. 1982. The United Nations University. Accessed at: http://www.unu.edu/unupress/unupbooks/uu39se/uu39se09.htm
101. David LeClaire. Building Bridges: Testosterone Surges! 1998. Issue 26 (of 43). Accessed at: http://www.sideroad.com/bridges/column26.html
102. Albert Camus. QuoteDB. Accessed at: http://www.quotedb.com/quotes/1939
103. Ambrose Bierce. ThinkExist.com. Accessed at: http://thinkexist.com/quotation/there_are-kinds_of_homicide-felonious-excusable/7017.html
104. Bill Maher. Thinkexist.com. Bill Maher Quotes. Accessed at: http://thinkexist.com/quotation/suicide_is_man-s_way_of_telling_god—you_can-t/200215.html
105. Cited in: Jaime Holguin. A Murder A Minute: WHO Report Says 1.6 Million People Met Premature Deaths In 2000. CBS News Health. 3 October 2002.

Accessed at: http://www.cbsnews.com/stories/2002/10/03/health/main524231.shtml

106. Lynne Forest. Dying to Live Again. The Times of India. Hyderabad, India. 6 July 2008. p. 17.

107. Cited in: Hara Estroff Marano. Not Always a Cry for Help: Suicide May be an Attempt to Exercise Power and Control. Psychology Today. 6 May 2003. Accessed at: http://www.psychologytoday.com/articles/200305/not-always-cry-help

108. Cited in: Hara Estroff Marano. Not Always a Cry for Help: Suicide May be an Attempt to Exercise Power and Control. Psychology Today. 6 May 2003. Accessed at: http://www.psychologytoday.com/articles/200305/not-always-cry-help

109. Cited in: Nicole Jackman. The Brains of Violent Males: the Homicidal & Suicidal Brain. Biology Paper 202. 2003. Serendip. Accessed at: http://serendip.brynmawr.edu/bb/neuro/neuro03/web2/njackman.html

110. The Deccan Chronicle. Hyderabad, India, 3 November 2004. p. 3.

111. Cited in: Matthew Price. Sinner Take All: Graham Greene's Damned Redemption. BookForum. Oct/Nov 2004. Accessed at: http://www.bookforum.com/archive/Oct_04/price_oct.html

112. Karma. Haryana-Online.com. Accessed at: http://www.haryana-online.com/Culture/karma.htm

113. Karma. Haryana-Online.com. Karma, Accessed at: http://www.haryana-online.com/Culture/karma.htm

114. Spiritual Science Research Foundation. Accessed at: http://www.spiritualresearchfoundation.org/articles/id/spiritualresearch/spiritualscience/lawofkarma/karma

115. Wendy Doniger and Brian K. Smith. The Laws of Manu. 1991. Penguin Classics. Penguin Books. London, UK. p. 286.

116. Sri Swami Sivananda. Prarabdha And Purushartha. September 1997. Accessed at: http://www.dlshq.org/discourse/sep97.htm

117. Cited in: David Godman. Hinduism Articles: Karma and Destiny. The Teachings of Sri Ramana Maharshi. Accessed at: http://www.indiaoz.com.au/hinduism/articles/karma_destiny_ maharshi.shtml

118. Cited in: David Godman. Hinduism Articles: Karma and Destiny. The Teachings of Sri Ramana Maharshi. Accessed at: http://www.indiaoz.com.au/hinduism/articles/karma_destiny_ maharshi.shtml

119. Cited in: Swami Muktananda. Readings in the Theory of Karma: Prarabdha Karma. Accessed at: http://baharna.com/karma/1_Readings.htm

120. Cited in: Ramesh S. Balsekar. Consciousness Speaks. VedicBooks.net. Accessed at: http://www.vedicbooks.net/consciousness-speaks-p-2649.html

121. Cited in: Bardor Tulku Rinpoche. Why We should Give up Anger. 2005. Densal, Issue 1703. June 2005. Karma Triyana Dharmachakra. Accessed at: http://www.kagyu.org/ktd/densal/archives/1703/anger.php

Chapter - 4
The Sacred, Secular and the Profane

1. Rodney Stark. Secularization. R.I.P. 1999. Sociology of Religion: a Quarterly Review. 60(3). p.270.
2. Cited in: University of St. Andrews. News and Events. Has Science Made Religion Redundant? 26 February 2008. Accessed at: http://www.st-andrews.ac.uk/news/Title,19733,en.html
3. Cited in: Steven Swinford. I've Found God, Says Man Who Cracked the Genome. The Times. UK. 11 June 2006. Accessed at: http://www.times online.co.uk/tol/news/uk/article673663.ece
4. Cited in: Wikipedia. Alfred Russel Wallace: Spiritualism. Accessed at: http://en.wikipedia.org/wiki/Alfred_Russel_Wallace
5. John Brockman (ed.). What We Believe but Cannot Prove: Today's Leading Thinkers on Science in the Age of Creativity. 2005. The Free Press. UK. p.85.
6. John Brockman (ed.). What We Believe but Cannot Prove: Today's Leading Thinkers on Science in the Age of Creativity. 2005. The Free Press. UK. p 41.
7. Cited in: Steven Swinford. I've Found God, Says Man Who Cracked the Genome. The Times. UK. 11 June 2006. Accessed at: http://www.timesonline.co.uk/tol/news/uk/article673663.ece
8. Cited in: Mahidol University. Approaching the Frontiers of Mind: the Limitations of Scientific Knowledge. Buddhist Scriptures Information Retrieval. Bangkok, Thailand. Accessed at: http://www.mahidol.ac.th/budsir/Toward/5_approaching_1.htm
9. Cited in: Mahidol University. Approaching the Frontiers of Mind: the Limitations of Scientific Knowledge. Buddhist Scriptures Information Retrieval. Bangkok, Thailand. Accessed at: http://www.mahidol.ac.th/budsir/Toward/5_approaching_1.htm
10. Cited in: Huston Smith. Religion in the Twenty-First Century. 2000. Vedanta Society of Southern California, USA. Accessed at: http://www.vedanta.org/reading/monthly/articles/2000/11.21st_ century.html
11. The Times of India. With Rat's Brain, Experts Develop a 'Frankenrobot'. Hyderabad, India. 16 August 2008. p.14.
12. Sam Wang and Sandra Aamodt. Your Brain Lies to You. The Times of India. Hyderabad, India. 5 July 2008. p.14.
13. Nick Bostrom. Transhumanist Values: What is Transhumanism? World Transhumanist Association. Accessed at: http://www.transhumanism.org/index.php/WTA/more/transhumanist-values
14. Cited in: Casey Kazan. Has Human Culture Replaced Biological Evolution? The Daily Galaxy. 4 March 2010. Accessed at: http://www.dailygalaxy.com/my_weblog/2010/03/has-human-culture-replaced-biological-evolution.html
15. Richard Heinberg. Cloning the Buddha: the Moral Impact of Biotechnology. 1999. Health Harmony. B. Jain Publishers, New Delhi, India. p.19.

16. Cited in: Neha Rathi. For Some Lonely Souls, Heart is Where the Gadget Is. The Deccan Chronicle. Hyderabad, India. 23 March 2008. p.II.
17. Cited in: C.E.M. Joad. Wikipedia. Accessed at: http://en.wikipedia.org/wiki/C._E._M._Joad
18. The Times of India. Hyderabad, India. 17 June 2008.
19. The Times of India. Hyderabad, India. 17 June 2008.
20. Cathryn M. Delude. Transfer Troubles. Scientific American. USA. October 2004. p.12
21. Albert Einstein. The Quotations Page. Michael Moncur's (Cynical) Quotations. Accessed at: http://www.quotationspage.com/quote/9.html
22. Pierre Baldi. The Shattered Self: The End of Natural Evolution. 2002. The MIT Press, USA. p.46.
23. Ralph Waldo Emerson. ThinkExist.com. Accessed at: http://thinkexist.com/quotation/things_are_in_the_saddle-and_ride/157703.html
24. Jacques Ellul (Joachim Neugroschel, tr.). The Technological System. 1980. The Continuum Publishing Corporation. New York, USA. p.1.
25. Michael G. Zey. Seizing the Future: The Dawn of the Macroindustrial Era. 1998. Transaction Publishers. New Jersey, USA. p.9.
26. John D. Barrow. Impossibility: the Limits of Science and the Science of Limits. 1999. Oxford University Press, USA.
27. Cited in: Michael Dirda. Wake Up and Dream. [Review of the book "Generosity: an Enhancement" by Richard Powers]. The New York Review of Books, USA. 14 January – 10 Febraury 2010. p.50.
28. The Future of Human Cloning. GlobalChange.com. Accessed at: http://www.globalchange.com/clonech.htm
29. The Deccan Chronicle. Hyderabad, India. 30 October 2004. p.13.
30. Michio Kaku. Visions: How Science Will Revolutionize the 21st Century. 1997. Anchor Books. New York, USA.
31. The New York Review of Books, USA. 14 November 2004. pp.87-96.
32. George Bernard Shaw. CreatingMinds.org. Accessed at: http://creatingminds.org/quotes/science.htm
33. Cited in: William S. Harris, et al. Response of Intelligent Design Network, Inc., to a Resolution by the Ohio Academy of Science Advocating the Teaching of Cosmic, Geological and Biological Evolution and the Censorship of "Intelligent Design" in Public School Science Education. 2002. Accessed at: http://www.intelligent designnetwork.org/OASresolutionRESPONSE.htm
34. David Adam. Is This the Answer to God, the Universe and All That? The Guardian. UK. 21 August 2004. Accessed at: http://www.guardian.co.uk/science/2004/aug/21/sciencenews. theguardianlifesupplement
35. Cited in: Wikisource. Omar Khayyam. Dmitri Smirnov (tr.). Accessed at: http://en.wikisource.org/wiki/Where_have_we_come_ from% 3F_Where_are_we_going%3F
36. Reader's Digest. Indian Edition. October 2003. p.86.

37. Caitrin Nicol. Brave New World at 75. The New Atlantis. No. 16, Spring 2007. Accessed at: http://www.thenewatlantis.com/publications/brave-new-world-at-75
38. Caitrin Nicol. Brave New World at 75. The New Atlantis. No. 16, Spring 2007. Accessed at: http://www.thenewatlantis.com/publications/brave-new-world-at-75
39. Statistics on the Blind. NewMedia Journalism. Accessed at: http://www.fims.uwo.ca/NewMedia2007/blindstats.aspx
40. Time Magazine. USA. 11 October 1999. pp.14-16.
41. Richard Dawkins. Wikiquote. The Selfish Gene (1976, 1989). Accessed at: http://en.wikiquote.org/wiki/Richard_Dawkins
42. Stephen L. Talbott. Owen Barfield and Technological Society. The Nature Institute. New York, USA. Accessed at: http://www.natureinstitute.org /txt/st/barfield.htm
43. Richard Soutar. Waking Up the Automatic Self. Futurehealth Winter Brain, Optimal Functioning and Positive Psychology and StoryCon Meeting. Accessed at: http://brainmeeting.com/maxspeakers/reports/speaker 2007_102.html
44. Dani Eder. What is This Singularity? Is it a Science-Fiction Thing Invented by Vernor Vinge? Can the Singularity be Avoided? Accessed at: http://www.aleph.se/Trans/Global/Singularity/singul.txt
45. Ravi Ravindra. Science and the Sacred. 2000. The Theosophical Publishing House. Adyar, Chennai, India. p.154.
46. Swami Prabhavananda and Frederick Manchester (trs.). The Upanishads: Breath of the Eternal. The Kena Upanishad. Spiritual Writings, Atma Jyoti Ashram. Accessed at: http://www.atmajyoti.org/up_kena_upanishad_text.asp
47. Allah: Both Transcendent and Imminent. Discover Islam. Accessed at: http://www.islamforall.net/is%20there%20a%20god.htm
48. Swami Vivekananda. Sayings. Accessed at: http://www.srira makrishna.org/vvksay.htm
49. Sigmund Freud. Quotations of Sigmund Freud. Atheism. Accessed at: http://atheisme.free.fr/Quotes/Freud.htm
50. Cited in: Robert Andrews. The Concise Columbia Dictionary of Quotations. 1989. Columbia University Press, USA. p.223.
51. Cited in: Robert Andrews. The Concise Columbia Dictionary of Quotations. 1989. Columbia University Press, USA. p.223.
52. R.D. Ranade. A Constructive Survey of Upanishadic Philosophy. 1968. Bharatiya Vidya Bhavan. Chowpatty, Bombay, India. p.241.
53. Cited in: StateMaster Encyclopedia: Spirituality. Accessed at: http://www.statemaster.com/encyclopedia/Spirituality
54. Cited in: David Pratt. John Eccles on Mind and Brain. [*Evolution of the Brain, Creation of the Self, p.241*]. Reprinted from Sunrise Magazine. June/July 1995. Theosophical University Press. Accessed at: http://www.theosophy-nw.org/theosnw/science/prat-bra.htm

55. How Science and Occult Science Work. ArticleNext. Accessed at: http://www.articlenext.com/Article/18133.html
56. Cited in: Alexandra Elizabeth Brichacek. Anthropomorphic Theater: Deep Ecology and the New Paradigm. Environmental Vegetarian Union (EVU) News. Issue 3/1997. Accessed at: http://www.euroveg.eu/evu/english/news/news973/anthropo.html
57. Swami Nirmalananda Giri. Commentary on the Katha Upanishad. The Divine Indwellers. Spiritual Writings. Atma Jyoti Ashram. Accessed at: http://www.atmajyoti.org/up_katha_upanishad_16.asp
58. Cited in: Andrew Wilson (ed.). World Scripture, a Comparative Anthology of Sacred Texts. The Sanctity of Nature. Accessed at: http://www.tparents.org/library/unification/books/world-s/WS-05-01.htm
59. Dean H. Hamer. The God Gene: How Faith is Hardwired Into Our Genes. 2004. Doubleday. New York, USA. p.212.
60. Dean H. Hamer. The God Gene: How Faith is Hardwired Into Our Genes. 2004. Doubleday. New York, USA. p.215.
61. Cited in: A Collection of Quotations on the Virtue of Compassion. The Virtues. Accessed at: http://www.thevirtues.org/site/10-Compassion.html
62. Cited in: Mahakankala Buddhist Center. What do Buddhists Believe? Compassion. Accessed at: http://meditatio ninsanta barbara.org/what-do-buddhists-believe
63. Cited in: Craig von Buseck. Christian Jihad: the Crusades and Killing in the Name of Christ. [Interview with Dr Ergun Caner]. Spiritual Life. CBN.com. Accessed at: http://www.cbn.com/spirituallife/churchandministry/churchhistory/crusades_caner christian jihad0505.aspx
64. Cited in: Craig von Buseck. Christian Jihad: the Crusades and Killing in the Name of Christ. [Interview with Dr Ergun Caner]. Spiritual Life. CBN.com. Accessed at: http://www.cbn.com/spirituallife/churchandministry/churchhistory/crusades_ canerchrist ianjihad0505.aspx
65. Cited in: Negation of Knowledge. Topic posted on 28 April 2006. Accessed at: http://astrotribe.tribe.net/thread/45406047-d687-470d-8372-c648467d4ca9
66. Cited in: Negation of Knowledge. Topic posted on 28 April 2006. Accessed at: http://astrotribe.tribe.net/thread/45406047-d687-470d-8372-c648467d4ca9
67. Osho. The Heart Sutra. Discourses on the Prajnaparamita Hridayam Sutra of Gautama the Buddha. 1978. Tao Publishing Pvt. Ltd. Pune, India. p.66.
68. Swami Nityaswarupananda (tr.). Ashtavakra Gita. 2001. Sri Ramanasramam. Tiruvannamalai, India. p.27.
69. Gary Zukav. The Seat of the Soul. 1995. MIT Press. London, UK. p.60.
70. Napoleon Hill. ThinkExist.com. Accessed at: http://thinkexist.com/quotations/desire/
71. Cited in: H.P. Blavatsky. The Voice of the Silence. 1998. The Theosophical Publishing House. Adyar, Chennai, India. pp.8-9.

72. Sri Aurobindo. The Future Evolution of Man. Chapter 5: The Development of the Spiritual Man. Accessed at: http://www. mountainman.com.au/auro_5.html
73. Sri Aurobindo. The Future Evolution of Man. Chapter 5: The Development of the Spiritual Man. Accessed at: http://www.mountainman.com.au/auro_5.html
74. Richard Bach. QuoteWorld.org. Accessed at: http://www.quote world.org/quotes/811
75. New Scientist. UK. 4 September 2004. p.30.
76. Mark Hamilton. God-Man: Our Final Evolution. 1998. Integrated Management Associates, Nevada, USA.
77. Mahatma Gandhi Speaks. Excerpt from the Woods/Greene collection of direct voice recordings with direct voice medium Leslie Flint. Accessed at: http://www.xs4all.nl/~wichm/gandhi.html
78. Satprem. Mind of the Cells. 1999. Institut de Recherches Evolutives. Paris, France. p.71.
79. Alister E. McGrath. Christian Literature: an Anthology. 2001. Wiley-Blackwell, USA. p.464.
80. Elaine Matthews. The Heartbeat of Intelligence. Trans4Mind. Accessed at: http://www.trans4mind.com/counterpoint/index-success-abundance/matthews.shtml
81. Ernest F. Pecci. In the Foreword to "Science and Human Transformation: Subtle Energies, Intentionality and Consciousness" by William A. Tiller. 1997. Pavior Publishers. USA. p.xvii.
82. William A. Tiller. Science and Human Transformation: Subtle Energies, Intentionality and Consciousness. 1997. Pavior Publishers. USA. p.ix.
83. William A. Tiller. Science and Human Transformation: Subtle Energies, Intentionality and Consciousness. 1997. Pavior Publishers. USA. p.ix.
84. Ernest F. Pecci. In the Foreword to "Science and Human Transformation: Subtle Energies, Intentionality and Consciousness" by William A. Tiller. 1997. Pavior Publishers. USA. p.xvii.
85. Percy B. Shelley. Positive Atheism's Big List of Percy Bysshe Shelley Quotations. Accessed at: http://www.positiveatheism.org/hist/quotes/shelley.htm
86. Cited in: Paths of Discovery. The Seventh Generation. Accessed at: http://www.pathsofdiscovery.com.au/
87. Kishor Gandhi. Lights on Life-Problems: Sri Aurobindo's Views On Important Life Problems. 1987. Sri Aurobindo Ashram. Pondicherry, India. p.70.
88. Ernest F. Pecci. In the Foreword to "Science and Human Transformation: Subtle Energies, Intentionality and Consciousness" by William A. Tiller. 1997. Pavior Publishers. USA. p.xviii.
89. Elaine Matthews. The Heartbeat of Intelligence. 2002. Writer's Showcase. New York, USA. p.108.

90. Elaine Matthews. The Heartbeat of Intelligence. 2002. Writer's Showcase. New York, USA. p.108.
91. Brian W. Harrison. Did the Human Body Evolve Naturally? A Forgotten Papal Declaration. Living Tradition: Organ of the Roman Theological Forum. No.73-74. January-March 1998. Accessed at: http://rtforum.org/lt/lt73.html
92. Annie Besant. The Bhagavad-Gita. 2003. The Theosophical Publishing House. Adyar, Chennai, India. p. 216.
93. The Times of India. Hyderabad, India. 31 October 2008. p.18.
94. The Times of India. Hyderabad, India. 7 December 2003. p.13.
95. James Hillman. The Soul's Code: in Search of Character and Calling. 1997. Warner Books. A Time Warner Company, USA. p.146-147.
96. Jack Kornfield. Reincarnation: the Karmic Cycle Karma. The Heart is our Garden. 2000. Chinmaya Publications. Chinmaya Mission West Publications Division. Piercy, USA. pp. 85-86.
97. Swami Vivekananda. God in Everything. Chapter VII. Complete Works of Swami Vivekananda. Vol.2. Jnana-Yoga. Accessed at: http://www.firehead.org/~pturing/occult/vivekananda/volume_2/jnana-yoga/god_in_everything.htm
98. Elaine Matthews. The Heartbeat of Intelligence. 2002. Writer's Showcase. New York, USA. p.vii.

Chapter - 5
From Mind to Heart — the Odyssey Within

1. Elaine Matthews. The Heartbeat of Intelligence. 2002. Writer's Showcase. New York, USA. p.102.
2. Cited in: Steve Cady. Selecting Methods: the Art of Mastery. The Change Handbook (Peggy Holman, Tom Devane, and Steven Cady, eds.). 2007. Berret-Koehler Publishers. California, USA. p.28.
3. James Berry. The Universe Story, as told by Brain Swimme and Thomas Berry. The Trumpeter (10)2. Accessed at: http://trumpeter.athabascau.ca/index.php/trumpet/article/viewFile/386/615
4. Raag Gauree. Shri Guru Granth Sahib. Section 07, Part 003. Internet Sacred Text Archive: Sikhism. Accessed at: http://www.sacred-texts.com/skh/granth/gr07.htm
5. Cited in: MegaEssays.com. The Mind is Its Own Place. Accessed at: http://www.megaessays.com/viewpaper/97915.html
6. Cited in: Adventus. A Method of the Discourse. 26 September 2008. Accessed at: http://rmadisonj.blogspot.com/2008/09/method-of-discourse.html
7. The Buddha. ThinkExist.com. Mind Quotes. Accessed at: http://thinkexist.com/quotes/with/keyword/mind/
8. Kathy Hurley and Theodorre Donson. The Enneagram: Key to Opening the Heart. The Enneagram in the Healing Tradition. Accessed at: http://www.hurleydonson.com/opening_heart.htm

9. Kathy Hurley and Theodorre Donson. The Enneagram: Key to Opening the Heart. The Enneagram in the Healing Tradition. Accessed at: http://www.hurleydonson.com/opening_heart.htm
10. Cited in: Robert Fripp. From Crimson King to Crafty Master. Chapter Seven: Sabbatical. Progressive Ears. Accessed at: http://www.progressiveears.com/frippbook/ch07.htm
11. The Times of India. Hyderabad, India. 6 July 2008. p.17.
12. Sri Ramana Maharshi. Sri Ramana Maharshi on Self-Enquiry. Self-Enquiry — Self-Enquiry vs. Other Means of Quieting the Mind. Accessed at: http://www.angelfire.com/space2/light11/diction/ramana.html
13. Sri Ramana Maharshi. Sri Ramana Maharshi on Self-Enquiry. Self-Enquiry — Self-Enquiry vs. Other Means of Quieting the Mind. Accessed at: http://www.angelfire.com/space2/light11/diction/ramana.html
14. J.P. Vaswani. Peace or Perish. Holistic Hong Kong. Accessed at: http://www.holistichongkong.com/Articles/Peace-or-Perish.html
15. Satprem. The Mind of the Cells or Willed Mutation of Our Species. 1982. The Institute for Evolutionary Research. New York, USA. p.77.
16. Roger Penrose. Shadows of the Mind: a Search for the Missing Science of Consciousness. 1994. Oxford University Press. New York, USA. p.9.
17. P.D. Ouspensky. The Psychology of Man's Possible Evolution. 1974. Vintage Books. [Random House]. New York, USA. p.86.
18. P.D. Ouspensky. The Psychology of Man's Possible Evolution. 1974. Vintage Books. [Random House]. New York, USA. p.88.
19. Immortal Words: an Anthology. 1963. Bharatiya Vidya Bhavan. Chaupatty, Bombay, India. p.71.
20. G. de Purucker. Man in Evolution. Chapter 16: The Pineal and Pituitary Glands. 1977. Second and Revised Edition. Grace F. Knoche (ed.). Theosophical University Press. Pasadena, California, USA. Accessed at: http://www.theosociety.org/pasadena/man-evol/mie-16.htm
21. Mother Teresa. BrainyQuote.com. Mother Teresa Quotes. Accessed at: http://www.brainyquote.com/quotes/quotes/m/mothertere 158106.html
22. Cited in: Jen Johans. Film Intuition. Woody Allen's Existential Crimes and Misdemeanors. 2002. Accessed at: http://www. filmintuition.com/Crimes.html
23. W. Somerset Maugham. BrainyQuote.com. W. Somerset Maugham Quotes. Accessed at: http://www.brainyquote.com/quotes/authors/w/w_ somerset _maugham.html
24. Elaine Matthews. The Heartbeat of Intelligence. 2002. Writer's Showcase. New York, USA. p.vii.
25. Elaine Matthews. The Heartbeat of Intelligence. Accessed at: http://www.trans4mind.com/counterpoint/index-emotional-intelligence/matthews.shtml
26. Elaine Matthews. The Heartbeat of Intelligence. Accessed at: http://www.trans4mind.com/counterpoint/index-emotional-intelligence/matthews.shtml

27. Cited in: Stephen Harrod Buhner. The Secret Teachings of Plants: The Intelligence of the Heart in Direct Perception of Nature. 2004. Inner Traditions. Vermont, USA. p.70.

28. Institute of HeartMath. Science of the Heart: Exploring the Role of the Heart in Human Performance. 2010. IHM. Boulder Creek, California, USA. Accessed at: http://www.heartmath.org/research/science-of-the-heart.html

29. Immortal Words: an Anthology. 1963. Bharatiya Vidya Bhavan. Bombay, India. p.194.

30. Mani Shankar. The Times of India. Hyderabad, India. 20 December 2009. p.II.

31. Kathryn S. Bennett. The Future of Mental Health Awareness: a Global Perspective. The Humanist Magazine. September/October 2001. Vol.61, no.5. Accessed at: http://www.thefreelibrary.com/The+Future+of+ Mental+ Health+Awareness:+A+Global+Perspective.-a078966505

32. Abraham H. Maslow. The Farther Reaches of Human Nature. 1993. Penguin. p.167.

33. Cited in: Annie Besant. The Coming Race. Adyar Pamphlets. Lecture delivered at the Theosophical Conference held at Chittoor on 17 March 1916. Theosophical Publishing House. Adyar, Chennai, India. Accessed at: http:// www.theosophical.ca/adyar_pamphlets/AdyarPamphlet_No76.pdf

34. Annie Besant. The Coming Race. Adyar Pamphlets. Lecture delivered at the Theosophical Conference held at Chittoor on 17 March 1916. Theosophical Publishing House. Adyar, Chennai, India. Accessed at: http:// www.theosophical.ca/adyar_pamphlets/Adyar Pamphlet_No76.pdf

35. G. de Purucker. The Esoteric Tradition. Theosophical University Press Online Edition. Pasadena, California, USA. Accessed at: http://www.theosociety.org/ pasadena/et/et-intro.htm

36. Ernest F. Pecci. In the Foreword to "Science and Human Transformation: Subtle Energies, Intentionality and Consciousness" by William A. Tiller. 1997. Pavior Publishers. USA. p.xvii.

37. Signs of Agni Yoga. Heart. 1932. Agni Yoga Society. New York, USA. Accessed at: http://www.agniyoga.org /ay_heart.html

38. Winifred A. Parley. A Blavatsky Quotation Book. 2000. The Theosophical Publishing House. Adyar, Chennai, India. p.27.

39. Winifred A. Parley. A Blavatsky Quotation Book. 2000. The Theosophical Publishing House. Adyar, Chennai, India. p.50.

40. Cited in: Andreas Ohrt. Dormant Powers of the Human Brain. Norman D. Livergood. Mind Power News. Saturday, 26 June 2004. Issue 49. Accessed at: http://www.mindpowernews.com/049.htm

41. Elaine Matthews. The Heartbeat of Intelligence. 2002. Writer's Showcase. New York, USA. p.87.

42. William A. Tiller. Science and Human Transformation: Subtle Energies, Intentionality and Consciousness. 1997. Pavior Publishers. USA. p.278.

43. Elaine Matthews. The Heartbeat of Intelligence. 2002. Writer's Showcase. New York, USA. p.102.
44. Cited in: HPS.Online.com. Mental health, a Tibetan Buddhist Perspective. Introduction: The Natural Bardo. The Wisdom of Egolessness. Accessed at: http://www.hps-online.com/sogyal.htm
45. Discourses of Meher Baba. Vol. III. 1954. Adi K Irani Meher Publications. Mumbai, India. p.95.
46. Anup Taneja. There is Nothing Inside the Cloak but God. The Times of India. Hyderabad, India. 18 January 2009. p.10.
47. Antoine de Saint Exupéry. Katherine Woods (tr.). The Little Prince. 1962. Penguin Books. London, UK. p.84.
48. G. de Purucker. The Buddhas of Compassion and the Pratyeka Buddhas. Extracts from Golden Precepts. Eclectic Theosophist. No.56. Accessed at: http://theosophy.katinkahesselink.net/purucker/buddha-compassion.html
49. Dave De Luca (ed.). Pathways to Joy: The Master Vivekananda on the Four Yoga Paths to God. 2003. Inner Occan Publishing. Makawao, Hawaii, USA. p.135.
50. Vedanta Kesari. Ramakrishna Math. Hyderabad, India. September 2004. p.9.
51. Vedanta Kesari. Ramakrishna Math. Hyderabad, India. September 2004. p.8.
52. Cited in: The Divine Lotus Flower, Kein Java, Manarayana Upanishad XII-16, Accessed at: http://www.harekrsna.de/Lotus-FLower.htm
53. Cited in: The Eternal Wisdom: Central Sayings of Great Sages of All Times. 1993. Sri Aurobindo Ashram Publications. Pondicherry, India. p.427.
54. Cited in: Power of Your Thoughts/Mind. SortLifeOut.co.uk. Discover Your True Purpose. Accessed at: http://www.meaningoflife.i12.com/Mind.htm
55. Khalil Gibran. The Voice of the Master. 1958. The Citadel Press. Secaucus, New Jersey, USA. p.79.
56. Cited in: The Real Essentials. Follow Your Heart. Accessed at: http://www.therealessentials.com/followyourheart.html
57. Cited in: Friedrich. Notes on the Word "Intellectual". 8 august 2003. Accessed at: http://www.2blowhards.com/archives/2003/08/notes_on_ the_word_intellectual.html
58. Cited in: SufiBlog.com. Ibn Arabi. Accessed at: http://www. sufiblog.com/ibn-arabi.html
59. Virginia Essene. Heart and Brain: How are Your Heart and Brain Connected to God? Global Onenness. Accessed at: http://www.experiencefestival.com/a/Heart_and_Brain/id/1961
60. The Heart's Mind. The Theosophical Movement. September 2001. Vol.71. No.11. Theosophy Company. Mumbai, India. Accessed at: http://www.ultindia.org/Mumbai/7111heart.html
61. Cited in: The Real Essentials. Follow Your Heart. Accessed at: http://www.therealessentials.com/followyourheart.html

62. Cited in: The Real Essentials. Follow Your Heart. Accessed at: http://www.therealessentials.com/followyourheart.html
63. Cited in: Flux64. Three Minds Into One. Adapted from 'Cosmic Healing I' by Matt Gluck. Accessed at: http://flux64.blogspot.com/2006_10_01_archive.html
64. Cited in: Message of Sri Ramakrishna. Ramakrishna Mission Vivekananda College (autonomous). Mylapore, Chennai, India. Accessed at: http://rkmvc.ac.in/mission/ramakrishna.html
65. Pravrajika Vrajaprana. Living Wisdom. 1995. Ramakrishna Math. p.215.
66. Cited in: Quotations by Blaise Pascal [Pensées 1670]. Accessed at: http://www-history.mcs.st-andrews.ac.uk/Quotations/Pascal.html
67. Cited in: Rumi's Mathnawi. Daylight. Accessed at: http://chippit.tripod.com/daylight.html
68. The Times of India. Hyderabad, India. 12 September 2004. p.15.
69. Cited in: Mind is Creation of Society; Heart Has No Logic. The Deccan Chronicle. Hyderabad, India. 22 June 2008. p.II.
70. Cited in: Speech Commonly Attributed To Chief Seattle. Accessed at: http://www.ilhawaii.net/~stony/seattle2.html
71. Cited in: The International Endowment for Democracy. Democracy Quotes. Accessed at: http://www.iefd.org/articles/demo cracy_quotes.php
72. George Orwell. Nineteen Eighty-Four. 1961. Penguin Publishers. USA. p. 249.
73. Scientific American. USA. January 2005. p. 22.
74. Avatar Meher Baba. Way to Spiritual Wisdom Through Heart. The Times of India. Hyderabad, India. 10 July 2007.
75. Avatar Meher Baba. Way to Spiritual Wisdom Through Heart. The Times of India. Hyderabad, India. 10 July 2007.
76. Cited in: The Eternal Wisdom: Central Sayings of Great Sages of All Times. 1993. Sri Aurobindo Ashram Publications. Pondicherry, India. p. 429.
77. Cited in: The Eternal Wisdom: Central Sayings of Great Sages of All Times. 1993. Sri Aurobindo Ashram Publications. Pondicherry, India. p. 430.

Chapter - 6
Contours of Consciousness Change

1. David Wilcock. The Energetic Engine of Evolution. In: The Reincarnation of Edgar Cayce? Interdimensional Communication & Global Transformation [Wynn Free, David Wilcock]. 2004. Frog Books. Berkeley, California, USA. p.337.
2. David Wilcock. The Ultimate Secret of the Mayan Calendar: an Imploding Cycle of Energy Increase, Culminating in 2010-2013. No Reason to Fear the Changes. Accessed at: http://divine cosmos.com/index.php?option=com_content& task=view &id=45 &Itemid=30

3. Albert Einstein. ThinkExist.com. Consciousness Quotes. Accessed at: http://thinkexist.com/quotes/with/keyword/consciousness/
4. Sol Luckman. Shift in Human Consciousness. 2007. Accessed at: http://www.2012warning.com/shift-in-human-consciousness-2012.htm
5. Annie Wood Besant. Study in Consciousness: a Contribution to the Science of Psychology. Chapter II: Consciousness. 1998. Kessinger Publishing. Montana, USA. p.32.
6. Stuart S. Sutherland. The International Dictionary of Psychology. 2nd edition.1995. Crossroad Publishing. New York, USA.
7. Miguel de Unamuno. BrainyQuote.com. Accessed at: http://www.brainyquote.com/quotes/quotes/m/migueldeun147359.html
8. P.D. Ouspensky. Tertium Organum: The Third Canon of Thought. A Key to the Enigmas of the World. 1922. Accessed at http://www.sacred-texts.com/eso/to/to02.htm
9. Paramahansa Yogananda. Ascension Gateway.com. Accessed at: http://www.ascensiongateway.com/quotes/paramahansa-yogananda/index.htm
10. Wikipedia. Julian Jaynes. Accessed at: http://en.wikipedia.org/wiki/Julian_Jaynes
11 . Cited in: Perry Smith. Excerpts from Dalai Lama's Book of Transformation. Accessed at: http://www.perryland.com/Noteworthy8.shtml
12. Cited in: Perry Smith. Excerpts from Dalai Lama's Book of Transformation. Accessed at: http://www.perryland.com/Noteworthy8.shtml
13. H.P. Blavatsky. The Secret Doctrine: the Synthesis of Science, Religion and Philosophy. Vol. II. Anthropogenesis. 1978. The Theosophical Publishing House. Adyar, Chennai, India. p.81.
14. Simone Weil. BrainyQuote.com. Accessed at: http://www. brainyquote.com/quotes/quotes/s/simoneweil147174.html
15. Dean H. Hamer. The God Gene: How Faith is Hardwired Into Our Genes. 2004. Doubleday, New York, USA. p.6.
16. Dean H. Hamer. The God Gene: How Faith is Hardwired Into Our Genes. 2004. Doubleday. New York, USA. p.6-8.
17. Piero Scaruffi. Quantum Consciousness. Thymos: Studies on Consciousness, Cognition and Life. Accessed at: http://www.scaruffi.com/science/qc.html
18. Piero Scaruffi. Quantum Consciousness. Thymos: Studies on Consciousness, Cognition and Life. Accessed at: http://www.scaruffi.com/science/qc.html
19. Cited in: Janna Lynn. Cry of the Hawk for Her Beloved. Poems. Accessed at: http://seven_directions.tripod.com/id7.html
20. Soren Kierkegaard. BrainyQuote.com. Accessed at: http://www.brainyquote.com/quotes/authors/s/soren_kierkegaard.html
21. Cited in: New Advent. Sermon 77 on the New Testament. Accessed at: http://www.newadvent.org/fathers/160377.htm

22. Samuel Johnson. ThinkExist.com. Accessed at: http://thinkexist.com/quotation/he_who_makes_a_beast_of_himself_gets_rid_of_the/263212.html
23. Wikipedia. Pain and Pleasure. Accessed at: http://en.wikipedia.org/wiki/Pain_and_pleasure
24. Cited in: Consequentialism. Wikipedia. Accessed at: http://en.wikipedia.org/wiki/Consequentialism
25. Robert C.W. Ettinger. The Prospect of Immortality. 1964. Accessed at: http://www.cryonics.org/book1.html
26. Jean Rostand. Preface to 'The Prospect of Immortality' by Robert C.W. Ettinger. 1964. Accessed at: http://www.cryonics.org/preface1.html
27. Cited in: Daniel Callahan. The Desire for Eternal Life: Scientific Versus Religious Visions. The 2002-03 Ingersoll Lecture. Harvard Divinity Bulletin. Harvard Divinity School. Accessed at: http://www.hds.harvard.edu/news/bulletin/articles/callahan.html
28. Swami Krishnananda. The Secret of the Katha Upanishad. 2nd edition. 2002. The Divine Life Society. India. p.138.
29. Cited in: Richard Pettinger. Sarada Devi. Write Spirit. Accessed at: http://www.writespirit.net/authors/sarada-devi
30. Swami Vivekananda. Famous Quotations of Swami Vivekananda. Accessed at: http://www.saha.ac.in/lib/a.malakar/quot.htm
31. Cited in: Other. Wikipedia. Accessed at: http://en.wikipedia.org/wiki/Other
32. Jeremy Griffith. Beyond the Human Condition. The Story of Homo. 1991. World Transformation Movement. Accessed at: http://www.worldtransformation.com/Beyond/StoryOfHomo.html
33. Cited in: Learn Peace, a Peace Pledge Union Project. Aldous Huxley. Ends and Means. The Nature of War. Accessed at: http://www.ppu.org.uk/learn/infodocs/people/pp-huxley1.html
34. Cited in: The Ministry of Truth. Wikipedia. Accessed at: http://en.wikipedia.org/wiki/Ministry_of_Truth
35. Cited in: Ernest F. Pecci. Foreword to "Science and Human Transformation: Subtle Energies, Intentionality and Consciousness" by William A. Tiller. 1997. Pavior Publishers. USA. p.xix.
36. Marcel Proust. ThinkExist.com. Accessed at: http://thinkexist.com/quotation/the_real_voyage_of_discovery_consists_not_in/144224.html
37. Cited in: Ralph Metzner. The Unfolding Self: Varieties of Transformative Experience. Introduction: From Caterpillar to Butterfly. Accessed at: http://www.greenearthfound.org/products/books_unfold_tus-intro.html
38. Dawson Church. The Genie in Your Genes: Epigenetic Medicine and the New Biology of Intention. Elite Books. California, USA. p.171.
39. Duane Elgin and Coleen LeDrew. Global Consciousness Change: Indicators of an Emerging Paradigm. New Horizons for Learning: Perspectives on the Future. Accessed at: http://www.newhorizons.org/future/elgin2.htm

Chapter - 7
Transformation and God

1. Cited in: Russell DiCarlo. Explorations in Consciousness. [Interview with Edgar Mitchell. Excerpted from 'Towards a New World View: Conversations at the Leading Edge' by Russell DiCarlo. 1996. Epic Publishing. USA]. Accessed at: http://www.healthy.net/scr/interview.asp?Id=208
2. The Economist. Synthetic Biology: And Man Made Life. 20 May 2010.
3. H.P. Blavatsky. The Secret Doctrine: the Synthesis of Science, Religion and Philosophy. Vol. I. Cosmogenesis. Part III. Cyclic Evolution and Karma. 1978. The Theosophical Publishing House. Adyar, Chennai, India. p.639.
4. R.D. Ranade. A Constructive Survey of Upanishadic Philosophy. 1968. Bharatiya Vidya Bhavan, Chowpatty, Bombay, India. p.118.
5. R.D. Ranade. A Constructive Survey of Upanishadic Philosophy. 1968. Bharatiya Vidya Bhavan, Chowpatty, Bombay, India. p.118.
6. Sri Chinmoy. Transformation, Liberation, Revelation, Manifestation. Accessed at: http://www.srichinmoy.org/resources/library/talks/transformation/transformation_liberation/
7. H.P. Blavatsky. The Secret Doctrine: the Synthesis of Science, Religion and Philosophy. Vol. I. Cosmogenesis. Part III. Cyclic Evolution and Karma. 1978. The Theosophical Publishing House. Adyar, Chennai, India. p.643.
8. Thomas McEvilley. The Shape of Ancient Thought: Comparative Studies in Greek and Indian Philosophies. 2002. Allworth Press. New York, USA. p.99.
9. Carlos Barrios. The Mayan Calendar – The World Will Not End. Accessed at: http://www.mayamysteryschool.com/pdf%20files/Carlos_Barrios.pdf
10. Duane Elgin and Coleen LeDrew. Summary: Global Consciousness Change: Indicators of an Emerging Paradigm. New Horizons for Learning: Perspectives on the Future. Accessed at: http://www.newhorizons.org/future/elgin1.htm
11. Duane Elgin and Coleen LeDrew. Summary: Global Consciousness Change: Indicators of an Emerging Paradigm. New Horizons for Learning: Perspectives on the Future. Accessed at: http://www.newhorizons.org/future/elgin1.htm
12. Leo Tolstoy. Patriotism and Government. Anarchy Archives. Accessed at: http://dwardmac.pitzer.edu/Anarchist_Archives/bright/tolstoy/patriotismandgovt.html
13. Gillian Ross. The Future. Quotations. Accessed at: http://www.kindness.com.au/quotations.htm
14. Michael Shermer. Captain Kirk Principle. Scientific American Magazine. USA. December 2002. p.1.
15. G.K. Chesterton. The Everlasting Man. 2008. Wilder Publications. Virginia, USA. p.5.
16. Cited in: Sailen Routray. The Mahimandala Gita of Tantric Saint Arakkhita Das. Anuvada of Mahimandala Gita. Chapter 66. Accessed at: http://www.indiadivine.org/articles/269-mahimandala-gita-tantric-saint-arakkhita-das.html

17. R.D. Ranade. A Constructive Survey of Upanishadic Philosophy. 1968. Bharatiya Vidya Bhavan, Chowpatty, Bombay, India. pp.92-93.

18. Erwin Schrodinger. What is Life? [with *Mind and Matter* and *Autobiographical Sketches*]. 1992. Canto. Cambridge University Press. Cambridge, UK. p.87.

19. James C. Swindal and Harry J. Gensler. The Sheed and Ward Anthology of Catholic Philosophy. 2005. Rowman & Littlefield Publishers. Maryland, USA. pp.204-205.

20. Soren Kierkegaard. Brainy Quote.com. Accessed at: http://www.brainyquote.com/quotes/authors/s/soren_kierkegaard.html

21. H.G. Wells. God: The Invisible King. Chapter I. The Cosmogony of Modern Religion. Section 5. God is Within. 1917. p.23.

22. Cited in: Wikipedia. Voltaire. Accessed at: http://en.wikipedia.org/wiki/Voltaire

23. Cited in: Tan Kheng Khoo. Ultimate State of Consciousness (Enlightenment). Accessed at: http://www.kktanhP.com/ultimate_state_.htm

24. Maurice Bloomfield (tr.). Sacred Books of the East. Vol.42: Hymns of the Atharva-Veda. Internet Sacred Text Archive. Accessed at: http://www.sacred-texts.com/hin/sbe42/av094.htm

25. Cited in: A. Rishi. Swami Vivekananda – The Importance of Being Indian. Life Positive. Accessed at: http://www.lifepositive.com/Spirit/masters/swami-vivekananda/chicago.asp

26. Cited in: The Eternal Wisdom: Central Sayings of Great Sages of All Times. 1993. Sri Aurobindo Ashram Publications. Pondicherry, India. p.66.

27. Emily Bronte. No Coward Soul is Mine. The Wondering Minstrels. Accessed at: http://www.cs.rice.edu/~ssiyer/minstrels/poems/262.html

28. Sri Aurobindo. The Poet Seers. Accessed at: http://www.poetseers.org/the_poetseers/sri_aurobindo/selected_poems/god/

29. George C. Mynchenberg. And Man Created God. 2000. Writers Club Press. Lincoln, Nebraska, USA. p.iii.

30. Cited in: Theology: The God is Dead Movement. Time Magazine. Friday, 22 October 1965. Accessed at: http://www.time.com/time/magazine/article/0,9171,941410-1,00.html

31. William Archer. Quotes. Man Created God. Accessed at: http://atheisme.free.fr/Quotes/Man_created_god.htm

32. Arthur C. Clarke. Quotes. Man Created God. Accessed at: http://atheisme.free.fr/Quotes/Man_created_god.htm

33. Friedrich Nietzsche. Quotes. Man Created God. Accessed at: http://atheisme.free.fr/Quotes/Man_created_god.htm

34. George Santayana. Quotes. Man Created God. Accessed at: http://atheisme.free.fr/Quotes/Man_created_god.htm

35. Pearl S. Buck. Wisdom Quotes. Accessed at: http://www.wisdomquotes.com/topics/faith/index2.html

36. Cited in: Paul Helm. Faith and Understanding. 1997. Edinburgh University Press. Edinburg, UK. p.92.

37. Swami Nikhilananda. The Gospel of Sri Ramakrishna. 1996. Sri Ramakrishna Math. Chennai, India. p.172.
38. Sikh Philosophy Network. Essays on Sikhism: Madness of Belief in Caste: Jaat-Paat. Accessed at: http://www.sikhphilosophy.net/essays-on-sikhism/14792-madness-of-belief-caste-jaat-paat.html
39. Cited in: Steven Pinker. Can You Believe In God And Evolution?.Time Magazine. USA. Sunday, 2 August 2005. Accessed at:http://www.time.com/time/magazine/article/0,9171, 1090921,00.html
40. B.L. Atreya. Samvid (tr.). The Vision and Way of Vasistha. 2nd edition. 2005. Samata Books. Chennai, India. p. 95.
41. P.D. Sharma. Immortal Quotations and Proverbs. 2003. Navneet Publications. Mumbai, India. p.42.
42. Fate and Free Will. Advaita. Accessed at: http://www.advaita.org.uk/discourses/real/freewill.htm
43. Sri Chinmoy. Fate and Free Will. Accessed at: http://www.srichinmoy.org/spirituality/god_the_supreme/the_cosmic_ game/fate_and_free_will/
44. H.P. Blavatsky. The Secret Doctrine: the Synthesis of Science, Religion and Philosophy. Vol. I. Cosmogenesis. Part.1. 1978. The Theosophical Publishing House. Adyar, Chennai, India. p.105.
45. Dhananjay Kulkarni. Life After Death. Buzzle. Accessed at: http://www.buzzle.com/editorials/6-14-2004-55447.asp
46. Ralph Waldo Emerson. ThinkExist.com. Accessed at: http://thinkexist.com/quotations/fate/
47. Sogyal Rinpoche. What is Karma? Law of Cause and Effect. Accessed at: http://www.meaningoflife.i12.com/karma.htm
48. Gerard Manly Hopkins. Bartleby. Accessed at: http://www. bartleby.com/122/7.html
49. Cited in: Richard Pettinger. Life of Ramana Maharishi. Accessed at: http://www.writespirit.net/authors/ramana_maharshi/life_of_ramana_maharshi
50. Sri Aurobindo. Savitri. Canto IV: The Secret Knowledge. 1993. Sri Aurobindo Ashram Trust. Pondicherry, India. p.67.
51. Sri Aurobindo. Savitri. Book VI: The Book of Fate. 1993. Sri Aurobindo Ashram Trust. Pondicherry, India. p.458.
52. Barbara Brown Taylor. Leaving Church: a Memoir of Faith. 2007. HarperCollins Publishers. New York, USA. p.106.
53. William James. The Varieties of Religious Experience: a Study in Human Nature. 2008. Arc Manor. Maryland, USA. p.302.
54. P.D. Sharma. Immortal Quotations and Proverbs. 2003. Navneet Publications. Mumbai, India. p.35.
55. I.V. Chalapati Rao. Triveni. India's Literary and Cultural Quarterly. Chikkadapally, Hyderabad, India. Vol. 74, no.2, April-June 2005. p.5.

56. Cited in: Tulsidas Sundarakand. Part 4. Saranaagathi - Surrender to the Divine. Accessed at: http://saranaagathi.wordpress.com/online-devotional-works/tulsidas-sundarakand/tulsidas-sundarakand-4/
57. Cited in: Wayne Blank. Why Isn't Infant Baptism Valid? The Church of God Daily Bible Study. Accessed at: http://www.keyway.ca/htm2007/20070210.htm
58. Annie Besant. The Bhagavad-Gita. 2003. The Theosophical Publishing House. Adyar, Chennai, India. p.255.
59. Peter Kreeft. Truth Journal. The Case for Life After Death. Accessed at: http://www.leaderu.com/truth/1truth28.html
60. Wikipedia. Antony Flew. Accessed at: http://en.wikipedia.org/wiki/Antony_Flew
61. Wikipedia. Atheism. Accessed at: http://en.wikipedia.org/wiki/Atheism
62. Annie Besant. The Doctrine of the Heart. 2003. The Theosophical Publishing House. Adyar, Chennai, India. p.v.
63. Annie Besant. The Doctrine of the Heart. 2003. The Theosophical Publishing House. Adyar, Chennai, India. p.x.
64. Annie Besant. The Doctrine of the Heart. 2003. The Theosophical Publishing House. Adyar, Chennai, India. p.xii.
65. Swami Nikhilananda. The Gospel of Sri Ramakrishna. 1996. Sri Ramakrishna Math. Chennai, India. p.635.
66. Mark Tully. Unfashionable Virtue of Heartfelt Humility. The Times of India. Hyderabad, India. 11 July 2007. p.12.
67. William A. Goddard III, et al. (eds.). Handbook of Nanoscience, Engineering, and Technology. 2003. CRC Press. Florida, USA. p.I-3.
68. Rabindranath Tagore. Sadhana: the Realisation of Life. Soul Consciousness. 1916. Internet Sacred Text Archive. Accessed at: http://www.sacred-texts.com/hin/tagore/sadh/sadh04.htm
69. Cited in: Woolf Abrahams. Reflecting on Judaism. Petitional Prayer, Determination & Freewill; Are They Compatible? Accessed at: http://www.reflectingonjudaism.com/?q=Petitional_Prayer
70. Alexander Pope. The Poetical Works of Alexander Pope. Volume 1. Full Books. Accessed at: http://www.fullbooks.com/The-Poetical-Works-Of-Alexander-Pope-Vol4.html
71. Parrinder Geoffrey. A Dictionary of Religious and Spiritual Quotations. 1989. Simon and Schuster. USA. p.140.
72. The Bible. New International Version. Bible Gateway. Accessed at: http://www.biblegateway.com/passage/?search=Romans%2012:2
73. Jiddu Krishnamurti. Commentaries on Living. Accessed at: http://www.jiddukrishnamurti.org/thought.htm
74. Ken Wilber. The Pocket Ken Wilber. 2008. Shambhala Publications. Massachusetts, USA. p.125.
75. P.D. Ouspensky. The Psychology of Man's Possible Evolution. 1974. Vintage Books. A division of Random House. New York, USA. pp.8.

76. Mewlana Jalaluddin Rumi. Masnawi. PoemHunter.com. Accessed at: http://www.poemhunter.com/poem/masnawi/
77. Shri Sai Satcharitra. Chapters 16 and 17. Accessed at: http://www.saibabaofshirdi.net/satcharita/sai16_17.html
78. Cited in: Ivan M. Havel. Remarks on Schrodinger's Concept of Consciousness. Accessed at: http://www.cts.cuni.cz/~havel/work/schroe94.html
79. Cited in: Matthew Price. Sinner Take All. Graham Greene's Damned Redemption. BookForum. Oct/Nov 2004. Accessed at: http://www.bookforum.com/archive/Oct_04/price_oct.html
80. Cited in: Transformation via the Human Algorithm. Order of the Great Diesis. Accessed at: http://www.harmonicresolution.com/Transformation.htm
81. The Bible. (King James Bible). Biblos. Accessed at: http://bible.cc/ecclesiastes/9-12.htm
82. Sri Aurobindo. Savitri. 1993. Sri Aurobindo Ashram Trust. Pondicherry, India. p.137.
83. Delbert D.Thiessen. Bittersweet Destiny: the Stormy Evolution of Human Behavior. 1996. Transaction Publishers. New Jersey, USA. p.287.
84. The Bible. New International Version. Bible Gateway. Accessed at: http://www.biblegateway.com/passage/?search=2+ Corinthians +3:18&version=NIV
85. Cited in: Kristen Nummi Nummerdor. The Dream Lives On: Student Group Leaders Speak On The Legacy Of Martin Luther King, Jr. Accessed at: http://mit.edu/activities/thistle/v9/9.02/8dream.html
86. Thomas Aquinas. Wikiquote. Accessed at: http://en.wikiquote.org/wiki/Thomas_Aquinas
87. Sri Aurobindo. Savitri. 1993. Book VI: The Book of Fate. Sri Aurobindo Ashram Trust. Pondicherry, India. p.448.
88. Sri Aurobindo. The Future Evolution of Man: The Divine Life Upon Earth. 1971. Sri Aurobindo Ashram Trust. Pondicherry, India. p.27.
89. Elaine Matthews. The Heartbeat of Intelligence. 2002. Writer's Showcase. New York, USA. p.83.
90. Omar N. Bradley. ThinkExist.com. Accessed at: http://thinkexist.com/quotes/omar_bradley/
91. M.K. Gandhi. An Autobiography or the Story of My Experiments With Truth. 2008. Navajivan Publishing House. Ahmedabad, India. p.15.
92. Sir Francis Younghusband. Dawn in India: British Purpose and Indian Aspiration. Chapter XIII: Indian Spirituality. Frederick A. Stokes Company. New York, USA. p.240.
93. Eknath Easwaran. The Lesson of the Humming Bird. In Context. No.26, Summer 1990. Accessed at: http://www.context.org/ICLIB/IC26/Easwaran.htm
94. Albert Einstein. BrainyQuote.com. Accessed at: http://www.brainyquote.com/quotes/quotes/a/alberteins130982.html

95. Charles Harrison and Paul Wood (eds.). Art in Theory: An Anthology of Changing Ideas 1900-2000. 2007. Blackwell Publishers. Massachusetts, USA. p.538.
96. Paramahamsa Yogananda. Consciousness. Ascension Gateway. Accessed at: http://www.ascensiongateway.com/quotes/subject/consciousness/index.htm
97. Remez Sasson. Quotes on Mind and Consciousness. Success Consciousness. Accessed at: http://www.successconsciousness.com/index_000017.htm
98. Rabindranath Tagore. Poetry. Acropolis. Accessed at: http://www.acropolis.org.au/poetry/Tagore.htm
99. Howard Martin. The Heart Math Method. Achievement Library. Accessed at: http://www.achievementlibrary.com/heartmath.htm
100. Cited in: Swami Nirmalananda Giri. The Dweller in the Heart. Katha Upanishad. Spiritual Writings. Atma Jyoti Ashram. Accessed at: http://www.atmajyoti.org/up_Katha_ Upanishad_ 23.asp
101. Absolute Shakespeare. Shakespeare Quotes. Accessed at: http://www.absoluteshakespeare.com/trivia/quotes/quotes.htm
102. Elaine Matthews. The Heartbeat of Intelligence. 2002. Writer's Showcase. New York. USA. p.87.

Chapter - 8
Models and Metaphors for Human Transformation

1. Michael N. Nagler. In the Foreword to "Gandhi, the Man: the Story of His Transformation" by Eknath Easwaran. 3rd edition. 1997. Nilgiri Press. California, USA. p. 6.
2. Satprem. The Mind of the Cells or Willed Mutation of Our Species. 1982. The Institute for Evolutionary Research. New York, USA. p.15.
3. Cited in: Timothy J. Madigan. Evolutionary Humanism Revisited: The Continuing Relevance of Julian Huxley. HUUmanists. Association of Unitarian Universalist Humanists. Accessed at: http://www.huumanists.org/publications/journal/1999/evolutionary-humanism-revisited-the-continuing-relevance-of-julian-huxley
4. Pat Roy Mooney. The ETC Century: Erosion, Technological Transformation, and Corporate Concentration in the 21st Century. 2001. Dag Hammarskjold Foundation (DHF, Uppsala, Sweden) and Rural Advancement Foundation International (RAFI, Winnipeg, Canada). Development Dialogue 1999:1-2. Accessed at: http://www.dhf.uu.se/pdffiler/DD1999_1-2.pdf
5. RAFI (Rural Advancement Foundation International) News Release. 11 April 2001. The 'ETC Century': Erosion, Technological Transformation, and Corporate Concentration in the 21st Century. Accessed at: http://www.ratical.org/co-globalize/ETCcent.html
6. RAFI (Rural Advancement Foundation International) News Release. 11 April 2001. The 'ETC Century': Erosion, Technological Transformation, and

Corporate Concentration in the 21st Century. Accessed at: http://www.ratical.org/co-globalize/ETCcent.html

7. Cited in: Brian T. Posser and Andrew Ward. Kierkgaard's 'Mystery of Unrighteousness' In The Information Age. University of Aberdeen. Accessed at: http://www.abdn.ac.uk/philosophy/endsandmeans/vol5no2/prosser_ward.shtml
8. RAFI (Rural Advancement Foundation International) News Release. 11 April 2001. The 'ETC Century': Erosion, Technological Transformation, and Corporate Concentration in the 21st Century. Accessed at: http://www.ratical.org/co-globalize/ETCcent.html
9. The Times of India. Hyderabad, India. 8 July 2008. p.1.
10. Mice Produce Human Sperm Give Hope For Infertile Men. News Archive: Tuesday, 8 July 2008. The Visible Embryo. Accessed at: http://www.visembryo.com/baby/NewsArchive68.html
11. Alec MacAndrew. What Does The Mouse Genome Draft Tell Us About Evolution? Molecular Biology. Accessed at: http://www.evolutionpages.com/Mouse%20genome%20home.htm
12. Wikipedia. Lemming. Accessed at: http://en.wikipedia.org/wiki/Lemming
13. Chuang Tzu. The Quote Garden. Accessed at: http://www.quotegarden.com/butterflies.html
14. Murray Stein. Transformation: Emergence of the Self. (No.7, Carolyn and Ernest Fay Series in Analytical Psychology, David H. Rosen, ed.). 2005. Texas A&M University Press. College Station, Texas, USA. pp.14-15.
15. Wikipedia. Sri Aurobindo. Accessed at: http://en.wikipedia.org/wiki/Aurobindo.
16. Genece Hamby. The Human Butterfly. Accessed at: http://www.selfgrowth.com/articles/Hamby2.html
17. K. Martin-Kuri. A Message for Humanity: the Call of God's Angels at a Time of Global Crisis. 2001. Clairview Books. East Sussex, UK.
18. Margaret Atwood. The Homer of the Ants. [Review of the book "Anthill: a Novel" by Edward O. Wilson]. The New York Review of Books, USA. 8 April 2010. p.6.
19. Manataka American Indian Council. Cree Prophecy. Warriors of the Rainbow. Accessed at: http://www.manataka.org/page235.html
20. Manataka American Indian Council. Hopi Prophesy. Warriors of the Rainbow. Accessed at: http://www.manataka.org/page235.html
21. Dorothea Soelle. Quotes about God. Religious Tolerance. Accessed at: http://www.religioustolerance.org/godquote2.htm
22. Hugh Ross. Evidence for Design in the Universe. Limits for the Universe. Does God Exist? Accessed at: http://www.doesgodexist.org/Charts/EvidenceForDesignInTheUniverse.html
23. Sri Aurobindo. The Future Evolution of Man: The Divine Life Upon Earth. 1971. Sri Aurobindo Ashram Trust. Pondicherry, India. p.56.

24. Paul Pearsall. The Heart's Code: Tapping the Wisdom and Power of Our Heart Energy. 1999. Broadway Books. New York, USA. p.xiii.
25. Wikipedia. All the World's a Stage. Accessed at: http://en.wikipedia.org/wiki/All_the_world's_a_stage
26. Brian Swimme. The Universe Is a Green Dragon: Reading the Meaning in the Cosmic Story. In Context. No.12, Winter 1985/86. Accessed at: http://www.context.org/ICLIB/IC12/Swimme.htm
27. Goethe. Quotes About God. Religious Tolerance. Accessed at: http://www.religioustolerance.org/godquote1.htm
28. David Anderson. Quotes About God. Religiou 1963. Bharatiya Vidya Bhavan. Chaupatty, Bombay, India. p.54.
29. Immortal Words: an Anthology. 1963. Bharatiya Vidya Bhavan. Chaupatty, Bombay, India. p.54.
30. Cited in: J.C Ryle. Self-Effort. Bible Bulletin Board. Accessed at: http://www.biblebb.com/files/ryle/PRACT2.TXT
31. Miguel de Unamuno. ThinkExist.com. Accessed at: http://thinkexist.com/quotation/those_who_believe_ that_they_ believe_in_god-but/174029.html
32. Miguel de Unamuno. Wikiquote. Accessed at: http://en.wikiquote.org/wiki/Miguel_de_Unamuno
33. Albert Einstein. Lost Pine. Accessed at: http://www.lostpine.com/quotes/wisdom_022.htm
34. Cited in: Steven Weinberg. Without God. The New York Review of Books, USA. 25 September 2005. p.73.
35. The Times of India. Hyderabad, India. 28 July 2008. p.18.
36. The Deccan Chronicle. Anantapur, Andhra Pradesh, India. 12 August 2007. p.4.
37. J.P Krol. The Global Mind and Human Brains. Accessed at: http://www.globalmind.info/global_mind_and_human_brains.htm
38. Cited in: Israel Rosenfield and Edward Ziff. How the Mind Works: Revelations. The New York Review of Books, USA. 26 June 2008. p.65.
39. Paul Pearsall. The Heart's Code: Tapping the Wisdom and Power of Our Heart Energy. 1999. Broadway Books. New York, USA. p.17.
40. Cited in: B.L. Bhola. Sharing Mystic Insights in Science and Spirituality. The Times of India. Hyderabad, India. 25 June 2008. p.16.
41. H.P. Blavatsky. The Voice of the Silence. 1998. The Theosophical Publishing House. India. p.111.
42. Peter Browne. A Surprise from St. Augustine. The New York Review of Books, USA. 11 June 2009. p.41.